MARSDEN HARTLEY

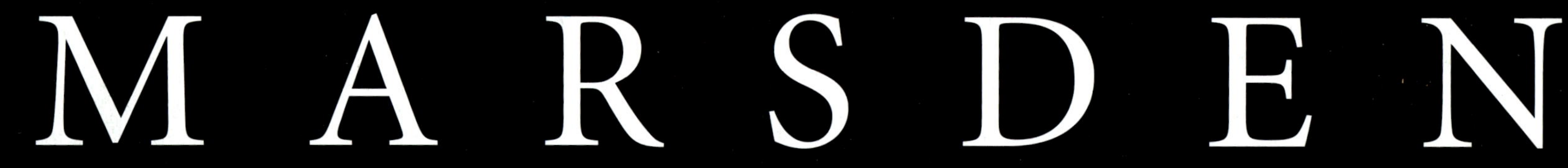

MARSDEN

Wadsworth Atheneum Museum of Art
in association with Yale University Press
New Haven and London

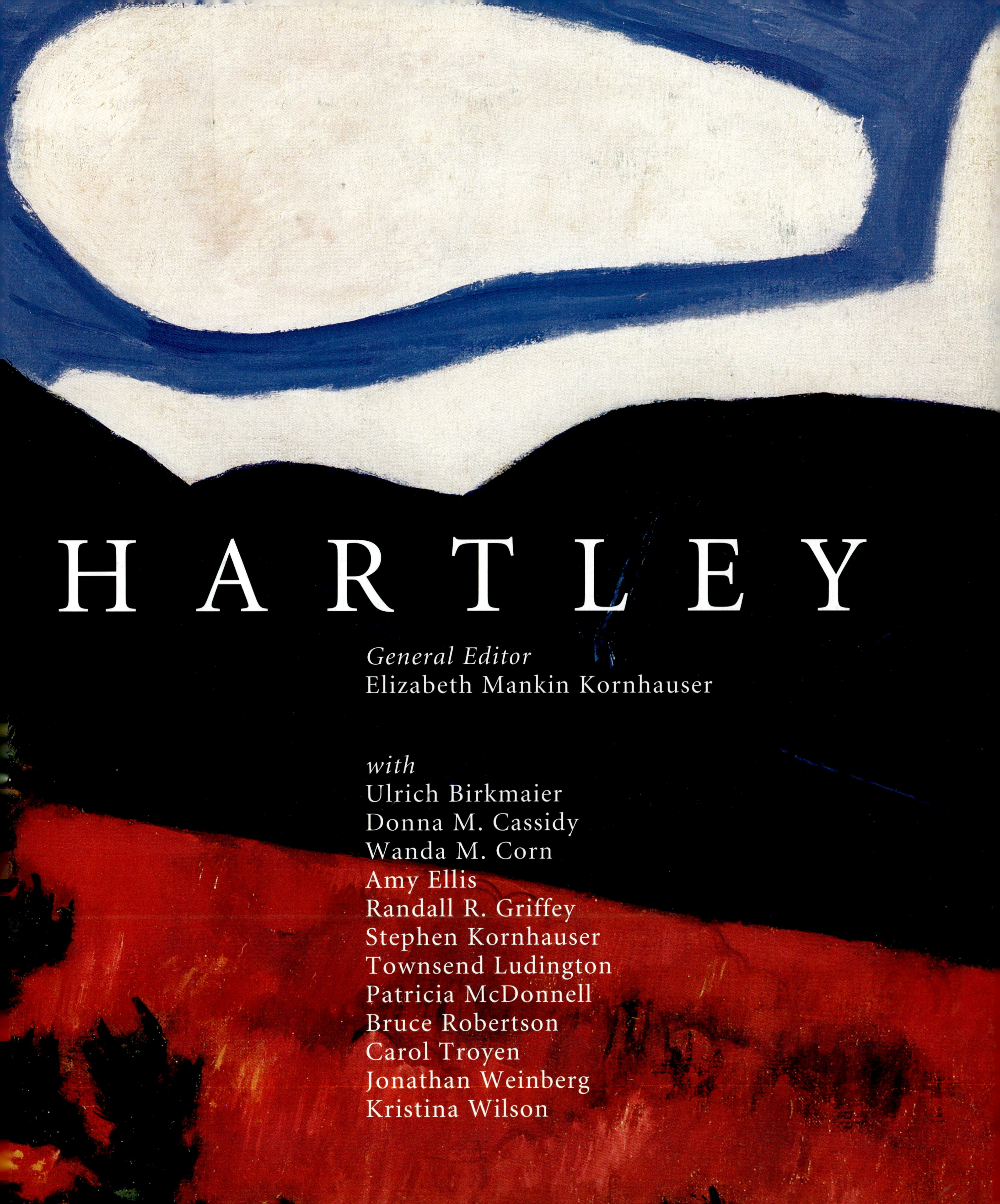

HARTLEY

General Editor
Elizabeth Mankin Kornhauser

with
Ulrich Birkmaier
Donna M. Cassidy
Wanda M. Corn
Amy Ellis
Randall R. Griffey
Stephen Kornhauser
Townsend Ludington
Patricia McDonnell
Bruce Robertson
Carol Troyen
Jonathan Weinberg
Kristina Wilson

The exhibition is made possible by
United Technologies Corporation and The Henry Luce Foundation, Inc.

The exhibition was organized by the
Wadsworth Atheneum Museum of Art, Hartford

Additional support for the catalogue was provided by Ed Shein

Exhibition dates

Wadsworth Atheneum Museum of Art, Hartford
17 January – 20 April 2003

The Phillips Collection, Washington, D.C.
7 June – 7 September 2003

The Nelson-Atkins Museum of Art, Kansas City
11 October – 11 January 2004

Published by Yale University Press, New Haven and London

Designed by Cummings & Good
Typeset in Adobe Minion
Printed in Singapore by CS Graphics

Library of Congress Cataloging-in-Publication Data
Kornhauser, Elizabeth Mankin, 1950–
Marsden Hartley / Elizabeth Mankin Kornhauser with contributions from
Patricia Mc Donnell...[et al.].
p. cm.
Includes bibliographical references and index.
ISBN 0-300-09767-0 (alk. paper)
1. Hartley, Marsden, 1877–1943—Exhibitions. I. McDonnell, Patricia, 1956- II. Title.

ND237.H3435 A4 2003
759.13—dc21 2002008215

Front Cover (Plate 12)
Marsden Hartley
Military, 1913
Oil on canvas, 39¼ × 39¼ in.
Wadsworth Atheneum Museum of Art, Hartford
The Ella Gallup Sumner and Mary Catlin Sumner Collection Fund

Back Cover (Plate 88)
Marsden Hartley
Lobster Fishermen, 1940–41
Oil on Masonite-type hardboard, 29¾ × 40 in.
The Metropolitan Museum of Art, New York
Arthur Hoppoch Hearn Fund, 1942
Photograph © 2002
The Metropolitan Museum of Art

Title Page (Plate 91)
Marsden Hartley
Mount Katahdin, Autumn No. 2, 1939–40
Oil on canvas, 30¼ × 40¼ in.
The Metropolitan Museum of Art, New York
Edith and Milton Lowenthal Collection, Bequest of Edith Abrahamson Lowenthal, 1991
Photograph © 1992
The Metropolitan Museum of Art

Contents

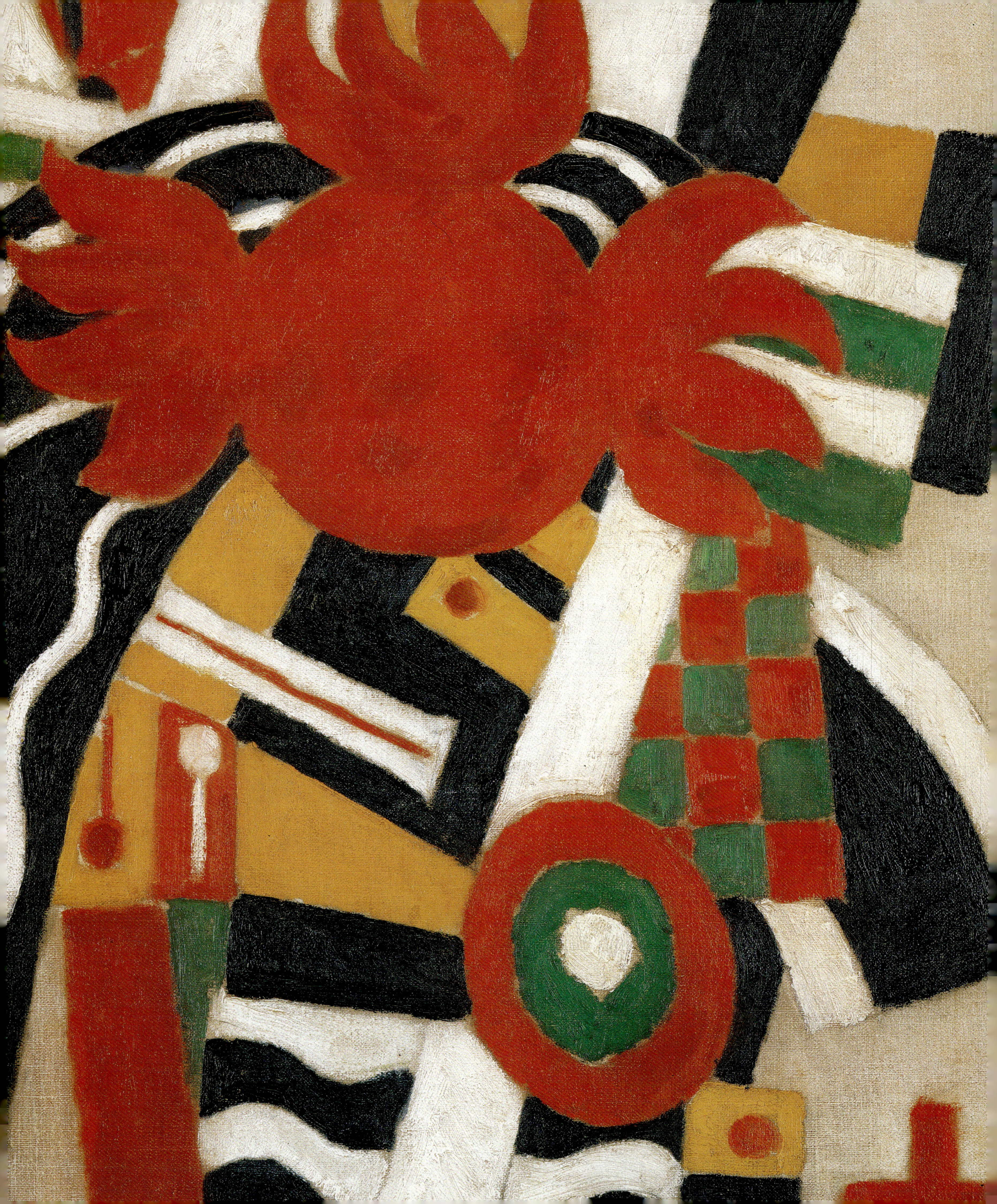

Sponsor's Foreword

Marsden Hartley's paintings inspired Gertrude Stein to write, "In some ways he has managed to keep your attention freshened and as you look you keep on being freshened."

Hartley was at once international and regional in scope. He made significant contributions to modern art, seeking throughout his career to portray abstraction and realism in new ways. From early innovative German abstract paintings to later powerful realistic depictions of Maine lobstermen, Hartley's capacity for growth and change in his work surprise and freshen us now as they did Gertrude Stein's *Lost Generation.*

We are pleased to bring the work of this important modernist to new audiences and generations in Hartford, Washington and Kansas City.

George David
Chairman and Chief Executive Officer
United Technologies Corporation

Detail, Plate 15

Foreword

The Wadsworth Atheneum Museum of Art has been committed to the presentation of American art since its opening in 1844, when works by then contemporary artists such as Thomas Cole, John Vanderlyn, and Rembrandt Peale graced the gallery. Founder Daniel Wadsworth collected the Hudson River School painters, followed by Atheneum patron Elizabeth Hart Jarvis Colt, whose collection was shaped by her advisor Frederic Edwin Church. Successive leadership of the Wadsworth continued interest in American painting and particularly in American Modernism, beginning with A. Everett ("Chick") Austin, the museum's legendary director from 1927 to 1944.

Austin acquired important American modernists such as Joseph Cornell, having purchased the *Soap Bubble Set,* the first Cornell box construction to enter an American museum collection, in 1938. Austin also began the museum's history of special exhibitions devoted to the field with *The Water Colors of Edward Hopper* in 1928.

Marsden Hartley (1877–1943) was a painter, poet, writer, and pioneer in American modernism. Born in Lewiston, Maine, Hartley led a peripatetic life, traveling to and living in Paris, Berlin, New York, Mexico, New Mexico, Bermuda, and elsewhere before returning to Maine in 1934. His landscapes, still lifes, portraits, and abstract works reflect his experience of the people and the environments he encountered. Hartley is admired today for his strength as a painter. The first Hartley to enter the museum's collection came in 1959 with the purchase of *Movement No. 8, Provincetown (*1916) with funds provided by Mrs. Robert E. Darling. In 1973 the pivotal *Military* of 1913 was purchased through The Ella Gallup Sumner and Mary Catlin Sumner Collection Fund that has made possible so many of the most important paintings in the Wadsworth's collection. Then in 1999 the late, powerful *Down East Young Blades* was acquired with support from a coalition of Atheneum patrons dedicated to enhancing the museum's already impressive American art collection. These three significant examples of Hartley's work give a glimpse into the shifting nature of Hartley's art that is much further explored in the present exhibition.

Incorporating over one hundred paintings and works on paper, this exhibition considers the range and depth of Hartley's entire career and pays attention to previously neglected portions of his oeuvre, such as his Cézanne-inspired paintings of France; his paeans to Mount Katahdin; his works connected with his time in New Mexico and Mexico; and his extraordinary paintings of the regional scenery and people of his native Maine from the last ten years of his life and career.

Elizabeth Mankin Kornhauser has been organizing this comprehensive reappraisal of Hartley's work for some six years, at a time when she has also served the Wadsworth as deputy director, chief curator, acting director (2000), and Krieble Curator of American Art.

The museum owes her an enormous debt of gratitude for all her dedicated service and especially for the current project. Throughout this time, she has been ably assisted by Amy Ellis, assistant curator of American art. We thank as well the team of scholars that has collaborated to bring the project to fruition.

Major traveling exhibitions are possible only through the generosity of the lenders, private individuals, corporations and our sister institutions, who have parted with their precious paintings so that they might be enjoyed by additional numbers of museum visitors. We thank all our lenders for sharing these wonderful objects with us. For their support of this project, I am grateful to our partner institutions: The Phillips Collection in Washington, D.C., and its director Jay Gates and the Nelson-Atkins Museum of Art in Kansas City, and its director Marc F. Wilson.

We were able to pursue this project because of the generosity of our sponsors. First and foremost is United Technologies Corporation and its chairman George David, who also serves as president of the Wadsworth's Board of Trustees. His support for the museum's ambitious exhibition program has led to its continued success, bringing important works of art and scholarly inquiry to a broad public here in Hartford and in the many communities where these exhibitions have traveled. The Henry Luce Foundation supported the catalogue, and the early stages of inquiry allowing us to bring together Hartley scholars to organize the exhibition. We are extremely grateful for their generous support for this project and many others in the field of American art. We are also pleased to thank Ed Shein for his contribution to the exhibition.

Marsden Hartley, who was born in Maine, traveled the world, and returned to his New England roots, created a body of work that remains provocative, powerful, and fresh to our contemporary eyes. We hope that you will derive from this exhibition and catalogue a new appreciation for his complexity and depth.

Kate M. Sellers
Director

Lenders to the Exhibition

Addison Gallery of American Art, Phillips Academy, Andover, Massachusetts
Allen Memorial Art Museum, Oberlin College, Ohio
Amon Carter Museum, Forth Worth, Texas
The Art Institute of Chicago
AXA Financial, Inc., through its subsidiary The Equitable Life Assurance Society of the United States
Babcock Galleries, New York
Baltimore Museum of Art
Bates College Museum of Art, Lewiston, Maine
The Beinecke Rare Book and Manuscript Library, Yale University, New Haven
Berry-Hill Galleries, New York
Brooklyn Museum of Art
The Carnegie Museum of Art, Pittsburgh
Colby College Museum of Art, Waterville, Maine
Curtis Galleries, Minneapolis, Minnesota
Mr. and Mrs. Barney A. Ebsworth
Carol and Maurice Feinberg
The Frances Lehman Loeb Art Center, Vassar College, Poughkeepsie
Frederick R. Weisman Art Museum, University of Minnesota, Minneapolis
Gerald Peters Gallery, New York
Hirshhorn Museum and Sculpture Garden, Smithsonian Institution, Washington, D.C.
Huntington Library, Art Collections, and Botanical Gardens, San Marino, California
Los Angeles County Museum of Art
The Metropolitan Museum of Art, New York
Milwaukee Art Museum
Minneapolis Institute of Arts

Museum of Fine Arts, Boston
Museum of New Mexico, Museum of Fine Arts, Santa Fe
National Gallery of Art, Washington
The Nelson-Atkins Museum of Art, Kansas City, Missouri
New Orleans Museum of Art
Roy R. Neuberger
North Carolina Museum of Art, Raleigh
The Ogunquit Museum of American Art
Barbara R. Palmer
Philadelphia Museum of Art
The Phillips Collection, Washington, D.C.
Private Collections
Rose Art Museum, Brandeis University, Waltham, Massachusetts
The Saint Louis Art Museum
Salander-O'Reilly Galleries, New York
Carol and Ted Shen
Shein Collection
Smith College Museum of Art, Northampton, Massachusetts
Smithsonian American Art Museum, Washington, D.C.
The University of Iowa Museum of Art, Iowa City
Wadsworth Atheneum Museum of Art, Hartford
Walker Art Center, Minneapolis
Washington University Gallery of Art, St. Louis
Whitney Museum of American Art, New York
Worcester Art Museum, Worcester, Massachusetts

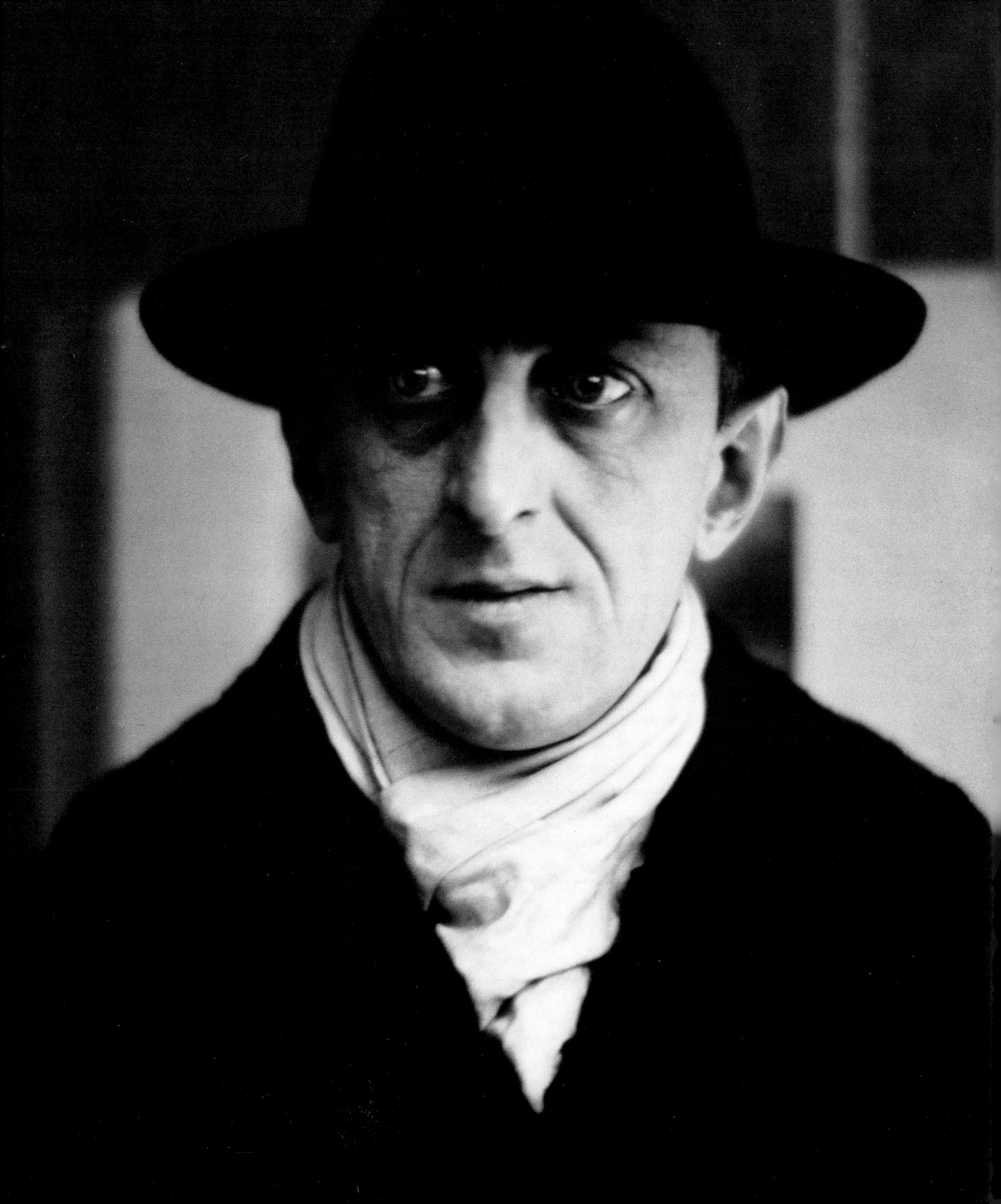

Preface

"The career of Marsden Hartley," Hilton Kramer wrote in 1969, "is one of the most interesting in the history of modern painting in America, but the very reasons that make it interesting have also made it difficult at times to keep his accomplishments clearly in focus."[1] With the exception of a Museum of Modern Art retrospective in 1944 and Barbara Haskell's seminal Hartley retrospective at the Whitney Museum of American Art in 1980, all of the exhibitions prior to this one concentrated on a single segment of Hartley's oeuvre. These smaller, focused shows made important contributions in elucidating those periods and helped "to keep [Hartley's] accomplishments in focus." But they also prevented the public from understanding the breadth and depth of Hartley's career as a whole.

With the current exhibition, we hope to change that. Taking advantage of the considerable scholarship that has been achieved since the Whitney show in 1980, we have gathered together a large selection of Hartley's works from every period of his long artistic career. A look back at what others have written, published, and exhibited with regard to Hartley helps position this retrospective in the history of Hartley studies. In 1910, at the outset of Hartley's career, a critic wrote, "Marsden Hartley makes you catch your breath."[2] It is hoped that this exhibition will recreate that excitement.

Two major studies begun in the 1940s and 1950s, largely unpublished, laid a foundation for Hartley scholarship. Elizabeth McCausland, an art critic well acquainted with the artist, spent the years 1944 until her death in 1966 preparing a book on Hartley that was never completed.[3] Robert Northcutt Burlingame's unpublished dissertation of 1953, "Marsden Hartley: A Study of His Life and Creative Achievement," focused on Hartley as a writer. Simultaneously, Hartley's own papers were placed in the Collection of American Literature in the Beinecke Library at Yale University.

In the 1940s and 1950s, as Marcia Brennan has demonstrated, the art critic Clement Greenberg launched a deliberate program of negative reviews denouncing the Stieglitz circle of artists, in particular Georgia O'Keeffe, as he attempted to unseat his rival, the elder prophet of modernism, Alfred Stieglitz. This effort was aimed at gaining recognition for the emerging New York School. Greenberg was critical of Hartley's retrospective at the Museum of Modern Art and effectively discounted Hartley's claim to being "the painter from Maine" by promoting the more popular John Marin and his art as the sole link between modernism and the emergence of Jackson Pollock.[4] (Marin had claimed Maine as his primary subject.) While in time Greenberg came to admire Hartley's art, his dismissal of the Stieglitz circle artists in the 1940s, with the exception of Marin, did little to advance Hartley scholarship.

When Barbara Haskell mounted the full-scale exhibition of Hartley's work at the Whitney Museum of American Art in 1980, she did so in the absence of a formal biography

Detail
Alfred Stieglitz
Marsden Hartley, 1915–16
Photograph, silver gelatin print, 22½ × 19 in.
The Museum of Fine Arts, Boston
Gift of Alfred Stieglitz, 24.1719

or catalogue raisonné.[5] The catalogue for the exhibition provided the initial attempt at a biography, including the earliest mention of Hartley's homosexuality, and presented for the first time the full range of Hartley's art in an effort to establish a chronology for his multiple stylistic shifts. It was a remarkable accomplishment and inspired new generations of admirers and an avalanche of writings on Hartley.

In recent decades, one biography and two monographs have appeared. Townsend Ludington's biography (1992) remains comprehensive. Gail Scott's monograph (1988) thoughtfully focuses on Hartley's art, and Bruce Robertson's (1995) combines a discussion of the artist's art and life, incorporating contemporary insights into his work.

Many scholars have chosen to approach this complex artist by isolating moments in his career and by presenting them as discrete. Hartley's penchant for painting in series has led to specific studies of his Berlin abstract paintings by Patricia McDonnell and others; his landscapes of Dogtown, Massachusetts; his elegiac archaic portraits of the Mason family in Nova Scotia; his portraits of heroes, including three of Abraham Lincoln; and his late male figure paintings.[6] Single aspects or themes of his biography as it influenced his art have been addressed in such books as Jonathan Weinberg's *Speaking for Vice: Homosexuality in the Art of Charles Demuth, Marsden Hartley, and the First American Avant-Garde,* and his iconography has been explored in, for example, Jeanne Hokin's *Pinnacles and Pyramids: The Art of Marsden Hartley.* The artist's prolific career as a poet and writer has been honored in a number of publications of his writings and poetry, edited by Gail R. Scott, and his autobiography, edited by Susan Elizabeth Ryan. In addition, Hartley has been dealt with as a member of the Stieglitz circle of artists in numerous articles, exhibitions, and books.[7] And yet, in the absence of a recent comprehensive overview of his work, he has remained the least known of the core group of Stieglitz circle painters, despite the fact that many perceive him to have been the most talented.[8]

While a great deal of biographical information exists, a complete understanding of the works of this artist has remained elusive. The fact that there are numerous Hartley biographies and yet no catalogue raisonné has resulted in excessive weight being placed on the eccentricities of his personality to the detriment of the appreciation and understanding of his work. While the fact remains, as Susan Elizabeth Ryan has stated, that "it is virtually impossible to banish biography from any discussion of [Hartley's] art," confusion still exists regarding the strict chronology of important series of paintings, particularly his Paris and Berlin paintings, as well as his works produced in Provincetown, Bermuda, Mexico, and Maine. One of the most prolific and successful periods of his career, his last eight years in Maine, requires focused attention and new thinking. Little concern has been paid to his working methods and materials despite the fact that he is acknowledged to have been a brilliant colorist and an adroit painter. His substantial body of works on paper, including pencil and charcoal drawings, watercolors, pastels, and prints, reveals a great deal about the artist's thinking process and clearly influenced his final oils, but have received only the most cursory attention. The links between his writings and paintings are profound and essential for an understanding of his art, and while important work has been done in this area, the richness and sheer quantity of Hartley's writings require further exploration. Hartley's position within the artistic circles of the era in which he worked, a most complex period in the history of art, has received little attention beyond his place within the Stieglitz circle. Hartley's response to the popularity of Thomas Hart Benton's brand of regionalism, and his connections to the German expressionists in the 1930s, Max Beckmann for instance, are important areas for exploration. The many artistic mentors, Picasso for example, and rivals, John Marin and Walt Kuhn, who shaped his art and inspired his work require further consideration. Finally, Hartley's influence on successive generations of artists has yet to be seriously considered.

This exhibition and book address many of these and other issues in an attempt to redress the imbalance in Hartley scholarship by focusing on the strength of his accomplishments as a painter. Beginning with a chronology of the artist's life, critical moments in his career and potent themes that run through his entire oeuvre are then explored in order to clarify the development and the diversity of his achievement as a painter. They are followed by a discussion of Hartley's working methods and materials and entries that provide detailed information for each work in the exhibition.

Acknowledgements

The work for this exhibition and book began six years ago, and from its inception, this project has benefited from the generous support of countless individuals. We are deeply grateful to all listed here, who responded to our many requests with enthusiasm. From its inception, this exhibition and catalogue received the support and encouragement of Peter C. Sutton, former director, Wadsworth Atheneum Museum of Art. The museum's current director, Kate M. Sellers, has continued that support and allowed this project to reach completion. I thank her along with the museum's Board of Trustees. The assistance of the museum staff over many years has made this project possible. In particular, we are grateful to our curatorial and conservation colleagues: Nicholas Baume, Deirdre Bibby, Thomas Denenberg, Zenon Ganziniec, Carol Krute, Linda Roth, and Eric Zafran. Many other departments including Education, Exhibition Design, and Registrar, among others, played critical roles, and we wish to acknowledge Cecil Adams, Gretchen Dietrich, Dana Deloach, Susan Hood, Mary Schroeder, and Nicole Wholean.

We set out to produce a definitive catalogue on Marsden Hartley and were blessed to have an inspired team of contributors: Ulrich Birkmaier, painting conservator, Wadsworth Atheneum Museum of Art; Donna M. Cassidy, associate professor, American and New England studies and art history, University of Southern Maine; Randall R. Griffey, assistant curator, Nelson-Atkins Museum of Art, Kansas City; Stephen Kornhauser, chief conservator, Wadsworth Atheneum Museum of Art; Townsend Ludington, Boshamer Distinguished Professor of American Studies and English, University of North Carolina at Chapel Hill; Patricia McDonnell, curator, Frederick R. Weisman Art Museum, and adjunct professor of art history, University of Minneapolis, Minnesota; Bruce Robertson, chief curator, American art, Los Angeles County Museum of Art; Carol Troyen, curator of paintings, Art of the Americas, Museum of Fine Arts, Boston; Jonathan Weinberg, independent scholar and J. Paul Getty Museum fellow; Kristina Wilson, Marcia Brady Tucker post-doctoral fellow, Yale University Art Gallery, New Haven. Marcia Hinckley helped us in the early stages of research, and Allison Hewey was indispensable in assisting with both object and general research for the project. Maureen Miesmer provided crucial editorial and curatorial help with the final stages of the catalogue and the exhibition. Joell Williams helped with photography permissions.

This project has benefited from earlier scholars who have studied Hartley. In addition to the authors of this catalogue, we are grateful for the accounts and advice provided by Gerald Ferguson, Thomas W. Gaehtgens, Sarah Greenough, Barbara Haskell, Jeanne Hokin, Gail Levin, Gail R. Scott, Susan Elizabeth Ryan, and James Voorhies. For assistance on matters concerning Hartley's working methods and materials and on framing issues, we are indebted to the following: frame historians William Adair, David Mandel, Charles Schreiber, Eli Wilner, and Suzanne Smeaton; scientists Professor Henry de Phillips, René de la Rie, Christopher Maines, James Martin, and Harold Moskowitz; curator Opal Baker;

and paintings conservators Albert Albano, Rita Albertson, Mark Aronson, Clark Bedford, Lucy Belloli, David Findley, Patricia Garland, Charlotte Hale, Kristin Hoermann, James Horns, Irene Konifil, Jay Krueger, Susan Lake, Lance Mayers, Gay Myers, Lenora Paglia, Suzanne Penn, Elizabeth Steele, Marcia Steele, Hubert von Sonnenburg, Isabelle Tokumaru, Jean Woodward, James Wright, and Frank Zuccari.

At Yale University Press, John Nicoll expressed early interest and support for this book, and Sally Salvesen guided us through the publication process very ably and cheerfully. The very large manuscript greatly benefited from the intelligent and sensitive editing of Faith Brabenec Hart. The talented design work of Cummings & Good, in particular Peter Good, ably assisted by Kirsten Livingston and Dawn Llaser, has made this a beautiful and useable volume.

The exhibition would not have been possible without the generosity of our lenders. We thank the following: Adam Weinberg, Addison Gallery of American Art, Phillips Academy; Sharon F. Patton, Allen Memorial Art Museum, Oberlin College; Patricia Junker and Rick Stewart, Amon Carter Museum; Daniel Schulman and James N. Wood, Art Institute of Chicago; Pari Stave, AXA Financial Gallery; John Driscoll, Babcock Galleries; Doreen Bolger and Kathy Rothkopf, Baltimore Museum of Art; Genetta McLean and William Low, Bates College Museum of Art; Barbara A. Shailor and Patricia Willis, Beinecke Rare Book and Manuscript Library, Yale University; Berta Walker, Berta Walker Gallery; Linda Ferber, Barbara Dayer Gallati, and Arnold Lehman, Brooklyn Museum of Art; Richard Armstrong and Louise Lippincott, Carnegie Museum of Art; Hugh Gourley, Colby College Museum of Art; Irvin M. Lippman, Columbus Museum of Art; Myron Kunin, Curtis Galleries; James Mundy, Frances Lehman Loeb Art Center, Vassar College; Patricia McDonnell, Frederick R. Weisman Art Museum, University of Minnesota; Lily Downing Burke and Gerald Peters, Gerald Peters Gallery; Gregory Hedberg, Hirschl & Adler Galleries; Ned Rifkin, Phyllis Rosenzweig, and Judith Zilscher, Hirshhorn Museum and Sculpture Garden, Smithsonian Institution; Shelley M. Bennett, Amy Myers, and Edward Nygren, Huntington Library, Art Collections, and Botanical Gardens; Irene Martin, Andrea Rich, and Bruce Robertson, Los Angeles County Museum of Art; Ida Balboul, Philippe de Montebello, William S. Lieberman, and Frances Redding Wallace, Metropolitan Museum of Art, New York; Russell Bowman, Milwaukee Art Museum; Evan M. Maurer and Patrick Noon, Minneapolis Institute of Arts; Elliot Bostwick Davis, Erica Hirshler, Malcom Rogers, and Carol Troyen, Museum of Fine Arts, Boston; Stuart Ashman, Museum of Fine Arts, Santa Fe, New Mexico; Sarah Greenough, Franklin Kelly, and Earl A. Powell III, National Gallery of Art, Washington; Margi Conrads, Randall Griffey, and Marc Wilson, Nelson-Atkins Museum of Art; Lucinda Gedeon, Neuberger Art Museum; E. John Bullard, New Orleans Museum of Art; John W. Coffey and Lawrence J. Wheeler, North Carolina Museum of Art; Michael Culver, The Ogunquit Museum of American Art; Anne d'Harnoncourt, Michael R. Taylor, Philadelphia Museum of Art; Jay Gates, Eliza Rathbone, and Beth Turner, Phillips Collection; Joseph Ketner, Rose Art Museum, Brandeis University; Brent R. Benjamin, Saint Louis Art Museum; Andrew Kelly, Leigh Morse, and Lawrence Salander, Salander-O'Reilly Galleries; Suzannah Fabing and Linda Muehlig, Smith College Museum of Art; Elizabeth Broun, Smithsonian American Art Museum; Howard Collinson and Pamela White Trimpe, University of Iowa Art Museum; Kathy Halbreich, Walker Art Center; Mark S. Weil, Washington University Gallery of Art; Maxwell Anderson and Barbara Haskell, Whitney Museum of American Art; David Brigham and James A. Welu, Worcester Art Museum; and the many private collectors including Mr. and Mrs. Barney A. Ebsworth, Carol and Maurice Feinberg, Mr. and Mrs. J.R. Hyde, Barbara Palmer, Roy R. Neuberger, Ed Shein, and Carol and Ted Shen.

This project would never have been accomplished without the early and enthusiastic sponsorship of United Technologies Corporation and its Arts and Culture Employee Committee. We are particularly indebted to George David, president and CEO of United Technologies and a most enlightened arts benefactor, who made it possible for this project to reach its ambitious goal. In addition, the Henry Luce Foundation has once again provided the Wadsworth Atheneum with critical support for this groundbreaking project. We are indebted to Henry Luce III, chairman and CEO, and to Ellen Holtzman, program director for the arts, for their extraordinary generosity. We are also grateful for the support received from Ed Shein.

Finally, and by no means least, thanks are due to Robert, Sara, and Stephen Kornhauser, who provided patience, humor, and support through each phase of this project.

Elizabeth Mankin Kornhauser with Amy Ellis

1 Hilton Kramer, "Marsden Hartley: The Return of the Native," *New York Times,* 21 September 1969, sec. 2, 29.

2 James Huneker in the *New York Sun,* quoted in *Camera Work,* no. 31 (July 1910): 43–47, and in *Alfred Stieglitz, Camera Work: The Complete Illustrations, 1903–1917* (Cologne: Taschen, 1997), 532.

3 McCausland Papers, Archives/Smithsonian; Elizabeth McCausland, *Marsden Hartley* (Minneapolis: University of Minnesota Press, 1952).

4 Clement Greenberg, *The Collected Essays and Criticism,* ed. John O'Brian, vol. 1 (Chicago: University of Chicago Press, 1986), 246–48; Marcia Brennan, *Painting Gender, Construction Theory: The Alfred Stieglitz Circle and American Formalist Aesthetics* (Cambridge: MIT Press, 2001), 236, 241.

5 Gail Levin is in the process of assembling a catalogue raisonné on Hartley's known works.

6 See Patricia McDonnell, *Dictated By Life: Marsden Hartley's German Paintings and Robert Indiana's Hartley Elegies* (Minneapolis: Frederick R. Weisman Art Museum, University of Minnesota, 1995); *Marsden Hartley: Soliloquy in Dogtown* (Gloucester, Mass.: Cape Ann Historical Society, 1985); Ferguson; Randall Griffey, "Marsden Hartley's Lincoln Portraits," *American Art* 15 (summer 2001): 34–51; Randall Griffey, "Marsden Hartley's Late Paintings: National Identity in the 1930s and '40s" (diss., University of Kansas, 1999).

7 Most recently, Hartley has been included in three exhibitions of Stieglitz and his circle: Beth Turner, *In the American Grain: Arthur Dove, Marsden Hartley, John Marin, Georgia O'Keeffe, and Alfred Stieglitz* (Washington, D.C.: Phillips Collection, 1995); Elizabeth Mankin Kornhauser and Amy Ellis, *Stieglitz, O'Keeffe, and American Modernism* (Hartford: Wadsworth Atheneum, 1999); Sarah Greenough, *Modern Art and America: Alfred Stieglitz and His New York Galleries* (Washington, D.C.: National Gallery of Art, 2001).

8 Robert Hughes has called Hartley "the greatest of early American modernists" in his landmark survey *American Visions: The Epic History of Art in America* (New York: Alfred A. Knopf, 1997), 365; Hilton Kramer declared that "among the first generation of modernist painters in this country . . . Hartley stands out as one of the strongest—perhaps *the* strongest," in Kramer, "Marsden Hartley, American Yet Cosmopolitan," *New York Times,* 20 January 1968, 25.

Notes to the Reader:

Essays:

Endnotes follow each of the ten essays, and a list of abbreviations for frequently used references in the essays and entries is provided here. Each essay is followed by a group of color plates of works in the exhibition, organized in roughly chronological order.

Entries:

The entries are listed chronologically, and each is illustrated by a full color plate. The catalogue numbers and plate numbers are identical. Entries include the media for each work including the following supports: canvas, composite board, composition board, fiberboard, Masonite-type board, and paper, and are discussed in the essay by Kornhauser and Birkmaier. The dimensions of the support are given in inches followed in parentheses by centimeters. Height precedes width. The initials of the author of each entry follow the entry.

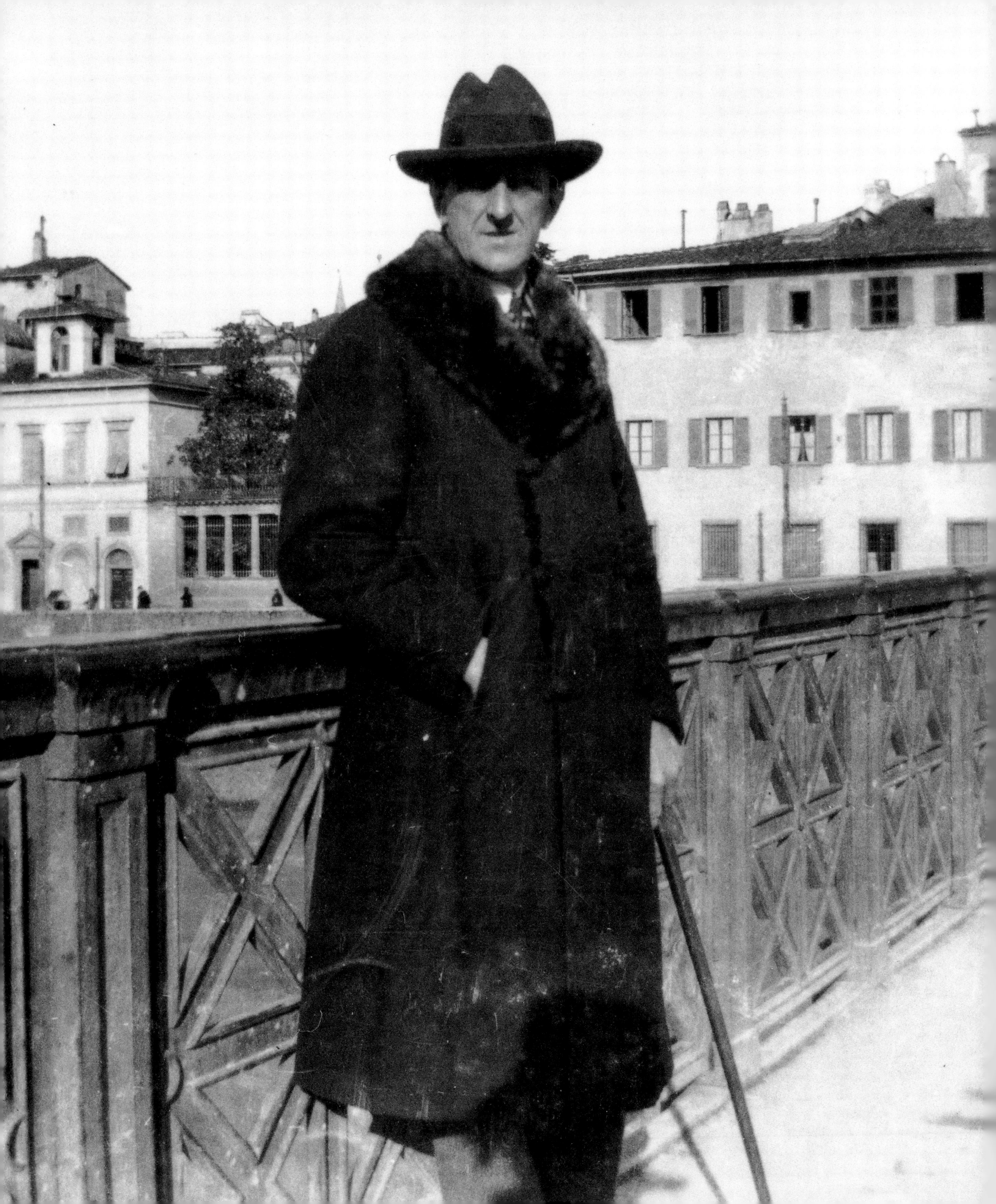

Chronology
Marsden Hartley, 1877–1943

This chronology and exhibition history is drawn from previous chronologies by Barbara Haskell, *Marsden Hartley* (New York: Whitney Museum of American Art, 1980); Gail R. Scott, *Marsden Hartley* (New York: Abbeville Press, 1988); Susan Elizabeth Ryan, ed., *Somehow a Past: The Autobiography of Marsden Hartley* (Cambridge: MIT Press, 1997); and Sarah Greenough, et al., *Modern Art and America: Alfred Stieglitz and His New York Galleries* (Washington, D.C.: National Gallery of Art in association with Bulfinch Press, 2000).

1877 Edmund Hartley born January 4 in Lewiston, Maine, to Thomas and Eliza Jane Hartley.

1885 Mother died on March 4.
Hartley's youngest sisters moved to Cleveland, Ohio, to live with his oldest sister.
Hartley moved to Auburn, Maine, to live with another, married sister.

1889 Father married Martha Marsden on August 20, and the couple moved to Cleveland to join some of Hartley's sisters.
Edmund stayed in Auburn, Maine.

1893 Hartley joined the family in Cleveland.

1896 Hartley began taking art classes weekly with Cleveland painter John Semon.

1898 Took an outdoor summer painting class with impressionist painter Cullen Yates.
Entered the Cleveland School of Art (Cleveland Institute of Art) in the fall on a scholarship.
Received copy of Ralph Waldo Emerson's *Essays* from Nina Waldeck, a teacher there.

1899 Anne Walworth, a trustee of the Cleveland School of Art, offered Hartley an annual stipend of $450 for five years of studying art in New York City.
Studied art at the Chase School, New York, for one year.

1900 Spent summer in Lewiston, Maine.
Transferred to the National Academy of Design, New York, studying there for four years.

1902 Spent summer in Center Lovell, Maine.
Awarded Honorable Mention in composition and the Suydam Silver Medal for still-life drawing at the National Academy of Design, New York.

Unknown Photographer
Marsden Hartley's postcard to Alfred Stieglitz from Florence, 1924
Photograph postcard
Yale Collection of American Literature, Beinecke Rare Book and Manuscript Library, Yale University, New Haven

1904 Worked part-time as an extra with Proctor's Theater Company, New York, through fall 1906.

1905 Painted *Walt Whitman's House, 328 Mickle Street, Camden, New Jersey* (plate 1) around this time.

1906 Moved to Lewiston, Maine, to teach painting.
Took stepmother's maiden name, calling himself Edmund Marsden Hartley.
Began painting *Storm Clouds, Maine* (plate 2).

1907 Painted impressionist-style landscapes in winter.
Spent time in the summer at Green Acre, a spiritualist retreat in Eliot, Maine.
Moved to Boston for the winter.

1908 Dropped his first name and became Marsden Hartley.
Used brighter palette and applied paint more thickly in impressionist-style landscapes.
Moved to North Lovell, Maine, in the fall.
Began making neo-impressionist paintings and drawings, including *Carnival of Autumn* (plate 3) and *The Ice-Hole, Maine* (plate 4), and self-portrait drawings, including *Self-Portrait as a Draughtsman* (plate 5).

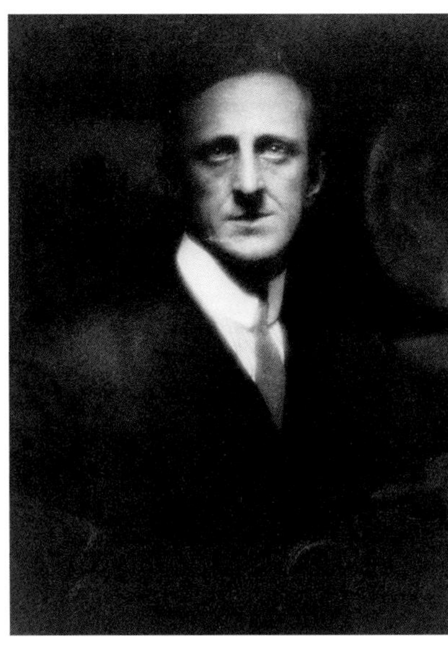

Unknown Photographer
Marsden Hartley, c. 1910
Photograph
Yale Collection of American Literature, Beinecke Rare Book and Manuscript Library, Yale University, New Haven

1909 Met Alfred Stieglitz in New York.
First solo exhibition at Stieglitz's 291 gallery in New York: *Exhibition of Paintings in Oil by Mr. Marsden Hartley of Maine.*
Met Albert Pinkham Ryder and began Dark Landscape series, including *Deserted Farm* (plate 6).

1910 Spent summer in North Lovell, Maine.
Began painting fauvist landscapes.

1911 Spent summer in North Lovell, Maine.
Experimented, drawing on the work of Picasso and Cézanne.
Returned to New York in fall.
Saw original Cézannes for the first time in late 1911 or early 1912.

1912 Second solo exhibition at 291: *Recent Paintings and Drawings by Marsden Hartley.*
Went to Paris and joined artistic community there. Met Gertrude Stein.
Painted still lifes influenced by Matisse and Cézanne, including *Still Life* (plate 7).
Introduced to writings and work by Wassily Kandinsky and Der Blaue Reiter. Began paintings that were influenced by Kandinsky, including *Musical Theme (Oriental Symphony)* (plate 8).
Began *Portrait Arrangement No. 2* (plate 9).

1913 Went to Berlin for three weeks.
Met Kandinsky and Gabriel Münter in Munich.
Returned to Paris, where Gertrude Stein visited his studio and chose four paintings to hang in her apartment.
Returned to Berlin, stopping in Sindelsdorf to see Franz Marc.
In Munich, met with Kandinsky, Münter, Marc, and Albert Bloch to discuss his paintings and tried to arrange exhibition at Galerie Goltz.
Began painting pre-war pageants, including *Portrait of Berlin* (plate 10), *The Warriors* (plate 11), and *Military* (plate 12).

Exhibited five paintings (Intuitive Abstractions) in the Erster Deutscher Herbstsalon (First German Autumn Salon) in Berlin.
Returned to New York in November; brought work back for exhibition at Stieglitz's 291.

1914 Solo exhibition at 291: *Paintings by Marsden Hartley.* Exhibition included paintings made in Paris and Berlin, and a bronze bust of Hartley by Arnold Rönnebeck.
Returned to Berlin in March, stopping in London and Paris first.
Painted *Himmel* (plate 13), *Berlin Ante-War* (plate 14), and *The Aero* (plate 15).
Began Amerika series, including *Indian Fantasy* (plate 16) and *Indian Composition* (plate 17), among others.
War declared.
Father died.
Karl von Freyburg killed in war on October 7.
Made drawings, including *Military Symbols I* (plate 18).
Began German Officer paintings, including *Portrait of a German Officer* (plate 19), *Painting No. 47, Berlin* (plate 20), *Painting No. 49, Berlin* (plate 21), *The Iron Cross* (plate 22), and *E. (German Officer—Abstraction)* (plate 23).

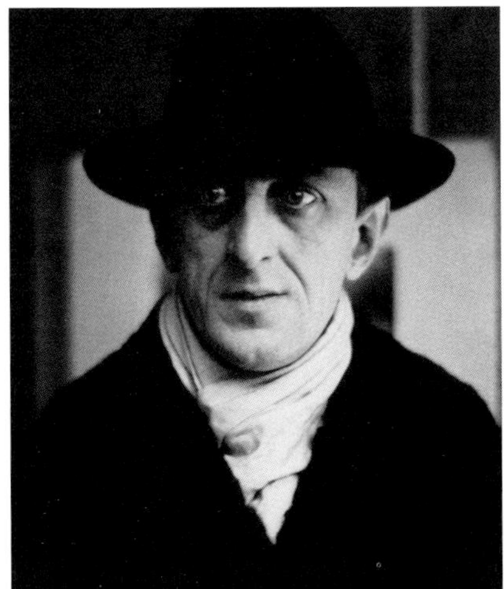

Alfred Stieglitz
Marsden Hartley, 1915–16
Photograph, silver gelatin print
The Museum of Fine Arts, Boston
Gift of Alfred Stieglitz, 24.1719

1915 Exhibited Mountain series at the Daniel Gallery, New York.
Stepmother, Martha Marsden, died.
Exhibited forty-five paintings and a group of abstract drawings made in Europe, in addition to some early 1908 drawings, at the Münchener Graphik-Verlag, Berlin.
Returned to New York in December.

1916 Visited Mabel Dodge (Luhan) in Croton-on-Hudson, New York.
Painted in synthetic cubist style, including *Handsome Drinks* (plate 24), *A Nice Time* (plate 25), and *One Portrait of One Woman* (plate 26).
Exhibited six paintings and three drawings in the Forum Exhibition at the Anderson Galleries, New York.
Solo exhibition at Stieglitz's 291 gallery included forty oils, most of which were painted in Berlin.
Spent summer in Provincetown, Massachusetts, as John Reed's guest.
Met Eugene O'Neill and the Provincetown Players.
Began painting Movements, such as *Movement No. 8, Provincetown* (plate 27).
Shared a house with artist Charles Demuth in Provincetown in fall.
Returned to New York in November before traveling with Demuth to Bermuda in December.

1917 In Bermuda, continued with Movements and painted *Elsa* (plate 28) and *Trixie* (plate 29).
Solo exhibition at Stieglitz's 291 gallery, New York: *Marsden Hartley's Recent Work, Together with Examples of His Evolution.*
Painted *Atlantic Window* (plate 30) and *Still Life with Eel* (plate 31).
Returned to New York in spring.
Went to Lewiston, Maine, in June, before traveling to Ogunquit, Maine, where he painted *Tinseled flowers* (plate 32) and stayed at the art colony founded by Hamilton Easter Field.
Returned to New York and lived in Brooklyn Heights apartment owned by Field.

1918 Went to Santa Fe, New Mexico, and then to Taos, where he spent June through October.
Made pastels of New Mexico landscape, including *Pueblo Mountain, New Mexico* (plate 33).
Moved to Santa Fe in November.

Painted *Blessing the Melon: The Indians Bring the Harvest to Christian Mary for Her Blessing* (plate 34), *Santos, New Mexico* (plate 35), and *El Santo* (plate 36).

1919 Went to La Cañada, California, to visit Carl Sprinchorn. Met Robert McAlmon and Arthur Wesley Dow.
Visited San Francisco.
Returned to Santa Fe in June. Began second series of pastels and oil paintings of the New Mexico desert.
Returned to New York and painted more pictures based on the New Mexico pastels.

1920 Solo exhibition at the Daniel Gallery, New York.
Appointed first secretary of the Société Anonyme, founded by Marcel Duchamp, Katherine Dreier, and Man Ray.
Spent summer in Gloucester, Massachusetts; Elie Nadelman and Stuart Davis were also there.
Returned to New York in October.
Made pastel *Calla Lilies* (plate 37).

1921 Delivered lecture titled "What is Dada?" at the Société Anonyme.
Participated in reading of works of Gertrude Stein in honor of the first anniversary of the Société Anonyme.
Published *Adventures in the Arts.*
Auctioned 117 of his works at the Anderson Galleries, New York, on May 17; raised enough money for a return to Europe.
Journeyed to Paris in July.
Moved to Berlin in November.

1922 Painted still lifes of food, bowls, and baskets in brown palette.
Began making still-life lithographs.

1923 Began New Mexico Recollections series, including *Landscape, New Mexico* (plate 38) and *New Mexico Recollections—Storm* (plate 39).
Began making pastel drawings of male and female nudes, including *Seated Male Nude* (plate 40).
Published *Twenty-five Poems.*
Traveled to Vienna.
Went to Italy: spent eight weeks in Florence, and Christmas in Rome with Maurice Sterne.

1924 Returned to New York in February.
Returned to Paris via London in summer.
Continued New Mexico Recollections.
Began fish still lifes and Paysage series (recollections of Maine).

1925 Moved to Vence, France, in August.
Painted series of images of the south of France, including *Landscape, Vence* (plate 41).

1926 Moved to Aix-en-Provence, where Cézanne worked.
Began *Fig Tree* (plate 42).

1927 Traveled to Paris, Berlin, and Hamburg in winter and spring.

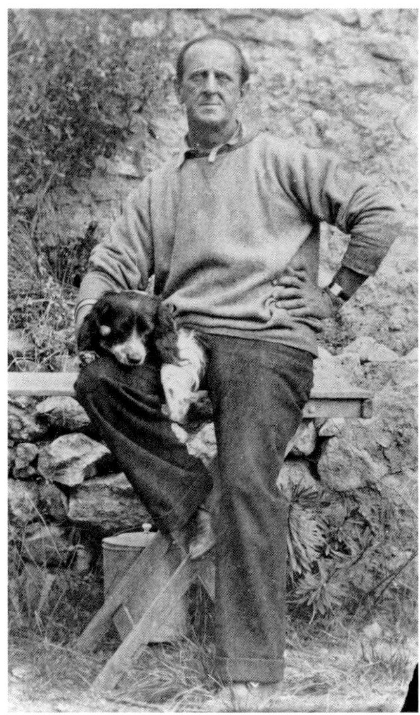

Unknown Photographer
Marsden Hartley at Aix-en-Provence with his dog, Toy, 1928
Photograph
Archives of American Art, Smithsonian Institution, Washington, D.C.

Returned to Aix-en-Provence in May.
Began Mont Sainte-Victoire paintings, including *Mont Sainte-Victoire, Aix-en-Provence* (plate 43); drawings, including *Mont Ste.-Victoire* (plate 44); and a series of silverpoint landscapes in the style of Cézanne.
Returned to Paris in December.

1928 Returned to New York in January.
Traveled to Chicago in March to see his exhibition at the Arts Club of Chicago: *Paintings and Watercolors by Marsden Hartley.*
Went on to Denver to see Arnold Rönnebeck, who had moved there.
Spent two weeks in August in Georgetown, Maine, with Paul and Rebecca Strand and Gaston and Isabel Lachaise.
Returned to Paris on August 20.
By December, began series of seashell still lifes.

1929 Stieglitz exhibited the Mont Sainte-Victoire landscapes and Parisian still lifes at his Intimate Gallery, New York, in January, 100 works in total, including works in oil, watercolor, silverpoint, and pencil.
Left Paris for Aix-en-Provence in spring.
Left for Paris, Hamburg, Berlin, and Dresden on November 21.

1930 Exhibited at Stieglitz's An American Place, New York: *Marsden Hartley—New Paintings—Landscapes—New Hampshire—Still Lifes—Paris and Aix-en-Provence.*
Returned to New York in March.
Spent summer in Sugar Hill, near Franconia, New Hampshire.
Painted New Hampshire landscapes, including *Franconia Notch* (plate 45).
Returned to New York in November.

1931 Received Guggenheim grant to paint for a year outside of the United States; decided to go to Mexico.
Spent summer in Gloucester, Massachusetts.
Began first series of Dogtown paintings, including *Mountains in Stone, Dogtown* (plate 46) and *Flaming Pool, Dogtown* (plate 47), set in Dogtown, a moraine on Cape Ann, near Gloucester.
Drawings include *Whale's Jaw Rock, Dogtown* (plate 48).
Returned to New York in December before leaving for Cleveland to spend Christmas with his family.

1932 Traveled to Mexico City in March.
Exhibition of Hartley's work at the Downtown Gallery, New York: *Pictures of New England by a New Englander: Recent Paintings of Dogtown, Cape Ann, Massachusetts.*
Hart Crane committed suicide on April 26.
Traveled to Cuernavaca, Mexico, in May.
Painted series of high-keyed, symbolic landscapes, including *Earth Cooling, Mexico* (plate 51), *Morgenrot* (plate 52), and *Popocatépetl, Spirited Morning—Mexico* (plate 53).
Returned to Mexico City in November.

1933 Solo exhibition at the Galeria de la Escuela Central de Artes Plasticas, Mexico City: *Exposicion Marsden Hartley.*

Painted *Eight Bells Folly, Memorial for Hart Crane* (plate 54).
Left Mexico for Germany in April.
Spent summer in Hamburg.
Moved to Garmisch-Partenkirchen in the Bavarian Alps in September or October.
Began a series of landscape paintings of the region, including *Waxenstein at Hamarsbach, Garmisch, Bavaria* (plate 55); lithographs; and drawings, including *Mountain Landscape, Church Steeple in Foreground* (plate 56), *Mountain Landscape with Pine Trees* (plate 57), and *Garmisch* (plate 58).
Wrote autobiography, *Somehow a Past,* in November and December.

1934 Returned to New York in February.
Employed by the federal government in the easel division of the Public Works of Art Project.
Spent much of the summer in Gloucester, Massachusetts.
Began second Dogtown series, including drawing *Untitled (Blueberry Patch)* (plate 49).
Painted *Sea View—New England* (plate 59).
Returned to New York in fall.

1935 Destroyed 100 paintings and drawings stored in a warehouse in order to consolidate and save storage fees.
Spent summer in Bermuda.
Painted Bermuda landscapes and bright gouaches and pastels of fish and flowers.
Traveled to Blue Rocks, Nova Scotia, in September.
Went on to Eastern Points, Nova Scotia, to live with Mason family in November.
Returned to New York in December.

1936 Employed by the Works Progress Administration from January to mid-May.
Exhibition at Stieglitz's An American Place: thirty paintings, including six panels "intended for use as focus motives in a convalescent pavilion," "four modern ikons for a wooden sea-chapel in the bitter north," and seven paintings from the New England series and seven Alpine views. *Flowers (Roses from Hispania)* (plate 60) is one of the "focus motives."
Returned to Eastern Points, Nova Scotia, in July to stay with the Masons.
Began third Dogtown series, including *The Old Bars, Dogtown* (plate 50), painted from memory, and painted still lifes of fishing-related subjects.
Two of the Mason boys and one of their cousins drowned at sea on September 19.
Painted dark, Ryderesque landscapes such as *Northern Seascape, Off the Banks* (plate 61).
Returned to New York in the winter.

1937 Last exhibition with Stieglitz at his gallery, An American Place, of recent paintings, primarily from Nova Scotia. Accompanying catalogue included essay by Hartley: "On the Subject of Nativeness—A Tribute to Maine."
Spent summer in Georgetown, Maine, and painted landscapes there.
Painted Smelt Brook Falls (plate 62).
Moved to Portland, Maine.

1938 Solo exhibition at the Hudson Walker Gallery, New York.
Began series of paintings of Vinalhaven, Maine.
Painted *Give Us This Day* (plate 63).
Began series of "archaic" portraits of the Masons from memory, including *Fishermen's*

Last Supper (plate 64), *Adelard the Drowned, Master of the "Phantom"* (plate 66), *Marie Ste. Esprit* (plate 67), and *Cleophas, Master of the "Gilda Grey"* (plate 68). Drawings include *Untitled (Three Men Standing Behind Two Women with Aprons)* (plate 65).
Painted archaic *Portrait of Albert Pinkham Ryder* (plate 71).
Traveled to Boston in mid-November.

1939 Returned to New York in February.
Solo exhibition at the Hudson Walker Gallery, New York.
Continued painting Mason portraits, including *The Lost Felice* (plate 69).
Returned to Portland, Maine, in June.
Moved to West Brookville, Maine, in July, and to Bangor, Maine, in September, where he taught painting at the Bangor Society of Art.
Took an eight-day trip to Mt. Katahdin in October.
Applied for a Guggenheim grant for writing, but was denied.
Began a series of paintings of Mt. Katahdin, including *Mount Katahdin, Autumn, No. 2* (plate 91) and *Mount Katahdin, Maine, First Snow, No. 1* (plate 92).
Painted self-portrait titled *Sustained Comedy* (plate 72) and a picture called *Flaming American (Swim-Champ)* (plate 75).
Drawings include *Untitled (Mt. Katahdin)* (plate 95).

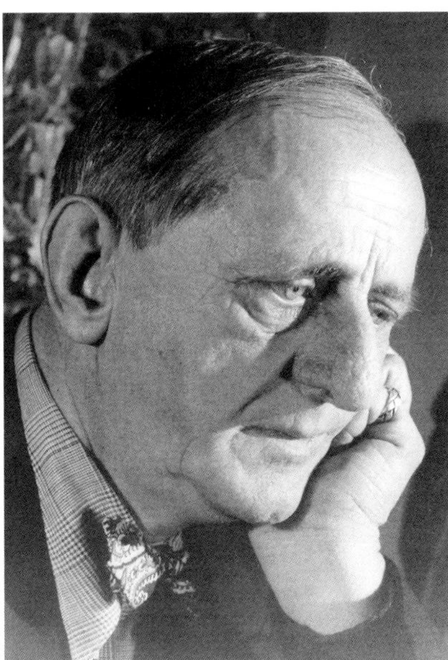

Alfred Valente
Marsden Hartley, 1940
Photograph
Archives of American Art, Smithsonian Institution, Washington, D.C.

1940 Returned to New York in the spring.
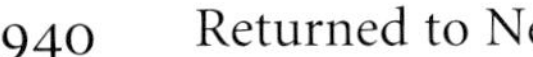
Exhibited for third and last time at the Hudson Walker Gallery, New York, before the gallery closed permanently: *Marsden Hartley: Recent Paintings of Maine.*
Traveled to Corea, Maine, in August, where he lived with Katie and Forest Young.
Began series of paintings of bathers, including *Canuck Yankee Lumberjack at Old Orchard Beach, Maine* (plate 81) and *On the Beach* (plate 82); of lobstermen, including *Down East Young Blades* (plate 85), *Lobster Fishermen* (plate 88); and of other male "types," including *Madawaska—Acadian Light-Heavy* (plate 76).
Drawings include *Untitled (Three Fishermen with Fish and Lobster)* (plate 83), *Down East Young Lobster Men* (plate 84), *Untitled (Six Lobstermen and Lobster Traps)* (plate 86), and *Study for "Lobster Fishermen"* (plate 87).
Began series of religious subjects, including *Christ Held by Half-Naked Men* (plate 80).
Drawings include *Untitled (Five Lobstermen and Christ Figure—Pietà Concept)* (plate 79).
Began series of Maine landscapes and seascapes, including *The Wave* (plate 96), *The Lighthouse* (plate 98), the drawing for *The Lighthouse* (plate 97), and the drawing *Church at Corea, Maine* (plate 90).
Painted *The Last Look of John Donne* (plate 77).
Published *Androscoggin,* a volume of poetry.

1941 Moved to Bangor, Maine, in January.
Returned to New York in March.
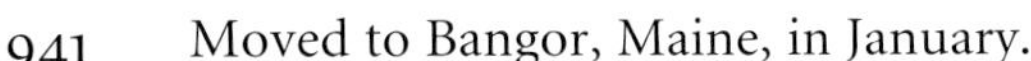
Began being represented by the Macbeth Gallery, New York.
Hudson Walker purchased twenty-three paintings from Hartley for $5,000.
Concentrated on writing poetry and essays.
Returned to Corea, Maine.
Painted still lifes with monochromatic backgrounds, including *Lobster on Black Background* (plate 101) and *Shells by the Sea* (plate 102).
Painted *Crow with Ribbons* (plate 100).

Began *Storm Down Pine Point Way, Old Orchard, Maine* (plate 105).
Published *Sea Burial,* a volume of poetry.
Traveled to Cincinnati for joint exhibition with Stuart Davis, and then on to Cleveland to spend Christmas with his family.

1942 Presented lecture titled "Is Art Necessary—What is Its Social Significance?" at the Cincinnati Art Museum in January.
Returned to New York.
Solo exhibition at Macbeth Gallery, New York.
Spent July through fall in Corea, Maine.
Paul Rosenberg became Hartley's dealer in August.
Began series of still lifes with landscape or seascape backgrounds, including *Sea Window—Tinker Mackerel* (plate 103) and *Summer, Sea, Window, Red Curtain* (plate 104).
Began landscape series, including *Hurricane Island, Vinalhaven, Maine* (plate 99), and a Mt. Katahdin series, including *Mount Katahdin* (plate 93) and *Blue Landscape* (plate 94).
Painted *The Great Good Man* (plate 78), his third portrait of Abraham Lincoln.
Received the Fourth Painting Purchase Prize in the exhibition *Artists for Victory* at the Metropolitan Museum of Art, New York.

1943 Returned to New York.
Solo exhibition at Paul Rosenberg Gallery, New York.
Painted in George Platt Lynes's photographic studio, and photographed by Lynes (Robertson figs. 9–10).
Returned to Corea, Maine, in July.
Painted *Roses* (plate 106).
Died of heart failure on September 2 in Ellsworth, Maine.

Abbreviations

Adventures — Marsden Hartley, *Adventures in the Arts* (New York: Boni and Liveright, 1921); reprinted as *Adventures in the Arts: Informal Chapters on Painters, Vaudeville, and Poets* (New York: Hacker Art Books, 1972).

Archives/Smithsonian — Archives of American Art, Smithsonian Institution, Washington, D.C. (Marsden Hartley Papers; Rockwell Kent Papers; Elizabeth McCausland Papers; Carl Sprinchorn Papers; Helen Stein Papers; Hudson Walker Papers)

Autobiography — Marsden Hartley, *Somehow a Past: The Autobiography of Marsden Hartley,* ed. Susan Elizabeth Ryan (Cambridge: MIT Press, 1997).

Beinecke/Yale — Yale Collection of American Literature, Beinecke Rare Book and Manuscript Library, Yale University, New Haven (Norma Berger Papers; Marsden Hartley Papers; Gertrude Stein/Alice B. Toklas Papers; Alfred Stieglitz/Georgia O'Keeffe Archive. All are cross-referenced under Hartley.)

Collected Poems — Marsden Hartley, *The Collected Poems of Marsden Hartley, 1904–1943,* ed. Gail R. Scott (Santa Rosa, Calif.: Black Sparrow Press, 1987).

Ferguson — Gerald Ferguson, ed., *Marsden Hartley and Nova Scotia,* (Halifax: Mount Saint Vincent University Art Gallery, in association with the Press of the Nova Scotia College of Art and Design, and the Art Gallery of Ontario, 1987).

Greenough — Sarah Greenough, et al., *Modern Art and America: Alfred Stieglitz and His New York Galleries* (Washington, D.C.: National Gallery of Art in association with Bulfinch Press, 2000).

Haskell — Barbara Haskell, *Marsden Hartley* (New York: Whitney Museum of American Art, 1980).

Hokin — Jeanne Hokin, *Pinnacles and Pyramids: The Art of Marsden Hartley* (Albuquerque: University of New Mexico Press, 1993).

Ludington — Townsend Ludington, *Marsden Hartley: The Biography of an American Artist* (Boston: Little, Brown, 1992); rev. ed. (Ithaca: Cornell University Press, 1998).

On Art — Marsden Hartley, *On Art,* ed. Gail R. Scott (New York: Horizon Press, 1982).

Robertson — Bruce Robertson, *Marsden Hartley* (New York: Harry N. Abrams in association with the National Museum of American Art, Smithsonian Institution, 1995).

Scott — Gail R. Scott, *Marsden Hartley* (New York: Abbeville Press, 1988).

Weinberg — Jonathan Weinberg, *Speaking for Vice: Homosexuality in the Art of Charles Demuth, Marsden Hartley, and the First American Avant-Garde* (New Haven and London: Yale University Press, 1993).

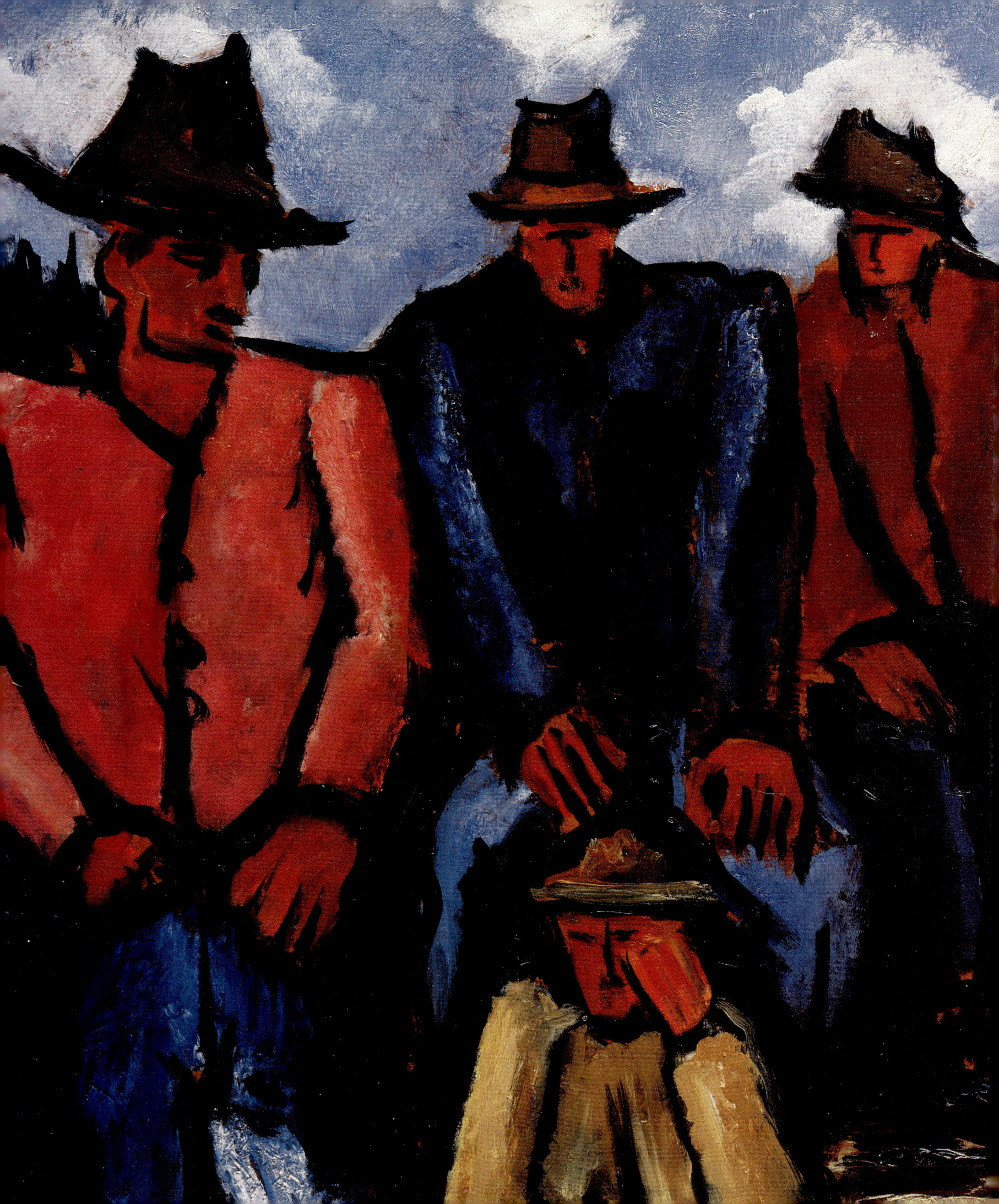

Marsden Hartley: "Gaunt Eagle from the Hills of Maine"

Elizabeth Mankin Kornhauser

Hartley was a sensation in Berlin before the last World War with the prescience of his wild canvasses. He is a new sensation today for those with eyes who will see here another, broader and deeper prescience, full of late courage and passion, of the sort of love that's not easy to kill or to understand either for that matter—lying at the base and under a shaken but unmoved world.[1]

William Carlos Williams, 1940

A friend and fellow writer, William Carlos Williams understood and admired the "prescience" of Marsden Hartley's art across his entire career.[2] In general, however, Hartley was never widely understood or properly recognized in his lifetime. As a modern artist, he was certainly not alone in this. Additionally, the complexity of his life and the times in which he lived influenced the reception of his art. Historic events more than once eclipsed his emergence as a leading modern artist. An American public possessed by growing anti-German sentiment first viewed Hartley's greatest early achievement—the "wild canvasses" of pre-war and wartime Berlin—in 1916 as war raged in Europe. While they were favorably received by a cadre of critics and artists, the public perceived them as pro-German in character, which overshadowed their critical reception for decades. Hartley's inability to return to Germany during the war to pursue this series (the United States entered the war in 1917) dealt a major blow to his career. He would spend the next decade and a half working his way back to a second great breakthrough, although with many high points along the way. His later primitivist depictions of his native New England, "full of late courage and passion," were unique and personal responses by this American artist to the Depression of the 1930s and the approach of a second world war. While Hartley gained stature and some commercial success with these paintings, their significance and meaning remained elusive. Accounts written by those who did not begin to understand the broad scope, complexity, and veiled meanings of his art continued to obscure the importance of his contributions to modernism. He was celebrated during his lifetime, however, but only among an international coterie of artists and intellectuals, as a painter of great visual strength and originality.

Hartley was a member of the group of artists that the photographer and dealer Alfred Stieglitz took under his wing in the first decades of the century. This group included Charles Demuth, Arthur Dove, John Marin, Georgia O'Keeffe, and Paul Strand, and they collaborated with Stieglitz to promote American modernism. Stieglitz offered Hartley his first solo exhibition in 1909 in New York City. Hartley's connection to Stieglitz was a

Detail, Plate 88

fortuitous one that introduced the young artist to European modernism. His exposure to the art of Matisse, Picasso, and Cézanne, among others, influenced Hartley's own work and soon spurred him to travel to Europe where, through Stieglitz and others, he gained access to the leading salons including that of Gertrude Stein.

Despite his obvious ambition and talent, Hartley was often on the periphery of the Stieglitz circle, set apart from the others by virtue of his pronounced admiration for European artists, his constant travel, including spending critical portions of his career in Paris and Berlin, and his penchant for experimentation. He continually sought new inspiration for his art in various regions in the United States, France, Germany, Mexico, and Canada. The sheer number of geographic locales and artistic directions revealed in his paintings was not perceived favorably at the time, and his reputation suffered. In the post–World War I mood of isolationism, Hartley's constant allusions to foreign places went against the grain. Continually traveling until his final return to Maine in 1937, Hartley's working habits, so unlike those of Dove, Marin, and O'Keeffe, who rooted themselves and their art in specific regional American landscapes, appeared to call into question his commitment to Stieglitz's modernist project. Stieglitz, who was able to promote his other American artists as "naturals" who arose from the American soil, faced a far more difficult challenge with Hartley. Furthermore, as Marcia Brennan has demonstrated, the circle of writers and critics around Stieglitz who became powerful proselytizers for his modernist agenda, including Paul Rosenfeld and Waldo Frank, "routinely interpreted Hartley's travels as a sign of the artist's own rootlessness, restlessness, and, more darkly, his personal sense of incompletion."[3] Because he was drawn to experimentation, and his art evolved and changed in ways that were difficult to categorize at the time, he posed a dilemma for his critics.

Hartley remains best known for his early German abstract paintings, specifically the War Motif series that he began in 1914, with a singular focus on one masterwork, *Portrait of a German Officer* (plate 19). He is also celebrated for his late Maine landscapes, begun in 1939. This exhibition explores these high points but takes issue with the assumption that what came in between is of less consequence. His entire artistic output warrants a comprehensive examination to appreciate fully Hartley's contributions to modern art, and to provide greater clarity of understanding for all of his work. More often than not, within his travels and aesthetic explorations, Hartley sought and achieved originality, compounding and expanding his knowledge as he moved to new subject matter and styles, navigating between abstraction and realism. As the works in this exhibition reflect, in addition to the acknowledged cornerstones that flank his career, Hartley consistently achieved remarkable single works and new series within each of the four decades of his career. Persistent themes, ranging from mysticism and spirituality to desire and death, and subjects ranging from mountains to masked self-portraits, can be traced throughout his career.

While frequently portrayed as the painter from Maine, he was in fact a cosmopolitan artist, returning again and again to New York to re-engage with his dealers, clients, fellow artists and writers. But at the same time, in keeping with the Stieglitz circle's spiritual and sensual approach to nature, he renewed himself through his love of the natural world. Hartley expressed it this way: "The inherent magic in the appearance of the world about me, engrossed and amazed me. No cloud or blossom or bird or human ever escaped me."[4] His life began and ended in Maine, and in between he lived in New York; Paris; Berlin; Provincetown, Massachusetts; Taos, New Mexico; various locales in France and Germany; Mexico; Gloucester, Massachusetts; and Blue Rocks, Nova Scotia. In each of these regions, Hartley found new inspiration for his paintings and his writings. With the benefit of hindsight, this exhibition and catalogue stake a claim for Hartley in the pantheon of leading modernists and seek to broaden audience familiarity with his art.

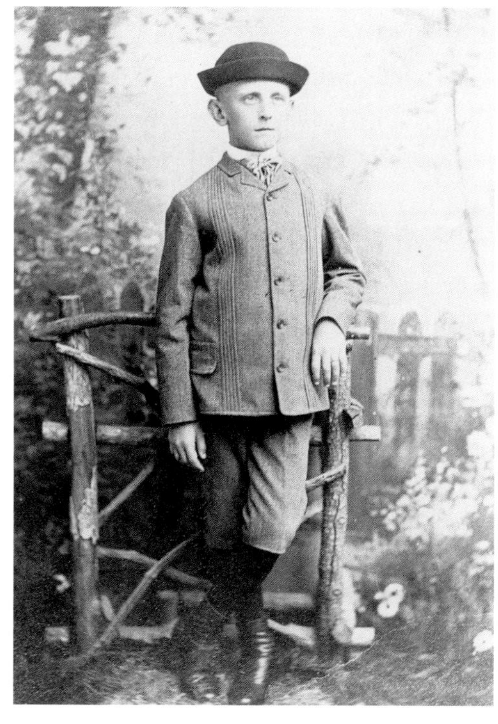

Figure 1
Unknown Photographer
Edmund (Marsden) Hartley, age 7 years
Marsden Hartley Memorial Collection
© Bates College Museum of Art, Lewiston, Maine

Figure 2
Unknown Photographer
Marsden Hartley on the banks of the Androscoggin River, Lewiston, c. 1910
Marsden Hartley Memorial Collection
© 1998 Bates College Museum of Art, Lewiston, Maine

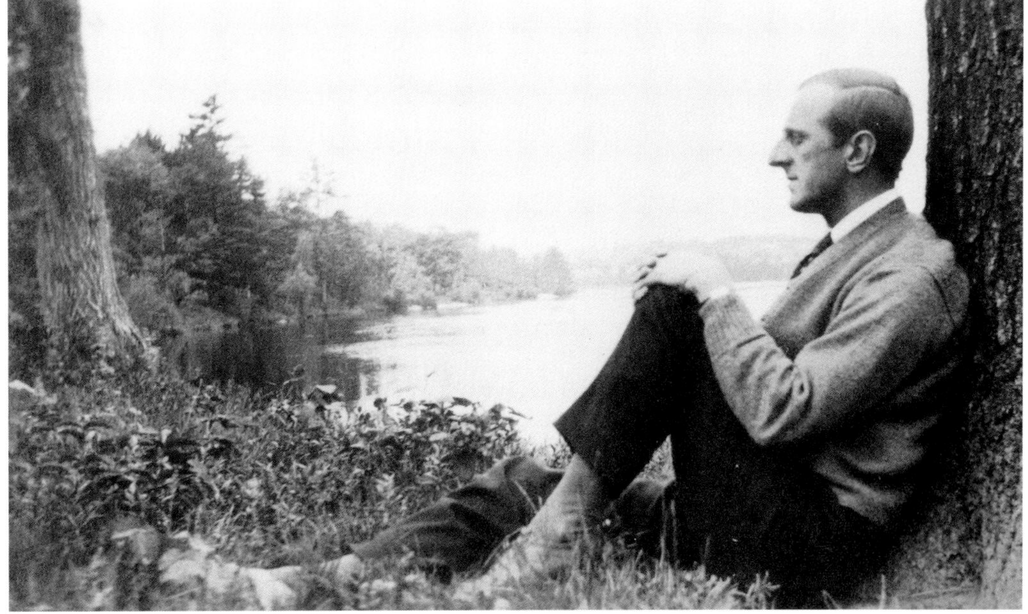

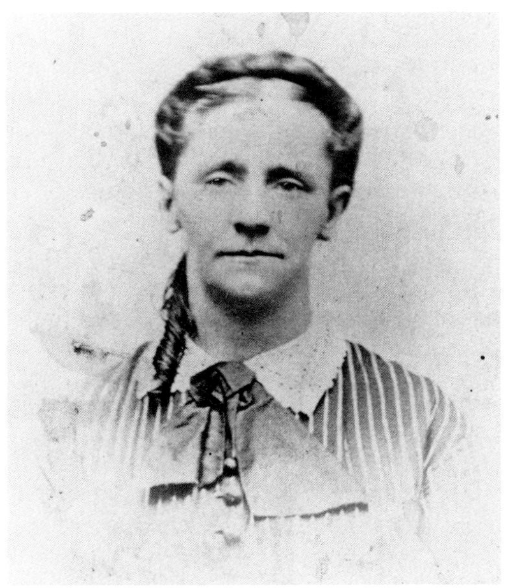

Figure 3
Unknown Photographer
Eliza Jane Horbury (Hartley's mother), c. 1880
Yale Collection of American Literature
Beinecke Rare Book and Manuscript Library
Yale University, New Haven

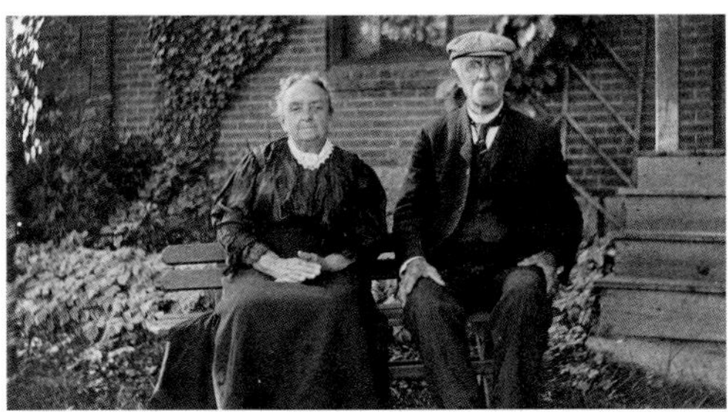

Figure 4
Unknown Photographer
Martha Marsden Hartley (stepmother) and Thomas Hartley (father), c. 1900
Yale Collection of American Literature
Beinecke Rare Book and Manuscript Library
Yale University, New Haven

Biography

Hartley was born in Lewiston, Maine, in 1877 to English immigrant parents. The hardships of his childhood spent in this inland mill town, hours from the coast, gave him a legitimate claim to a true Yankee heritage that was quite different from that of the artists he would compete with later in his career, the painters of New England and Maine, including Winslow Homer, John Marin, and Carl Sprinchorn. It would also inspire in him a fierce desire to overcome his provincial roots through self-education and the pursuit of an intellectual life.

Christened Edmund, he was the youngest of eight children, later remembering himself as "the most obstreperous, spiritually speaking, the last and least found, the most troubled."[5] Growing up amidst the "harsh grinding of the mills," Hartley also recalled the soothing sound of "the running of the water over the stones" of the Great Falls of the Androscoggin River that ran through Lewiston (fig. 2).[6] His father worked in the cotton mills and later posted bills for the local theater, which was run by his brother-in-law. Hartley would later describe his mother in his autobiography as the "last of a long line of sturdy, simple people," a type he greatly admired and would incorporate into his late paintings of the Mason family of Nova Scotia, and other Maine down east types (fig. 3).[7] Despite the hardships of his surroundings, Hartley's lifelong fascination with the circus, as well as theater, opera, and parades of all sorts, was engendered in Lewiston through his exposure to the town theater; as he later admitted, "I am as all my life have been a parade hound."[8]

In 1885, when he was eight, Hartley's mother died. At the end of his life he wrote, somewhat melodramatically, "I was to know complete isolation from that moment forward" (fig. 1).[9] Four years later, his father remarried and moved with his bride to Ohio, leaving his youngest child behind with an older sister. Hartley's sense of isolation fed his artistic disposition, and as a lonely child, he turned to nature for companionship, establishing a lasting pattern of retreating to the healing solitude of the natural world to escape the hardship and uncertainties of life.

Despite the upheaval caused by these early events, he remained close to his family throughout his lifetime. While living for eight years with his older sister Elizabeth in Auburn, Maine, he left school at the age of fifteen to work in a shoe factory. In 1893 Hartley moved to Cleveland, Ohio, to join his father and second wife, Martha Marsden (whose name he later adopted and which would eventually replace his given name, Edmund), and there he began art lessons (fig. 4).

Jonathan Weinberg has observed that "the instability of Hartley's childhood and his sense of repeated abandonment were played out when he matured," evident in the fact that he never stayed in one place for more than a year or two, establishing a peripatetic pattern he would follow for the rest of his life. While "he often found himself separated from family, lovers, and friends by untimely deaths," he just as often "severed relationships through his own restlessness. He was always leaving town in hopes of finding a place that was more conducive to his art and life."[10]

Hartley first pursued his artistic career at the Cleveland School of Art. There he was given a copy of Ralph Waldo Emerson's *Essays,* which he read in search of religious and spiritual inspiration. Emerson's transcendentalism struck a chord with this struggling young artist who had begun to commune with nature as a boy in the pastures and woods around Lewiston. Hartley's predisposition toward the search for spiritual truth, first evidenced in his youth, became a lifelong pursuit and influenced his painting and writing. Hartley moved to New York City, where in 1899 he began classes at the New York School of Art run by William Merritt Chase. Many other modernists, including Charles Sheeler, Georgia O'Keeffe, and Morton Schamberg, began their careers at one of the many art schools run by Chase. Hartley transferred to the National Academy of Design where he first met fellow students and future modernists Abraham Walkowitz and Maurice Sterne and was impressed by the landscape paintings of John Twachtman and George Inness.

It was in New York that Hartley began to find his way as an artist and a man. As he later recalled: "I began somehow to have curiosity about art at the time when sex consciousness is fully developed and as I did not incline to concrete escapades, I of course inclined to abstract ones, and the collection of objects which is a sex expression took the upper hand."[11] Hartley funneled his sexual/creative energy into aesthetic pursuits. His personal effects, now at Bates College in Lewiston, attest to his desire to collect beautiful and meaningful objects that despite his transient lifestyle were carefully preserved.

In the early years in New York, Hartley could be found at Kriel's Bakery, where he was allowed to eat for free along with other impoverished artists and writers. One of these, Alfred Kreymborg, who met Hartley around 1903, provided an insightful description of the young artist at this time, dressed as a dandy, and cultivating the aura of an intellectual:

> *When spring came, if he could afford nothing else, Marsden managed to buy a gardenia for his buttonhole. The others thought him a snob; his ways were so superior; his devotion to William Blake and Francis Thompson seemed a little mad; and his exquisite tastes, the exotic longing he had for warm, and precious stones, aggravated the impression. These predilections and starved mystical obsessions tended to give him a place apart. And he wrapped his coat like a toga about his spare form, held his extraordinary nose in the air, used his aristocratic cough as a warning not to come too close. But his friends learned to know Marsden better before many years elapsed. Among them all, he was easily the loneliest.... None of the young men ever froze so bitterly, or looked as frozen as the eagle from the state of Maine.*[12]

He would later assume for himself the form of an eagle in his painting *Indian Fantasy* (plate 16) and in a poem he wrote in the late 1920s (as related in the essay by Wanda Corn); and in an obituary for the artist, Paul Rosenfeld described Hartley as the "gaunt eagle from the hills of Maine."[13]

While in New York, Hartley found inspiration in the poetry of Walt Whitman and was encouraged in his study of the poetry by Whitman's greatest champion, Horace Traubel, who befriended Hartley and offered him support. The artist was drawn to Whitman's ideas of manly camaraderie and sexual intimacy, paying homage to his muse in an early view of Whitman's house in Camden, New Jersey (plate 1; discussed in the essay by Jonathan Weinberg). From this time forward, Hartley mingled an impressive array of artistic and literary influences in his art. His extensive personal library, now housed at Bates College, is a testament to the broad reach of his intellectual curiosity. The approximately 180 books, many inscribed by Hartley, include volumes of poetry, philosophy, literature, religion, art, military and circus history, travel, and music.[14]

In the summer and fall of 1907, at the suggestion of Thomas Moser, the publisher and Whitman disciple, Hartley worked at Green Acre in Eliot, Maine, a utopian religious community where he was exposed to a world of theosophical mysticism, including discourse among the artists, theologians, and mystics that he encountered there. This rural retreat was founded by Sarah Farmer, a member of a New England transcendentalist family, and it eventually became a center for the Bahai World Faith. Green Acre attracted a number of artists including Arthur Dow, the teacher of Georgia O'Keeffe and Max Weber, and later, Mark Tobey, who shared Hartley's interest in spiritualism.[15] He continued to explore mysticism in France, Germany, and Mexico, where he pursued his readings and began incorporating mystical signs and symbols in his art.

Hartley came of age as an artist at the very beginning of the twentieth century and rapidly identified himself with the modernist movement. An early moment in his exposure to European modernism took place in 1903 when he discovered the Segantini "stitch," an overlapping and interweaving of small, brightly colored strokes of paint distinctive to the works of the contemporary Italian painter Giovanni Segantini, reproduced in the January 1903 issue of *Jugend.*

Three years later, at age twenty-nine, Hartley formally announced himself as an artist, with cards that stated his newly adopted name: Edmund Marsden Hartley (he dropped Edmund in 1908). In the fall of that year, with Emerson, Thoreau, and Whitman as inspiration, he pursued his interest in nature and landscape painting by returning to his native state to establish a studio in Lewiston. Hartley also sought isolated regions in the Stoneham Valley near North Lovell, where he lived in a desolate, abandoned shack in order to develop his artistic vision as a landscape painter. He executed his first accomplished works, employing a neo-impressionist style in his landscapes of mountains and overhanging cloud forms (see plates 2–3), which became a favorite subject for his art for the rest of his career. The subject matter and "stitch" technique of these works show Hartley's adaptation of the brushwork of Segantini, whom he later recalled as "the only artist who has ever put a mountain spirit on canvas."[16] His commitment to the decorative quality of overall surface pattern was also influenced by the Japanese prints he had been interested in while a student, and several examples hung in his Lewiston studio. Many of the titles of his landscapes at this time evoke music and mystical experiences, such as *Cosmos* (1908–9; Columbus Museum of Art) and *Hall of the Mountain King* (fig. 5). In his landscapes, he favored the winter season—"I think nature is never quite so dramatic as when she is bared to the brow and shows her face in sturdy acceptance of the coming cold and dreariness"—seen in such bold paintings as *Winter Chaos, Blizzard* (fig. 6).[17]

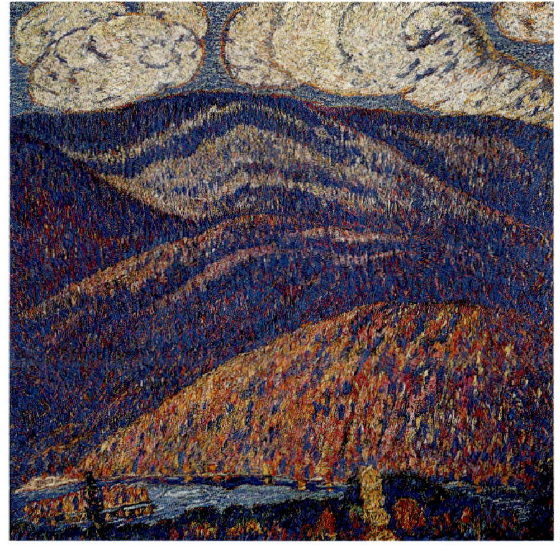

Figure 5
Marsden Hartley
Hall of the Mountain King, 1908–9
Oil on canvas, 30 × 30 in. (76.2 × 76.2 cm)
Private Collection

From this remote area in inland Maine, Hartley established a pattern of seeking unconventional regions for his artistic subjects: Berlin rather than New York or Paris; Dogtown rather than Gloucester, Massachusetts; and Cape Breton, Canada, and Corea, Maine, rather than the popular tourist centers along the Maine coast. Hartley also produced a series of self-portrait drawings (plate 5) in the winter of 1908–9, while living in the bleak surroundings of North Lovell. In nervous, wiry strokes, he began to explore his own self-image (as discussed in the essay by Bruce Robertson).

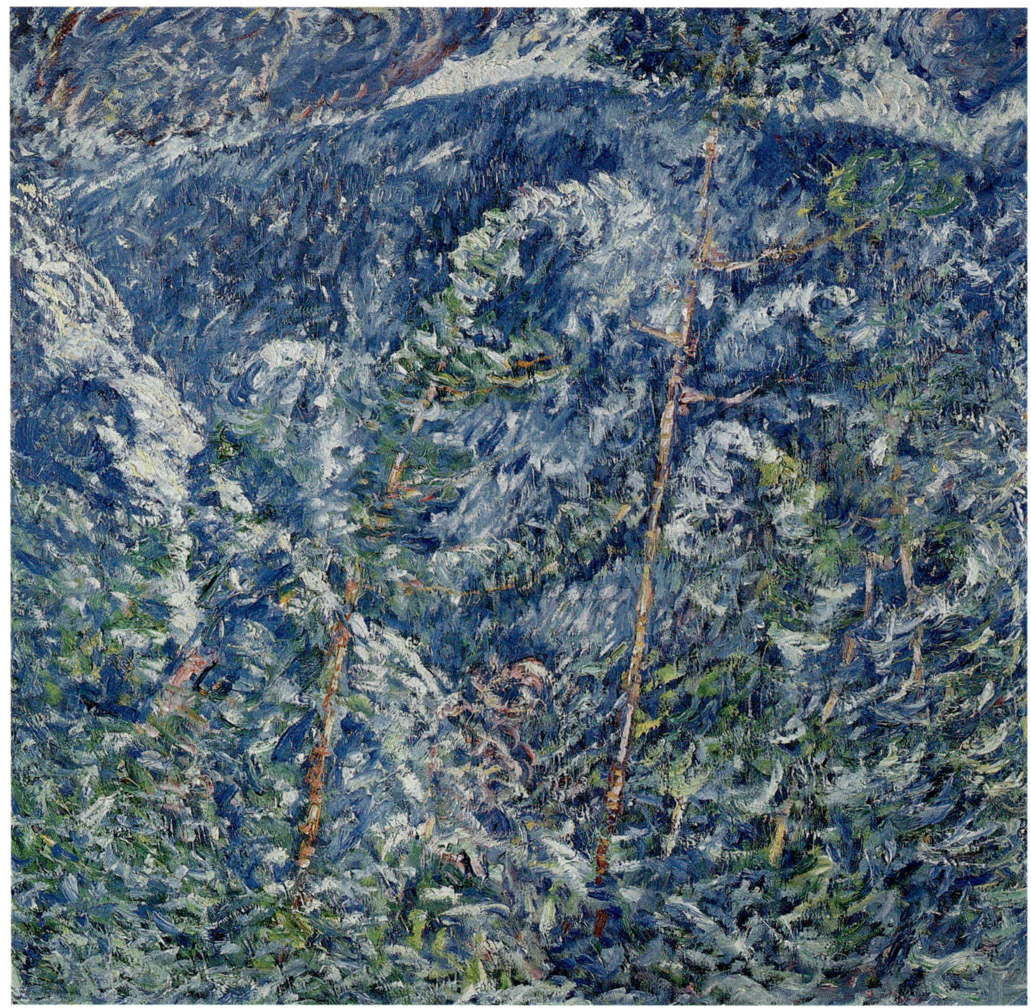

Figure 6
Marsden Hartley
Winter Chaos, Blizzard, 1909–11
Oil on canvas, 35½ × 35½ in. (90.2 × 90.2 cm)
Philadelphia Museum of Art
The Alfred Stieglitz Collection

In 1909 Hartley returned to New York and was introduced by the poet Shaemas O'Sheel to the most magnetic arts figure in America, Alfred Stieglitz, who, only days after seeing Hartley's daring landscapes, offered him an exhibition at his gallery 291. Thus began a lifelong relationship between the two men that, while often strained, was based on respect and admiration.[18] Stieglitz accelerated Hartley's swift turn toward modernism, and he would support Hartley for thirty years as his dealer, friend, and intellectual sounding board. As Hartley explained to his niece Norma Berger in 1911, "[Mr. Stieglitz] owns and operates the little gallery where I exhibited my pictures.... I don't attempt to exhibit my work elsewhere as I belong to the school of 'modernists' as they call them—and am considered a little unusual—a little different—or to say—individual in my work."[19] He reveals an artistic ambition to single himself out among the avant-garde of his time (fig. 7).

After viewing Hartley's landscapes at 291, the dealer N. E. Montross felt that Hartley should see the work of the visionary American painter Albert Pinkham Ryder. The painting, *Moonlight Marine* (fig. 8), that Hartley saw at this time had a profound impact: "It was a picture that so affected me that I in all truth was never the same after the first moment," he later wrote. "I was a convert to the field of imagination into which I was born. I had been thrown back into the body and being of my own country as by no other influence that had come to me."[20] Hartley's series of so-called Black or Dark Landscapes, such as Deserted Farm (plate 6), which Stieglitz exhibited at gallery 291 in the 1910 *Younger American Painters* exhibition, shows Ryder's influence on Hartley's art. He later paid tribute to his mentor by painting his portrait from memory in 1938 (plate 71). By 1911, after Stieglitz sent him several photographs of still-life paintings by Cézanne, Hartley abandoned landscape and

Figure 7
Unknown Photographer
A group of young American artists of the modern school, 1911
Back row, left to right: Marsden Hartley, Lawrence Fellows, John Marin;
Front row: Jo Davidson, Edward Steichen, Authur B. Carles
Marsden Hartley Memorial Collection
© Bates College Museum of Art, Lewiston, Maine

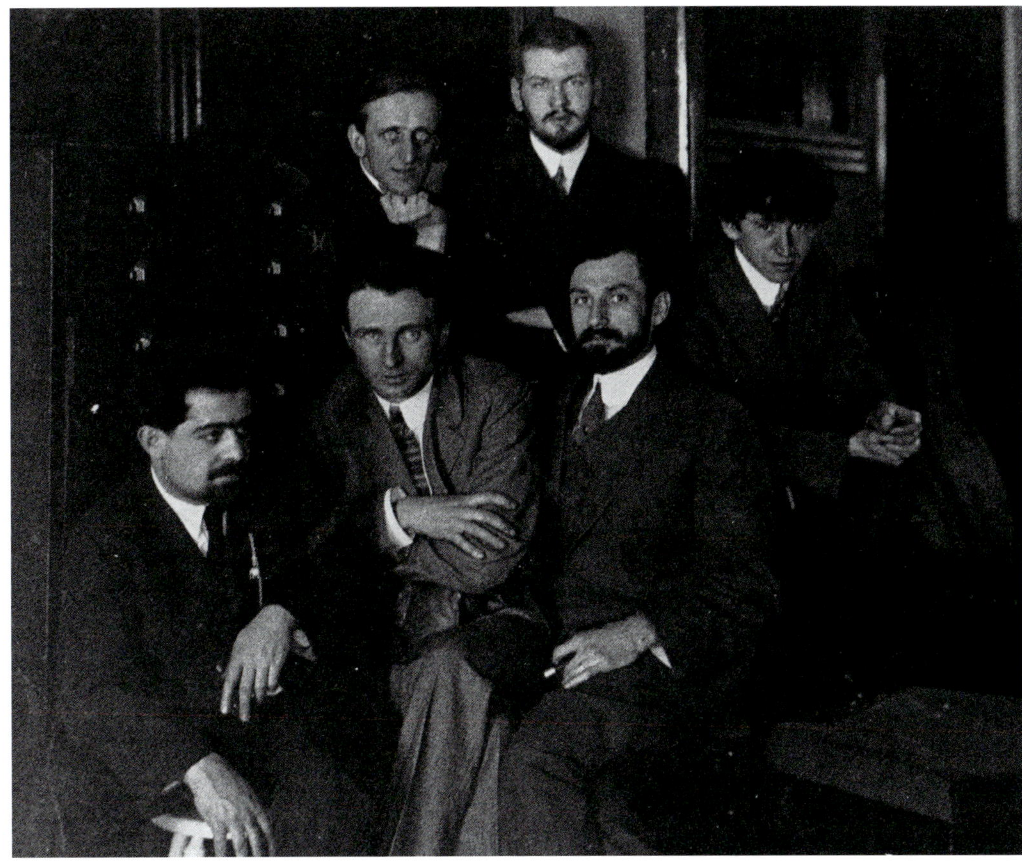

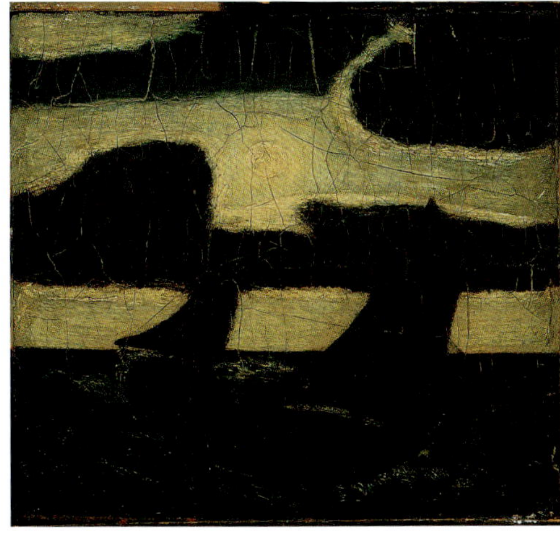

Figure 8
Albert Pinkham Ryder
Moonlight Marine, probably 1870s or 1880s
Oil on possibly wax on wood, 11½ × 12 in. (29.2 × 30.5 cm)
The Metropolitan Museum of Art, New York
Samuel D. Lee Fund, 1934 (34.55)
Photograph © 1980
The Metropolitan Museum of Art

produced a number of monochromatic still lifes of fruit, for example *Pears* (1911; Frederick R. Weisman Art Museum, University of Minnesota, Minneapolis).

With Stieglitz and his gallery 291 at the center, Hartley participated in the debate that led to revolutionary ideas about art in the twentieth century concerning, as Sarah Greenough has suggested, "the interrelationships between painting, sculpture, photography, and music; about abstraction versus realism; about Western versus non-Western art; about art by men versus women and art by children; about European versus American art; about the role of commerce and commercialism in art; and about the function of the machine and the place of nature in the modern age."[21] Hartley's understanding of modern art grew through his exposure to the exhibitions held by Stieglitz at 291 where he viewed works by Cézanne, Matisse, Rodin, and Picasso, as well as photographs by Stieglitz, Paul Strand, and others. He participated in important theoretical discussions in which the artists and critics connected to Stieglitz formulated a critical vocabulary for the new work. They promoted, for example, the idea of equivalence: Marius de Zayas asserted in his 1911 essay on Picasso that the artist "receives a direct impression from external nature," which he analyzes, develops, and translates "with the intention that the picture should be the pictorial equivalent of the emotion produced by nature."[22] Furthermore, as Stieglitz and others around him defined what they had come to call "the idea of photography," Hartley saw the ways in which the camera compressed space and stacked planes one on top of another. Stieglitz succeeded in placing photography at the very center of the evolving discourse on modernism. Gail Levin has explored the importance of photography in Hartley's creative process, including the fact that he took photographs with his own camera and often used these or photographs taken by others as tools for his painting process throughout his career (see plates 78, 88, 96, 98).[23] He revealed a great deal about his involvement with the medium in his essay "The Appeal of Photography," which appeared in his first book, *Adventures in the Arts,* writing, "I have always said for myself that the Kodak offers me the best substitute for the picture of

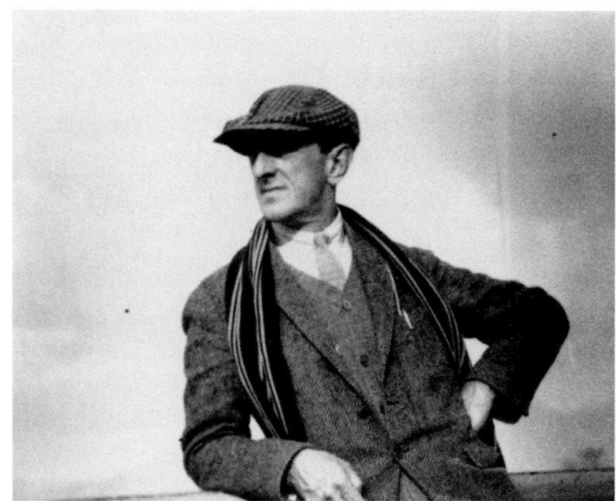

Figure 9
Unknown Photographer
Hartley on board ship: "First Trip Abroad," 1912
Yale Collection of American Literature
Beinecke Rare Book and Manuscript Library
Yale University, New Haven

life, that I have found. I find the snapshot, almost without exception, holding my interest for what it contains of single registration of and adherence to facts for themselves."[24] Hartley was present during the most intense years of activity at 291, preparing him for his direct exposure to European modernism upon his arrival in Paris in 1912 (fig. 9).

Paris and Berlin, April 1912–December 1915

With contacts and financial support provided by Stieglitz, Hartley quickly became a frequent visitor at the famous salon of Gertrude Stein, 27 rue de Fleurus, where he viewed the latest Parisian art. He recalled seeing the walls filled with paintings by Picasso and Matisse: "they seemed to burn my head off—I felt indeed like a severed head living off itself by mystical excitation" (fig. 10).[25] In Paris he was befriended by two Germans, Arnold Rönnebeck and Karl von Freyburg, who introduced him to the recently published book by Wassily Kandinsky, *On the Spiritual in Art,* and to *Der Blaue Reiter,* the almanac produced by the German expressionists centered in Munich, including Kandinsky and Franz Marc. Hartley began to explore cosmic cubism in his work, what he termed "intuitive abstractions," and continued to read broadly, from William James and the philosopher Henri Bergson to the medieval mystic Jakob Böhme. But he never felt at ease in Paris and was soon drawn to Germany, writing to Stieglitz, "It is with Germans I have always found myself both in New York and Paris—and now it is in Germany that I find my creative conditions—and it is there I must go."[26] After an initial trip in 1912, he returned in the spring of 1913, where he remained until December 1915, when the escalation of World War I forced him to leave Berlin.

During this period, Hartley produced a powerful and original body of work (discussed in the next two essays). These paintings gained him recognition and approval from his German colleagues, who encouraged him to exhibit his work alongside their own. In October he was one of only a few Americans included in the largest avant-garde exhibition in Berlin (the others were Patrick Henry Bruce, Lyonel Feininger, and Albert Bloch), with five of his paintings hung near works by Kandinsky and Henri Rousseau. In such paintings as the 1913 *Military* (plate 12), Hartley employed a near-abstract language that celebrated his infatuation with German soldiers, reducing their representation and paraphernalia to a complex of triangles, circles, and mystical symbols and numbers. After heeding Stieglitz's pleas for him to return to New York in order to raise money with exhibitions at 291 and elsewhere, Hartley returned to Berlin and began his series based on Native American objects and designs. Painted for a German audience, the series became known as his Amerika paintings. These were followed by the renowned War Motif series that he began painting in response to the news that his friend and possible lover Karl von Freyburg had been killed in battle on October 7, 1914. He began with a group of charcoal drawings (plate 18) that depict elements of a German officer's uniform—a sleeve and epaulets—in an abstract pattern that led him to the larger oils. These paintings serve as memorials to a modern hero—von Freyburg, whom Hartley later described as "the one idol of my imaginative life."[27] *Portrait of a German Officer* is considered the first in the series and, significantly, is Hartley's largest painting.[28] In this work, pictorial elements are assembled on the tall narrow canvas to form the headless body of von Freyburg. In the works that followed, such as *Painting No. 47, Berlin* (plate 20), the size of the canvas becomes smaller, and the elements form a portrait of von Freyburg's head. The final works in the series are executed in a square format of more generalized military symbols and forms. Two years later, Hartley began a writing project entitled "Letters Never Sent," originally titled "Letters to the Dead," and included one written to von Freyburg, which serves, as Jonathan Weinberg has suggested, as a verbal equivalent of the portraits.[29]

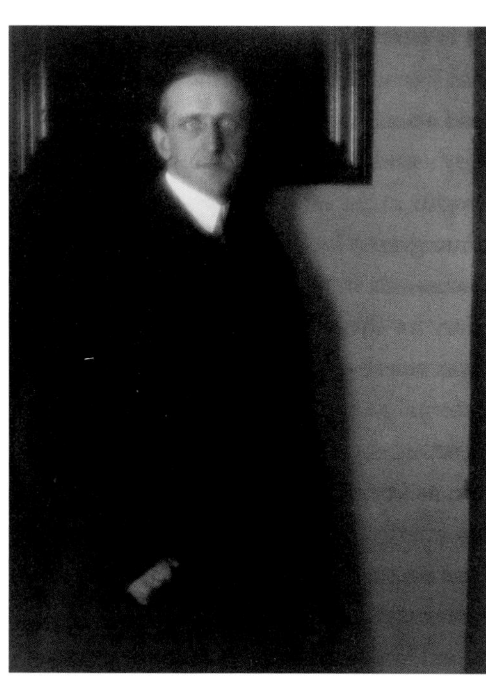

Figure 10
Unknown Photographer
Marsden Hartley, c. 1912
Yale Collection of American Literature
Beinecke Rare Book and Manuscript Library
Yale University, New Haven

As his grief began to subside, Hartley returned to his earlier pre-war Berlin and Amerika paintings in preparation for an exhibition. In October 1915, in an atmosphere of growing tension between the United States and Germany, Hartley had the only major solo exhibition of his art in Europe, with forty-five paintings and drawings on display at the prestigious Münchener Graphik-Verlag in Berlin. In the "Artist's Prologue" to a pamphlet for the show, Hartley moved to allay suspicions that these works held covert references to the war in Europe, writing, "Pictures that I exhibit are without titles and without description. They describe themselves."[30] This statement was expanded by Hartley to accompany the exhibition held at Stieglitz's 291 gallery in April 1916:

> *The Germanic group is but part of a series which I had contemplated of movements in various areas of war activity from which I was prevented, owing to the difficulties of travel. The forms are only those which I have observed casually from day to day. There is no hidden symbolism whatsoever in them; there is no slight intention of that anywhere. Things under observation, just pictures of any day, any hour. I have expressed only what I have seen. They are merely consultations of the eye—in no sense problem; my notion of the purely pictorial.*[31]

One American critic at the Berlin show wrote a supportive review entitled "American Artist Astounds Germans: Marsden Hartley's Exhibition in Berlin Surprises, Pains, and Amuses" in which he speculated about Hartley's pro-German sympathies, including the possibility that the paintings were celebratory images of the German military. In the end, he remained non-committal, suggesting that Hartley was likely neutral, or may, as some thought, have even intended to satirize the Germans: "there was here and there just a suspicion that these critics thought German battles were being ridiculed."[32] But as Jonathan Weinberg has noted in a discussion of Hartley's pro-German stance, as seen in the War Motif series: "Hartley's officer is a hero who is killed fighting for the fatherland, and Hartley's painting, for all its modernist form, is part of the tradition of military memorials."[33] While Hartley was politically naïve and surely abhorred the horrors of war, he felt a strong affinity for Germany that he expressed in a letter to Stieglitz in 1915: "I have achieved a nearness to the primal intention of things never before accomplished by me. The Germans have helped me to this—therefore I am loyal."[34]

New York, Provincetown, Bermuda, and Ogunquit, 1916–1917

Hartley's return to New York City in December 1915 was devastating in many respects. He was forced to abandon his German abstractions, and he suffered the loss of his growing European career and the admiration of his German colleagues. Considered to be the most audacious American artist of his generation in Europe, he now found himself on uncertain ground, facing an American audience that did not share his admiration for German art and culture. While continuing to mourn the death of von Freyburg, he had also lost his father, who died in August 1914, and his stepmother, who died the following May. The exhibition of his German paintings at 291 generated tepid reviews and few sales. The four paintings that did sell went to prestigious buyers, however: Arthur B. Davies, John Quinn, Paul Rosenberg, and Mabel Dodge (Luhan). Stieglitz, who had willingly taken the risk of showing Hartley's German paintings at this time and who shared Hartley's admiration for German culture, later recalled: "Much of the enthusiasm that had existed at 291 gradually disappeared because of the war. Close friends seemed to fall by the wayside. I could not turn 291 into a political institution, nor could I see Germany as all wrong and the Allies as all right. The work going on at the gallery, I felt, was universal."[35]

In search of a new direction and in an effort to find an American audience, Hartley, in a deliberate attempt to distance himself from the German methods and subjects with which he was currently too-closely associated, looked to Paris to inform his style. In particular, the formal abstraction seen in Picasso's latest paintings inspired Hartley's art. He likely saw in New York several of these in an exhibition held at Marius de Zayas's Modern Gallery during December 1915.[36] Hartley painted some of his most daring, abstract works in Provincetown, Massachusetts, in the summer of 1916, which he called his Movement series (discussed in the essay by Amy Ellis). "I want my work in both writing and painting to have that special coolness, for I weary of emotional excitement in art, weary of episode, of legend and of special histories," he wrote to his friend and fellow artist Carl Sprinchorn.[37]

Hartley continued his pattern of following prominent patrons and of traveling to the various colonies established by New York artists. He did not remain in one place for long, traveling with Charles Demuth to Bermuda, where they joined fellow American artists Charles Hawthorne, Ambrose Spencer, Georgia O'Keeffe, and Albert Gleizes. There Hartley painted a number of still lifes with objects placed in front of a window (plate 30), and a symbolic portrait, *Still Life with Eel* (plate 31). His restlessness and desire to go his own way are revealed in a letter to Stieglitz written from the house of his patron Mabel Dodge (Luhan) in New York: "I had to keep on the outside as I get simply frantic when many disciples of a common idea get together for talking—It seems to give me a physical pain."[38] The following summer, he moved on to another colony, led by Hamilton Easter Field, in Ogunquit, Maine. Field and the Ogunquit school artists were prominent collectors of American folk art, and in this community, Hartley renewed his interest in folk art by completing several reverse glass paintings, a folk technique he had seen in Bavaria (plate 32).

New Mexico and New York, 1918–1921

In search of new inspiration, Hartley wrote to Stieglitz: "I want an open space for my eyes to regain their vision and my mind to feel itself free again."[39] In June 1918 he traveled to New Mexico, drawn to the southwestern region as were so many of his contemporaries. He first stayed in Taos near Mabel Dodge (Luhan) but quickly moved to nearby Santa Fe for an eighteen-month stay. He was not impressed with the artists he found there and kept his distance. Hartley was intrigued, however, by the landscape and the many cultures in the region: Hispanic, Native American, and Anglo. "I want the bigness and the sense of giving of this big country in my system and it is the one way to recreate myself" (fig. 11).[40]

He first painted the landscape in pastel; the dryness of this medium paralleled the dry, hard quality of the arid landscape (plate 33). While he chose not to depict the Indian, his recent interest in folk art was rekindled by the primitive qualities he associated with the regional folk art of the Southwest. He produced a number of still lifes that include Hispanic religious paintings and sculpture, or *santos,* native pottery, and cactus (plates 34–36). Hartley's writings informed his southwestern paintings and, as was true at other points in his career, he found greater success at this time with his writings, which included six essays about New Mexico and native culture (discussed in the essay by Wanda Corn). Hartley left the Southwest in November 1919, never to return, but he revisited the region through the veil of memory in paintings and writings he executed in New York and Europe during the 1920s.

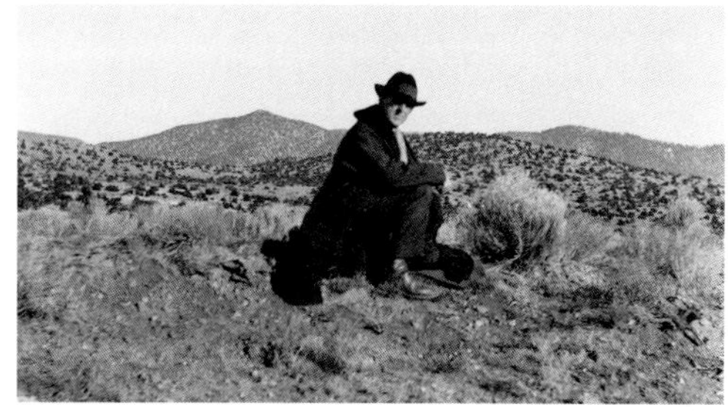

Figure 11
Unknown Photographer
Marsden Hartley in New Mexico, c. 1918
Yale Collection of American Literature
Beinecke Rare Book and Manuscript Library
Yale University, New Haven

Back in New York, Hartley reconnected with the Stieglitz circle. At the same time, responding to the multifaceted art scene of New York with its influx of European artists and styles, he was appointed secretary of the Société Anonyme, the modern art museum recently founded by Katherine Dreier, Marcel Duchamp, and Man Ray. With this appointment

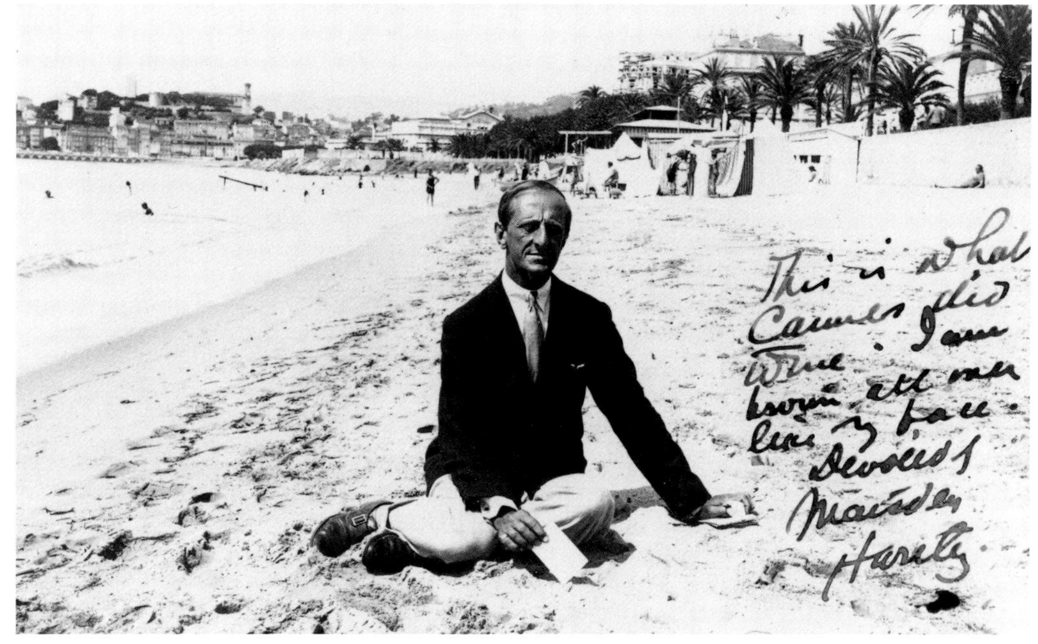

Figure 12
Unknown Photographer
Marsden Hartley on the beach at Cannes, 1925
Postcard
Yale Collection of American Literature
Beinecke Rare Book and Manuscript Library
Yale University, New Haven

and his participation as a lecturer for this group, he signaled his affiliation with the New York Dada group. His Dada poetry was published in the *Dial* in the spring of 1921; his first book, *Adventures in the Arts,* which included an essay entitled "The Importance of Being Dada," received favorable reviews. Despite his involvement in the various artistic circles in New York at the time, Hartley was desperate to return to Europe and succeeded in convincing Stieglitz to arrange for an auction of 117 of his paintings and works on paper, which was held at the Anderson Galleries in May 1921. Nearly five thousand dollars was raised, a huge sum for the time, which allowed Hartley a rare sense of financial security, and he sailed for Europe in July of that year.

France and Germany, 1921–1929

Hartley spent most of the 1920s in Berlin and France (fig. 12) painting still lifes inspired by Georges Braque and Juan Gris, landscapes of New Mexico from memory while living in Berlin, important series of drawings, pastels, and lithographs, and, returning to his admiration of Cézanne, a series of landscapes of Provence. While these years were difficult ones in Hartley's personal life, it was a period of bold experimentation and important achievement. His return to his favorite city, Berlin, was at first thrilling, but Hartley soon felt the changes that had taken place in post-war Germany and, lacking the camaraderie of his old friends, felt isolated and lonely.

In 1922, while settled in Berlin for two years, Hartley revisited his memories of the southwestern landscape, writing to Stieglitz:

> *I am working on some New Mexican landscape recollections.... it is really astonishing how states of being revive themselves upon request. These landscapes are more vivid in the sense of nature than they were when I worked from the same thoughts in New York. I think you will like the simplicity of the works.... they are for the first time in my life—almost without me in them.*[41]

Hartley often chose to paint subjects that he had faithfully studied and considered after he had left them behind and moved away; now in Berlin, he conjured up his memories of the Southwest. Hartley had written earlier in one of his essays on New Mexico that painters had to understand that "the country of the southwest is essentially a sculptural country."

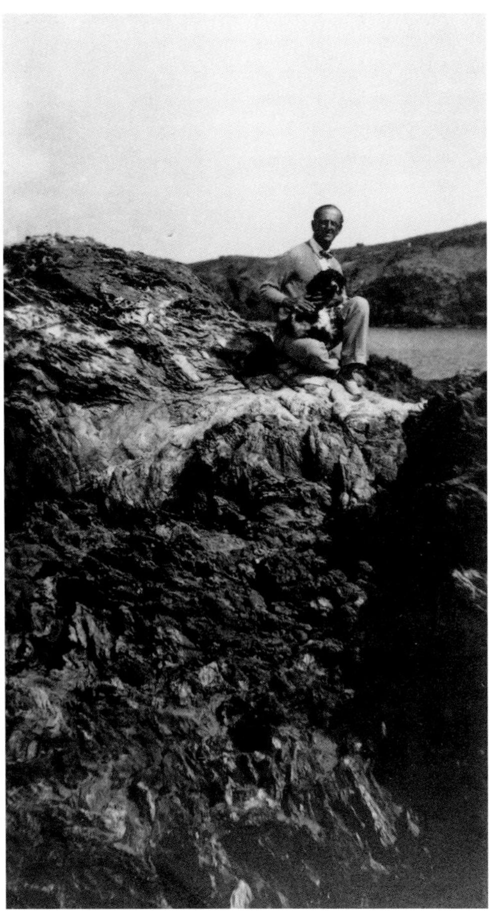

Figure 13
Unknown Photographer
Marsden Hartley with his dog, c.1925
Yale Collection of American Literature
Beinecke Rare Book and Manuscript Library
Yale University, New Haven

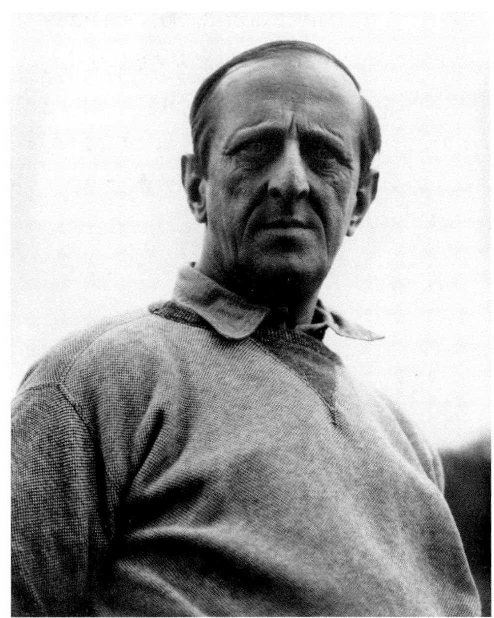

Figure 14
Paul Strand
Marsden Hartley, 1928
Yale Collection of American Literature
Beinecke Rare Book and Manuscript Library
Yale University, New Haven

In such works as *Landscape, New Mexico* (plate 38) and *New Mexico Recollections—Storm* (plate 39), both of 1923, Hartley used a somber palette that recalls his earlier landscapes of Maine. The large, horizontal format and undulating, sensual movement of the landscape elements produce a haunting and monumental effect. In the following year, he returned to the earlier Dark Landscapes inspired by Ryder, painting from memory the stark, wild, lonely scenery of Maine in larger paintings such as *Paysage* (1924; New York University Art Collection, Grey Gallery).

At this time, Hartley took up life drawing, creating over twenty pastels of mainly male nudes, using as his model a twenty-two-year-old former wrestler (plate 40). He also experimented with lithography, creating a set of still lifes of fruit. After a trip to Italy and a stay in Paris, Hartley went to the countryside in Vence (fig. 13), where he assimilated the techniques and subject matter of Cézanne, including a series of landscapes of Mont Sainte-Victoire (plate 43). He spent two more years in Aix-en-Provence and lived in Maison Maria, once occupied by Cézanne himself. This was a prolific period for the artist as he created oils, watercolors, pencil drawings, silverpoints, and lithographs—all directly from nature—in preparation for exhibitions in Chicago and New York.

Hartley faced disappointment at the end of the decade when in 1929 Stieglitz gave him a show at the Intimate Gallery of "one hundred paintings in oil, water-color, silver point, and pencil: still-life, landscape—mountains—trees—etc.—by Marsden Hartley, painted in Paris and Aix-en-Provence—France—1924–1927," as well as earlier New Mexico landscapes.[42] The show was not successful and was poorly received by the critics, one of whom, Henry McBride, labeled Hartley's landscapes "reminiscent of too many others." McBride insisted, somewhat unreasonably, that "American artists should not flee their country but should work in America even though the conditions for the artists be impossible here."[43] Hartley's relationship with Stieglitz, who concurred with McBride's sentiments, became strained from this point forward, and he began to search for new dealers to represent him.[44]

New Hampshire, Dogtown, Mexico, Bavaria, 1930–1934

Returning to America in March 1930, Hartley, now fifty-three, faced the harsh economic climate caused by the stock market crash and the beginning of the Great Depression. In a conservative artistic environment in which American Scene painting reigned, Hartley searched for a new style for the time (fig. 14). He finally satisfied his critics, turning his attention to the American landscape during the summer of 1930, first painting the White Mountains of New Hampshire in a Cézannesque style. Still, he sought a new vision for his art and for the times. On a visit to Gloucester, Massachusetts, a popular tourist destination that had attracted artists for generations, Hartley discovered the stark, primeval landscape of Dogtown, an eighteenth-century settlement in the hills behind the port of Gloucester. In the direct sketches and canvases he produced from 1931 to 1936 (plates 46–50), he found an original artistic voice (as discussed in the essay by Carol Troyen). In the midst of painting the first series in October 1931, he wrote to Adelaide Kuntz, his closest woman friend and confidante, whom he had known since the 1920s, that he had focused his efforts on "this extraordinary stretch of almost metaphysical landscape—it cannot appeal to dull painters because it calls for deep contact and study and I am capable of both, and while my pictures are small—they are more intense than ever before, and I have for once (again) immersed myself in the mysticism of nature."[45] The originality and power of these small paintings that seem to burst from the canvas led him on to his later paintings of Maine.

In what appears to have been a carefully crafted campaign to mark Hartley's turn toward native subject matter, Edith Halpert organized in April 1932 an exhibition of twenty of his Dogtown landscapes at her Downtown Gallery in New York. She titled the show *Pictures of New England by a New Englander*. It was accompanied by Hartley's poem "The Return of the Native":

Rock, juniper and wind,
and a sea gull sitting still—
all these of one mind.
He who finds will
to come home
will surely find old faith
made new again,
and lavish welcome.

Old things breaketh
new, when heart and soul
lose no whit of old refrain;
it is a smiling festival
when rock, juniper and wind
are of one mind;
a seagull signs the bond—
makes what was broken, whole.[46]

He had taken the first step toward his return to his native roots.

Before he made his final move to Maine, however, Hartley took a number of detours along the way that would lead to new artistic discoveries and inspiration. He received a Guggenheim travel grant that required him to spend a year or so out of the country, and he chose Mexico, arriving in Mexico City in March 1932. He began by devoting time to "archeological research in the museum" there, confirming that "the Aztec remains are astounding in beauty and nobility."[47] Hartley moved on to Cuernavaca, where he read extensively from a substantial collection of books about mysticism. As he reported to Edith Halpert, "I have accomplished... something which I have wished to do for years... that is to read heavily upon abstruse philosophical matters.... I have wanted to get back to a state of mind which I had in Paris in 1912–1913, and then again in 1914–1915 when I did some abstractions." He announced that he had completed twenty paintings for an exhibition for the Ministry of Education,

> *all of a mystical nature, all of them fiery in colour, for I have returned to the "gaudy flame" of earlier pictures.... Mexico has done this for me, for it is the most profound mystical space I have ever been privileged to live in, the others being my own native Maine with its northern edge, New Mexico with its southern, and now Mexico with its ultra southern obliqueness.*"[48]

A number of the works Hartley referred to in this letter, including *Morgenrot* (plate 52) and *Popocatépetl, Spirited Morning—Mexico* (plate 53), are part of a series that Hartley defined as "Murals for an Arcane Library,"[49] and rank among his finest works. As Bruce Robertson has noted, these "mystical paintings effect a conjunction between his two most important periods: Maine and Berlin."[50] He constructed a carefully conceived thematic program for these panels, which were intended as a series to hang in a library, that included symbols of Aztec legend and tributes to the three great mystics that Hartley rediscovered, Paracelsus (Yliaster), Jakob Böhme, and Richard Rolle (discussed in the essay by Jonathan Weinberg). In these paintings, Hartley's sources included architectural ruins of Ancient Mexico and the symbolism and mannerisms that he saw in the art of the Mexican muralists, including José Clemente Orozco, David Alfaro Siqueiros, and Diego Rivera.[51] He particularly admired Orozco, writing in his autobiography, "There is a deeper nature in Orozco—for there is a greater degree of pure Indianism in this man. He is rebellious, he is cruel—bitter—majestic in his deepest thoughts and touches depths of Blake and Dante in his simple planes."[52] The mystical nature of these paintings, the carefully constructed theme for an architectural program, and the boldness of the works themselves opened the door for his great achievements in Maine. Influenced by Orozco and the Mexican muralists, he continued to conceive important series as panels for specific public buildings including churches, libraries, and gymnasiums. Hartley also created a single masterwork that commemorated the suicide off the coast of Mexico of his friend the poet Hart Crane (plate 54). Painted in 1933, a year after Crane's death, the commemorative nature of the work recalls the earlier War Motif paintings, and he revisited the theme again a few years later in his archaic portraits of the Mason family (plates 66–70), where death and the sea re-emerge in his art. From this point forward, mysticism, symbolism, and bold color defined his paintings.

In April 1933 Hartley set sail from Mexico for his beloved Germany, where he spent time in Hamburg. This would be his last trip to Germany, and he found the country greatly changed from the earlier Weimar period. He arrived only four months after Hitler had been swept into power, with the Nazi party on the rise. Hartley retained his apolitical stance and was likely unaware of the most sinister aspects of the Nazis, but he did not relinquish his attraction to German culture, including his fascination with Hitler and an admiration for the beautiful Aryan youths he encountered at this time.[53]

In Hamburg, Hartley became captivated by a movie by Franz Schmidt set in the Bavarian Alps, watching it four times. Inspired by the scenery in the film and, as Susan Elizabeth Ryan has suggested, intent on retracing the steps of his 1913 trip to the Alpine home of Franz Marc, he headed for the mountains, moving to Partenkirchen in the Bavarian Alps.[54] There he set about making detailed studies of the mountains, a favorite subject that he had

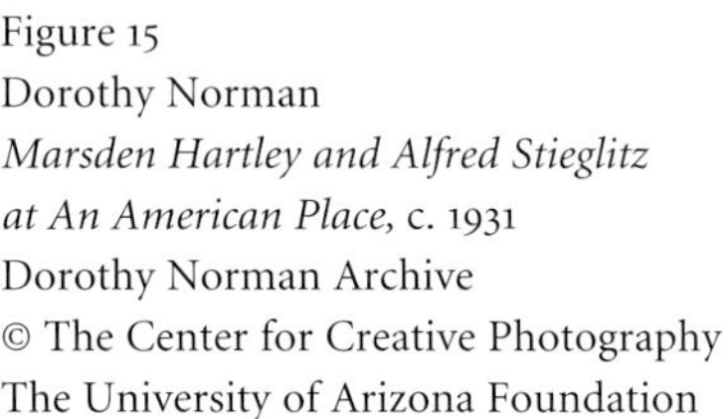

Figure 15
Dorothy Norman
Marsden Hartley and Alfred Stieglitz at An American Place, c. 1931
Dorothy Norman Archive
© The Center for Creative Photography
The University of Arizona Foundation

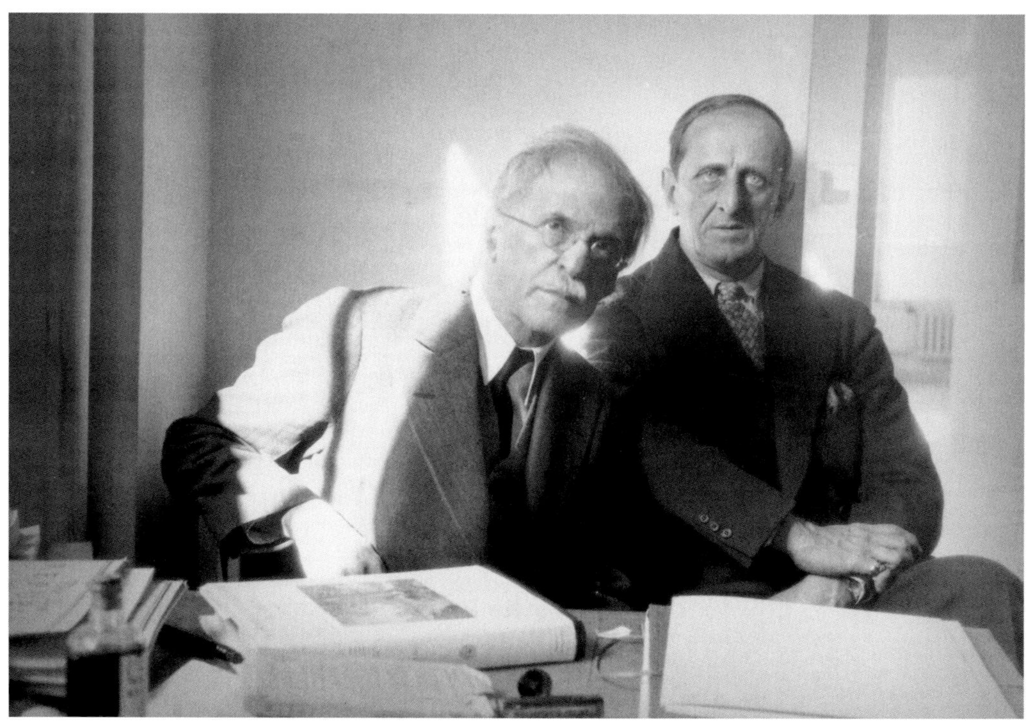

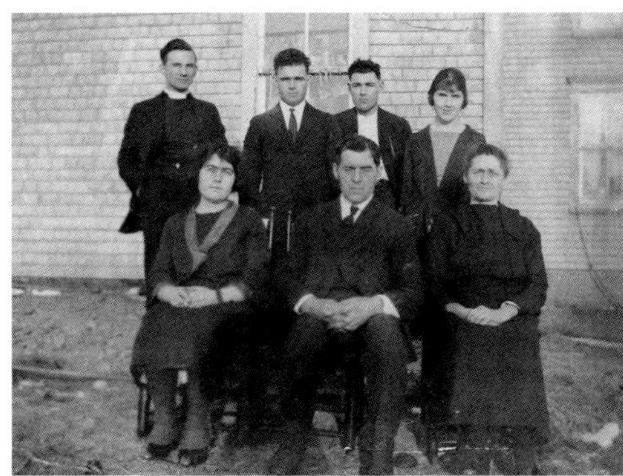

Figure 16
Unknown Photographer
Francis Mason family, c. 1930s
Yale Collection of American Literature
Beinecke Rare Book and Manuscript Library
Yale University, New Haven

pursued in every locale since his earliest works in Maine. "As a painter," he insisted at the time, "I *have* to have a mountain."[55] Hartley began by making silverpoint drawings (plates 56-57) and pastels. He wrote his niece Norma Berger that he had "nearly finished 15 paintings and walked over 100 miles to make drawings and observations." During his extensive physical explorations of the mountains, he experienced a moment of rapturous "cosmic consciousness" that would inspire his paintings.[56] He later wrote to Stieglitz of his epiphany:

> *The singular experience in the Alps—during a walk in the afternoon snow up the valley at Garmisch-Partenkirchen—seeing the keystone drop…[the feeling was of a] conversion—or equal to what St. Augustine's followers called the "mystery of opening," and the whole vision of life was opened and I knew the work of my life had been completed.*[57]

Shortly after receiving a copy of Gertrude Stein's newly published *Autobiography of Alice B. Toklas,* Hartley wrote the first and most complete version of his autobiography, *Somehow a Past,* in November and December of 1933, describing it to his niece as an "exercise in memory."[58] This was the beginning of a writing project "to recover a verbal vision" of his past that he was engaged in until the end of his life (discussed in the essay by Bruce Robertson).

Hartley's return to America in 1934 was again marked with financial hardship and personal setbacks. He worked briefly for the new federal government arts programs, in the easel division of the Public Works of Art Project, but lasted only one month before quitting. Offered a mural commission for Radio City Music Hall, he turned it down. Unable to afford to store all of his art, he used the occasion of his fifty-eighth birthday to destroy one hundred of his paintings and drawings (though he admitted they "were too tentative, and most of them incomplete").[59] While Stieglitz disapproved of Hartley's recent European stay, he exhibited thirty of his paintings at An American Place in March 1936 (fig. 15). This show included several groups of works that, like the earlier Mexican paintings for the "Arcane Library," were presented as architectural mural projects, including six panels "intended for use as focus motives in a convalescent pavilion" (see plate 60), "four modern ikons for a wooden sea-chapel in the bitter north" (see plate 69), and seven paintings from the New England series and Alpine series.[60] The critical reception was disappointing and he sold only six works. Hartley had only one more show with Stieglitz, in April 1937, which included twenty-one paintings and drawings from his Dogtown series and from the powerful new works he had painted in his next locale, Nova Scotia, in the summers and falls of 1935 and 1936.

Gail Scott has made the point that Hartley vacillated between "a desire to be left alone in remote locations to pursue his art, and a yearning for the stimulus of art centers like New York, Paris, and Berlin.… His movements from one location to the next were often a matter of a chance invitation or some unexpected income."[61] Hartley's fortuitous discovery of the Mason family, who lived on the island of East Point across from Blue Rocks, Nova Scotia, occurred at the suggestion of his Canadian friend the novelist Frank Davison, who inspired Hartley to visit his native Nova Scotia. Hartley's creative imagination was sparked by this French-Canadian fishing family, by their remote island setting, and eventually, and sadly, by the tragic drownings at sea of the Mason sons, whom Hartley had come to love (fig. 16). The archaic portraits, as Hartley called them, of the family, painted from memory in 1938 and 1939, and the landscape elegies and other works that resulted from Hartley's experiences during the summers with this family in 1935 and 1936, rank among his finest works (and are discussed in the essays by Amy Ellis, Jonathan Weinberg, and Carol Troyen). Hartley managed to present the Masons as modern primitive heroes.

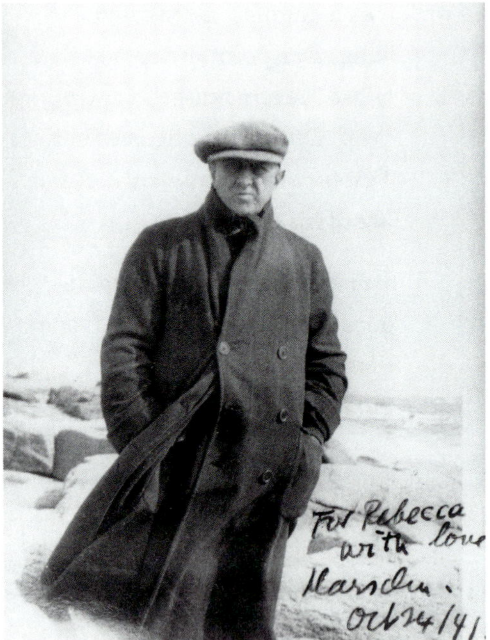

Figure 17
Unknown Photographer
Marsden Hartley in Maine, 1941
Museum of New Mexico,
Museum of Fine Arts, Santa Fe

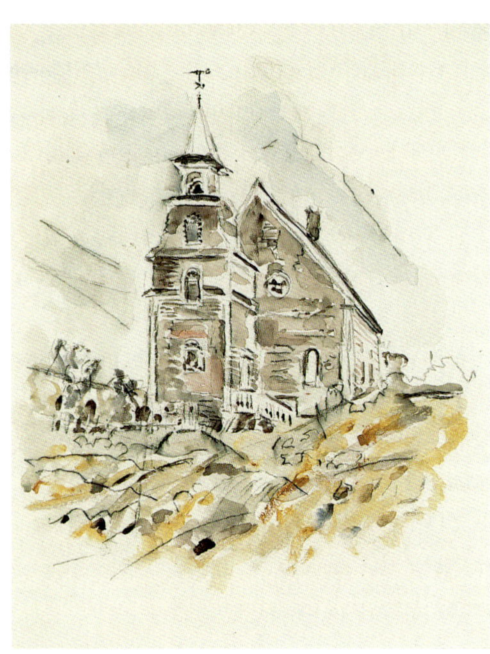

Figure 18
John Marin
Where Marsden Hartley Had His Studio, 1945
Watercolor and charcoal, 18⅝ × 14½ in.
(47.3 × 36.8 cm)
Richard York Gallery, New York

Maine and New York, 1937–1943

> *Someday, perhaps some day not so far distant, Hartley will have to go back to Maine. For it seems that flight from Maine is in part flight from his deep feelings. It was down east that he was born and grew and lived a great many years. There dwell the people whom he is closest akin; there is the particular landscape among which his decisive experiences were gotten; there every tree and mountain wall is reminiscent of some terrible or wonderful day. And when he has to make his peace with life, it is to this soil, so it would appear, that he must return. Here are his own people; the ones he must accept and understand and cherish. For among them only can he get the freedom of his own soul.*[62]
>
> Paul Rosenfeld, 1924

For the catalogue of his last show with Stieglitz at An American Place, Hartley wrote an essay entitled "On the Subject of Nativeness—A Tribute to Maine" in which he asserted, "I wish to declare myself the painter from Maine."[63] After twenty-five years of constant travel, Hartley returned to Maine in the summer of 1937, coming full circle to settle in his native land, where he reconciled memories from his early childhood as he revisited the writing of his autobiography. Drawing on all that had come before in his artistic explorations, or as Susan Elizabeth Ryan has put it, "his dogged pursuit of the meaning of artistic practice," Hartley applied his energy once again and created an extraordinary body of regional works that represent one of the most successful and prolific periods in his career. In addition to the portraits of the Mason family, he created romantic and often haunting landscapes of coastal and inland Maine, turbulent paintings of the sea, a series of iconic male figure paintings, portraits of heroes and fishermen, enigmatic self-portraits, monumental stark still lifes of sea creatures, shells, and birds, and elegiac landscapes of Mount Katahdin (these works are discussed in the final three essays).

During the last four summers of his life, Hartley stayed in the remote lobster-fishing village of Corea, Maine, located over an hour beyond the tourist region of Mount Dessert. He boarded with Katie and Forest Young, a lobster-fishing family (fig. 17). While suffering ill health, he nevertheless worked tirelessly in studios he fashioned in the town's church (fig. 18) and in a converted chicken coop behind the Youngs' house. His paintings from this period rank among the finest and most original works by any American artist.

Upon viewing an exhibition of Hartley's late paintings of Maine at the Hudson Walker Gallery in New York in 1940, William Carlos Williams proclaimed that "Hartley is painting better today than he ever could have hoped to do formerly and the reason, a basic reason, it has to do with the mind, the body and the spirit drawn gradually together into one life and finally flowering, once."[64] In his final years, Hartley benefited from the attention of a number of prominent new dealers, including Hudson Walker, William MacBeth, and Paul Rosenberg. The powerful primitive style that Hartley developed for his Maine subjects was a brilliant compilation drawn from a lifetime of artistic exploration. Hartley applied paint to board in rough, broad strokes, and he used bright, primary colors, outlining forms in thick, black pigment. His distinctive primitive style even inspired a new frame type made of wormy chestnut wood that bore his name, designed for Hartley's paintings by the renowned New York framer Henry Heydenryk (as discussed in the essay by Kornhauser and Birkmaier). He often chose traditional subjects for his paintings, for example *Fishermen's Last Supper* (plate 70), *Church at Head Tide* (plate 89), and *The Lighthouse* (plate 98), but in his treatment he intentionally distorted the perspective, tilting his subjects at an angle. For his late male figure paintings, such as *Down East Young Blades* (plate 85) and *Lobster Fishermen* (plate 88), Hartley developed a self-consciously primitive portrayal that at once exudes masculinity and homoeroticism, creating a powerful and engaging tension. Hartley successfully employed his primitive style for his landscapes of the coast, such as *The Wave* (plate 96), to evoke the turbulent energy of the sea, and for his extensive series of Mt. Katahdin (plates 91–95), shown in all moods and seasons.

At the end of his life, Hartley summed up his importance in a letter to his niece: "I am not a 'book of the month' artist and do not paint pretty pictures; but when I am no longer here my name will register forever in the history of American art and so that's something too."[65] In September 1943 his heart gave out, and he died alone in a small hospital in Ellsworth, Maine.

Critical Reception

Several months after Hartley's death, a writer for *Newsweek* reported that "the ashes of Marsden Hartley were scattered at his request over the river he celebrated in his painting and poetry—the Androscoggin of his native Maine. It was the end of a lonely, frustrated life." The writer took comfort, however, in the fact that Hartley knew in his final days that he was to have a retrospective exhibition at the Museum of Modern Art, noting that it was "one of the greatest honors that can be accorded an American artist."[66]

Hartley's retrospective was combined with a show of paintings by his friend and colleague Lyonel Feininger (1871–1956). A courageous act on the part of the museum, the joint exhibition of these two American artists, who were linked by the fact that they had spent crucial periods of their careers in Germany, opened in New York in an atmosphere of anti-German sentiment at the height of World War II. While an important landmark in Hartley's career, once again the show was poorly timed to allow for a true appreciation of the artist's vital contribution to early modern art, namely his abstract paintings of wartime Berlin.

Of the seven hundred existing works then known by Hartley, the exhibition included an impressive number—eighty-seven paintings and nineteen works on paper—covering the artist's nearly four-decade career. What was excluded from the selection, however, is significant. Only three of more than forty-five known Berlin paintings from the 1912–15 period were shown. *Himmel* (plate 13) and *Forms Abstracted* (whereabouts unknown) and only one example, *Painting No. 5* (Whitney Museum of American Art), from Hartley's now renowned War Motif series appeared. Thus twice were major showings of paintings that should have been celebrated as singular achievements by an American modernist, thereby securing Hartley's place as a major international artist, overshadowed by public sentiment surrounding the two world wars.

Also absent from the retrospective were examples of Hartley's late series of male figure paintings. Only *Young Hunter Hearing Call to Arms* (fig. 19), with its patriotic 1939 wartime title, was shown. Hartley's male figure paintings (here the subject of an essay by Randall Griffey) were not widely exhibited during his lifetime or following his death. Encoded with both masculine and veiled homosexual content, they have required the distance of time to be fully appreciated. In addition, the artist's enigmatic self-portraits, including the 1939 *Sustained Comedy* (plate 72; discussed in the essay by Bruce Robertson), were also missing. Hartley's determination to mask his identity as a gay man during his lifetime prevented him from publicly identifying these works as self-portraits. Furthermore, the conflict that arose in the 1930s between Alfred Stieglitz and his modernist circle on the one hand, and Thomas Hart Benton's conservative regionalist school on the other, did not allow for a true appreciation of Hartley's paintings. Stieglitz and Benton vied for popular

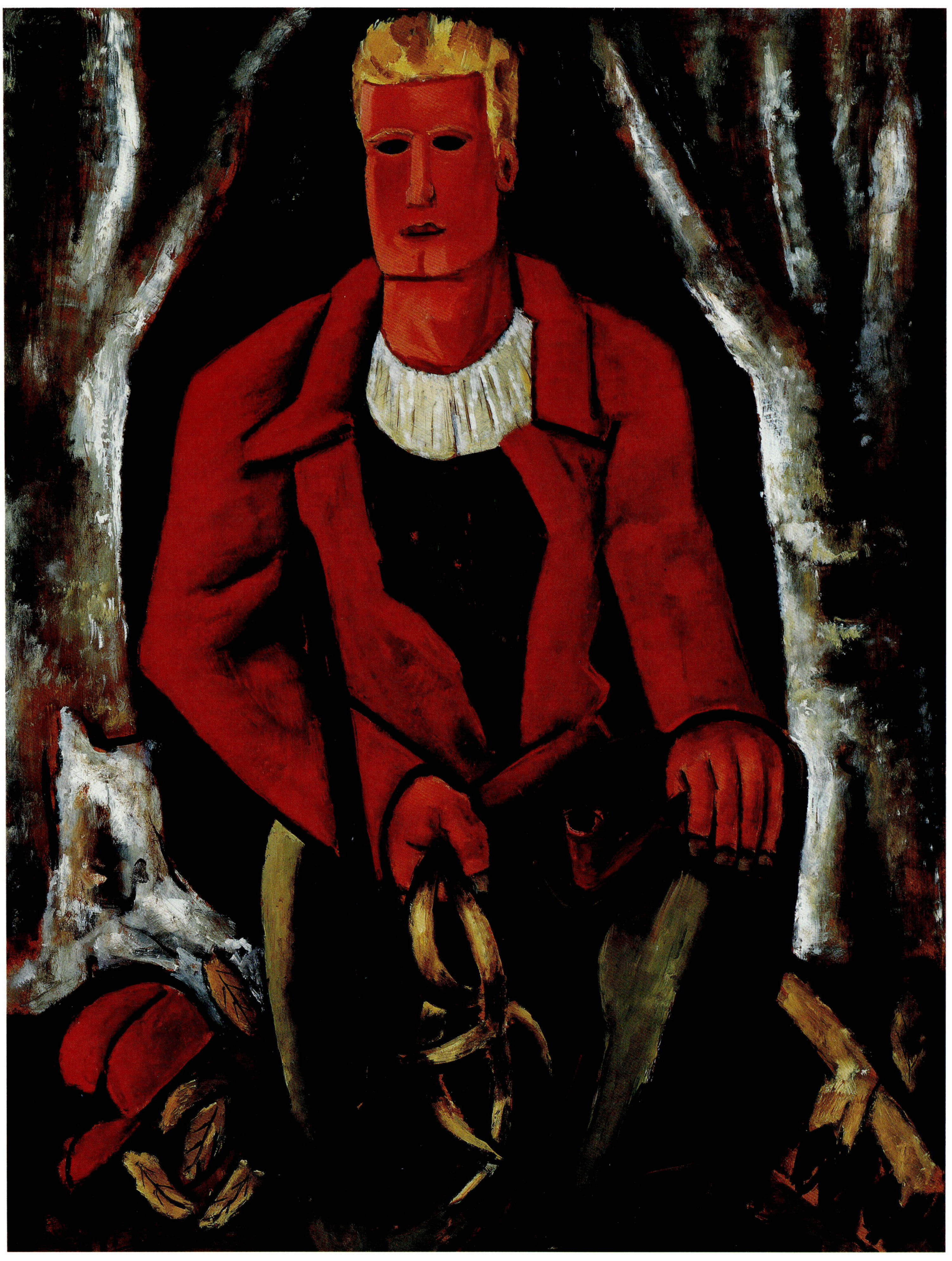

Figure 19
Marsden Hartley
Young Hunter Hearing Call to Arms, 1939
Oil on Masonite, 41 × 30¼ in. (104 × 76.8 cm)
Carnegie Museum of Art, Pittsburgh, Pennsylvania
Patrons Art Fund, 1944

supremacy in the 1930s in a contest of masculinity, with each group of adherents proclaiming to be the "true" painters of American character.[67] The critic Thomas Craven joined forces with Benton, waging antimodernist, anti-Semitic, and homophobic attacks in the media against the Stieglitz circle.[68]

In the small catalogue for the retrospective, the brief introduction by the museum curator Monroe Wheeler proclaimed that Hartley "has become a kind of prototype and legendary personality, inspiring to younger artists," and yet, he concluded, "the full scale will have to wait, for our subject is unusually complex, and should afford excellent material for a long line of critics and biographers." He acknowledged that, "while the past ten years has seen the artist's reputation grow by leaps and bounds, ... there are still many whose sensibilities are bruised by the power of his work, which they think crude."[69] Wheeler's prediction was correct, as it took over thirty-five years for the next major exhibition to be mounted, at the Whitney Museum of American Art, with only sparse attention paid during the interim.

The 1980 Whitney show inspired new generations of admirers and an avalanche of new research and writings on Hartley. This exhibition and catalogue draw on recent scholarship and consider the full range and depth of Hartley's entire career. A new appreciation for the many contributions Hartley made to modern art is revealed in a comprehensive examination of the stylistic shifts and growth in his art, and the overall strength and power of his work over the course of his thirty-five-year career. In a tribute to Hartley's remarkable life as a modern artist, Monroe Wheeler noted: "Hartley's death did not come too soon to allow him satisfaction and realization. It was too soon for the world, for it terminated a still vigorous and clearly visioned painting career. Hartley was apt to say, when commended on a show, 'Oh, but just wait and see what I will paint *next* year!'"[70]

Notes

This essay benefited from the advice provided by the following readers: Amy Ellis, Townsend Ludington, Patricia McDonnell, and Carol Troyen.

1 William Carlos Williams, unpublished review for Hartley exhibition at the Hudson Walker Gallery, New York, April 1940: Archives/Smithsonian, reel 1368, frames 548–49.

2 Williams acquired a number of works by Hartley including *Still Life with Eel* (plate 31); a pastel of New Mexico, *Mountains in Mexico* (1919; collection of Mr. and Mrs. Paul Williams); and a drawing, *Shell Contours* (1936; Museum of Art of Ogunquit, Maine; Gift of Mrs. William Carlos Williams). He greatly admired Hartley's painting *New England Sea View—Fish House* (1934; see plate 59) but could not afford it, thus Hartley gave him an inscribed reproduction; see Dickran Tashjian, *William Carlos Williams and the American Scene, 1920–1940* (New York: Whitney Museum of Art in association with the University of California Press, 1978), 50, 52.

3 Marcia Brennan, *Painting Gender, Construction Theory: The Alfred Stieglitz Circle and American Formalist Aesthetics* (Cambridge: MIT Press, 2001), 157.

4 *Adventures,* 6.

5 Quoted in Ludington 1992, 16.

6 Marsden Hartley, *Adventures,* 4.

7 *Autobiography,* 199.

8 Hartley to Adelaide Kuntz, 12 December 1933, McCausland Papers, Archives/Smithsonian, roll D268.

9 *Autobiography,* 49.

10 Weinberg, 121.

11 *Autobiography,* 56.

12 Quoted in Ludington 1992, 44; Alfred Kreymborg, *Troubadour: An Autobiography* (New York: Boni and Liveright, 1925), 112–13.

13 The poem, included in a poetry manuscript, "Bach for Breakfast," Beinecke/Yale, is reproduced in *On Art,* 21. See obit., Paul Rosenfeld, "Marsden Hartley," *Nation* 157, no. 12 (18 September 1943): 326–27.

14 Inventory of the Library of Marsden Hartley, Bates College, Lewiston, Maine.

15 For a discussion of Hartley's involvement with mysticism, see Gail Levin, "Marsden Hartley and Mysticism," *Arts* 60, no. 3 (November 1985): 16–21.

16 Hartley to Adelaide Kuntz, 24 June 1933, quoted in Ludington 1992, 231.

17 Hartley to Horace Traubel, postmarked 29 October 1907; reproduced in *Heart's Gate: Letters Between Marsden Hartley and Horace Traubel, 1906–1915,* ed. William Innes Homer (Highlands, N.C.: The Jargon Society, 1982), 57.

18 While Hartley and Stieglitz had a tumultuous friendship, and their artist/dealer association formally ended in 1937, they remained acquaintances until Hartley's death.

19 Hartley to Norma Berger, September 1911, Beinecke/Yale.

20 *Autobiography,* 67.

21 Greenough, 23.

22 Ibid., 37–38.

23 The influence of photography on Hartley's art is discussed in Gail Levin, "Photography's 'Appeal' to Marsden Hartley," *Yale University Library Gazette* 68 (1994).

24 Hartley, "The Appeal of Photography," in *Adventures,* 102.

25 Quoted in Robertson, 37.

26 Hartley to Alfred Stieglitz, 3 November 1913, Beinecke/Yale, quoted in Weinberg, 141.

27 Marsden Hartley, "Letters Never Sent," in "A Life in the Arts", ed. Gail R. Scott, typescript, Beinecke/Yale, 48–49.

28 Regarding its scale and significance, see Bruce Robertson, "Marsden Hartley, 1916, Letters to the Dead," in Greenough, 229–41.

29 Ibid., 161.

30 Marsden Hartley, "Foreword," *Camera Work,* no. 48 (October 1916): 12.

31 Marsden Hartley, *Paintings by Marsden Hartley* (New York: Photo Secession Galleries, 1916); foreword reprinted in *Camera Work,* no. 48 (October 1916): 12.

32 The review appeared in the *New York Times,* 19 December 1915, 4.

33 Weinberg, 154.

34 Ibid.; Hartley to Alfred Stieglitz, 15 March 1915, Beinecke/Yale.

35 Quoted in Dorothy Norman, *Alfred Stieglitz: An American Seer* (New York: Random House, 1973); repub. (New York: Aperture, 1990).

36 A lecture (publication forthcoming) given by Michael Taylor, at the Pennsylvania Academy of the Fine Arts, Philadelphia, entitled "Marsden Hartley: The 'Movement' Series," discusses Picasso's influence on Hartley's Provincetown paintings including *Man with Pipe* (1915) and *Guitar Player* (1915).

37 Quoted in Roberston, 69; Hartley to Carl Sprinchorn, 1917, McCausland Papers, Archives/Smithsonian, roll D267, frame 1260.

38 Hartley to Alfred Stieglitz, February 1916, Beinecke/Yale.

39 Hartley to Alfred Stieglitz, 24 May 1918, Beinecke/Yale.

40 Hartley to Alfred Stieglitz, 1 August 1918, quoted in Lois Palken Rudnick, *Utopian Vistas: The Mabel Dodge Luhan House and the American Counterculture* (Albuquerque: University of New Mexico Press, 1996), 84.

41 Hartley to Alfred Stieglitz, 28 April 1923, Beinecke/Yale.

42 *Hartley Exhibition,* The Intimate Gallery, New York, January 1929.

43 Quoted in Townsend Ludington, "Marsden Hartley: On Native Ground," in Greenough, 401–2.

44 For a detailed discussion of Hartley's relationship with Stieglitz at this time, see ibid., 401–21.

45 Quoted in Townsend Ludington, *Seeking the Spiritual: The Paintings of Marsden Hartley* (Ithaca: Cornell University Press, 1998), 54.

46 *Collected Poems,* 251.

47 Hartley to Edith Halpert, 3 May 1932, quoted in Garnett McCoy, "South of the Border with Marsden Hartley: Letters to Edith Halpert, 1931–1933," *Archives of American Art Journal* 37, nos. 1–2 (1997): 12.

48 Quoted in Hokin, 91.

49 Ibid., 16.

50 Robertson, 94.

51 Hokin, 88.

52 *Autobiography,* 151.

53 Hartley's political views are discussed in Weinberg, 172–73; Robertson, 101–2.

54 *Autobiography,* 13.

55 Quoted in Hokin, 104; Hartley to Adelaide Kuntz, 4 November 1933, Archives/Smithsonian.

56 Quoted in Hokin, 91.

57 Hartley to Alfred Stieglitz, 21 November 1934, Beinecke/Yale.

58 *Autobiography,* 25; see Susan Elizabeth Ryan's Introduction for a comprehensive discussion of the various manuscripts that make up Hartley's autobiography.

59 Quoted in Robertson, 103.

60 Elizabeth McCausland described them as "large wall panels, painted as projects for murals… the fact that Hartley, after 60, has sufficient vital and creative energy to break away from his lifelong routine of easel painting and think in terms of the wall is most hopeful." McCausland, "Marsden Hartley Shows His Recent Paintings," *Springfield (Mass.) Sunday Union and Republican,* 17 March 1940, 6.

61 Gail R. Scott, "Cleophus and His Own: The Making of a Narrative," in Ferguson, 55.

62 Paul Rosenfeld, *Port of New York* (New York: Harcourt, Brace, 1924), reprint, 1966.

63 Marsden Hartley, "On the Subject of Nativeness—A Tribute to Maine," in *Marsden Hartley: Exhibition of Recent Paintings, 1936* (New York: An American Place, 20 April–17 May 1937), 5.

64 William Carlos Williams, unpublished review for Hartley exhibition at the Hudson Walker Gallery, New York, April 1940: Archives/Smithsonian, roll 1368, frames 548–49.

65 Quoted in Robertson, 9.

66 John Marin was the first Stieglitz circle artist to be so honored during his lifetime, in 1936; followed by Hartley's memorial retrospective in 1944–45, and a show of Georgia O'Keeffe's work in 1946.

67 Brennan, *Painting Gender,* 206.

68 Ibid., 202–32.

69 *Lyonel Feininger, Marsden Hartley,* ed. Dorothy C. Miller (New York: Museum of Modern Art, 1944), 56.

70 Monroe Wheeler, "Death Takes Hartley," *Art Digest* (1 October 1943): 29.

PLATES 1–6

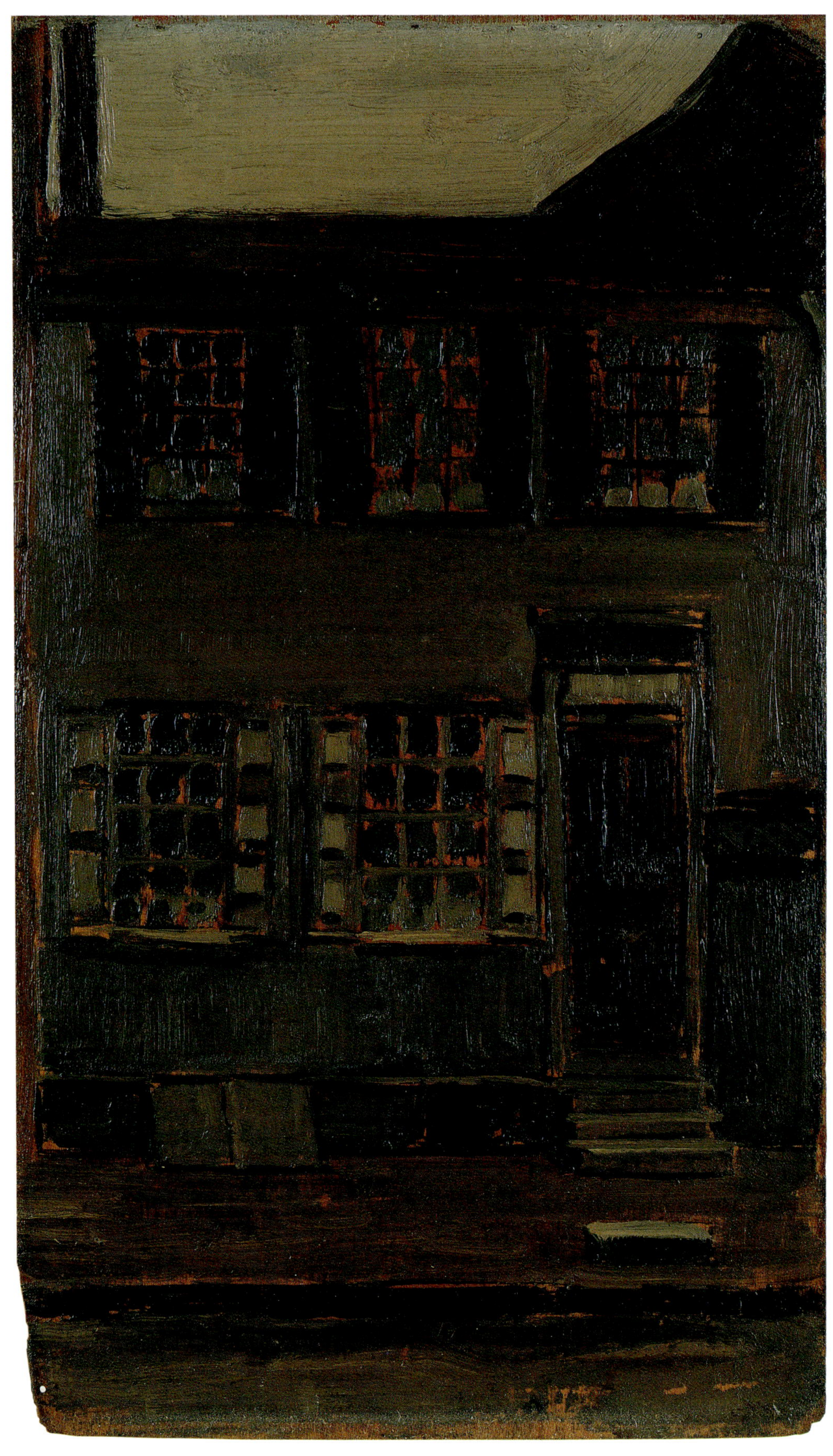

1
Walt Whitman's House, 328 Mickle Street, Camden, New Jersey, c. 1905
Oil on board, 10 × 8 in.
Private Collection

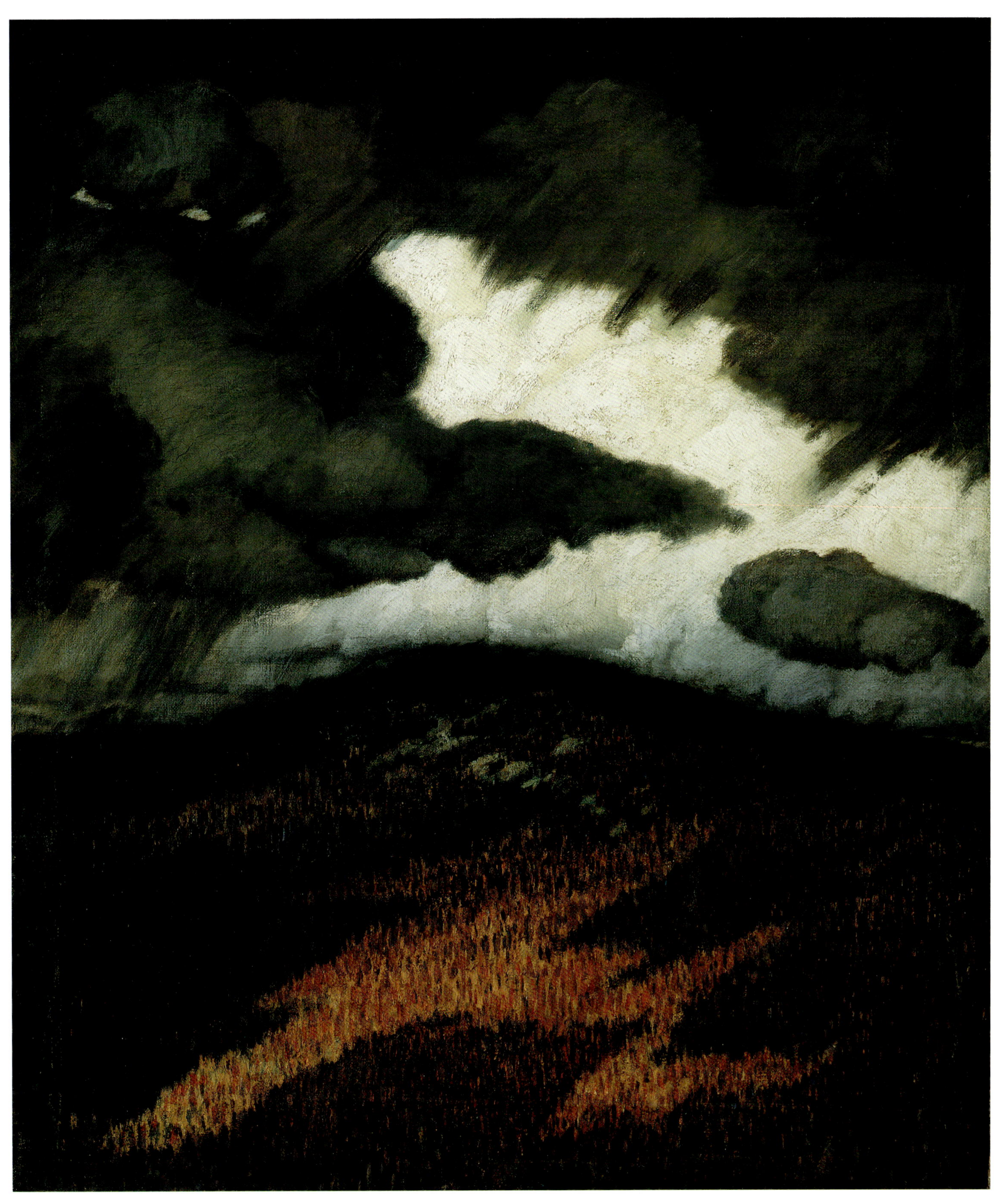

2
Storm Clouds, Maine, 1906–7
Oil on canvas, 30⅛ × 24$^{15}/_{16}$ in.
Collection of Walker Art Center, Minneapolis
Gift of the T. B. Walker Foundation, Hudson Walker Collection, 1954

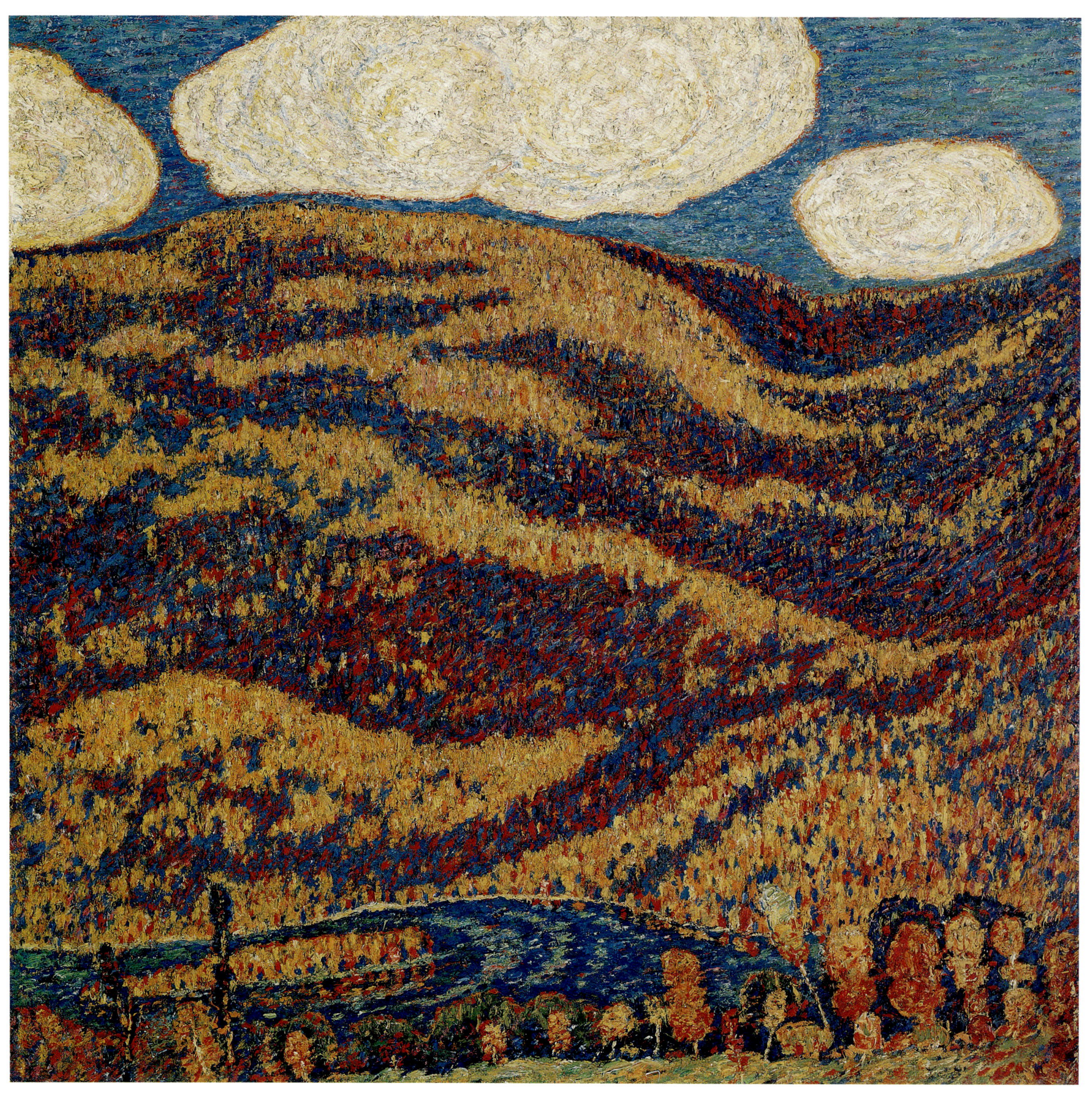

3

Carnival of Autumn, 1908
Oil on canvas; 30¼ × 30⅛ in.
Museum of Fine Arts, Boston
The Hayden Collection
Charles Henry Hayden Fund, 1968

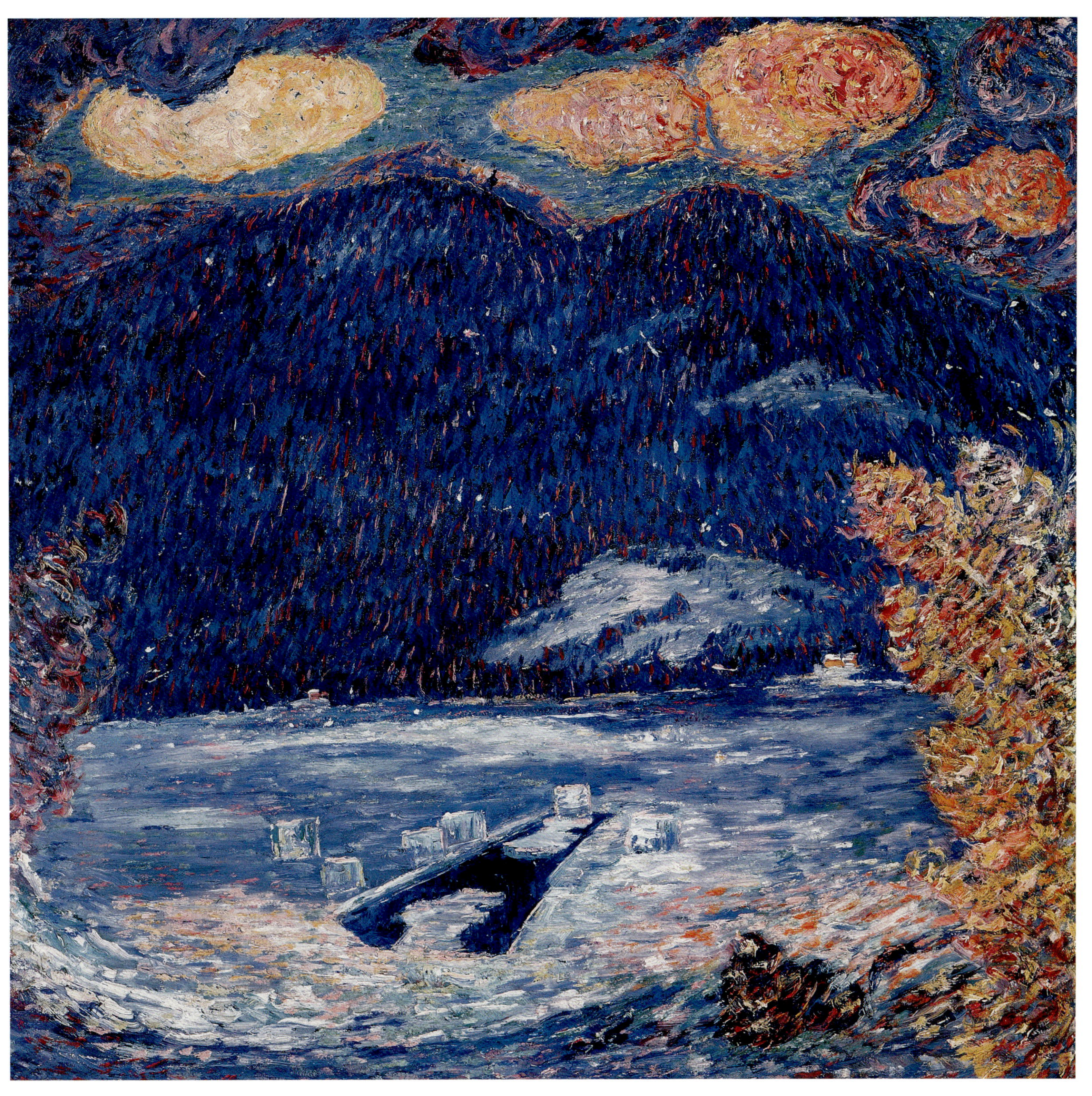

4
The Ice-Hole, Maine, 1908–9
Oil on canvas, 34 × 34 in.
New Orleans Museum of Art
Museum purchase; Ella West Freeman Matching Fund

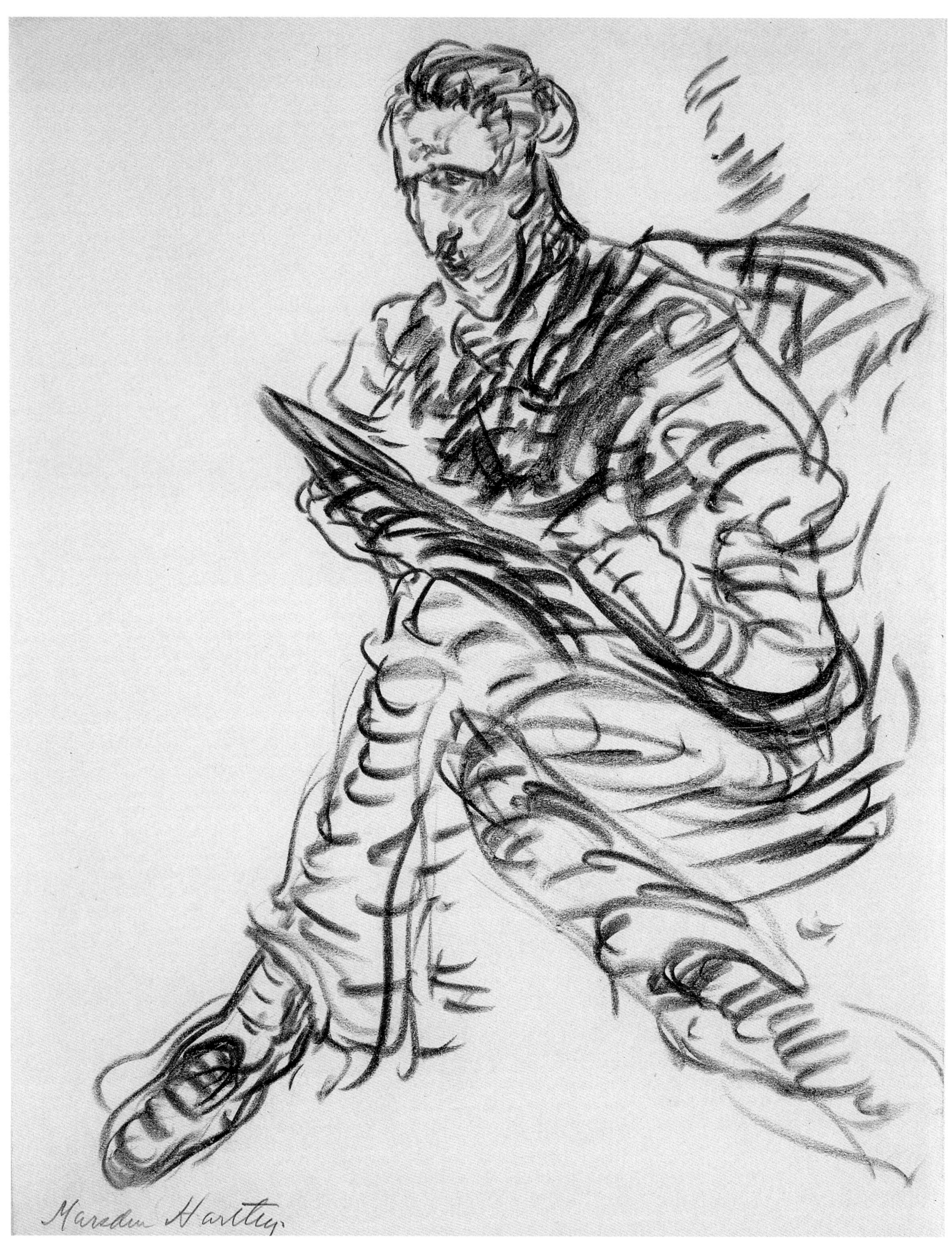

5

Self-Portrait as a Draughtsman, 1908–9

Crayon on paper, 12 × 8 15/16 in.

Allen Memorial Art Museum, Oberlin College, Ohio

Gift of the Oberlin College Class of 1945

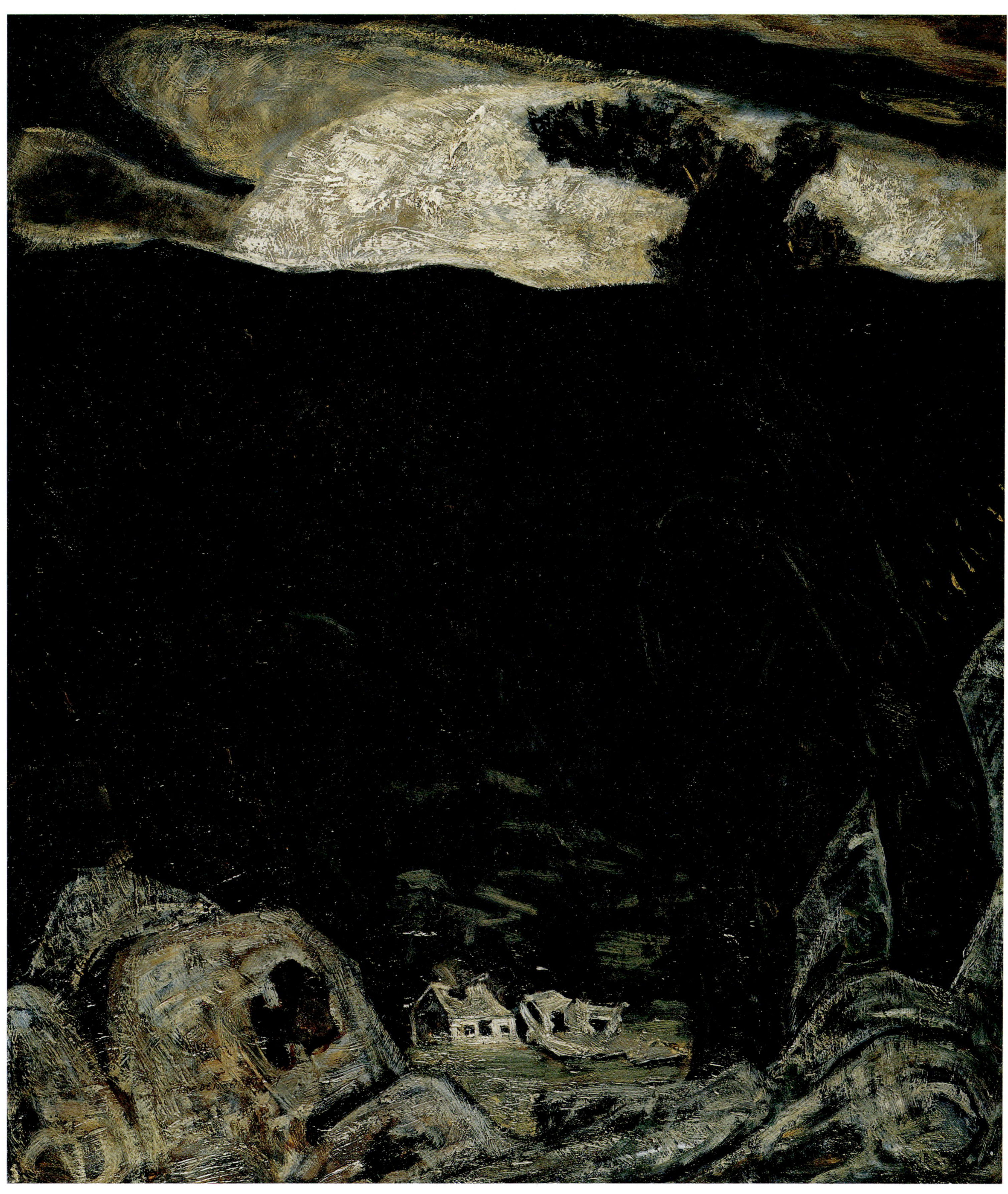

6
Deserted Farm, 1909
Oil on fiberboard, 24 × 20 in.
Frederick R. Weisman Art Museum,University of Minnesota, Minneapolis
Gift of Ione and Hudson Walker

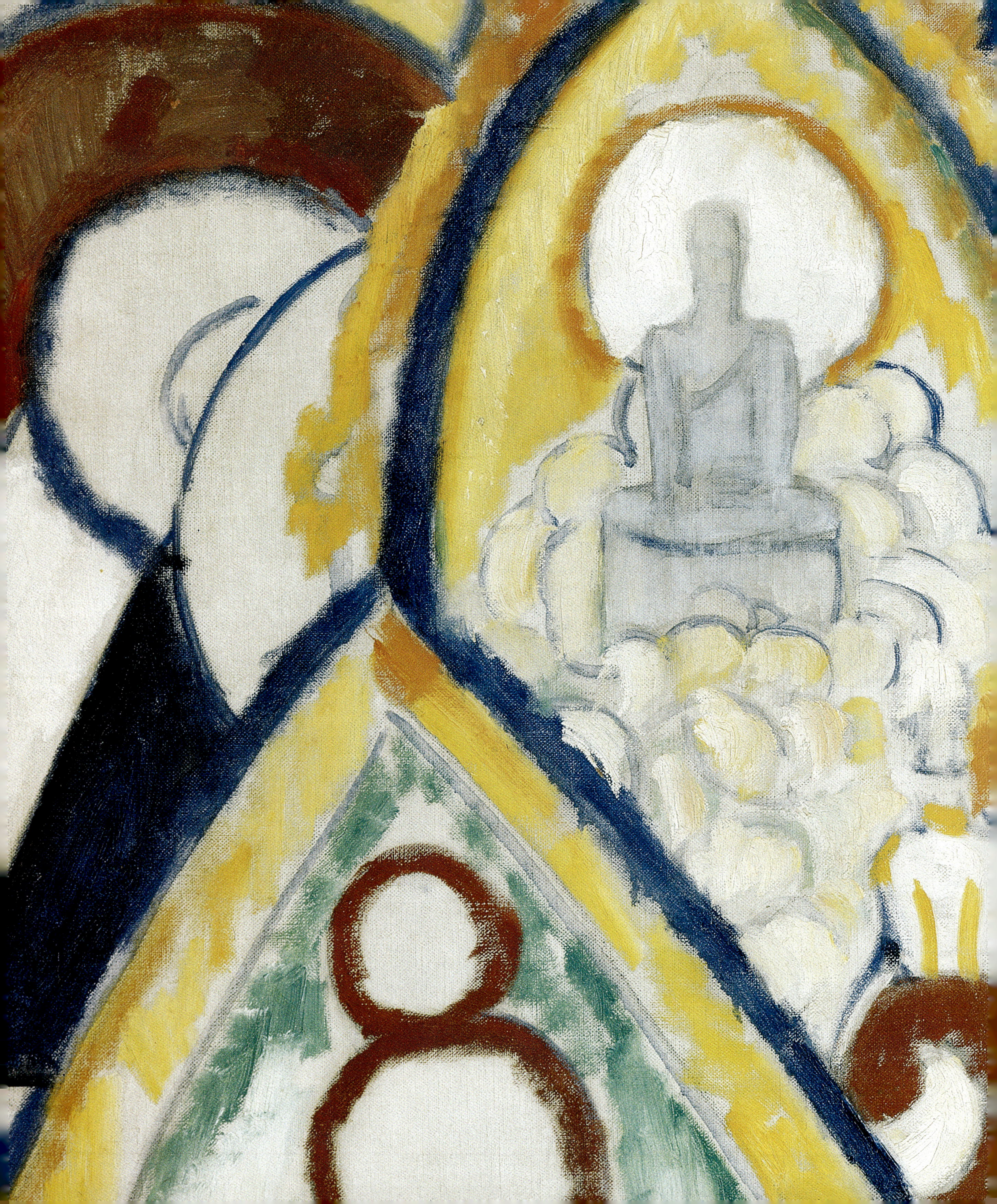

"Portrait of Berlin": Marsden Hartley and Urban Modernity in Expressionist Berlin

Patricia McDonnell

I like Berlin extremely.... For me artistically it is stimulating strange to say. I find it full of mystical ideas + colors + I have begun to paint them—.[1]

Marsden Hartley, 1913

At the age of thirty-five, in April 1912, Marsden Hartley set out for Europe. His motives for going abroad were clear—he wanted "an artist's education," as he called it.[2] As critic Van Wyck Brooks wryly noted of his and Hartley's generation, "it was understood in the world I knew that a voyage to Europe was the panacea for every known illness and discontent."[3] Hartley initially settled in Paris and quickly entered the lively international mix of artists, writers, and performers living there. In his short ten months in France from spring 1912 to early 1913, he penetrated the scene and visited the studios of Pablo Picasso, Robert Delaunay, Frantisek Kupka, and Gertrude Stein. All but Picasso returned the compliment and came to see Hartley's paintings. Working assiduously to explore Europe and its art capitals, he made a trip to Berlin in January 1913 with German friends he had made in Paris. Immediately upon returning to Paris that winter, he was fevered with plans to get back to Berlin just as soon as he could manage. Berlin was, he wrote buoyantly, "without question the finest modern city in Europe."[4] Its "great activity of life" convinced him that "it is in Germany that I find my creative conditions—and it is there that I must go—" (fig. 1).[5]

Hartley lived in the imperial German capital from May 1913 to December 1915, a two-and-a-half year stretch that extended deep into World War I. Discussions of his Berlin paintings have overwhelmingly focused on the artist's War Motif series, twelve masterful canvases begun in late 1914 as a memorial to Hartley's friend and possible lover, the German lieutenant Karl von Freyburg, who died in early campaigns on the western front. The emphasis on these paintings is warranted, because they are widely thought to be the best in Hartley's entire career.[6] Further, they place Hartley—and through him American modernism—toe to toe with the most advanced painting of any country at that date. With the War Motif paintings in mind, art critic Robert Hughes ranked Hartley as "the most brilliantly gifted of the early generation of American modernists."[7]

In comparison, little focused scholarship has addressed the pictorial and conceptual advances in Hartley's German paintings in 1913 and 1914—that is, before he began the War Motif oils in November 1914.[8] Not a prescribed series, the strong body of work that grew from Hartley's initial time in the imperial capital attempted something quite new in his career—he made paintings that characterize, abstractly and imaginatively, the tenor of modern Berlin.

Detail, Plate 10

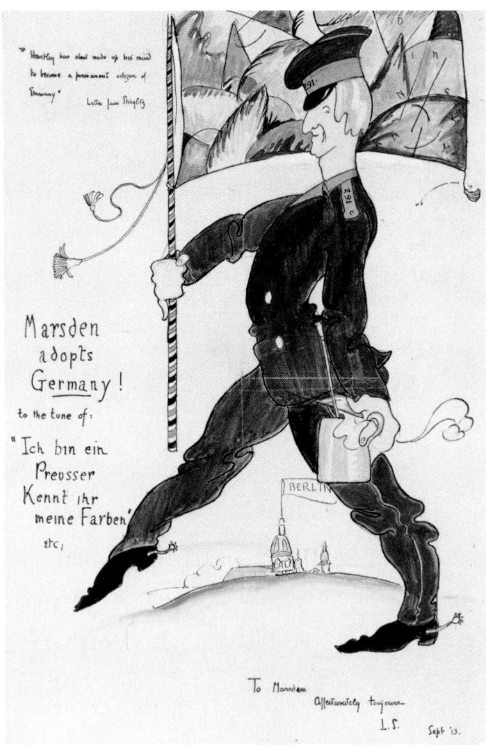

Figure 1
Lee Simonson
Hartley Adopts Germany, 1913
Watercolor on paper
Yale Collection of American Literature
Beinecke Rare Book and Manuscript Library
Yale University, New Haven

These early German canvases are forceful city paintings or *Grossstadtbilder.* And the degree to which they function as art registering the kaleidoscope of modern life has been obscured by the fact that they are such unconventional and, as a consequence, daring city paintings.

Hartley did not take imposing architecture as his subject matter—the skyscrapers, towers, or bridges newly arrayed in city centers thanks to technological advances. The hyperstimulus of outward sensations in the metropolis encouraged him, instead, to look inward to his subjective responses. As he explained to his friend the writer Gertrude Stein in the fall of 1913, his art "express[ed] a fresh consciousness of what I see + feel around me—taken directly out of life + from no theorist formulas as prevails so much today."[9] The 1913 *Military* (plate 12) might have been on the easel as Hartley penned this conviction. In it, as in related early Berlin paintings, a complex matrix of forms, motifs, and numbers animate the canvas. The whole is a jumble of bold colors and disconnected parts, made even livelier by quickly applied muscular paint. Areas of color are not modeled with shading, the result of which is a forceful two-dimensionality that presses the image flush against the picture plane. Upon seeing many Berlin paintings by Hartley in modest-size galleries, Georgia O'Keeffe aptly commented years later that "it was like a brass band in a small closet."[10] *Military* and its companions are clamorous, blaring tributes to modern city experience—appropriately, they knit frenetic disjunctiveness with a moving pictorial inventiveness.

In turning to the modern metropolis, Hartley aligned his art with a tradition of modernism quite well established by the second decade of the twentieth century. French critic and poet Charles Baudelaire was the first to call persuasively for "the painter of modern life," the title of his famous 1863 essay.[11] He encouraged artists to abandon the tired pictorial formulas and historical subjects of the academy and to create work that explored contemporary experience. The hustle of crowded streets, the character of city living, was what he meant by "painting modern life."[12] French impressionism of the late nineteenth century creatively chronicled the vast changes then under way with increasing industrialization and urbanization. Scenes of urban transport, bustling boulevards, city parks and cafés, and bourgeois leisure activities filled their canvases. Their pictorial arsenal also changed—from the mannered polish and precision of academic art to more disorderly, often improvisational, systems of visual representation. Explaining the new approach decades later, the Paris-based sculptor Jacques Lipchitz quipped, "One cannot live on a visual diet of skyscrapers and produce the same sort of art as one who fed visually on the Acropolis."[13]

A host of critics and sociologists worked to formulate a framework for the "new," for modernity as it was lived in recently industrialized cities. Baudelaire and George Simmel, Walter Benjamin, and Sigfried Kracauer after him, all agreed that "the ephemeral, the fugitive, [and] the contingent" defined the essential contours of the new, urban conditions.[14] The idea that human experience and perception operated in a rationally ordered continuum was jettisoned for the notion that perception was fleeting, mutable, and arbitrary. Life experience in the industrial city was and is governed by a persistent barrage of temporal, fragmentary stimuli. George Simmel, the eminent sociologist who lived in Berlin and based his trenchant essays on it, famously characterized the jarring urban scene in 1903 as "the rapid crowding of changing images, the sharp discontinuity in the grasp of a single glance, and the unexpectedness of onrushing impressions."[15] By the 1900s, the experience of cities—Simmel's "intensification of nervous stimulation"—was seen as paradigmatic of the new century.[16] As historian Jonathan Crary intelligently demonstrated, a unifying system of visual representation that presented reality as an illusory but graspable whole within a single view no longer squared with lived experience. Nonetheless, illusory realism continued to dominate pictorial representation. In assessing the changed understanding

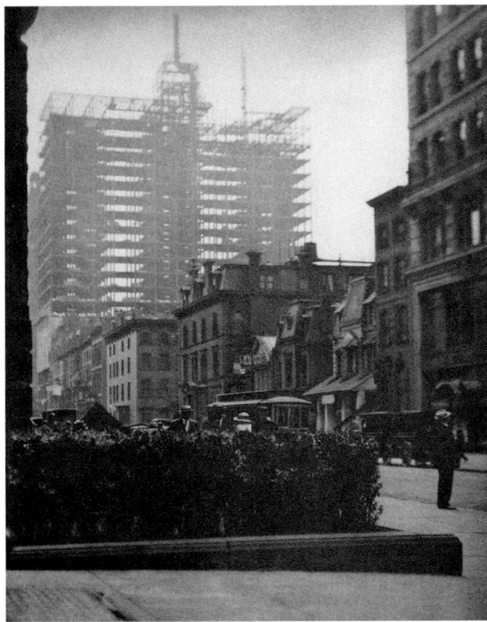

Figure 2
Alfred Stieglitz
Old and New New York, 1910
Photogravure on Japanese tissue
mounted on paperboard
The Art Institute of Chicago
Alfred Stieglitz Collection, 1949.3.311
Photograph © 2002, The Art Institute of Chicago,
All Rights Reserved

of visual perception, Crary focused on the modern observer, the city dweller who encounters a virtual minefield of sensory stimuli when navigating the metropolis.[17]

Disjunction, in a word, conditioned the daily interchange in modern cities. Over time, creative responses to the new urban circumstances developed, and whole new literary, musical, and pictorial vocabularies emerged to evoke its fragmentary, discontinuous verve. In the distinguished scholarship on the changing metropolis and its cultural impact, some historians propose that modern art as a whole arose from the basic characteristics of urban modernity and modernization.[18] That overstates the case, unfortunately, and leaves too many fascinating artists unaccounted for even though the experience of cities could be profoundly alluring in this era.

Hartley had a wealth of models close at hand inspiring him to consider the city and take it up in his art. On both sides of the Atlantic, forward-looking artists were making city paintings. In New York, Ashcan school artists drew attention to their progressive work that chronicled the urban scenes and behaviors entirely new in the early twentieth century—vaudeville shows, teeming immigrant tenements, window shopping, elevated commuter rail transit, and skyscraper construction sites filled their canvases. The work of Robert Henri, John Sloan, William Glackens, Everett Shinn, and others represented a leading form of rebellious modernism in the States in these years, and only now are the intelligence and daring of these artists and their portrayals of city life coming to be understood.[19] Although Ashcan art did not directly inspire Hartley in Berlin, he could scarcely forget its importance within the New York art world.

In his own circle of friends and colleagues in Manhattan, Hartley would have been familiar with the experiments with city pictures made by Alfred Stieglitz and John Marin. Hartley's mentor and dealer, the photographer Stieglitz turned to the subject of the city in the 1890s. His initial pictures of New York, abreast of trends at the time, were pictorialist and presented a soft-focus romanticized view of the metropolis. Even the titles for these photographs make clear that they acted as metaphoric celebrations of the city—for example *The Hand of Man* (1902), a railyard obscured by billowing steam. The pictorial rhetoric drew from late-nineteenth-century conventions "to describe what was novel by using terms that were timeworn and familiar," as art historian Wanda Corn put it.[20] By roughly 1910, however, the vocabulary of Stieglitz's city images had changed. In the intervening years, he had exhibited and embraced prime adherents of the European avant-garde—Paul Cézanne, August Rodin, Henri Matisse, and Pablo Picasso. Coming to terms with Picasso and cubism, in particular, photography historian Sarah Greenough maintains, fostered a new direction in Stieglitz's understanding and art; it inspired his move from pictorialism to radical modernism.[21] He developed a greater concern with compositional structures and formal devices. He adopted straight photography with crisp focus and sharp detail to throw each component into high relief. *Old and New New York* (fig. 2) represents this new body of work well. The city view is a web of graphic shapes and lines that resist quick comprehension. The impact of cubism's abstraction is clear in this photograph, wherein an agitated knot of architectural elements stands as the important content, and not the street scene itself. And Stieglitz offered pointed commentary on the "new" in this image by juxtaposing the rising scaffolding of a Manhattan skyscraper under construction with the nineteenth-century brownstones at the fore—the old and new in his title. The comparison signals the celebratory nature of the image. His photography grew increasingly abstract—cropping elements from view, zooming in on sparer compositions, creating sharply two-dimensional effects by compressing the pictorial space. Although Stieglitz did not exhibit his city pictures in his New York gallery until February/March 1913 when Hartley, as an intimate of the Stieglitz circle, was already in Europe, Hartley would have been well aware of his developing eye.

John Marin, too, in the first years of the second decade was at work innovating new ways to capture the energy and frenetic dimension of city experience. With many artists of the era, Marin depicted the obvious icons of New York's growing modernity. His art includes repeated views of the Brooklyn Bridge, the Woolworth Building (tallest building in the world from 1913 to 1930), and Fifth Avenue shopping. Formally, his metropolitan watercolors are an advance from turn-of-the-century models. The quick dash of his brush, the wobbling buildings, the heaving sidewalks all convey the animated energy of the city streets. Although these images do considerably deconstruct conventional modes of representation, they still present vistas and viewpoints that offer a full, not fragmentary, scene and, thus, a totalizing, illusory vision of the city. As Corn correctly analyzed, Marin's city pictures retain traces of the picturesque (fig. 3).[22]

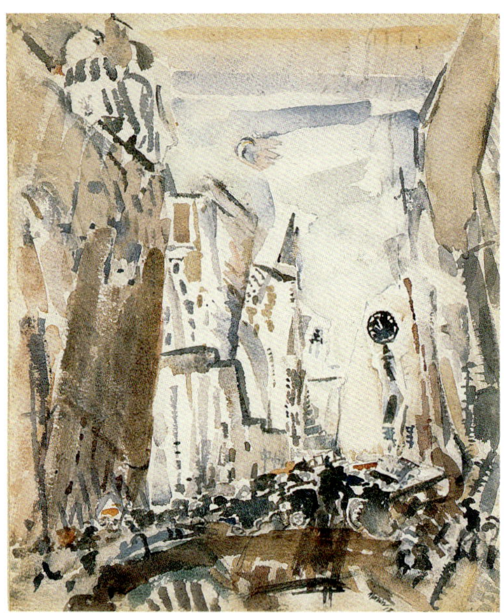

Figure 3
John Marin
Movement, Fifth Avenue, 1912
Watercolor, with traces of black crayon, over charcoal, on off-white watercolor paper, $16\frac{7}{8} \times 13\frac{11}{16}$ in. (42.8 × 34.8 cm)
The Art Institute of Chicago
Alfred Stieglitz Collection, 1949.554
Photograph by Kathleen Culbert-Aguilar, Chicago
Photograph © 2002, The Art Institute of Chicago, All Rights Reserved
© 2003 The Estate of John Marin/Artists Rights Society (ARS), New York

Robert Delaunay and his well-known paeans to the modernity of Paris would have been the next body of city paintings Hartley encountered at close hand. In Paris, Hartley met Delaunay one evening at the salon of writer Gertrude Stein.[23] At the time, Delaunay was midstream with an extended cycle of evolving paintings on Paris. Hartley might have seen *The City of Paris* (fig. 4) on view at the spring 1912 Salon des Indépendants. In a cubist fracture, it combines the Eiffel Tower, three classical graces, and lower-lying buildings of old Paris along the Seine. On the one hand, Delaunay portrayed the modernity of Paris through its signal engineering achievement. On the other, he also looked to the city's illustrious past. About a year later, Hartley visited Delaunay at his studio with his German friend the sculptor Arnold Rönnebeck. In a letter recounting the gathering to Stieglitz, Hartley clearly described Delaunay's *The Cardiff Team* (fig. 5), a painting that combined pictorial motifs in a more haphazard fashion than *The City of Paris*.[24] We know from letters that Delaunay rubbed Hartley the wrong way. To Hartley's mind, he seemed both arrogant and overly interested in conceptual constructs for his art.[25] Nonetheless, there are compelling reasons why Hartley would have paid close attention to the French painter.

Hartley was often beset with doubts regarding how things would turn out for him, but he rarely doubted his own importance as an artist. In his many letters home, he made it clear that he longed to make a name for himself in Europe, something he set about with determined purpose. Delaunay, in the years approaching World War I, was admired,

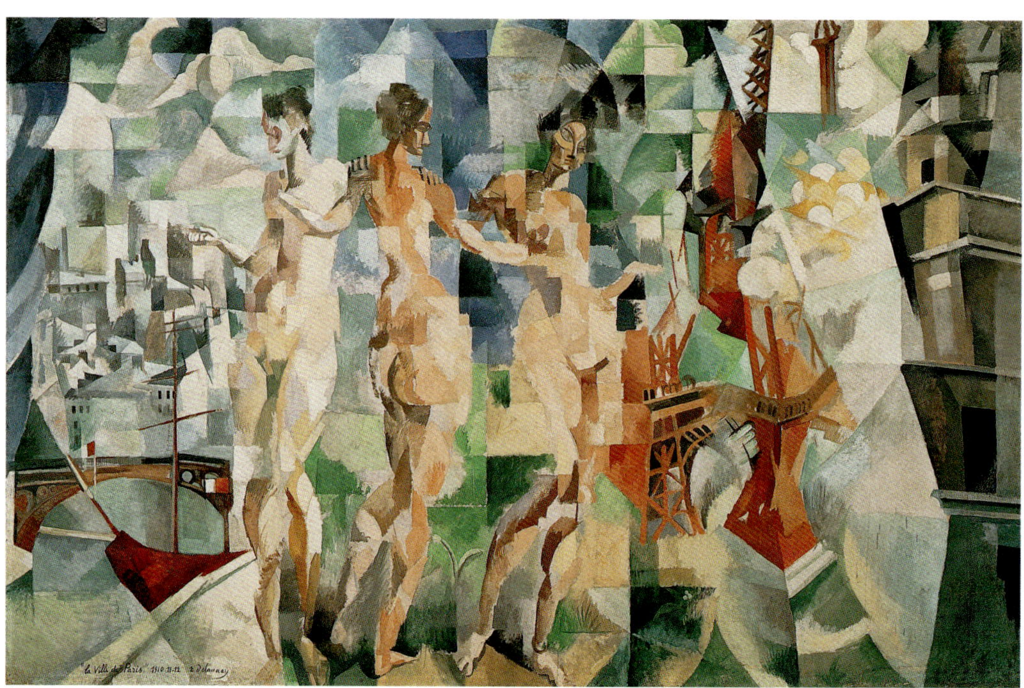

Figure 4
Robert Delaunay
La Ville de Paris (The City of Paris), 1910–12
Oil on canvas
Musée National d'Art Moderne, Centre Georges Pompidou, Paris
© L & M Services B.V. Amsterdam 20020510
CNAC/MNAM/Dist. Réunion des Musées Nationaux/Art Resource, N.Y.

Figure 5
Robert Delaunay
L'Équipe de Cardiff (The Cardiff Team), 1912–13
Oil on canvas
Musée d'Art Moderne, Paris
© L & M Services B.V. Amsterdam 20020510
© Photothèque des Musées de la Ville
de Paris (ou PMVP)/Cliché: Joffre

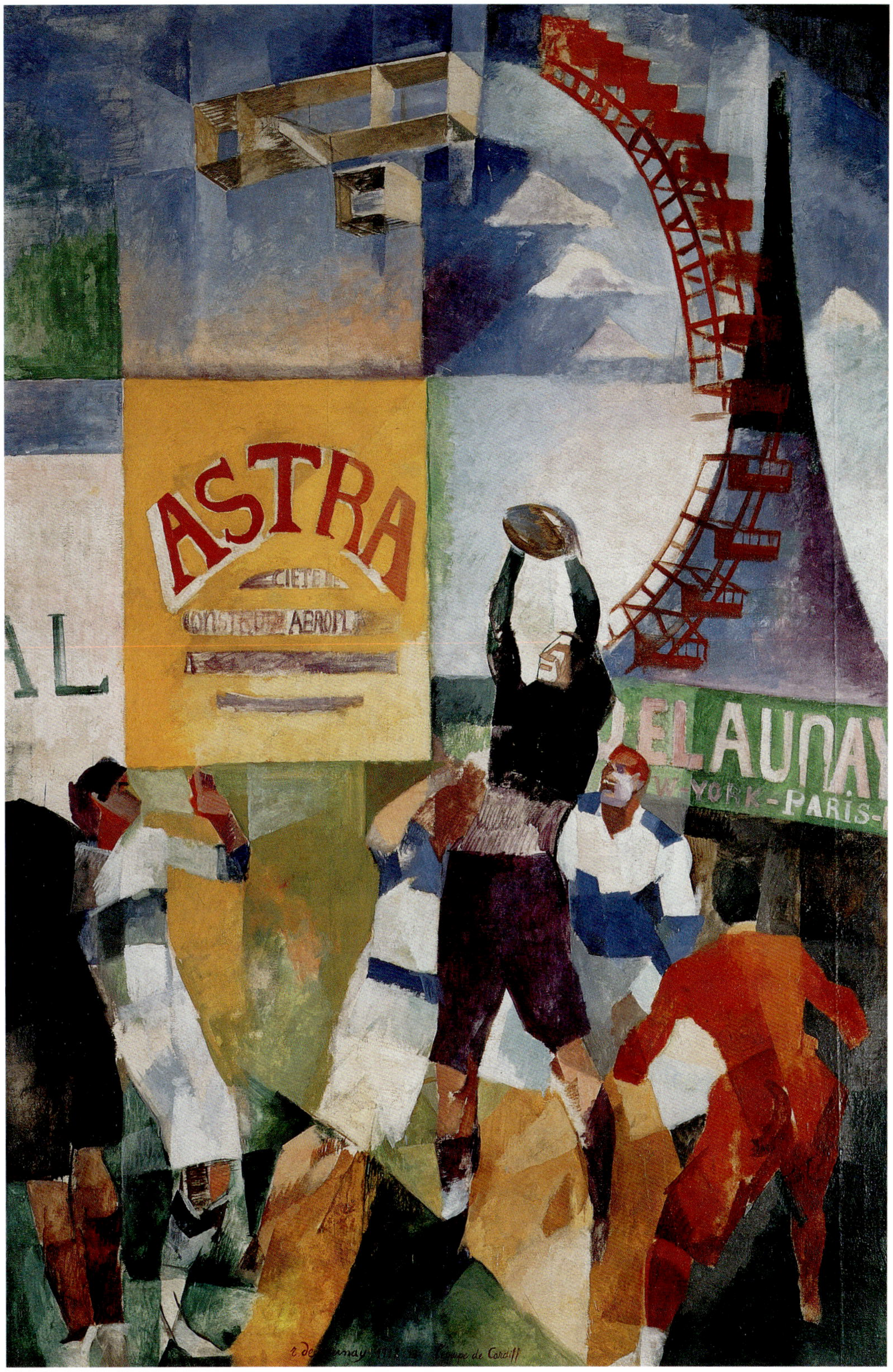

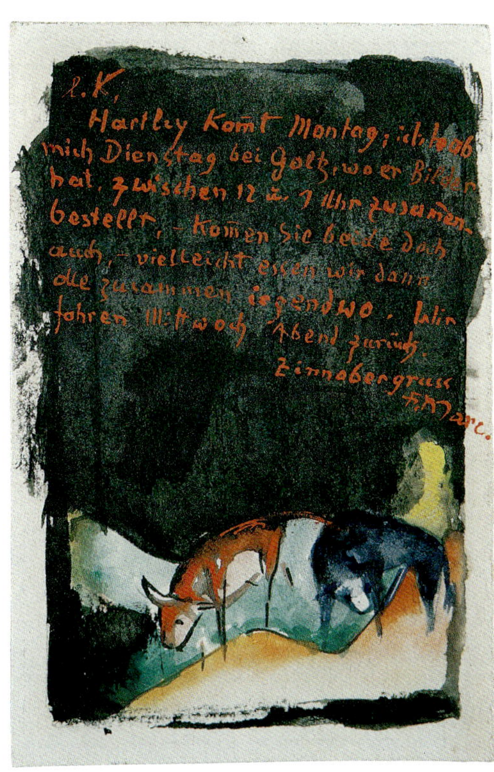
l. K,
Hartley komt Montag; ich hab
mich Dienstag bei Goltz, wo er Bilder
hat, zwischen 12 u. 1 Uhr zusamen-
bestellt, – komen Sie beide doch
auch, – vielleicht essen wir dann
alle zusammen irgendwo. Wir
fahren Mittwoch Abend zurück.
Zinnobergruss
F. Marc.

Figure 6
Franz Marc
Zinnobergruss, 1913
Postcard from Franz Marc to Wassily Kandinsky, 19 April 1913. Marc wrote to arrange a meeting between himself and Kandinsky, Gabriele Münter, and Hartley
© Stadtische Galerie im Lenbachhaus, Munich

exhibited, and collected in precisely the settings where Hartley also settled or had significant contacts—Paris, Munich, and Berlin. Hartley routed his travels to Berlin through Bavaria to examine the scene in Munich. There he met many of the expressionist Blaue Reiter artists and was taken under the wing of Franz Marc (fig. 6) and Wassily Kandinsky, the primary leaders of the group. Marc in particular corresponded regularly and helped Hartley to find exhibition opportunities in Germany.[26] Delaunay was already well established with this group and popular with their patrons. When Delaunay showed with the first Blaue Reiter exhibition in Munich in December 1911, three of his four paintings sold.[27] Delaunay was also well integrated in Berlin. During Hartley's initial visit to Berlin in January 1913,

Figure 7
Robert Delaunay
Soleil, Tour, Aéroplane (Sun, Tower, Airplane), 1913
Oil on canvas, 52 × 51⅝ in. (132.1 × 131.1 cm)
Collection Albright-Knox Art Gallery,
Buffalo, New York
A. Conger Goodyear Fund, 1964

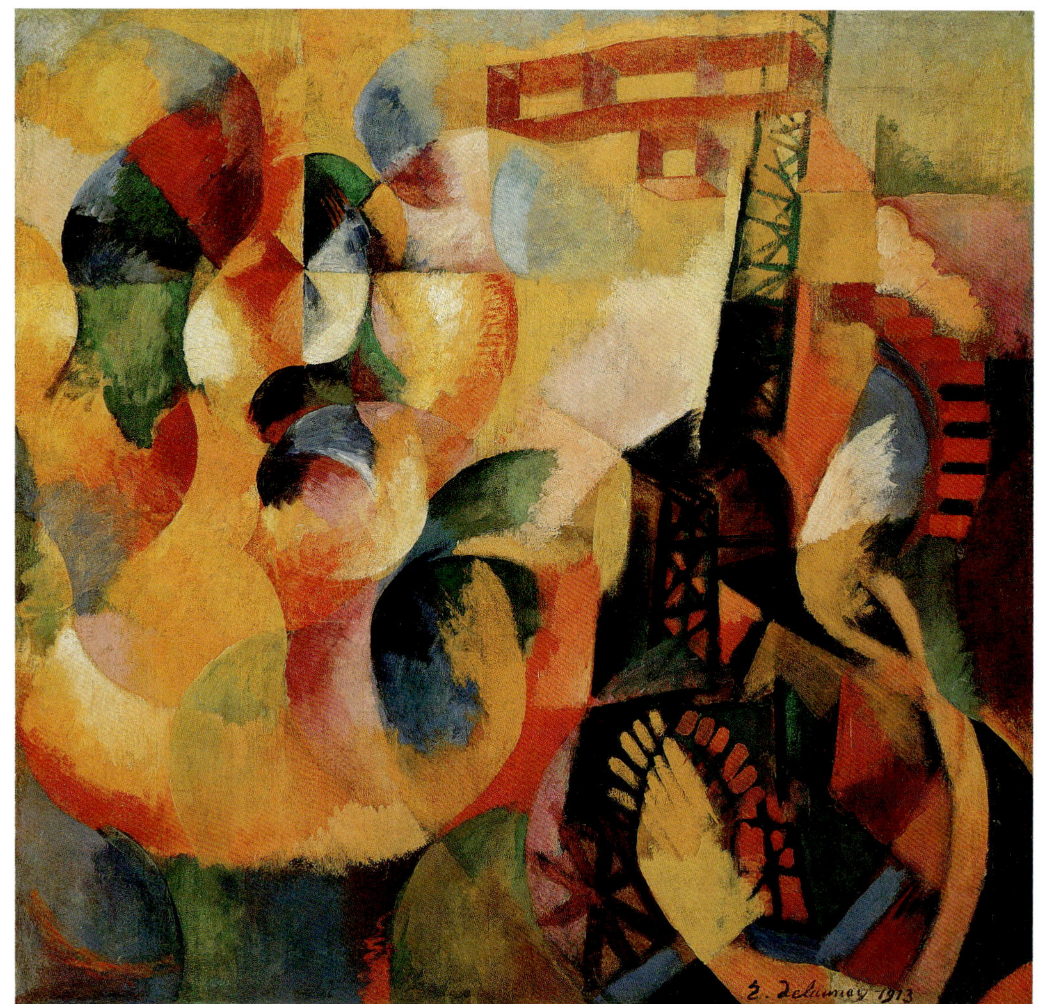

Delaunay's solo exhibition was on at Der Sturm. Led by impresario and one-time concert pianist and composer Herwarth Walden (born Georg Lewin), Der Sturm was Berlin's center for the most daring art.[28] In the fall of 1913, Walden organized a landmark exhibition that surveyed Europe's leading avant-garde art at the time, the Erster Deutscher Herbstsalon (First German Fall Salon). To accommodate the 366 works, additional gallery space was rented on Potsdamerstrasse. Through Marc's and Kandinsky's intercession, Hartley exhibited in the Herbstsalon. He was tremendously pleased to be included, represented in his first showing ever in Europe by four paintings. By contrast, Robert Delaunay had twenty-one paintings on display, second only to the special memorial tribute to the recently deceased French painter Henri Rousseau.[29]

The Cardiff Team was exhibited at the Erster Deutscher Herbstsalon as well as *Sun, Tower, Airplane* (fig. 7). Parisian architectural motifs appear again, notably the striking Eiffel Tower. But the web of purely pictorial construction gradually erases the conspicuous city imagery. Color in patches of forceful unmodulated hue can be seen moving the representational elements off the canvas. Fragmented remnants of a green Eiffel Tower are still in evidence at the right.[30] A prop plane also appears in spare outline in the upper right corner, yet its colors blend so well with the adjacent hues that it is hard to decipher immediately as a representational motif. Delaunay's demonstration would have been important for Hartley. In the course of a year, Delaunay effectively turned from symbolic, representational images—their clear modernity notwithstanding—to a far more innovative form of pictorial expression. The visual drama of color contrasts and a swirling arabesque of shifting prismatic forms now evoked the dynamism of the city.

At least one other painting caught Hartley's eye at the Erster Deutscher Herbstsalon, although his enthusiasm for the project revealed in his letters suggests that many others did as well. Earlier in that year, French artist Francis Picabia had traveled to New York to see the Armory show, another massive exhibition of more than one thousand works demonstrating international artistic trends, a first on American shores. Picabia responded enthusiastically to the throbbing crowds and looming towers of Manhattan, and he began a series of exceptional watercolors that abstractly translated his sensations of the city. Alfred Stieglitz, convinced by that time that abstraction was "a new medium expression—the true medium," appreciated the symbolic equation between Picabia's pulsing shapes and excited city haste.[31] Ten works by Picabia on the theme of New York City went on display at Stieglitz's gallery from March 17 through April 5, 1913.[32] Of course, Hartley missed the show. But he was able to see one of these watercolors, because Walden included it in the Herbstsalon. *New York* (fig. 8) achieves what remains a direction in Delaunay's city paintings—clear-cut references to the cityscape or urban scenes have been jettisoned. Picabia's *New York* tightly knits geometrical blocks with looser, undulating forms. The compression of small parts merged together and then set against sweeping vertical lines vaguely recalls the city's physical architectural setting—a grid of smaller buildings that stand in relief against one of the newer vast highrises. Yet usual cues to this kind of reading don't exist. The compacted composition evokes the jostling of rush hour or the dense thicket of city structures.

The Italian futurists exhibited at the Erster Deutscher Herbstsalon too, and Hartley wrote that he had also seen examples of their work in Paris. A core theme for futurist art was the passioned, hectic pace of city life. The futurists invented "lines of force" that convey both movement and energy and applied this pictorial device to individual objects, humans, and entire cityscapes. Such city pictures at Der Sturm's Herbstsalon must have struck Hartley.

Living in Berlin, Hartley also made his own survey of the scene, his research aided by Arnold Rönnebeck, the Berliner whom Hartley initially befriended in Paris.[33] Beyond Der Sturm, he visited the progressive galleries of Paul Cassirer and Hans Gurlitt, where more German modernism would have been on view. As a whole, the German expressionists were

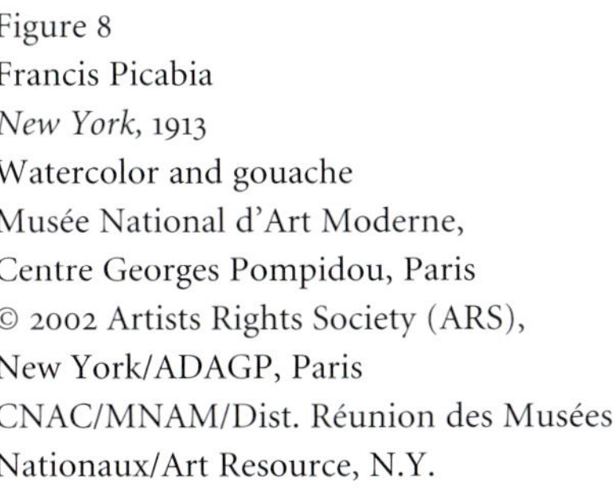

Figure 8
Francis Picabia
New York, 1913
Watercolor and gouache
Musée National d'Art Moderne,
Centre Georges Pompidou, Paris
© 2002 Artists Rights Society (ARS),
New York/ADAGP, Paris
CNAC/MNAM/Dist. Réunion des Musées
Nationaux/Art Resource, N.Y.

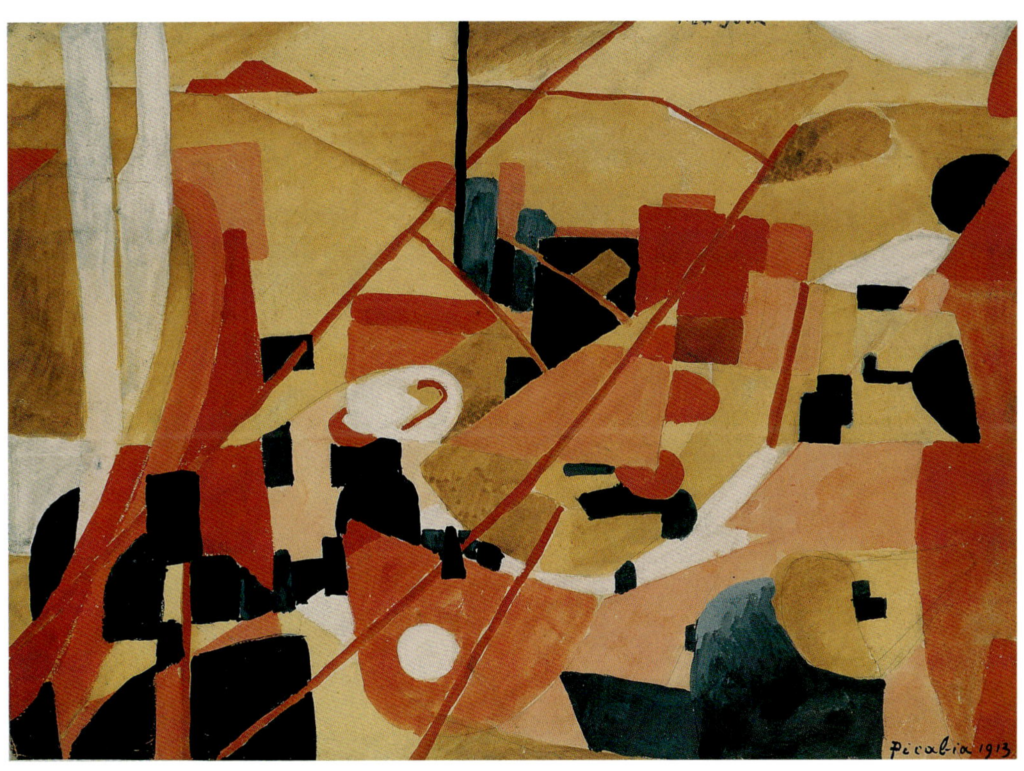

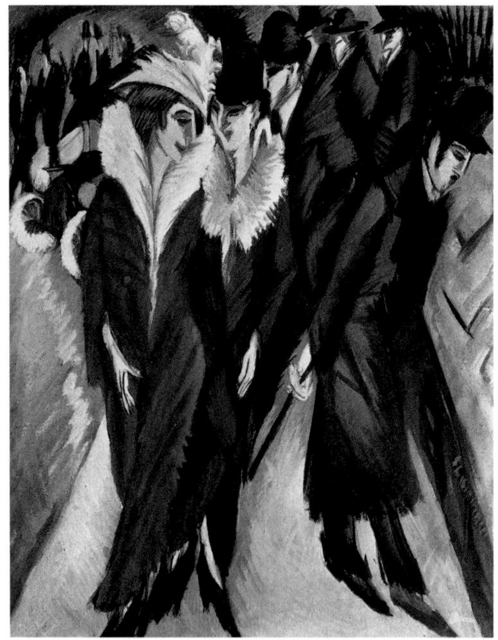

Figure 9
Ernst Ludwig Kirchner
Street, Berlin, 1913
Oil on canvas, 47½ × 35⅞ in. (120.7 × 91.1 cm)
The Museum of Modern Art, New York
Purchase
Digital File © 2002
The Museum of Modern Art, New York

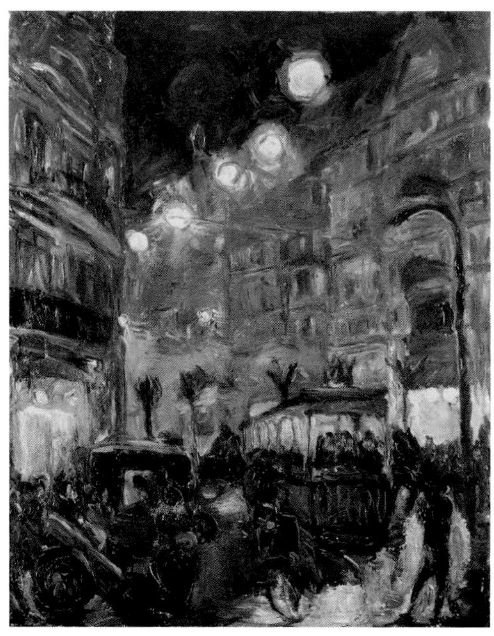

Figure 10
Max Beckmann
Strasse bei Nacht (Street at Night), 1913
Oil on canvas
Private Collection
Photograph by Hans Joachim Bartsch, Berlin

keenly interested in the metropolis in which they lived. A generation before them, the German impressionists had depicted the sites of leisurely pleasure in Berlin, when they represented it in their work at all.[34] Beginning especially around 1910, the expressionists eagerly turned to their burgeoning new *Weltstadt.*[35] Ernst Ludwig Kirchner's *Street, Berlin* (fig. 9), Ludwig Meidner's *Apocalyptic Landscape (Near the Halensee Railroad Station)* (fig. 12), Heinrich Richter-Berlin's *Our Dear Lady of Tauentzien Street* (fig. 11), or Max Beckmann's *Street at Night* (fig. 10) exemplifies the range of *Grossstadtbilder* these Berlin modernists formulated. Like the New York Ashcan artists, in investigating city experience, they examined new and evolving forms of social exchange and urban activities. Kirchner made a series of paintings creatively depicting the showy presence of prostitutes along Berlin's bustling shopping corridors. Richter-Berlin's *Tauentzeinstrasse* shows a busy boulevard flanked by the swankiest Berlin department stores and leading to the Kaiser Wilhelm Memorial Church. These and other expressionist images offer a fevered language of slashing strokes, jarring colors, and heavy, gestural paint that imbue their canvases with the clamor of the streets. For Hartley, it would have been quite important that the metropolis attracted such artistic interest by many of Germany's leading new talents. Yet Hartley wanted to make an original contribution and to be known. When he adopted city painting, his art would necessarily take a different tack.

What was it about Berlin that first caused Hartley to adopt the metropolis as the subject of his art when he moved there from New York, perhaps the only other city whose pace of growth and change outstripped all other major urban centers in the late nineteenth and early twentieth centuries? Why hadn't he taken up this subject in Manhattan? The answer involves many factors, but is tied especially to timing, context, and the artist's drive. As the foregoing suggests, many within Europe's leading avant-garde were active with city painting. It wasn't enough for Hartley that progressive artists stateside looked to the metropolis as an avenue to make their art modern. But when this subject became widespread and a source of innovation for Europeans, Hartley wanted to be counted in their league. In addition, from his correspondence, it is clear that Berlin mesmerized Hartley. The Wilhelmine capital was not a city of skyscrapers like New York. But as an industrial power, it visibly paraded its modernization in ways that Paris or London did not in this period. Observing other key artists abroad and at home wrestle with creative representations of city experience, Hartley decided in Berlin to paint the place and its phenomena that newly fascinated him.

Berlin was a tremendously exciting city in the early decades of the twentieth century. A blossoming of culture, industry, technology, and politics made the city unique. Berlin was the brand new capital city of the German Reich. The principalities of Germany united to form a collective nation only in 1871, following the German victory in the Franco-Prussian War, and Berlin was designated its new center. As the former nucleus of Prussia, Berlin had been a formidable industrial strength for some time by 1871. The German companies that remain familiar business names to this day—including Agfa, Borsig, Schering, and Siemens—were founded in Berlin before 1870.[36] Berlin was Germany's center for the iron and coal manufacturing characteristic of the first industrial revolution. After 1870 Berlin, like New York, led the managerial and technical developments that enabled the transmission and distribution of electrical power so necessary for ongoing modernization of all kinds.[37] Electrical engineering, chemical production, and the creation of technical infrastructure characterized the second industrial revolution, in which Berlin and New York excelled.

One measure of the pace of continual industrial expansion in turn-of-the-century Berlin lies in the city's population statistics, as workers were attracted to factory jobs. In 1849 Berlin had 412,000 inhabitants. A little more than twenty years later, in 1871 after the

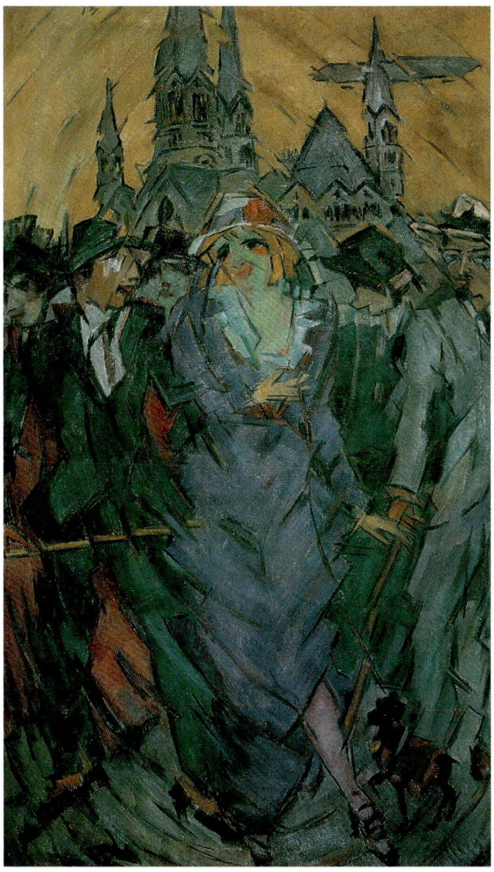

Figure 11
Heinrich Richter-Berlin
Unsere liebe Frau von der Tauentzienstrasse (Our Dear Lady of Tauentzien Street), 1913
Oil on canvas, 58⅝ × 31¼ in. (149 × 79.5 cm)
Berlinische Galerie, Landesmuseum für Moderne Kunst, Photographie und Architektur, Berlin

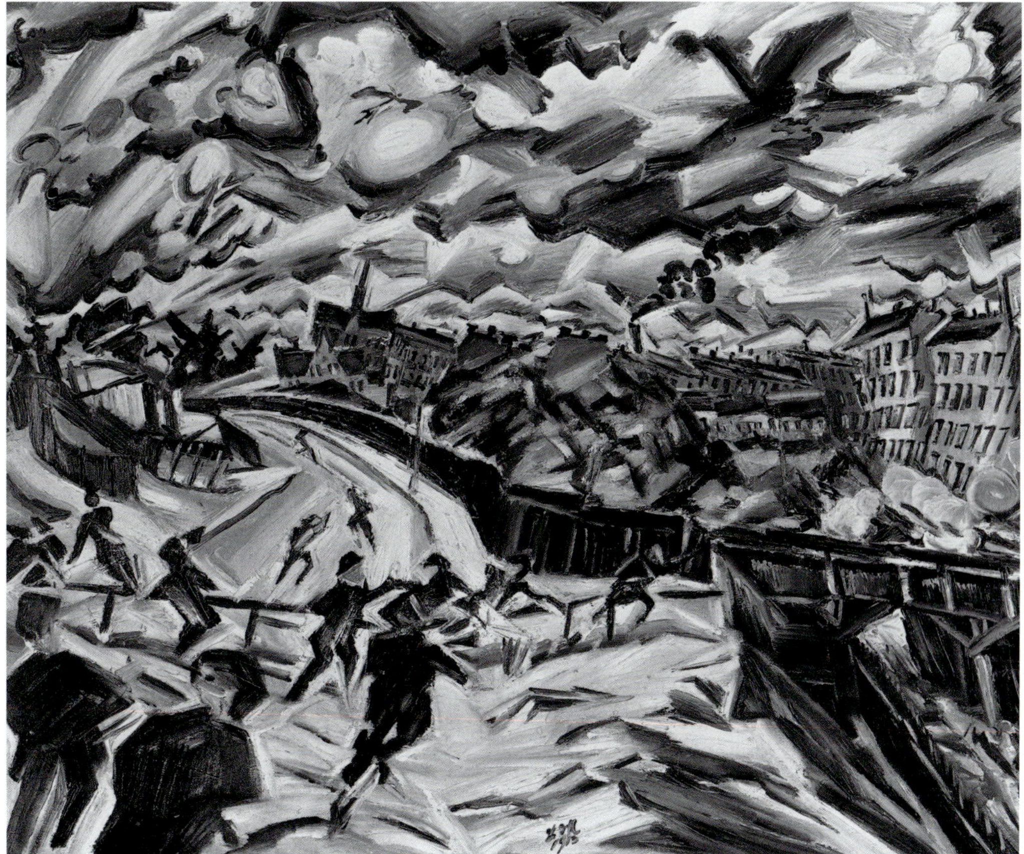

Figure 12
Ludwig Meidner
Apocalyptic Landscape (Near the Halensee Railroad Station), c. 1913
Oil on canvas, 37½ × 31⅝ in. (95.3 × 80.3 cm)
Los Angeles County Museum of Art
Gift of Clifford Odets

city became the German capital, that figure doubled to 826,000. In 1877 the city hit the one million mark; in 1905 it had two million; by 1914 the count grew to four million city dwellers.[38] The incorporation of Grossberlin in 1920, drawing adjacent municipalities together, made the city the third largest metropolis after London and New York.[39] Berliner street slang dubbed the place a *Buddelstadt,* or sand box city, after the continuous construction to accommodate this rapid growth.[40] In 1910 the city's leading art critic wrote a book about Berlin in which he claimed that it was "damned always to perpetual becoming, never to being."[41] Transitory or fleeting experiences in Berlin happened any day on the street, yet "transitory" is also a word that aptly described the ever-evolving cityscape of buildings.

To enable city dwellers to move from home to work to play, networks of commuter transit grew around the city. Horse-drawn streetcars were introduced in 1865 and replaced by electric ones in 1895. A city railway began operation in 1882 and was supplemented by the first subway line in 1902. A large city of people bustling to and fro was part of the *Schnellebigkeit* (fast living) that became both actual fact and the preferred mythos of the city (fig. 13).

In Berlin, movement about town was also conditioned by the imperial presence. Wilhelm II, Germany's monarch from 1888 to 1918 and a man of highly conservative tastes, demanded an ostentatious show of his rule. Accordingly, imperial guards and military units paraded through town and escorted aristocracy and court officials from palace to court to Potsdam, the Kaiser's country residence and main garrison for troops. As historians Sabine

Figure 13
Berlin. Unter den Linden, Ecke Friedrichstrasse, Kranzler Ecke
Postcard from Marsden Hartley to Alfred Stieglitz, postmarked July 19, 1914
Yale Collection of American Literature
Beinecke Rare Book and Manuscript Library
Yale University, New Haven

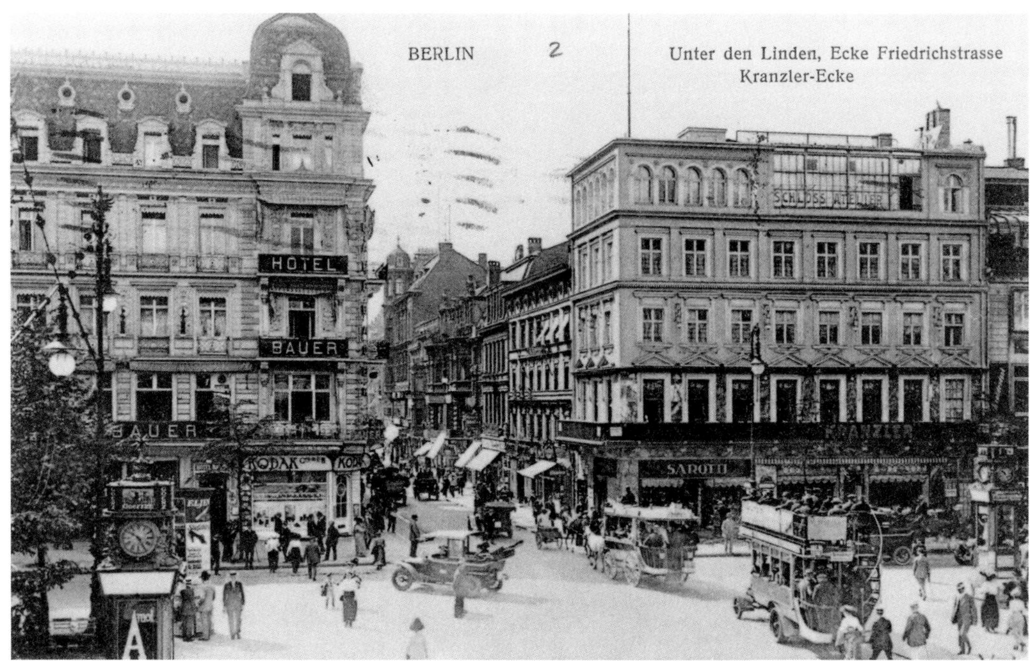

Hollburg and Gottfried Korff explained: "One talked about the 'metropolis in guard uniform' during the Kaiser's rule and thereby underscored that social life in Berlin was intoxicated with the spirit and color of the military as no other European capital."[42] Hartley simply loved this pomp and circumstance and said in 1913, "it stimulates my child's love for the public spectacle."[43] In his autobiography, he nostalgically recalled:

> *The military life provided the key and clue to everything then— … Of course in the Kaiser time there was always a parade of some kind coming down the Unter den Linden— … there was always the changing of the watch before the castle in Berlin every morning between ten thirty and eleven— … I had arrived in Berlin at the right time to get the richness of the pageantry idea. There was a sense of magic in seeing royalty pass—.*[44]

Hartley also arrived at the right time to enjoy Berlin's dramatic urban spectacle, confirming that "there was so much to regale the eye with" in this city.[45] In recent years, urban scholars and cultural historians have examined the transition of cities into fantastic consumer showcases from roughly 1890 to 1920. A heightened emphasis on visual sensation developed that had the power to intoxicate urbanites by its voltage and newness. Electrical lighting brightened the night sky and enticed people to "go out" in new numbers, an activity chronicled by Beckmann in *Street at Night* (fig. 10). In the eerie palette, Beckmann conveys the intense, garish glow of the first electrical arc lamps. Novel urban amusements—music halls and moving picture shows—offered visual delights and quick-tempoed variety acts.[46] The invention and manufacture of plate glass in the 1890s enabled stores to display their wares attractively in vast gleaming windows while lighting them dramatically for the first time with electricity. Major department stores appeared that presented a sumptuous encyclopedia of consumer goods, often in opulent architectural settings. The main shopping boulevards were always overcrowded, and "just shopping" became a definitive urban pastime.[47] In 1910 noisy protest finally extinguished a Berlin ordinance that required store windows to be shuttered on Sundays, and thereafter window shoppers were free to browse leisurely seven days a week.[48] Advertising markedly changed the look of cities when newly invented inexpensive printing methods and electrical lighting made provocative posters, bills, and signs ubiquitous. Coincidentally, the street-corner column to which people affix a changing array of bills was invented in Berlin. In German, they are called *Littfasssäulen* after Ernst Littfass, the savvy printer who first installed them.[49] In the urban milieu, ever more, ever larger, and ever bolder advertising signage competed for the passerby's attention. Speeding elevated or subterranean streetcars also offered exhilarating vistas onto the city's commotion. This potpourri of city experience increasingly intensified visual stimuli, and recent studies have emphasized that a new mode of exaggerated visual experience—"an unabashed display of visuality," according to scholar Miriam Hansen—arose in this era.[50] "Alles 'fürs Auge'" (everything for the eye) were the words Berlin critic and politician Walther Rathenau used to characterize the changed dimension of his city in 1902.[51]

Artists were not immune to the appeals of this vibrant new visual culture. Beyond the caffeinated pace of modern city life, visual artists appreciated its new level of spectacle. The very fact that Hartley began painting the city in Berlin indicates that he too saw and valued the extraordinary showcase it had become. "Berlin is helping me much," he wrote shortly after settling in Germany. "I am getting a something from the German life impulse which is most excellent for me. It gives a new crescendo to my sensations—."[52]

Hartley was a new convert to abstraction when he arrived in Berlin. While in Paris, he had begun a series of works initially devoted to a creative visual transcription of music to canvas. *Musical Theme (Oriental Symphony)* (plate 8) of 1912–13 includes musical notation in a tapestry of exotic motifs and emblems. Steeped in reading mystical literature at the time, Hartley inserted a seated Buddha at the upper right and the Indian sign *abhaya mudra* (have no fear) of three raised hands at the top center. He executed these paintings, he explained, "in the style of automatic writing."[53] In shifting his residence to Berlin in 1913, Hartley initially maintained a similar pictorial vocabulary, but the drama of the Berlin streets replaced his musical reveries as subject matter.

Portrait of Berlin (plate 10) is likely Hartley's first Berlin city painting, for it is a key transitional work building on his development in Paris. The work orchestrates a complex of recognizable motifs, numerals, and abstract forms within an energized image. Pictorial elements press against one another, crowding every inch of the tightly compacted canvas to convey an animated force. Drawing from recent precedents in Paris, Hartley inserted a Buddha figure (to the left of center), and he retained his basic color scheme of bold primary yellow, red, blue, and green punctuating a luminous field of white. In addition to circles, stars, and triangles, Hartley peppered the canvas with German guards mounted on horseback. The plume-helmeted soldier on his red steed is easily recognized in the circle at the canvas's lower right corner. Strewn across the canvas, however, Hartley also included similar military guards viewed from behind that are less immediately identifiable.

Though an uncommon likeness for its subject, Hartley titled the painting *Portrait of Berlin.* Assimilating the dynamic spectacle of the imperial capital, he sorted his perceptions and offered them back in a pictorial language abstracted from the street. Hartley explained that "Berlin is packed with that live-wire feeling—."[54] He later remembered that "the whole scene was fairly bursting with organized energy and the tension was terrific and somehow most voluptuous in the feeling of power—a sexual immensity even in it."[55] Hartley translated his enthusiasm for the pace and spirit of Berlin onto his canvases. He confirmed as much by writing to Gertrude Stein that "there is an interesting source of material here—numbers + shapes + colors that make one wonder—and admire—It is essentially mural this German way of living—big lines + and large masses—always a sense of pageantry of living. I like it."[56] And he began to paint the so-called pageantry of living.

The most direct explication Hartley provided for his Berlin paintings centers on *The Warriors* (plate 11). In his autobiography, he described the scene, writing:

those huge cuirassiers of the Kaiser's special guard—all in white—white leather breeches skin tight—high plain enamel boots—those gleaming blinding medieval breast plates of silver and brass— ... There were the inspiring helmets with the imperial eagle and the white manes hanging down—there was six foot of youth under all this garniture—everyone on a horse—and every horse white—that is how I got it—and it went into an abstract picture of soldiers riding into the sun—.[57]

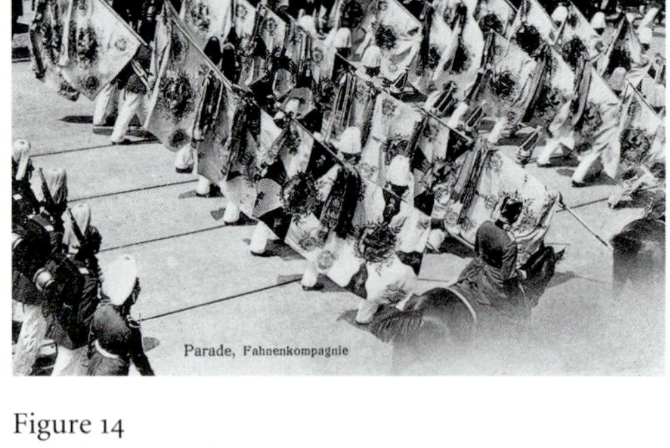

Figure 14
Parade, Fahnenkompagnie, 1913
Postcard from Marsden Hartley to Gertrude Stein, postmarked September 5, 1913
Yale Collection of American Literature
Beinecke Rare Book and Manuscript Library
Yale University, New Haven

The large expanse of canvas depicts the impressive German imperial cuirassiers on parade, white manes and flags flying. The quotation makes clear the homoerotic appeal for Hartley of these stunning German soldiers with skin-tight breeches (fig. 14).

As Hartley continued to formulate and refine his artistic vocabulary, he also deepened his conceptual approach. His friendship with Gertrude Stein, an author whose concrete writing captured the spirit of her ostensible subjects but never approached conventional description of them, encouraged Hartley toward more radical painting. She lent him a book by the philosopher William James, the novelist's brother.[58] The reading and discussions with Stein about James inspired Hartley. James argued for the undeniable value and consequence of one's subjective experience, bold claims when he articulated them in the years before Sigmund Freud published his ideas and they were popularized. The authority of Stein and James and the timing of Hartley's acquaintance with their beliefs propelled him toward key conceptual advances in his own art. His claim in 1913 that "I do not think first but after" signals the shift he undertook to develop a deeper sensitivity to his subjective side and use it to fuel his art.[59] In Germany, he emphasized repeatedly that his

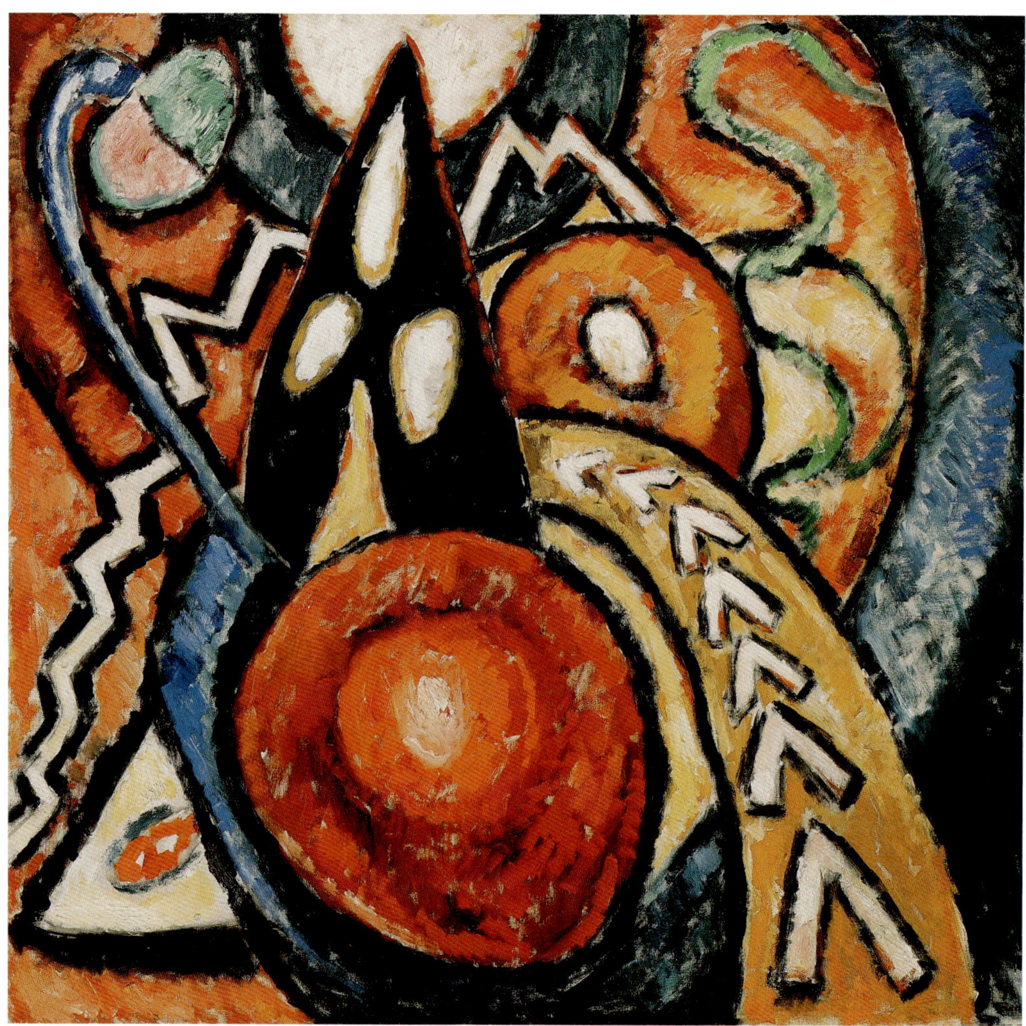

Figure 15
Marsden Hartley
Movements, c. 1915
Oil on canvas, 47⅛ × 47¼ in. (119.7 × 120 cm)
The Art Institute of Chicago
Alfred Stieglitz Collection, 1949.544
Photograph © 2002, The Art Institute of Chicago, All Rights Reserved

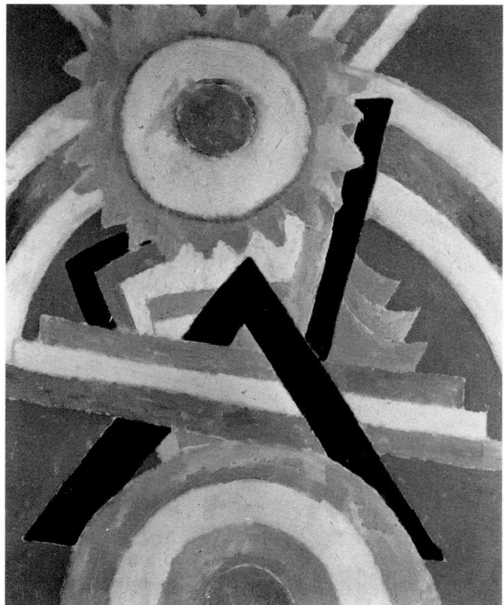

Figure 16
Marsden Hartley
Pre-War Pageant, 1914
Oil on canvas, 40 × 32 in. (101.6 × 81.3 cm)
Columbus Museum of Art, Ohio
Gift of Ferdinand Howald, 1931.175

painting arose from concrete experiences and that his intuitive perception was paramount. "Everything I do is attached at once + directly to personal experiences," Hartley affirmed. "It is dictated by life itself."[60] This approach prompted Hartley to focus on Berlin, and yet to use the city as a foil and enable his own sensitive perceptions of stimulating urban experiences to stand as the true content of his painting.

Consequently, *Movements* (fig. 15) and *Pre-War Pageant* (fig. 16) along with the 1913 *Military* (plate 12) are unusual city paintings. They capture with great originality and pictorial power that quality of Berlin that Hartley called "the intense flame-like quality of life."[61] Their bold color, writhing forms, and gestural, active paint condense the vigor and cacophony of the metropolis. They concentrate and reformulate the artist's sensations from this sensually provocative milieu.

German expressionist artist Ludwig Meidner was simultaneously engaged in making *Grossstadtbilder* in Wilhelmine Berlin. In 1911 he wrote a passionate essay on the topic and called for "a deeper insight into reality," one defined in modern times by "a bombardment of whizzing rows of windows, of screeching lights between vehicles of all kinds and a thousand jumping spheres, scraps of human beings, advertising signs, and shapeless colors."[62] Paintings like *Movements* achieve what Meidner encouraged and on a level that Meidner himself, whose work remained conventionally representational, did not. Scholar Philip Fisher formulated a useful distinction, in an essay about modern literary expression of the city, between city mind and city matter. More daring creations move beyond direct mimesis, he suggested; they are *of* the city rather than *about* the city and recast human perception of urban experiences, not its physical settings. Hartley's Berlin paintings were clearly *of* the city, not directly representational, conveying what Fisher termed its "structure of consciousness."[63]

Hartley enjoyed the appeal of Berlin and wrote about it in letters home. One especially poignant moment is his mention of a zeppelin passing overhead in 1914. One can imagine him seated at one of the city's sidewalk cafés. Hartley interrupts his line of thought and then returns to his letter and writes, "The Luftschiff L.V. has just passed over us here as I write—a fascinating thing which transports me somehow every time one sees any of them—."[64] Because Hartley dedicated himself to recording his experiences of the modern city, it isn't a stretch to suggest that *The Aero* (plate 15) is a work that arose from this or similar moments. Whether an airplane or airship, Hartley's *The Aero* offers a contemplation of one of modernization's more amazing inventions. The pictorial language that Hartley uses is jubilant. Flag patterns—flowing stripes and checkerboards—and graphic color juxtapositions spread across the canvas, the center of which depicts the fireburst of a flying machine's engine.

Himmel (plate 13) is a later addition to Hartley's city paintings.[65] It returns to the layered matrix of motif, emblems, and shapes first started in *Portrait of Berlin*. Hartley had made a quick trip back to the States in 1914 to hold an exhibition and raise more money for living expenses. On his return he made four paintings on the theme of Amerika, with Germanized spelling and Native American imagery (discussed in the essay by Wanda Corn).[66] Those paintings used a hieratic compartmentalization of the image, strongly geometric following the vivid patterns of American Indian art. The pictorial structure of the Amerika series informed other work Hartley made simultaneously in 1914, and his interest in Indian design elements encouraged him to include more recognizable imagery again in his city paintings.

The military figure on horseback reappeared in Hartley's treatment of Berlin. A statue of a German officer in *Himmel* and the idealized cuirassier in other 1914 paintings are signature elements. Abstracted solar orbs, flower bursts, flag patterns, eight-pointed stars,

Figure 17
Marsden Hartley
Painting No. 5, 1914–15
Oil on canvas, 39½ × 31¾ in. (100.3 × 80.6 cm)
Whitney Museum of American Art, New York
Gift of an anonymous donor (58.65)
Photograph © 1997: Whitney Museum
of American Art, New York
Photograph by Sheldon C. Collins, N.J.

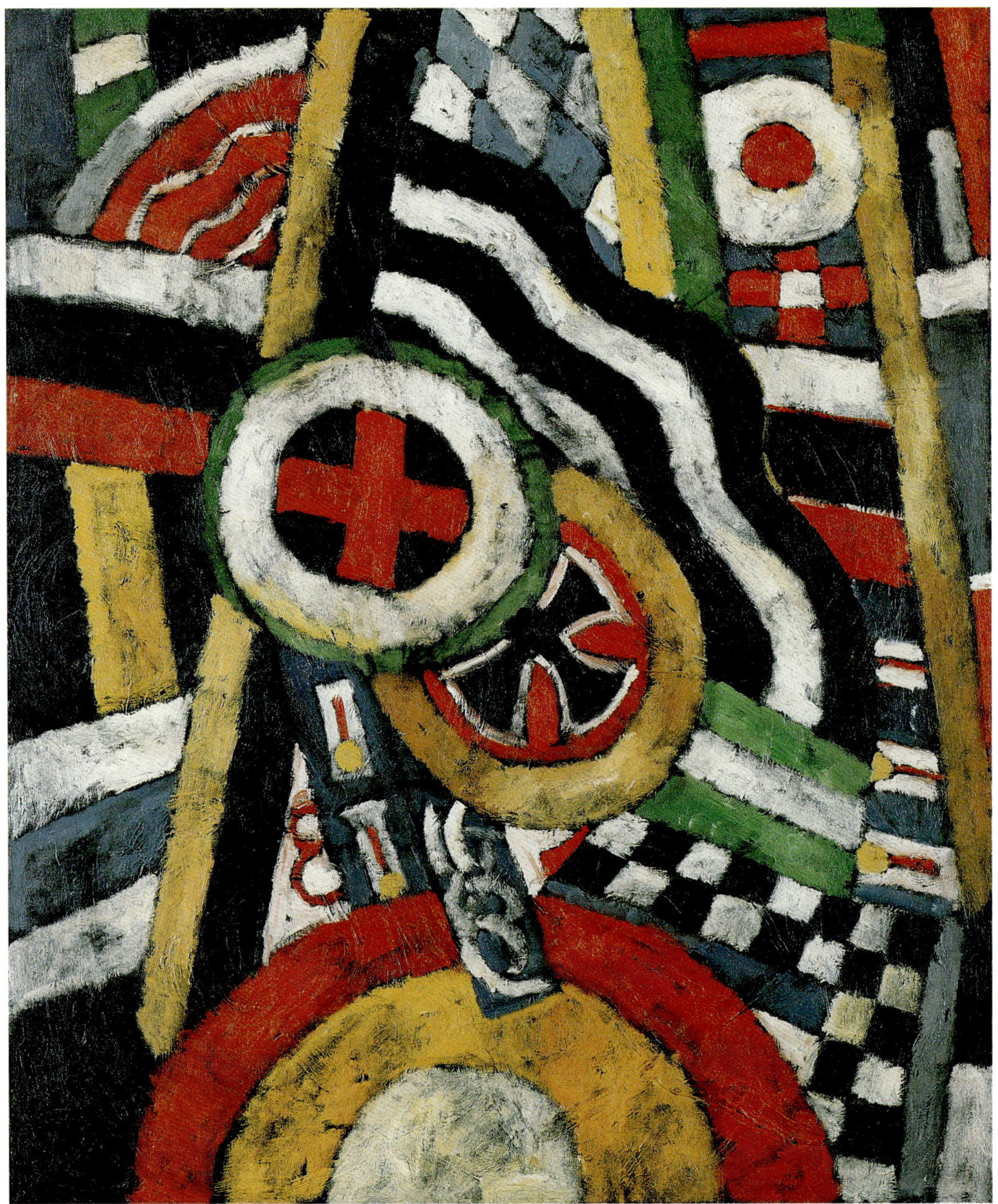

an equestrian's spur, abstracted insignia—these elements jostle for space in the compacted image and replicate the disjunctive but invigorating experience of the urban environment.

In describing his latest paintings for his New York show in January 1914, Hartley wrote: "A picture is but a given space where things of moment which happen to the painter occur.... The present exhibition is the work of one who sees—who believes in what is seen—and to whom every picture is as a portrait of that something seen."[67] For Hartley, *seeing* meant more than simple sight, and his paintings involved more than literal transcription. *Seeing* symbolized the requisite creative powers to assimilate intense sensual stimuli. His clear artistic mission was to discover a language that could convey such sensations. His resulting work needed to be compelling, unfettered from convention, and free from effected mannerism. He told German expressionist painter Franz Marc, "I am by nature a visionary," and his project at this point was certainly influenced by a resolute belief in subjectivity.[68] Nonetheless, he emphasized again and again—in his art and writings—that his direct encounters with the world around him provided his creative source. For his 1915 show at the Haas-Haye Galerie, prominently located in Berlin just steps away from the Brandenburg Gate, he said of his paintings, "they are characterizations of the 'Moment,' everyday pictures of every day, every hour."[69] The abstract, agitated forms and vibrant colors transform Hartley's experience of exhilaration in Berlin's teeming metropolis into groundbreaking art. They offer subjective, perceptual snapshots of the electric but chaotic and disjunctive environment of "the finest modern city in Europe."

There is one other essential way that these paintings speak of Berlin. The persistent depiction of the German military during these years covertly points to a defining aspect of Hartley's *and* Berlin's identity. Hartley was a gay man, and Berlin supported a thriving homosexual subculture. Historically, the city had been tolerant of homosexuals and a pioneering force for gay culture the world over. In Germany and Europe, its homosexual subculture became a magnet and haven. The first studies of, petitions to legalize, and journals that served homosexual men and culture all started in Berlin.[70] When Hartley wrote that he felt so at home in Berlin, in significant ways that feeling had to do with the welcoming community he found himself in.[71] He wrote Stieglitz that "I have lived rather gayly in the Berlin fashion—with all that implies."[72] The phrase "with all that implies" clues us to the fact that Hartley was satisfying his sexual needs, even if we cannot be certain about the specific meaning of the word "gay" in 1915.

During the time that Hartley lived in Berlin, the German military symbolized homosexuality. It was a deeply rooted trope on the street as well as in the popular press and international journalism. A considerable contingent of Berlin's gay male population lived as part of the German military. Starting in 1909, an international scandal involving the Kaiser's closest friends erupted and brought that fact in graphic detail to the public. The headlines and comics of the mainstream media, at the time of the affair and long after, cemented the equation between the German soldier and homosexuality.[73] Hartley had friends in the military, especially Lieutenant Karl von Freyburg. He lamented to artist friend Charles Demuth, a man who also was gay and spent time in Berlin, that he could no longer go out to Potsdam, garrison for the troops, since World War I began. There was simply "too much there to remember."[74] In short, Hartley handled imagery with loaded meaning in prewar Berlin. By adding the German military to his artistic repertoire, Hartley covertly acknowledged an essential piece of his milieu and identity. This reading was lost to recent audiences, but the commonplace association would have been glaringly apparent to Wilhelmine Berliners.

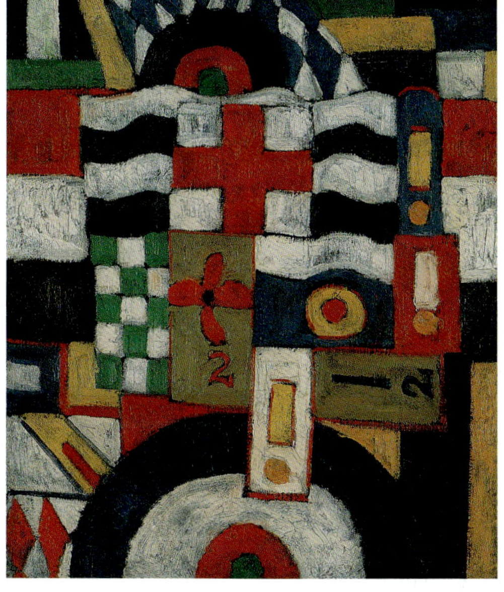

Figure 18
Marsden Hartley
Military, 1914–15
Oil on canvas, $23\frac{3}{4} \times 19\frac{7}{16}$ in. (60.3 × 49.4 cm)
© 2002 The Cleveland Museum of Art
Gift of Professor Nelson Goodman, 1981.83

While the flair of the military pervaded the imperial city, militarism as a whole went into high gear with the war. For several months at least, Hartley did not paint after the Guns of August began. Emotional disaster struck when Karl von Freyburg was killed on October 7, 1914. Von Freyburg's cousin Arnold Rönnebeck returned injured from the front. Hartley wrote long, lamenting letters back home to Stieglitz and, in them, made clear that his grasp of the world events and politics whirling around him was uninformed. Finally, in November, he went back to the easel. "I am working out some war motifs which people praise highly," he wrote in early November 1914, and the title of Hartley's famous series, the War Motifs, derives from this line.[75]

Portrait of a German Officer (plate 19) is considered the first of this remarkable series. The paintings began as a memorial to von Freyburg, for he is abstractly pictured in this unconventional portrait. The knot of pictorial elements congeals in a vertical alignment that suggests the presence of a human torso. Further, many of the military insignia and patterns contain associations to von Freyburg. The initials "Kv.F" at lower left are his, and at lower right, the number 24 gives his age at death. The spur just below the 24 alludes to his equestrian unit. The Iron Cross medal for bravery bestowed posthumously on von Freyburg is depicted in the upper center of the painting. The blue and white flag pattern stems from Bavaria, the German region of von Freyburg's origin. Numerous other clues of this kind exist to build an accumulative though cryptic system that points to Hartley's friend.[76] Over time, the pictorial elements loosened—they spread across the entire canvas, and they lost their specific association to von Freyburg. *Painting No. 5* (fig. 17) and *Military* (fig. 18) clearly demonstrate these changes. As this occurred, Hartley's use of the vibrant designs of the German military continued, but the distinct cachet of eulogy waned.

The War Motif paintings build upon Hartley's earlier city paintings in many ways. Formally, the progression is easy to see as the amalgam of motifs from *Portrait of Berlin* or the 1913 *Military* finds a fresh arrangement and restricted design source in a work like *Painting No. 5*. The graphic matrix and bold hues of 1913 mature to yield a unique style that achieves a subtle, sophisticated tension between two and three dimensions in 1915. The War Motif paintings also richly develop the conceptual premise of Hartley's art. In Paris when he first ventured into abstract painting, he said that he operated "in the style of automatic writing." To pursue more fully the range of his subjective perceptions and give them voice in his art, he suspended his analytic reasoning skills and abandoned representational realism. As he continued on this course, he talked of his art as "portraits of moments" in 1914 and as "characterizations of the 'Moment'" in late 1915. Hartley's profound enthusiasm for the Berlin metropolis first led him to make his subconscious response to the city the focus of his art. With the war, he shifted to concentrate on the vocabulary of the military uniform. This, too, he argued, was based first and foremost on his direct perceptual experiences. The greater militarism of a country at war and on the offensive coupled with the painful reality of so many lives lost now conditioned Hartley's sense of the world about him. "The forms are only those which I have observed casually from day to day.... I have expressed only what I have seen," he emphasized about his later paintings from Berlin.[77] These claims follow the sure conceptual path Hartley charted for himself while abroad. He worked persistently to formulate a visual language that captured, distilled, and translated onto canvas his intuitive impressions. He explained this most succinctly in 1913 when he wrote, "There are sensations in the human consciousness beyond reason—and painters are learning to trust these sensations and make them authentic on canvas. This is what I am working for."[78]

Like all artists, Hartley defined the parameters of an artistic challenge and worked assiduously to realize it. His experiments sometimes stumbled, and the swerves and changes in Hartley's art during his time abroad before the Great War show him trying very hard to discover what he would contribute. In this effort, Berlin and the drama of its noisy, stimulating, jarring modernity fueled his creativity. His experiences of its chaotic energy became the subject matter *and* content of his art. Hartley's city paintings and his War Motif series draw from Berlin, and they collectively demonstrate why this artist is so admired. Hartley rarely settled for the usual choices, intending to set himself apart. So in picturing the city, he shunned the obvious. His city paintings don't depict Potsdamerplatz or the Brandenburg Gate. They don't address the architectural vocabulary of the city or street at all. Further, they avoid the social dimension of prostitutes, shoppers, or tenement dwellers. Instead, the impressive formal power of these canvases translates the modern city's heightened emphasis on the visual into artistic scripts. His syntax of starbursts, vivid patterning, chance numerals, intense hues, flowing lines, and surging forms calls forth a symbolic and abstracted equivalent for Simmel's "intensification of nervous stimulation."

Hartley knew that he accomplished something significant in these German paintings. His achievement in expressionist Berlin finds more praise as every year passes. Nonetheless, he was hard pressed to find an audience for these pictures. When he could no longer receive cables of money as an American in wartime Berlin, Hartley was forced to leave the city in

December 1915. He left reluctantly. He returned to New York expecting a hero's welcome, he was so confident in his art. Yet his timing could not have been worse. Sentiment in the United States, though the country did not officially enter the war until April 1917, had sharply turned against Germany. A strong xenophobia gripped the land. Hartley's artistic imagery relied on the military uniform of "the enemy." He sold few paintings and received tepid critical reviews.

The immense tragedy of Hartley's German paintings is that the artist had to abandon them even though he knew well that they were a signal achievement, works that presented a commanding and original voice within the international avant-garde. In 1916 Hartley returned to representational landscape and still-life painting, taking a sharp turn from the work that now is applauded. Hartley's city paintings from expressionist Berlin captured the pulse of distinctly new experiences. They did so through an evocative pictorial language that consciously, rigorously pursued what it meant to be modern. Today we are able to see the paintings Hartley made in 1913 and 1914 as he intended—as portraits of Berlin.

Notes

1 Hartley to Alfred Stieglitz, August 1913, Beinecke/Yale.

2 *Autobiography,* 66.

3 Van Wyck Brooks, *Scenes and Portraits* (New York: Dutton, 1954), 81.

4 Hartley to Alfred Stieglitz, 1 February 1913, Beinecke/Yale.

5 Hartley to Alfred Stieglitz, February 1913, Beinecke/Yale.

6 See Patricia McDonnell, *Dictated by Life: Marsden Hartley's German Paintings and Robert Indiana's Hartley Elegies* (Minneapolis: Frederick R. Weisman Art Museum in association with D.A.P., 1995).

7 Robert Hughes, "American Visions," *Time,* special issue (spring 1997): 74.

8 See Thomas W. Gaehtgens, "Paris–München–Berlin: Marsden Hartley und die europäische Avantgarde," in *Kunst um die Folgen, Werner Hofmann zu Ehren* (Munich: Prestel Verlag, 1988), 367–82. See also Gail Levin, "Wassily Kandinsky and the American Avant-Garde, 1912–1950" (Ph.D. dissertation, Rutgers University, 1976).

9 Hartley to Gertrude Stein, 18 October 1913, Beinecke/Yale.

10 Calvin Tompkins interview with the artist, 24 September 1973, quoted in Roxana Robinson, *Georgia O'Keeffe: A Life* (New York: Harper & Row, 1989), 136.

11 Charles Baudelaire, "The Painter of Modern Life," in *The Painter of Modern Life and Other Essays,* trans. and ed. Jonathan Mayne (London: Phaidon Press, 1964), 1–40.

12 Michele Hannoosh, "Painters of Modern Life: Baudelaire and the Impressionists," in *Visions of the Modern City: Essays in History, Art, and Literature,* ed. William Sharpe and Leonard Wallock (Baltimore: Johns Hopkins University Press, 1987), 168–88.

13 Jacques Lipchitz quoted in George H. Roeder, Jr., "What Have Modernists Looked At? Experiential Roots of Twentieth-Century American Painting," *American Quarterly* 39, no. 1 (spring 1987): 56.

14 Baudelaire, "The Painter of Modern Life," 13. For analysis of these authors' shifting definitions of modernity, see David Frisby, "Modernité," in *Fragments of Modernity: Theories of Modernity in the Work of Simmel, Kracauer, and Benjamin* (Cambridge: MIT Press, 1986), 11–37.

15 George Simmel, "The Metropolis and the Mental Life," in *Classic Essays on the Culture of Cities,* ed. Richard Sennett (New York: Appleton, Century, Crofts, 1969), 48.

16 Ibid.

17 Jonathan Crary, *Techniques of the Observer: On Vision and Modernity in the Nineteenth Century* (Cambridge: MIT Press, 1990). See also his *Suspensions of Perception: Attention, Spectacle, and Modern Culture* (Cambridge: MIT Press, 1999).

18 Raymond Williams, "Metropolitan Perceptions and the Emergence of Modernism," in *The Politics of Modernism* (London and New York: Verso, 1989), 37–48. William Sharpe and Leonard Wallock, "From 'Great Town' to 'Nonplace Urban Realm': Reading the Modern City," in *Visions of the Modern City,* 5.

19 See especially Rebecca Zurier, Robert W. Snyder, and Virginia Mecklenburg, *Metropolitan Lives: The Ashcan Artists and Their New York* (Washington, D.C.: National Museum of American Art in association with W. W. Norton, 1995); Rebecca Zurier, *Picturing the Urban City: Urban Vision and Representation in the Art of the Ashcan School* (Berkeley and Los Angeles: University of California Press, forthcoming).

20 Wanda M. Corn, "The Artist's New York, 1900–1930," in *Budapest and New York: Studies in Metropolitan Transformation, 1870–1930,* ed. Thomas Bender and Carl E. Schorske (New York: Russell Sage Foundation, 1994), 284. See also Patricia Hills, "The Art World in New York, 1900–1919," in *Berlin–New York, Like and Unlike: Essays on Architecture and Art from 1870 to the Present,* ed. Josef Paul Kleihues and Christina Rathgeber (New York: Rizzoli, 1993), 194–209; Elizabeth Sussman, *City of Ambition: Artists and New York, 1900–1960* (New York: Whitney Museum of American Art in association with Flammarion, 1996).

21 Sarah Greenough, "Alfred Stieglitz and 'Idea' Photography," in *Alfred Stieglitz: Photographs and Writing* (Washington, D.C.: National Gallery of Art, 1983), 12–32. My thanks to Sarah Greenough for reminding me that Stieglitz illustrated his city photographs with Picasso's drawing in *Camera Work,* no. 36 (October 1911). See also Joel Smith, "How Stieglitz Came to Photograph Cityscapes," *History of Photography* 20, no. 4 (winter 1996): 320–31.

22 Wanda M. Corn, *The Great American Thing: Modern Art and National Identity, 1915–1935* (Berkeley and Los Angeles: University of California Press, 1999), 175.

23 Ludington, 79; *Autobiography,* 82–83.

24 Hartley to Alfred Stieglitz, 13 March 1913, Beinecke/Yale.

25 "Delaunay spends most of his time talking about Delaunay and his gifts." Hartley to Alfred Stieglitz, 13 March 1913, Beinecke/Yale.

26 For information on Hartley's exchanges with Blaue Reiter artists, see Patricia McDonnell, "American Artists in Expressionist Berlin: Ideological Crosscurrents in the Early Modernism of America and Germany, 1905–1915," (Ph.D. dissertation, Brown University, 1991), 177–214. See also idem, "Marsden Hartley's Letters to Franz Marc and Wassily Kandinsky, 1913–1914," *Archives of American Art Journal* 29, nos. 1–2 (1980): 35–44. Marc characterized Hartley to Kandinsky as "not mature but nonetheless fine." Marc to Kandinsky, 23 July 1913, in *Wassily Kandinsky, Franz Marc Briefwechsel,* ed. Klaus Lankheit (Munich: Piper, 1983), 235.

27 Peter-Klaus Schuster, *Delaunay und Deutschland* (Cologne: DuMont Buchverlag, 1985), 30. Paintings were purchased by Berlin businessman and collector Bernhard Koehler and Munich artists Adolf Erbslöh and Alexej von Jawlensky. Delaunay made a gift of the fourth work to Wassily Kandinsky.

28 The scholarship on Walden and Der Sturm is vast. For a recent study of Der Sturm in the second decade of the century, see Barbara Alms and Wiebke Steinmetz, eds., *Der Sturm: Chagall, Feininger, Jawlensky, Kandinsky, Klee, Kokoschka, Macke, Marc, Schwitters, und viele andere im Berlin in der zehner Jahre* (Delmenhorst: Städtische Galerie Delmenhorst Haus Coburg, 2000).

29 *Erster Deutscher Herbstsalon* (Berlin: Der Sturm, 1913). See also Mario-Andreas von Lüttichau, "Erster Deutscher Herbstsalon, Berlin 1913," in *Stationen der Moderne: Die bedeutenden Kunstausstellungen des 20. Jahrhunderts in Deutschland* (Berlin: Berlinische Galerie, 1988), 130–53. Peter Selz, "Emergence of the Avant-Garde: Erster Deutscher Herbstsalon of 1913," in Peter Selz, *Beyond the Mainstream: Essays on Modern and Contemporary Art* (Cambridge and New York: Cambridge University Press, 1997), 43–54.

30 Green was a brash, arbitrary color choice for the Eiffel Tower. It was originally painted graduating shades of orange and yellow, deeper hues at the base and lighter ones at the spire to redouble the effect of its imposing height. In other Delaunay paintings, this original color scheme is represented. See Mark Roskill, *Visions of Paris: Robert Delaunay's Series* (New York: Solomon R. Guggenheim Museum, 1997).

31 Alfred Stieglitz to Heinrich Kühn, 14 October 1912, quoted in *Stieglitz: Photographs and Writings,* 194.

32 See Charles Brock, "The Armory Show, 1913: A Diabolical Test," in Greenough, 127–43.

33 See Betsy Fahlman, *Arnold Rönnebeck, 1885–1947* (New York: Conner-Rosenkranz Gallery, 1998).

34 See Charles W. Haxthausen, "'A New Beauty': Ernst Ludwig Kirchner's Images of Berlin," in *Berlin: Culture and Metropolis,* ed. Charles W. Haxthausen and Heidrun Suhr (Minneapolis: University of Minnesota Press, 1991), 58–93; Katharina Henkel and Roland März, *Der Potsdamer Platz: Ernst Ludwig Kirchner und der Untergang Preussens* (Berlin: Nationalgalerie, 2001).

35 See Christoph Brockhaus, "Die ambivalente Faszination der Grossstadterfarhung in der deutschen Kunst des Expressionismus," in *Expressionismus, Sozialer Wandel und Künstlerische Erfahrung* (Munich: W. Fink Verlag, 1982), 89–106; Dominik Bartmann, "Das Grossstadtbild Berlins in der Weltsicht der Expressionisten," in *Stadtbilder: Berlin in der Malerie vom 17. Jahrhundert bis zur Gegenwart* (Berlin: Berlin Museum, 1987), 243–59; Bernhard Schulz, "Natursehnsucht und Grossstadthektik: Der deutsche Expressionismus zwischen 'Brücke' and Berlin," in *Ich und die Stadt: Mensch und Grossstadt in der deutschen Kunst des 20 Jahrhunderts,* ed. Eberhard Roters and Bernhard Schulz (Berlin: Berlinische Galerie, 1987), 15–34; Charles W. Haxthausen, "Images of Berlin in the Art of the Secession and Expressionism," in *Art in Berlin, 1815–1989* (Atlanta: High Museum of Art, 1989), 61–82.

36 Hans-Christian Täubrich, "Industrielandsort Berlin," in *Berlin, Berlin: Die Ausstellung zur Geschichte der Stadt* (Berlin: Nicolai, 1987), 157–70.

37 Thomas P. Hughes, "The City as Creator and Creation," in *Berlin–New York,* 13–31.

38 Reinhard Rürup, "Berlin—Umrisse der Stadtgeschichte," in *Berlin, Berlin,* 39; Sabine Hollburg and Gottfried Korff, "Metropole in Gardeuniform," in *Berlin, Berlin,* 255.

39 Peter Hielscher, "Gross-Berlin: Entwürfe und Probleme," in *Berlin, Berlin,* 365–86.

40 John Czaplicka, "Pictures of a City at Work, Berlin, circa 1890–1930: Visual Reflections on Social Structures and Technology in the Modern Urban Construct," in *Berlin: Culture and Metropolis,* 31.

41 Karl Scheffler, *Berlin: Ein Stadtschicksal* (Berlin: Reiss, 1910), 267; as translated in Peter Jelavich, "Berlin's Path to Modernity," in *Art in Berlin,* 23.

42 "Berlin war die Bühne für ein pracht- und wirkvolles Ineinander von imperialer Selbstbestätigung, Behauptung des Weltgestus, aristokrater Traditionspflege, und der Demonstration nationalen Ehrgeizes. Dabei war das Erscheinungsbild der Stadt wesentlich vom Parade-, Manöver-, und Soldatenspiel in visuelle-zeremonieller Form bestimmt.... Man sprach in der Kaiserzeit von der 'Metropole in Gardeuniform' und unterstrich damit, dass das gesellschaftliche Leben in Berlin wie in keiner anderen der europäischen Hauptstädte vom Geist und von der Couleur des Militärs durchertränkt war." Hollburg and Korff, "Metropole in Gardeuniform," in *Berlin, Berlin,* 256.

43 Hartley to Rockwell Kent, March 1913, Kent Papers, Archives/Smithsonian, quoted in Ludington 1992, 97.

44 *Autobiography,* 86–87.

45 Ibid., 87.

46 See Peter Jelavich, *Berlin Cabaret* (Cambridge: Harvard University Press, 1993).

47 See Peter Stürzebecher, *Das Berliner Warenhaus* (Berlin: Archibook, 1979); Siegfried Gerlach, *Das Warenhaus in Deutschland* (Stuttgart: Steiner Verlag, 1988). See also William Leach, *Land of Desire: Merchants, Power, and the Rise of a New American Culture* (New York: Pantheon, 1993).

48 Peter Fritzsche, "The City as Spectacle," in *Reading Berlin 1900* (Cambridge: Harvard University Press, 1996), 155.

49 Ibid., 149–50.

50 Miriam Hansen, *Babel and Babylon: Spectatorship in American Silent Film* (Cambridge: Harvard University Press, 1991), 45.

51 Walther Rathenau quoted in Lothar Müller, "Modernität, Nervosität, and Sachlichkeit: Das Berlin der Jahrhundertwende als Hauptstadt der 'neuen Zeit,'" in *Mythos Berlin: Zur Wahrnehmungsgeschichte einer industriellen Metropole* (Berlin: Ästhetik und Kommunikation, 1987), 80.

52 Hartley to Alfred Stieglitz, August 1913, Beinecke/Yale.

53 *Autobiography,* 83.

54 Hartley to Gertrude Stein, 9 May 1913, Beinecke/Yale.

55 *Autobiography,* 87.

56 Hartley to Gertrude Stein, 7 August 1913, Beinecke/Yale.

57 *Autobiography,* 90.

58 William James, *The Varieties of Religious Experience* (1902). For the impact of Stein and James on Hartley's development, see McDonnell, *Dictated by Life.* For a discussion of James's relevance to the artist, see Gail R. Scott's Introduction to *On Art,* 19–57.

59 Hartley to Alfred Stieglitz, May or June 1913, Stieglitz/O'Keeffe Archive, Beinecke/Yale.

60 Hartley to Alfred Stieglitz, August 1913, Beinecke/Yale.

61 *Autobiography,* 86.

62 Ludwig Meidner, "An Introduction to Painting Big Cities," in *Voices of German Expressionism,* ed. Victor H. Miesel (Englewood Cliffs, N.J.: Prentice-Hall, 1970), 111.

63 Philip Fisher, "City Matters: City Minds," in *The Worlds of Victorian Fiction* (Cambridge: Harvard University Press, 1975), 377.

64 Hartley to Alfred Stieglitz, June 1914, Beinecke/Yale.

65 See David Cateforis, "Marsden Hartley's *Himmel,*" in *American Paintings to 1945 at the Nelson-Atkins Museum of Art* (Kansas City: Nelson-Atkins Museum of Art, forthcoming).

66 See Patricia McDonnell, "Marsden Hartley's Myth of *Amerika* in Expressionist Berlin," *North Carolina Museum of Art Bulletin* 16 (1993): 50–64.

67 Marsden Hartley, "Foreword," *Camera Work,* no. 45 (dated January 1914, published June 1914): 17; quoted in *On Art,* 62–63.

68 Hartley to Franz Marc, 13 May 1913, quoted in McDonnell, "Marsden Hartley's Letters to Franz Marc and Wassily Kandinsky," 38.

69 Hartley quoted in "American Artist Astounds Germans," *New York Times,* 19 December 1915, sec. 6, p. 4.

70 For landmark studies of Berlin's gay culture, see James Steakley, *The Homosexual Emancipation Movement in Germany* (New York: Arno Press, 1975); Michael Bolle and Rolf Bothe, eds., *El Dorado: Homosexuelle Frauen und Männer in Berlin, 1850–1950* (Berlin: Frölich und Kaufman, 1984); Andreas Sternweiler and Hans Gerhard Hannesen, eds., *Goodbye to Berlin? 100 Jahre Schwulenbewegung* (Berlin: Verlag rosa Winkel, 1997). For a key study of Hartley's experience in Germany, see also Weinberg.

71 "I have every sense of being at home among the German + I like the life color of Berlin." Hartley to Alfred Stieglitz, May or June 1913, Beinecke/Yale.

72 Hartley to Alfred Stieglitz, 15 March 1915, Beinecke/Yale.

73 James Steakley, "Iconography of a Scandal: Political Cartoons and the Eulenburg Affair in Wilhelmine Germany," in *Hidden from History: Reclaiming the Gay and Lesbian Past* (New York: New American Library, 1989), 233–63; Isabel Hull, "Kaiser Wilhelm and the 'Liebenberg Circle,'" in *Kaiser Wilhelm II: New Interpretations* (Cambridge: Cambridge University Press, 1982), 193–220; John C. G. Röhl, "Phillipp Eulenburg, the Kaiser's Best Friend" in *The Kaiser and His Court: Wilhelm II and the Government of Germany* (Cambridge: Cambridge University Press, 1994), 28–69. See also Patricia McDonnell, "El Dorado: Marsden Hartley in Imperial Berlin," in *Dictated by Life,* 14–55.

74 Hartley to Charles Demuth, n.d. [1915], Beinecke/Yale.

75 Hartley to Alfred Stieglitz, 3 November 1914, Beinecke/Yale.

76 For iconographic analysis of the series, see Roxana Barry, "The Age of Blood and Iron: Marsden Hartley in Berlin," *Arts Magazine* 54, no. 2 (October 1979): 166–71; Gail Levin, "Hidden Symbolism in Marsden Hartley's Military Pictures," *Arts Magazine* 54, no. 2 (October 1979): 154–58; and William H. Robinson, "Marsden Hartley's Military," *Bulletin of The Cleveland Museum of Art* 76, no. 1 (January 1989): 1–26.

77 Marsden Hartley, "Foreword, Paintings by Marsden Hartley," *Camera Work,* no. 48 (October 1916): 12; quoted in *On Art,* 67. We shouldn't take this quotation by Hartley entirely at face value, however. Robert K. Martin was the first to point out that this disavowal of any deeper content may have been Hartley's attempt to ward off revelations of the artist's homosexuality via this art. See his "Reclaiming Our Lives," *Christopher Street* 4 (June 1980): 34.

78 Hartley to Alfred Stieglitz, 28 September 1913, Beinecke/Yale.

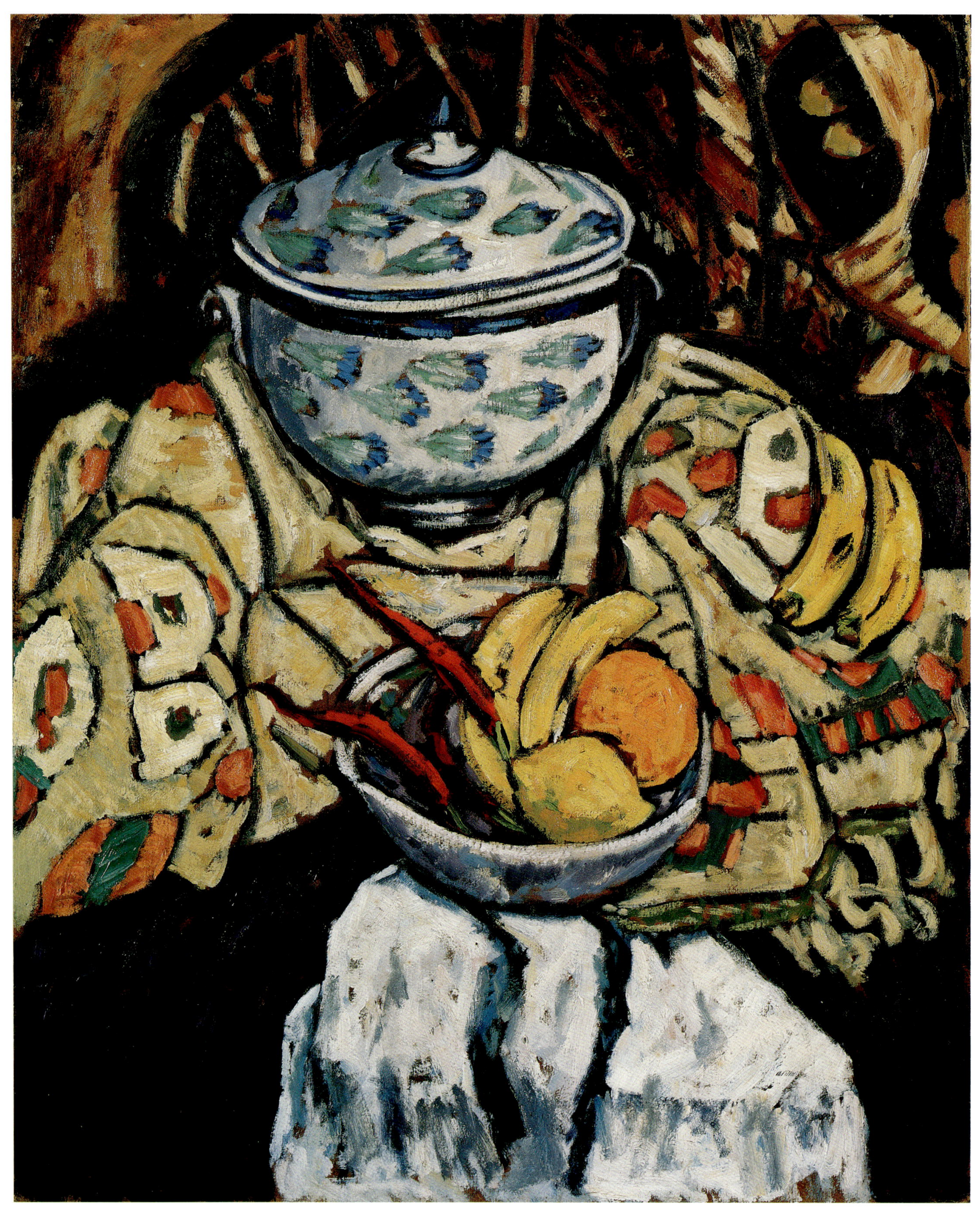

7

Still Life, 1912

Oil on fiberboard, 32⅛ × 25⅝ in.

Frederick R. Weisman Art Museum, University of Minnesota, Minneapolis

Bequest of Hudson Walker from the Ione and Hudson Walker Collection

(Right) Detail, Plate 7

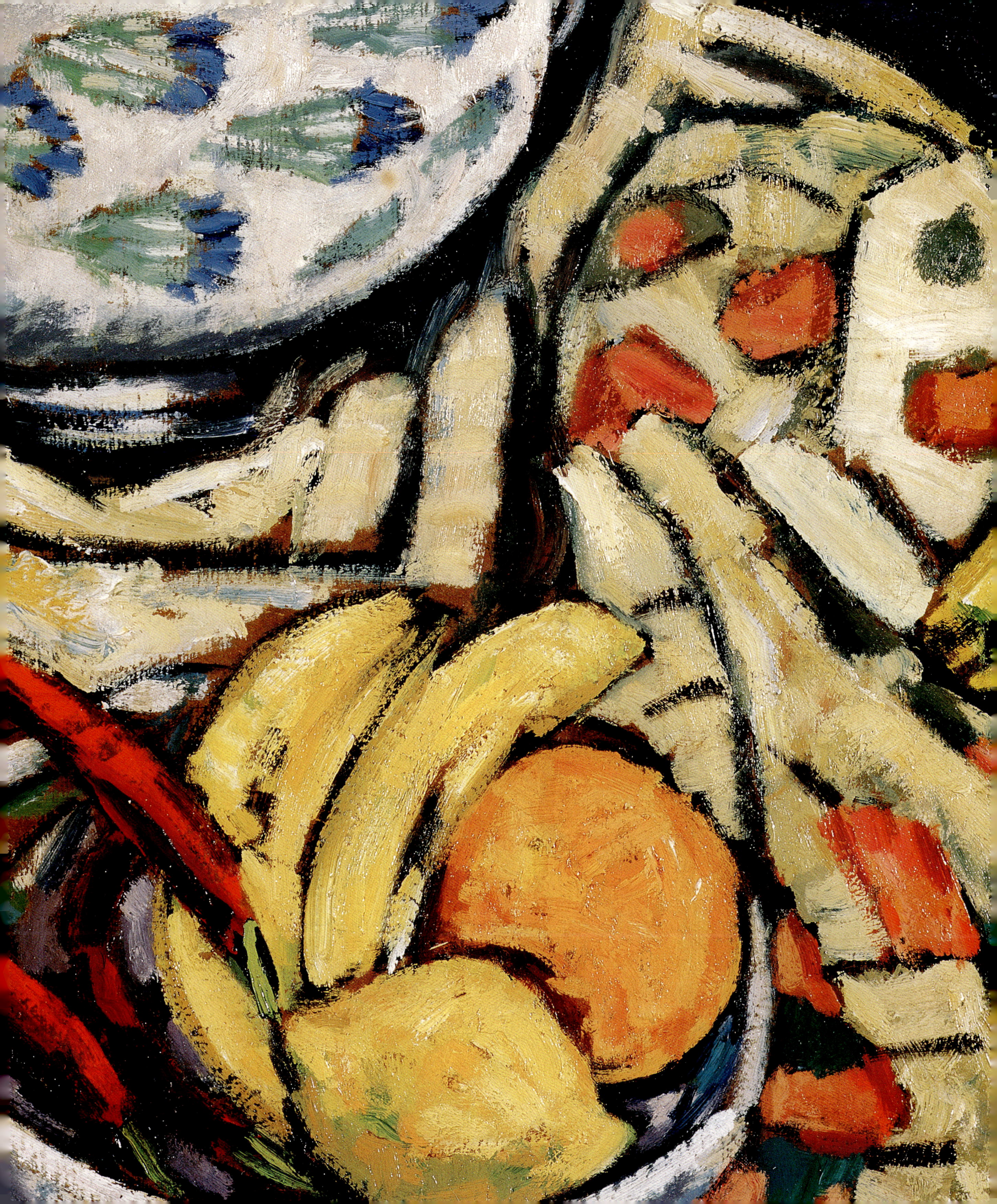

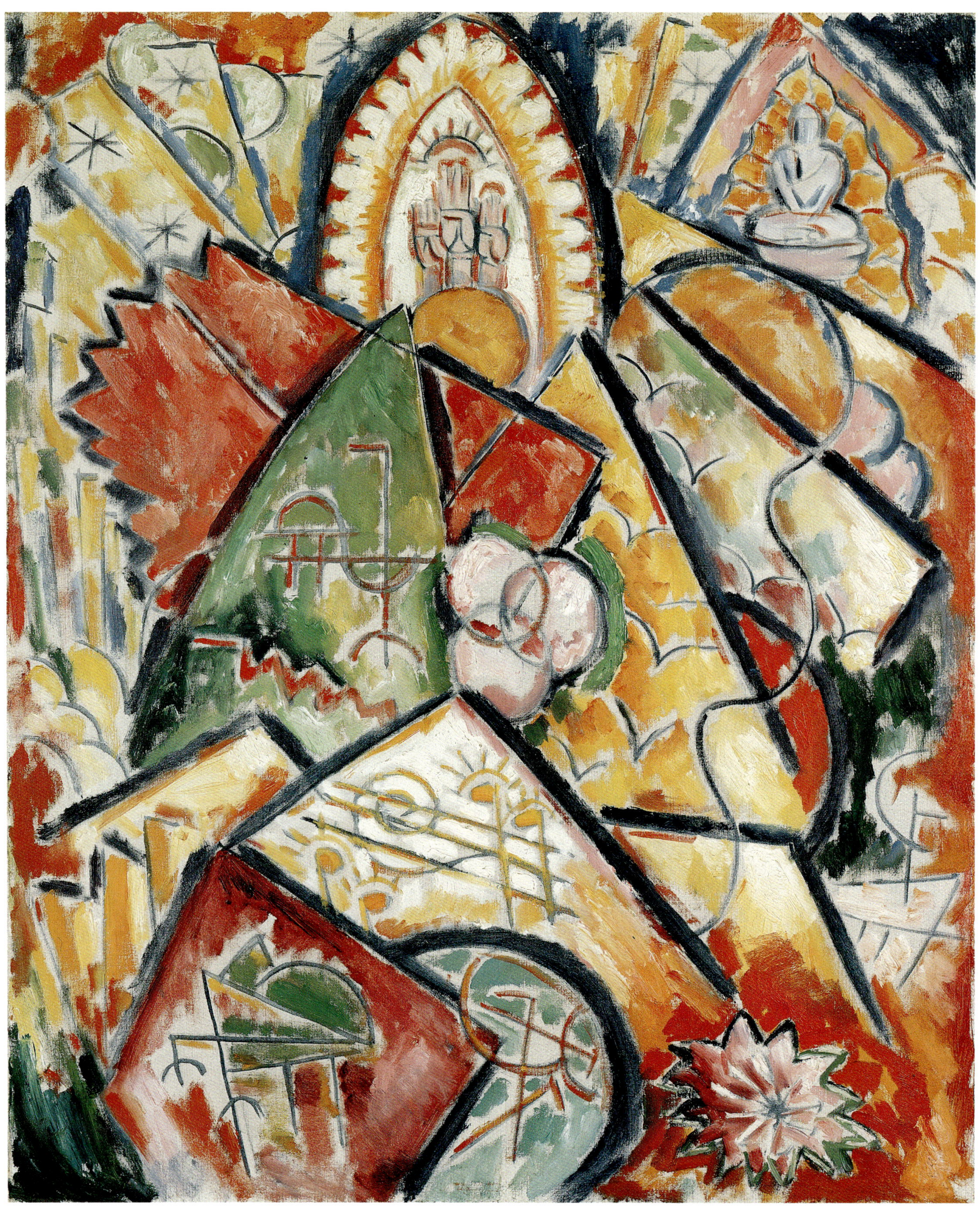

8

Musical Theme (Oriental Symphony), 1912–13
Oil on canvas, 39⅜ × 31¼ in.
Rose Art Museum, Brandeis University, Waltham, Massachusetts
Gift of Samuel Lustgarten, Sherman Oaks, California

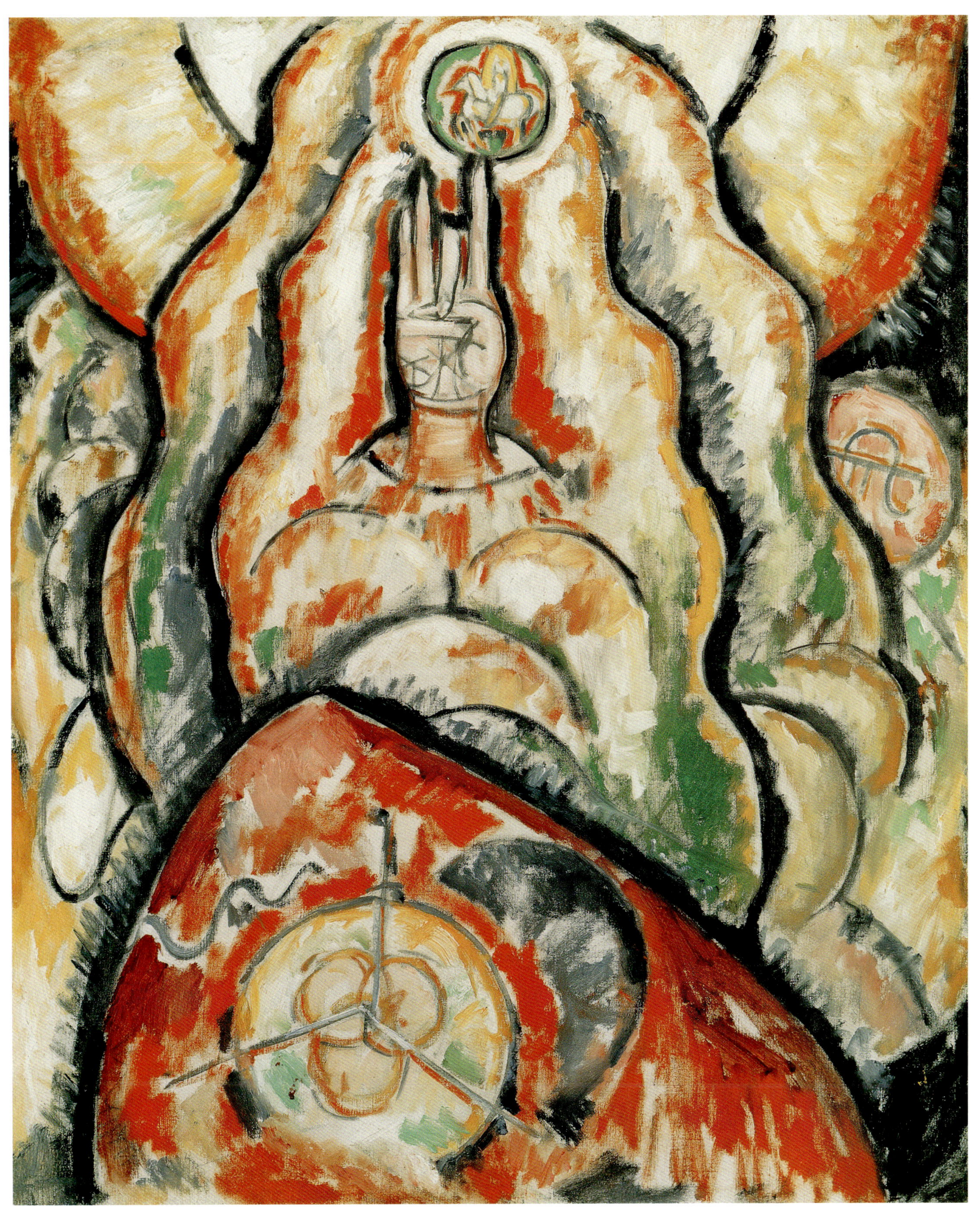

9
Portrait Arrangement No. 2, 1912–13
Oil on canvas, 39½ × 31¼ in.
Private Collection
Courtesy of Babcock Galleries, New York

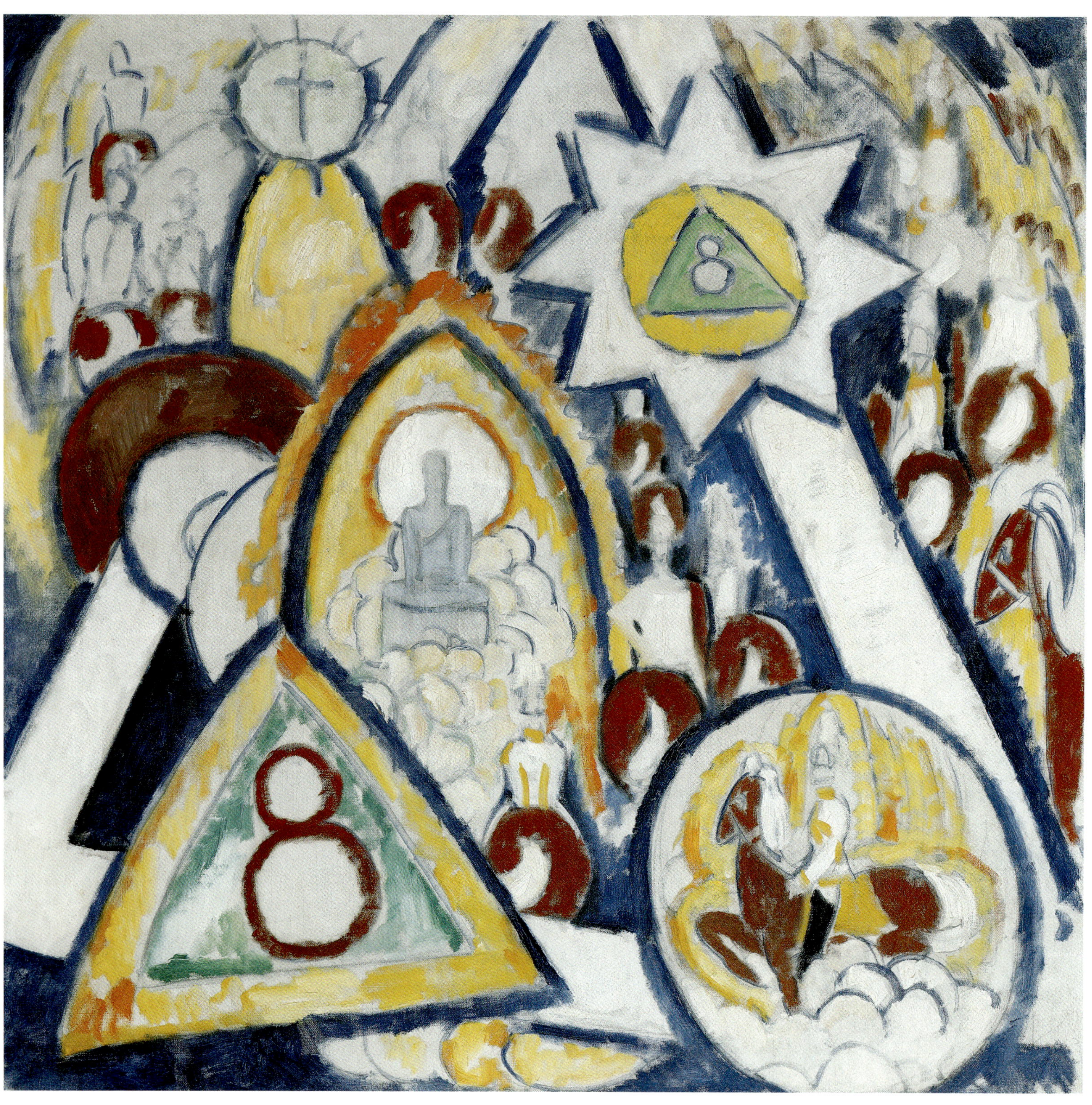

10
Portrait of Berlin, 1913
Oil on canvas, 39¼ × 39⅜ in.
Yale Collection of American Literature, Beinecke Rare Book and Manuscript Library, Yale University, New Haven
Gift of Mabel Dodge Luhan to the Collection of American Literature, University Library

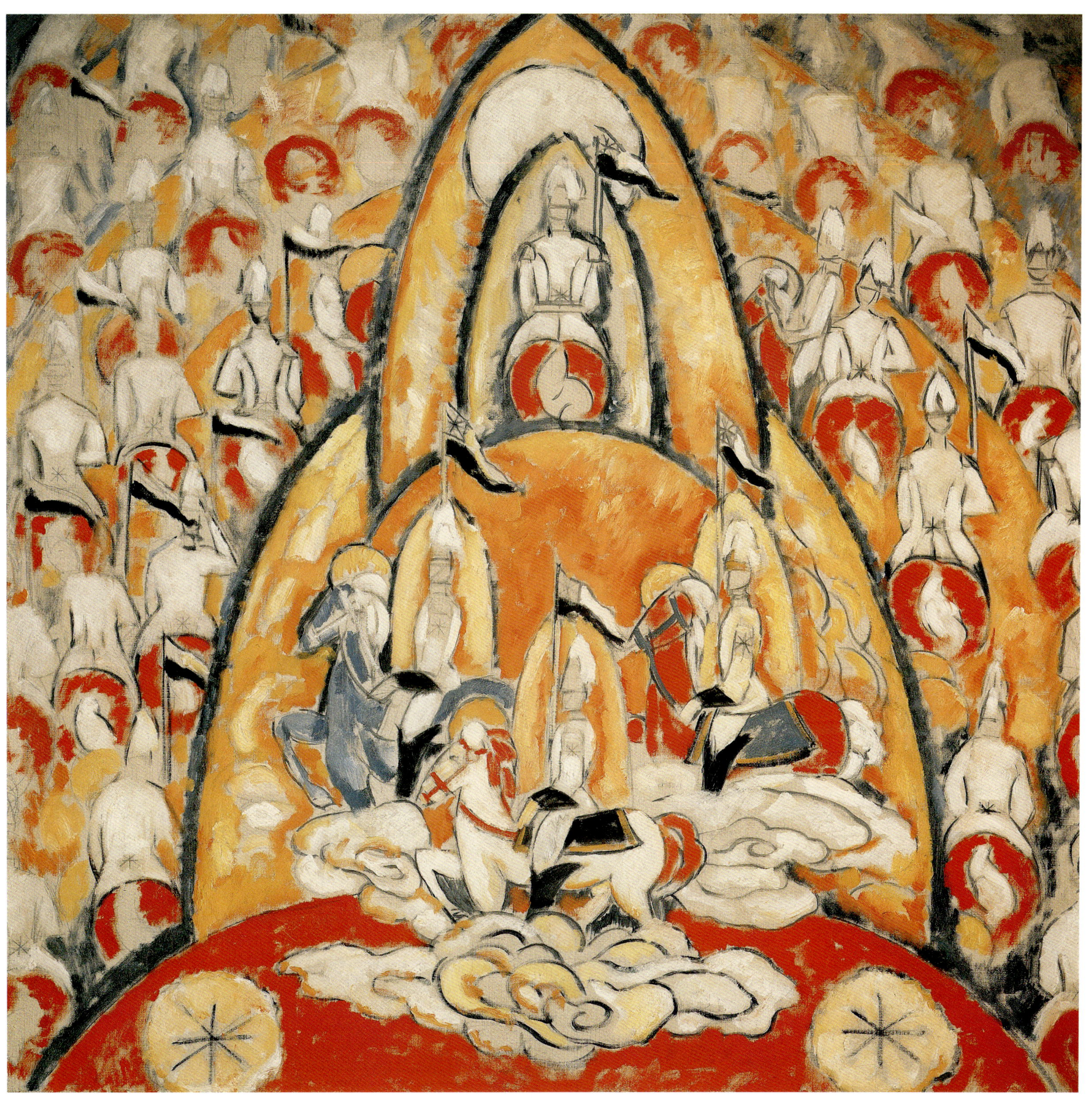

11

The Warriors, 1913

Oil on canvas, $47^{1/2} \times 47^{1/4}$ in.

Private Collection

Courtesy of Salander-O'Reilly Gallery, New York

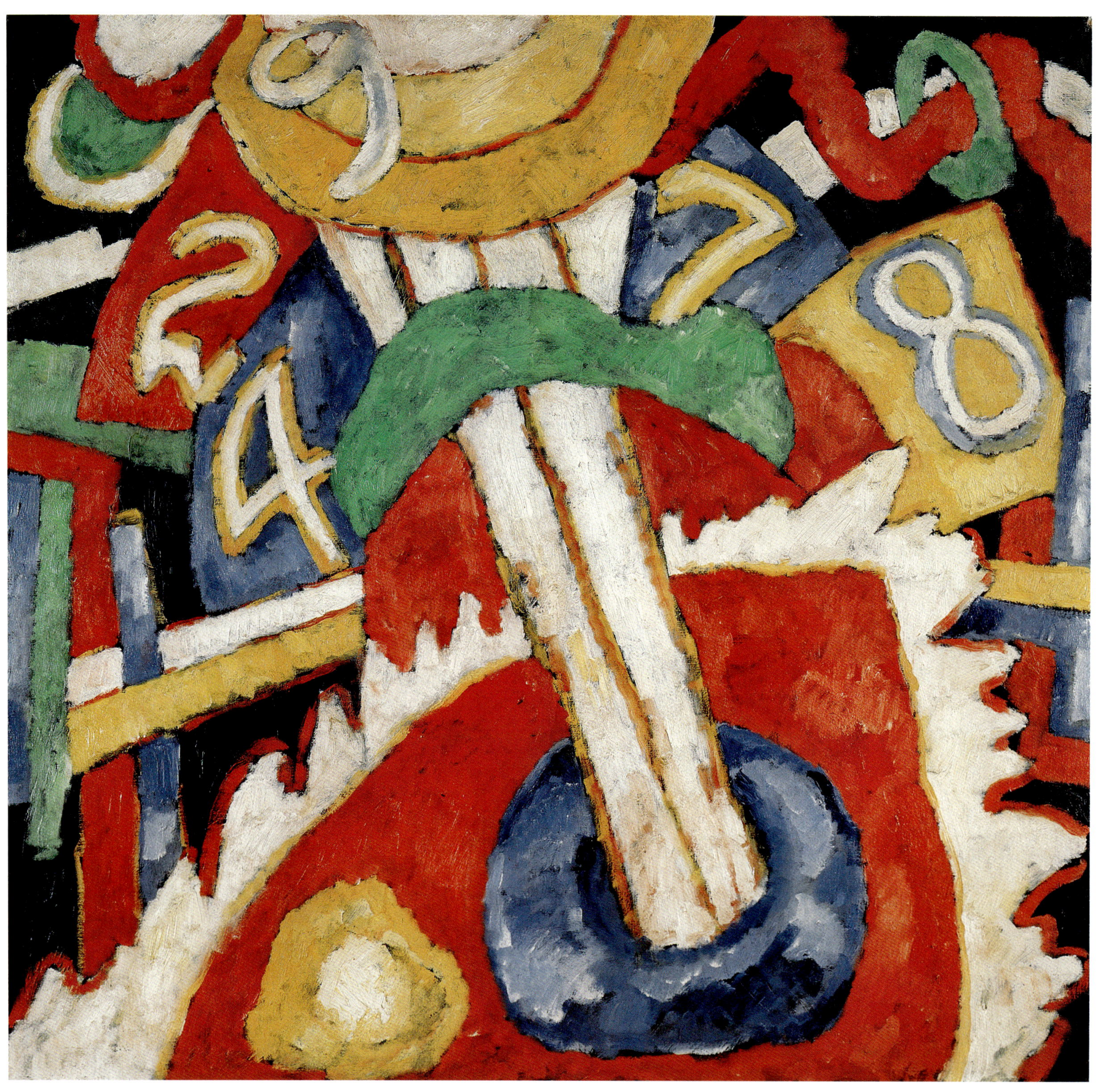

12

Military, 1913

Oil on canvas, 39¼ × 39¼ in.

Wadsworth Atheneum Museum of Art, Hartford

The Ella Gallup Sumner and Mary Catlin Sumner Collection Fund

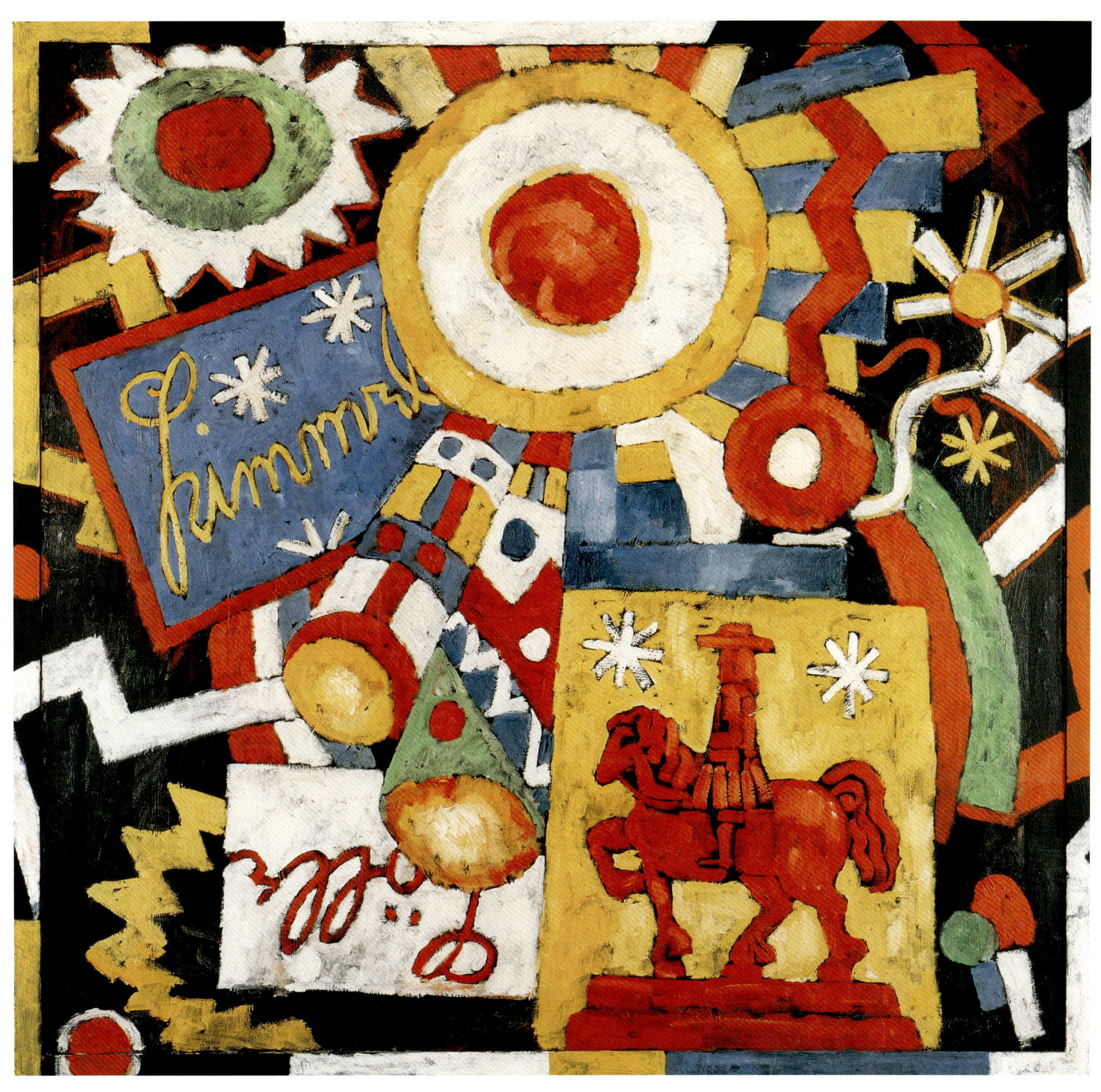

13

Himmel, c. 1914–15
Oil on canvas with painted frame, 47⅜ × 47⅜ in.
The Nelson-Atkins Museum of Art, Kansas City, Missouri
Gift of the Friends of Art

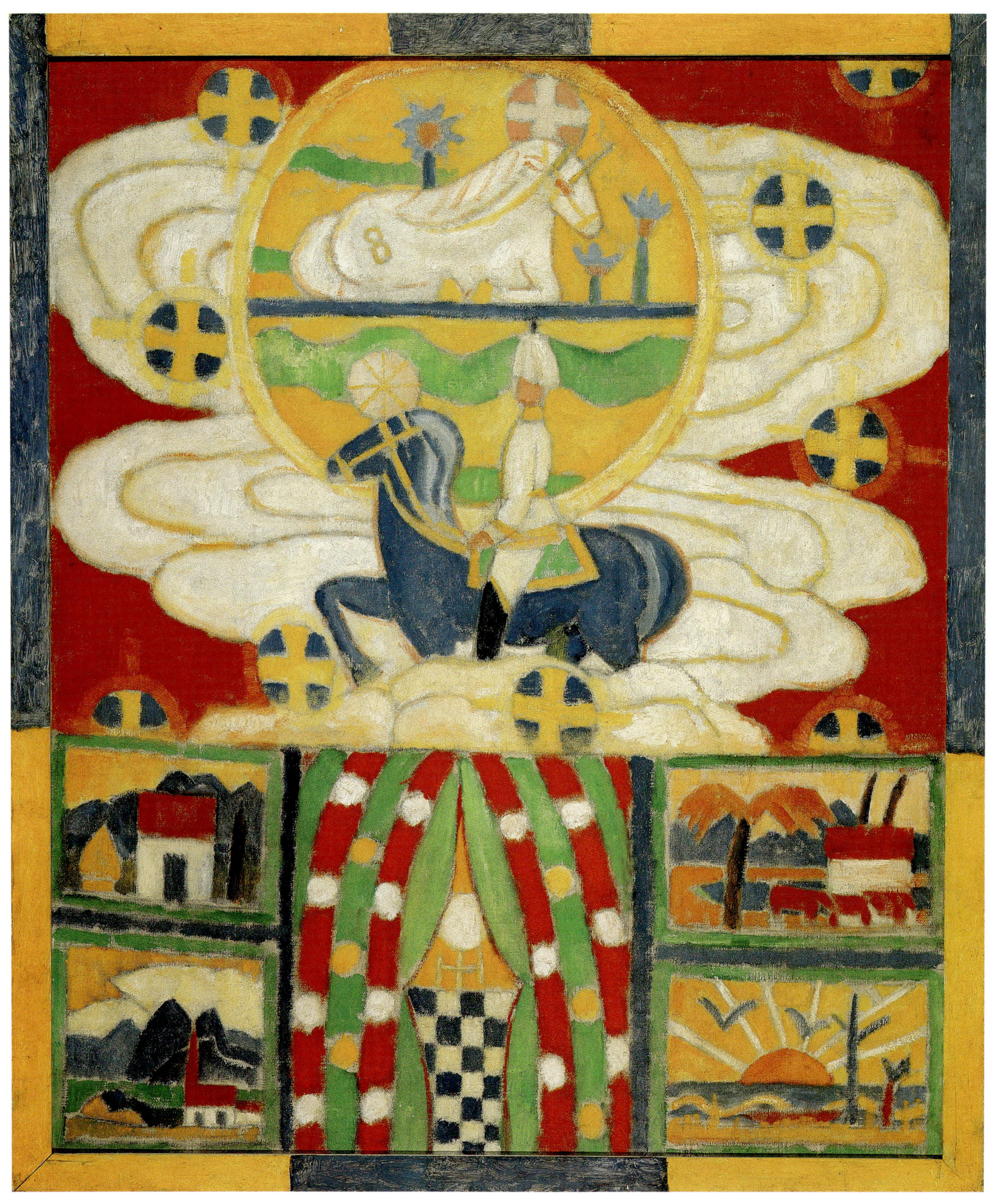

14
Berlin Ante-War, 1914
Oil on canvas with painted frame, 41¼ × 34½ in.
Columbus Museum of Art, Ohio
Gift of Ferdinand Howald

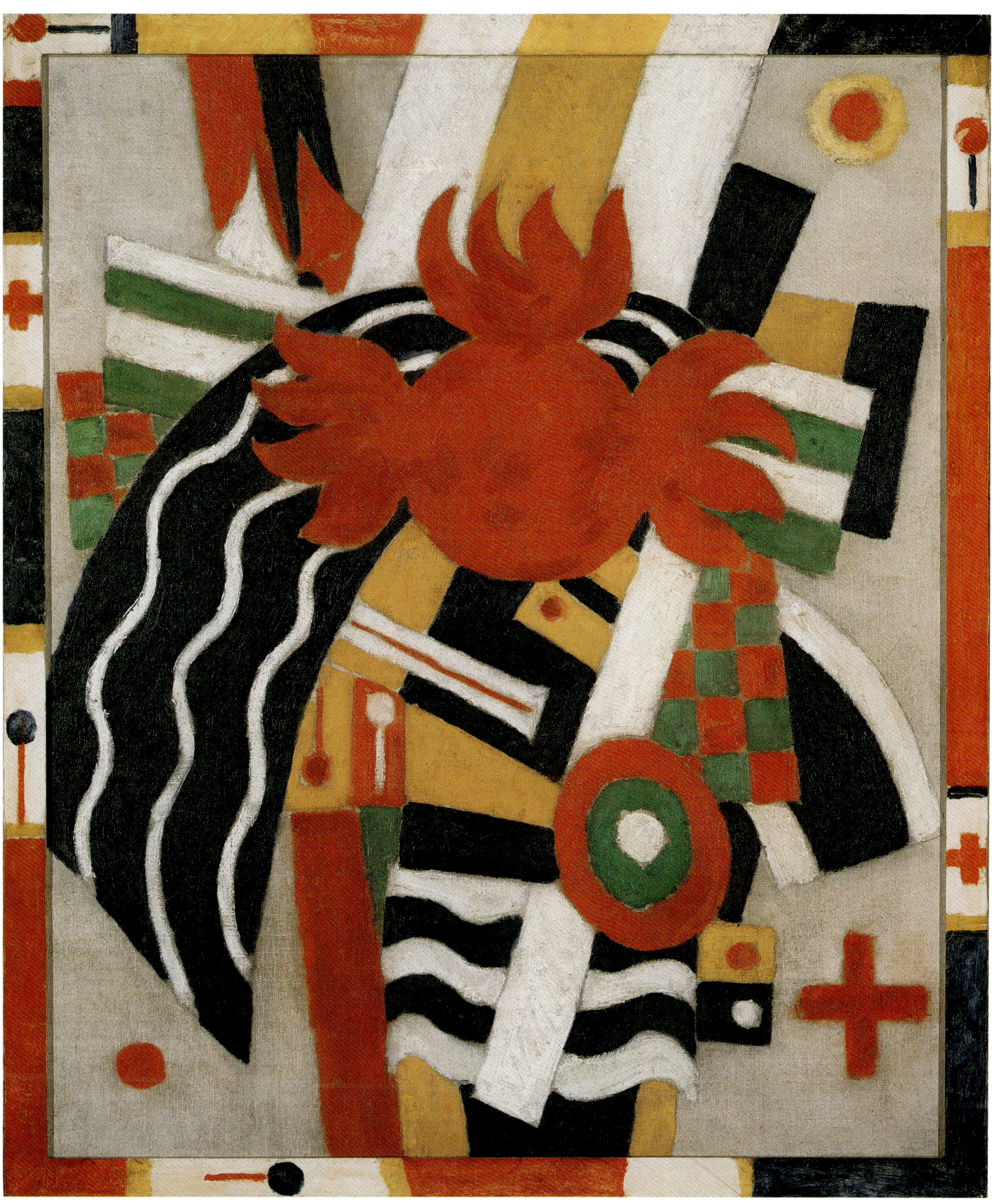

15
The Aero, c. 1914
Oil on canvas with painted frame, 42 × 34½ in.
National Gallery of Art, Washington
Andrew W. Mellon Fund, 1970.31.1

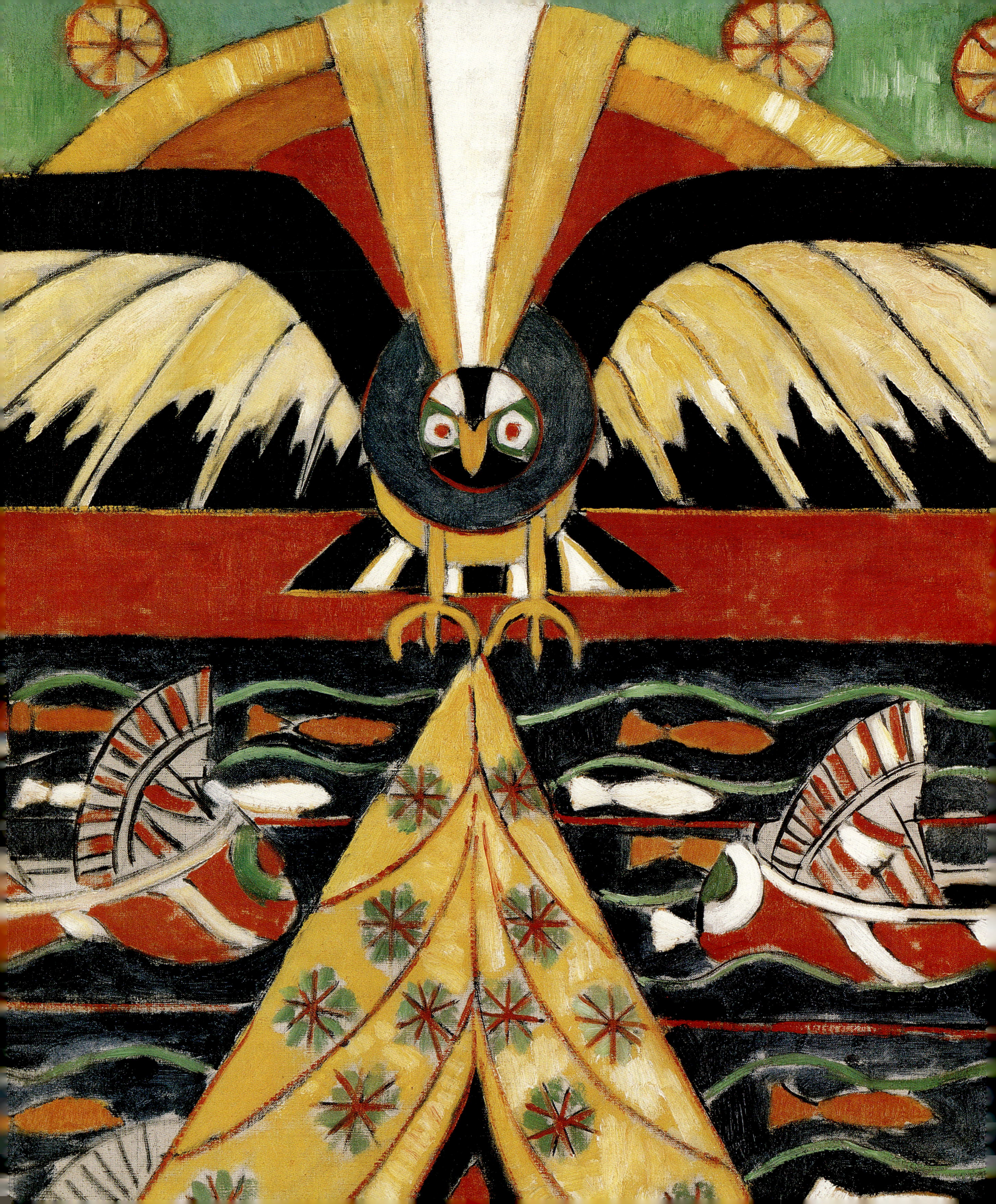

Marsden Hartley's Native Amerika

Wanda M. Corn

Writing from Berlin in November 1914, Marsden Hartley told Alfred Stieglitz of a fantasy: "I find myself wanting to be an Indian—to paint my face with the symbols of that race I adore[,] to go to the West and face the sun forever—that would seem the true expression of human dignity."[1] Such an ecstatic and self-absorbed declaration—fanciful but intensely felt—was typical of Hartley when he wrote letters about a current painting enthusiasm or engagement with the writings of a new thinker. He dramatized both his moods and his newest passions. In this case he projected himself into the body of a romantic other, conjuring himself as a proud Indian, war paint on his cheeks, facing the setting sun in the American West. It was a poster-like image, common to those found in contemporaneous travel illustrations or film advertisements.

Hartley's desire to go native also inspired some of his paintings of that year. While living in Berlin, he created a number of brightly colored abstractions made up of Native American motifs. He called these paintings his Amerika series, spelling America as Germans do, with a *k*.[2] While the paintings that comprise the series have never been definitively catalogued, the three that have engaged scholars the most will also be the focus of my discussion here (fig. 1, plates 16–17).[3] More or less of the same dimensions (in the neighborhood of three to four feet high and wide), *American Indian Symbols, Indian Fantasy,* and *Indian Composition* all include Indian figures and still lifes; if hung cheek by jowl, their brilliant reds, yellows, blues, and greens would sound, to quote Georgia O'Keeffe on remembering Hartley's work of this period, "like a brass band in a small closet."[4]

Each of these three large paintings is based on a few Indian motifs, all of them fairly standard storybook and filmic images. All have a large pyramidal tepee at the center of the composition, sometimes enclosing smaller tepees. Small-scaled tepees also trail out from either side of the central dwelling. In the sky areas, there are rising orbs of color, recalling suns and moons, accompanied, in two of them, by eight-pointed stars. In all the paintings, small male figures sit impassively in or next to the tepees, wrapped like mummies in blankets and wearing long feather headdresses. Baskets, bowls, campfires, and bows and arrows accompany them. Serpentine bands of color suggest water, and round forms recall battle shields.

Stylistically, the three Amerika paintings are not only brightly colored but intensely patterned. Like many traditional designs for rugs, they have a dominant center with smaller elements left and right mirroring one another. Most components cling to the surface with passages of shallow depth created by overlapping forms or change in scale. This rigorous and flat symmetry is so pervasive, and so unusual in Hartley's work, that I will have more to say about it shortly.

Detail, Plate 16

Figure 1
Marsden Hartley
American Indian Symbols, 1914
Oil on canvas, 39¼ × 39¼ in. (99.7 × 99.7 cm)
Amon Carter Museum, Fort Worth, Texas

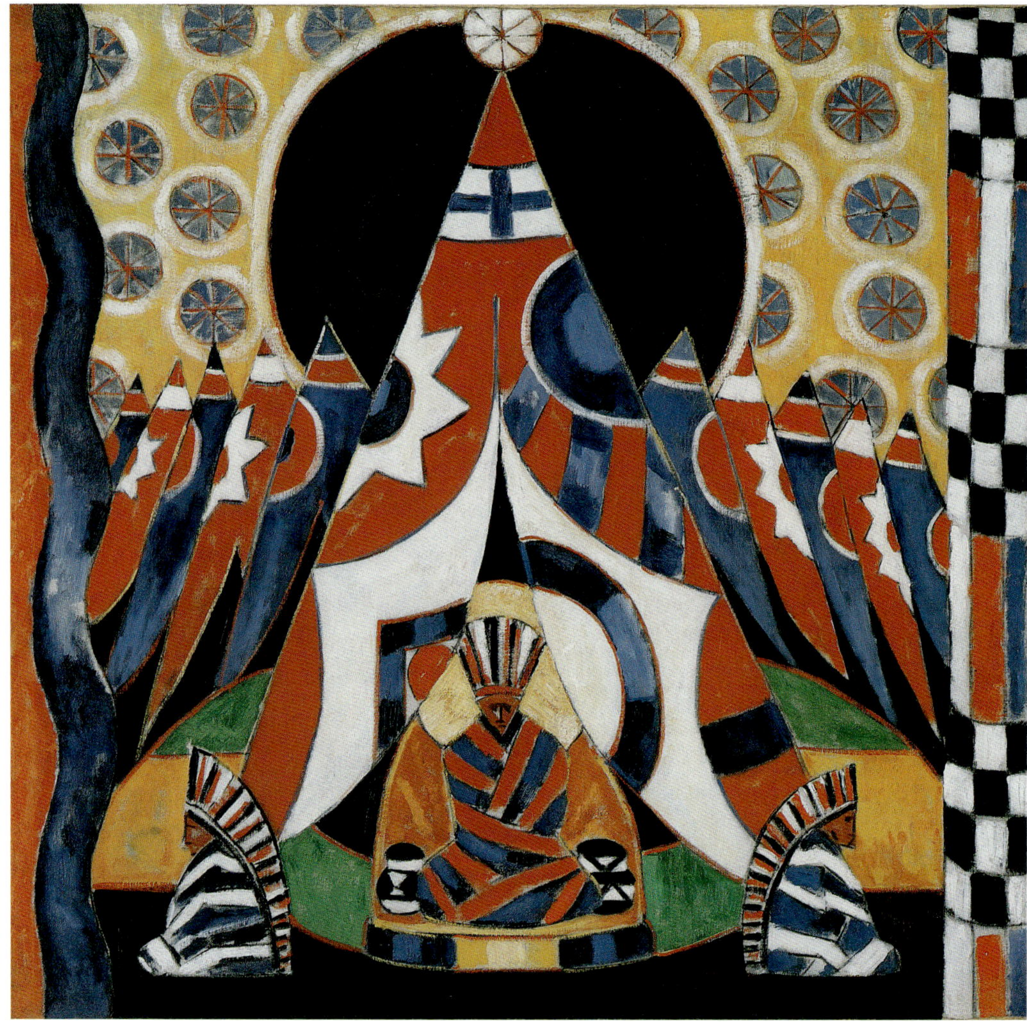

Overall, the paintings feel laden with secrecy. It seems as if tribal rituals are under way, without their particulars being available to us. Here and there are cryptic pictographs or hieroglyphic signs like those found on ancient scrolls or prehistoric rock paintings. Since only men appear in the canvases, these appear to be fraternal rites, embodying visions of life in paradisiacal landscapes of order, harmony, and pleasure. They reformulate Matisse's languid, heterosexual *Joie de vivre* landscape paintings of the previous decade into all-male, homoerotic, and communal fantasies on the same theme.

With these general observations in mind, a closer look at one Amerika painting will ground my analysis. *Indian Fantasy* is structured by three horizontal bands of activity: a yellow ground along the bottom edge, a black waterway in the middle, and a green sky above (plate 16). A large yellow tepee soars up and out of the ground level and crosses the middle band to touch the horizon. It is a complicated, multi-layered dwelling. The outermost layer is a yellow canopy dotted with stars and sheltering a smaller red tepee with geometric designs. Inside the red tepee is a mandorla enclosing an eight-pointed star and a cross—pictorial signs that are richly suggestive of religious rites. On either side of the red tent, other tepees march back into space with a regularity that conjures up a military encampment. The eye is led to these tents by following the edge of a green orb of grass crossed by two red paths. At the center of the canvas, two men wrapped in green striped blankets sit motionless on a black ground evoking a number of art historical tropes. Facing each other, and focused upon the mandorla within the red tepee, they suggest guardian figures; they also recall Buddha figures and Egyptian mummies. Noting the attentiveness of the figures to the mandorla, Gail Levin saw in them recollections of the Christian nativity scene, the accompanying bowls and baskets akin to offerings brought to the Christ child.[5] Outside the tepees we see other Indian attributes: to the left a campfire, a bow and arrows; to the right a campfire, a bowl, and several white and red fish.

Moving up the canvas, a broad block of black water is richly stocked with flat red and white fish, like those that swim in Persian carpets. This is a land of plenty. Subdivided by thin red lines, the water zone alternates a band of fish with a band of men in canoes, each element moving in synch from left to right. The stylized Indians do not paddle or fish but sit passively (and a bit absurdly) like wise men in toy canoes.

In the sky zone, a green ground with yellow stars, the painting moves from small elements to large, emphatic ones. This sky is dominated by a heraldic bird, most certainly a stylized eagle, whose large wings are symmetrically splayed across the canvas. The bird's head and tail feathers are shaped like crowns, and its talons are symmetrically placed at the tip of the tepee below; it is as if the bird has just landed or, conversely, that it is taking flight. A semicircular orb of red with yellow and orange edges provides a dramatic solar throne for the bird, its visual heat pushing the imperial creature into our space and consciousness. As viewers we face both the commanding bird and the sun, enacting Hartley's fantasy of going Indian and traveling "to the West [to] face the sun forever."

This then is the picture's iconography: an encampment of tepees; cookie-cutter men in blankets and headdresses; canoes, campfires, bowls, fish, eagle, sun, and stars. It is all storybook material; Hartley did not invent so much as recirculate Indian motifs that he knew from popular cowboy and Indian illustrators, early moviemakers, and romantic storytellers. Like most of his artist counterparts, Hartley was not a serious student of Indian history. He cavalierly fused the woodland tribes who used canoes with the plains Indians who were migratory and lived in tepees and on important occasions wore feather bonnets. Furthermore, for a series dedicated to the American Indian, Hartley freely mixed in motifs from other cultures: the Buddha from the East; mummies and pyramids from Egypt; the mandorla and cross from Christianity; and the eight-pointed stars and the eagle from multiple cultures, including America and the Imperial German military.[6] The Amerika series is very multicultural.

If eclectic and even hackneyed in imagery, *Indian Fantasy* is extremely inventive in visual and optical effects, as are the other two paintings in the series. Hartley's hot reds and yellows, and orchestrated patterns, create what quilt-makers call an "eye dazzler": a surface of small chunks of strong color tightly patterned for eye-grabbing effects.[7]

Besides color, the most prominent characteristic of the Amerika series, we have noted, is a self-consciousness of design. As in traditional rugs, wallpapers, and fabrics, symmetry and patterns are Hartley's guiding principles here. If a line is drawn down the middle of *Indian Fantasy,* the forms on one side all but mirror the other. There are also subtle cubist dynamics, proving Hartley to be intimately informed about Parisian avant-garde painting. The large central tepee encompassing all the smaller tepees is a collage of pushing and pulling pyramidal shapes. The red tepee is optically within the yellow tent and simultaneously in front of it. And the large yellow tepee is both a parent tepee and a stylized stream of light radiating from the bird or pointing up to it. The bird's headdress, an inverted triangle, also functions as a piece of the sun, both radiating out and pointing down to the eagle.

The bird's headdress contributes to the calculated flow of visual energy both downwards and upwards to the bird—with the canoes and fish providing a lighter countermovement from left to right. Ultimately, our focus as viewers is drawn to that majestic and soaring bird, the visual climax of the painting; it is king of the mountain, or, in a Christian metaphor, god-the-father commanding his kingdom below.

What close looking reveals, then, is a set of clichéd images of American Indians rendered in highly calculated, decorative, symmetrical, and cubistic compositions. It is within this odd combination of storybook kitsch and modernist inventiveness that I want to suggest the operations of culture manifest themselves. To tease them out, let me ask three different questions of the artist and this series. Since Hartley made the series abroad, several years before his first contact with Native Americans in a visit to New Mexico in 1918–19, why did he, as an American expatriate living in Berlin, select such a theme? Why the meticulous concern for balance and decorative patterns in a painter whose aesthetic both before and after this series was much more dynamic and explosive? And why are there such forceful pictorial hierarchies in the Amerika paintings, with some parts much larger and more visually powerful than others?

These last two questions highlight the strangeness of this series in the artist's oeuvre. Hartley had already made a serious turn towards abstraction when he painted this picture, so its collage-like and expressionist simplifications are not surprising. But the tight, almost classical symmetry and uniformity of small parts are. His abstractions of the previous years, such as his *Musical Theme (Oriental Symphony)* of 1912–13 (plate 8), and the *Grossstadtbild* that Patricia McDonnell discusses, exhibit large baroque movements where forms implode and move in and out from a highly energized surface without concern for symmetries (plates 10, 15; McDonnell fig. 15). In moving to a restrained patterned style, Hartley was exploring what was for him a new aesthetic principle, but one that he would quickly discard in the War Motif series that followed.

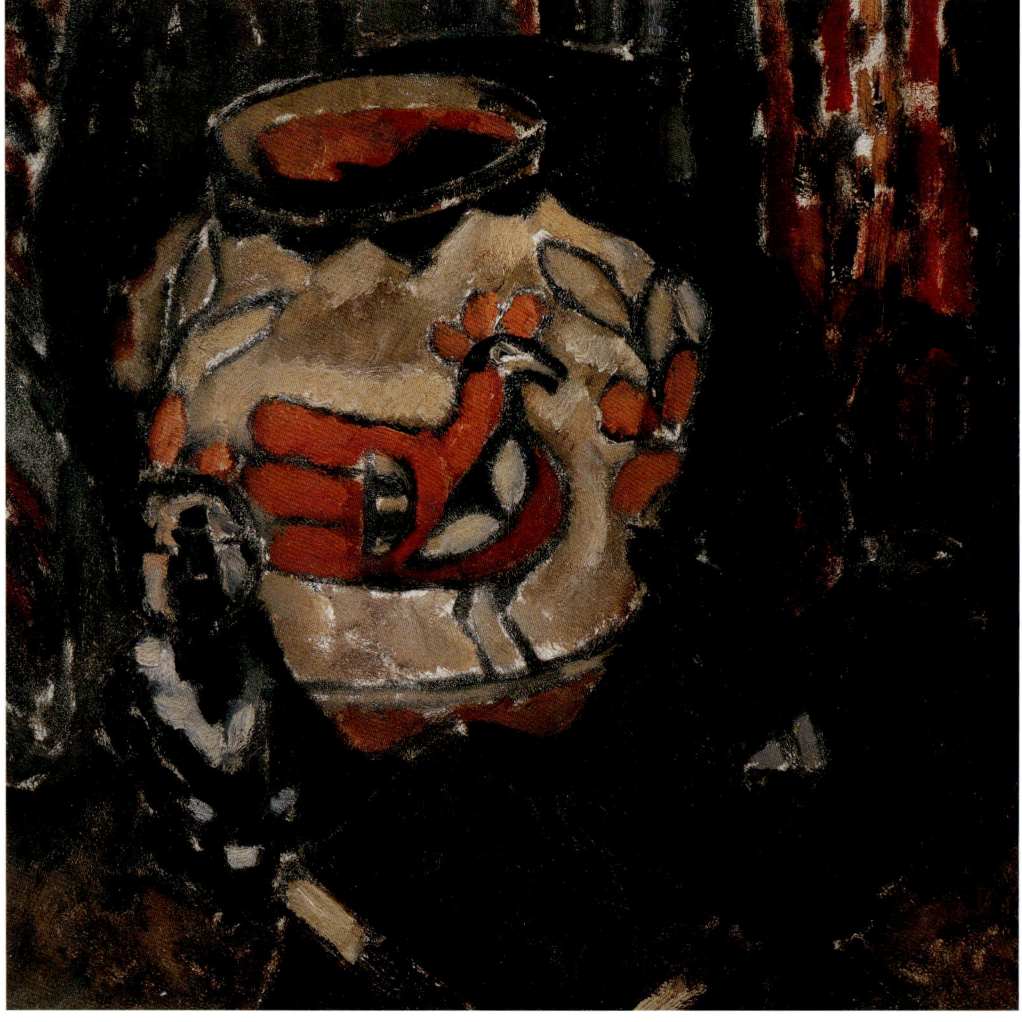

Figure 2
Marsden Hartley
Indian Pottery (Jar and Idol), 1912
Oil on canvas, 20¼ × 20¼ in. (51.4 × 51.4 cm)
Private Collection

Furthermore, there is an organizational structure in the Amerika series that is built upon power relationships and upon visual cues of the ways power is distributed. This too is different from the abstractions that preceded and followed the Amerika paintings, which tended to be based upon an equality of visual weight and parts; whereas in *Indian Fantasy*, the large bird and the yellow tepee represent those in power at the top, while the rank and file membership of those below paddle or swim in formation or, if tepees, march in parade behind the monarchical dwelling. Neither men nor fish nor smaller tepees have any pronounced individuality of their own. One is reminded of corporate or military activities organized by strict rules and traditions where the hierarchy of leadership is clearly identified. While this imparts popular Euro-American beliefs that tribal cultures were organized along similar lines—a chief or elder leading his people—it also suggests Western practices, especially in Germany where rank and place in society were finally tuned. This hunch will take us to 1914 Berlin, to its gay subculture, and to the central presence of the Kaiser and the military within the urban fabric.

Why would an American artist living in Berlin take on Native Americans as his subject? The easiest answer to this question is the most obvious one: that Hartley had become a primitivist, following in the footsteps of Picasso and Braque, who had initiated the practice of modern artists drawing from objects produced by tribal peoples whose art did not adhere to academic traditions. Hartley had been in Paris for a number of months before coming to Berlin, and he had directly experienced the artists' excitement over African and Oceanic ethnographic collections and become familiar with the avant-garde's rhetorical view of these arts as "natural," "simplified," childlike," "uncorrupted," and "authentic." Indeed, it was in 1912 in Paris that Hartley first included Native American artifacts in still-life paintings, drawing his images from Native American pottery and kachina dolls at the Musée Trocadero (fig. 2).[8]

But that said, one must still ask why Hartley did not, like his European colleagues, focus on African or Oceanic art forms, but turned instead to American Indian artifacts? Certainly there were some personal motivations. By taking on Indian themes, Hartley briefly laid claim to a subject that was sanctioned by the primitivists but that also gave him identity abroad as an American artist. He did so at the very moment other American writers and artists were beginning to celebrate the Indians as America's "antiquity" and golden age, and as the country's first artists.[9] Working within the colonialist discourse of primitivism, but replacing negrophilia with Indianism, Hartley joined other American modernists in constructing the Indian to be their spiritual and stylistic ancestor. To create such a genealogy was an act of cultural nationalism, whereby modernists structured for themselves a family tree that was consciously non-European and native. Sometimes the flag-waving was quite literal. In two of Hartley's Amerika paintings—*Indian Composition* and especially *American Indian Symbols*—red, white, and blue strike an unmistakably dominant color chord.

But the story is more complicated still and ultimately cross-cultural. In the Amerika paintings, Hartley was also courting German artists with whom he wished to be associated, particularly those in Munich such as Wassily Kandinsky and Franz Marc. Incorporating Indian motifs in his art provided Hartley with a way to articulate a distinctive identity abroad as an American painter. Within his circles in Germany, who had more right to the subject than he did? In letters, Hartley wrote of his pride in having been one of the few Americans to make connections to the avant-garde artists in Der Blaue Reiter. In the fall of 1913, through the influence of Kandinsky and Marc, Hartley was invited to exhibit in Europe for the first time as one of the four Americans chosen for the Erster Deutscher Herbstsalon held in Berlin (Albert Bloch, Lyonel Feininger, and Patrick Henry Bruce were the other Americans). Featuring nearly four hundred works, the Herbstsalon was a grand survey of modern art, and Hartley was

Figure 3
Paolo Salviati
Buffalo Bill: "The Only Indians Ever in Venice"
Hand-tinted photograph, 10½ × 13½ in. (26.7 × 34.3 cm)
Buffalo Bill Historical Center, Cody, Wyoming

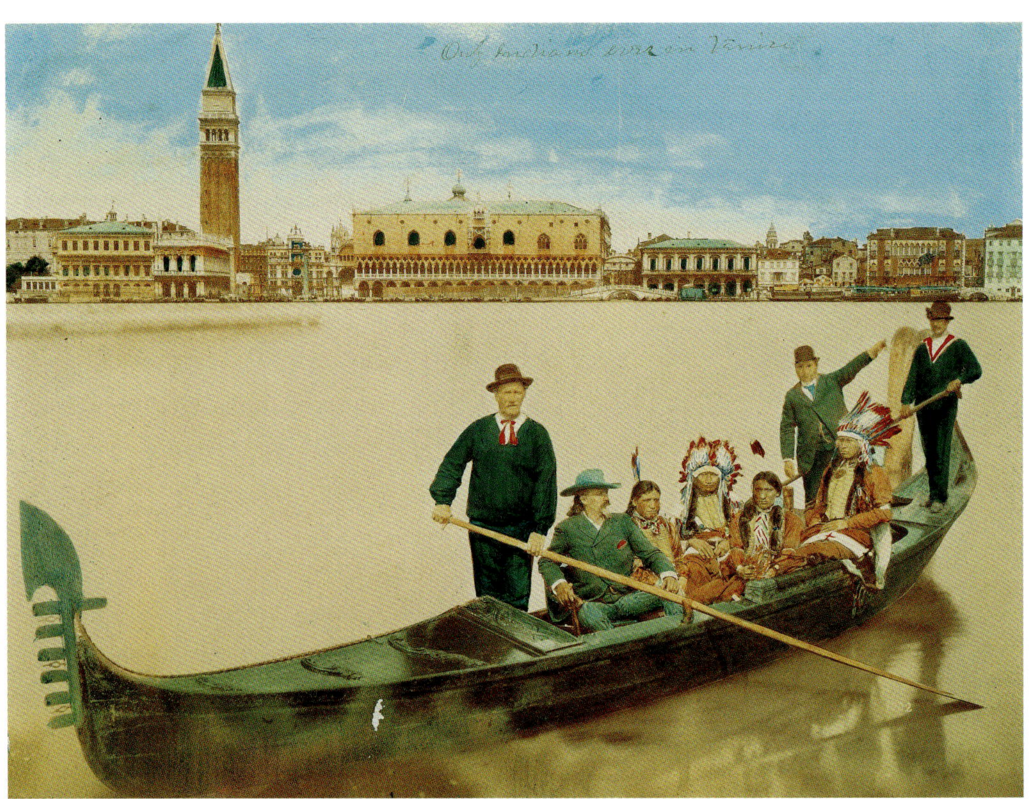

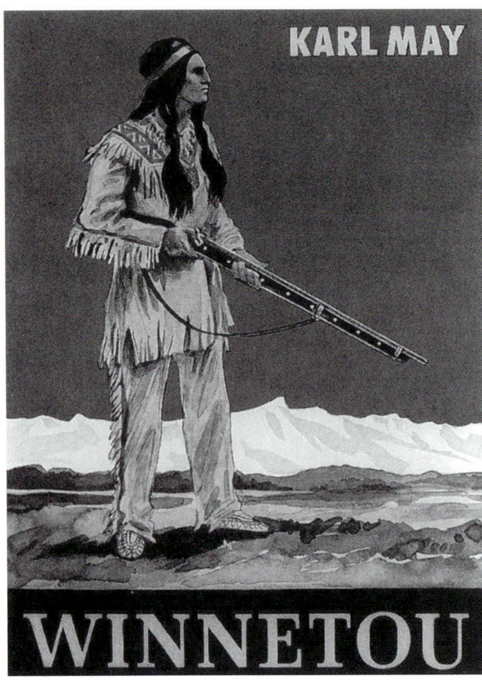

Figure 4
Unknown Photographer
Winnetou with "silver rifle" in the outfit of a Plains Indian, as described by Karl May
Cover of a one-volume edition of Karl May's Winnetou stories, c.1975
Location Unknown

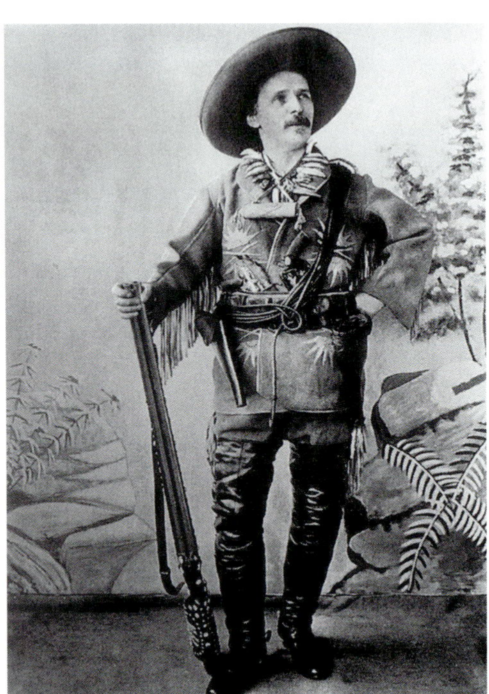

Figure 5
Alois Shießer
Karl May as Old Shatterhand with Winnetou's "silver rifle" in his hand, 1896
Location Unknown

proud to be a part of it. He bragged to Stieglitz that at the opening he "was the only American present, Germany—Swiss—Austria—Armenia—France, America. Kandinsky not there but Marc—Macke—& many I did not know."[10] In a letter of 1915, he told Stieglitz he was "the only so-called 'ultra-modern' American artist in Germany."[11]

To adopt Indian motifs was a powerful signifier of Americanness in the Germany of 1914. In doing so, Hartley not only claimed these materials as his rightful national heritage, but he played directly into a longstanding love affair Germans had with Native Americans. Germany's "Indianism" goes back to early European teams that explored the American West before it was fully colonized and brought back depictions of what they had seen and native arts they had acquired. Deeply interested in ethnology, German scholars were among the first serious collectors of Native American objects, from both North and South America. By the mid-nineteenth-century, they were producing major studies of these objects and in 1886, when the new Königliches Museum für Völkerkunde opened in Berlin, the largest display halls were devoted to American objects. When Hartley began his Amerika series, these collections were well known and readily at hand to study and draw upon.[12]

In addition, Germans were (and still are) avid consumers of Indian entertainments that popularized stereotypes of Indian men in feather headdresses living in tepees. In the late nineteenth century, showmen like Buffalo Bill regularly brought groups of American Indians to perform Wild West Shows in European cities. These natives wore full ceremonial Plains Indians dress on their European tours, not only in their staged battles on horseback, but when they toured cities and visited tourist sites abroad (fig. 3). In Germany, Buffalo Bill performances were so popular that the appearance of native Indians and reenactments of battles became standard acts in circuses, carnivals, and fairs.[13]

Fascination with New World natives was also deeply nourished by a string of late-nineteenth-century novels written by Karl May (1842–1912), who became, and still is, a top seller in Germany. Karl May is a phenomenon hard to grasp in the United States, where there is no storyteller quite like him. He was recently described by Carol Krinsky as "a

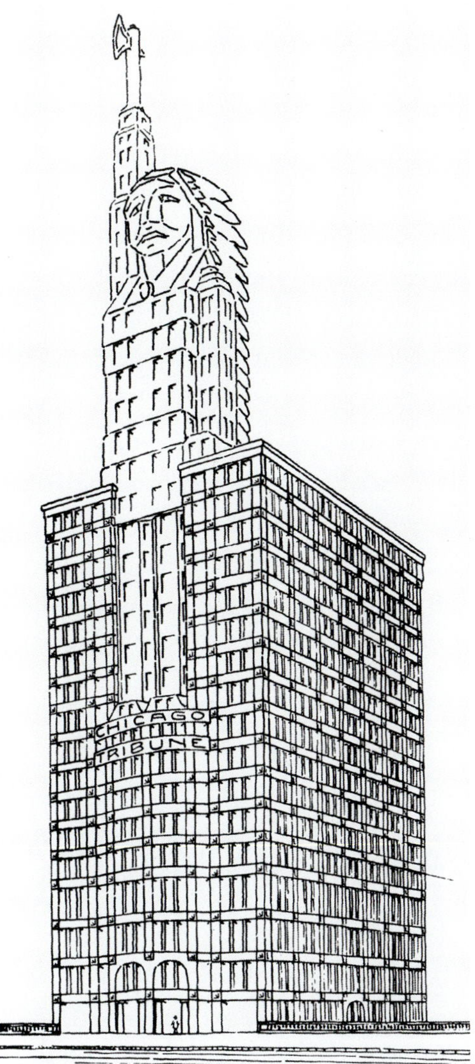

Figure 6
Heinrich Mossdorf, Hans Hahn, and Bruno Busch
Entry for the Chicago Tribune Competition, 1922
Drawing reproduced in *The International Competition for the New Administration Building for the Chicago Tribune MCMXXII* (Chicago: 1923), pl. 232
Location Unknown

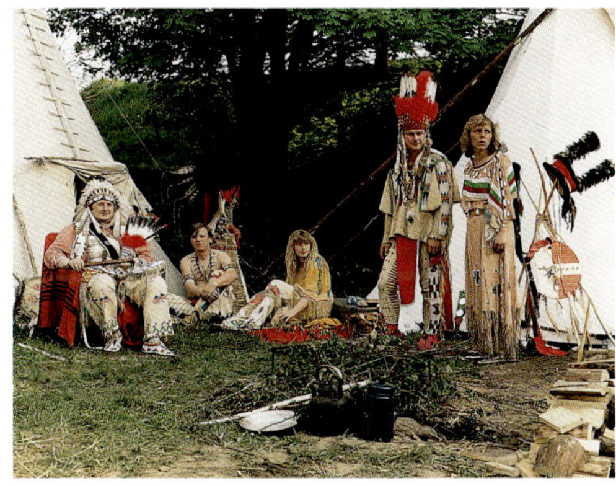

Figure 7
Andrea Robbins and Max Becher
Campfire, 1997–98
Color photograph
© Andrea Robbins, Max Becher

prolific charlatan who never visited the American West." Though he was famous for telling of trips and adventures in the Wild West, in fact he never got further west than Buffalo, New York, on his first, brief, late-life trip to the States in 1908.[14] May might be characterized as a cross between James Fenimore Cooper and Walt Disney. Like Cooper, he created Wild West adventure stories about a white frontiersman, in May's case, a fictional German immigrant called Karl, or "Old Shatterhand"—the latter name because he fought his enemies with his fists, not with a gun. Karl takes up with a brave and good Apache named Winnetou, "der Rote Gentleman," who mentors him in ways of living with nature and on the frontier (figs. 4–5). Like the Lone Ranger and Tonto long popular in the United States, the two men get themselves in an unending set of adventures and predicaments. Representing the forces of good over evil (be it a corrupt gold prospector, the U.S. Calvary, or violent Indians), they invariably succeed. May's literary skills were quite ordinary, yet he went far as a popularizer. Rivaling Walt Disney's success in marketing a pantheon of cartoon characters Americans commonly recognize, May went to such lengths in cultivating his two characters—Winnetou and Old Shatterhand—that they are known today to every adult and child in Germany. Furthermore, May's novels have been translated into twenty-eight languages. Speaking of May's phenomenal presence, Krinsky writes: "The only German writing that has been more often translated is Luther's Bible.... May's volumes have even outsold Goethe's with more than 80 million copies printed so far."[15]

Such Indianphilia helps explain the design three German architects submitted in 1922 to the Chicago Tribune competition, one that reworked the Statue of Liberty into a tower shaped as an Indian with tomahawk in hand (fig. 6). It also gives some insight into the sustained presence of German Indian clubs—*Indianistikgruppen*—which flourish throughout Germany, and the popularity there of American western and country music. In the 1920s, after May's death, his widow, Klara May, opened an Indian Museum at the Villa Shatterhand in Radebeul, where they lived, about five miles from Dresden. On May's birthday, hundreds of Indian club members in costume descend upon Radebeul for a two-day festival. They dress up in feather headdresses and deerskin shirts, erect tepees, and enact powwow-styled dances and ceremonies, powerfully captured recently in a photographic essay by Andrea Robbins and Max Becher (fig. 7).[16] "Accuracy" of dress is important to these hobbyists, who go to great lengths to masquerade as Plains Indians, using late-nineteenth- and early-twentieth-century photographs and paintings as their guides.

While Buffalo Bill and Karl May conditioned Germans to revere and mythologize the American Indian and inculcated the desire to act out their Indianism in annual events, what is most crucial to understanding Hartley's investment in native motifs was the participation of the German avant-garde in Indian-mania. Wanting to negotiate a place for himself within the European avant-garde community, Hartley was surely aware that some of his German artist peers also worked within the Indianist discourse. For painters, modernist primitivizing made it possible to cast Indians as a tribal folk who, like the Bavarian glass painters admired by the Munich moderns, made their arts (and their warfare) out of pure instinct rather than school learning. Indians were constructed as unassimilated and non-modern; they were romantic figures who rode on horses, inhabited temporary dwellings, and lived in close harmony with the land.

Indianism also played a prominent place in the *Amerikanismus* that surfaced in avant-garde Germany around the years of World War I and sustained a number of art projects and enthusiasms in the 1920s. In its simplest form, *Amerikanismus* was cultural envy and critique, a love–hate relationship to things in the United States that Germans felt their older, and more tradition-bound society did not have. Within the early-twentieth-century avant-garde, Americanophilia took many forms—heightened enthusiasm for skyscrapers, jazz, Charlie Chaplin, and black Harlem, for instance—and in Germany, as in no other country, deep-seated Indianism.[17] In Hartley's own Berlin, artist George Grosz installed a tepee in his studio, decorated it with tomahawks and buffalo skins, and entertained his friends by wrapping up in a blanket and smoking a white clay pipe.[18] Both Grosz and his contemporary Otto Dix made numerous paintings and drawings of Indians, usually in war paint, with feathers in their headdresses and tomahawks in hand (figs. 8–9). Often they included an American flag.

Grosz's and Dix's Indians were warriors—tough and violent Indians, often more like Chicago gangsters (another admiration of theirs) than smokers of peacepipes. Other members of the German avant-garde depicted gentler Native Americans, good Indians rather than bad ones. This was especially true of August Macke, a Blaue Reiter painter Hartley admired, who pictured Indians much like Gauguin represented Tahitians, as living close to the natural world. In Macke's *Indians on Horseback,* natives are rendered as akin to trees and flowers, a part of nature, not separate from it (fig. 10). And lest we mistake their origins, the Indian on foot carries a staff with a red, white, and blue decoration. In a wall

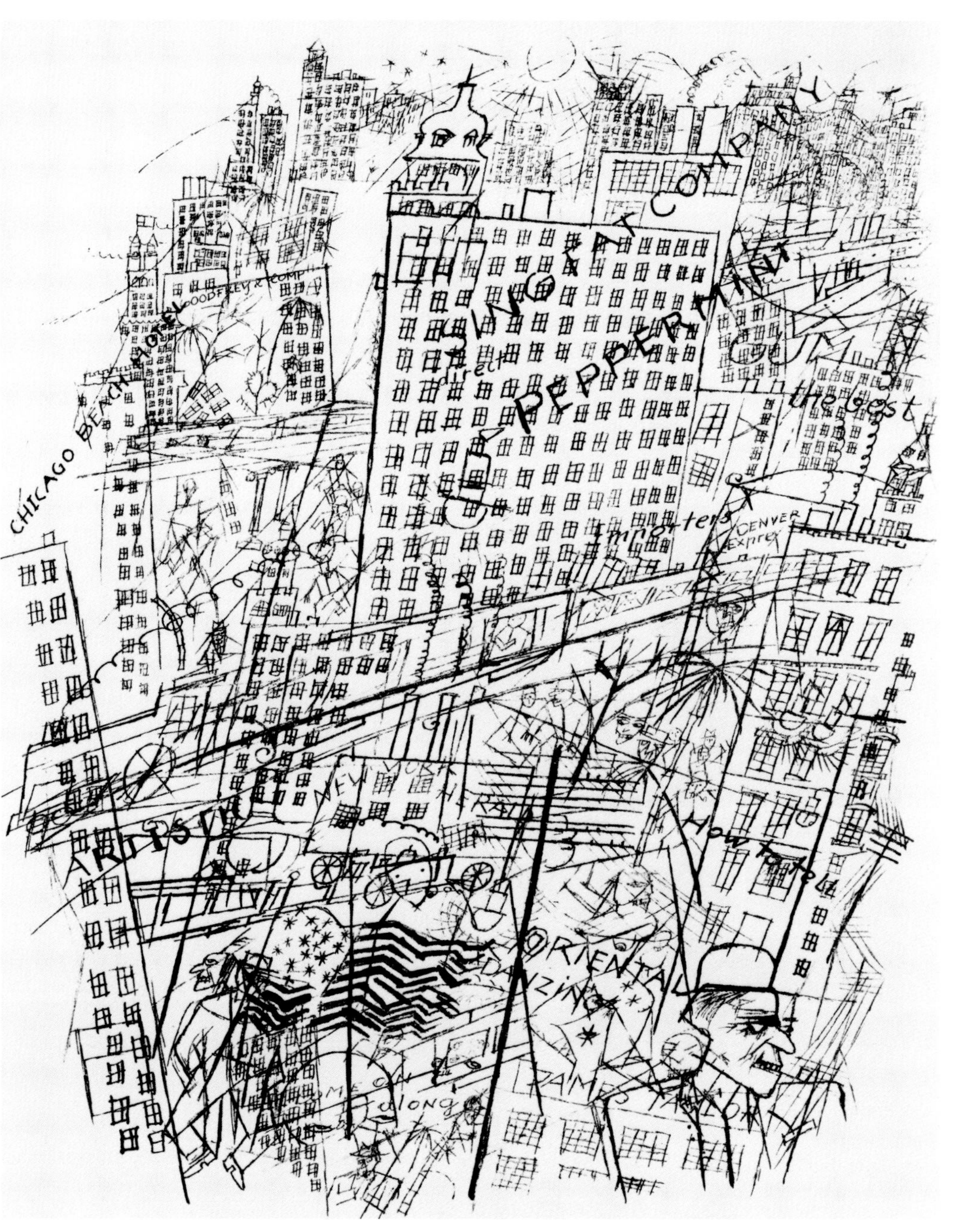

Figure 8
George Grosz
Memory of New York, from "The First George Grosz Portfolio," 1915–16
Black ink on off-white Japan paper, 19 9/10 × 15 3/8 in. (50.5 × 39.1 cm)
Courtesy of the Busch-Reisinger Museum, Harvard University Art Museums
Museum Purchase
Photograph by David Mathews
© President and Fellows of Harvard College/Estate of George Grosz/Licensed by VAGA, New York

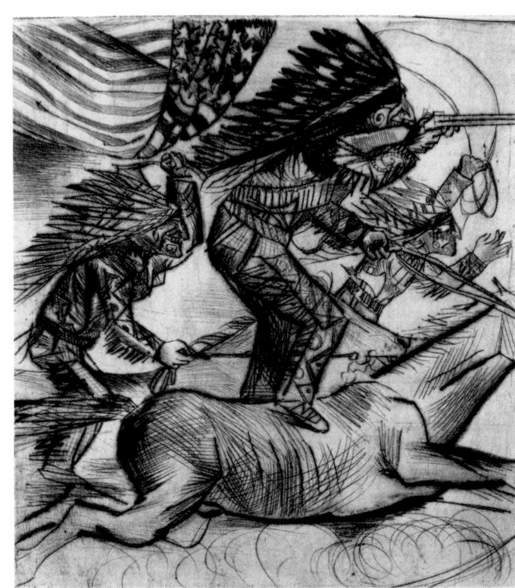

Figure 9
Otto Dix
American Riding Act, 1922
Etching and drypoint from the *Zirkus Mappe,* 19 5/8 × 16 7/8 in. (49.8 × 43 cm)
Los Angeles County Museum of Art
© 2002 Artists Rights Society (ARS), New York/VG Bild-Kunst, Bonn

Figure 10
August Macke
Indianer auf Pferden (Indians on Horseback), 1911
Stadtische Galerie im Lenbachhaus, Munich

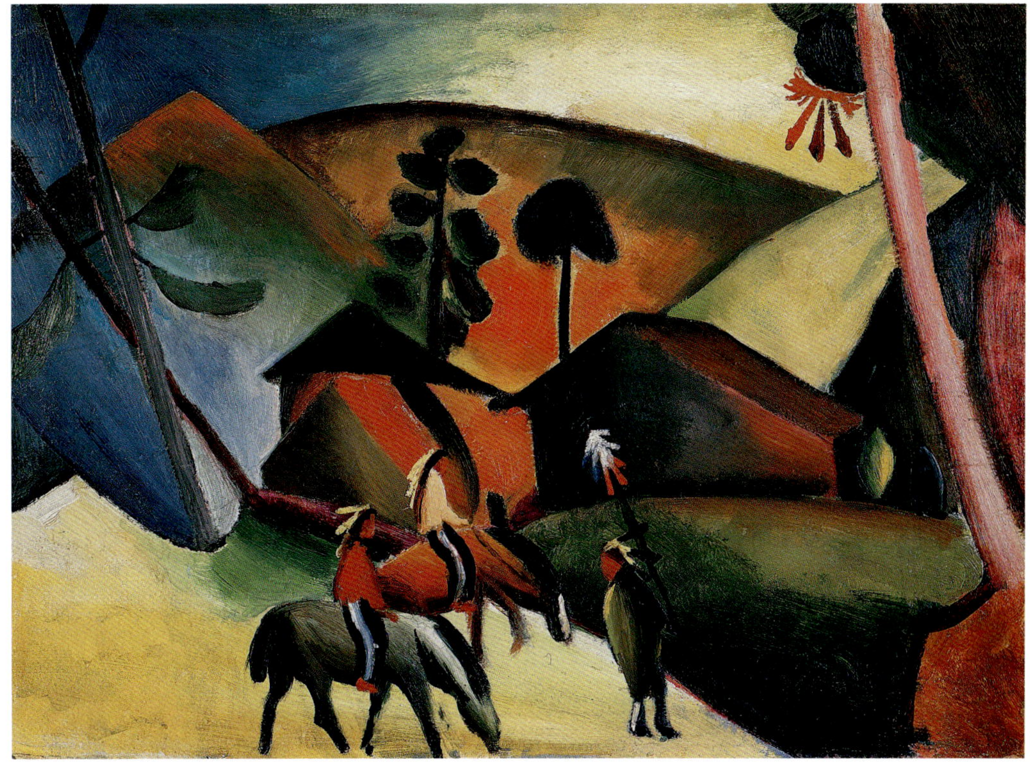

hanging by Ernst Ludwig Kirchner created for a tobacco merchant in 1914, the same year Hartley painted his Amerika series, the central image is a dark dancing native whose body is silhouetted against a long headdress; native figures in similar headdresses are to either side and Indian-like patterns radiate from the dancer (fig. 11). To the far left, native figures smoke, and to the right a native gives a pipe to a man dressed in European dress. This exchange establishes Indians as the original smokers who gave the gift of tobacco to the world.

Both bad, war-mongering chiefs and good, nature-loving Indians, then, peopled the German modernists' repertoire, just as they did Karl May's adventure stories. Hartley's Indians, entombed in blankets and seated like paperweights, perpetuated the good, peaceful Indian type. In 1914 Hartley had not yet visited an American Indian village or reservation and had never, in fact, been west of the Mississippi. And before coming to Europe, he had never taken Indian motifs as his subject. He took up this new subject aware of the heightened presence of Indian lore in Germany, especially among the avant-garde artists with whom he wished to associate. His Amerika series strengthened his identity as an American while simultaneously playing to the Germans' exaggerated stereotypes of Indian life.

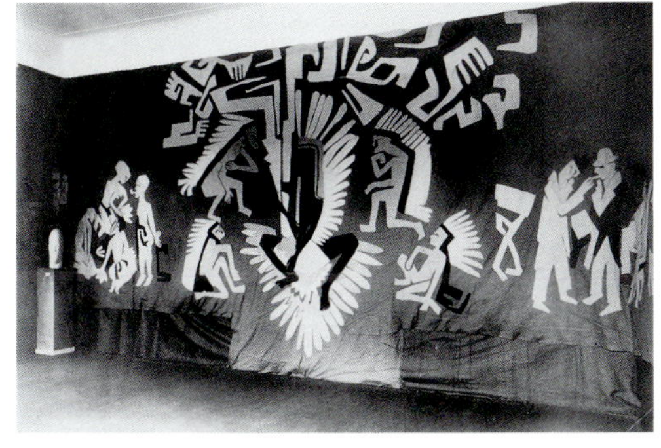

Figure 11
Ernst Ludwig Kirchner
Wanddekoration: "Die Kunst in Tabakgewerbe?"
Archiv Kirchner Museum Davos
Photograph by Hildegard Naser, Davos
© Works of Kirchner by Ingeborg and Dr. Wolfgang Henze-Ketterer, Wichtrach/Bernz

Furthermore, Hartley could "research" his subject at the Museum für Völkerkunde, where he found tepees, canoes, and totem poles on display as well as a wide selection of handcrafted Indian clothing, weapons, furnishings, or tools. The holdings were impressive and it was surely here that Hartley gained his fullest appreciation for the material culture and arts of the American Indian. Gail Levin, an art historian who has looked carefully at the Berlin collection, has identified a wooden eagle from Vancouver that may have inspired the bird form in *Indian Fantasy,* for instance, and miniature tepees like those in which Hartley's Indian chiefs sit. She has also pointed out the various abstract and pictographic signs that Hartley favored in the Amerika series that are commonly found in native vocabulary: crosses, eight-pointed stars, mandorlas, and checkerboard patterns.[19]

What Hartley also drew from studying these objects was an aesthetic. Earlier in this essay I remarked upon the intensely colored patterning and symmetry in the Amerika series and asked why Hartley submitted to such a visual regime for this series as he did not for

Figure 12
Yakima Peoples
Parfleche Envelope, c. 1900
Rawhide and paint, 12 × 26½ in. (30.5 × 67.3 cm)
The University of Iowa Museum of Art, Iowa City
(1986.58b)

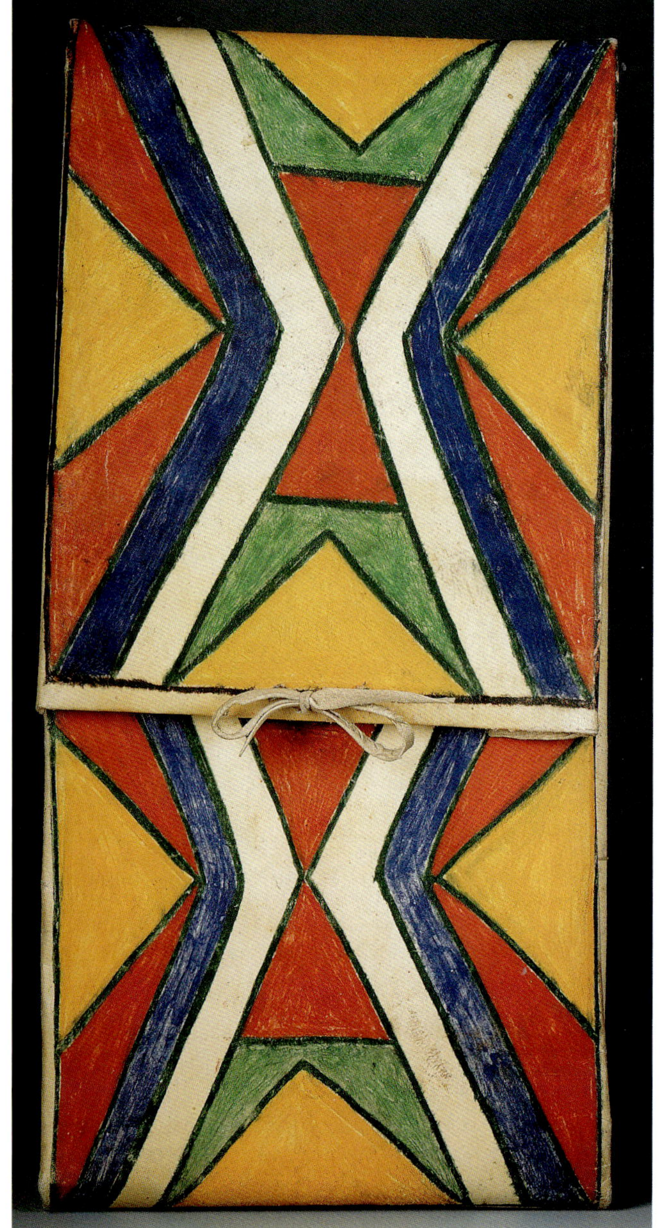

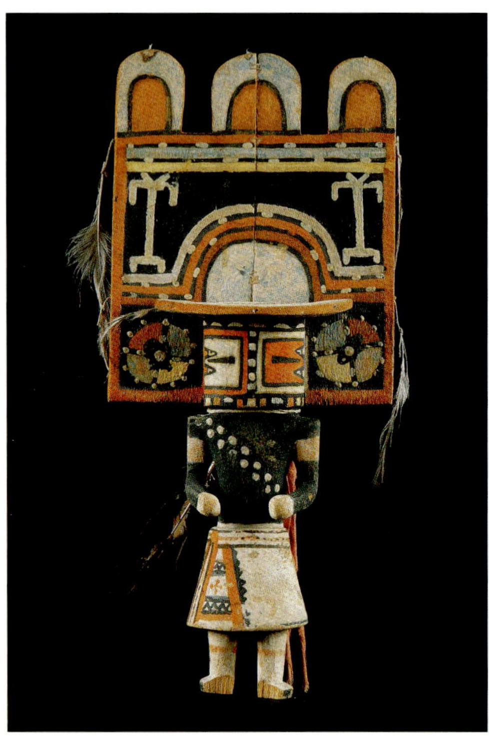

Figure 13
Zuni-Hemis Kachina, 1899
Hopi figure
Staatliche Museen zu Berlin, Preussischer
Kulturbesitz Ethnologisches Museum
Inv. Nr. IV 2292
Photograph by Dietrich Graff 1999

others. Given that so much Indian beadwork, featherwork, and painted parfleches were similarly dependent on repeated, small-scale patterns of concentric circles, bands, stripes, zig-zags, triangles, squares, and boxes, and that color in many tribal traditions is dense and dazzling, it seems clear that Hartley drew some of his compositional strategies from this work (figs. 12–13). He was fusing what he deemed an Indian aesthetic of color and decoration to a modern style of abstraction.

But that said, it is also clear that Hartley grafted this decorative Indian aesthetic onto some strong European painting conventions. He organized his Amerika canvases into a foreground, middle ground, and sky above, and he made little still-life arrangements near his seated figures, giving them attributes. His figures have vestiges of modeling and are not at all the schematic stick figures found in Indian paintings. And above all, the pictorial hierarchies I pointed out in the opening remarks are decidedly European and not Indian: the small tepees on parade behind the lead tent; and the commanding bird lording over the smaller village of tepees and Indians below.

Hartley's preoccupation with hierarchy—and with decoration—is deeply rooted in the artist's personal life in Berlin, something we know a great deal about because his letters in these months to friends in Paris and the States have been preserved. In his autobiography, written later in his life, he also wrote about his time in Berlin.[20] Temperamentally, Hartley was generally a moody and unhappy man, but he loved the Berlin he came to know in 1913–15; he was so satisfied with his life there that he ventured he might live in Europe for the rest of his days.[21]

Hartley's happiness, McDonnell writes in her essay, was rooted in a number of Berlin's urban offerings in the ante-war years. The capital of Imperial Germany and home to Kaiser Wilhelm II and his court, Berlin had an elegance and exploding modernity that Hartley found thrilling. The city held liberal attitudes toward homosexuality, and he had two important male friendships: with Arnold Rönnebeck, a sculptor and military man, and with Rönnebeck's cousin, Lieutenant Karl von Freyburg. Hartley also liked the city's overall orderliness. He lauded what he called the "well-keptness and healthful system" of Germany as compared to the gray "sickliness of the French." Berlin, he wrote, was "ultra-modern" with "a unique sense of order and cleanliness," a place where "health and order and gaiety prevails." Using the highly gendered descriptions typical of that time, he characterized France as "utterly feminine in its essence while Germany is essentially masculine with masculine ruggedness and vitality."[22] Masculine was good; feminine was bad.

For Hartley to make so much of the masculinity of his adopted city is indicative of the deep pleasures the gay artist found in Berlin's male culture. Hartley confessed in a letter to Stieglitz that he "lived rather gayly in the Berlin fashion—with all that implies."[23] And when he recalled Berlin and its pageantry in his later autobiography, he used sexual imagery to evoke his pleasure. "The whole scene was fairly bursting with organized energy and the tension was terrific and somehow most voluptuous in the feeling of power—a sexual immensity even in it—when passion rises to the full and something must happen to quiet it."[24] As Patricia McDonnell has explained in this book and elsewhere, Berlin was a remarkably liberal city and supported entertainment, societies, and journals dedicated to same-sex partnerships. Furthermore, she tells us, homosexuality was rife in the military as well as within Kaiser Wilhelm's court. The Kaiser himself, some maintain, was a bisexual, who loved pageantry and fancy dress and hosted parties for men where, as John Rohl put it, he could indulge his "love of uniforms, of jewelry, of dressing-up, and of childish games played in all-male company."[25]

Hartley, too, loved pomp and men in costumes, especially in the public spectacles and large formal parades the Kaiser ordered up to show off Germany's military and the members of his own court. He found the military men so handsome and becoming that he sent postcards to friends of the German military on parade in full regalia (McDonnell figs. 13, 15). "Of course the military system is accountable for many things," he wrote to Rockwell Kent, "and to some this military element is objectionable—but it stimulates my child's love for the public spectacle—and such wonderful specimens of health these men are—thousands all so blond and radiant."[26]

So intensely public was he about his pleasure in uniformed male bodies on parade that one of his artist friends, Lee Simonson, drew a parody of Hartley as a German soldier. He pictured the artist in military uniform and goose-stepping with pointed toes; he carries a German parade flag in one hand, with a design based on Kandinsky's style of abstraction, and the insignia 291 for his New York gallery is painted onto his epaulets. In his left hand the artist carries a beer mug, and in the top corner Simonson wrote: "Hartley has about made up his mind to become a permanent citizen of Germany" (McDonnell fig. 1).

The Amerika series was bookended by paintings about German military pomp, coming after Hartley's first major painting about German soldiers on parade—*The Warriors,*

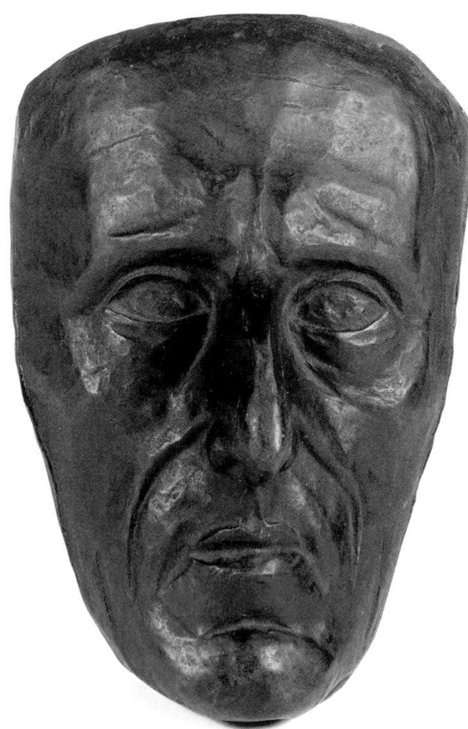

Figure 14
Arnold Rönnebeck
Portrait Mask of Marsden Hartley, 1912
Bronze, life-size
Location Unknown
Yale Collection of American Literature
Beinecke Rare Book and Manuscript Collection
Yale University, New Haven

painted in 1913 upon Hartley's arrival in Berlin—and before the War Motif series created after the war had begun. Commonly, art historians have interpreted *The Warriors* and the War Motif series as pictorial equivalents for what the artist tells us about his sensuous excitement at seeing military men in dress uniform on horseback. But no one has yet remarked upon the ways in which Hartley's passion for Berlin's pageantry, and for men in dress-up, also shaped his Amerika series. The Amerika paintings, like all of Hartley's war paintings, covertly express the homoerotic pleasures Hartley took in all-male gatherings and in seeing military men dressing up and parading in choreographed formations. The photographic postcards Hartley sent Gertrude Stein of these parades picture them as chorus-line formations, lines of soldiers in dress uniforms marching or riding on horseback with flags and banners aloft or at their backs.

The Warriors (plate 11) was Hartley's first important work to employ an abstract aesthetic of symmetry and pattern, and in this respect it initiates the Amerika series that began the following year. *The Warriors* is made up of small repeated units, most of them horse rumps, and it is also spectacularly colorful, dazzling the eye in ways similar to the Amerika series. In all of these works, Hartley utilized the theory of equivalents, using color and abstraction to express the childlike wonder and homoeroticism he was experiencing. Indeed, in retrospect it seems a rather simple act of transference for Hartley to have moved from a painting of all male soldiers on parade to a painting of all male Indians set into patterns. The Indian paintings are all militaristically ordered, the powerful "commanders" at the center and the troops to either side. In *The Warriors,* the foot soldiers are pictured in rote formation to either side of a golden dome of ascending forms that enclose the four haloed leaders. In *Indian Fantasy,* the Indians in canoes are distributed equally on either side of the luminous mountain of tepees upon which the majestic bird alights.

Noting the militaristic order Hartley imposed on his Amerika compositions returns us to *Indian Fantasy* and to its commanding eagle backed by the fiery hues of the sun. Some have plausibly argued that the stylized form of the bird is taken from objects Hartley could have seen at the ethnological museum in Berlin.[27] Furthermore, along with the water, fish, and campfires, the bird conveys one of the core elements of the white man's Indianism: an idealization of the Indian as a "natural" being, rather than a civilized being, who knows and lives within the ways of nature. The bird here helps characterize the landscape as unspoiled, uncorrupted, and paradisiacal.

But these are the most literal or manifest meanings of the bird, and they say nothing about the bird's enormous scale and power position in the composition. Nor do they take into account that Hartley, because of his very distinctive aquiline nose, was often referred to as the Eagle or Albatross.[28] In profile, his nose looked to some, including Rönnebeck who sculpted him, like a beak (fig. 14). The "gaunt eagle from the hills of Maine," Paul Rosenfeld, writing Hartley's obituary, called him.[29] When Hartley first arrived in Berlin in 1913, he used the image of a bird flying high over the landscape in his letters as a literary metaphor for his happiness: he described himself as "the eagle having raised my wings and leapt off the precipice into space and in my circlings . . . having found something which is my own and no other's."[30] A couple of months later, in a postcard to Gertrude Stein, he wrote, "I think it must be fine to be a Himalayan Condor and just sit on the topmost tops and condescend occasionally to consider things beneath one's wings in the valley places."[31] The eagle spreading his wings over the entire landscape in *Indian Fantasy* was Hartley's self-image. In soaring over the Indian landscape, Hartley envisioned himself as an artist transcendent, in command of his life and his adopted city. This was a rare moment for Hartley, who for once felt at the top of his powers.

Hartley's happiness soon ended, and so too did his Indian fantasies, though not his military ones. In the fall of 1914, when Hartley learned that the German lieutenant he loved, Karl von Freyburg, had been killed on the western front, and Rönnebeck wounded, he began to supplant his Indian motifs with military ones. A new series emerged with references to Karl, Arnold, and the German militia, with increased attention to costumes, flags, and insignia. The new paintings were different—the aesthetic was one of overlapping collage-like planes not patterned symmetry—of throbbing and grand movements rather than quiet storybook idylls. But there was a continuum with the Amerika series, as the very first paintings in the War Motif series were built along a symmetrical model before they evolved into their more dynamic and imploding set of forms that characterize the best of them (plates 19–21). Most importantly, the War Motif series did not break with but continued the artist's process of working out his being an American expatriate in an adopted city and being so absorbed by military pageantry. This Berlin—partially real, partially fantasy—began to unravel in wartime; and the conditions forced Hartley home in December 1915. When Hartley returned to Berlin after the war, it was not the same city, and he was no longer enamored of it in the same way; he never painted such rapturous paintings again.[32]

The paintings in the Amerika series, then, are densely layered cultural texts. They are "expatriate" canvases, so to speak, created by an American abroad seeking connection with his birthplace while simultaneously trying to be noticed by the German avant-garde. Primitivist in their fusing of the native artist's use of repetitious patterns with avant-garde European ideas about abstraction, the Amerika paintings are also nationalist in Hartley's presuming that the Indian material would give him an American identity abroad. They give a rich cross-cultural account of Hartley's American love affair with Berlin and Germany's romance with Native America. Hartley so closely identified with Indians at this moment and felt so jubilant and self-confident that he projected himself in the painting as the all-embracing, all-powerful eagle.

But most surprisingly, the Amerika paintings are urban paintings, evoking Berlin's modernity and its military showmanship at the onset of World War I. Militarist in their compositions, the paintings evoke the soldier culture of Berlin and anticipate the War Motif series where Hartley mourns his dead lover. The War Motif series openly expresses Hartley's psychological and emotional absorption in military parades, in decorations such as flags and ornaments, and in uniforms standing in for the male body. His desire for male companionship and his delight in the costumed male body is equally embedded in the Amerika series, albeit disguised and displaced, not yet "out," rendered as storybook decorations about Indian warriors and hunters.

Coda

There is a sequel to Hartley's Berlin foray into Indianism. Returning to New York in 1915, Hartley stayed in the United States for six years. In 1918 he made his first trip west, going first to Taos, New Mexico, where Mabel Dodge (Luhan) had settled and encouraged her artist-friends to come, and a few months later, to Santa Fe. In New Mexico he experienced living Native American culture for the first time, finding, of course, no one bearing resemblance to the romantic stereotypes he had evoked in his Amerika series. The Pueblo peoples of northern New Mexico had for centuries lived in long-established villages, not on the plains, and were great farmers, not hunters. The men often wore white blankets, but not highly colored feathered bonnets and striped blankets. They lived in adobe homes, not tepees, and they traveled by horse and car, not by canoe. Sensing some of these differences, Hartley wrote that the Taos Indians "did not have perhaps the appearance of monoliths against the morning sky with delicately chiseled profiles as has the Apache.... [Y]ou get the oriental touch in the Taos Indians through the white blanket which they affect in all weather, covering themselves to the eyes in the manner of orientals." He went on to compare the "very old men of the tribe who sit in the sun and expose their worn ribs to the warmth" to carved Chinese idols. In characterizing them as "the little wise men who sit pondering on the immensities" of life, the artist was clearly thinking back to the squat little Indian figurines he had pictured in the Amerika series.[33]

Perhaps it was because he did not find what he expected at the Taos pueblo, or because he realized how overdrawn his earlier Indian imagery had been, that Hartley never painted another series of Indian-based works. He painted primarily landscapes in the Southwest, without reference to native culture (plates 38–39). He disliked paintings that the Taos and Santa Fe Euro-American artists created of the local Indians, finding them to be academic paintings of the worse sort. And he was not that enthusiastic about Pueblo pottery and blankets.[34] The only allusions he made to Indians in his New Mexico paintings were in an occasional still life where he put together Hispanic *santos* and Pueblo pottery (plates 34–36).

Recalling the enthusiasm Kandinsky and other Blaue Reiter painters had taught him for Bavarian *hinterglasbilder,* a religious folk-painting tradition, Hartley was drawn to the simply painted and sculpted *santos,* made by Hispanic artists for use in churches and home altars, and collected by Mabel Dodge (Luhan). But he was unnerved to discover Catholic churches and *santos* of Christian crucifixes and saints on the Indian reservations and criticized "the catholic adherence among this original people."[35] Like so many of his generation, Hartley wanted the Indian to be forever "pagan," living in nature with an "unquestionable goodness in things around him."[36]

He spoke to this issue by putting together still lifes that combined Christian and Indian motifs, often, it seems, to critique the "foreign invasion" of Catholicism upon native peoples. *Blessing the Melon: The Indians Bring the Harvest to Christian Mary for Her Blessing* pictures the dissonance between belief systems (plate 34). For Hartley, the large imposing Madonna *santo* most likely represented the prevailing Catholic faith in the Southwest, while the watermelon, smaller and more humble, signified the Indian's faith in the natural world.

While Hartley painted very little of Indian culture in the Southwest, he was attentive to it in a series of articles he published between 1918 and 1922. Essay writing was new to Hartley in the post-Berlin years, and he became particularly impassioned about defining what he conceptualized as the "redman" aesthetic and what he now took to be the Native American's most important art form: their dances and related ceremonies. These essays were his effort to theorize a position towards Native Americans and to contribute his voice to the anthropological and literary discourse about American Indians that was beginning to circulate widely in intellectual circles.[37] As was common among many writers, Hartley saw the "redman" as a doomed and vanishing race. He primitivized Indians as "the beautiful children of the world," idolizing their pagan, pre-Christian culture and comparing their antiquity to the Egyptians, Assyrians, Greeks, Abbysinians, and Chinese. Along with others in these years, Hartley claimed the American Indian as "our first artistic relative."[38] "We have nothing more native at our disposal," he wrote, "than the beautiful creations of this people."[39] Not surprisingly, given the aesthetic he employed in the Amerika series, he also characterized the Indian as "one of the essential decorators of the world."[40]

One of the most interesting threads in his essays, particularly given Hartley's preoccupation with male bodies on parade in Berlin, is the focus on Indian bodies in movement. He was completely taken with the dances and footraces at the puebloes in northern New Mexico and went to a good number of them. Indeed, he was one of the first outsiders to focus on and argue for the Indian dance as an art form. He was not interested in anthropological description but rather in defining the aesthetic beauty of their dances, just as he had once grappled with the decorative aesthetic of native objects in Berlin. Indeed, the Indian dances and the footraces became for Hartley what the military parade had been for him in Berlin, a site of sensuous and emotional pleasure. The dances were "pageants" and "beautiful spectacles." The dancers had the gift for "masquerade."[41] And as in Berlin, it was the male body in movement that would draw his attention. (He barely mentioned the many women and children who regularly participated in dances.) He complimented the males for their "notable athleticism... so strong of muscle and of sinew." And he described the male footracers further as "fine specimens of manly vigor, superbly painted in earth hues of deep Indian red."[42]

Not far beneath the surface of Hartley's praise for Indian ceremonies lay his own despair with machine age culture and modern American art, which seemed so limp, weak, and disengaged by comparison. He mourned that modern artists were becoming "mechanical brained" and had no religion or any deep attachment to the earth.[43] In the native dancer, Hartley found an allegorical figure for the modern artist; and in the sincerity and rootedness of native dancing he uncovered a standard by which modern art should be judged. He found the dances to be deeply spiritual but also indigenous, related to American soil. In their fusion of music, dance, and poetry, the dances modeled what Hartley yearned to achieve in his own art: an authentic expression from deep within, an American art expressing a deep and harmonious relationship to the land and culture.

Hartley did not have the same confidence in his New Mexico paintings that he had in the Berlin ones; he was writing more and painting less. The years from 1915 through the 1920s were rough years for Hartley as a painter, stronger for him as an essayist. His writings about the Indian poignantly express his own unhappiness as an artist and his unfulfilled yearnings to achieve the same wholeness in his art that he found in native dances.

In New Mexico, Hartley returned to landscape painting, moving away from the dramatically abstract vocabulary he had practiced so inventively before the war. Being back in the States and among the Stieglitz artists who always talked about the invention of a new Americanized painting, he characterized his turn to the New Mexico landscape as a quest for national identity. "I am an American discovering America," he began an early essay from New Mexico, sounding for all the world like Stieglitz himself. "I like the position and I like the results. As a painter, I am impressed with the fact that America as landscape is, one may rightly say untouched."[44]

When Hartley returned to Berlin in late 1921, he once again faced identity issues being an American abroad. This time he expressed his Americanness in a series of landscapes he called his New Mexico Recollections, harking back to his work in the Southwest (plates 38–39). These landscapes of deserts and sagebrush, he must have hoped, might once again appeal to the German's absorption in stories from the Wild West. Vigorously painted, these compositions picture fallen trees, sage, cactus, or skeletal bones in the foreground; and rolling mesas, foothills, and mountains in the distance. The skies are thick with paint, pulsating with clouds that look like twisted cloth. They are strong paintings but their mood is dark and gloomy, their spaces desolate and remote. They give us an older, more troubled and somber Hartley than the artist enraptured by Berlin seven years earlier.

Notes

1 Hartley to Alfred Stieglitz, 12 November 1914, Beinecke/Yale.

2 Hartley scholarship to date has not sorted out precisely when the Amerika series begins and ends and which paintings belong to it. Besides the three images I am considering here, there are another seven or eight paintings, large and small, that have definable Indian imagery but are more abstract. All of them date from 1914–15 and some of them may overlap with the making of the War Motif series. Two large paintings with Indian details are solidly dated 1915. First published by Gail Levin, they are in the collection of the Staatliche Galerie, Moritzburg, Halle, Germany, the only Amerika paintings in a collection abroad. See Gail Levin, "Marsden Hartley's 'Amerika': Between Native American and German Folk Art," *American Art Review* 5, no. 2 (winter 1993): 120–25, 170–71.

3 Most particularly Ann Temkin, "Marsden Hartley's 'America': The 1914 Indian Compositions," unpublished seminar paper, Yale University, January 1983; and Patricia McDonnell, "*Indian Fantasy*: Marsden Hartley's Myth of Amerika in Expressionist Berlin," *North Carolina Museum of Art Bulletin* 16 (1993): 49–64. I am grateful to Patricia for the many times she has shared her files and insights with me on Hartley.

4 O'Keeffe quoted in Roxana Robinson, *Georgia O'Keeffe: A Life* (New York: Harper & Row, 1989), 136.

5 Gail Levin, "Marsden Hartley, Kandinsky, and Der Blaue Reiter," *Arts Magazine* 52 (November 1977): 160. Levin relates how close some of Hartley's compositional choices were to those used in Bavarian glass paintings he and other modernists in Germany, especially Wassily Kandinsky, revered and collected.

6 In Hartley to Alfred Stieglitz, August 1913, Beinecke/Yale, the artist wrote about the stars: "everywhere in Berlin one sees the eight pointed star—all the kings wore it over their heart—the soldiers on the forehead—I find also the same stars in the Italian Primitives."

7 Knowing of his color innovations in this period, Gertrude Stein paid Hartley the strongest of compliments, finding him more inventive in color than either Matisse or Picasso. In a letter to Stieglitz in 1913 (Beinecke/Yale), she wrote: "He is the only one working in color, that is considering the color as more dominant than line, who is really attempting to create an entity in a picture which is not a copy of light. He deals with his color as actually as Picasso deals with his forms. In this respect he is working in a very different way from the new impressionists…and Matisse [who] are really producing a disguised but poverty stricken realism; the realism of form having been taken away from them they have solaced themselves with the realism of light. Hartley has not done this; he deals with color as a medium for creation." Quoted in Donald Gallup, "The Weaving of a Pattern: Marsden Hartley and Gertrude Stein," *Magazine of Art* 41, no. 7 (November 1948): 259.

8 See Gail Levin's discussion of Hartley in Paris in "American Art," in *Primitivism in Twentieth Century Art* (New York: Museum of Modern Art, 1984), 455–57.

9 For a broad-based discussion of the modern artist's relationship to Native American art, see W. Jackson Rushing, *Native American Art and the New York Avant-Garde: A History of Cultural Primitivism* (Austin: University of Texas Press, 1995). For Hartley, see pp. 34–39, 55–58. For my own discussion, see Wanda M. Corn, *The Great American Thing: Modern Art and National Identity* (Berkeley and Los Angeles: University of California Press, 1999), 250–56.

10 Hartley to Alfred Stieglitz, 22 September 1913, Beinecke/Yale.

11 Hartley to Alfred Stieglitz, 5 August 1915, Beinecke/Yale.

12 For a new study of these collections, today housed in the renamed Ethnologisches Museum Berlin, see Peter Bolz and Hans-Ulrich Sanner, *Native American Art: The Collections of the Ethnological Museum Berlin* (Seattle: University of Washington Press), 1999.

13 The literature on Buffalo Bill is extensive and cited in Joy S. Kasson, *Buffalo Bill's Wild West: Celebrity, Memory and Popular History* (New York: Hill and Wang, 2000). I thank Joy Kasson for her fine study and her help in locating an appropriate Buffalo Bill image for this essay.

14 Carol Herselle Krinsky, "Karl May's Western Novels and Aspects of Their Continuing Influence," *American Indian Culture and Research Journal* 23, no. 2 (1999): 53. Krinsky cites other bibliographic sources.

15 Ibid., 54.

16 My thanks to Corey Keller, Patricia McDonnell, and others for alerting me to the photographs by Andrea Robbins and Max Becher and the publication of some of their work in *Contact Sheet 98*, published by Light Work, in Syracuse, New York.

17 For a broad examination of *Americanismus* in German visual arts, see Beeke Sell Tower, *Envisioning America: Prints, Drawings, and Photographs by George Grosz and his Contemporaries, 1915–1933* (Cambridge: Busch-Reisinger Museum, Harvard University, 1990).

18 Beth Irwin Lewis, *George Grosz: Art and Politics in the Weimar Republic* (Madison: University of Wisconsin Press, 1971), 25–29.

19 Levin, "American Art," 457–61. These signs also appear in other cultures. The checkerboard pattern may be an early reference in Hartley's painting to Karl von Freyburg who loved to play chess. Arnold Rönnebeck writes about this in a letter to Duncan Phillips, after 1943, Beinecke/Yale, quoted in Gail Levin, "Hidden Symbolism in Marsden Hartley's Military Pictures," *Arts Magazine* 54 (October 1979): 156.

20 *Autobiography,* 86–92.

21 He wrote of "becoming a European gradually because of no encouragement at home." Hartley to Rockwell Kent, April 1913, Kent Papers, Archives/Smithsonian.

22 Hartley to Rockwell Kent, March 1913, Kent Papers, Archives/Smithsonian.

23 Hartley to Alfred Stieglitz, 15 March 1915, Beinecke/Yale.

24 *Autobiography,* 87.

25 John C. G. Rohl, "The Emperor's New Clothes: A Character Sketch of Kaiser Wilhelm II," *Kaiser Wilhelm II: New Interpretations* (Cambridge: Cambridge University Press, 1982), 36; quoted in Patricia McDonnell, "El Dorado: Marsden Hartley in Imperial Berlin," in *Dictated by Life* (Minneapolis: Frederick R. Weisman Art Museum, University of Minnesota, 1995), 35. This essay by McDonnell offers a richly textured discussion of gay culture in the German military and in pre-war Berlin, a subject first opened up by Weinberg, 141–45.

26 Hartley to Rockwell Kent, March 1913, Kent Papers, Archives/Smithsonian.

27 See Levin, "American Art," 459–60.

28 Ludington 1992, 89.

29 Paul Rosenfeld, "Marsden Hartley," *Nation* 157, no. 12 (18 September 1943): 326.

30 Hartley to Rockwell Kent, April 1913, quoted in Ludington 1992, 97.

31 Hartley to Gertrude Stein, 19 June 1913, Beinecke/Yale. See also the poem Hartley wrote in the late 1920s about himself as an eagle in *On Art,* 21.

32 Two months before leaving Germany in December 1915, Hartley had an exhibition of forty-five paintings and some drawings at the Münchener Graphik-Verlag in Berlin. In April 1916 Stieglitz showed Hartley's Berlin paintings at 291 in New York. From reviews, one can ascertain that at least some of the Amerika paintings were included in both exhibitions.

33 Marsden Hartley, "The Scientific Esthetic of the Red Man, Part II: The Fiesta of San Geronimo at Taos," *Art and Archaeology* 14, no. 3 (September 1922): 138.

34 Hartley characterized the Taos school of painters as "following the Indian around, applying Parisian literary poses to him, [and] attaching redman titles" to their paintings. Marsden Hartley, "America as Landscape," *El Palacio* (21 December 1918): 340. On Pueblo pots and weavings, he wrote: "If his pottery and his blankets offer the majority but little, his ceremonials do contribute to the comparative few who can perceive a spectacle

we shall not see the equal of in history again." Marsden Hartley, "Red Man Ceremonials: An American Plea for American Esthetics," *Art and Archaeology* 9, no. 1 (January 1920): 13.

35 Hartley, "Fiesta of San Geronimo at Taos," 137.

36 Marsden Hartley, "The Scientific Esthetic of the Redman, Part I: The Great Corn Ceremony at Santo Domingo," *Art and Archaeology* 13, no. 3 (March 1922): 114.

37 From 1918 to 1922, Hartley published six essays about New Mexico. The second and third essays appeared in *El Palacio,* a bulletin published by the Museum of New Mexico, in December 1918. These essays were relatively short and evidenced Hartley's sorting out his response to the striking southwestern landscape and what an "ultra modern" artist could paint there. Hartley published the first of his essays on the Southwest in the *Dial,* a literary journal, when living in New Mexico; the other three appeared after he was back in New York in *Art and Archaeology,* published by the Archaeological Institute of America. These four essays were about the beauty and ancient values inherent in Native American dance and ceremonies, such as the footraces. In each, Hartley presents Native American rituals as significant art forms.

In order of their publication: "Tribal Esthetics," *Dial* 65 (16 November 1918): 399–401; "Aesthetic Sincerity," *El Palacio* 5 (9 December 1918): 332–33; "America as Landscape," *El Palacio* (21 December 1918): 340–42; "Red Man Ceremonials: An American Plea for American Esthetics," *Art and Archaeology* 9, no. 1 (January 1920): 7–14; "The Scientific Esthetic of the Redman, Part I: The Great Corn Ceremony at Santo Domingo," *Art and Archaeology* 13, no. 3 (March 1922): 113–19; "The Scientific Esthetic of the Red Man, Part II: The Fiesta of San Geronimo at Taos," *Art and Archaeology* 14, no. 3 (September 1922): 137–39. Hartley reprinted "Red Man Ceremonials," as "The Red Man" in his book of essays, *Adventures,* 13–29.

38 Hartley, "Red Man Ceremonials," 7.

39 Ibid., 12.

40 Ibid., 10.

41 Ibid., 8–11.

42 Hartley, "Fiesta of San Geronimo at Taos," 137–38.

43 Hartley, "Great Corn Ceremony at Santo Domingo," 115.

44 Hartley, "America as Landscape," 340.

PLATES 16–23

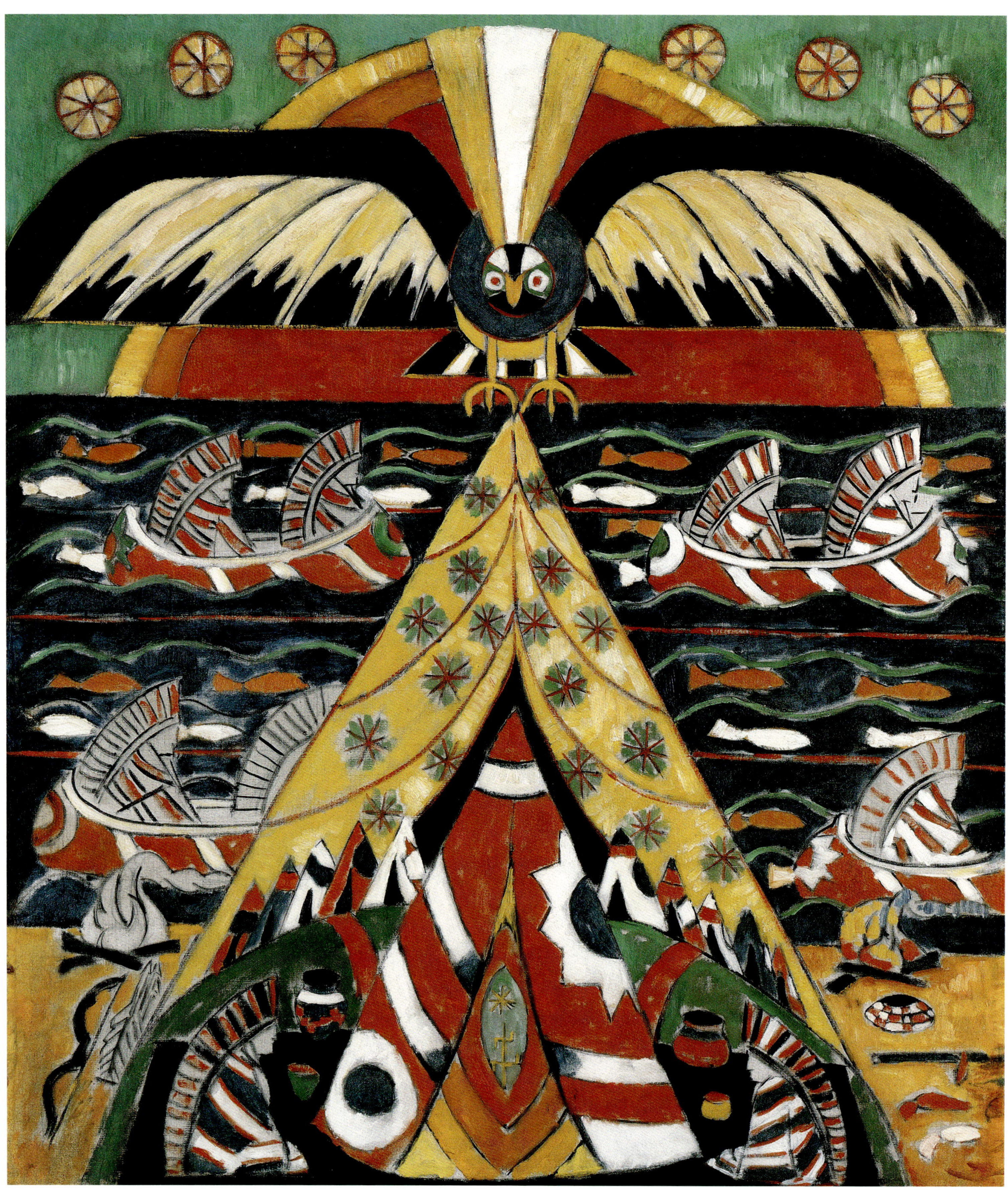

16

Indian Fantasy, 1914

Oil on canvas, 46⅝ × 39⅜ in.

North Carolina Museum of Art, Raleigh

Purchased with funds from the State of North Carolina

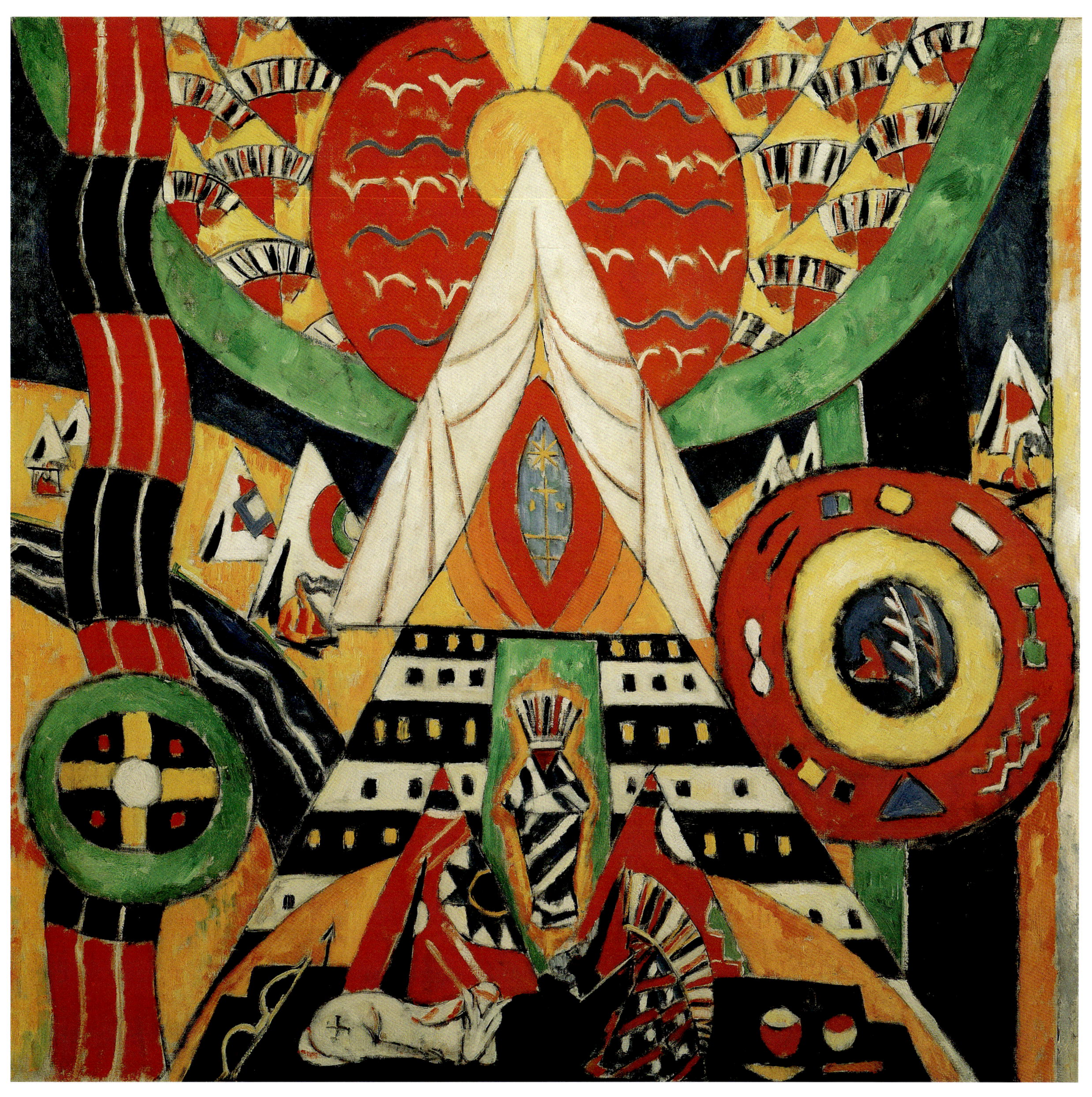

17
Indian Composition, 1914
Oil on canvas, 47¾ × 47¾ in.
Frances Lehman Loeb Art Center, Vassar College, Poughkeepsie, New York
Gift of Paul Rosenfeld (through Edna Bryner '07), 1950

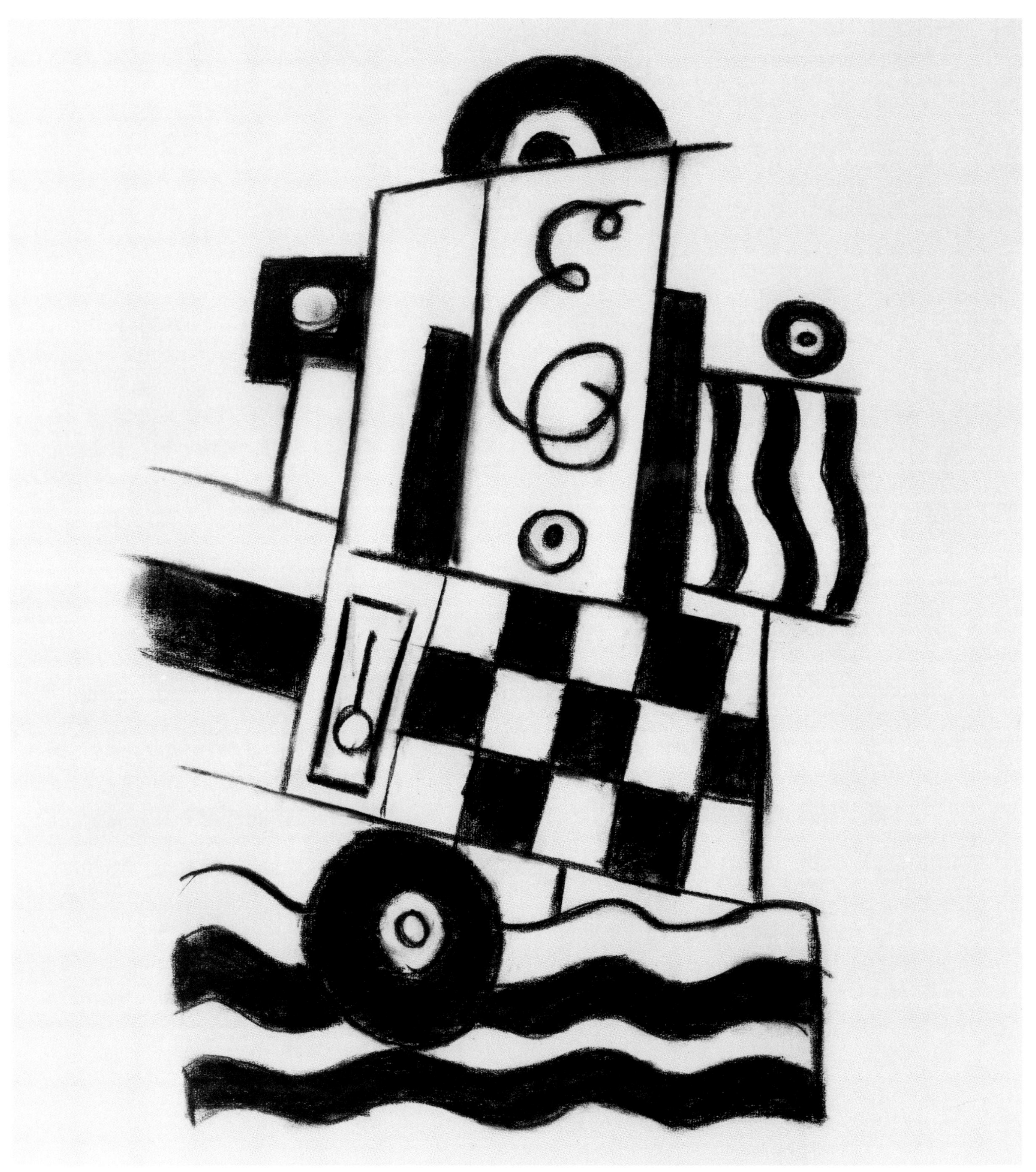

18

Military Symbols I, 1914
Charcoal on paper, 24¼ × 18¼ in.
The Metropolitan Museum of Art, New York
Rogers Fund, 1962

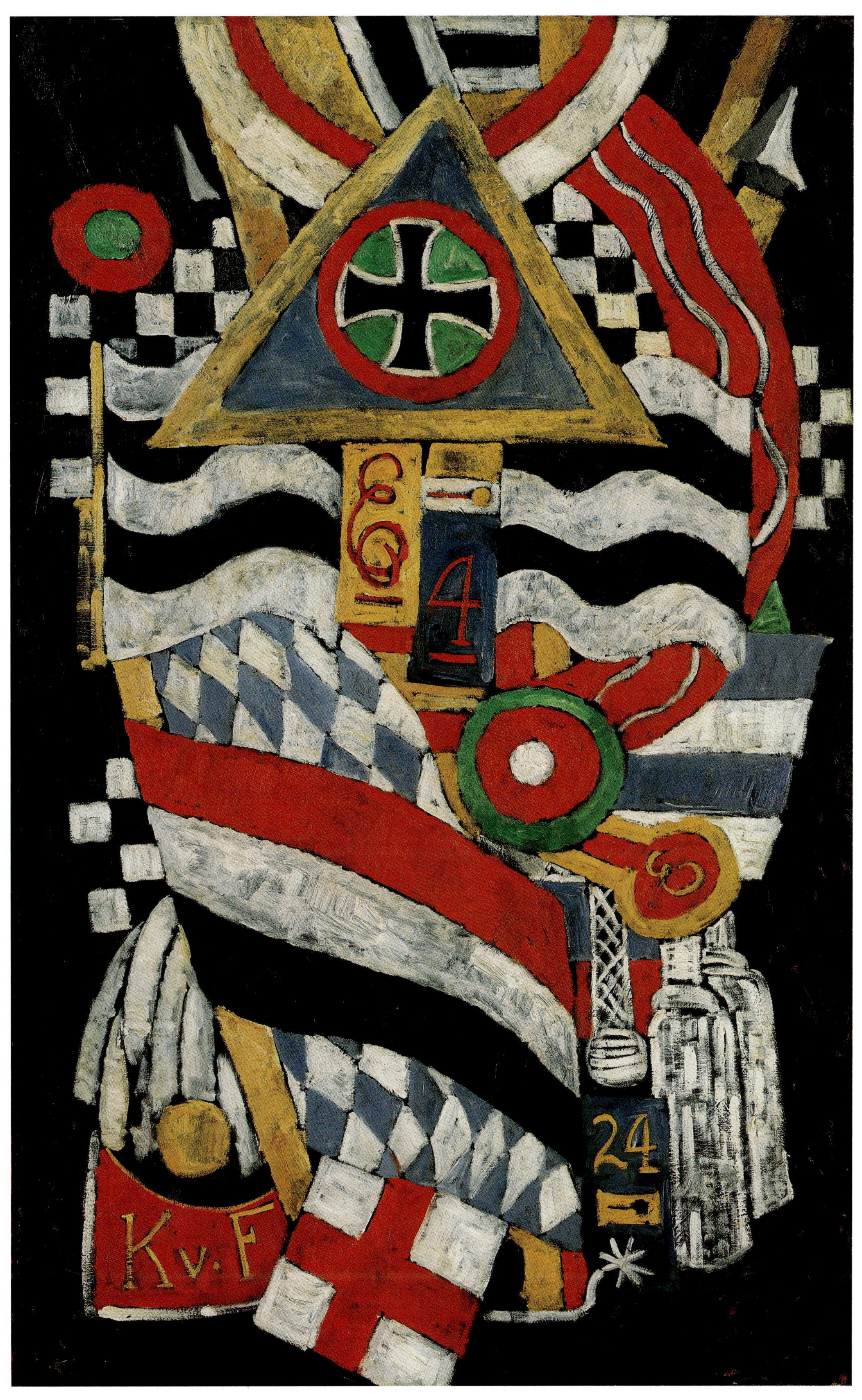

19

Portrait of a German Officer, 1914

Oil on canvas, 68¼ × 41⅜ in.

The Metropolitan Museum of Art, New York

The Alfred Stieglitz Collection, 1949

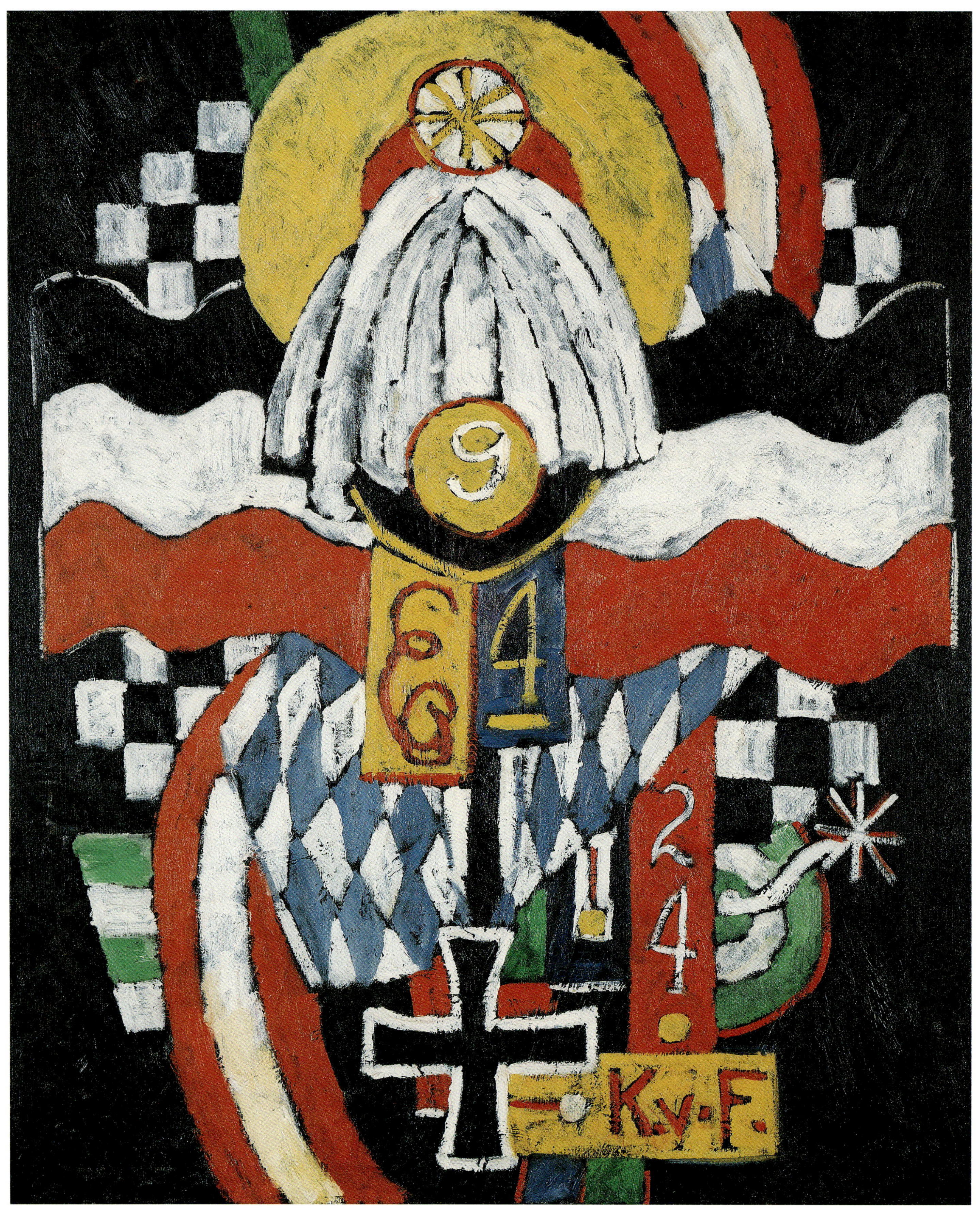

20

Painting No. 47, Berlin, 1914–15

Oil on canvas, $39\frac{1}{2} \times 31\frac{5}{8}$ in.

Hirshhorn Museum and Sculpture Garden, Smithsonian Institution, Washington, D.C.

Gift of Joseph H. Hirshhorn, 1972

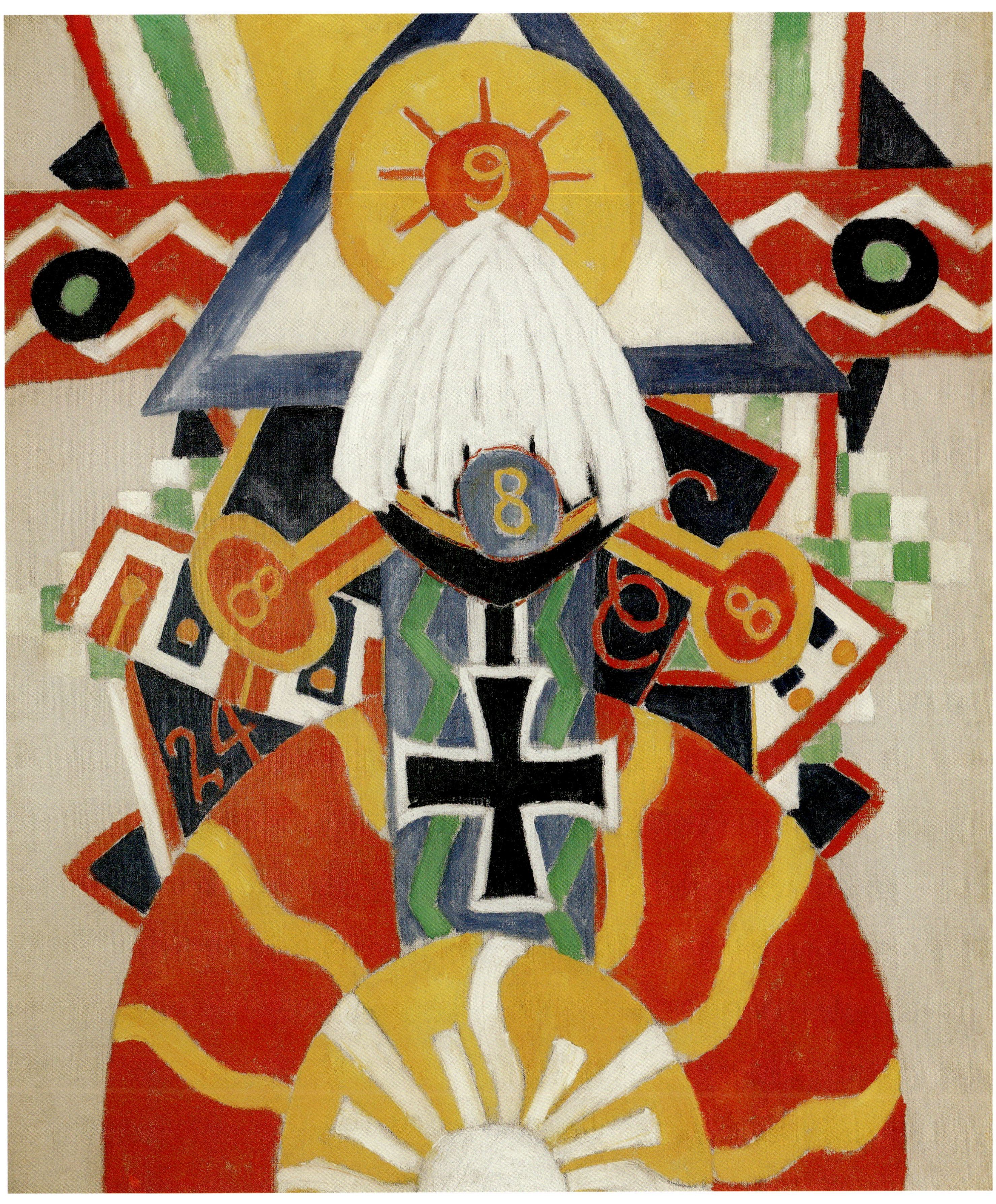

21
Painting No. 49, Berlin, 1914
Oil on canvas, 47 × 39½ in.
Collection of Mr. and Mrs. Barney A. Ebsworth
Partial and Promised Gift to the Seattle Art Museum

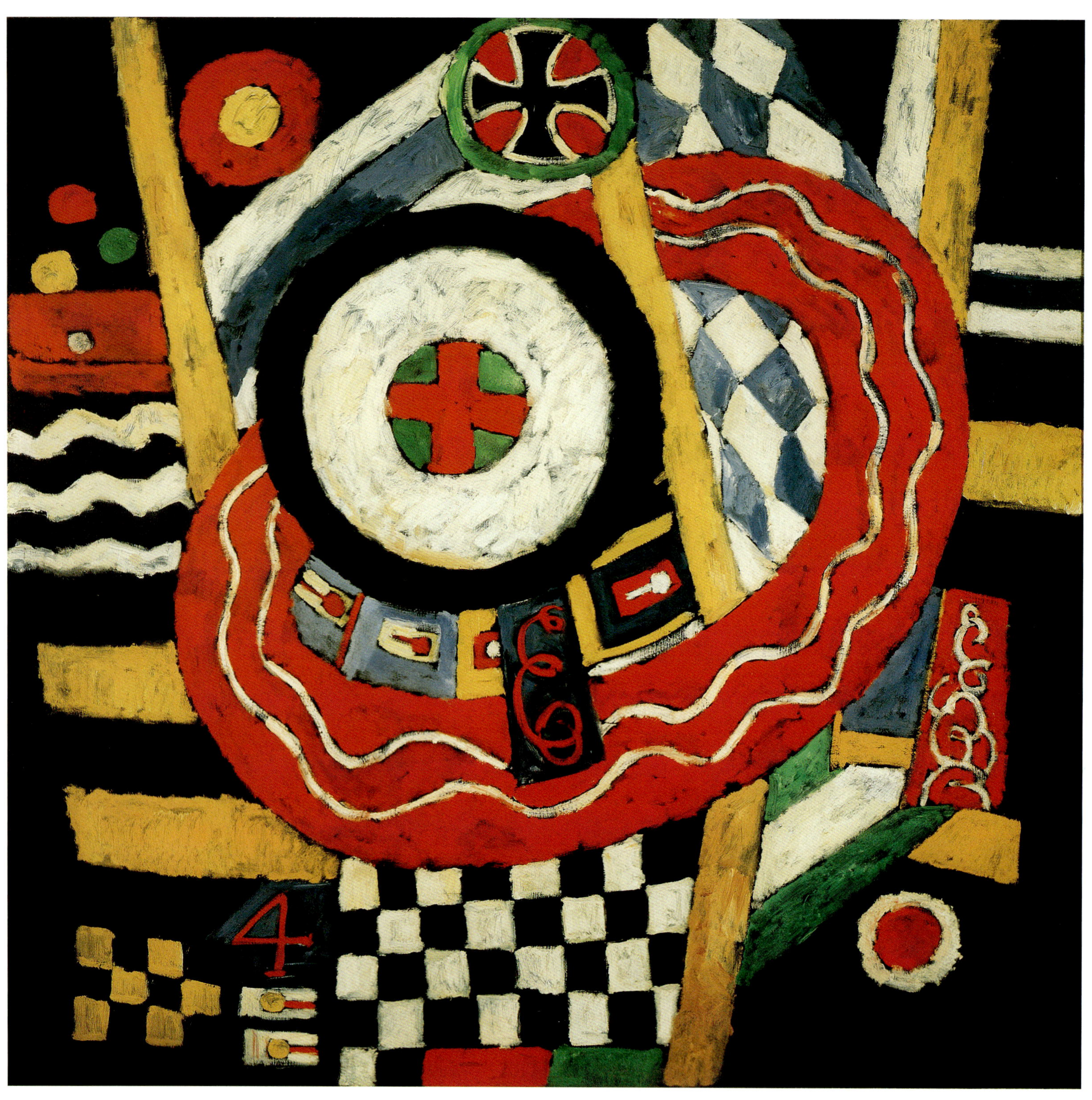

22

The Iron Cross, 1914–15

Oil on canvas, 46¾ × 46¾ in.

Washington University Gallery of Art, St. Louis

University Purchase, Bixby Fund, 1952

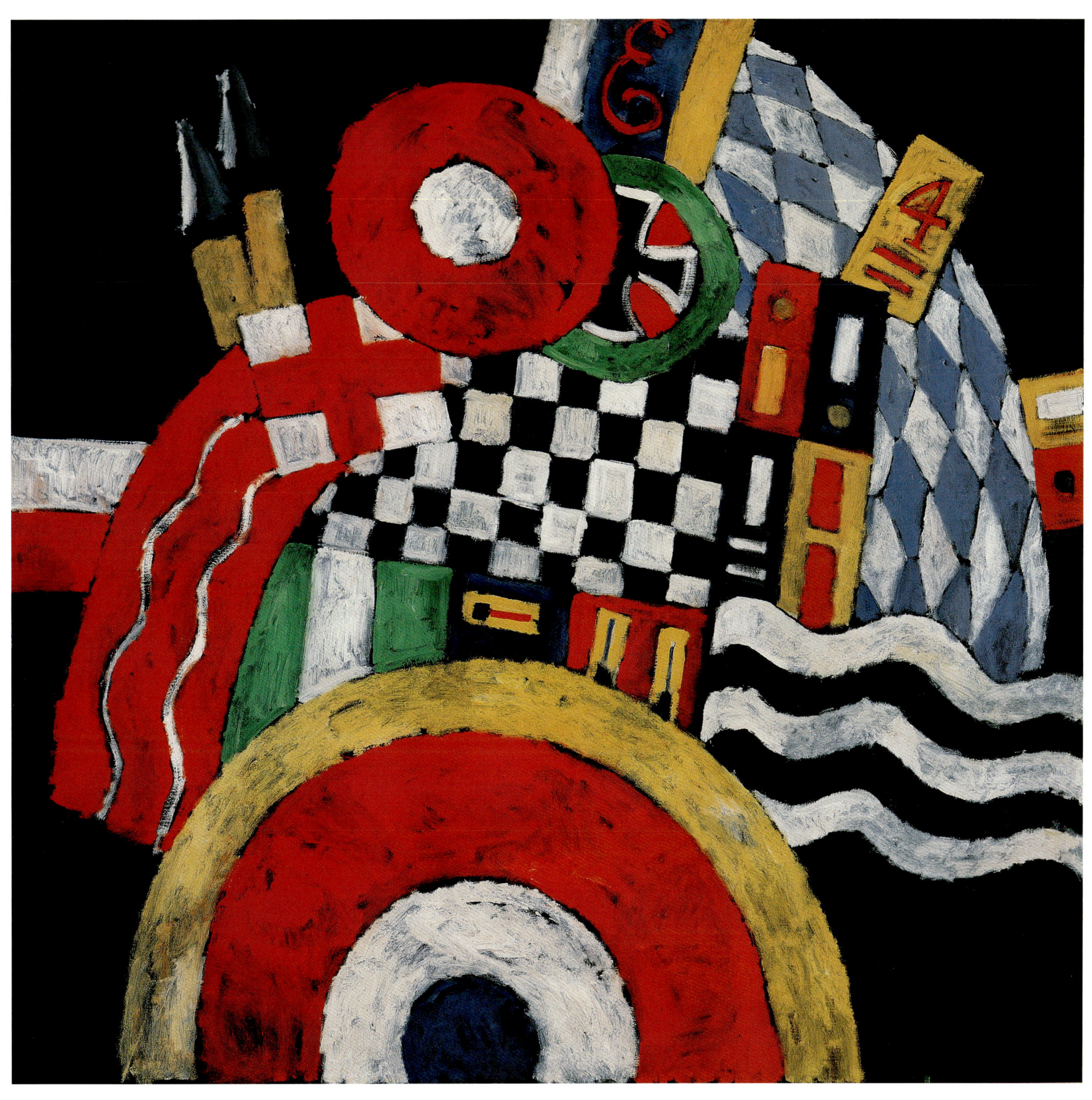

23

E. (German Officer—Abstraction), c. 1915
Oil on canvas, 47⅛ × 47⅛ in.
The University of Iowa Museum of Art, Iowa City
The Mark Ranney Memorial Fund (1958.1)

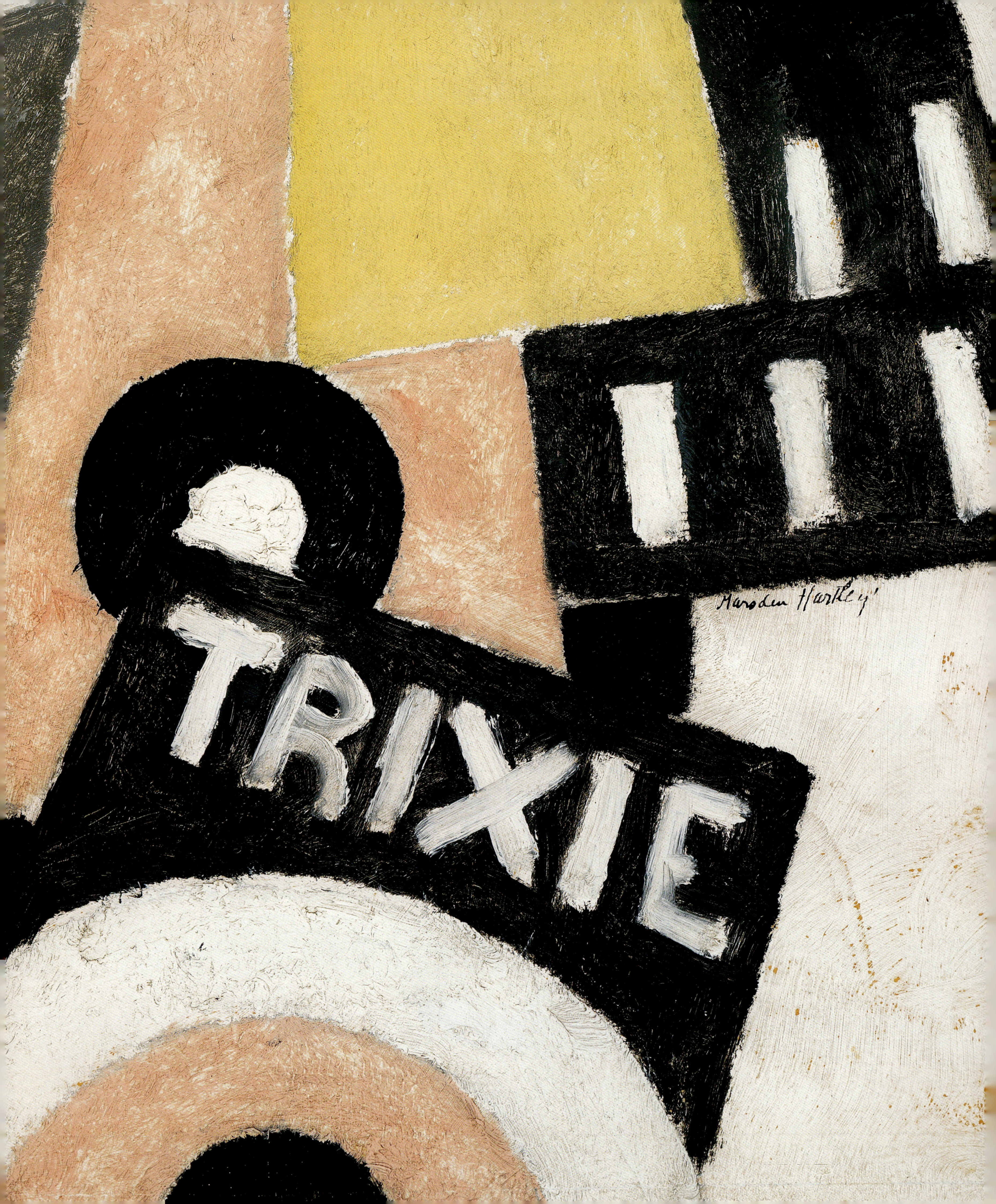
TRIXIE
Marsden Hartley

"The Great Provincetown Summer": The Impact of Eugene O'Neill on Marsden Hartley

Amy Ellis

Marsden Hartley spent the summer of 1916 in Provincetown, Massachusetts. It was a stay that he documented in a short piece called "The Great Provincetown Summer" written as part of his autobiography, *Somehow a Past.* In it he recalled the summer as "that period in the history of Provincetown which has made more history than any other," saying that "more of real consequence was taking place," and crediting the Provincetown Players' theater with that. Hartley wrote about those who were there: Charles Demuth, John Reed, Louise Bryant, Susan Glaspell, George Cram Cook (founder of the Provincetown Players), Hutchins and Neith Hapgood, and, best known of the group today, Eugene O'Neill. When the fledgling playwright O'Neill arrived in Provincetown in the summer of 1916, he came with a group of one-act plays. During the summer the Players performed O'Neill's *Bound East for Cardiff* and *Thirst* at the Wharf Theatre. Both plays were set at sea, and death played a central part, two themes that were later conjoined in some of Hartley's most powerful paintings, *Eight Bells Folly* (plate 54) and the portraits of the Masons from the 1930s (plates 66–69).

Hartley arrived in Provincetown in July 1916, staying in John Reed's house, and then, at the end of the summer, moving with Demuth to other rent-free quarters. They remained in Provincetown through October. Declared the "biggest art colony in the world" by the *Boston Globe* on August 27, 1916, Provincetown drew artists, writers, and theater people who sought to recreate something of the intellectual atmosphere enjoyed in Europe.[1] In this lively milieu, Hartley painted the quietest works of his career, the ironically titled Movement series.

The Provincetown Movement paintings include such pictures as *Movement No. 1 (Provincetown)* (fig. 1) and *Provincetown Abstraction* (fig. 2). *Movement No. 1,* with its curving, flame-like sail atop a bull's-eye hull, exhibits more "movement" than others in the series, and yet the thin and controlled, almost texture-free, application of paint starkly contrasts with Hartley's earlier paintings, particularly one like *Musical Theme (Oriental Symphony)* (plate 8), inspired by Kandinsky's work.[2]

In November 1916 Hartley and Demuth left Provincetown for Bermuda. From there, Hartley wrote to his friend, fellow artist Carl Sprinchorn: "I know they [the paintings] will look fairly well for they are all subdued, and of the same quietude and intensity, which is gratifying to me, for I want my work in both writing and painting to have that special coolness, for I weary of emotional excitement in art, weary of episode, of legend and of special histories, which most painters occupy themselves with."[3] At the same time, Hartley was looking forward to O'Neill's arrival on the island. He wrote to Stieglitz: "Eugene O'Neill, the son of the actor [James O'Neill] who was with us in Provincetown last year is on the next boat, and so we will have a little life of our own."[4]

Detail, Plate 29

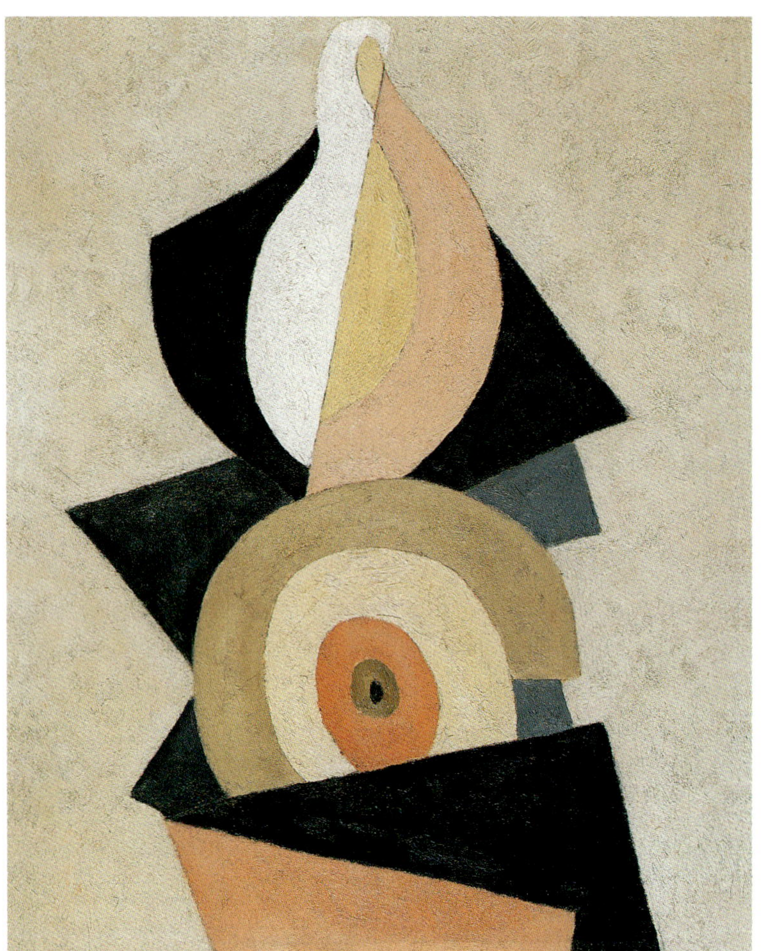

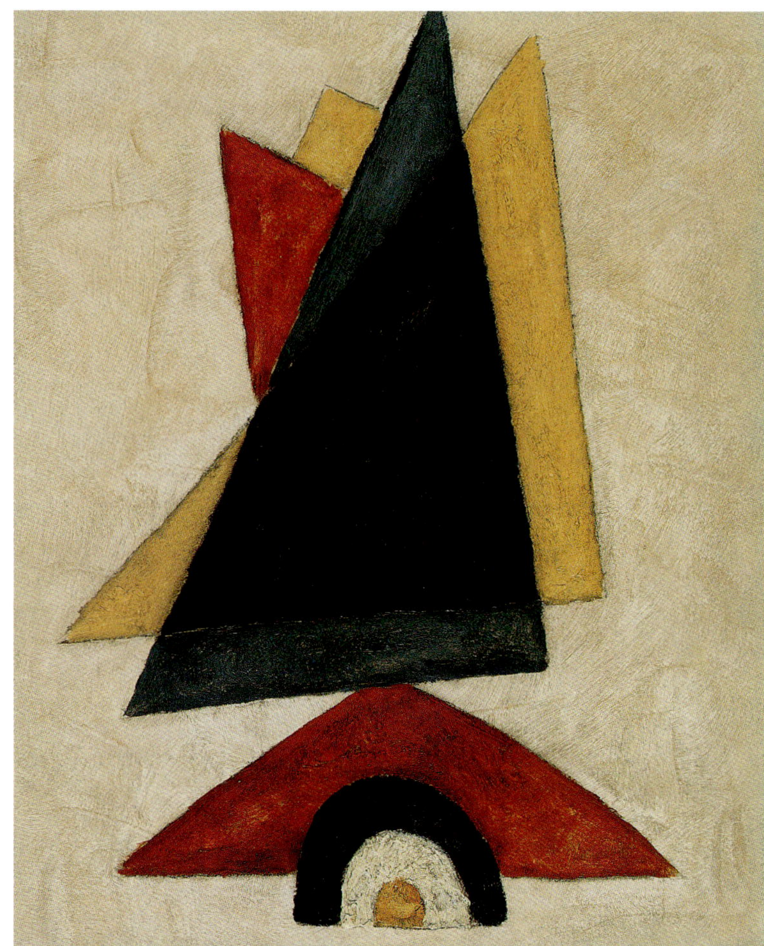

Figure 1
Marsden Hartley
Movement No. 1 (Provincetown), 1916
Oil on composition board, 20 × 15¹⁵⁄₁₆ in.
(50.8 × 40.5 cm)
Philadelphia Museum of Art
The Alfred Stieglitz Collection

Figure 2
Marsden Hartley
Provincetown Abstraction, 1916
Oil on composition board, 19⅞ × 15⅞ in.
(50.5 × 40.3 cm)
Amon Carter Museum, Fort Worth, Texas
1983.169

Hartley continued with the Movement series in Bermuda, though moving away from the most abstract of the first Movement paintings. *Trixie* (plate 29) employs a more colorful palette, using a warm reddish orange tone with yellow, and an arrangement of forms that make up the hull, sails, and pennant in such a way as unmistakably to suggest a boat. Compared with *Movement No. 1, Trixie* is far less abstract. Hartley's brushwork in *Trixie* is more varied and more discernible but continues to show the restraint of the Provincetown Movement paintings. Despite the changes, there is still a "coolness" to this painting and the other Bermuda works that makes them stand apart from the rest of Hartley's artistic career, before and after.

Scholars have criticized Hartley's work from 1916 and 1917 in Provincetown and Bermuda as being a retreat from the boldness of his Berlin paintings and, as a group, derivative of the work of the French cubists. As a result, scant attention has been paid to the artist's time there. And indeed, Hartley's paintings from this period are characterized by their reliance on synthetic cubism and a comparatively muted palette, primarily of grays, pinks, browns, and blacks. Within most of these abstract paintings have been identified the various ships that came into the Provincetown and Bermuda harbors, but some among them have fewer recognizable shapes and references than even the Berlin paintings before them (plates 11 and 13, for example, and see the essay by Patricia McDonnell).[5]

Certainly, the bad press that Hartley received for the poorly timed 291 exhibition in 1916 of his German paintings may have spurred him to turn from the emotional, expressionist style of those works to cubism, an intellectual style, perhaps less legible for an American audience but tied to Paris rather than Berlin. Upon his return to New York, he painted three works with specifically French allusions: *Handsome Drinks* (plate 24), *A Nice Time* (plate 25), and *One Portrait of One Woman* (plate 26, and see the essay by Jonathan Weinberg).[6]

Figure 3
Marsden Hartley
Movement No. 5, Provincetown Houses, 1916
Oil on composition board, 20 × 16 in. (50.8 × 40.6 cm)
The Metropolitan Museum of Art, New York
The Alfred Stieglitz Collection, 1949 (49.70.43)
Photograph © 1986 The Metropolitan Museum of Art

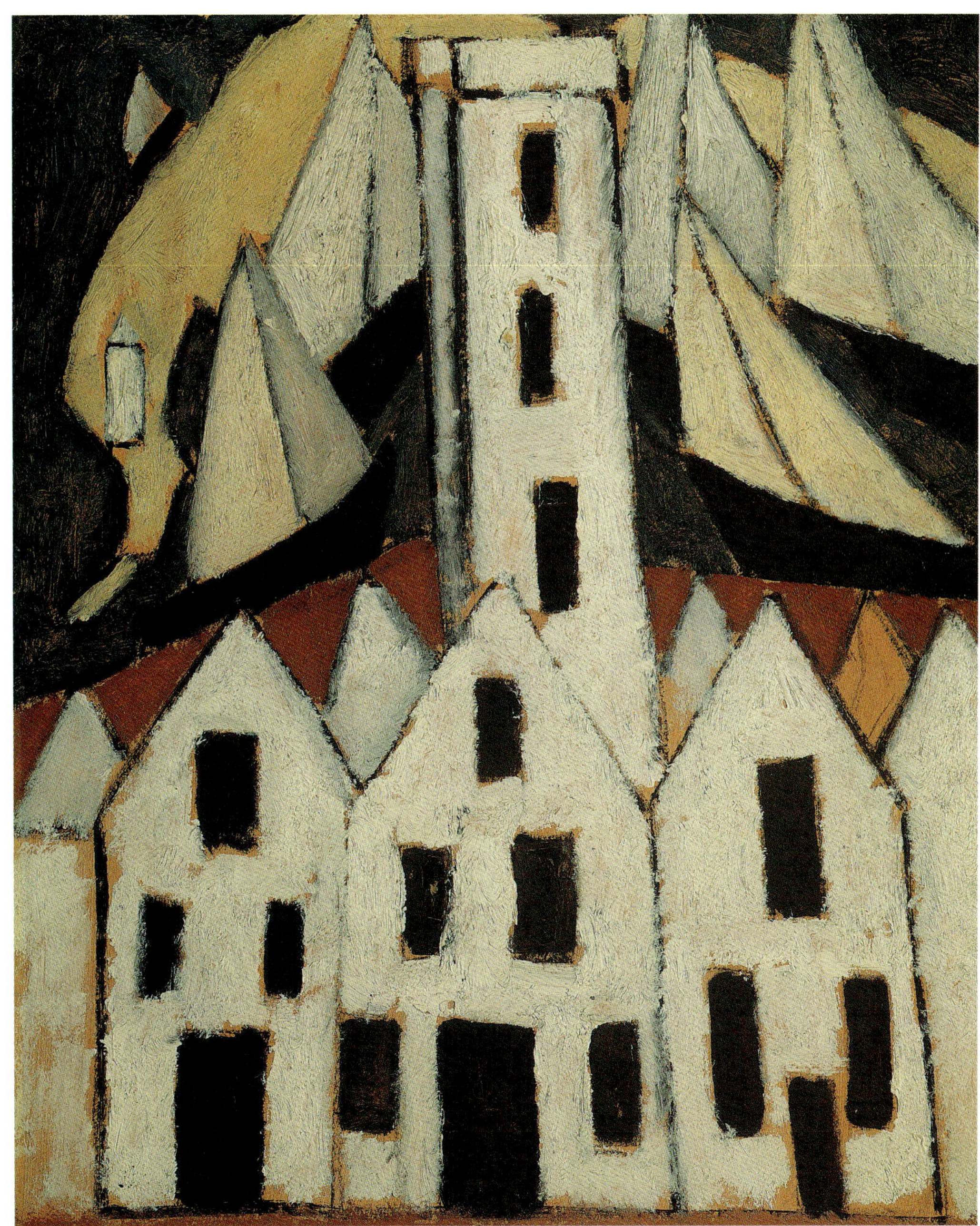

While in Provincetown, Hartley vacillated between representational and abstract work, finally returning to figurative work after leaving Cape Cod, never to revisit pure abstraction in his painting in any sustained way. While some of the paintings in his Movement series painted in Provincetown in 1916 are clearly representational (although not realistic), such as *Movement No. 5, Provincetown Houses* (fig. 3), they share ascetic and, despite the series title, primarily static qualities with those that are abstract. They lack the emotional verve and activity of the Berlin paintings and of even the early Maine landscapes. After leaving Provincetown for Bermuda in December, where he and Demuth lived until May 1917, Hartley began incorporating the names of the ships into his compositions (see, for example, *Elsa,* plate 28), and he painted still lifes and window paintings, such as *Atlantic Window* (plate 30).[7]

Bruce Robertson has attributed the core of Hartley's Provincetown abstract subject matter—ships and related instruments, such as sextants—to the artist's sexual attraction to sailors. But O'Neill also had a strong affinity for the sea.[8] O'Neill's play *Bound East for Cardiff,* for example, was based in part on the playwright's experience as a seaman on a variety of ships, including in 1910 the Norwegian barque *Charles Racine* and in 1911 the British

Figure 4
Unknown Photographer
Hartley at costume ball, 1916
Courtesy of the Provincetown Art Association and Museum, Provincetown, Massachusetts

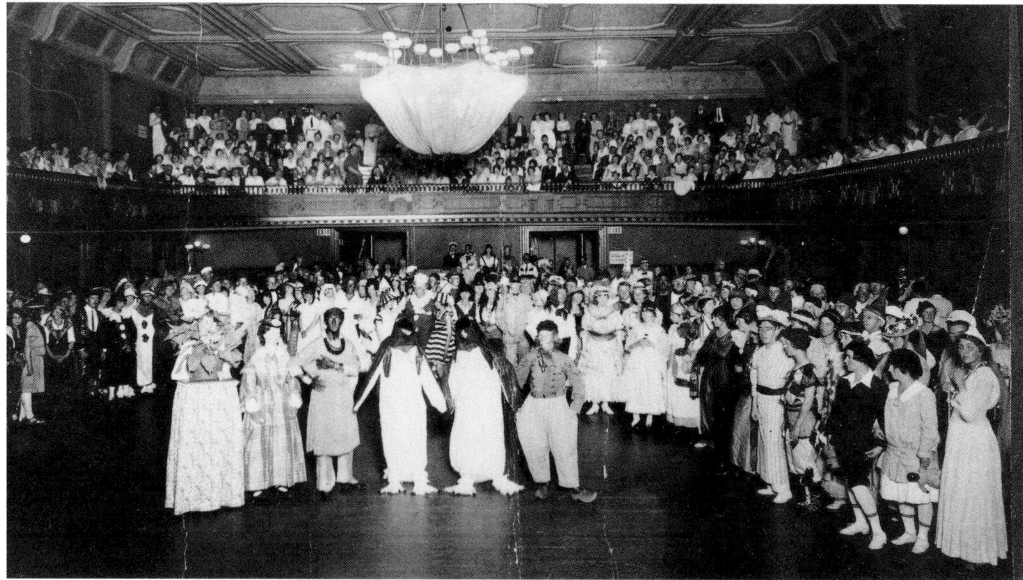

freighter *Ikala,* and the people he met at sea.[9] And yet, the emotion that Hartley revealed in *Eight Bells Folly* (plate 54) or in *Northern Seascape, Off the Banks* (plate 61), for example, is not yet evident in the Provincetown works.

Hartley's marked stylistic shift after arriving in Provincetown was in part due to his introduction to the uncompromising emotional realism of O'Neill's early plays and the work of the Provincetown Players. Hartley continued to follow O'Neill's career and, later in the 1930s in particular, drew on O'Neill's work—both the early works and the later, expressionist plays. The motivating force behind Hartley's most compelling works is tragedy, just as it was for Eugene O'Neill's.

Characteristically evasive, Hartley in "The Great Provincetown Summer" seemed to dismiss the importance of the theater for his own work and experience. He wrote:

> *Having little or no feeling for the theatre and no huge respect outside of the strictly amusement field, I did not become involved in the theatrical project which has since become so well known, but the air was full of it then, and it was amazing in all truth what this group accomplished in not more than twelve or fifteen feet of space for the stage, and not much more for the benches arranged in circus fashion, but the idea caught on, and the outcome of it all is now a matter of general amazement.*[10]

Despite his dismissive tone, Hartley indirectly acknowledged the influence of the Provincetown Players in this quote. While Hartley did not get as involved as some artists—including Demuth and the Zorachs—in the Players' theatrical activities, he did participate in modest ways and was, as always, a part of social events (fig. 4). Hartley was involved enough with the group to design a stock-market ticker for the set of a play by John Reed called *The Eternal Quadrangle.*[11] Although he claimed a lack of feeling and respect for serious theater, in the 1930s Hartley singled out *Bound East for Cardiff* and *Moon of the Caribees* (which was actually produced in 1918) as two of Eugene O'Neill's one-act plays dating from that summer. And in an earlier and broader version of "The Great Provincetown Summer" called "Summer Art Colonies," Hartley devoted paragraphs to descriptions of rehearsals; an appearance of Eugene's father, the actor James O'Neill; and the activities of the Players. He wrote, "I used to hang on the edges of the McDougall playhouse [the Players' winter quarters] because I knew everybody connected with it, and since you never can tell what you may get out of an idea."[12] Finally, in 1935 Hartley published "Farewell, Charles," dedicated to Demuth, who had just died, in which he recounted their time in Provincetown:

Charles, like so many of us, became a part of a certain epoch in phase of art history in America, beginning with that remarkable and never repeated summer at Provincetown where the "Provincetowns" began their first memorable attempt at little theatre movement which was to produce one famous playwright, Eugene O'Neill.[13]

What distinguished O'Neill's work—and that of the Players in general—was a rejection of commercial theater (which they deemed romantic, shallow, and trite) and an attempt to explore psychological and emotional reality, inspired by tragedy.[14] The early plays featured dialogue that was blunt and direct in a way that had not been seen before on the American stage. Although these aspects of O'Neill's work seem not to have affected Hartley's work immediately, in the 1930s they helped Hartley tackle subjects that were supremely emotional for him.

An experimenter like Hartley, O'Neill first used the mask in *The Hairy Ape* (1921) but in 1926 reintroduced masks in his play *The Great God Brown,* which ran for eight months in New York. He continued to use masks in different ways in a variety of plays. He reserved them not for his blue-collar characters, but for the bourgeoisie and the aristocracy. It was members of these classes that O'Neill found most hypocritical and most detached from their true emotions.

In 1932–33 O'Neill published three short essays in the *American Spectator*—"Memoranda on Masks," "Second Thoughts," and "A Dramatist's Notebook"—outlining his theories concerning the use of masks in theatrical productions. In "Memoranda on Masks," he stated that he saw the "idea of mask as a symbol of inner reality," and as "a necessary, dramatically revealing, new convention," and not as a "'stunty' resurrection of archaic props." Using the mask was a way in which to "express those profound hidden conflicts of the mind which the probings of psychology continue to disclose to us."[15]

In 1932 or 1933 Hartley finished a painting titled *Masks* (fig. 5).[16] *Masks* is composed of six "floating" masks, three arranged vertically with one at the left and two to the right. Three of the masks have round, staring eyes; the eyes are cut out from the other three. One of the masks without eyes, at the top of the vertical three, is full face, with two round spots for cheeks looking like clown make-up. The other two cover the eye and nose region only. One of these resembles the masks Demuth used in his portrait of O'Neill, *Longhi on Broadway* (fig. 6).[17]

Hartley's palette in *Masks,* in contrast with his other 1930s paintings, is of muted grays, blues, blacks, browns, whites, and pinks, and so resembles his work from 1916–17. In addition, the composition—masks arranged vertically and asymmetrically against a background of patches of color—compares with some of the more abstract Provincetown paintings (see plate 27, for example). All of this suggests that Hartley was alluding to the source of his inspiration, his time in Provincetown, and by extension O'Neill, through color and composition in *Masks.*

Furthermore, the single pink mask at the left, with the eyes cut out to reveal the blue of the background, in conjunction with the mask at the top, with its striking features, foreshadows a self-portrait Hartley painted in 1939, *Sustained Comedy* (plate 72, and see the essay by Bruce Robertson). In this work, Hartley simultaneously masks and reveals his own identity through a combination of symbols. The figure is pink, recalling the single pink mask in the earlier painting, and features Hartley's piercing blue eyes, which are framed by the pink mask in the earlier painting. The make-up on the face of the figure in *Sustained Comedy* compares with the uppermost mask in its accentuation of the facial features. Hartley masked his identity as a gay man and frequently masked his identity in his self-portraits. He never made a painting that he titled unambiguously "Self-Portrait."

Figure 5
Marsden Hartley
Masks, 1931–32
Oil on Masonite, 36 × 20 × ⅛ in.
(91.4 × 50.8 × 0.3 cm)
Walker Art Center, Minneapolis
Gift of Mrs. Joshua B. Cahn, New York, 1973

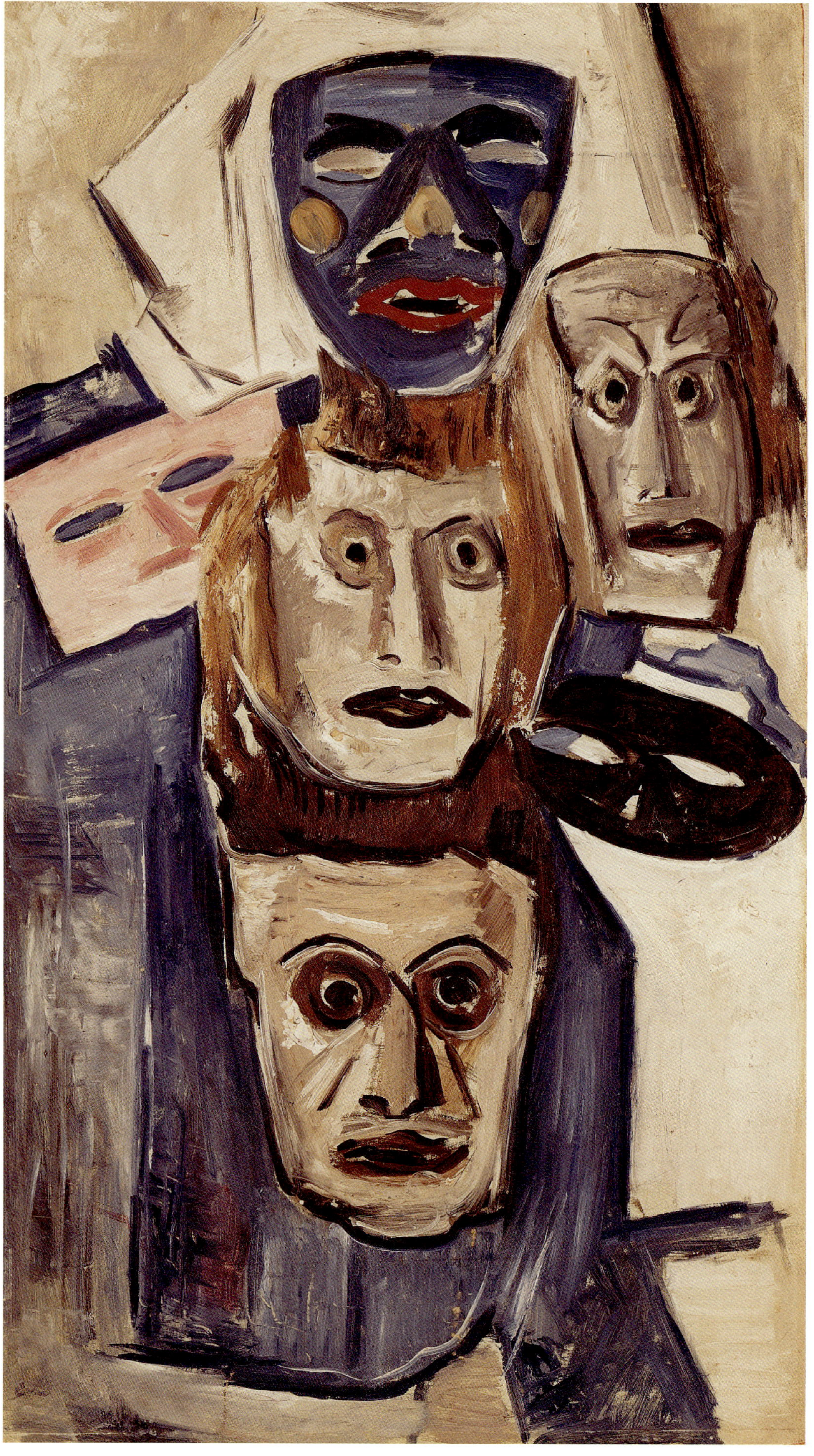

In turn, O'Neill may have incorporated Hartley into his own work. Others have noted that O'Neill's Pulitzer Prize–winning *Strange Interlude* (1928) features a character named Charles Marsden, a novelist, who is said to be a composite of Demuth and Hartley. Marsden is described in the stage directions as follows:

> *He is a tall thin man of thirty-five, meticulously well-dressed in tweeds of distinctly English tailoring, his appearance that of an Anglicized New England gentleman. His face is too long for its width, his nose is high and narrow, his forehead broad, his mild blue eyes those of a dreamy self-analyst, his thin lips ironical and a bit sad. There is an indefinable feminine quality about him, but it is nothing apparent in appearance or act. His manner is cool and poised. He speaks with a careful ease as one who listens to his own conversation. He has long fragile hands, and the stoop to his shoulders of a man weak muscularly, who has never liked athletics and has always been regarded as of delicate constitution. The main point about his personality is a quiet charm, a quality of appealing, inquisitive friendliness, always willing to listen, eager to sympathize, to like and to be liked.*[18]

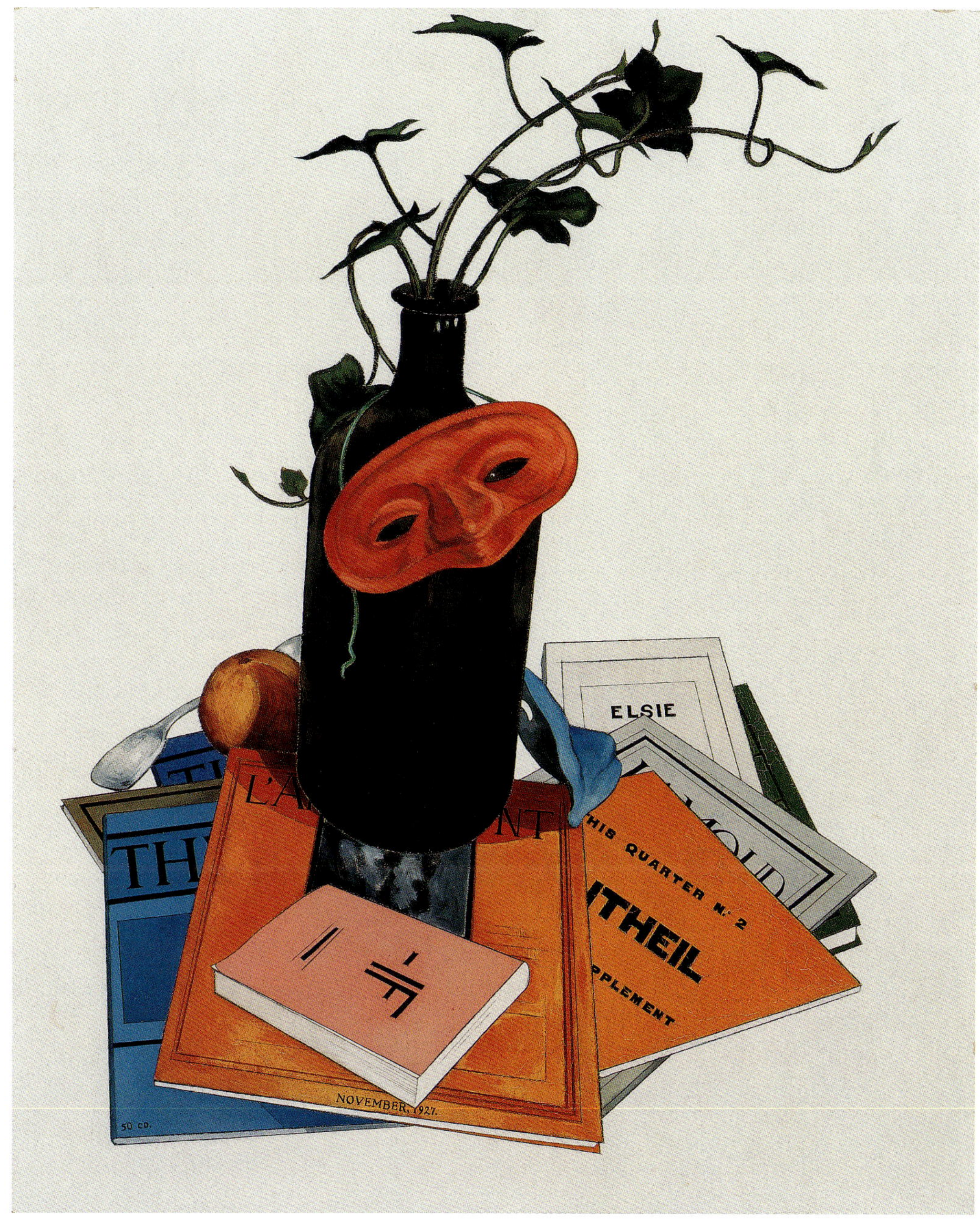

Figure 6
Charles Demuth
Longhi on Broadway, 1928
Oil on ¼-inch thick pulp-board, 34 × 27 in.
(86.4 × 68.6 cm)
The Museum of Fine Arts, Boston
Gift of the William H. Lane Foundation, 1990.397

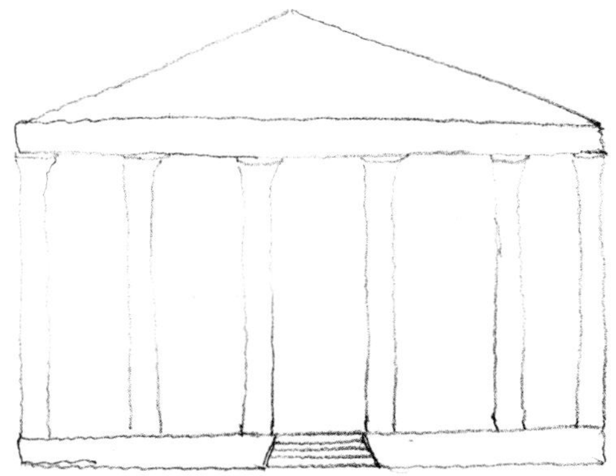

Figure 7
Eugene O'Neill
Drawing of Mannon House
From the Eugene O'Neill Papers
Yale Collection of American Literature
Beinecke Rare Book and Manuscript Library
Yale University, New Haven

Marsden suffers from an unresolved Oedipal complex and so is unable to pursue sexual relations, leading Louis Sheaffer, one of O'Neill's biographers, to speculate that the character is meant to be homosexual, as both Demuth and Hartley were.[19] Significantly, perhaps, in a letter to Isabel Lachaise in 1928, Hartley referred to his time in Europe as a "strange interlude." He had just returned to New York in January, after a three-year stint abroad.[20]

In the last decade of his life and career Hartley made a group of figurative works related to an event that affected him profoundly. These are the memory portraits of the Masons, painted after the deaths in 1936 of the two sons and a cousin at sea. The Masons were a working-class family in Nova Scotia—primarily involved with fishing and building boats—with whom Hartley boarded in the summers of 1935 and 1936. He claimed he had never felt more comfortable in his life than with the Masons, writing to his friend Adelaide Kuntz, "The experience has been so rich.... I do have such a sense of home and relatedness—true relatedness—as perhaps never experienced before—save in earlier Germany, perhaps."[21]

Hartley not only painted the Mason family, he wrote a lament for them called "Cleophas and His Own: A North Atlantic Tragedy." Divided into sections devoted to the various members of the family, this elegy is comprised of a series of prose portraits, for the most part, lyrical and literarily sophisticated, in contrast to their realistic and stoic painted counterparts.[22] Hartley gave each family member a symbolic name—identified by the artist as French-Canadian, but having other resonances as well—in order to mask their true identities.[23]

After the Masons' deaths, Hartley wrote to Adelaide Kuntz:

> *I have been working on my last efforts—two wild ducks which I so wanted &d were brought me thoughtfully by one of the couriers and I am working on them in the blacksmith's shop because it is now particularly so quiet—no hammers, no anvil tones, no blustering boys, no rich thick flavors of manly energy in labour there which made last year such a social delight and privilege. I wondered if I could endure the vacant space, but like the lady in Morning [sic] Becomes Electra, who on deciding to leave everything, stands in the outer steps and declares, "Now I can live here. I can live with the dead"—or almost those words, I decided I could work there, and if every plane and hammer, the anvil, the forge, the tool chest, and the general debris of such labours—all but shouted at me, I decided I could live with it all and make them ring true again. And so after going in one day alone to test myself, the first shock being a little painful I decided I could make everything now so silent have life through associations of memory, and so I have managed to work there not too disturbed.*[24]

The play Hartley cites, O'Neill's *Mourning Becomes Electra* (1931), loosely based on Aeschylus's *Oresteia* and set in Civil War–era United States, would seem an odd analogy for him to employ. The words Hartley remembered incorrectly are Lavinia Mannon's in the play, spoken after her mother and brother have committed suicide:

> *Don't be afraid. I'm not going the way Mother and Orin went. That's escaping punishment. And there's no one left to punish me. I'm the last Mannon. I've got to punish myself!... I'll live alone with the dead, and keep their secrets, and let them hound me, until the curse is paid out and the last Mannon is let die!*[25]

In the play, O'Neill uses the mask[26] to signal a level of deceit, a superficial layer covering the "hidden life forces" beneath.[27] Even the house wears one: "The temple portico is like an incongruous white mask fixed on the house to hide its somber gray ugliness" (fig. 7).[28] In his stage directions, O'Neill describes the gardener as having "a gaunt face that in repose gives one the strange impression of a life-like mask. It is set in a grim expression, but his small, sharp eyes still peer at life with a shrewd prying avidity and his loose mouth has a strong suggestion of ribald humor."[29] O'Neill describes Lavinia as follows:

> *She is twenty-three but looks considerably older. Tall like her mother, her body is thin, flat-breasted and angular, and its unattractiveness is accentuated by her plain black dress. Her movements are stiff and she carries herself with a wooden, square-shouldered, military bearing.... Above all, one is struck by the same strange, life-like mask impression her face gives in repose.*[30]

For his own grief over the Mason tragedy as well as for his depictions of the victims and the surviving family members, Hartley found the mask a useful tool. He assigned the mask the positive value of stoicism, and did not see it having the destructive qualities that O'Neill perceived. He painted the Masons with mask-like faces—almost expressionless, except for tears that roll down the cheeks of the figure of the mother in *Marie Ste. Esprit* (plate 67). Before the deaths of the Masons, Hartley expressed his admiration for their emotional restraint. He wrote to Kuntz, "I fell in love with the most amazing family of men & women the like of which I have never in my life seen—veritable rocks of Gibraltar in appearance the very salt of salt—how I would love to paint a series of them all."[31]

Hartley painted Alty Mason (plate 66) with a mask-like expression similar to the others. The artist's description of his subject is at variance with the image he created. In "Alphonse Adelard," the section of "Cleophas" that Hartley devotes to Alty, he writes: "What a spectacle is Adelard, if I hadn't known he was a human being, I should have thought him some devouring beast from the caverns and the caves, all of his thoughts emotionalized and dramatized by magnificent, opulent, voluminous body action."[32] Alty, in Hartley's prose description, seems to approximate the level of emotion one sees in O'Neill's early plays in particular. The language Hartley uses—"emotionalized and dramatized"—necessarily recalls O'Neill's theater. In addition, Hartley's splitting of Alty's character between his public stoicism as shown in the painting and his private side, as revealed in the prose poem, bears direct correlation to the manner in which O'Neill originally intended to represent the central character in *The Great God Brown.* In that play, the character Dion Anthony was both Dionysos and Saint Anthony, or excess and asceticism. In the final version, the mask served to suggest the alter ego.[33]

Hartley described the Masons—plain, working-class people—as "archaic" and used the same term for his portraits of them. Archaic for Hartley meant simple and direct, positive qualities, and he evoked these qualities in his portraits through thick outlines, heavy paint application, and stiff poses.[34] The characters in O'Neill's early plays—many of them working class—rage and express their emotions. They too are simple and direct, but there is a rawness that is exposed. They don't wear masks. In O'Neill's mid-career *Mourning Becomes Electra,* the mask is used to hide the emotions; the rawness is still there, but it is not always visible. In the end, it is the mask—the refusal to deal directly with what lies beneath—that brings the downfall of the Mannons. In Hartley's portraits of the Masons, the mask represents control and a stoicism that the artist admired. Rather than a curse, it is an asset and protects the wearer from emotional destruction. And yet, like O'Neill's mask-wearing Mannons, the Masons seem to be in repose. Only Alice in *The Lost Felice* (plate 69) appears to have active hands; the others' are all crossed at the wrist and resting in their laps. The figures stare blankly at or just past us, revealing little of the agony of grief in death.

It is not surprising that O'Neill's work would have seemed particularly relevant to Hartley in the 1930s. As other scholars have noted, tragedy in the form of death was the impetus for some of Hartley's best work, and this was also true for O'Neill. Hartley's powerful German officer paintings were the result of his reaction to the news of Karl von Freyburg's death. Similarly, the deaths of the Mason brothers and cousin galvanized Hartley to paint his archaic portraits of the Mason family—as well as seascapes and still lifes that reflect his mourning.[35]

Notes

I would like to thank Carol Troyen, Betsy Kornhauser, and Ken McDaniel for their critical readings of this essay.

1 See Tony Vevers, "75 Years Ago: Marsden Hartley in Provincetown," *Provincetown Arts* (1991), 111. I am grateful to Stephen Borkowski for bringing this article and contemporary photographs of Provincetown to my attention.

2 Michael R. Taylor's discussion of the Provincetown and Bermuda paintings is the most complete to date. Taylor, assistant curator of modern and contemporary art at the Philadelphia Museum of Art, delivered a paper at the University of Pennsylvania on 7 December 2000 titled "Marsden Hartley: The 'Movement' Series." In this paper, Taylor discusses the iconography of the Provincetown and related Bermuda paintings in great detail. I thank him for sharing his work with me prior to publication by the Philadelphia Museum of Art.

3 Hartley to Carl Sprinchorn, winter 1917, excerpted in McCausland Papers, Archives/Smithsonian, roll D267.

4 Hartley to Alfred Stieglitz, 8 February 1917, partial transcript in McCausland Papers, Archives/Smithsonian, roll D267.

5 See Taylor, "Marsden Hartley."

6 *One Portrait of One Woman* is interesting for its own connection to theater. This painting, a portrait of Gertrude Stein, is said to be the counterpart to Stein's incorporation of a portrait of Hartley into her play *IIIIIIIII*. See catalogue entry for *One Portrait of One Woman* in *American Paintings and Sculpture in the University Art Museum Collection* (Minneapolis: University of Minnesota, 1986), 162. See also Robertson, 69.

7 See Taylor, "Marsden Hartley," for a detailed discussion of these paintings.

8 Robertson, 72.

9 See Louis Sheaffer, *O'Neill: Son and Playwright* (Boston and Toronto: Little, Brown, 1968), 185–87.

10 Marsden Hartley, "The Great Provincetown Summer," Beinecke/Yale. A version of this piece also appears in *Autobiography,* 94–96.

11 Leona Rust Egan, *Provincetown as a Stage: Provincetown, The Provincetown Players, and the Discovery of Eugene O'Neill* (Orleans, Mass.: Parnassus Imprints, 1994), 174. Furthermore, Hartley had a long personal history of involvement with the theater. See Ludington 1998, 46 and 47, for example.

12 Marsden Hartley, "Summer Art Colonies," from Hartley Papers—Writings and Poems, Archives/Smithsonian, roll 1370, frame 2745.

13 Marsden Hartley, "Farewell, Charles," reprinted in *On Art,* 95.

14 See Joel Pfister, *Staging Depth: Eugene O'Neill and the Politics of Psychological Discourse* (Chapel Hill: University of North Carolina Press, 1995), for a context for O'Neill's work.

15 Eugene O'Neill, "Memoranda on Masks," *American Spectator* (November 1932): 3; reprinted in Oscar Cargill, N. Bryllion Fagin, and William J. Fisher, eds., *O'Neill and His Plays: Four Decades of Criticism* (New York: New York University Press, 1961), 116–18.

16 There is some question about the dating of this painting. Elizabeth McCausland saw the work in Adelaide Kuntz's storage and noted that Kuntz dated it 1933 and said it was painted in Mexico. McCausland also noted that Kuntz "found a carton containing the masks used for this painting in storage the day we were there," and that Kuntz acquired the painting directly from Hartley. See McCausland Papers, Photos of Marsden Hartley Work 1933, Archives/Smithsonian, roll D269. The Walker Art Center, which now owns the painting, dates the work to 1931–32, based on a letter from Kuntz to Georgette Passedoit of the Passedoit Gallery (which handled the painting at one point), reading: "I can absolutely authenticate it as being an original work of Marsden Hartley painted in Mexico during 1931–32 when he was there on a Guggenheim Fellowship." My thanks to Betsy Carpenter, Walker Art Museum, for this information. Hartley received the fellowship in 1931, but did not go to Mexico until March 1932. He remained in the country until April 1933, when he returned to Germany, so I am inclined to date the painting 1932 or 1933.

17 See Robin Jaffee Frank, *Charles Demuth: Poster Portraits, 1923–1929* (New Haven: Yale University Art Gallery, 1994), 90–100, for an excellent discussion of Demuth's portrait of O'Neill. See also Timothy Anglin Burgard, "Charles Demuth's 'Longhi on Broadway: Homage to Eugene O'Neill,'" *Arts Magazine* 58 (January 1984): 110–13. Demuth also used a similar mask in *Love, Love, Love (Homage to Gertrude Stein),* 1929. Stein wrote a play called *IIIIIIIII* (1922, in *Geography and Plays*) in which Hartley appears as "M—N H—." See Frank, 101–6.

18 Eugene O'Neill, *Strange Interlude,* in O'Neill, *Complete Plays, 1920–1931* (New York: Library of America, 1984), 633–34.

19 See Doris Alexander, *Eugene O'Neill's Creative Struggle: The Decisive Decade, 1924–1933* (University Park: Pennsylvania State University Press, 1992), 108, for this analysis of O'Neill's character Charles Marsden. However, Alexander does not believe that Charles Marsden is a composite of Demuth and Hartley; nor does she believe that O'Neill intended the character Charles Marsden to be homosexual, as O'Neill's biographer Louis Sheaffer did. See Alexander, 263, and Sheaffer, *O'Neill: Son and Artist,* 242.

20 Hartley to Isabel Lachaise, 29 August 1928, quoted in Ludington 1998, 186.

21 Hartley to Adelaide Kuntz, quoted in Ferguson, 53.

22 See Gail R. Scott, "Cleophas and His Own: The Making of a Narrative," in Ferguson, 55–73.

23 Robertson, 112. Cleophas, for example, was husband to one of the Marys who stood at the foot of the Cross at the Crucifixion.

24 Hartley to Adelaide Kuntz, 30 October 1936, quoted in Ferguson, 52.

25 From Act 4 of O'Neill's *Mourning Becomes Electra,* reprinted in Eugene O'Neill, *Three Plays: Desire Under the Elms, Strange Interlude, and Mourning Becomes Electra* (New York: Vintage Books, 1995), 423.

26 In a letter to George Jean Nathan, O'Neill writes that "the mask idea has also gone by the board.… All that is left of it is the masklike quality of the Mannon faces in repose, an effect that can be gained by acting and makeup." See Nancy L. Roberts and Arthur W. Roberts, eds., *"As Ever, Gene": The Letters of Eugene O'Neill to George Jean Nathan* (Rutherford, N.J.: Fairleigh Dickinson University Press, 1987), 121.

27 Alexander, *Eugene O'Neill's Creative Struggle,* 151.
28 O'Neill, *Mourning Becomes Electra,* 263.
29 Ibid., 264.
30 Ibid., 267.
31 Hartley to Adelaide Kuntz, quoted in Ludington 1998, 244.
32 Ibid., 98.
33 Stephen A. Black, *Eugene O'Neill: Beyond Mourning and Tragedy* (New Haven and London: Yale University Press, 1999), 322–27.
34 Ibid., 191.
35 Hartley himself made the connection between the death of the Masons and that of von Freyburg, writing: "I haven't felt anything like it since the death of Karl von F." Hartley, quoted in Haskell, 101.

PLATES 24–37

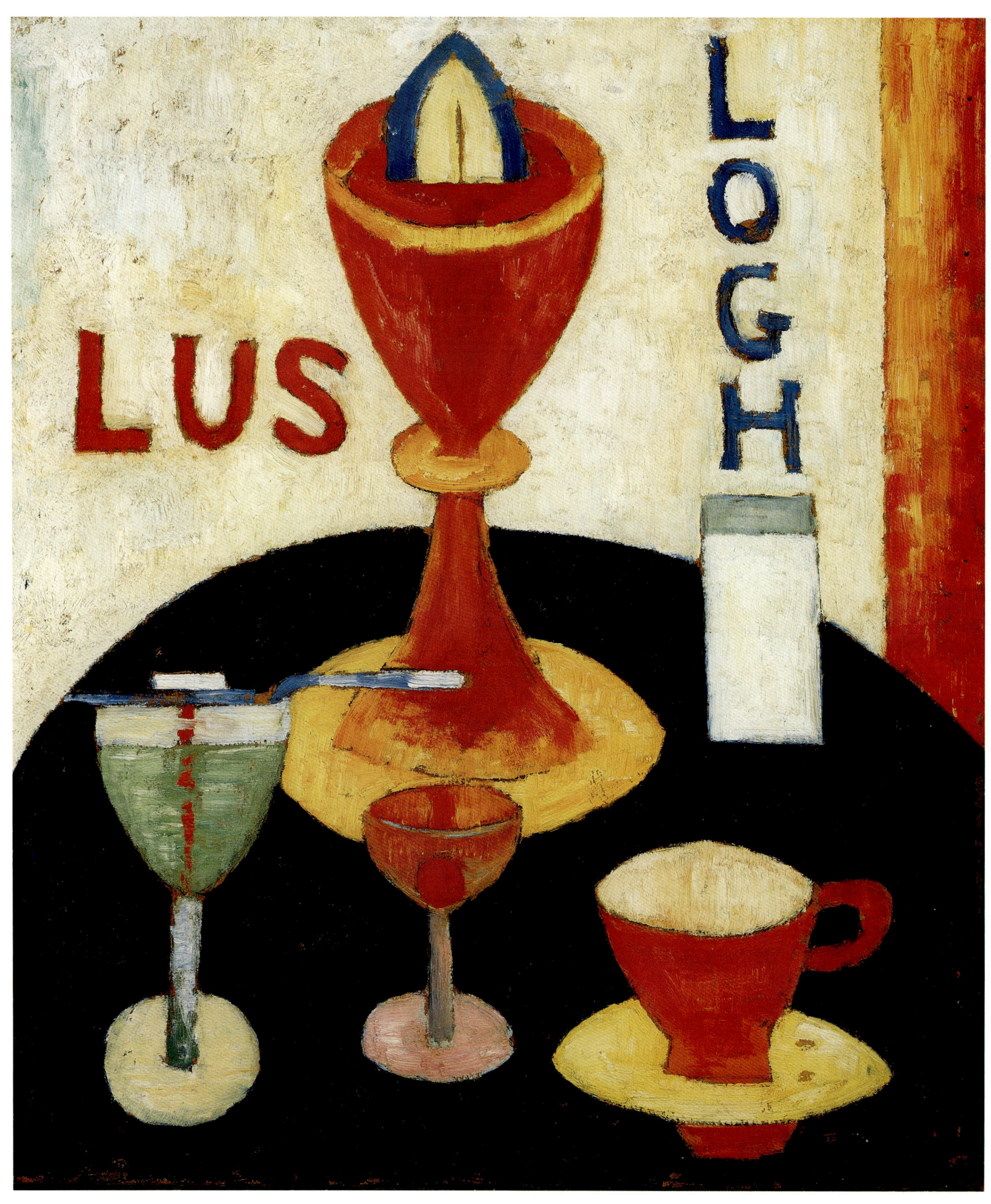

24
Handsome Drinks, c. 1916
Oil on composite board, 24 × 20 in.
Brooklyn Museum of Art
Gift of Mr. and Mrs. Milton Lowenthal

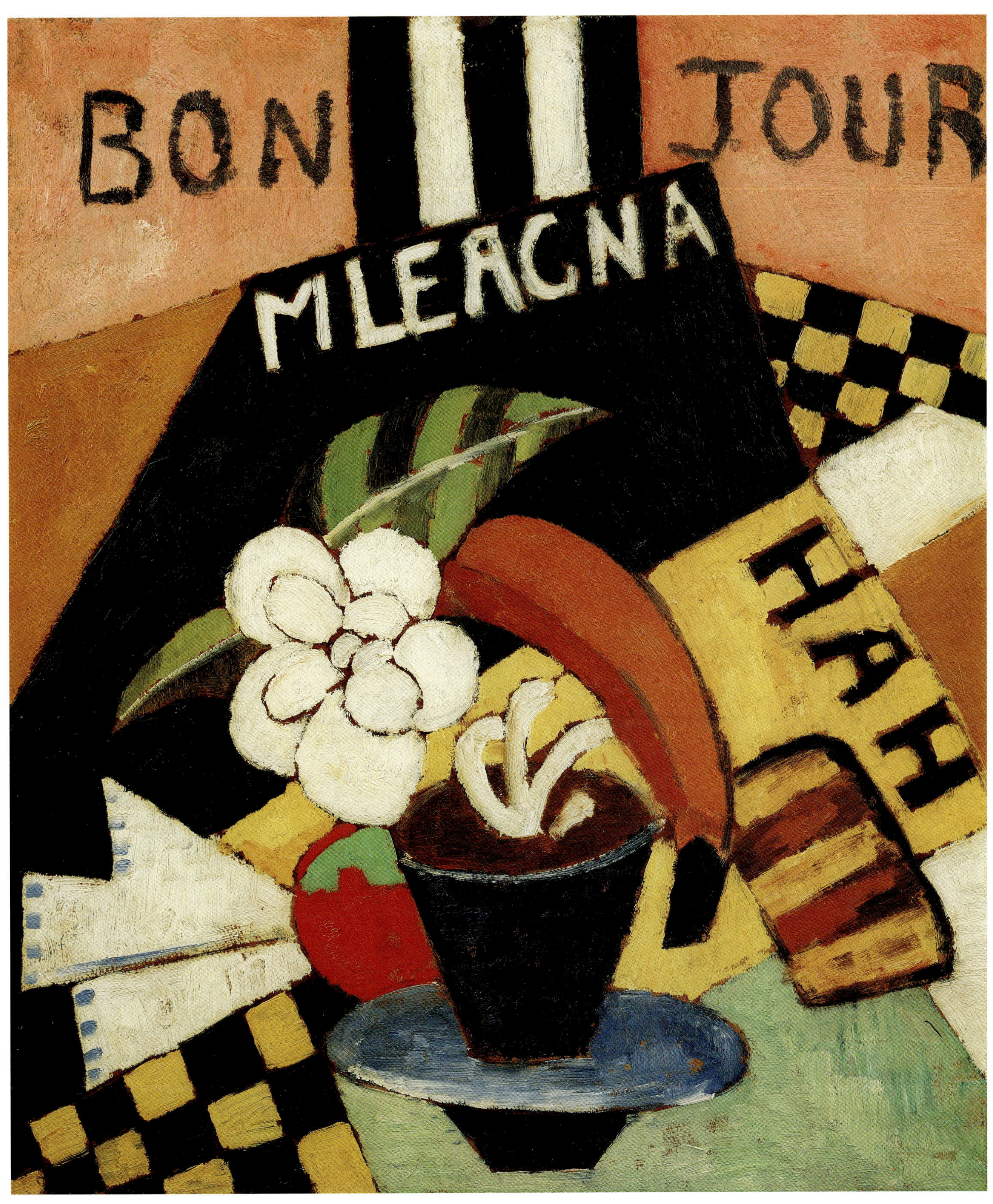

25
A Nice Time, c. 1916
Oil on board, 24 × 20 in.
Curtis Galleries, Minneapolis, Minnesota

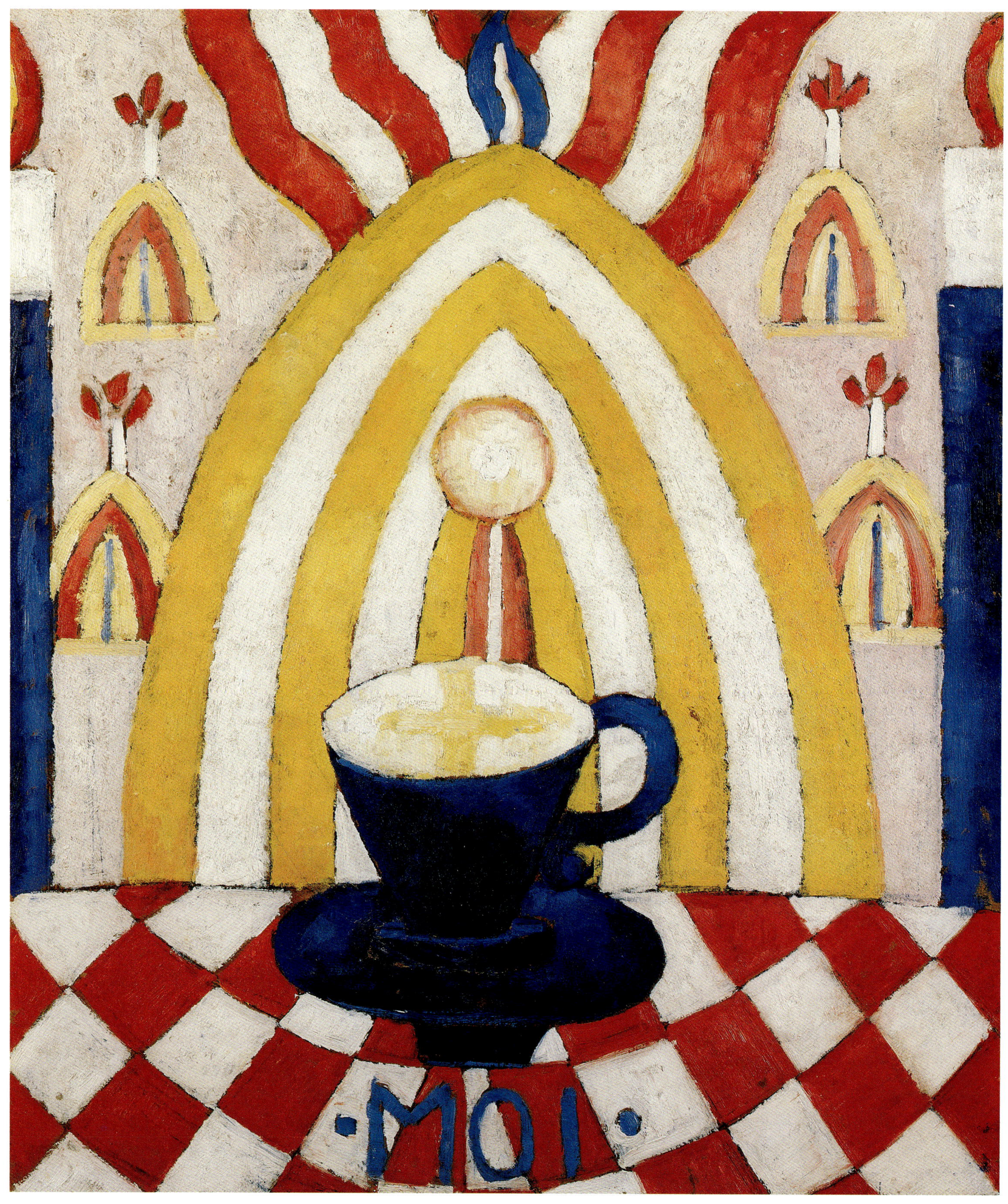

26

One Portrait of One Woman, c. 1916

Oil on fiberboard, 30 × 25 in.

Frederick R. Weisman Art Museum, University of Minnesota, Minneapolis

Bequest of Hudson Walker from the Ione and Hudson Walker Collection

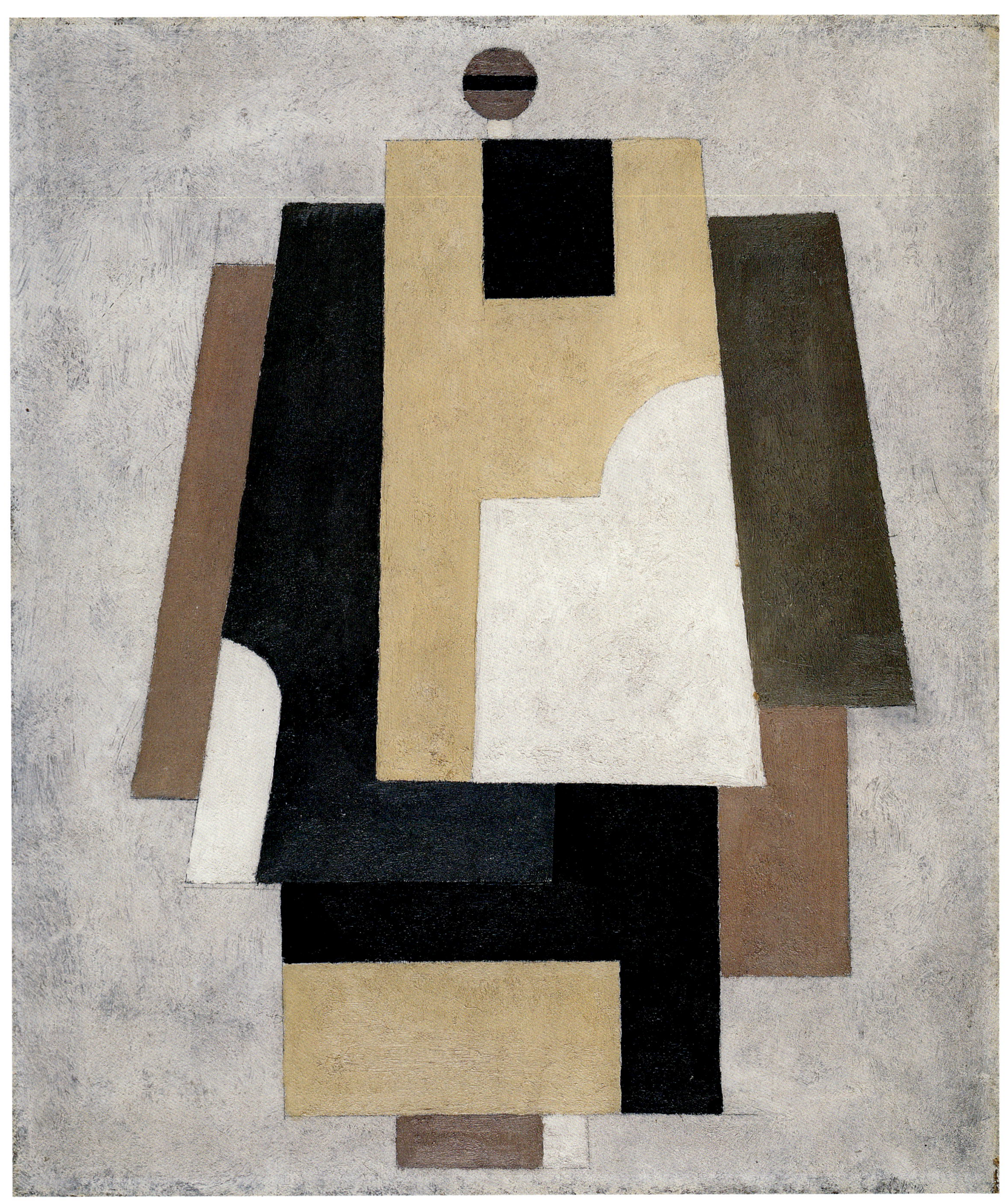

27
Movement No. 8, Provincetown, 1916
Oil on composite board, 23¼ × 19¼ in.
Wadsworth Atheneum Museum of Art, Hartford
Gift of Mrs. Robert E. Darling, 1959.5

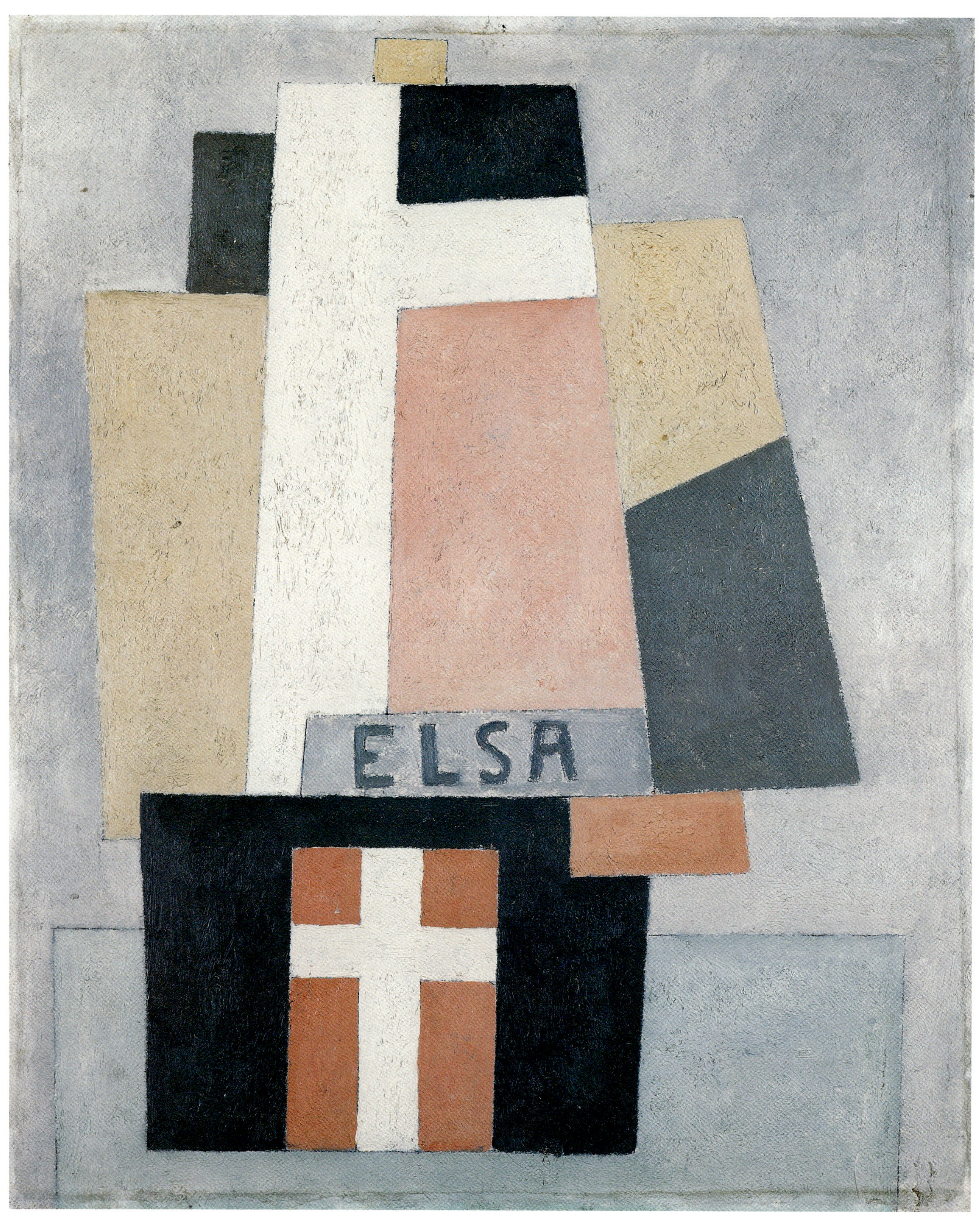

28
Elsa, 1917
Oil on composite board, 20 × 16 in.
Frederick R. Weisman Art Museum, University of Minnesota, Minneapolis
Bequest of Hudson Walker from the Ione and Hudson Walker Collection

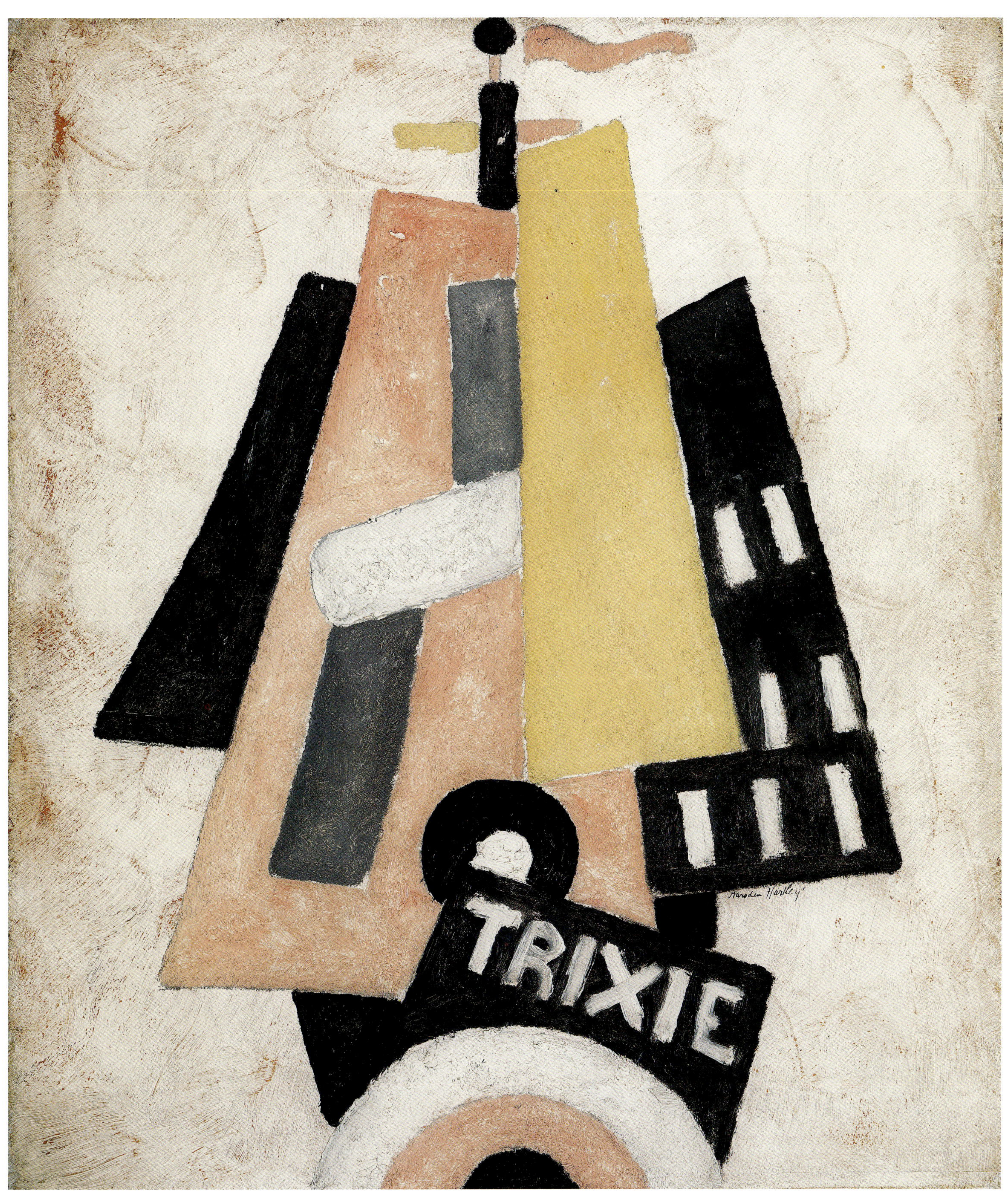

29
Trixie, c. 1916–17
Oil on composite board, 24 × 20 in.
Private Collection

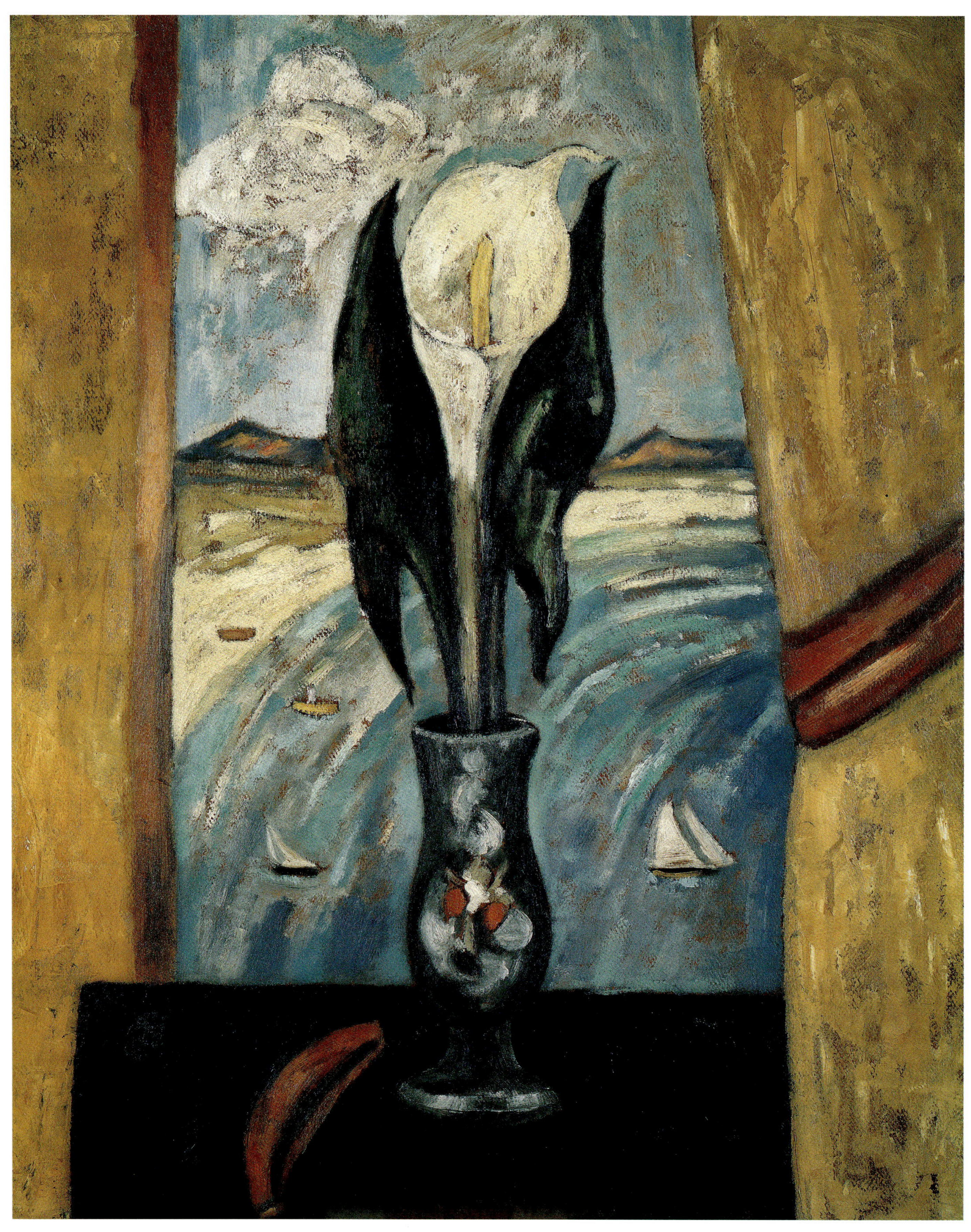

30
Atlantic Window, 1917
Oil on board, 32 × 25¾ in.
Private Collection
Courtesy of Gerald Peters Gallery, New York

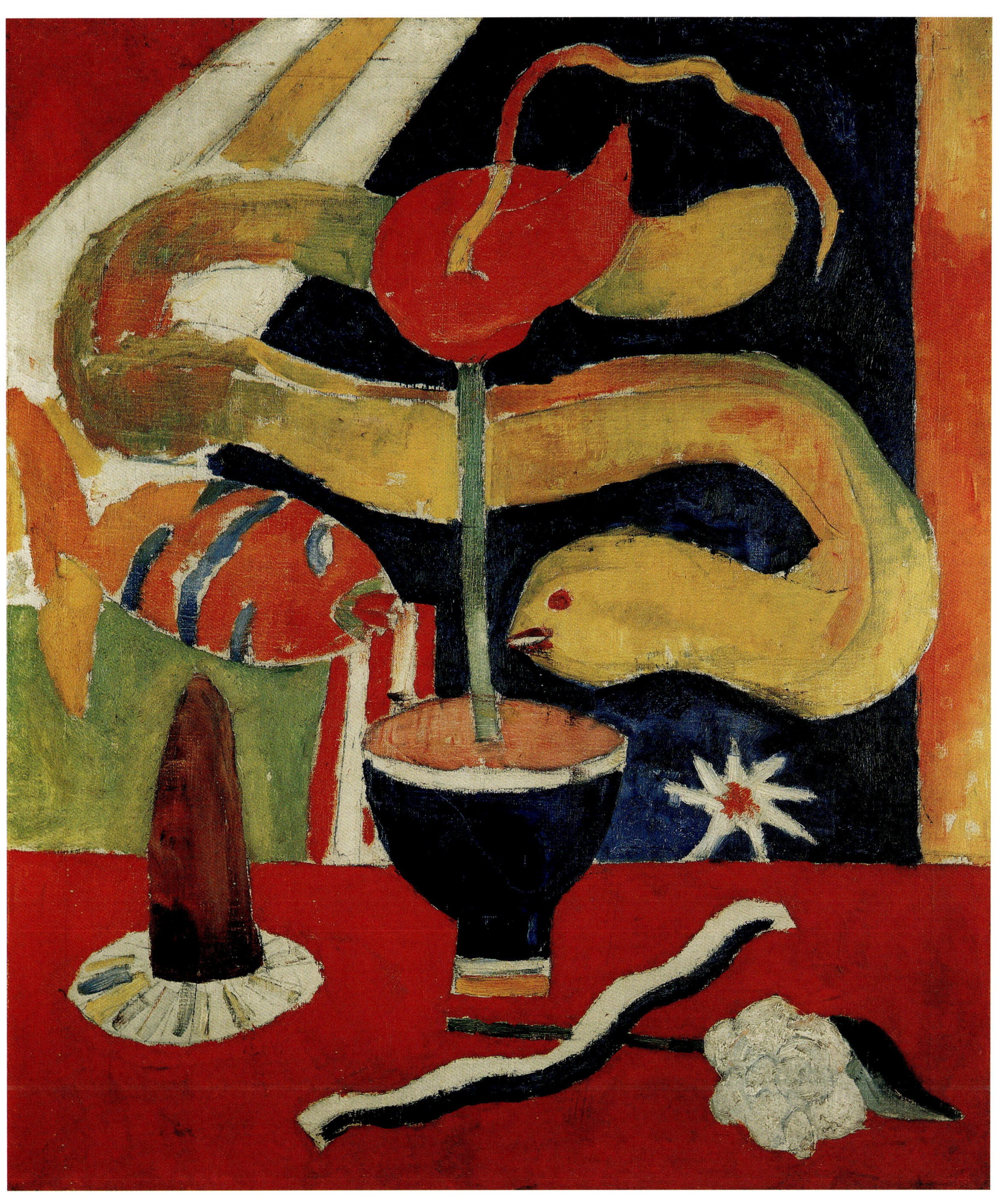

31
Still Life with Eel, c. 1917
Oil on canvas, 30 × 25 in.
The Ogunquit Museum of American Art
Permanent Collection, 58.4
Gift of Mrs. William Carlos Williams

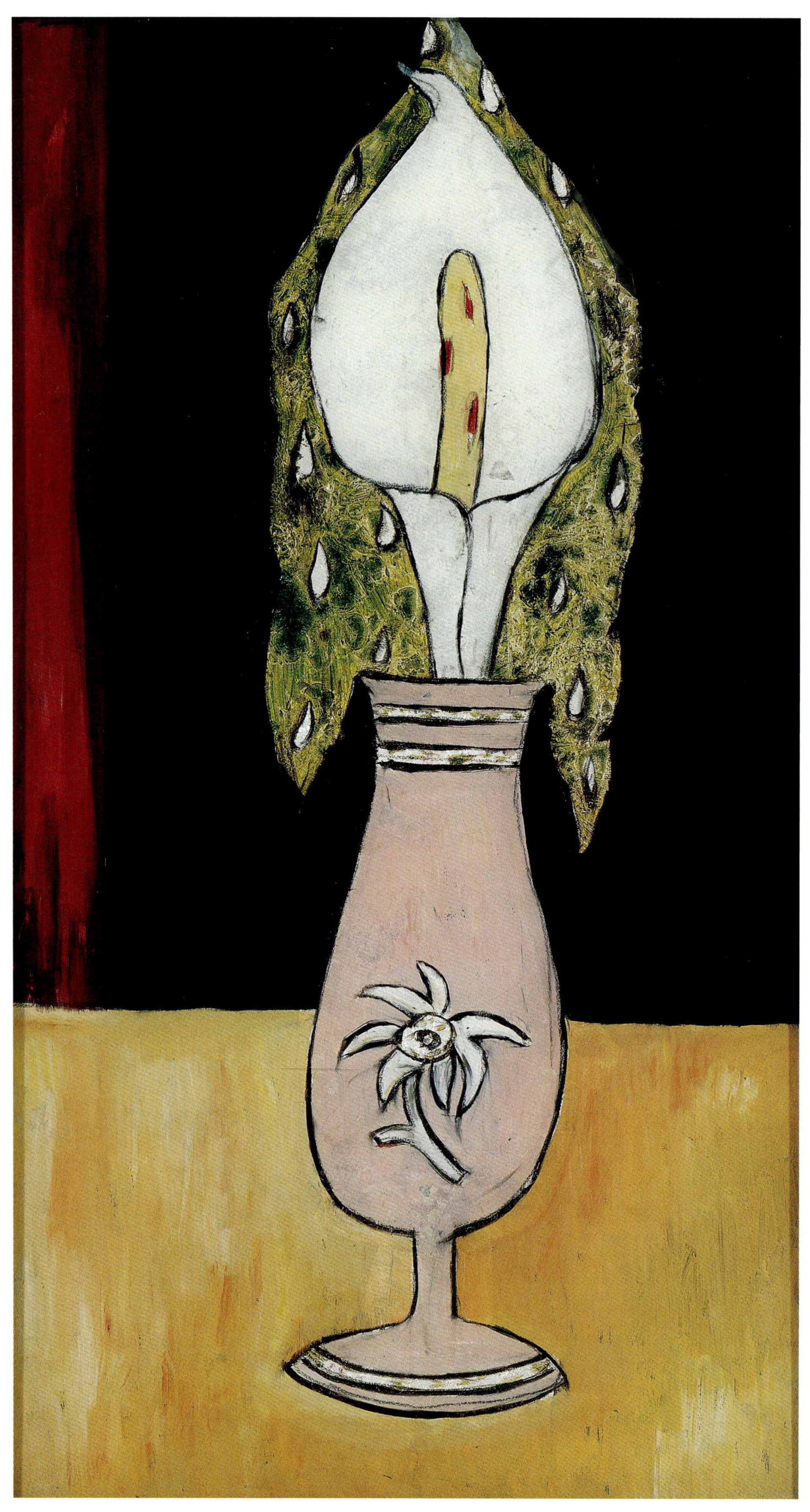

32
Tinseled Flowers, 1917
Tempera, silver foil, and gold foil on glass, 16⅞ × 9¼ in.
The Museum of Fine Arts, Boston
Gift of the William H. Lane Foundation

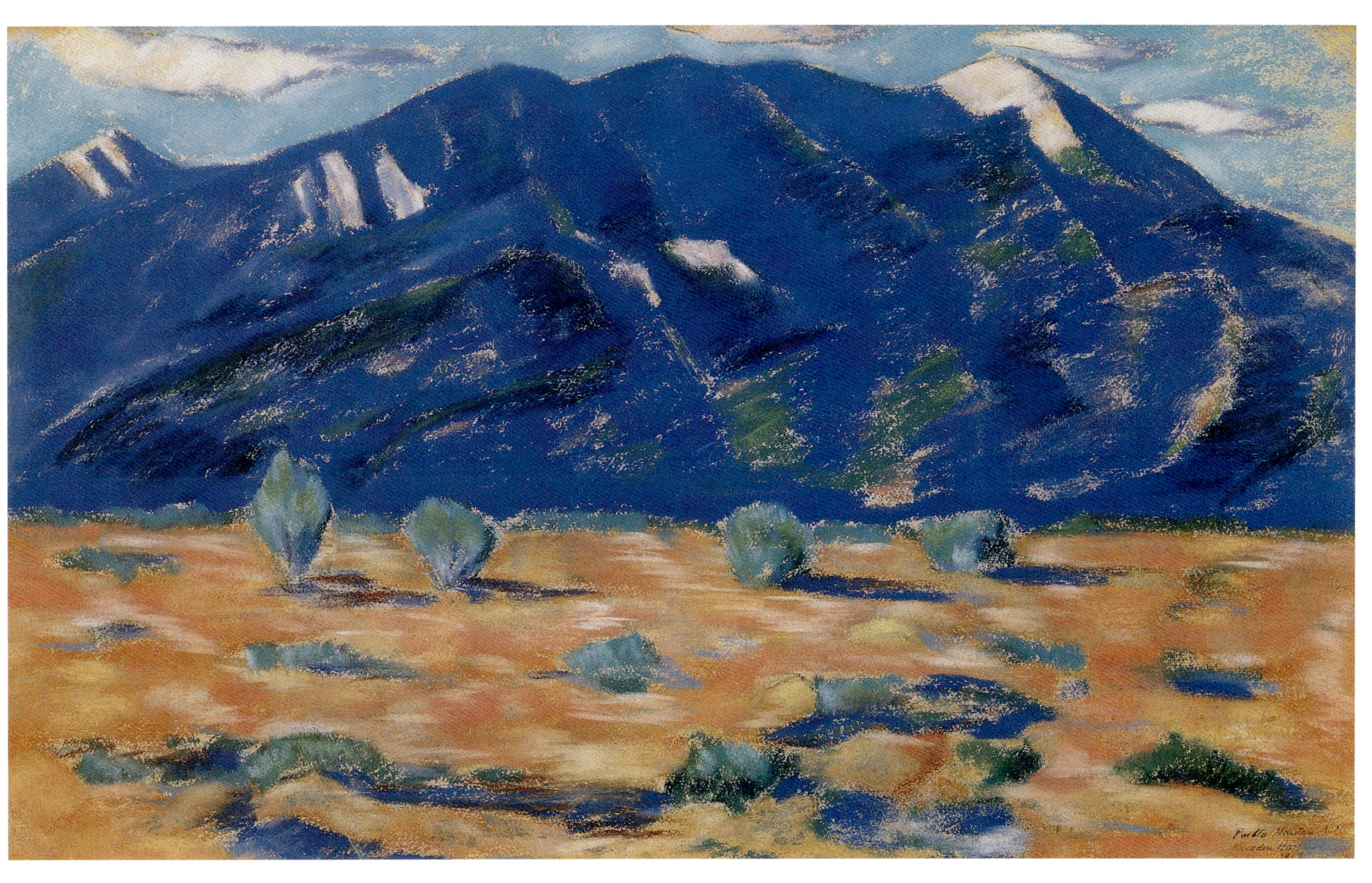

33
Pueblo Mountain, New Mexico, 1918
Pastel on paper, $17\frac{1}{2} \times 27\frac{7}{8}$ in.
Babcock Galleries, New York

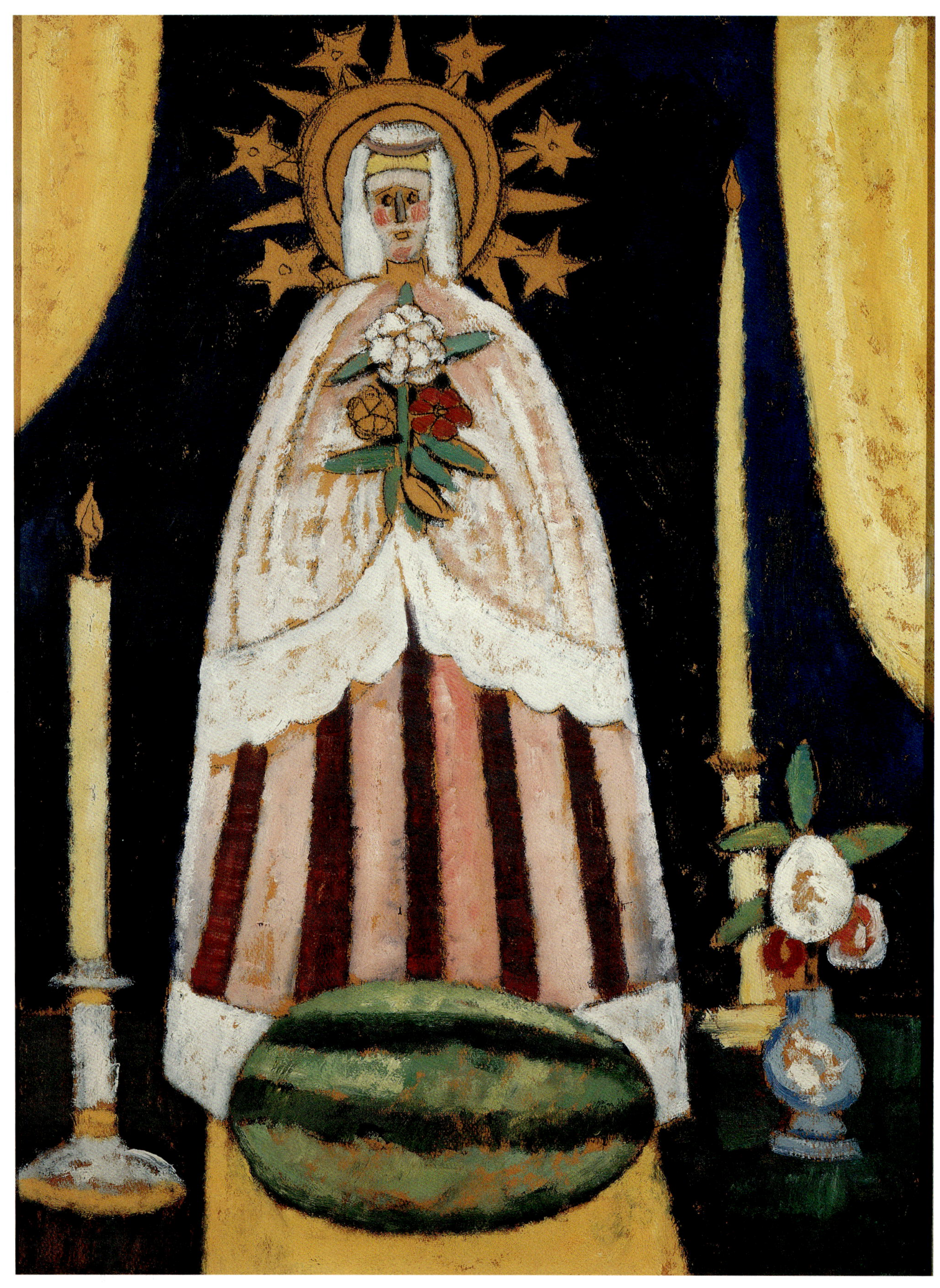

34
Blessing the Melon: The Indians Bring the Harvest to Christian Mary for Her Blessing, 1918
Oil on cardboard, 32½ × 23⅞ in.
Philadelphia Museum of Art
The Alfred Stieglitz Collection

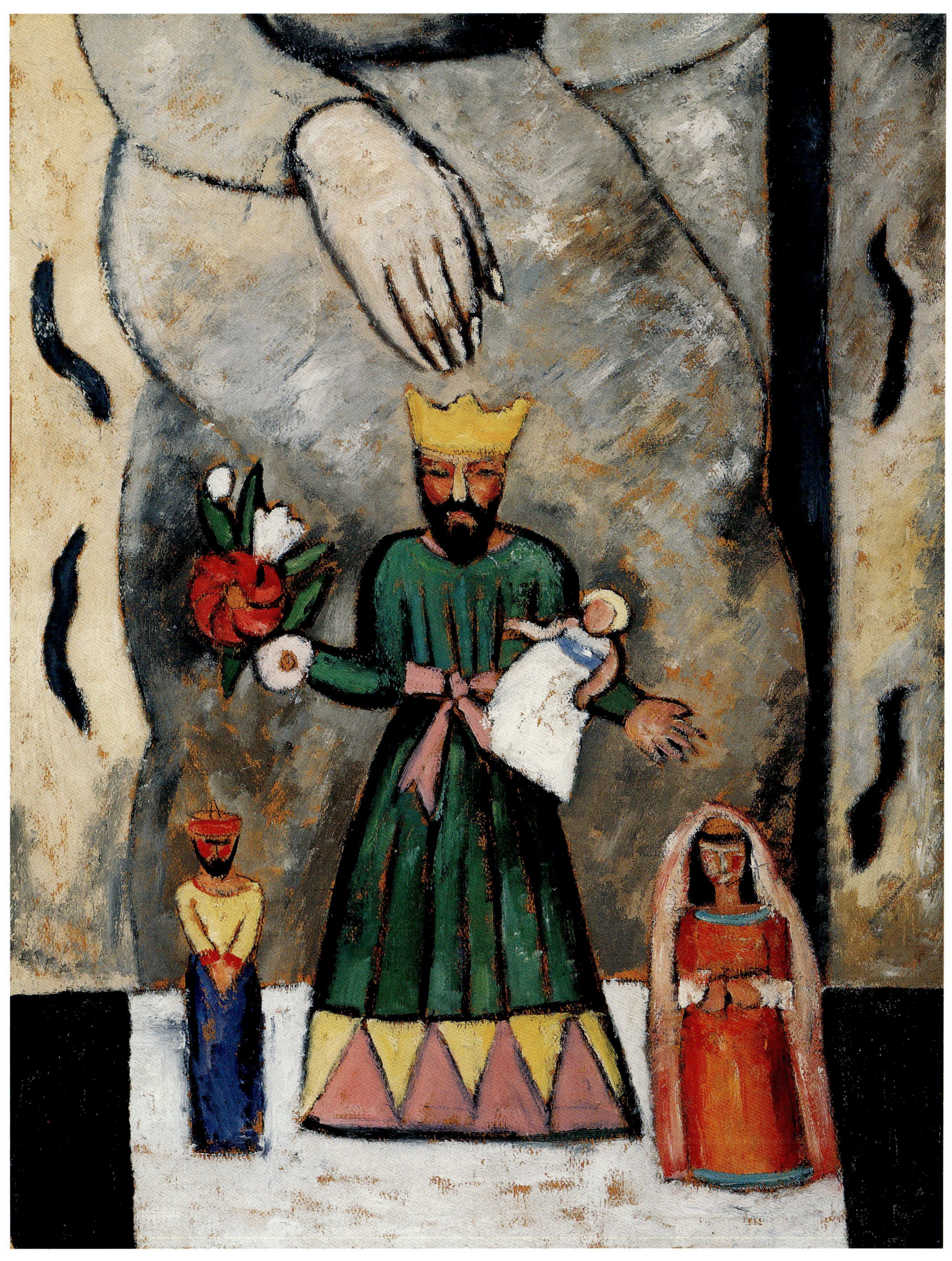

35
Santos, New Mexico, c. 1918–19
Oil on cardboard, 31¼ × 23¾ in.
Frederick R. Weisman Art Museum, University of Minnesota, Minneapolis
Bequest of Hudson Walker from the Ione and Hudson Walker Collection

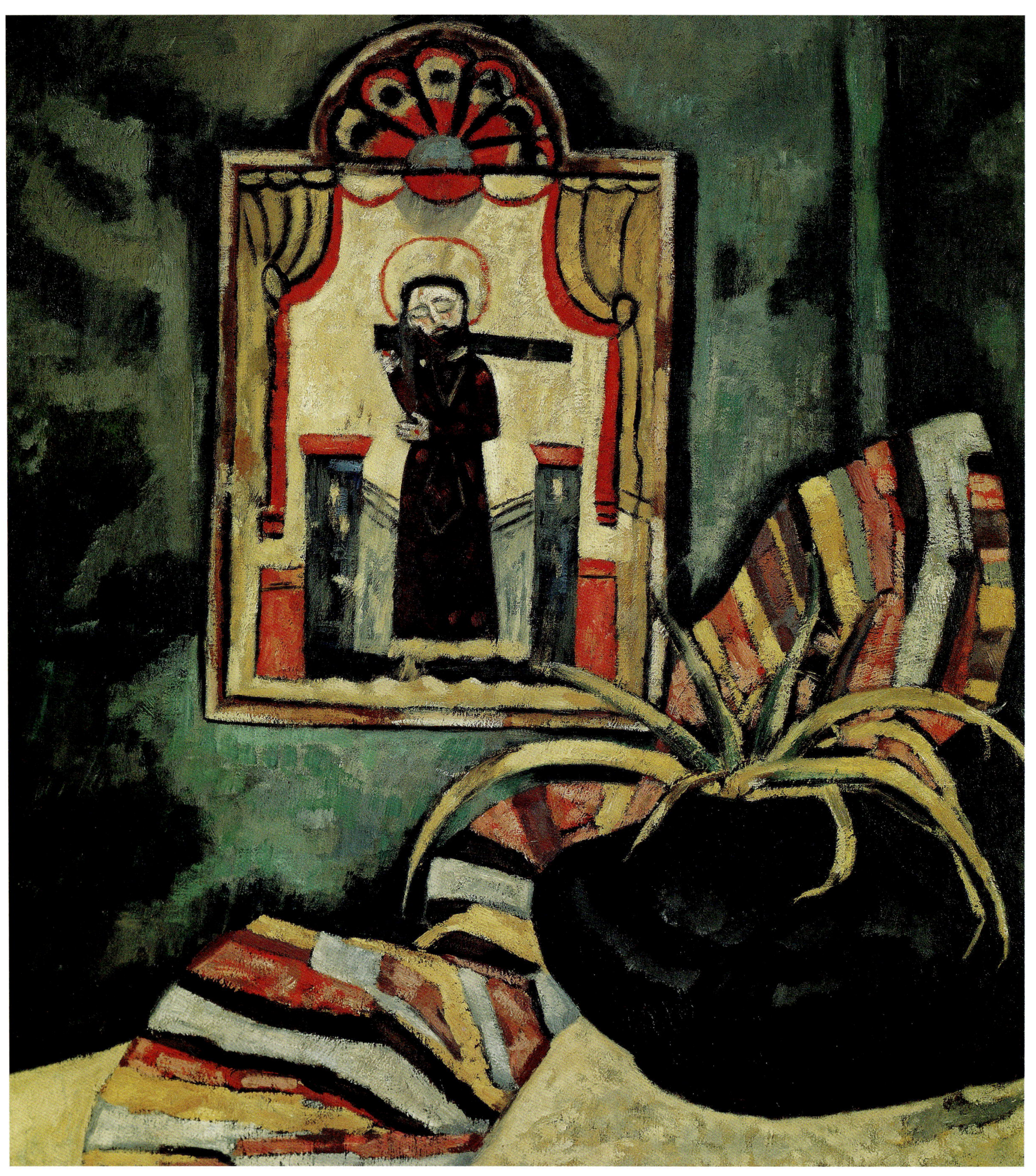

36
El Santo, 1919
Oil on canvas, 36 × 32 in.
Museum of New Mexico, Museum of Fine Arts, Santa Fe
Anonymous Gift of a Friend of Southwest Art, 1919

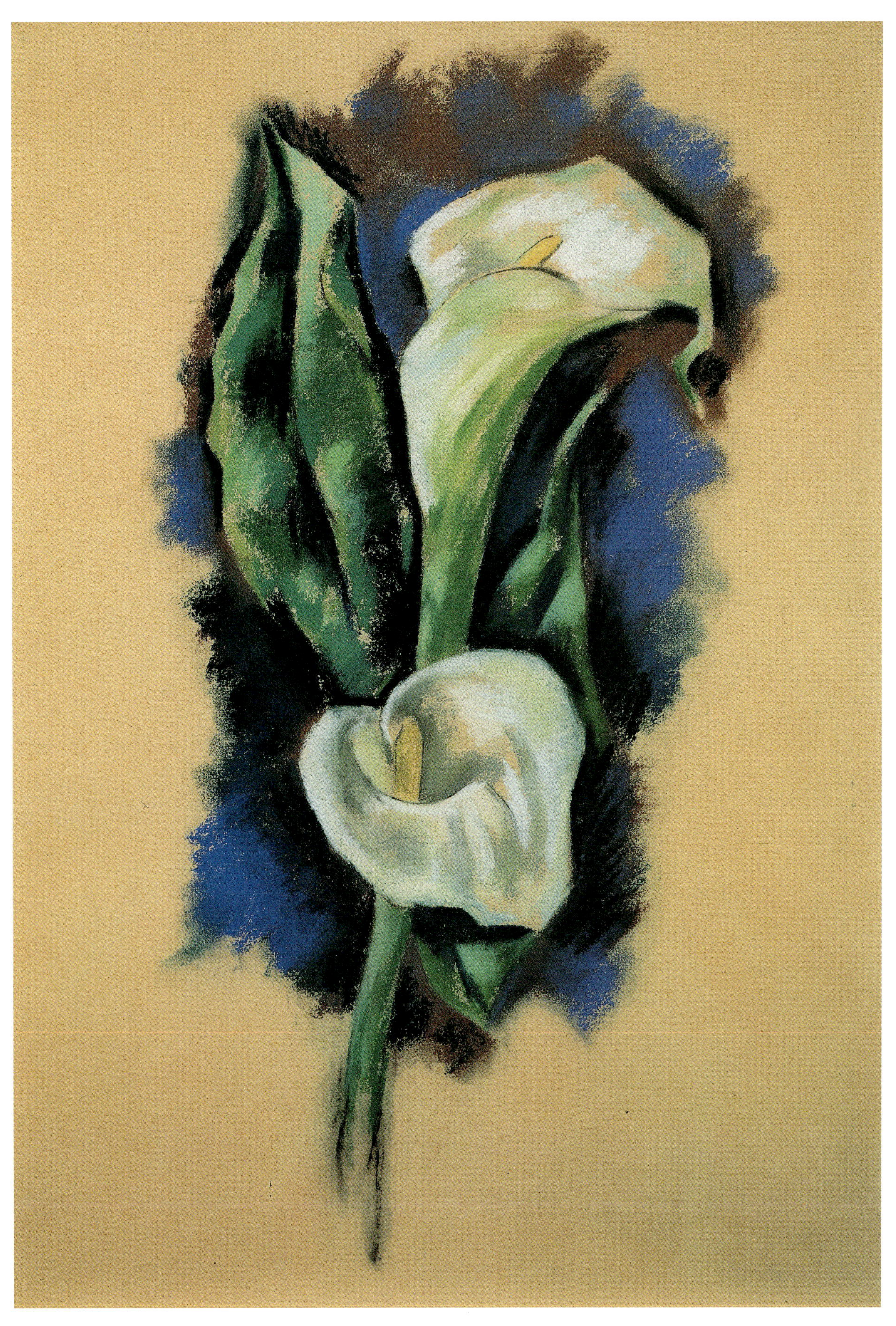

37
Calla Lilies, 1920
Pastel on paper, 24½ × 16¼ in.
Gerald Peters Gallery, New York

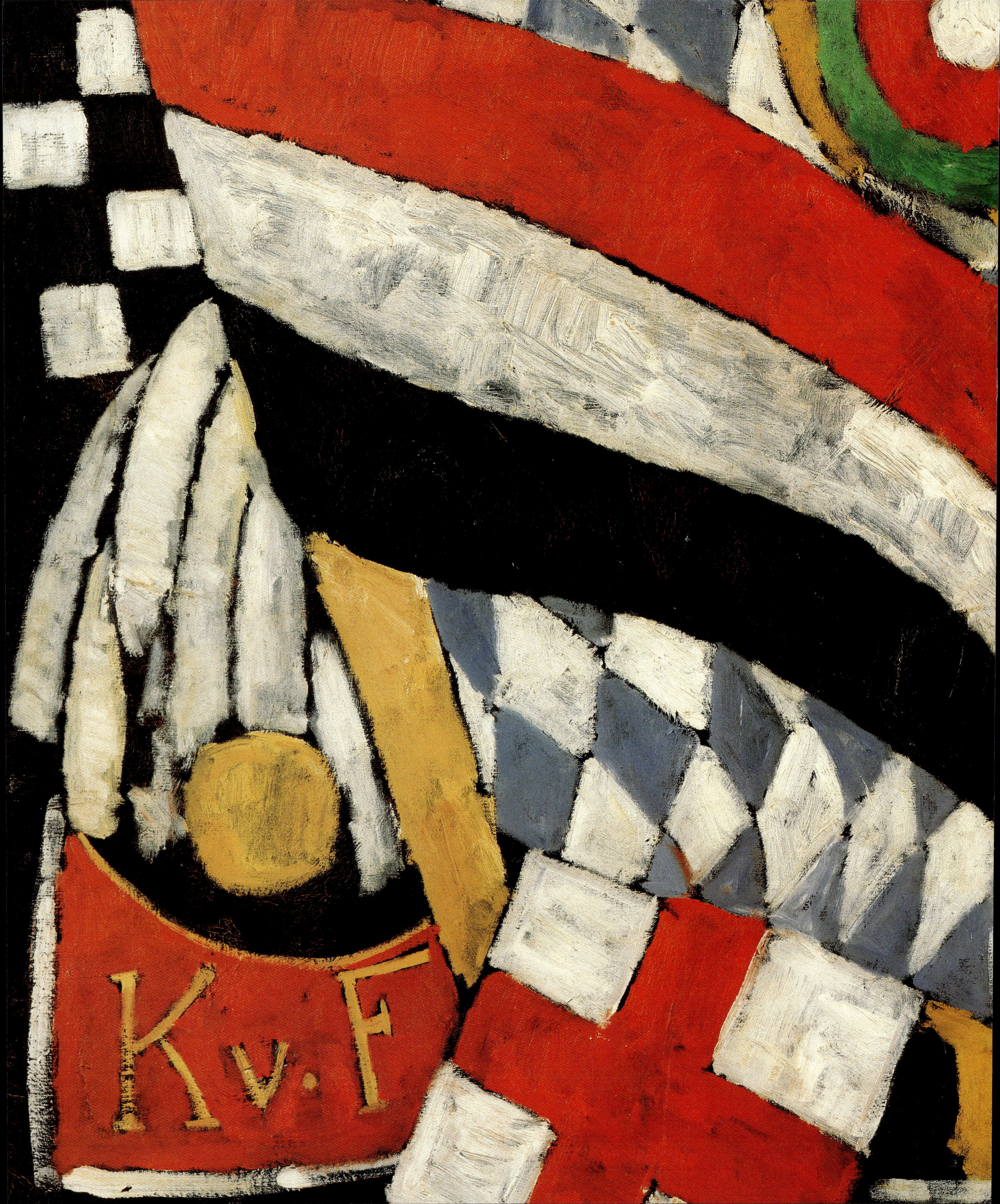
Kv.F

Marsden Hartley: Writing on Painting

Jonathan Weinberg

Marsden Hartley was an accomplished writer and poet as well as a painter. Hartley's art criticism and poetry appeared in some of the most prestigious journals of his day, including *Camera Work, Contact, Dial, Nation, Poetry,* and *Seven Arts.* In 1921 Hartley published *Adventures in the Arts,* a book of seventeen essays on art and culture, followed by three volumes of poetry: *Twenty-five Poems* in 1923, *Androscoggin* in 1940, and *Sea Burial* in 1941. After his death many of his published and unpublished manuscripts were gathered together in *On Art* (1982), edited by Gail R. Scott. Scott did the same for his poetry in *The Collected Poems of Marsden Hartley* (1987). His extended prose poem "Cleophas and His Own: A North Atlantic Tragedy" was also published in 1987 (in Gerald Ferguson's *Marsden Hartley and Nova Scotia*), and in 1997 Susan Elizabeth Ryan edited Hartley's unfinished autobiography, *Somehow a Past.* Yet much of Hartley's output remains unpublished. Scott counts six hundred poems and three hundred essays in the Hartley archive housed at the Beinecke Rare Book and Manuscript Library at Yale University.

Several scholars—Robert Northcutt Burlingame, Townsend Ludington, and Scott to name the most notable—have written eloquently about Hartley's art criticism and poetry. Art historians have mined his words as crucial guides to the meaning of his visual production. His poetry in particular has been a rich source of iconographic clues to his pictures, even though Hartley once told Leon Tebbetts that he did not want his poetry and pictures published together.[1] Rather than retrace these paths, the focus of this essay is on Hartley's paintings that are about writing, those works in which Hartley represents an author's life and work or in which he literally writes numbers and letters. When Hartley included the title of *Raptus* on the canvas itself, or incorporated the initials of a departed lover into the military regalia of *Portrait of a German Officer,* he was effectively writing and painting at the same time.

Although Hartley wrote copiously, he worried about relying on language to interpret paintings: "A true art needs no speech—it speaks itself."[2] He wrote Alfred Stieglitz that what he had "to express is not handled with words—it must 'come' to the observer—it must carry its influence over the mind of the individual into that region of him which is more than mind."[3] Such a distrust of language to convey adequately an aesthetic response to pictures was widespread among the Stieglitz circle and a cornerstone of modernist theory in general. Hartley's close friend the artist and sometime writer Charles Demuth echoed the same idea: "Across a Greco, across a Blake, across a Rubens, across a Watteau, across a Beardsley is written in larger letters than any printed page will ever dare to hold, or, Broadway façade or roof support, what its creator had to say about it. To translate these painted sentences, whatever they may be, into words—well, try it."[4] Yet for all of Demuth's fear of

Detail, Plate 19

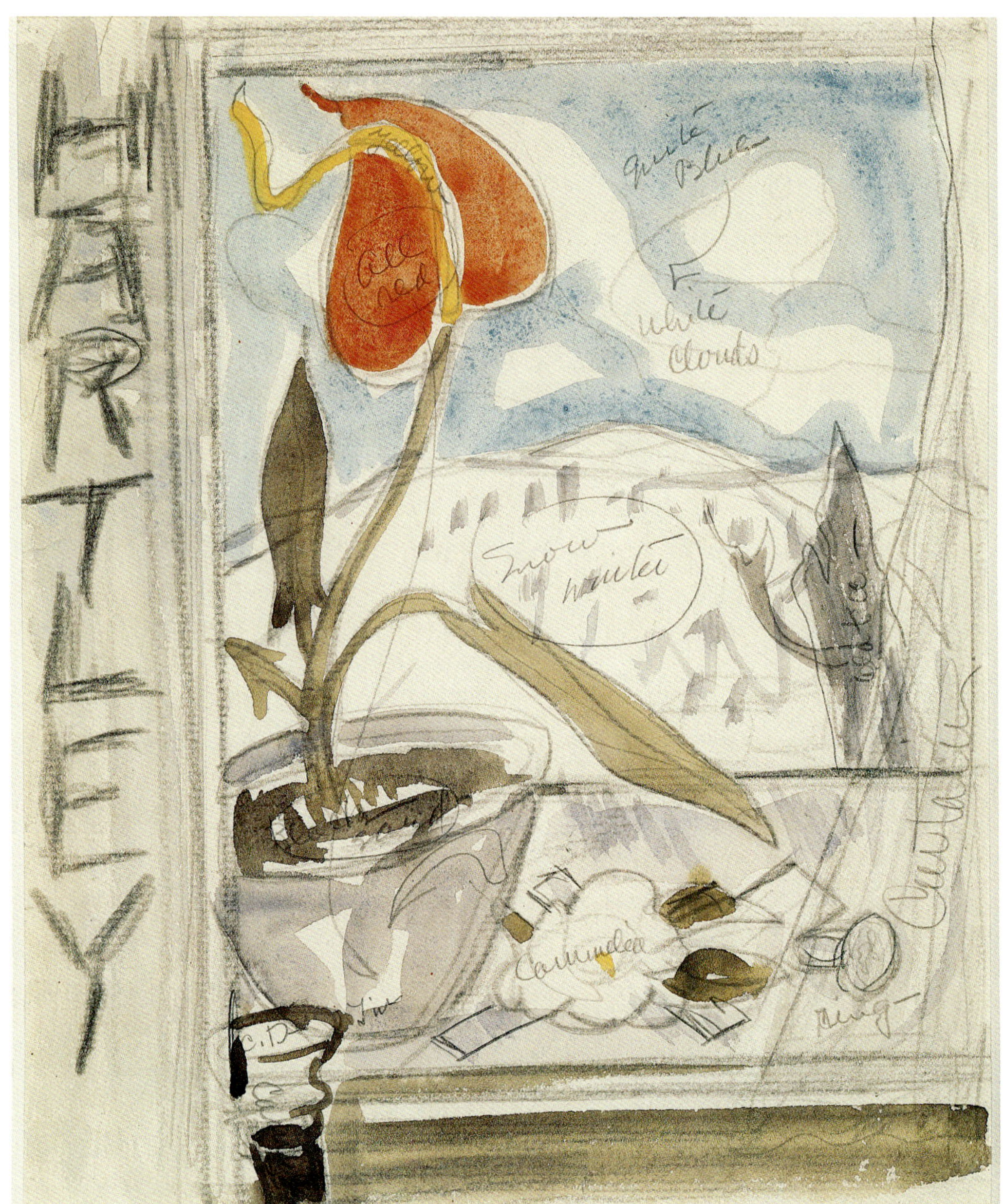

Figure 1
Charles Demuth
Study for Poster Portrait: Marsden Hartley, 1923-24
Watercolor and graphite, 10⅛ × 8⅛ in.
(25.7 × 20.6 cm)
Yale University Art Gallery, New Haven

words, he can only conceive of the work of art as written "in larger letters than any printed page will dare to hold." Indeed, this very confusion of looking at a picture and reading is built into Demuth's most ambitious paintings, his portrait posters of John Marin and Georgia O'Keeffe and his watercolor sketch *Study for a Poster Portrait: Marsden Hartley* (fig. 1). Instead of capturing likenesses, Demuth combined objects, signs, and names to evoke the subjects. These abstract portraits were themselves influenced by Hartley's paintings like the *Portrait of a German Officer,* in which letters and numbers invite the viewer to *read* the painting.

For all of Hartley's worries about interpreting art with words, he wrote Stieglitz in 1915 that he was about to send him a packet of manuscripts to be considered for publication in *Camera Work,* Stieglitz's magazine devoted to the artists of 291 and the cause of modern art. Hartley wrote: "I don't know how much I shall ever write—I shall never deteriorate into a *writer* any more than I shall deteriorate into just a painter. I believe too well in stopping this side of the mechanical aspect of anything."[5] The phrase *deteriorate into a writer* conveys Hartley's suspicion of professional critics. In his essay "The Dearth of Critics" published in *Adventures in the Arts,* he was blunt: neither journalists nor art historians were capable of a "serious approach to the current tendencies in art." Hartley implied that the typical newspaper critic was ignorant of aesthetic matters, while art historians were too interested in dry facts. "The journalist is frank and says that he doesn't know but that he must write; the other writes books that are well suited for reference purposes, but have scant bearing upon the actual truth in relation to pictures."[6] Hartley declared that his own words on culture gathered in *Adventures in the Arts* were "not intended in any way to be professional treatises."[7] In his various autobiographical writings, Hartley turned his lack of an advanced education into an asset, claiming to be entirely self-taught. In a rather pompous tone that belies his own claim for a kind of primitive authenticity, Hartley claimed to have "no culture in the academic forms. I have never felt it necessary to acquire all that baggage—I have let the divine mother of poetry itself show me the way, and if the real forms are there it is only because I must have absorbed them like a sponge."[8] Given his lack of a college degree and the supposed knowledge of poetic craft it might bring, he fell back on the power of intuition. He boasted to Robert McAlmon that "All my poems are written first draft and left."[9] The distinguished poet Robert Creeley attributes Hartley's bravado to a "vulnerability" because "he had only his own interests and instincts to guide him."[10] Yet if Hartley did not attend classes in poetry, he was frequently in the company of poets and writers. As a young man he was part of the literary circle of Horace Traubel, the biographer and disciple of Walt Whitman. And he counted among his friends many of the most important American writers of his day, including Djuna Barnes, Hart Crane, Marianne Moore, Robert McAlmon, Ezra Pound, Gertrude Stein, and William Carlos Williams. He was influenced not only by his heroes Ralph Waldo Emerson, William James, Henry David Thoreau, and Whitman, but also by fellow art critics in the Stieglitz circle, including Paul Rosenfeld and Waldo Frank. In other words Hartley was no literary naïf. The range of topics covered by *Adventures in the Arts*—it included not only essays on artists as different as Winslow Homer and Odilon Redon, but also discussions of examples of contemporary culture as varied as vaudeville, the acting of John Barrymore, and the poetry of Rupert Brooke—projected an image of Hartley as an intellectual with sophisticated and decidedly modernist tastes.

The term "intellectual" is key, because it explains Hartley's other worry that he voiced to Stieglitz, about deteriorating into being just a painter. Hartley took considerable pride in escaping the working-class roots of his father and the provincialism of his birthplace, Lewiston, Maine. If writing was an alternative mode of artistic expression for Hartley, it was also a means to establish his credentials as a member of a cosmopolitan aesthetic and intellectual elite. Indeed, Hartley countered a feeling of inferiority about his lack of education and social standing in the world by recounting in his various autobiographic sketches and letters all the artistic celebrities he knew throughout his life.

When Hartley wrote about art, he avoided the issues of stylistic development and historical context that troubled art historians. He said of his own essays, "they must be viewed in the light of entertaining conversations. Their possible value lies in their directness of impulse, and not in weight of argument."[11] His discussions of the works of his favorite artists—Ryder, Cézanne, Rembrandt, and Leonardo—rarely include sustained descriptions of their individual paintings, since presumably the greatness of their works speaks for itself. Hartley's art criticism, while useful as a means of charting the influences on his own painting and his changing theories about the nature of creativity, is not terribly revealing about its ostensible subject matters. To put it bluntly, if Hartley were not such a great painter, we would probably not be interested in what he had to say about the artists he prized.

Hartley's published statements about his own art-making are more revealing, yet only on a few occasions did he provide great detail into the processes that went into making specific paintings. Although he was profoundly influenced by Kandinsky's paintings and writings, he claimed that Kandinsky was too reliant on written theories and that his pictures tended merely to illustrate those theories: "Kandinsky has a most logical and ordered mind which appeals so earnestly to the instinct which has been over-mastered. In other words in my heart of hearts I think he is not creative—I think he is an interpreter of ideas."[12]

The urge to bring writing and painting together can be identified in the earliest extant picture by Hartley, his small canvas of Walt Whitman's house (plate 1). In his memoirs Hartley wrote about his feeling of abandonment when his mother died and his father left him to be cared for by an elder sister; he claimed he had been "left alone on the doorstep of the world."[13] In this little painting, Hartley imagines himself literally at the doorstep of his favorite poet, longing to become part of Whitman's spiritual family. But the door and windows are closed shut; the façade is impenetrable. Years later, Hartley used Whitman to forge a link between writing and painting in the essay "Whitman and Cézanne." "Cézanne's fine landscapes and still-lifes, and Whitman's majestic line with its gripping imagery are one and the same thing, for it reaches the same height in the mind."[14] Indeed, Hartley's aesthetic ambitions are neatly summarized in his conjoining of these two names. He wanted to combine Whitman's poetry of masculine comradeship and ecstatic love of the American landscape with the solidity and luminosity of Cézanne's paintings of mountains and bathers. It was only in his late paintings of lifeguards, lumberjacks and fishermen, such as *Down East Young Blades* (plate 85) that Hartley was fully able to recast Whitman's characters in Cézanne's form. Yet already in this early picture Hartley was thinking of how to convert Whitman's literary influence into paint. The resulting tiny painting, so seemingly empty of human presence, may appear to be the very opposite of Whitman's celebration of companionship, but Hartley claimed that Whitman, despite his gregariousness, kept his door "heavily padlocked against the intrusion of the imaginary outsider."[15]

The feelings of alienation that Hartley projects onto Whitman and his house are echoed in an apologetic letter he wrote Mabel Dodge (Luhan) ten years later: "I must never do more, at most, than walk in as graciously as possible, sit a little, and pass out again for there is always the quality of wonder in being really not quite anywhere at all times."[16] The phrase "not quite anywhere at all times" evokes Hartley's restlessness—throughout his career he traveled incessantly and never had a permanent home (his frequent shifts in styles of painting mirrored this restlessness). But it is possible that Hartley is also hinting at his homosexuality, which he shared with Whitman, and which made him feel always an outsider. Hartley rarely wrote overtly about his sexual attraction to men. Even at his most confessional, he tended to be circumspect. He wrote Stieglitz:

> *I am not happy interiorly and this as far as I can see cannot be changed[—]like every other human being I have longings which through trick of circumstances have been left unsatisfied and I am not the kind to brush them by—I feel them and feel the loss of them. These are the things which few in this world but myself know—it is not necessary now to begin telling them they would help no one—but it leaves me with an inner-need unsatisfied and the pain grows stronger instead of less and it leaves one nothing but the role of spectator in life watching life go by.*[17]

Given Hartley's seeming unwillingness to write directly about his unsatisfied urges, we might be tempted to say that he was in the closet. Indeed, the row house depicted in *Walt Whitman's House,* with its dark windows and closed door, is an apt metaphor for the pain of being forced to keep silent about sexual identity and love. Yet the evidence suggests that Hartley did not go out of his way to hide his homosexuality—he never married, nor did he invent romantic relationships with women in his correspondences to keep his friends off the track. On the contrary, Hartley made a concerted effort to express his homosexuality in his art.[18] Yet like many other homosexuals who lived before gay liberation, he was loathe to speak or write of his erotic attachments directly.

Walt Whitman's House links painting to writing by imaging a place where poetry was created. A few years later, Hartley actually wrote a poem on the back of *Landscape No. 16,* a small painting from 1908–9 of birch trees in autumn. The beauty of Hartley's painting is not particularly enhanced by such lines as "October Lies—Dying / The dead dance frantically!"[19] Yet in the act of writing on the back of the canvas, Hartley revealed the desire to heighten the painting's meaning, making explicit an obsession with death that runs through his most significant works. It is as if he were saying, this is more than a tiny landscape. However, by putting the words on the back, he could not guarantee that the audience would be aware of them. Such writing was a kind of secret message intended for the artist himself, or for whomever was fortunate enough to have the painting in his possession. But even when writing appears on the face of Hartley's canvases, it usually takes on a secretive quality. Writing bestows significance, even as its ultimate meaning remains elusive.

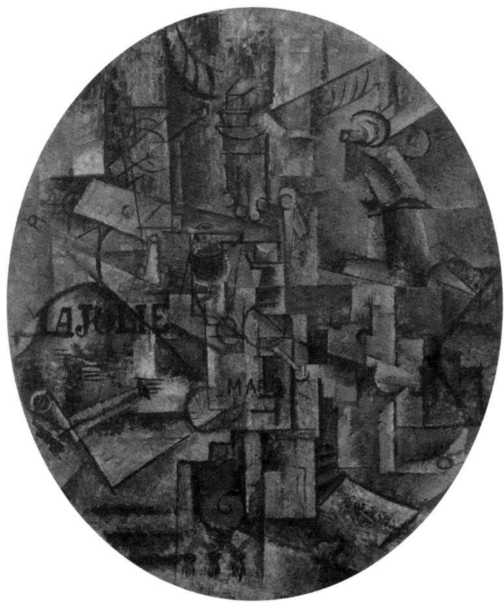

Figure 2
Pablo Picasso
The Architect's Table, 1912
Oil on canvas mounted on oval panel, 28⅝ × 23½ in.
(72.7 × 59.7 cm)
The Museum of Modern Art, New York
The William S. Paley Collection (697.71)
© 2002 Estate of Pablo Picasso/Artists Rights Society (ARS), New York
Digital Image © The Museum of Modern Art/Licensed by SCALA/Art Resource, N.Y.

The impetus for Hartley to use letters, numbers, musical notations, and other symbols on his canvases probably came from his first visits in 1912 to Gertrude and Leo Stein's famous home at 27 rue de Fleurus, where he was able to study closely several cubist works by Pablo Picasso (he also saw Picasso's work at Daniel-Henry Kahnweiler's gallery). In July 1912 he wrote Stieglitz that Picasso's newest work was "not as interesting." Nevertheless, he included a short description of one of Picasso's paintings, perhaps *The Architect's Table* (fig. 2): "just now he is doing things that have running over and across these network designs—names of people and words like jolie or bien and numbers like 75."[20] To illustrate "the new Picasso effect," he included a little sketch from memory of the Picasso painting (fig. 3)—this was a rare tribute from Hartley. What is interesting about the sketch is the way in which it dramatically simplifies and flattens the characteristic forms of Picasso's analytic cubism, even as it exaggerates the legibility of the number 75, the word "jolie" and the name "Marie." Indeed, it seems like an antecedent of *Portrait of a German Officer* and of the War Motif series in general.

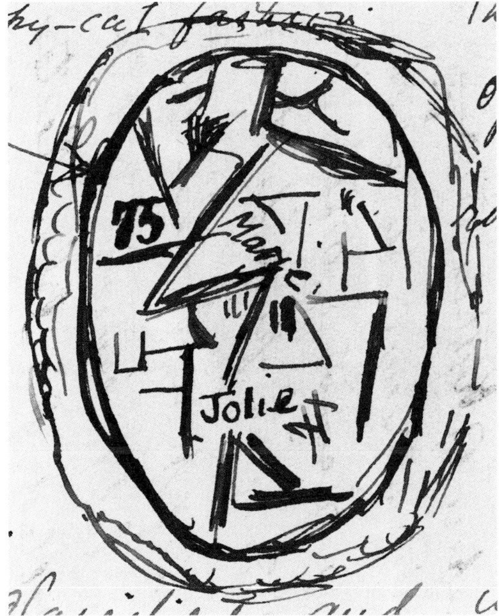

Figure 3
Sketch of Picasso Painting, July 12, 1912
Ink on paper in letter to Alfred Stieglitz
Yale Collection of American Literature
Beinecke Rare Book and Manuscript Library
Yale University, New Haven

In 1946 the modernist critic Clement Greenberg complained that Hartley "flirted with cubism and a kind of abstractionism . . . almost completely misunderstanding both."[21] Yet it is precisely in misunderstanding or, to use Harold Bloom's term for the mechanism of the anxiety of influence, *misreading* Picasso's style that Hartley finds his own voice.[22] The exact chronology of the abstract paintings that Hartley began to produce in 1912 and 1913 is impossible to establish, but it seems the earliest pictures are a series based on musical themes. *Musical Theme No. 2* (fig. 4) is remarkably close to Hartley's sketch of Picasso's painting. As the series progressed in paintings like *Musical Theme (Oriental Symphony)* (plate 8), Hartley moved away from a sense of a clear cubist grid and introduced broad washes of bright colors, producing work which he claimed was "not like Picasso—it is not like Kandinsky not like any 'cubism.'"[23] Writing was key to the pictures on a number of levels. He claimed to be inspired by Kandinsky's treatise *On the Spiritual in Art,* in which Kandinsky wrote about creating a visual language of color and line that would appeal directly to the emotions in the manner of music. Such a theory of synesthesia, in which color relationships operate like musical chords, would seem to take Hartley away from the written word as he tried to, as he wrote, "paint music—or the equivalent of sound in color."[24] After all, the 1912 almanac *Der Blaue Reiter,* which Hartley's German friends translated for him, included Arnold Schönberg's denunciation of those who insisted on understanding music by resorting to texts that were outside the direct musical experience.[25] Bruce Robertson

Figure 4
Marsden Hartley
Musical Theme No. 2 (Bach Préludes et Fugues), 1912
Oil on canvas mounted on Masonite, 24 × 20 in. (60.9 × 50.8 cm)
© Museo Thyssen-Bornemisza, Madrid

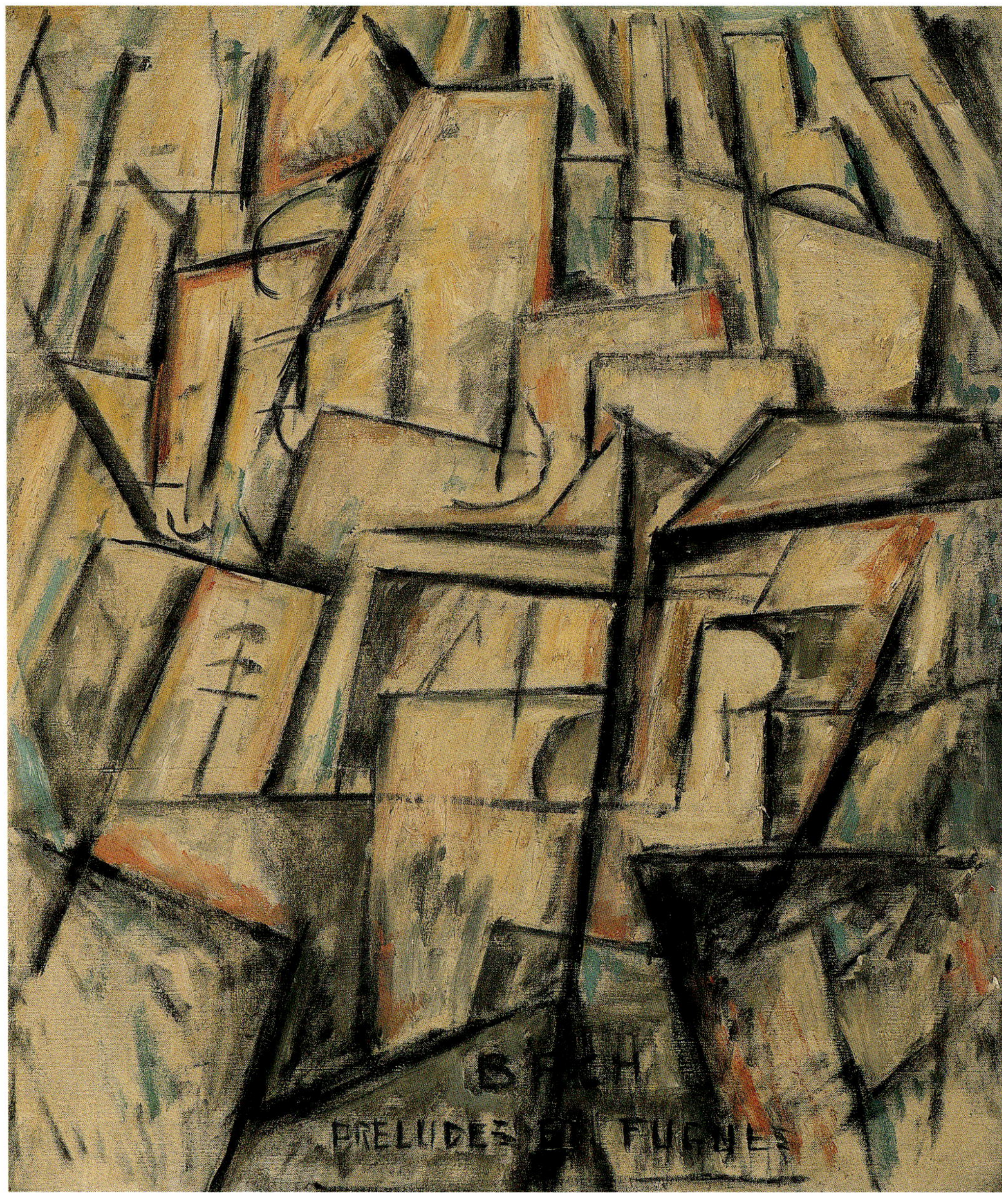

has noted the way in which the formal relationships in Hartley's abstractions imitate the rhythms of specific pieces of music by Bach.[26] And yet Hartley's evocation of music in *Musical Theme (Oriental Symphony)* relies less on color or spatial relationships to convey sound than on the inclusion of musical staffs, notes, and clefs. On the bottom of *Musical Theme No. 2,* Hartley actually wrote the words "BACH PRELUDES ET FUGUES," as if he were afraid the musical analogy would be missed.[27] Equally important in conveying sound are the works' titles, which ask the viewer to consider how painting might be analogous to music. This carries over into the later Provincetown "Movements" of 1916. However, in these paintings of boats and still lifes, there are no obvious musical elements such as notes—only the title suggests an analogy between painting and music.

In his autobiography, *Somehow a Past,* written in the 1930s, Hartley talked of the abstractions of 1912–13 as a kind of "automatic writing."[28] Hartley was undoubtedly aware that surrealists such as the poet André Breton and the painter Max Ernst experimented with forms of automatic writing—the use of stream of consciousness and the accident—as a means of access to the unconscious. However, in using the phrase, Hartley meant to connect his art to an earlier mystical tradition. Automatism was the means by which one of his favorite writers, the German Christian mystic Jakob Böhme, was inspired. Böhme said of his own writings, "Art has not written here, neither was there any time to consider how to set it down punctually, according to the understanding of the letters, but all was ordered according to the direction of the Spirit.... And though I could have wrote in a more accurate, fair, and plain manner, yet the reason was this, that the burning fire often forced forward with speed."[29] As if echoing Böhme, Hartley wrote Stieglitz: "I do not think first but after—allowing the spirit to do its own dictating—as the particular sphere I live in when I work has a language of its own and is not allied to aesthetics as much as related to itself."[30] He referred to his new abstractions in a letter to Rockwell Kent as a "cosmic dictation applied aesthetically to produce a harmony of shapes & colors." Dictation implies words, but Hartley instead refers to the visual elements in *Musical Theme (Oriental Symphony)*: "things that look like stars—birds' wings—sun rays—suns themselves at the sundown time—moon shapes and star beams all radiant together."[31] Hartley fails to mention the seated Buddha in the right corner and the three hands at the center giving the Indian sign *abhaya mudra* (have no fear).[32] These religious elements from Asia infuse the picture with a quality of spirituality and other-worldliness. He boasted to Stiegltiz, "I am told... that I succeed in bringing mysticism and art together."[33] Although his means were primarily visual, he suggested that the pictographic elements of his paintings evoked the origins of written language itself. "I am told by symbologists that there are forms in my pictures which occur in the earliest languages—that which I know nothing of because I read nothing."[34] Paradoxically, the authenticity of this "language" was guaranteed by Hartley's claiming that he *read nothing*.

In truth, Hartley was not only reading the writings of religious mystics like Böhme, but scholarly works like William James's *The Varieties of Religious Experience*. Writing retrospectively in 1932, Hartley said that his 1913 painting *Raptus* (fig. 5) was directly related to James's work.[35] James quotes at length Saint Theresa's claims of perceiving "in one instant how all things are seen and contained in God." According to James, "the deliciousness of some of these states seems to be beyond anything known in ordinary consciousness. It evidently involves organic sensibilities, for it is spoken of as something too extreme to be borne, and as verging on bodily pain." The word "raptus" suggest a rapturous transportation into a spiritual realm, but it also means ravishment or even rape. James discretely alludes to the erotic quality of Theresa's transports: "it is too subtle and piercing a delight for ordinary words to denote. God's touches, the wounds of his spear, references to ebriety and to nuptial union have to figure in the phraseology by which it is shadowed forth." Hartley conveys the sensation of divine knowledge as a triangle superimposed over circles, out of which come sword-like rays of light. The triangle, as well as the three overlapping circles at the bottom and center, refer to the Trinity, but James also mentions Theresa's vision where it was "as if the Deity were an enormous and sovereignly limpid diamond, in which all our actions were contained in such a way that their full sinfulness appeared evident as never before."[36]

Hartley hinted to Kent that he had some sort of mystical experience of his own: "I have enjoyed certain illuminations of late which are of too personal a nature to write down."[37] Perhaps he kept them secret because they involved an erotic component, or maybe Hartley found it embarrassing to admit that he had religious visions. He wrote Stieglitz vaguely of "religious attitudes" "too intimate and personal" to share. Yet if his mystical encounter remained vague, he suggested an equivalence to it in his perception of the ideal geometries that are part of the fabric of *Raptus:* "when the thought 'golden triangle' comes into my mind—I 'see' that triangle—I have a real vision of it—and so with the other shapes."[38] And yet as Robertson points out, Hartley probably knew illustrations of Böhme's work in which many of the geometric and symbolic elements of his paintings appear in diagrammatic form.[39]

Figure 5
Marsden Hartley
Raptus, c. 1913
Oil on canvas, 39⅜ × 32 in. (100 × 81.3 cm)
Currier Museum of Art, Manchester, New Hampshire
Gift of Paul and Hazel Strand in Memory of Elizabeth McCausland, 1965.4

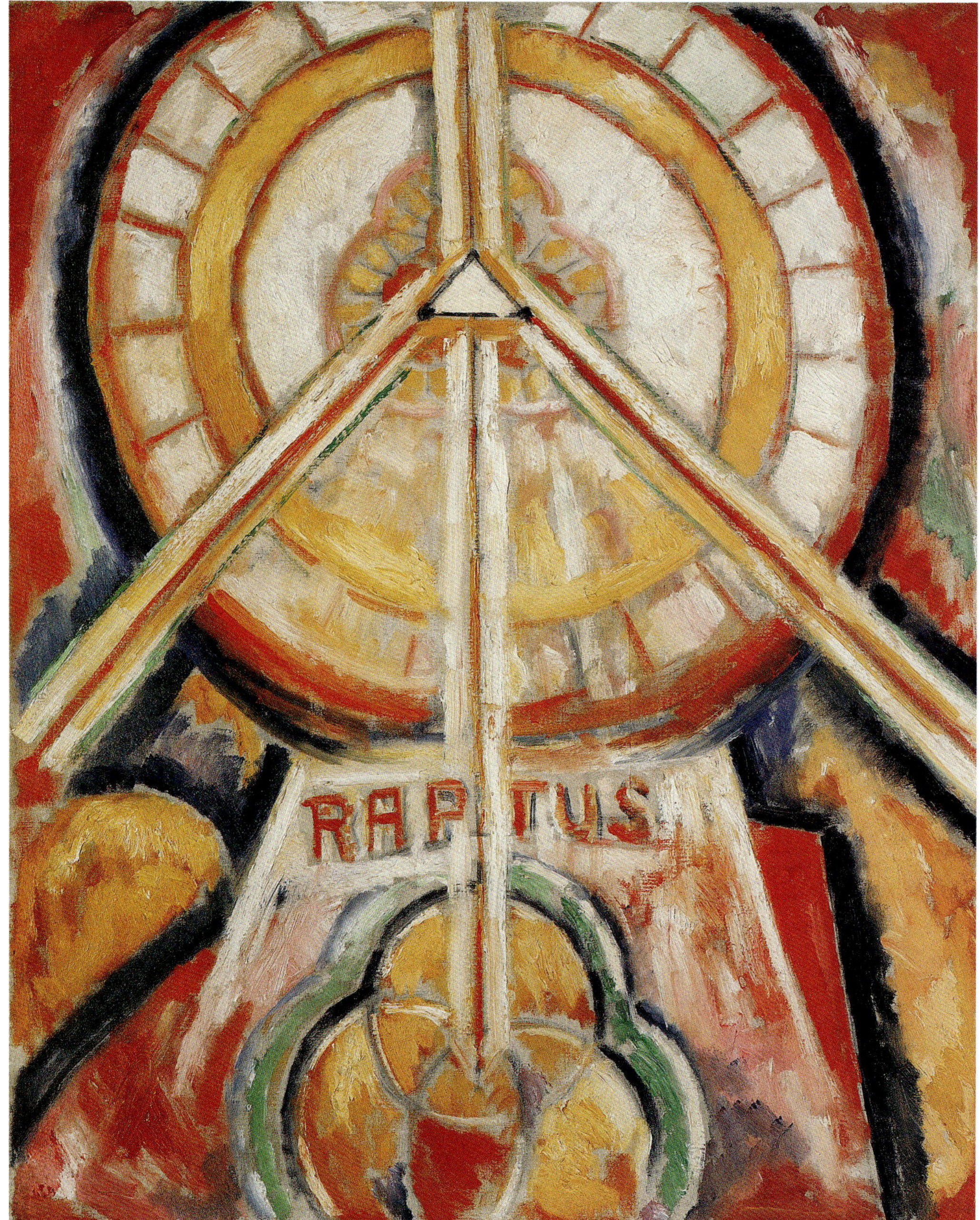

James admits in The *Variety of Religious Experiences* that he cannot share in mystical states: he can "speak of them only at second hand." Nevertheless his goal is convincing the reader "of the reality of the states in question."[40] He believes in the validity of visions like those of Saint Theresa even though the "incommunicableness of the transport is the keynote of all mysticism. Mystical truth exists for the individual who has the transport, but for no one else.... it resembles the knowledge given to us in sensations more than that given by conceptual thought."[41] Yet if such a state of "raptus" could not be conveyed in words, perhaps it could be expressed visually, or so Hartley hoped: "I seek only to arouse the self as I myself am stirred."[42] And yet without the word "Raptus" painted on Hartley's canvas it is doubtful if the picture's connection to mystical transport would be understood. In fact, Hartley later referred to this painting as a portrait of a word, as if the picture were less a record of a real mystical experience, and more an illustration of a psychological phenomenon described by writing.[43] Such a rarified Latin word invites exactly the kind of intellectual exegesis that is the very opposite of the spiritual rapture it promises. Long after the fact, Hartley seemed to remember the painting in the short poem "8 Words":

To
spin
a
rapture
high
is
solar
sanctity.[44]

The generalized abstractness of Hartley's mystical paintings of 1912–13—abstract in the geometry of their forms and the vagueness of the words he used to describe mystical states of consciousness—gives way to the more concrete, secular and finally more *ecstatic* Berlin paintings. God's spears of mystical union that are only hinted at in *Raptus* become the swords and assorted paraphernalia of the military parades that delighted Hartley's eye. Ideal geometries are replaced by shapes he found in the city, such as the eight-pointed stars he saw everywhere on the streets of Berlin.[45] The initial inspiration for *The Warriors* (plate 11) was a royal wedding in one of the central squares of the city. But such pageantry takes on a mystical glow. The soldiers on horseback seem to ascend to heaven, or Valhalla; Hartley's Christian-inspired mysticism fuses with Norse mythology in the manner of Wagner.

In the years 1914–15, Hartley's paint handling becomes thicker and more physical, even as the space in his painting becomes more compressed and less atmospheric. *Portrait of a German Officer* (plate 19) is one of the most corporeal pictures of the period in terms of its painterliness and its suggestion of an actual body. The application with a dry brush of color pigment so that the black underground is never entirely covered up (a technique called scumbling) both intensifies the colors through contrast, and makes us hyperaware of the paint's specific density: thick where it covers, thin where the underpainting peaks through. It is as if we were allowed to follow the process of Hartley's brush; we sense the quality of Hartley's touch visually. With the entire War Motif series of 1914–15 Hartley continues to rethink cubism. Perhaps he derived his brightly colored and patterned version of cubism after seeing Picasso's own synthetic cubist paintings of 1914 the first of which, such as *Man at a Bar,* predated the War Motif series by a few months. Although Hartley did not paste paper and other found materials onto his canvases, their shapes and flattened space suggest that he closely scrutinized Picasso's and Braque's collages of 1912–13 in which word or word fragments play such a large role.

How important are these words in understanding the abstract paintings of this time? Is it a mistake to try to read them? Clement Greenberg, in his famous essay on cubist collage, ignores the literal meaning of such text elements and instead sees the use of letters as a means for asserting the flatness of the picture plane: "the declaration of the surface became so vehement and so extensive as to endow its flatness with far greater power of attraction. The trompe-l'oeil lettering, simply because it was inconceivable on anything but a flat plane, continued to suggest and return to it."[46] Hartley's use of text in the War Motif paintings certainly helps to assert the flatness of his paintings. It is also important to remember that when an artist paints numbers and letters on a canvas, he is doing something very different from when he paints a motif such as a still life. No matter how convincingly he paints an apple, the painted fruit cannot be eaten. But the initials that appear in *Portrait of a German Officer,* even if based on letters found on von Freyburg's possessions, function independently; like any other letters written or printed, they are capable of forming words and being read. But if such a use of text might suggest that Hartley was breaking with traditional means of mimesis, he was not interested in what Rosalind Krauss calls cubism's "representation of representation," that is "the systematic exploration of the conditions of representability entailed by the sign."[47] There is little evidence in Hartley's War Motif series of cubist visual puns that raise doubts about the edges of things and their placement in space. Typically in a synthetic cubist work by Picasso it is difficult to tell what elements are collaged and what are painted. But Hartley's thick paint application assures that the flags, medals, crosses, and stars of the War Motif series will not be mistaken for actual collaged elements made of paper or cloth. For all of its radical flattening of form, most of the objects in *Portrait of a German Officer* are represented straight on; they are securely delimited and identifiable. Finally, Hartley refuses cubism's cutting up of bodies and things. Indeed, what is surprising about *Portrait of a German Officer* is the way it conveys a human presence in its arrangement of shapes and objects without any obvious allusions to fragments of a human body.

Ironically, this presence occurs in a painting that is eloquently about absence. The officer in question was Hartley's beloved friend and possible lover Karl von Freyburg, who died in the early days of World War I.[48] Von Freyburg's initials can be seen in the lower left corner of the painting, as can the number 24, his age at death. Hartley's use of initials and numbers harkens back to his thumbnail sketch of a Picasso painting in which the phrase "Ma Jolie" figures so prominently. Including *Ma Jolie*, the title of a popular song, in such works was a way for Picasso to refer to his lover Eva Gouel. Picasso wrote in 1912 that Eva "is very sweet. I love her very much and I will write this in my paintings."[49]

Von Freyburg's cousin the sculptor Arnold Rönnebeck insisted years later that he was actually half of the portrait. Both Rönnebeck and von Freyburg had been awarded the Iron Cross, which is seen at the center of the image, and Rönnebeck had lent his medal to Hartley to serve as a model. Yet Rönnebeck himself admitted that the cross was more a symbol of his fallen cousin: "Hartley admired its beautiful shape, designed by the great German architect Schinckle in 1813 and asked me to leave it on his palette table as something like a silent symbol of a silent friend who had left us." Rönnebeck also claimed that the *E* that appears on an epaulet stands for Queen Elizabeth of Greece, who was the patroness of the guard in which he served.[50] Yet the *E* also stands for Hartley, whose given name was Edmund (he changed it some ten years earlier). Given the nature of initials to both suggest and withhold full names, it is inevitable that there should be confusion and argument about the significance of the letters in Hartley's War Motif paintings. Hartley's *Portrait of a German Officer* addressed different audiences. Those who were among Hartley's inner circle might be privy to Hartley's erotic longing for von Freyburg. A more general audience, if not completely baffled by the picture's abstraction, might take it to be a celebration of the German war effort. The American avant-garde was overwhelmingly sympathetic to the French and British side. An exception was Hartley's dealer Stieglitz, who had been educated in Germany. Stieglitz alarmed his circle of friends with the vehemence of his defense of Germany and his seeming welcoming of the conflict.[51] Hartley himself was disturbed by how war meant the end to "one of the finest expressions of life impulse and universal intuition anywhere in the world."[52] As if to avoid any controversy, political or biographical, Hartley used words to head off all interpretations. When the War Motif pictures were shown at 291 in 1916 they were accompanied by Hartley's statement that read: "There is no symbolism whatsoever in them; there is no slight intention of that anywhere.... They are merely consultations of the eye—in no sense problem; my notion of the purely pictorial."[53]

Certainly, Hartley's act of focusing on the uniform and flag of a fallen hero has the potential to glorify war. The very attraction of military men is inseparable from the violence of their profession. And yet knowing that the War Motif series was inspired by a love that was deemed threatening to masculine authority undercuts the paintings' militaristic theme. The loud noise of military pomp—the empty public rhetoric of war and patriotism—is transformed into an elegy. Their gorgeous colors and patterns are finally more expressive of affection than the mere presence of the lover's initials or his age when he died: it suggests love's fulfillment. Above all, the picture's, union of bits and pieces of military regalia into an image of formal beauty is the very opposite of the annihilation that characterized World War I.

And yet we cannot forget that Hartley's use of text in the War Motif series imbues his pictures with a significance that most of his contemporaries would not understand. Naming Hartley's friend as the subject of *Portrait of a German Officer* might be falling into the trap identified by Krauss in her essay "In the Name of Picasso." Krauss attacks the use of biographical information to reduce a work of art to "the actual people who lie behind a set of fictional characters":

> *It is as though the shifting, changing sands of visual polysemy, of multiple meanings and regroupings, have made us intolerably nervous, so that we wish to find the bedrock of sense. We wish to achieve a type of signification beyond which there can be no further reading or interpretation. Interpretation, we insist, must be made to stop somewhere. And where more absolutely and appropriately than in the act of what the police call "positive identification"?*[54]

This attack on the search for a proper name precedes Krauss's discussion of cubism cited above. It is interesting that when Hartley described Picasso's work in 1912, he said that "there is everything classified and unnamable here,"[55] as if for Hartley cubism was a process of signification that withholds the names of things and people. By using initials, Hartley was playing his own game of naming and refusing to name. Yet there is no reason that the naming of von Freyburg should end the process of interpretation, as Krauss might predict. On the contrary, it raises a whole series of questions about the relationship of representation to issues of sexuality, identity, and form. Indeed, the issue of homosexuality, or "the love that dare not speak its name," puts into play the mechanisms by which meanings and feelings are expressed or not expressed, or to use Krauss's own terms, why certain names are proper or improper.

The unnamable or unreadable seems to be the very subject of a still life entitled *Handsome Drinks* (plate 24), painted just after the War Motif series upon his return to New York. Its assorted glasses and goblets evoke the cafés that Hartley frequented in Paris. The glass in the left corner is used for absinthe, which is traditionally poured over the spoon and sugar cube that rests on its lip. Absinthe, now illegal in the United States, was a favorite drink of the late-nineteenth-century artists and poets who valued its supposed hallucinogenic and creative properties. It is less easy to identify the contents of the goblet in the center with its tongue-like protrusion, or the purpose of the white box on the right. The word fragments "LUS" and "LOGH" are even more puzzling. "Lus" suggests lust, the *T* being hidden by the goblet, and "LOGH" could be "low" as in behaving in a decadent manner. "Logh" used to mean lake or pool, and it was also once an alternate spelling for "laugh."[56] But would Hartley know this? Perhaps, as in the case of Karl von Freyburg, these letters are a code for possible male friends. In this sense the handsome drinks would refer not only to beverages, but also to handsome drinking companions. *Handsome Drinks* is closely related to two other still lifes from the same period, *A Nice Time* (plate 25) and *One Portrait of One Woman* (plate 26). *A Nice Time* depicts a flowerpot on a table, and includes the words "BON JOUR" and "HAH," and the cryptic "MLEAGNA." Scholars connect *One Portrait of One Woman* with Gertrude Stein, who was a strong supporter of Hartley's work, and who wrote a symbolic portrait of Hartley in the play *IIIIIIIII* that seems to have inspired this picture. The picture focuses on the ritual of tea that was such an important part of Hartley's visits to Stein. The *I* of the play's title, which is both the personal pronoun and the roman numeral one, has been converted into the word "MOI" in the painting, as well as the digit-like candles that give the tea ceremony the quality of a religious experience (this is reinforced by the yellow cross that mystically appears in the cup).[57] Interpolating from *One Portrait of One Woman,* Robertson has suggested that all three of these still lifes are portraits, but if so, the identities of the other two subjects remain unknown.[58] The key word in the trilogy is "HAH," which appears in *A Nice Time.* It evokes not only the first syllable of Hartley's name, but laughter as well. The nonsensical quality of the words suggests the influence of the Dadaist Francis Picabia, whose 1915 caricatures of Stieglitz and Marius De Zayas were known to Hartley. In *Adventures in the Arts,* Hartley went so far as to declare himself a Dadaist. In the concluding essay, "The Importance of Being 'Dada,'" he criticized the seriousness and religious fervor in which people treated works of art: "Dada is irritated by those who write 'Art, Beauty, Truth', with capital letters, and who make of them entities superior to man," and he quotes without attribution: "Dada scoffs at capital letters, atrociously."[59]

One of the strangest things about the three cryptic still lifes is how *atrociously* Hartley fashions the actual capital letters. Unlike the work of the cubists, or the later poster portraits of his friend Demuth, Hartley makes no attempt to imitate the look of printed text in the signs or newspapers that could actually have been seen in a café. These letters are quite different too from the beautiful fashioned script and numbers that appear in the War Motif series. Nevertheless, the capital letters of the three strange paintings, while difficult to understand, and crudely written, bestow significance on the paintings. They insist that the images are more than decorative arrangements of objects and shapes. They ask the viewer to *read,* even if they say nothing.

Words appear in a less cryptic fashion in *Elsa* (plate 28) and *Trixie* (plate 29), two of the Provincetown and Bermuda paintings of 1916. The names "Elsa" and "Trixie" written across the bows of the boats give specificity to otherwise highly abstracted vessels. Robertson attributes such subject matter to Hartley's attraction to sailors, yet these paintings' muted colors and linear geometry negate any sense of desire. It is as if such names were a mere remnant of the specific experiences that had inspired the images, rather than central to their overall meaning, which is now a matter of composition and color.

With the exception of his signature, text disappeared in Hartley landscapes and still lifes of the twenties. One might expect that the move away from painting words would announce a less intellectual and more intuitive way of painting, one more connected to emotions. But this was the period in which Hartley claimed to banish the biographical from his art. He insisted that working from nature was an intellectual process, perhaps because it involved dealing with issues of form rather than with emotional attachments. He would have nothing to do with "private extra versions or introversions of specific individuals": "I have made the complete return to nature, and nature is as we all know, primarily an intellectual idea. I am satisfied that painting also is like nature, an intellectual idea, and that the laws of nature as presented to the mind through the eye—and the eye is the painter's first and last vehicle—are the means of transport to the real mode of thought: the only legitimate source of esthetic experience for the intelligent painter."[60] Yet for all of Hartley's emphasis on the intellectual aspects of painting from nature, many of his landscapes from this period have a decidedly emotional quality. This is particularly true of his series of "recollections" of New Mexico painted in Berlin in 1923 (plates 38–39). In dark rust reds, murky blacks, and grays they depict the Southwest as a bleak place. Contrary to Hartley's claim, nature in these landscapes seems less a matter of an intellectual concept than a reflection of the artist's loneliness and anxiety. Yet even when Hartley self-consciously pursued a formal experiment, as in his attempt to repaint Cézanne's beloved mountain, Mont Sainte-Victoire (plate 43), the results were characteristically expressionistic. Cézanne's blues and greens become hot pinks, and Cézanne's subtle overlapping of transparent planes of color, Hartley's anxious crosshatching.

In the end, Hartley's attempt at being an "intellectual experimentalist" did not last. It is significant that when his art returned to an emphatic expressionism, he began to bring words and painting together again as well. On the back of one of his first Dogtown canvases, *In the Moraine, Dogtown Common, Cape Ann* from 1931—a picture filled with hulking boulders that suggest precisely "private introversions"—he copied three lines of a T. S. Eliot poem, "Ash Wednesday," which Scott claims characterized "his own mental and physical situation":

> *Teach us to care and not to care*
> *Teach us all to sit still*
> *Even among the rocks.*[61]

Words also appear as graffiti on a huge boulder in *Whale's Jaw, Dogtown Common* (1934). Yet the use of language in the Dogtown paintings, whether on the front or back, is incidental to the expressive force of the pictures. This is not the case of an extraordinary series of paintings Hartley envisioned would decorate an "Arcane Library." Completed in 1932–33, when Hartley was living in Mexico, they were conceived as "word pictures" or portraits of words in the manner of his earlier *Raptus* painting.[62] Like that picture, they were an attempt to come to terms with the mystic writers that Hartley was reading again. *Morgenrot* (plate 52) illustrates Jakob Böhme's book *Aurora or Morning Redness.* Hartley tried to imagine what the divine word, as mediated through Böhme's vision, would look like. Ludington writes: "For Böhme, the seventh realm of divine corporeality—or the materialized word—was where individual sounds contributed to the divine harmony of the spheres. In *Morgenrot* the seventh sphere is on God's divine hand made corporeal, *7* being a symbol of perfect order and completeness."[63] His painting dedicated to Paracelsus, *Yliaster (Paracelsus),* uses a volcano and a divine ray of light to suggest the powerful cosmic forces that this alchemist and physician believed emanated from below and above the earth. *The Transference of Richard Rolle* (1932) is an homage to the fourteenth-century British author of *The Fire of Love.* Hartley clearly identified with Rolle's hermetic and wandering existence out of which came an ecstatic experience of God. Rolle's work seemed to hold out the promise of finding even in intense isolation a sensation of love and well-being. Rolle wrote: "I had never thought that we exiles could possibly have known such warmth, so sweet was the devotion it kindled. It set my soul aglow as if a real fire was burning there."[64] At the center in the midst of a fluffy cloud, a triangle frames Rolle's initial. It is fused with the letter *Y,* to stand for his union with God, that is YHESU, a derivative of Jesus. The letter *R* repeats in the clouds that hang over the red desert, symbolizing his ascension into the heavens. Hartley wrote a poem to Rolle on the back of the picture one line of which reads "His home is in a morning cloud."[65]

Hartley wrote to Adelaide Kuntz about his combining of "two expressions" in *The Transference of Richard Rolle*—poetry and painting. He hoped that "if it comes out of it all might come a fresher kind of self-expression." Unfortunately, Hartley's problem is encapsulated in his planned title for the entire series, "Panels for an Arcane Library." Arcane means "mysteriously obscure," implying not the immediate experience of God that was central to Rolle's experience, but the study of ancient texts housed in a dusty library. Hartley admitted to Kuntz that it was "A pity that I can't feel these things for myself (or perhaps not) for I can't image a personal deity—it all seems so sort of irrelevant to me—but I enjoy having the mystics tell of this experience nonetheless and what's more—I believe they had them."[66] The results are pictures whose very crudeness and iconic compositions, heavily influenced by the Mexican muralist José Clemente Orozco, are meant to be expressive of a primitive intensity of experience that Hartley only read about.

Far more successful is another visionary painting that Hartley completed a year later and which deals with yet another writer, *Eight Bells Folly, Memorial for Hart Crane* (plate 54). In this case, Hartley knew his subject. Hartley had met Crane several times, but they probably only became good friends a few months before Crane committed suicide off the coast of Mexico. Crane's death effected Hartley profoundly—he wrote several versions of elegies.[67] Like Hartley, Crane was homosexual and deeply unhappy about it. More importantly, Crane's writer's block following the completion of *The Bridge* raised for Hartley the specter of an artist who had seemingly lost his inspiration. Given Hartley's own travails, his loneliness and restless shifting of styles and subject matters with little critical success, Crane's fate must have been terrifying.[68] Hartley described his plan for the memorial in this way: "It has a very mad look as I wish it to have—there is a ship foundering—a sun, a moon, two triangular clouds—a bell with '8' on it—symbolizing eight bells—or Noon when he jumped off—and around the bell are a lot of men's eyes—that look up from below to see who the new lodger is to be—on one cloud will be the number 33—Hart's age—and according to some occult beliefs is the dangerous age of man—for if he survives 33—he lives on—Christ was supposed to be 33."[69] Although *Eight Bells Folly* shares with the mystical paintings of the previous year a similar use of symbols, its apocalyptic vision is not redemptive or transcendent. Crane's art did not save him. Yet in working through an artist's death, Hartley rediscovered his own subject matter. The shark in the foreground links the painting to Winslow Homer's *Gulf Stream* in which a beautiful male is about to be devoured. The turn to this quintessentially American artist was a crucial step in Hartley's return to the Northeast where he was born and his conscious decision to take up Homer's role as the painter from Maine.

The great late paintings based on Hartley's experience of Nova Scotia and Maine rarely include text. In so many of the earlier works, text was a means of investing a still life or landscape with a connection to a person whom Hartley prized. Hartley had almost never painted people, although he did some drawings and pastels of nudes in the 1920s (plate 40). However, in the late 1930s Hartley began to paint monumental figures. Instead of referencing his heroes symbolically, he made direct representations of John Donne, Abraham Lincoln, and Albert Pinkham Ryder. And he painted Alty Mason as a strapping youth with a flower in his hair and his shirt open to reveal his hairy chest so that there is no way to mistake his affection. And yet if he did not have to paint words onto his canvas to give them added significance, at no other time in Hartley's career is there such a seamless relationship between his poetry and his painting. It diminishes neither production to say that Hartley's portraits of the Mason family, with their monumental stoic faces, and his prose poem "Cleophas and His Own," which tells the tragic story of the deaths of the Mason sons, enrich each other. Compare his highly erotic description of Francis Mason, alias Cleophas, and his wonderful portrait *Cleophas, Master of the "Gilda Grey"* (plate 68):

His body is as hard as the rocks and his hands being huge look as if they could take trees in twos and twist them together like rope.
I look at him as we walk among the pyrites glistening in the iron bound shale on one shore of the island, the which he digs out with his fingers, dislocates them with the press of his strong digits, see him break out of what seems to be like stolen sleep of thought into articulation and a boy's smile, feeling the translucence of his spirit covering me, I feeling myself growing bigger. I can't help this, neither of us can, we are two human beings together who have learned much in the university of the imagination, he from the sea—I from the little things on the edge of the sea, intricately enfolding, binding us together and I know it is a case of true unspoken love.[70]

The poem reminds us that Hartley was physically attracted not only to the Mason sons, but to the father as well, whom he converts into a Whitmanesque patriarch, both wise and sensuous. The flower that the father holds in his hand in the portrait is a token of that "unspoken love" between two men which Hartley, at the end of his life, now has the courage to speak.

Words and paint come together one final time in the 1938 version of *Fishermen's Last Supper* (plate 64). Even before the Mason sons and their cousin had died at sea, Hartley wrote that he planned to do a picture of his newfound family: "The table is long and narrow. I'm in the center, Donny right, Alty left, and sister on the other side—walls blue, furniture black—Mama always in black with white apron—boys and papa in overalls and mystic looking."[71] After the accident, he made a picture that is something like the description, removing himself from the scene, as if the two boys' deaths also severed him from such domestic bliss. Across the bottom are the words "Mene Mene." They refer to the Book of Daniel in the Old Testament, and the story of Belshazzar's Feast. As the Babylonian king's guests drink from gold and silver vessels confiscated from the Jewish temple in Jerusalem, a mysterious disembodied hand appears and writes the words "Mene, Mene, Tekel, Upharsin" on a wall. Daniel interprets these Aramaic words to mean "God hath numbered thy kingdom and finished it. Thou art weighed in the balances, and art found wanting."[72] Belshazzar was defeated and killed the next day. According to Scott, the presence of the words was Hartley's way of alluding to "Alty's impetuous bravado—for his pride and defiance of God,"[73] which lead not only to his own death, but the deaths of his younger brother and cousin. But the words also promise divine salvation, evoking both God's liberation of the Jews from Belshazzar's tyranny and the Last Judgment, when the dead will rise and their souls will be weighed. In inscribing the words "Mene Mene" on his painting, Hartley was in effect mimicking a moment when God, the ultimate artist, is driven to write on the world. Indeed, Daniel, in interpreting the message, is a precursor of the modern critic or art historian whose job is to interpret "the handwriting on the wall." Nevertheless, Hartley decided to eliminate these words from his later and larger version of the painting (plate 70). He also removed his favorite eight-pointed stars from above their heads. Such literary and symbolic references now seem extraneous. Each of the family members is rendered with the simplest of means—crude black outlines, and thick patchy paint. But their crudely painted bodies are set off against a marvelously deep blue background—a blue that suggests the stormy waters that claimed the two boys, and the promise that in such a death there is redemption.

Hartley no longer needed to write words on his canvas to suggest spirituality; he claimed to have found God's handwriting all around him in the landscape of Maine: "I know I have seen God now. The occult connection that is established when one loves nature was complete."[74] He had only to paint that landscape with his newfound confidence to suggest mystical states. And yet right up to the last Hartley continued to write incessantly. As Ludington movingly writes, "living alone and often lonely, he found a sort of companionship in the voice on the page that spoke to him."[75] Although his words never reached the level of his visual production, his late writing, like the late paintings, is more direct and powerful than what came before. He continued to doubt language's ability to explain art and to express emotions. In the poem "A Word and Its Meaning," he decried the way the perfect word falls into "that terrible old cause of confusion—conversation."[76] But to the last, he alternated between painting and writing. Among his effects are a portfolio of photographs, press clippings, and programs he had gathered in preparation for writing a book on the circus. No matter how sublime his pictures, Hartley had no intention of deteriorating into just a painter.

Notes

I want to thank James Timothy Voorhies for sharing his manuscript of *My Dear Stieglitz: Letters of Marsden Hartley and Alfred Stieglitz, 1912–1915* (Columbia: University of South Carolina Press, forthcoming). I would also like to thank Nicholas Boshnack, Esther da Costa Meyer, Amy Ellis, Randall Griffey, Elizabeth Kornhauser, and Townsend Ludington for their advice and suggestions.

1 According to Gail R. Scott, "Hartley told Leon Tebbetts that he didn't want his poems to be illustrated with his paintings, that he wished to maintain the integrity of the two art forms." However, Scott goes on to say that "there are, indeed, many enlightening and beautiful parallels between poems and pictures... and it is generally *expected* that these be shown together." Gail R. Scott, "Editor's Preface," in *Collected Poems*, 27.
2 Hartley to Alfred Stieglitz, 13 June 1913, Beinecke/Yale.
3 Hartley to Alfred Stieglitz, October 1913, Beinecke/Yale.
4 Charles Demuth, "Across a Greco is Written," *Creative Art*, no. 5 (September 1929): 634.
5 Hartley to Alfred Stieglitz, 15 March 1915, Beinecke/Yale.
6 Hartley, "The Dearth of Critics," in *Adventures*, 237–40.
7 Hartley, "Prefatory Note," in *Adventures*, iii.
8 Quoted in Scott, "Editor's Preface," in *Collected Poems*, 22.
9 Quoted in Robert Creeley, "Foreword," in *Collected Poems*, 18.
10 Creeley, in *Collected Poems*, 18.
11 Hartley, "Prefatory Note," in *Adventures*, iii.
12 Hartley to Alfred Stieglitz, May 1913, Beinecke/Yale.
13 *Autobiography*, 180.
14 Marsden Hartley, "Whitman and Cézanne," in *Adventures*, 36.
15 Ibid., 32.
16 Hartley to Mabel Dodge (Luhan), 1916, Beinecke/Yale.
17 Hartley to Alfred Stieglitz, June 1913, Beinecke/Yale.
18 See Weinberg.
19 See Ludington 1992, 55–56.
20 Hartley to Alfred Stieglitz, July 1912, Beinecke/Yale.
21 Clement Greenberg, "Review of Two Exhibitions of Marsden Hartley," *Nation*, 30 December 1944; reprinted in Greenberg, *The Collected Essays and Criticism*, ed. John O'Brian, vol. 1 (Chicago: University of Chicago Press, 1986), 247.
22 See Harold Bloom, *The Anxiety of Influence: A Theory of Poetry* (New York: Oxford University Press, 1973).
23 Hartley to Alfred Stieglitz, received 20 December 1912, Beinecke/Yale.
24 Hartley to Norma Berger, 30 December 1912, Beinecke/Yale. Despite his use of musical terminology to describe his color theory, Kandinsky himself insisted that he was not painting music. See Wassily Kandinsky, "Cologne Lecture," in *Kandinsky: Complete Writings on Art*, ed. Kenneth C. Lindsay and Peter Vergo (New York: Da Capo Press, 1994), 400. I want to thank Esther da Costa Meyer for this citation.
25 See Wassily Kandinsky and Franz Marc, eds., *The Blaue Reiter Almanac*, ed. Klaus Lankheit (New York: Viking, 1974). See also Ludington, 84–86.
26 Robertson, 43.
27 As Esther da Costa Meyer reminds me, both George Braque and August Macke did paintings in 1912 dedicated to Bach's music.
28 *Autobiography*, 83.
29 Quoted in Evelyn Underhill, *The Mystics of the Church* (New York: Schocken Books, 1964), 217.
30 Hartley to Alfred Stieglitz, week of 18 May 1913, Beinecke/Yale.
31 Hartley to Rockwell Kent, 24 December 1912, Kent Papers, Archives/Smithsonian.
32 See Scott, 42.
33 Hartley to Alfred Stieglitz, week of 18 May 1913, Beinecke/Yale.
34 Ibid.
35 See Scott, 39. Hartley to Adelaide Kuntz, 17 February 1933, Hartley Papers, Archives/Smithsonian.
36 William James, *The Varieties of Religious Experience* (New York: Collier Books, 1961), 323–24.
37 Hartley to Rockwell Kent, 24 December 1912, Kent Papers, Archives/Smithsonian.
38 Hartley to Alfred Stieglitz, week of 18 May 1913, Beinecke/Yale.
39 Robertson, 45.
40 James, *Varieties of Religious Experience*, 299.
41 Ibid., 318.
42 Hartley to Alfred Stieglitz, week of 18 May 1912, Beinecke/Yale.
43 Hartley to Adelaide Kuntz, 17 February 1933, Hartley Papers, Archives/Smithsonian.
44 Hartley, "8 Words," in *Collected Poems*, 199. The number *8* was particularly important for Hartley, appearing in different guises throughout his career. It symbolized power and transcendence.
45 Hartley to Alfred Stieglitz, August 1913, Beinecke/Yale.
46. Clement Greenberg, "The Pasted-Paper Revolution," in Greenberg, *Collected Essays*, vol. 4 (1993), 63.
47 Krauss writes "in the great, complex cubist collages, each element is fully diacritical, instantiating both line and color, closure and openness, plane and recession.... What is

systematized in collage is not so much the forms of a set of studio paraphernalia, but the very system of forms." Rosalind E. Krauss, *The Originality of the Avant-Garde and Other Modernist Myths* (Cambridge: MIT Press, 1989), 34–37.

48 As Patricia McDonnell points out, the exact nature of Hartley's friendship to Von Freyburg is unclear. See her "El Dorado: Marsden Hartley in Imperial Berlin," in Patricia McDonnell, *Dictated by Life: Marsden Hartley's German Paintings and Robert Indiana's Hartley Elegies* (Minneapolis: Frederick R. Weisman Art Museum, University of Minnesota, 1995).

49 Picasso wrote this in a letter to D. H. Kahnweiler, dated 12 June 1912. The letter is cited in Kirk Varnedoe and Adam Gopnik, *High & Low* (New York: Museum of Modern Art, 1990), n. 21.

50 Arnold Rönnebeck to Duncan Phillips, n.d. [after March 1944], Beinecke/Yale.

51 Stieglitz's pro-German stance and his initial welcoming of World War I is discussed in Penelope Nixon, *Steichen: A Biography* (New York: Clarkson Potter, 1997), 405.

52 Hartley to Alfred Stieglitz, 29 October 1914, Beinecke/Yale.

53 Hartley, "1916 Catalogue Statement, 291," in *On Art*, 67.

54 Krauss, *Originality of the Avant-Garde*, 28.

55 Hartley to Alfred Stieglitz, July 1912, Beinecke/Yale.

56 According to the *Oxford English Dictionary* "Logh" is related to "lough," which is an Anglo-Irish obsolete variant for "loch," meaning a body of water. It is also an obsolete variant for "low" and "laugh." *Oxford English Dictionary* (Oxford: Clarendon Press, 1989), 1107. I want to thank Amy Ellis for bringing this citation to my attention and for help on trying to decipher the word fragments in Hartley's painting.

57 See Lyndel King, *Marsden Hartley, 1908–1942: The Ione and Hudson D. Walker Collection* (Minneapolis: University Art Museum, University of Minnesota, 1984), 22. Gertrude Stein's word portrait of Hartley was published in *Camera Work*, no. 45 (January 1914): 17, 19–20. See also Ludington 1992, 7–8.

58 See entry 121 in Christie's, *Important American Paintings, Drawings and Sculpture*, 30 November 1999.

59 Hartley, "The Importance of Being 'Dada,'" in *Adventures*, 252.

60 Hartley, "Art and the Personal Life," in *On Art*, 71. The essay was originally published in *Creative Art*, June 1928.

61 Scott, 90.

62 Hartley to Adelaide Kuntz, 17 February 1933, Hartley Papers, Archives/Smithsonian.

63 Townsend Ludington, *Seeking the Spiritual: The Paintings of Marsden Hartley* (Ithaca: Cornell University Press, 1998), 58.

64 Richard Rolle, *The Fire of Love*, trans. from Old English by Clifton Wolters (London: Penguin Books, 1972), 45.

65 Hartley, "Richard Rolle," in *Collected Poems*, 295. See Scott, 98.

66 Hartley to Adelaide Kuntz, 28 July 1932, Hartley Papers, Archives/Smithsonian.

67 See, for example, Hartley, "Un Recuerdo—Hermano—Hart Crane" and "To H.C.," in *Collected Poems*, 119, 151.

68 Hartley's relationship to Crane and his poetry are discussed at length in Weinberg.

69 Hartley to Adelaide Kuntz, 5 December 1933, Hartley Papers, Archives/Smithsonian.

70 Marsden Hartley, "Cleophas and His Own: A North Atlantic Tragedy," in Ferguson, 94.

71 Hartley to Adelaide Kuntz, 6 November 1935, Hartley Papers, Archives/Smithsonian.

72 This discussion of the Old Testament story is indebted to David Bjelajac's book on Washington Allston's *Belshazzar's Feast*, in his *Millennial Desire and the Apocalyptic Vision of Washington Allston* (Washington, D.C.: Smithsonian Institution Press, 1988). According to Scott, Hartley was interested in Allston's doomed painting. Scott, 161 n 9.

73 Scott, 110.

74 Hartley to Elizabeth Sparhawk Jones, 23 October 1939, Beinecke/Yale, quoted in Ludington, *Seeking the Spiritual*, 23.

75 Ludington, *Seeking the Spiritual*, 8–9.

76 Hartley, "A Word and Its Meaning," in *Collected Poems*, 199.

PLATES 38–50

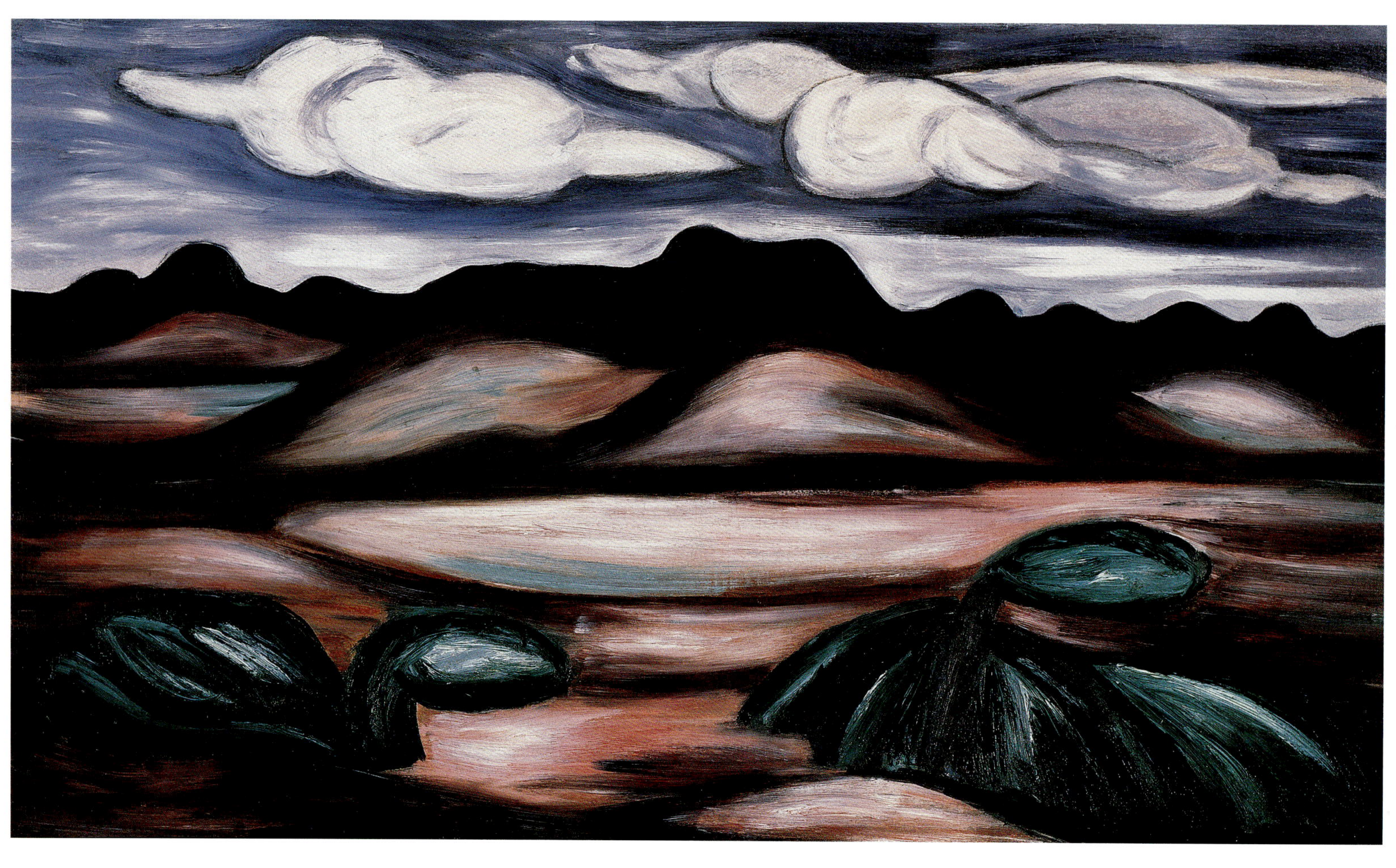

38
Landscape, New Mexico, 1923
Oil on canvas, 21¾ × 35¾ in.
Collection of AXA Financial, Inc., through its subsidiary
The Equitable Life Assurance Society of the United States

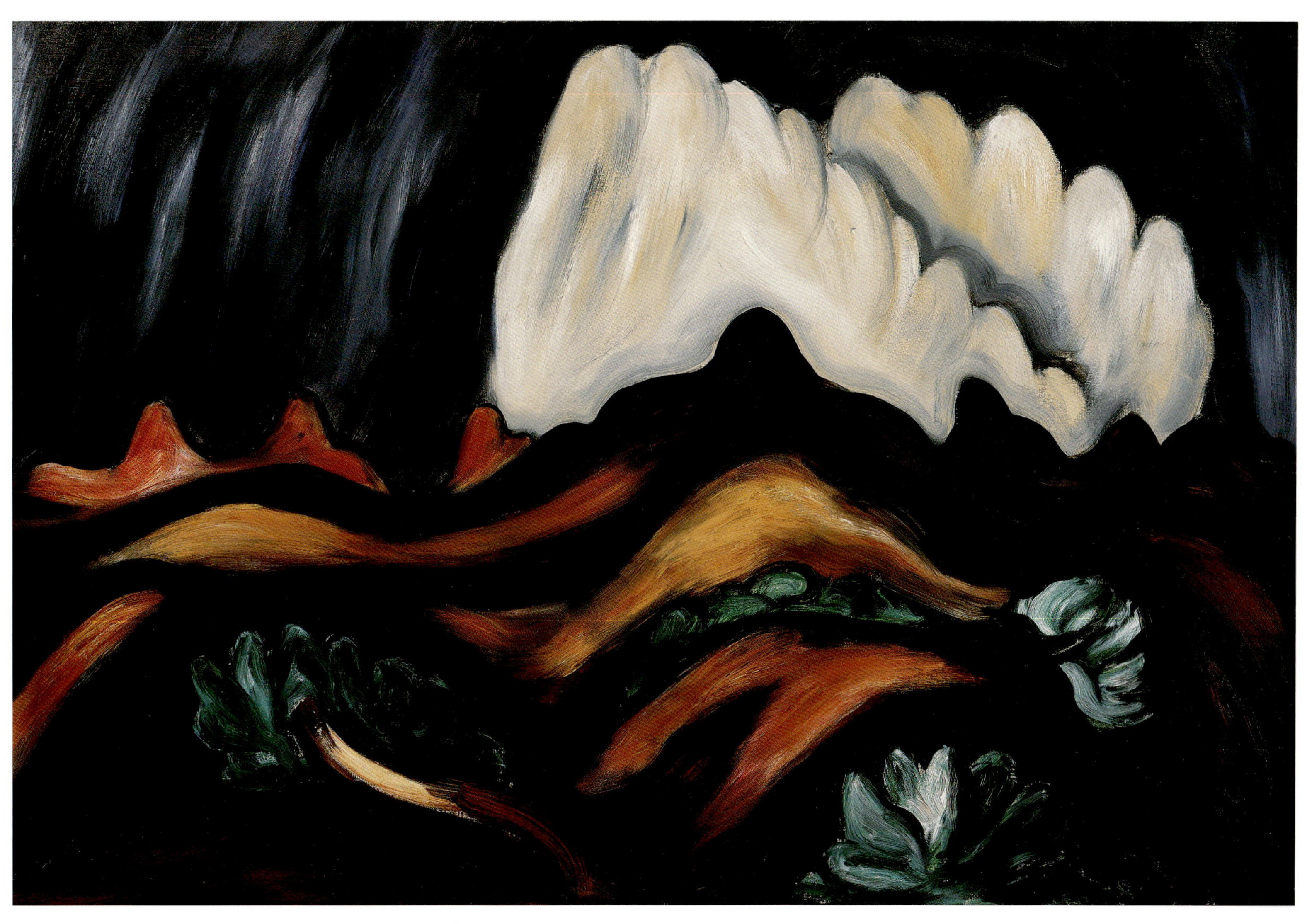

39

New Mexico Recollections—Storm, 1923

Oil on canvas, 29 × 41½ in.

Private Collection

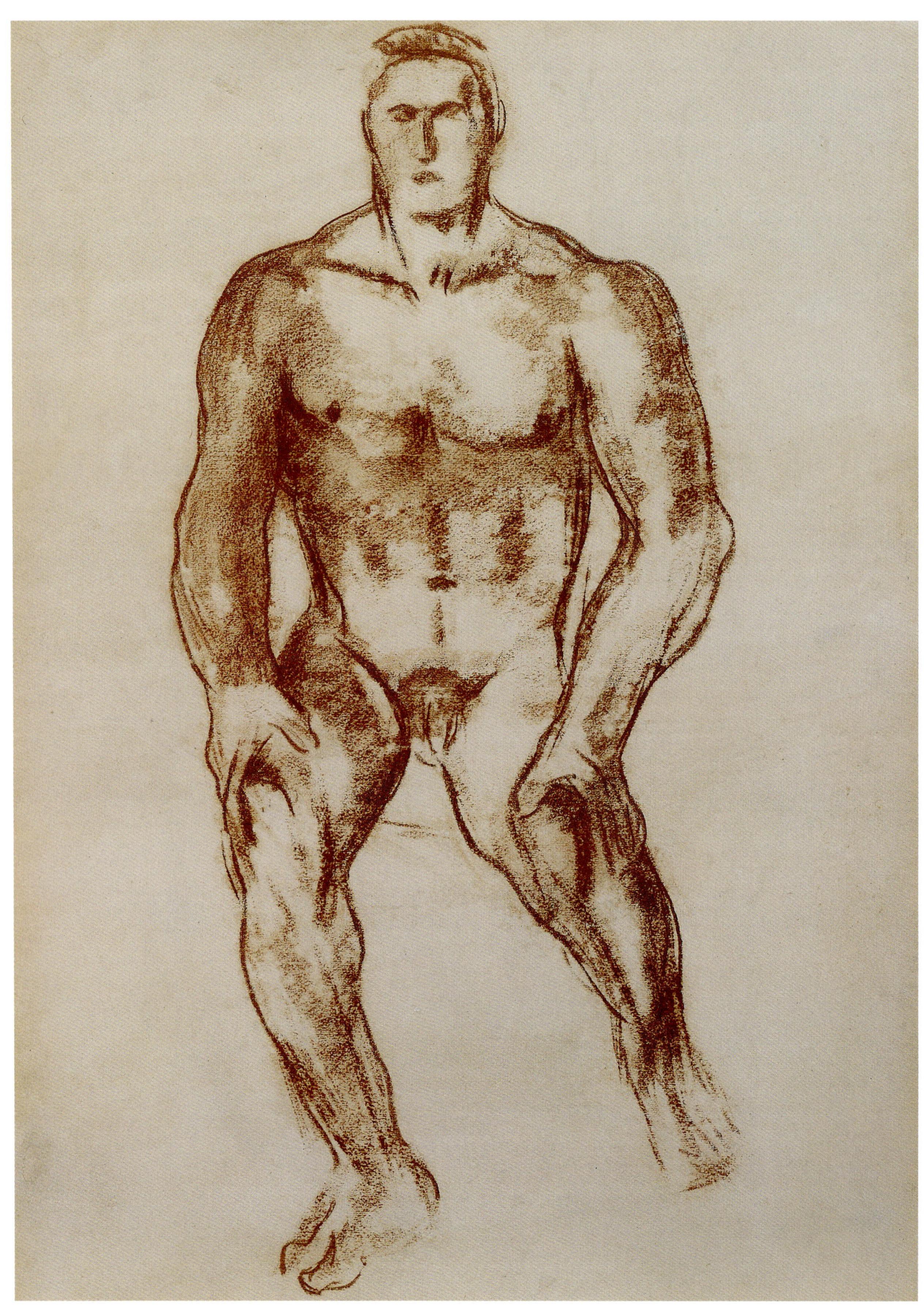

40
Seated Male Nude, 1922
Sanguine pastel on paper, 24 × 17 in.
Babcock Galleries, New York

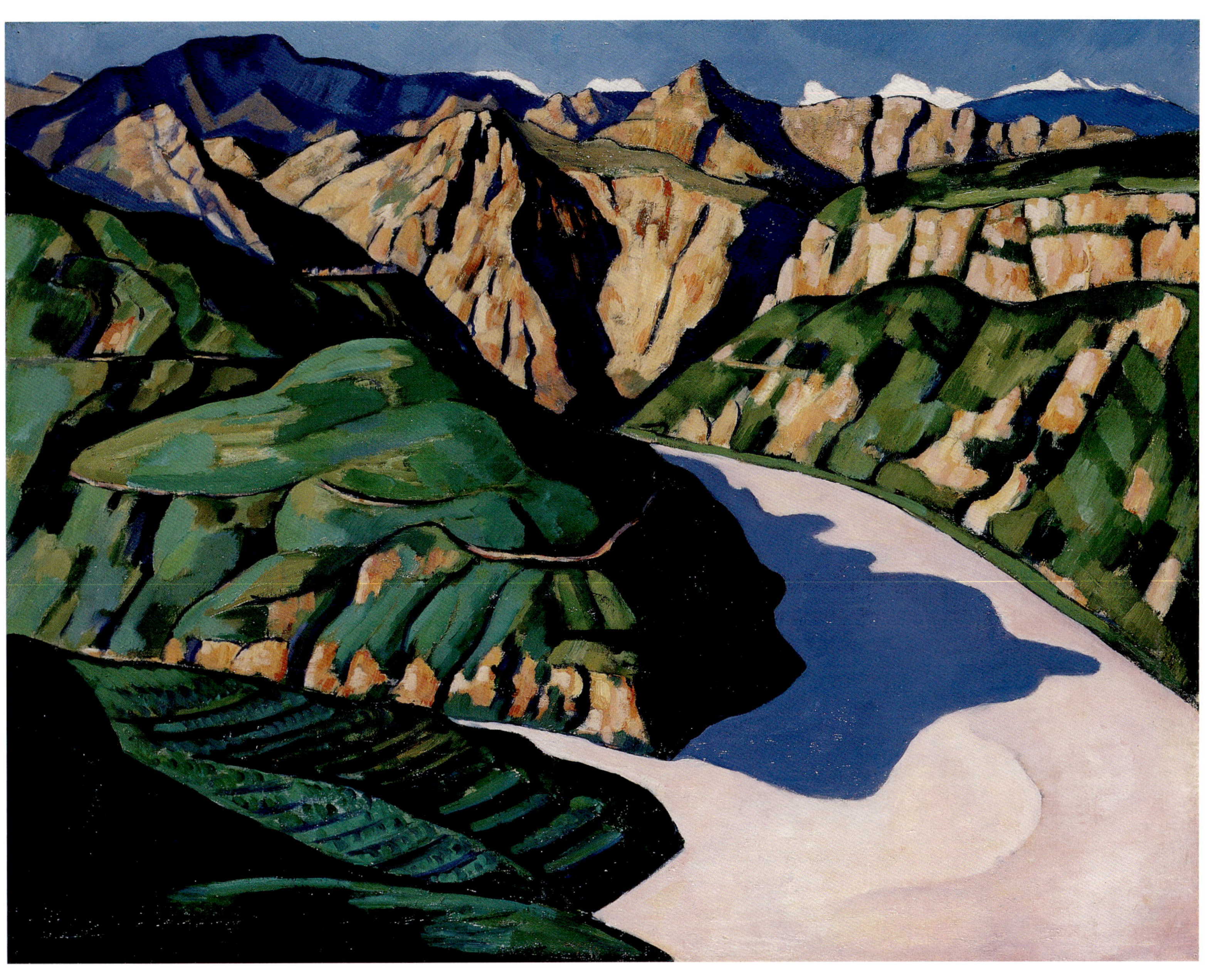

41

Landscape, Vence, 1925–26

Oil on canvas, 25⅝ × 31⅞ in.

Frederick R. Weisman Art Museum, University of Minnesota, Minneapolis

Bequest of Hudson Walker from the Ione and Hudson Walker Collection

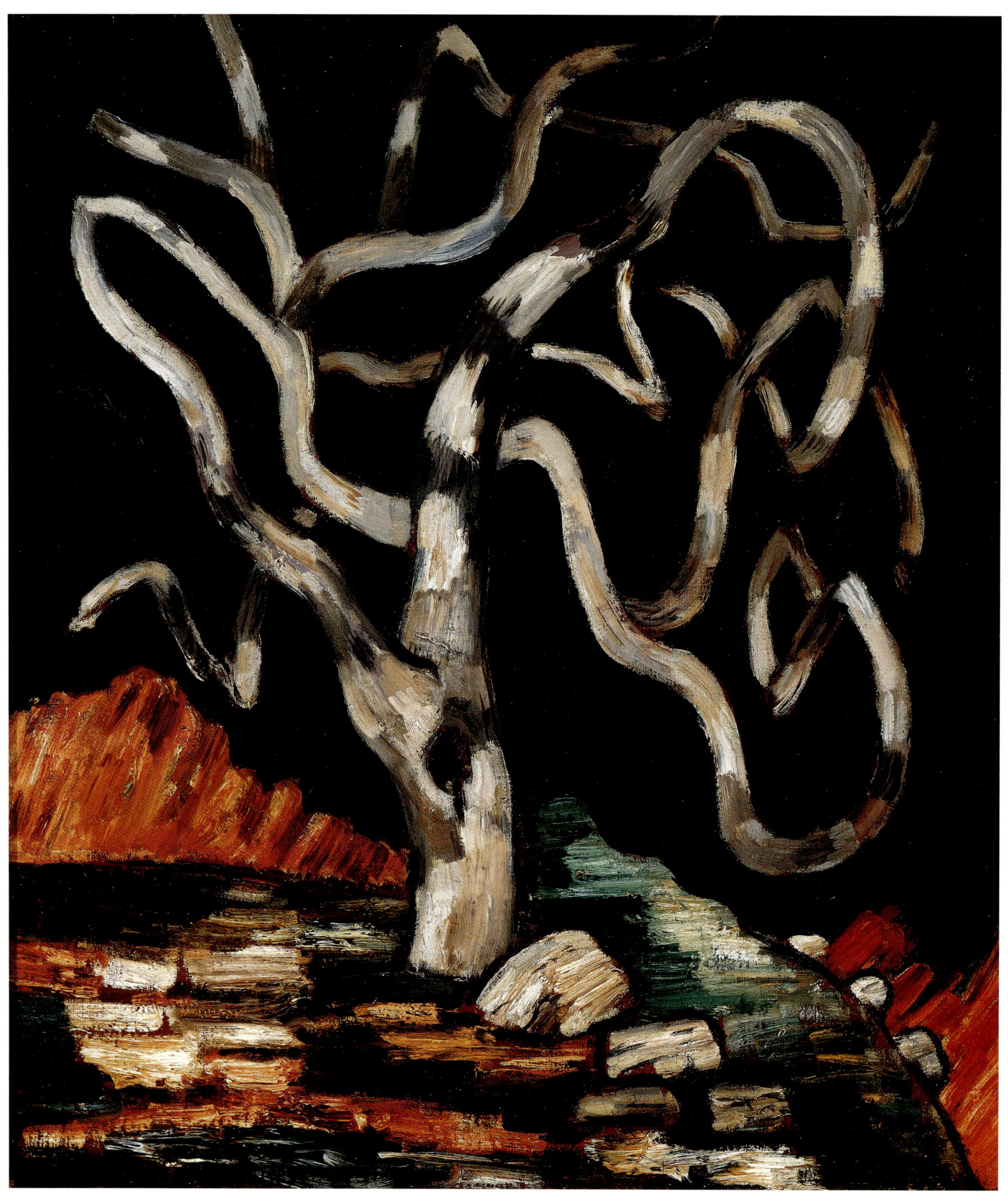

42

Fig Tree, c. 1926–28

Oil on canvas, 24¼ × 20½ in.

Private Collection

Courtesy of Martha Parrish & James Reinish, Inc., New York

(Right) Detail, Plate 42

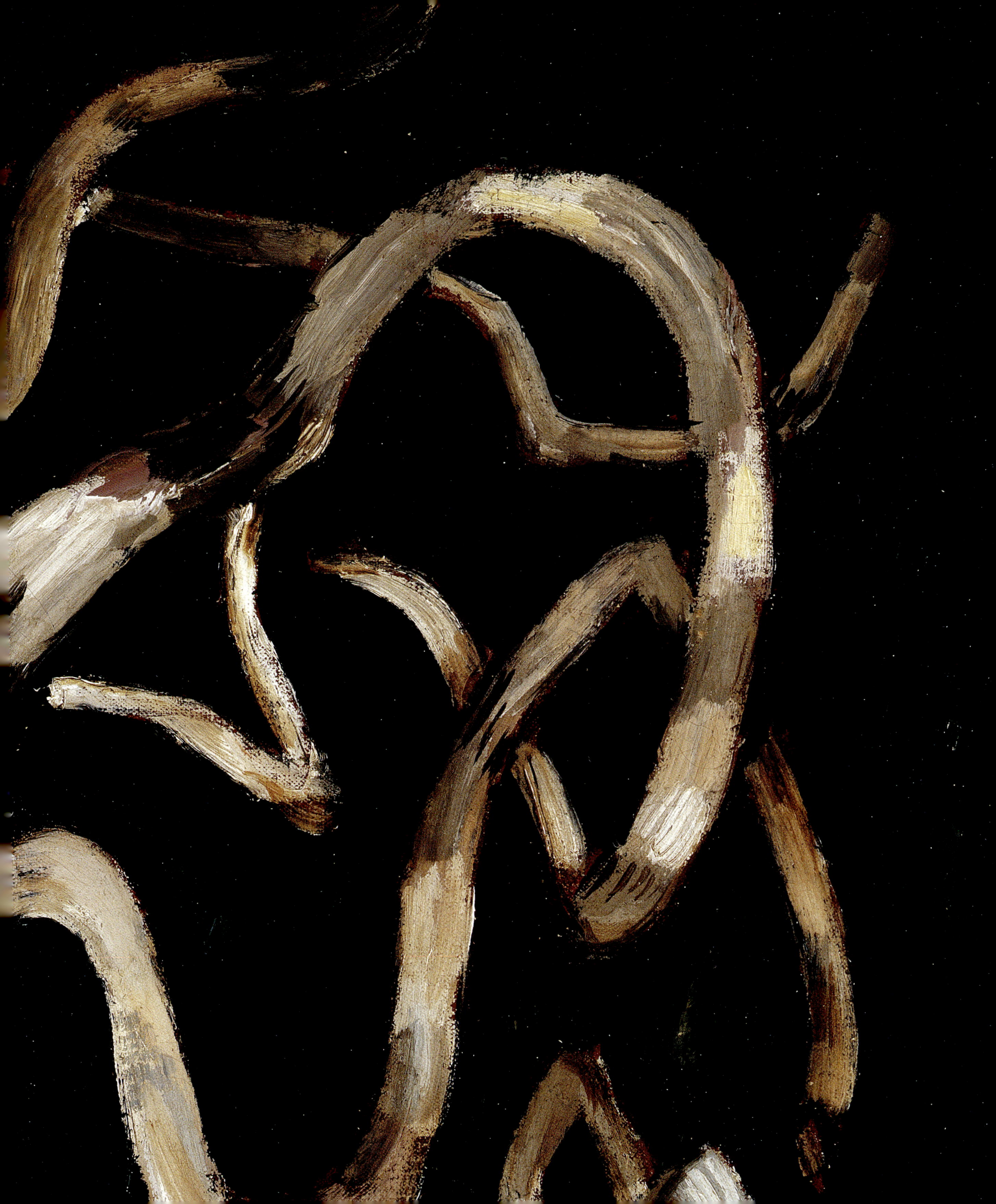

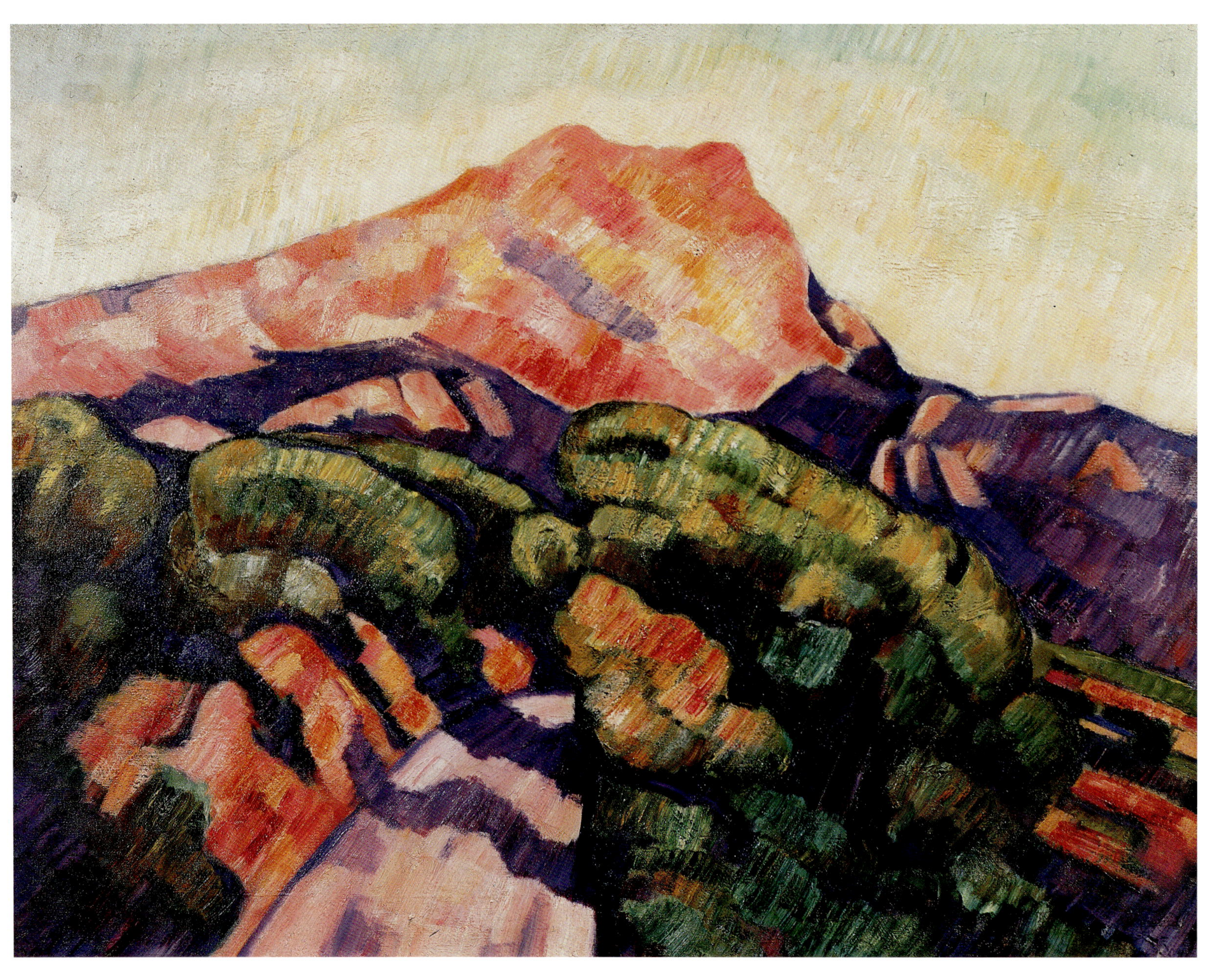

43
Mont Sainte-Victoire, Aix-en-Provence, 1927
Oil on canvas, 25½ × 31⅞ in.
Private Collection
Courtesy of Martha Parrish & James Reinish, Inc., New York

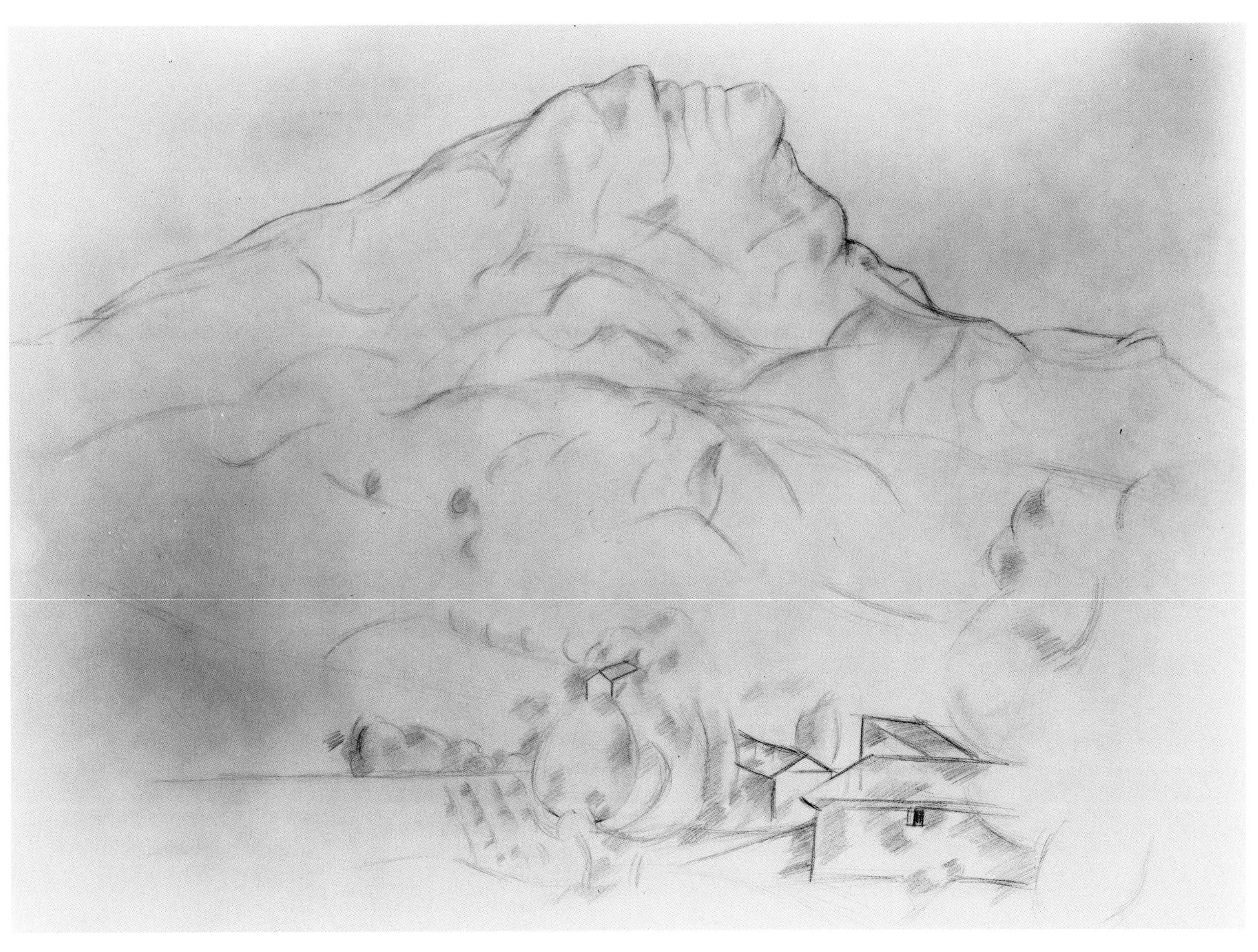

44
Mont Ste.-Victoire, 1927
Pencil on paper, 21 × 24 in.
Babcock Galleries, New York

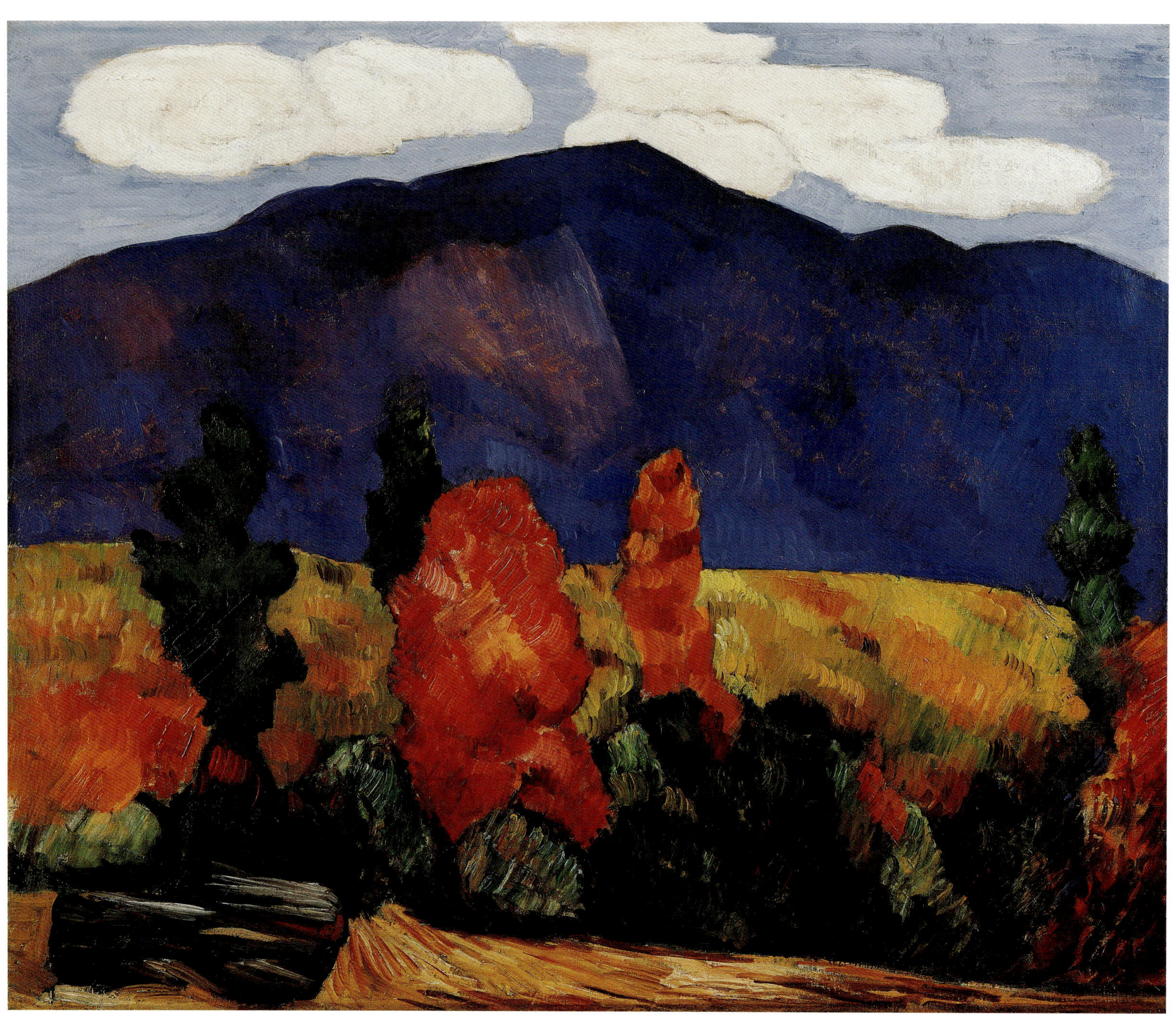

45
Franconia Notch, 1930
Oil on canvas, 30 × 36 in.
Curtis Galleries, Minneapolis, Minnesota

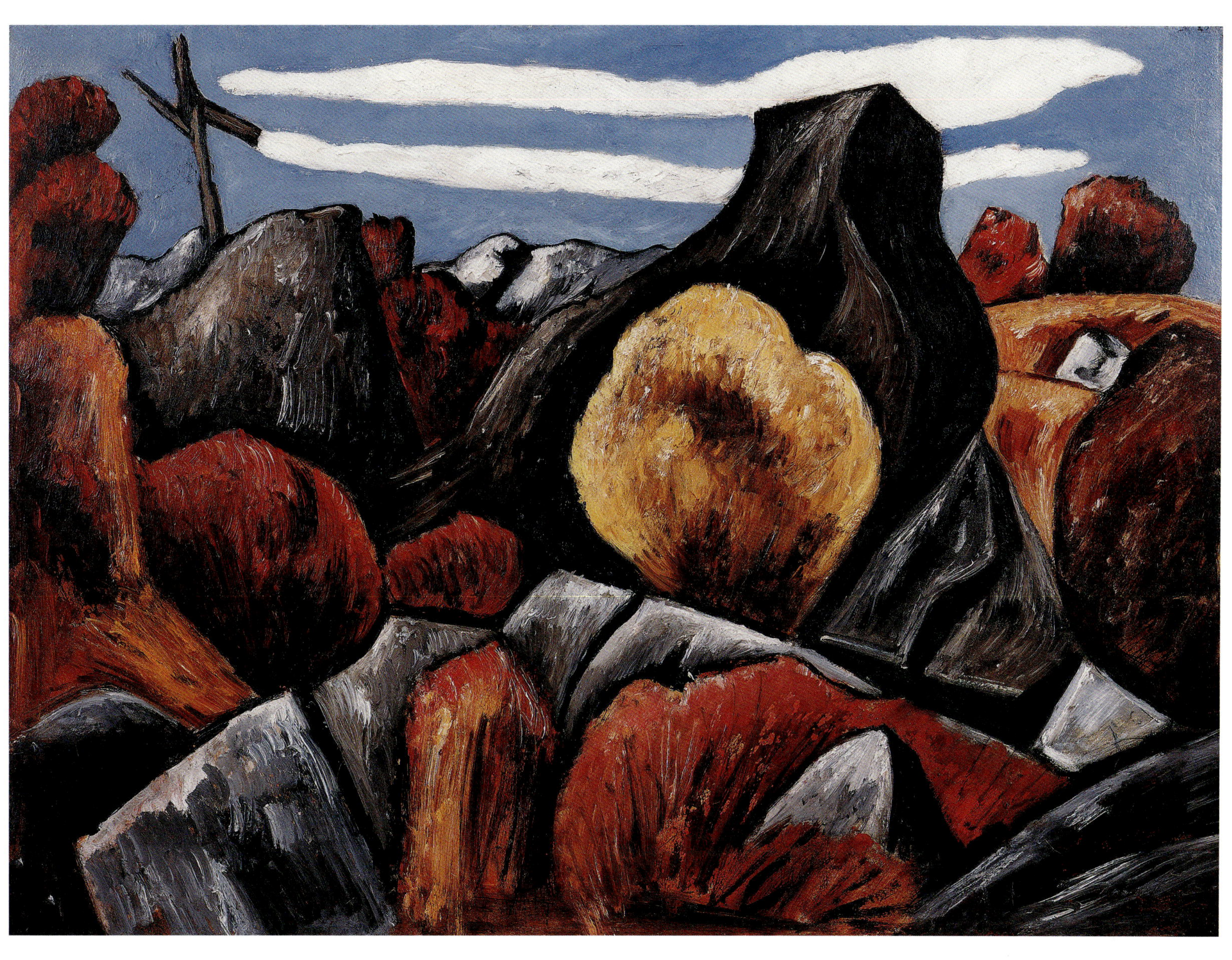

46
Mountains in Stone, Dogtown, 1931
Oil on academy board, 18 × 24 in.
Collection of Barbara R. Palmer
Courtesy of Babcock Galleries, New York

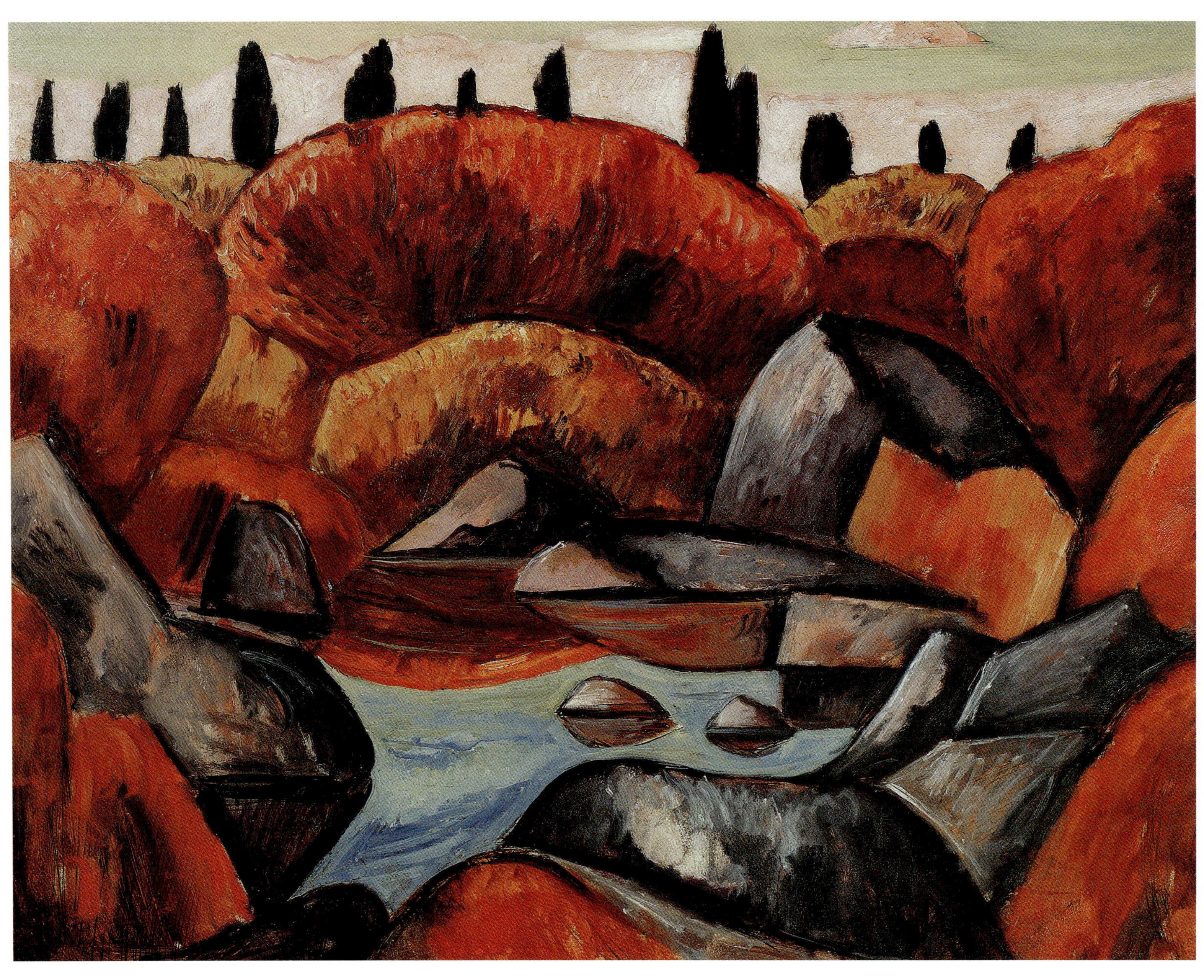

47
Flaming Pool, Dogtown, 1931
Oil on academy board, 18 × 24 in.
Yale Collection of American Literature, Beinecke Rare Book and Manuscript Library, Yale University, New Haven
Gift of Adelaide Kuntz

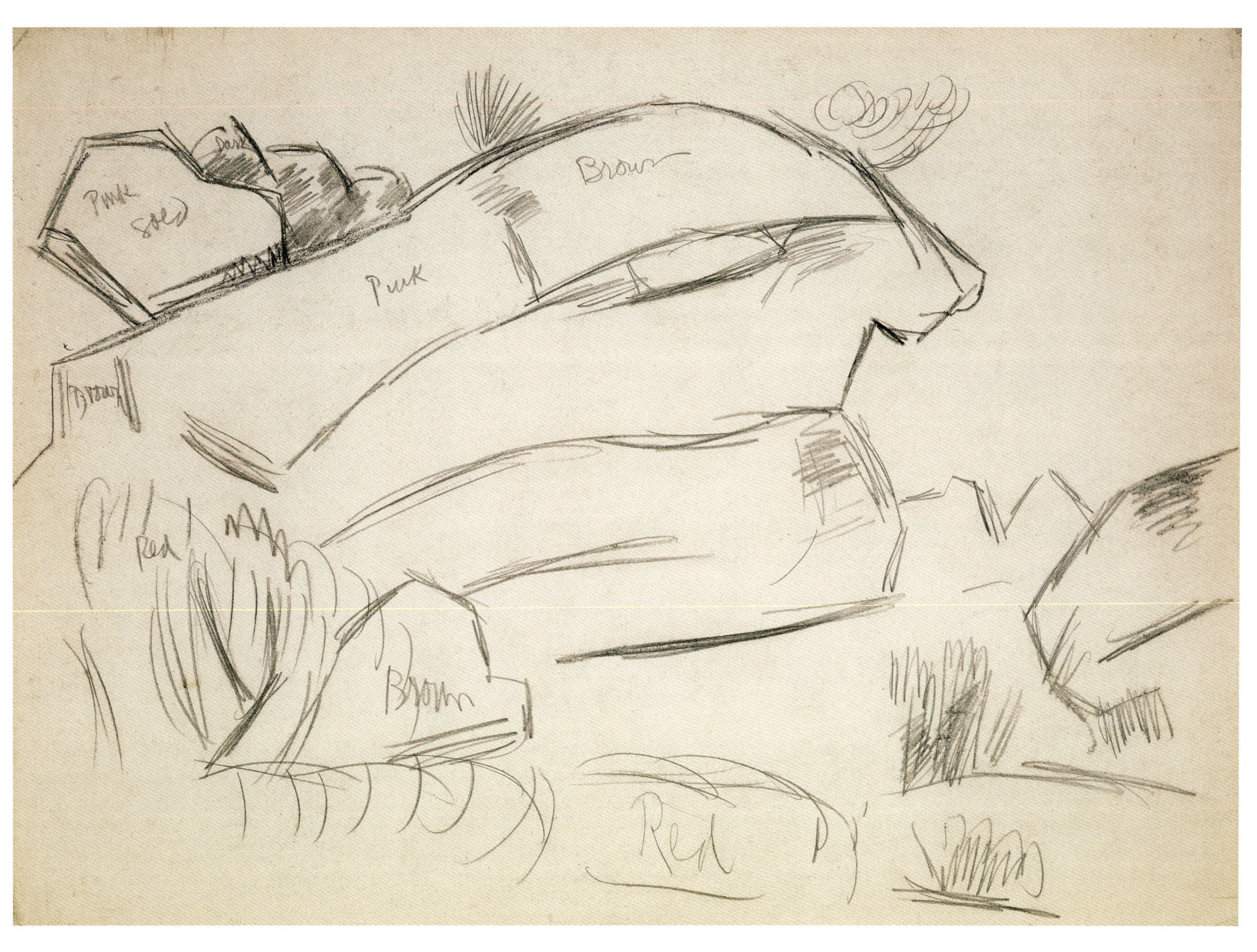

48

Whale's Jaw Rock, Dogtown, c. 1931–34

Pencil on academy board, 18 × 24 in.

Salander-O'Reilly Galleries, New York

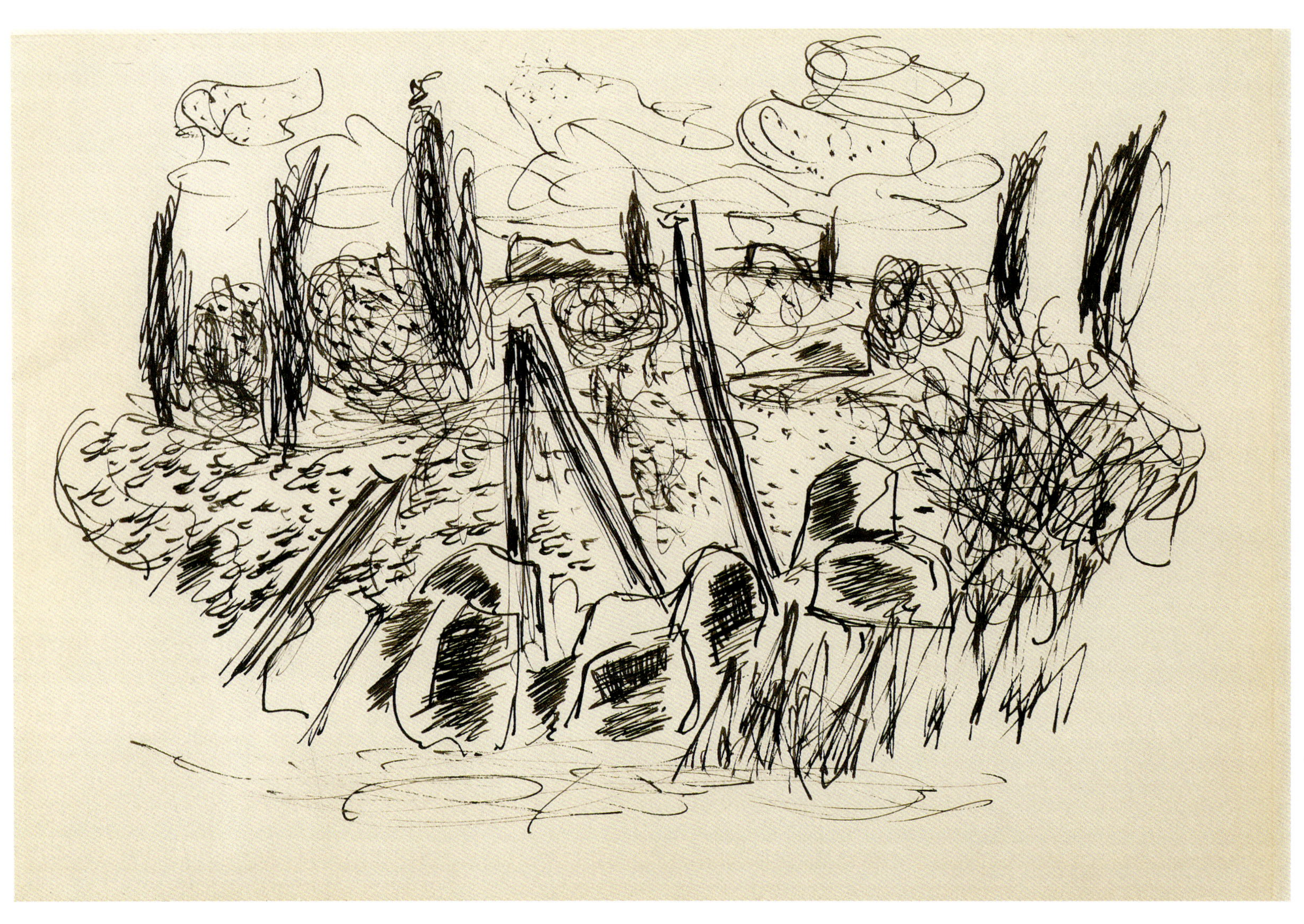

49
Untitled (Blueberry Patch), c. 1934–35
Pen and black ink on white paper, 6⅞ × 9⅞ in.
Bates College Museum of Art, Lewiston, Maine

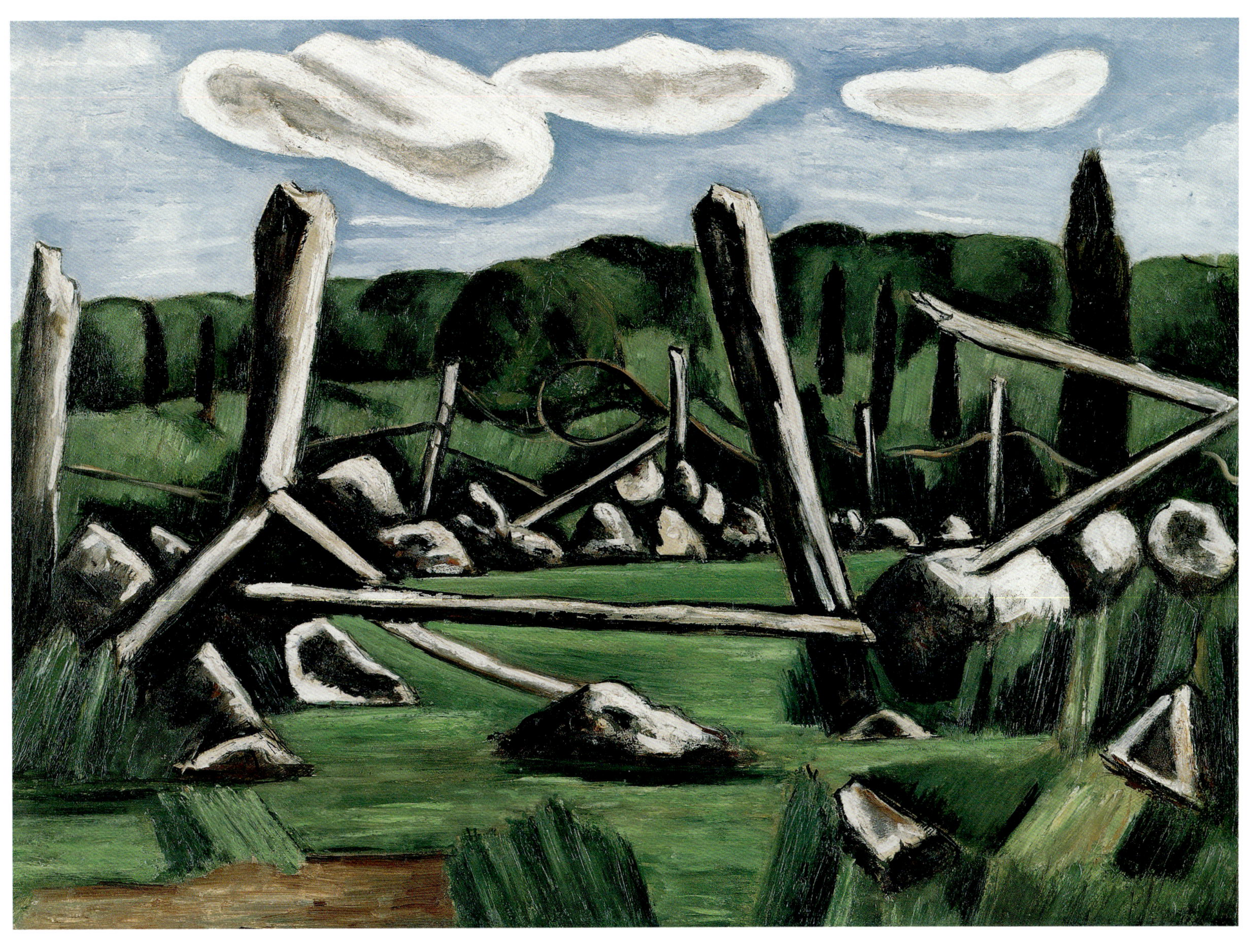

50

The Old Bars, Dogtown, 1936

Oil on academy board, 18 × 24 in.

Whitney Museum of American Art, New York

Purchase

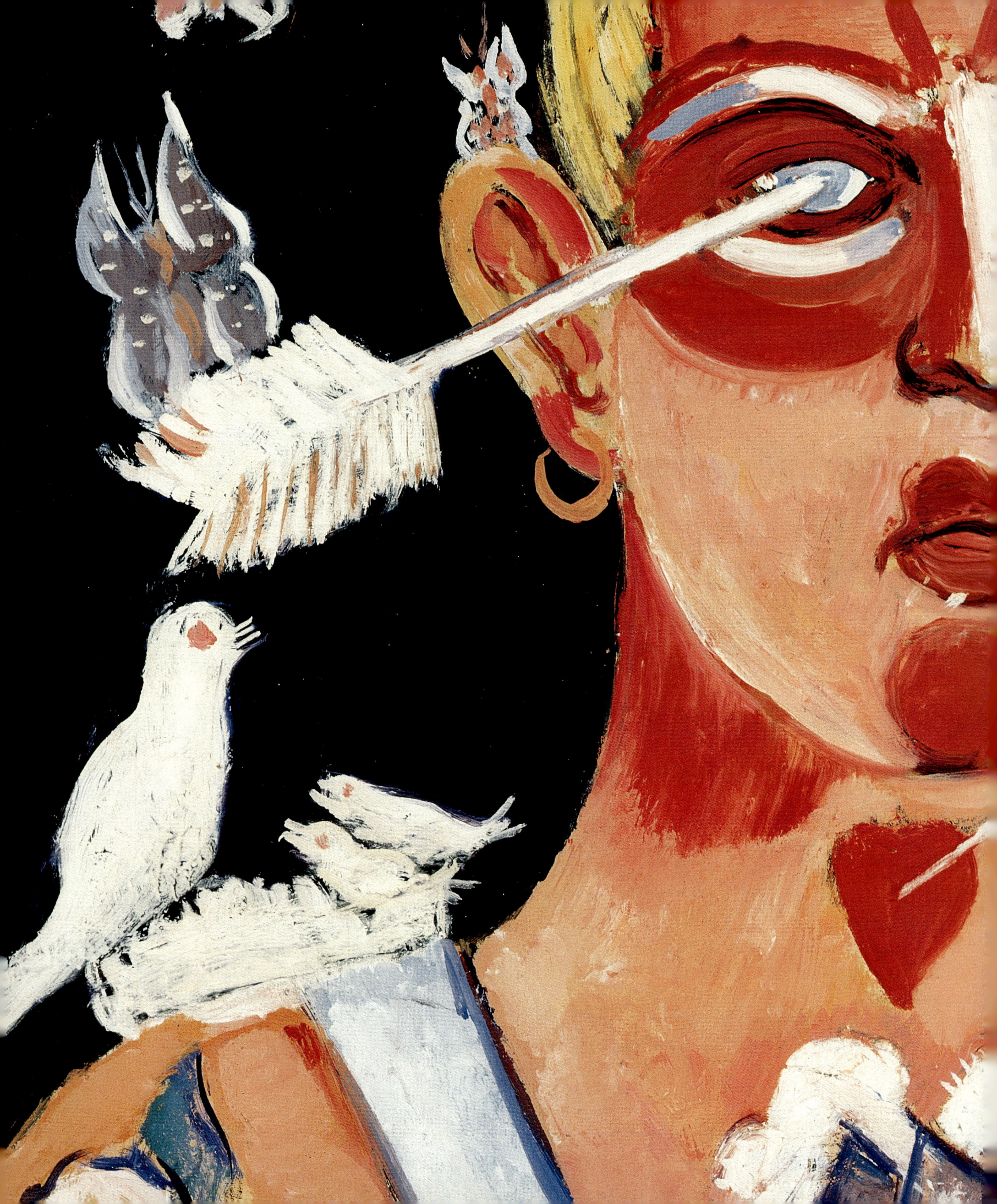

Marsden Hartley and Self-Portraiture

Bruce Robertson

Hartley was engaged in the project of portraiture all his life. A fundamental concern of his art was the need to create a true likeness between the visible world and his internal experience of it. He announced his philosophy in his catalogue essay for a solo exhibition at Alfred Stieglitz's gallery in 1914: "True modes of art are derived from modes of individuals understanding life.... The present exhibition is the work of one who sees—who believes in what is seen—and to whom every picture is a portrait of that something seen."[1] The exhibition, which constituted a first survey of Hartley's encounter with contemporary avant-garde painting in France and Germany, preceded by just a few months his first great symbolic, abstract portraits of an individual, those of Karl von Freyburg (plates 19–21). At the end of his life he was still talking of portraits. Writing for advice on how to get to Mt. Katahdin in 1939, he explained that he had "wanted all my life... to do a kind of official portrait of the mountain, as I feel I am now the 'authorized' painter to do that painting."[2] However, Hartley seldom painted self-portraits, and his first identifiable one dates from the same year he painted portraits of Mt. Katahdin. This work, *Sustained Comedy* (plate 72), is one of his most complex paintings and, even though it ultimately resists interpretation, it reveals much about Hartley's image of himself and how his self-portraits divulge the crucial relationship between memory and likeness. The act of looking was always mediated by the screen of memory; it is in the conjunction of the two that Hartley's art operates.

However different it initially appears, *Sustained Comedy* belongs to the group of "archaic portraits" that includes the paintings of Adelard, Marie, and Cleophas (respectively, Alty, Martha, and Francis Mason, plates 66–68) and the portrait of Albert Pinkham Ryder (plate 71). These five works constitute the first significant figurative paintings Hartley had ever produced, a radical departure for him; they are all the same size and the same basic half-length format. They were exhibited in 1939 by his dealer Hudson Walker, with the exception (perhaps for reasons of discretion) of *Sustained Comedy,* which is also the most visually complicated.[3] We know that the subject is Hartley because the physiognomy is his—his eyes and features—but it is Hartley transformed into a younger blond man in a T-shirt, covered in tattoos.[4] Conventionally the figure is described as a sailor, because of the tattoos, bared biceps, and the ring in his right ear. But the face paint and make-up suggest other contradictory identities: Native American, clown, or cross-dresser.[5] Looking more closely, the elements of the painting continue to challenge each other. On his right arm he appears to have tattoos of a butterfly and a white flower, on his left a woman and a starfish; at his chest above the T-shirt he has a sailing ship. There is a heart at his throat and a triangle on his forehead. On his right shoulder, above the gardenia, sits a bird's nest with mother and two babies; on the left two flowers appear to grow. Arrows project from both

Detail, Plate 72

eyes, with butterflies resting on their feathers, and other butterflies float above him. Out of his forehead, protruding from the triangle, is a thunderbolt.

At the center of this self-portrait are acts of transformation. Hartley is changed into a younger, more attractive man; the man is transformed into a symbol or set of symbols. In other words, the painting exists at the intersection of two of Hartley's dominant interests: on the one hand, his life-long fascination with mysticism and the use of symbolic language, which had appeared in his painting for over twenty-five years; on the other, his attraction to beautiful young men, which had just emerged visibly in his art that same year, in the context of this painting. The self-portrait performs the job of uniting two elements of his art at a critical juncture; balanced in a self-image, Hartley unites both his past and present artistic selves. At the same time, the painting speaks of private desires and longings—to be young, to be handsome, to be loved. Most interpretations have focused on the issue of self-revelation, and it is seen most convincingly as a kind of Saint Sebastian figure. The martyrdom of Saint Sebastian, because the subject presented a rare opportunity to depict an almost naked young man, was a favorite homoerotic subject.[6] Although Sebastian is not shot in the eye, the idea of martyrdom and the reference of the arrows to those of Cupid are clearly embedded in the image. Hartley's perennial sense of loss and alienation are memorialized.

But *Sustained Comedy* is also a meditation on Hartley's artistic and symbolic past. The references to his early Berlin paintings are plentiful, from the thunderbolts and arrows in the Amerika paintings to the birds and boats that appear in such symbolic German paintings as *Portrait Arrangement* (McNay Art Museum, San Antonio) and *Berlin Ante-War* (plate 14), both painted in 1914. The ship is reminiscent of *Eight Bells Folly* (plate 54) or *Northern Seascape, Off the Banks* (plate 61). The gardenia flower figured throughout Hartley's career—from the days of his first success in New York to his Guggenheim year in Mexico. Gardenias are, he claimed, "the perfect flower of all the white ones—the perfect white."[7] This emphasis echoes one of his earliest memories—of the death of a white kitten—but also the many other instances of the color white as an image of perfection and transcendence. In the same fashion, the butterfly is a familiar symbol of the psyche. Through these symbols, the painting collapses the present into the past, but not easily: the image wars with itself. At the very center of the sailor's chest, opened up like a window or triptych, is a figure of the crucified Christ, who stands before not a cross but another male figure who holds a ball of light in his hands directly above the Christ-figure's head.[8] The effect is rather like Leonardo's diagram of an ideal man inscribed in a circle and square, both Christianized and mysticized. The symbols tattooed on the skin of the sailor or resting on his shoulders open up at his heart to an image of the heroic, sacrificed male; the inner reality and vision are stronger than the outward signs. The portrait presents a more extreme version of the other archaic portraits—more symbolic and recondite, more difficult, more perverse—and it passes under their cover. The other paintings depict the Mason family, actors in a drama of faith under the indifferent hand of nature, and the artist Albert Pinkham Ryder, a visionary who had sacrificed himself for his art. Hartley's self-image rests between the two and completes the equation of these sacrifices for love and art. And it acts as a memory device, a form of continuity with his earlier art, retrieving in the present the passions and losses of the last thirty-five years.

The painting is inscribed on the back: "Sustained / Comedy—[*crossed out*] / Portrait of an object [*crossed out*] / "O Big Earth"— / or—the sustained travesty." The words "object" and "travesty" may be an indication of self-loathing, a grotesque or burlesqued likeness. Certainly, the title "sustained comedy" suggests nothing light but rather the grimness of human existence: incarceration on the "big earth" rather than the afterlife in the "divine comedy." But other transformations are signaled in the title. "Travesty" roles are those in which the performer cross-dresses. In addition, Hartley had frequently produced symbolic portraits based on personal objects associated with the sitter. In this fashion, Hartley again signals the ways in which the painting condenses his past life and art. At the same time, the inscription serves as a reminder of the importance of Hartley's own writings. Few if any of his important paintings from the last decade of his career exist independently from some poem or essay, and generally the literary texts amplify the meaning or redirect it; they seldom explain ecphrastically the content of the painting. Among his writings, two poems are most relevant. One seems to be a word portrait, equivalent to the painting. "He Too Wore a Butterfly" describes many of the same tattoos—the butterflies, woman, ship, and Christ—on a muscle-bound man, a "smiling morning of a man" who lives in the present "staving off for later years the pale textures of immitigable distance." This is a man utterly unlike Hartley, who always existed in another dimension than the here and now—but it is just like the impetuous, strong character of Alty Mason. Another, "Trapezist's Despair," concerns the trapeze artist Alfredo Codona who killed his wife, Vera Bruce, in 1937. Hartley describes the butterflies on his costume and asks: "Who could have for a moment thought that under this / very set of wings / there burned the battered centaur upon a raging hill, / all shot with spears from heaven-attack."[9] In these poems, Hartley suggests that beneath these hedonistically beautiful young men exist greater depths of pain, caused by both the fortunes of love lost and the erosion of time. His self-portrait endows his own image with these traits. He is yet another performer or sailor—an outsider—who beneath the surface suffers redemptively.

Sustained Comedy works to explicate the relationship of Hartley's current state with his past. It is not a depiction of his features so much as a record of his path to the present. At the same time, it was produced in a stressful period that demanded amelioration. The self-portrait knits together Hartley's identity at a point at which it might have been dangerously frayed. This function was one that self-portraiture fulfilled several times in his life, none more so than at its end. Hartley's idea of what constituted portraiture and thus self-portraiture was virtually all-inclusive and certainly without set boundaries. He attempted one definition in a letter to his friend Carl Sprinchorn, another Maine artist, in 1942: "But there again what is a portrait—for me it can truly be what you yourself see—if you are doing it—therefore a likeness."[10] He takes the position that a portrait's real likeness lies in what the artist decides to see in a subject. But Hartley immediately complicates the idea by adding: "and only Memling and a few others ever did get a portrait. I always feel when one looks at Memling—his people were like that—and Stieglitz years ago called him the first photographer." Here he seems to say that Memling manages to combine photographic accuracy with likeness, and is thus one of the few ever to paint a true portrait. In effect, Hartley distinguishes two kinds of portraits, the photographic and the likeness; few painters combine both and most, like Hartley himself, produce portraits that are likenesses, that match the inner vision of truth with the outer surface of the world. His self-portraits, the product of the most intense scrutiny he could give anyone or anything, we may presume are the most truthful likenesses of all his works.

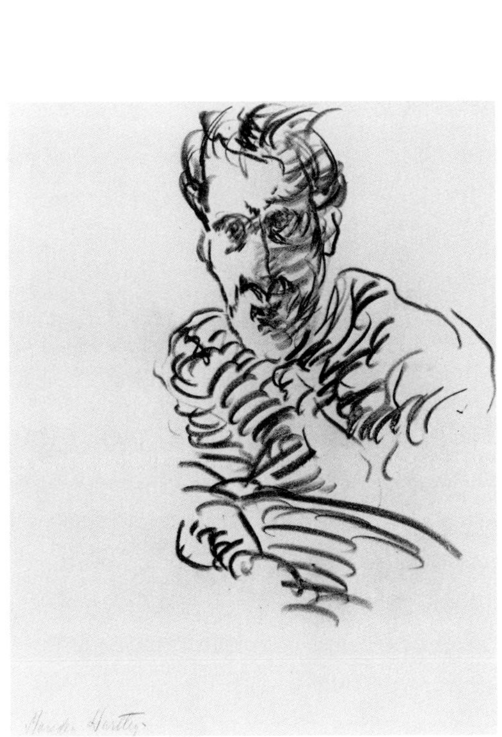

Figure 1
Marsden Hartley
Self-Portrait, 1908
Crayon on paper mounted on paperboard, 12¹⁄₁₆ × 8¹⁵⁄₁₆ in. (30.6 × 22.7 cm)
Smithsonian American Art Museum, Washington, D.C.
Museum purchase through the Robert Tyler Davis Memorial Fund

Fittingly, Marsden Hartley created his first self-portraits at the same time he produced his first mature paintings. As he worked during the fall and winter of 1908–9 in an isolated farmhouse in North Lovell, Maine, he repeatedly sketched himself, fixing his features on paper at the same time that he successfully fixed his ecstatic response to nature on canvas. Night after night in the only room he could keep heated, he sat at table and drew himself in the lantern light (fig. 1, plate 5). It was a time of great exhilaration and great stress—joy at his command of his art allied with a real fear of starvation—and his

Figure 2
Marsden Hartley
Christ, c. 1941–43
Oil on board, 28 × 22 in. (71.1 × 55.9 cm)
Collection of Mr. and Mrs. Barney A. Ebsworth

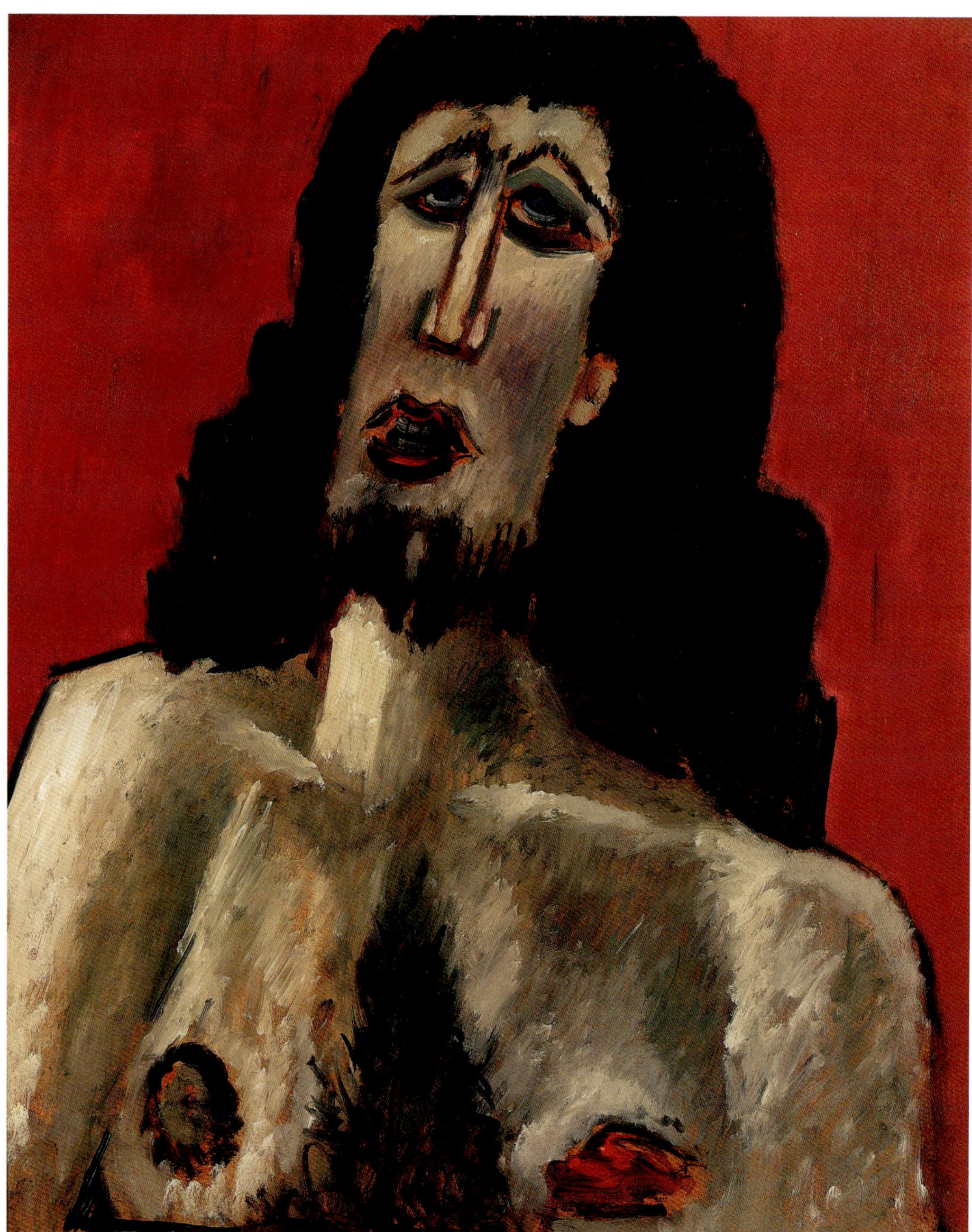

self-portrait drawings were an integral aspect of this intense examination of his own visual experience that he translated into art. The agitated and aggressive hatched strokes of his pencil are the counterpart to the energetic brush strokes of the paintings; but on paper, as just thin lines unsupported by color, they lay bare the almost desperate quality of his attempt to capture his reactions to nature. The poetic energy of the distant line of mountains in the paintings becomes frenzied close-up when he examines his own features. The self-portrait drawings seem cathartic, a private admission of what his art cost him.

Hartley's fellow artists hailed the landscapes that he painted that winter, and he was taken up by Stieglitz. He put aside the making of any overt or recognizable self-portraits at that point and did not return to the idea until the midst of the Depression. During that decade, from 1933 until his death, Hartley engaged in an ongoing, complex project of self-portraiture in all the genres he practiced as an artist. His first effort, his unfinished autobiography, *Somehow a Past*, led to a great number of autobiographical poems and several paintings. Three painted images dominate this production: *Sustained Comedy* from 1939 (plate 72); a half-length figure of the artist as Christ from 1941–43 (fig. 2); and *Young Seadog with Friend Billy* from 1942 (fig. 3). These years were another period of affliction and turmoil, marked by a long period of rejection by the public and critics and with success achieved only in the last few years of his life. Just as his career suffered remarkable reversals and new directions, so did his art; most importantly, Hartley transformed himself into a figure painter. Self-portraiture again, as in 1908, became a means to sort through the issues surrounding his identity as an artist.

Hartley's concern with this essence of identity and self-identity, the recording of the singular characteristics of an individual's selfhood, has been a hallmark of Western thought from its beginnings, but it had become deeply problematic just as he began his career. The index of that difficulty was the invention of an entirely new way of seeing the world, cubism. These same years saw the development of symbolic portraits, where the artist might abandon direct representation and present instead a cluster of symbols or objects that would represent the sitter. Within Stieglitz's circle, the most famous are Marius de Zayas's satirical portraits

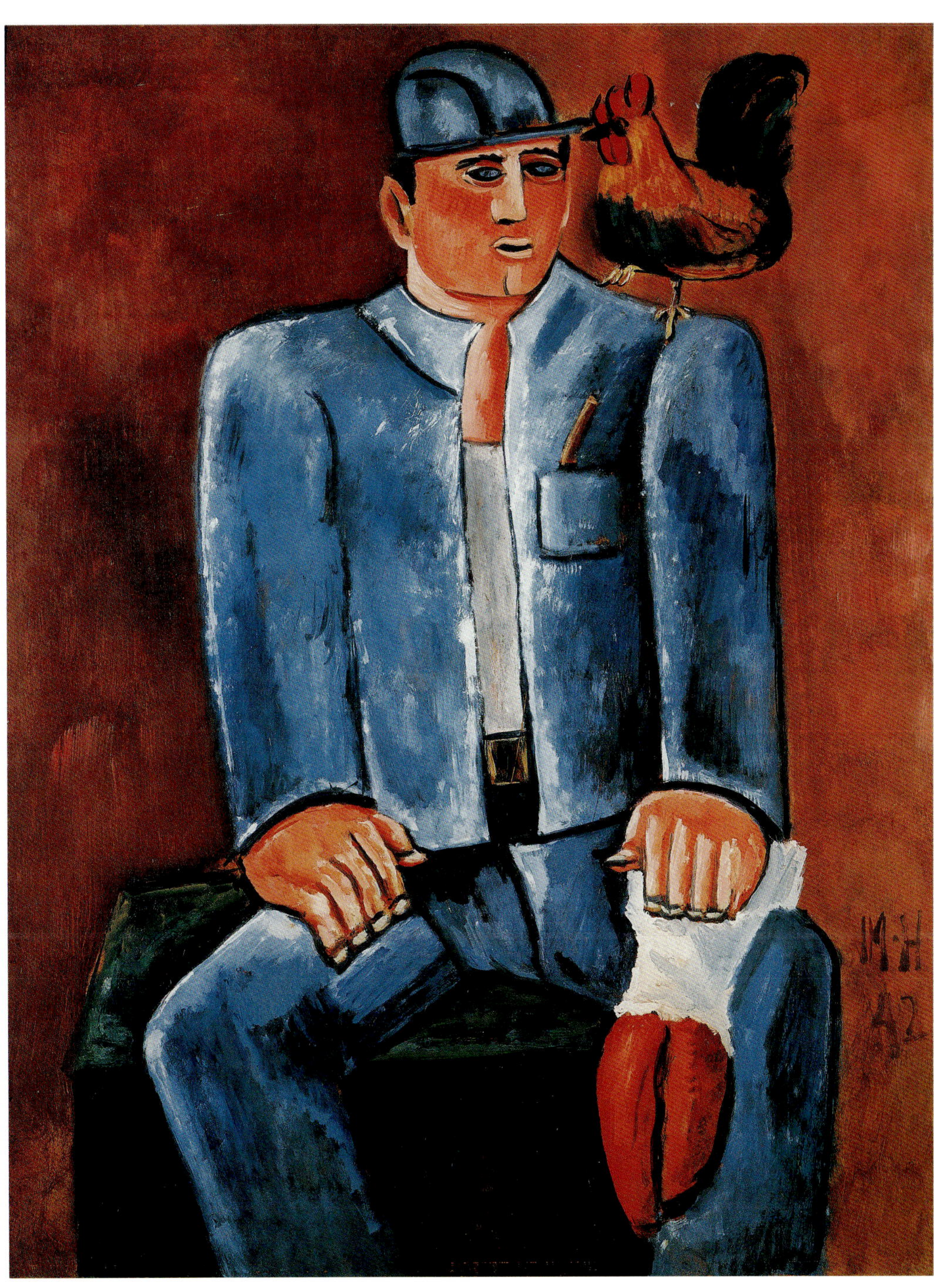

Figure 3
Marsden Hartley
Young Seadog with Friend Billy, 1942
Oil on canvas, 40 × 30 in. (101.6 × 76.2 cm)
Curtis Galleries, Minneapolis, Minnesota

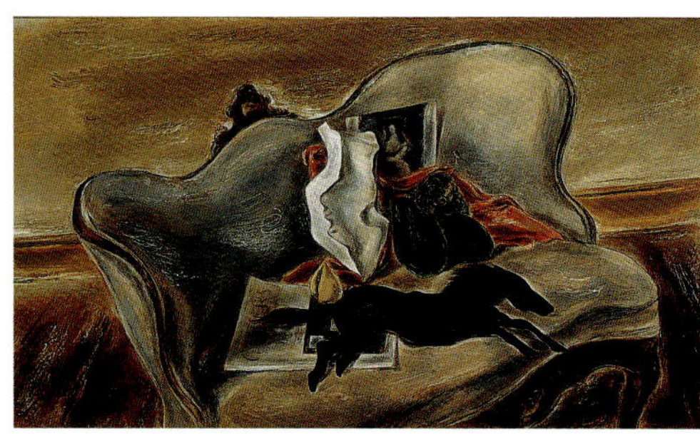

Figure 4
Yasuo Kuniyoshi
Weather Vane and Objects on a Sofa, 1933
Oil on canvas, 34 × 60 in. (86.4 × 152.4 cm)
Santa Barbara Museum of Art
Gift of Wright S. Ludington

of Stieglitz himself as a deflating camera, and Charles Demuth's poster portraits of John Marin, Georgia O'Keeffe, Marsden Hartley (see Weinberg, fig. 1), and others. But the experimentation extended well beyond Stieglitz's artists, ranging back in time to the trompe-l'oeil painter John Peto's paintings of his studio door to Yasuo Kuniyoshi's depiction of a couch in his studio, loaded down with objects that represent the phases of his career in America (fig. 4).[11] Even the purely representational Walt Kuhn produced a symbolic self-portrait within the context of his circus subjects: *Portrait of the Artist as a Clown (Kansas)* (fig. 5).[12] Hartley's portraits and self-portraits occupy the same diverse range of stylistic possibilities these artists explored. Hartley's motivation, however, was much more purely and single-mindedly memory.

In this, Hartley was influenced by the work of the philosopher and psychologist William James, who suggested to many modernists a way to connect what one saw with what one experienced. James related identity to memory, to the remembrance of experience: "The sense of sameness is the very keel and backbone of our thinking. We saw... how the consciousness of personal identity reposed on it." As the philosopher Wendy Steiner remarks, quoting this passage in her study of Gertrude Stein: "Comparison and memory are thus essential factors in identity."[13] Remembering and seeing were both essential for the success of making art. Hartley spent the last decade of his life remembering what he had seen. He wrote in his journal in 1936, quoting the French author Elizabeth de Graumont: "Memories are the only steadfast fixtures of our being."[14] The key to his memories was the power of his startlingly blue eyes to see more clearly than those around him; these were his best feature.[15] Thus in all his portraits he strove to reveal more than others saw, achieved both through his empathy and his memory.[16]

But painting clearly did not necessarily result from seeing and remembering distinctly, and his claim to be able to record and depict the truth of likeness more fully than other artists faced an almost insurmountable obstruction, his sexual orientation. Self-portraits in particular were a more difficult project to undertake for a gay man who could not ever draw fully open the curtain that hid his homosexuality from straight society. And for most of his life Hartley avoided such revelation. During the trying times of World War I, when he was forced to renounce the very things that had inspired his most intense and successful work, and then the long decade or more that followed it, largely spent wandering in Europe, he tried to distance himself from the portrait aspect of his art. In 1928, in an essay entitled "Art—and the Personal Life," he claimed: "Personal art is for me a matter of spiritual indelicacy. Persons of refined feeling should keep themselves out of their painting."[17] This claim resurfaced periodically for the rest of his career, but never very convincingly. And in times of real stress, he returned to his greatest concern: the nature of his relationship to others and to nature.

In 1933 he was again at such a point. Living in miserly frugality, in a small hotel in the town of Garmisch-Partenkirchen in the Bavarian Alps, far from anyone he knew, without income or prospects, he was forced to consider the meaning of his life. In this struggle, he was presented with a model: Gertrude Stein's *The Autobiography of Alice B. Toklas*. He had heard about its publication and success and had begged her for the loan of a copy. Receiving it early in November, he had devoured it and had immediately begun to write his own autobiography. Within a month he finished a draft, titling it "Somehow a Past." Hartley's response was prompted by both an intense sense of rivalry with Stein and a sudden recognition of the need to come to terms with himself and his life. Later he would write to Stieglitz that he had had a "singular experience in the Alps... the whole vision of life was opened and I knew the work of my life had been completed."[18] While he phrased this experience as mystical, the spark had been provided by Stein.

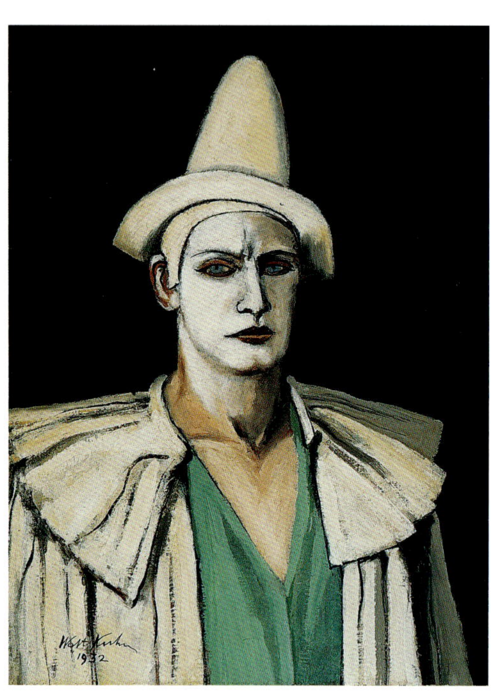

Figure 5
Walt Kuhn
Portrait of the Artist as a Clown (Kansas), 1932
Oil on canvas, 32 × 22 in. (81.3 × 55.9 cm)
Collection of Mr. and Mrs. Barney A. Ebsworth

Stein's autobiography is a deliberately literary construction in a way that Hartley's is not.[19] She refashioned the genre by producing an autobiography in another voice, that of Toklas, valuing the seemingly secondary position of "wife" more than that of "genius." Hartley read the autobiography, however, as history, an account that underscored the critical importance of the moment when Gertrude Stein played cultural impresario to the birth of cubism, as she made the fateful choice between Picasso and Matissse. Hartley had a role in that history—but it is one that Stein slights. Hartley rates two lines, and worse, his friend Arnold Rönnebeck, whom he had introduced to Stein, gets more than three pages.[20] Hartley, in contrast, had always seen his connection to Stein as critical to his achievement. In 1916, with war at his heels, he had announced his return to New York from Berlin with the exhibition of a symbolic portrait of Gertrude Stein.[21] *One Portrait of One Woman* (plate 26) is a response to a portrait she had written of him just three years before, published in the catalogue of his 1914 exhibition. Hartley's image of Stein would serve to position him, he hoped, as the most important and sophisticated American artist returning from Europe before America entered the war. Yet it is also a portrait of a moment in Hartley's life, when Stein had come to his apartment for tea and had declared: "At last, an original American."[22] The painting might be a portrait of Stein, but it is about Hartley and serves to portray Hartley's identity as much as it does Stein's.

Hartley immediately set out to redress Stein's oversight with his own autobiography. The narrative that he produced is no oblique rethinking of the position of the self, as Stein's is. It is rather an attempt to pin down the self, to elaborate it, to capture it whole. He claimed to his niece Norma Berger that "There has been no trace of drama in my life save the inner one, the spirit piercing through stone walls kind of thing."[23] But the story he tells is almost entirely concerned with exterior events, things and people. The memories of his childhood are focused most clearly on flowers, the colors of rocks, the furniture of his home: from the very start, Hartley has the eye of an artist which responds without thinking or analysis to the beauty and colors of the world as they present themselves. His narrative voice is slightly naïve, unrestrained by rules of time and guided by emotion instead. The written self-portrait Hartley created is one of a natively artistic creature who struggles mightily against his blighted childhood to achieve a place in the art world that, while it may not be the highest, is redeemed by its honesty and authenticity. He, like Stein, has seen and met the people who count: he manages to touch on as impressive a group as she, since he can bring in Americans from playwright Eugene O'Neill and journalist John Reed from "the big summer at Provincetown"[24] to the poet Hart Crane in Mexico. He also can produce many more interesting settings, from pre-war Berlin to Mabel Dodge (Luhan's) salons in New York and Santa Fe and so on. Above all, he presents himself as a sophisticated American who has seen it all and yet still is a simple being who finds nature and great art calling to his soul.

Hartley set aside the autobiography by the end of 1933. It seems to have fulfilled its immediate purpose (primarily of reassuring himself that his life was significant), and he turned to more pressing needs, namely surviving the Depression. But henceforth, the project of self-image making was never far from his mind.[25] Around 1938 he picked the autobiographical sketch up again and began to elaborate it, filling in the story of his first years, the ones that establish most obviously his credentials as an authentically grounded artist. In this later version, he adds a new incident, the death of the white kitten, which seems to foreshadow the greater death of his mother. The memory revolves around the funeral that he and his sister conduct, burying the kitten in the nearby woods filled with flowers, "and it was among the latter in a little knoll surrounded by boxbury leaves that the early symbol was buried." Hartley joined his love of nature—first flowers, then mountains.

and finally the sea ("delicacy, strength, moving power")—with this death as the defining features of his character, one marked by both impersonal love and personal loss.[26]In a still later version, both deaths of his mother and the white kitten are explicitly joined in the contemplation of a photograph of himself at age eight, poised on the steps. Hartley asks: "I look at this little lad and say: why did you want to do all that I have had to do to be you?"[27] This collapsing of memory and identity suggests, in the written self-portrait, a stable and continuous identity, a comparison of sameness, as William James would put it. His paintings would be less obvious.

Just as he returned to "Somehow a Past," Hartley began to produce figure paintings for the first time, and, within this group, his first painted self-portraits. These related developments came on the heels of one of the most stressful and rewarding periods of his life. After twenty-eight years with Stieglitz, Hartley was let loose. In 1938 a young dealer named Hudson Walker had expressed interest in handling Hartley's work, and Stieglitz had happily turned him over. More importantly, Hartley had discovered a family in Nova Scotia to live with—the Masons—during the summer of 1935. Hartley had grown particularly close to the two sons, Donny and Alty. Returning the next summer with the high hopes of perhaps making the relationship long-term, his first such hope since knowing the Rönnebeck family in Berlin before the war. But before the summer was over, both boys were dead, drowned in a boating accident. Hartley was crushed and took years to recover. His first response was to turn to landscape painting, producing several elegiac seascapes, such as *Northern Seascape, Off the Banks* (plate 61). Two years later he was able to develop a different response, in figurative paintings (plates 66–68). These were first shown in his second exhibition for Hudson Walker in 1939. The extended meditation on the Mason family that these archaic portraits represent was based on literary figures, the actors in the fictionalized story of the family Hartley had written in 1936, "Cleophas and his Own." The self-portrait he contributed to this group, *Sustained Comedy,* was based on the figure created in his autobiography.

Picking up the project of self-portraiture, reworking "Somehow a Past," and turning to poetry and painting as well, was part of a general turn to re-establish himself in the two halves of his professional and personal life, Maine and Manhattan. Stein remained on his mind: his lecture in conjunction with the historical survey of cubism at the Museum of Modern Art in 1936 pivoted on his experience with Stein in her famous salon. This was a year after her own triumphal tour of the United States (Hartley did not see her). In 1937 she published her account of the tour in *Everybody's Autobiography.* It is not clear that Hartley read this sequel, but he knew about it; and, in revising "Somehow a Past," he slipped in a reference to "everybody's autobiography."[28] Other accounts of those expatriate years may also have challenged him to return to his own. For example, Robert McAlmon, whose account of the 1920s, *Being Geniuses Together,* was published in 1938, had first appeared in Hartley's coterie in 1919 as a life model in drawing classes at the Cooper Union. Appearing in Paris in 1921, he had published modernist writers like Stein, Joyce, and Hartley. By 1940 McAlmon was stuck in Texas and began corresponding with Hartley, both of them dwelling on the good old days. In the same year, Hartley published a book that contained a great number of autobiographical poems about Maine, *Androscoggin,* named after the river that flowed through Lewiston. The landscapes he painted can be seen as another autobiographical expression, records of both his immediate and direct experience of particular sites but also summations of his life-long history with the state, much like the poems. To reinforce this history, he began a correspondence with the State Library in order to make sure that the Maine Authors Collection had a full representation of his work: he was going to establish

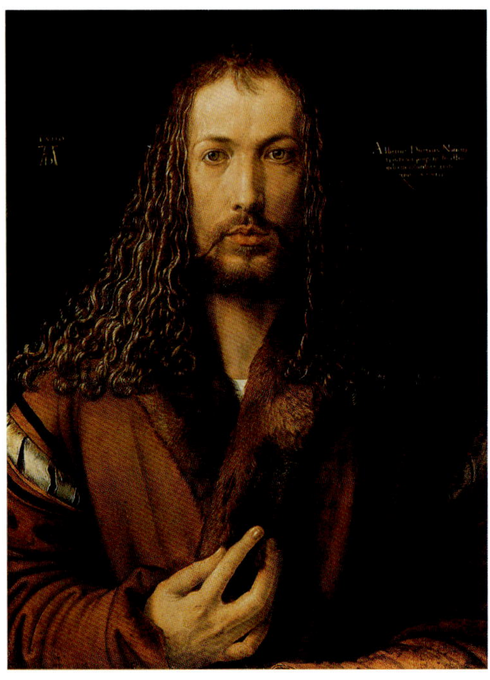

Figure 6
Albrecht Dürer
Self-Portrait in Fur Coat
Oil on panel, 26⅜ × 19¼ in. (67 × 49 cm)
Alte Pinakothek, Munich

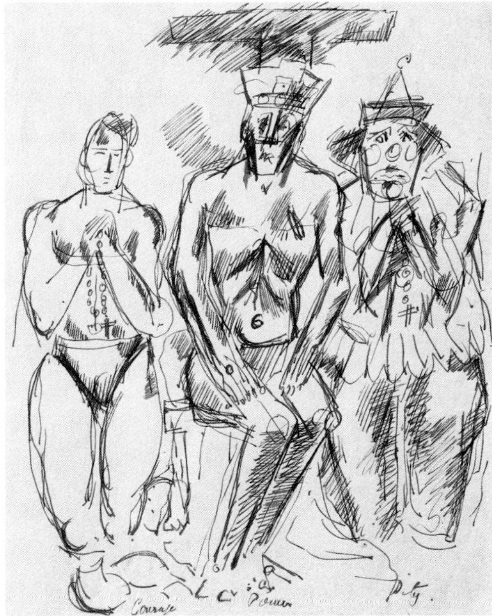

Figure 7
Marsden Hartley
Courage, Power, Pity, c. 1941
Pen and black ink on paper, 10¾ × 8¼ in. (27.3 × 21 cm)
Marsden Hartley Memorial Collection
© Bates College Museum of Art, Lewiston, Maine
Photograph by Melville McLean

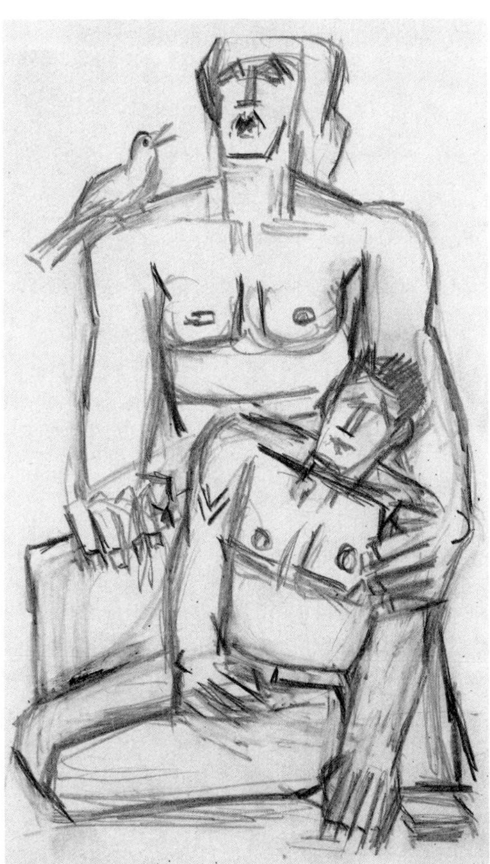

Figure 8
Marsden Hartley
Study for *"O Bitter Madrigal"*
Marsden Hartley Memorial Collection
© Bates College Museum of Art, Lewiston, Maine

himself publicly and permanently as "the painter from Maine," so that he would have that settled at least. Typically, however, he followed up his collection of Maine poems with one that attempted to meld this persona with his New York and European identities; *Sea Burial,* published in 1941, did not sell as well.

Hartley's painted self-portrait arises, then, out of his written autobiography and his attempt to establish a clear public profile as the painter from Maine. It is a phenomenon of memory and identity (a stabilization of the present self by comparison with the remembered self), and also a part of his general discovery of figure painting. *Sustained Comedy* and his other self-portraits must be understood as actors within the theater of these other paintings and writings, each one character among many. But by appearing within this crowded field (and never publicly identified as self-portraits), the other paintings serve not only as a way to contextualize and place Hartley's identity, but also as cover. Hartley submerges his sense of himself, specific to that moment and liable to alteration, within the context of the group he identifies with at that moment. As the subject of his figure paintings changed in the next few years—from archaic portraits to religious subjects to regional color—so did his self-portraits. At the same time, he remained afraid that too much would be revealed in the paintings and still protested: "I have no interest in the subject matter of a picture, not the slightest."[29] Given the integration of his self-portraits with the other figure paintings, it is generally hard to see where one stops and the other begins. Since the self-portraits were never exhibited or named as such in his lifetime, we guess their identity from the "burning spots of blue" for the eyes, generally the most important feature of Hartley's physiognomy, and other clues.[30] But these simple criteria are very broad. For example, one could argue that the central figure in *Down East Young Blades* (plate 85) represents Hartley, indulging in a moment of fantasy, flanked on either side by fantasy figures of sailors who have the character of dancers, not hardworking laborers. The central figure has the blue eyes and long face and nose that are the essential signs. But, then again, perhaps these really are portraits of fishermen Hartley has actually seen.

But within this ambiguous and shifting field of likeness, it is possible to identify two more paintings as self-portraits with some certainty. They share not only the blue eyes but Hartley's distinctive physiognomy, or are explicitly identified by him privately as self-portraits; they suffice to map out the functions of his painted self-portraits. *Sustained Comedy* has already been discussed; it was followed by *Christ* (fig. 2) in 1941–43. This self-portrait is more direct, an homage to Dürer's famous self-portrait of 1500 in Munich (fig. 6). Hartley visited the painting in the middle of writing the initial draft of his autobiography. "It is all around the best portrait that has ever been done by anyone at any time.... Dürer seemed to have all that the eye can have, he saw things exactly as they were, and knew how to convey that impression."[31] The painting represents Dürer frontally, his long hair parted to both sides, staring penetratingly directly out at the world: the artist takes on the likeness of Christ, as was generally understood and celebrated.[32] Hartley continued to extol the painting as the greatest portrait—and thus likeness of any artist—ever painted in later writings. The half-length image of Christ may be understood as another self-portrait because it is given Hartley's characteristic features—a long face and prominent blue eyes and nose—but also because of its references to the Dürer self-portrait. But the self-portrait also stands among a great many other works of Christ and Christ-like figures done by Hartley at the same time. These include single figures of Christ as well as more complex compositions like *Christ Held by Half-Naked Men* (plate 80) and *Courage, Power, Pity* (fig. 7) and more allusive conceptions like the *Study for "O Bitter Madrigal"* (fig. 8), all from the 1940s. Like *Sustained Comedy,* its meaning may be found within the company it keeps. The images of Christ by Hartley tend to endow the surrounding figures with greater strength; Christ is often weak and pitiable.

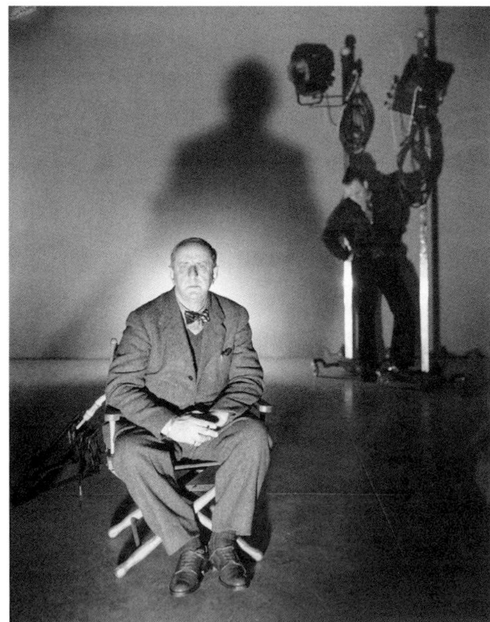

Figure 9
George Platt Lynes
Marsden Hartley
Archives of American Art
Smithsonian Institution, Washington, D.C.
Photograph by Lee Stalsworth

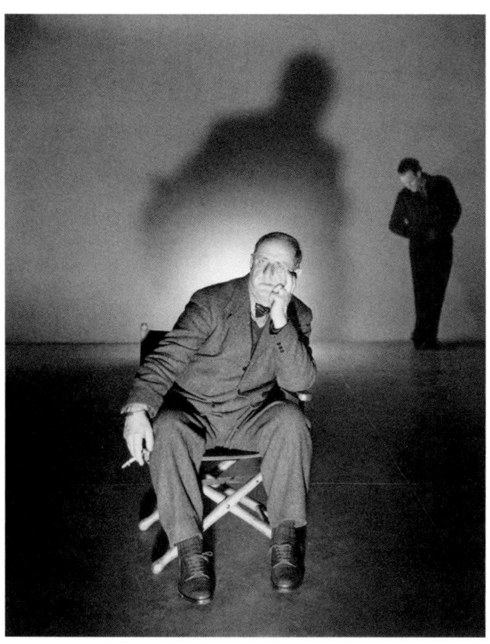

Figure 10
George Platt Lynes
Marsden Hartley
Archives of American Art
Smithsonian Institution, Washington, D.C.
Photograph by Lee Stalsworth

In *Courage, Power, Pity,* for example, "a small thin pale Christ" rests between a prizefighter and a clown, both of whom, Hartley says, have suffered as heroically. In adapting his own image of Christ to his self-portrait, Hartley turns the Dürer on its head, metaphorically. Dürer's figure is a monumental, heiratic, almost elegant image—Christ as a Prince of Men. Hartley's Christ is bearing the pain of the world, twisting with his mouth half-open in pain or ecstasy—Christ in agony. The artist takes on the sacrifice of Christ, not his power. The body of Christ is also less classical, less beautiful. This is no Renaissance idealized figure but thinner, less muscular, and marked by the imperfection of body hair. Hartley's Christ is one who has fallen into the world and has been hurt by it; there seems little possibility of either redemption or resurrection.

The third self-portrait is different again. Writing to Sprinchorn, Hartley explained that Hudson Walker had wanted a self-portrait of him for an exhibition that opened in December, but he couldn't do it in time.[33] "But I would have one—a likeness [of] one seated, my beautiful blue and black plaid cap on—some burning spots of blue for eyes—Billy the Bantam on my shoulder which is a daily trick and a lobster hanging down from left hand or left knee—all very typical and I have every reason to believe will be a *likeness,* that is for *me.*"[34] The painting *Young Seadog with Friend Billy* of 1942 (fig. 3) matches Hartley's description almost exactly. But without the evidence of his letter to Sprinchorn we would never think of it as a self-portrait. The painting shows a virile young man, an epitome of healthy outdoor living. It belongs to the group of representative figures of Maine that occupied Hartley from 1941, all of them brawny young men. In this painting, Hartley becomes one of them, the young man he never was, blending in with the local community, part of a family. "Foreground being the fruition of background,"[35] as he had once written, the background, in this case, is both his present community of local fishermen in Corea, Maine, and his childhood in Lewiston; the foreground is this fantasy image of himself.

While Hartley was completing this self-portrait, he became a portrait subject himself. He was using, in exchange for a painting (presumably *O Bitter Madrigal*), the New York studio of the photographer George Platt Lynes to finish paintings for his latest exhibition at Rosenberg's gallery, and he was photographed by Lynes (figs. 9–10). He had been photographed the year before by Alfred Valente, who had presented him as a serious figure of due aesthetic weight, seen against medieval tapestry and sculpture at the premises of the dealer Dikran Kelekian.[36] But within Lynes's studio, Hartley permitted a very different image of himself to be created. Lynes was a much younger gay photographer who actively created homoerotic images for circulation within a well-defined and prominent circle of gay artists and allied figures. Within this safe circle, Hartley could relax, and what had been hidden or symbolically covered could now be represented much more openly. Lynes's photographs act out a different story of Hartley's life, suggesting a world of bodily experience that Hartley almost always had transposed into the metaphysical. This sequence of some fifteen images positions Hartley in the foreground, calmly and somewhat imperiously seated on a director's chair. But behind him a young man hangs out, loitering by a pair of photographer's lights on stands; he is approached by other men, he talks intimately to one. Lynes suggests a classic pickup scene, with a hustler standing under the streetlight making himself available; it is a situation Hartley knew well and mentioned in veiled terms in letters but never depicted. Nonetheless, this sexualized male world is implicit in the self-portrait *Young Seadog,* in Hartley's "likeness" of himself as a handsome young buck.

Hartley complained that Lynes's photographs made him look too "chi-chi."[37] Hartley no doubt enjoyed the circle of younger gay men that surrounded Lynes, living again in the kind of society he had enjoyed in Berlin after the previous war.[38] Monroe Wheeler, a much younger contemporary of Hartley's and a member of the circle of gay artists and writers that included Lynes, described Hartley as young: "Even in old age, he spoke of his life work as a struggle, a discipline, a research and an evolution, as if he were still, in his own opinion, a promising youth ... already he has become a kind of prototype and legendary personality, inspiring to younger artists."[39] Hartley may well have seen photographs by Lynes of a nude man displaying his body on Lynes's bed, under Hartley's pietà *O Bitter Madrigal.* He would have enjoyed the transposition of the painted naked son into the living flesh of the young man on the bed.[40] But his own image directly placed in such an overtly gay context was too revealing. Hartley preferred not to have this aspect of himself pinned down.

Many of Hartley's contemporaries essayed descriptions of him, in addition to those who depicted him visually.[41] These are as various and contradictory as his own attempts: Hartley was sweet, miserly, puritanical, bitter, spinsterish, generous, etc.[42] Like his self-image, the reception of his persona was difficult to label or contain. What everyone did agree on, however, was his importance as an artist. There, Hartley would concur: "When I am no longer here my name will register forever in the history of American art."[43] But as Gertrude Stein explained in *Everybody's Autobiography,* the book she wrote in response to the success of her "autobiography" of Alice Toklas: "identity is funny being yourself is funny as you are never yourself to yourself except as you remember yourself and then of course you do not believe yourself. That is really the trouble with an autobiography."[44] Hartley certainly experienced that problem as he tried to paint himself. His self-portraits dramatize vividly the difficulty both for him and for us in discovering either an internal coherence to Hartley's oeuvre or a stable artistic persona. At the moment at which we think we have "remembered" Hartley, we know that the Hartley we have willed into being is a partial thing at best and a distortion at worst. The three self-portraits—a symbolic sailor, a harrowed Christ, and a guileless Maine fisherman—neither add up to a single "Hartley" nor contain the whole complexity of the artist. He aimed at "likeness" in his portraits, as he wrote to Sprinchorn, but viewing his self-portraits it is impossible to find the likeness that binds them together. Hartley's project of self-portraiture is a failure if we judge it in terms of self-revelation, and by this very failure, Hartley succeeded, much like his goad and inspiration, Gertrude Stein, in questioning the very terms of self-identity.

In the preface to his 1936 exhibition at Stieglitz's An American Place, entitled "An Outline in Portraiture of Self," in a letter addressed to Aurelie Cheronne, a woman he had met in France before World War I, he recalled his birth in the nineteenth century and his progress since:

> *All that is coming to the surface again.... life being a matter of successive and hopingly intelligent detours, foreground being the fruition of background, you would readily fill out the edges of this portrait for yourself, a life spent in plain beliefs, in despairs, understanding, and with more or less sudden vision accepting experience, made cautious with the need of reasonableness, denying the importance of anything at all but the quality and principle of life itself. Silence, solitude, two of the most exciting agencies I can think of, with certain degrees of representative laughter are sufficient.... You will understand more than anyone the meaning therefore, of Video and Gaudeo.*[45]

Out of the silences and solitudes of his life, Hartley, with the piercing vision conferred by his extraordinary blue eyes, saw, and he rejoiced: "Eyes speak.... Let us live forever, seeing things going on living forever, all the time, seeing."[46]

Notes

1 Hartley, "Gallery Statement," republished in *On Art,* 63.

2 Hartley to Miss McLeod, Maine State Library, 16 September 1939, Maine State Library Archives. He remarks in an earlier letter (10 September 1939) that he is satisfied calling them portraits "since they were recognized clearly by natives."

3 *Sustained Comedy* belongs to the same painting campaign, from the end of 1938 through most of 1939, and shares the basic format and size of these other paintings. The decision not to exhibit it may have been Hartley's (out of his continuing fear of exposure) or his dealer's: it is a very odd painting. The first owner claimed that Walker wanted to suppress it. See Weinberg, 190.

4 Weinberg, 145.

5 A number of these suggestions are derived from Diana Strazdes, *American Paintings and Sculpture to 1945 in the Carnegie Museum of Art* (New York: Hudson Hills Press, 1992), 230–31. See also Weinberg, 185–90; and Robertson, 8–9.

6 See James M. Saslow, *Pictures and Passions* (New York: Viking Penguin, 1999), 99, 210, 215.

7 *Autobiography,* 72–73. The painter George Luks had commended his painting of gardenias, and Hartley was always sensitive to his qualities as a flower painter—and to the way Georgia O'Keeffe had encroached on some of his favorite blooms.

8 Strazdes, *American Paintings and Sculpture,* 231, suggests the figure is Atlas.

9 *Collected Poems,* 170–71.

10 Letter to Carl Sprinchorn, 5 October 1942, excerpted in McCausland Papers, Archives/Smithsonian, roll D268, frame 1043.

11 Peto, *My Studio Door* (1895; Santa Barbara Museum of Art).

12 The success of Kuhn's paintings influenced Hartley's turn to figure painting.

13 Wendy Steiner, *Exact Resemblance to Exact Resemblance: The Literary Portraiture of Gertrude Stein* (New Haven and London: Yale University Press, 1978), 30.

14 Ferguson, 75.

15 See Susan Elizabeth Ryan's Introduction to *Autobiography,* 28.

16 After arguing with Georgia O'Keeffe, for example, about the truth of his portrait essay of Charles Demuth, he wrote to a friend that she of course would never have seen his "naughty-nasty side" the way Hartley had. What he did not say, of course, was that Hartley would have seen that side of Demuth as one gay man to another. Ludington 1992, 247.

17 Republished in *On Art,* 71.

18 Hartley to Alfred Stieglitz, 21 November 1934, quoted in *Autobiography,* 15. See also Gail R. Scott's Introduction to *On Art,* 50–51.

19 For recent discussions of *The Autobiography of Alice B. Toklas,* see Charles Caramello, *Henry James, Gertrude Stein and the Biographical Act* (Chapel Hill: University of North Carolina Press, 1996); Anne Herrmann, *Queering the Moderns* (New York: Palgrave, 2000); Margaret Norris, "The 'Wife' and the 'Genius': Domesticating Modern Art in Stein's Autobiography of Alice B. Toklas," in Liza Rado, ed., *Modernism, Gender, and Culture* (New York: Garland Publishing, 1997); Barbara Will, *Gertrude Stein, Modernism, and the Problem of "Genius"* (Edinburgh: Edinburgh University Press, 2000).

20 *Autobiography of Alice B. Toklas,* 122–25. For Hartley's public reaction, see "And the Nude has Descended the Staircase," a lecture given at the Museum of Modern Art in 1936, published in *On Art,* 268–74.

21 See Bruce Robertson, "Marsden Hartley, 1916: Letters from the Dead," in Greenough, 229–46

22 *Autobiography,* 84.

23 Hartley to Norma Berger, 13 November 1933, quoted in ibid., 171.

24 Table of Contents, reproduced in *Autobiography,* 8.

25 For example, both his journal entries and his prose-poem "Cleophas and His Own," produced in the summer of 1936, may be seen as an attempt to bring "Somehow a Past," which ends in 1934, up to the present. This time one of his models is Proust, as can be seen in his extended flashback prompted by the fragrance and *idea* of "Northern honey." Ferguson, 76.

26 *Autobiography,* 180.

27 Ibid., 197.

28 Ibid., 179.

29 Hartley, "Pictures," in *On Art,* 116.

30 "I always offer two signs of recognition: a vast nose and ultra blue eyes—the rest is nothing much." Hartley to Gertrude Tiemen, 8 February 1928, McCausland Papers; Archives/Smithsonian, roll D268, frame 761.

31 Hartley to Norma Berger, 13 November 1933, quoted in *Autobiography,* 171.

32 See Joseph Leo Koerner, *The Moment of Self-Portraiture in German Renaissance Art* (Chicago: University of Chicago Press, 1993), 72–78.

33 Presumably the exhibition at the Metropolitan Museum of Art, where Hartley exhibited *Lobster Fishermen* and won a prize.

34 Letter to Carl Sprinchorn, 5 October 1942, excerpted in McCausland Papers, Archives/Smithsonian, roll D268, frame 1043.

35 Hartley, "An Outline in Portraiture of Self from Letters Never Sent," in *On Art,* 111.

36 Milton Avery's 1943 painting replaces the pens in Hartley's jacket pocket seen in Valente's photograph with a white gardenia, a flower that Hartley loved but felt was possibly too obviously "gay" to wear. The photograph is reproduced in Ludington 1992, opp. p. 154.

37 Hartley to Hudson Walker, 8 October 1938, McCausland Papers, Archives/Smithsonian, roll 272, frame 815. Hartley must be referring to an earlier set of portraits.

38 As Robert McAlmon hinted to Elizabeth McCausland: "Marsden always wanted to keep in touch with youth, and all the modern movements, some of them by no means esthetic." 18 December 1951, McCausland Papers, Archives/Smithsonian, roll 271, frames 800–801.

39 Monroe Wheeler, *Feininger/Hartley* (New York: Museum of Modern Art, 1944), 55–56. Monroe Wheeler, one of Lynes's partners, arranged to have "The Spangle of Existence," the most complete collection of his late essays, professionally typed in 1942.

40 Kinsey Archives. My thanks to Keith Holt for bringing these to my attention.

41 Two of the photographers—George Platt Lynes and Alfred Valenti—are discussed below. Jacques Lipschitz sculpted him in 1942; Milton Avery's portrait, which is based on a photograph by Valenti, may be posthumous.

42 See Ludington 1992, 6–14; and Robertson, 8.

43 Hartley to Norma Berger, 20 December 1942 Beinecke/Yale.

44 Gertrude Stein, *Everybody's Autobiography,* 68, quoted in Steiner, *Exact Resemblance to Exact Resemblance,* 190.

45 Hartley, "An Outline in Portraiture of Self from Letters Never Sent," in *On Art,* 111.

46 "Testament Finals," unpublished poem, Hartley Papers, Archives/Smithsonian, roll 1371, frames 40–42.

PLATES 51–58

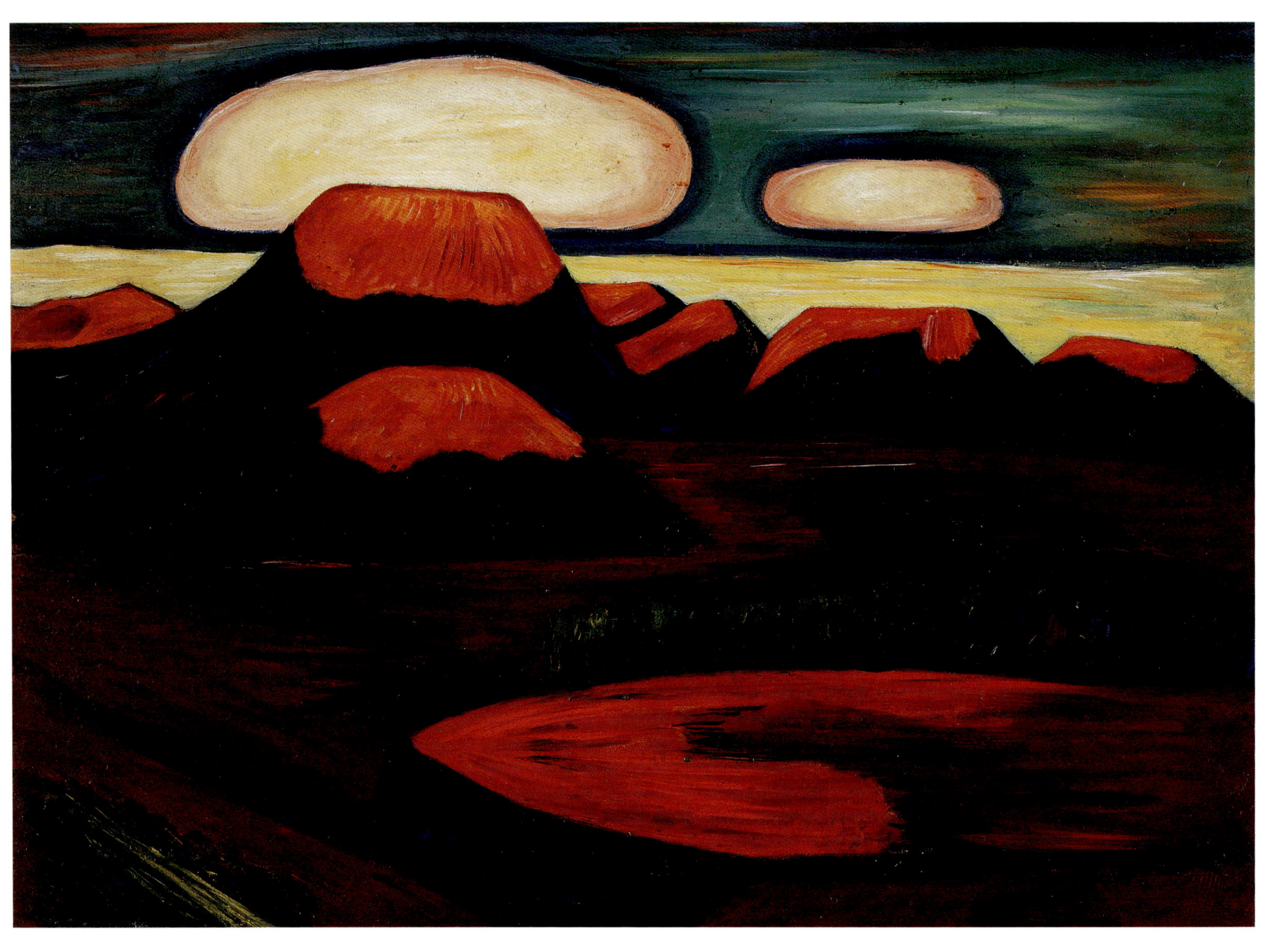

51

Earth Cooling, Mexico, 1932

Oil on cardboard, mounted on Masonite, 24½ × 33⅞ in.

Amon Carter Museum, Fort Worth, Texas

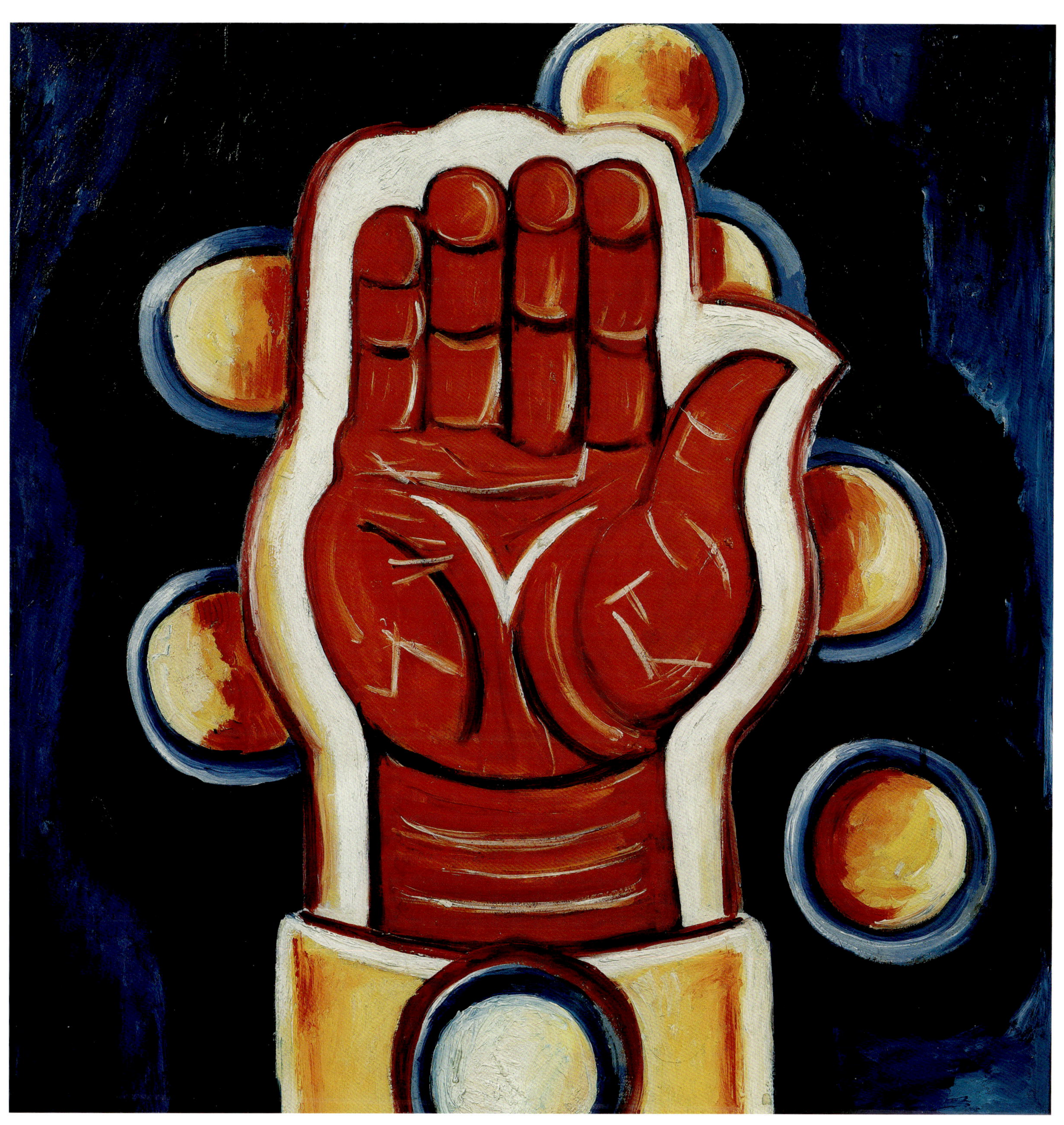

52
Morgenrot, 1932
Oil on canvas, 25 × 23 in.
Private Collection
Courtesy of Babcock Galleries, New York

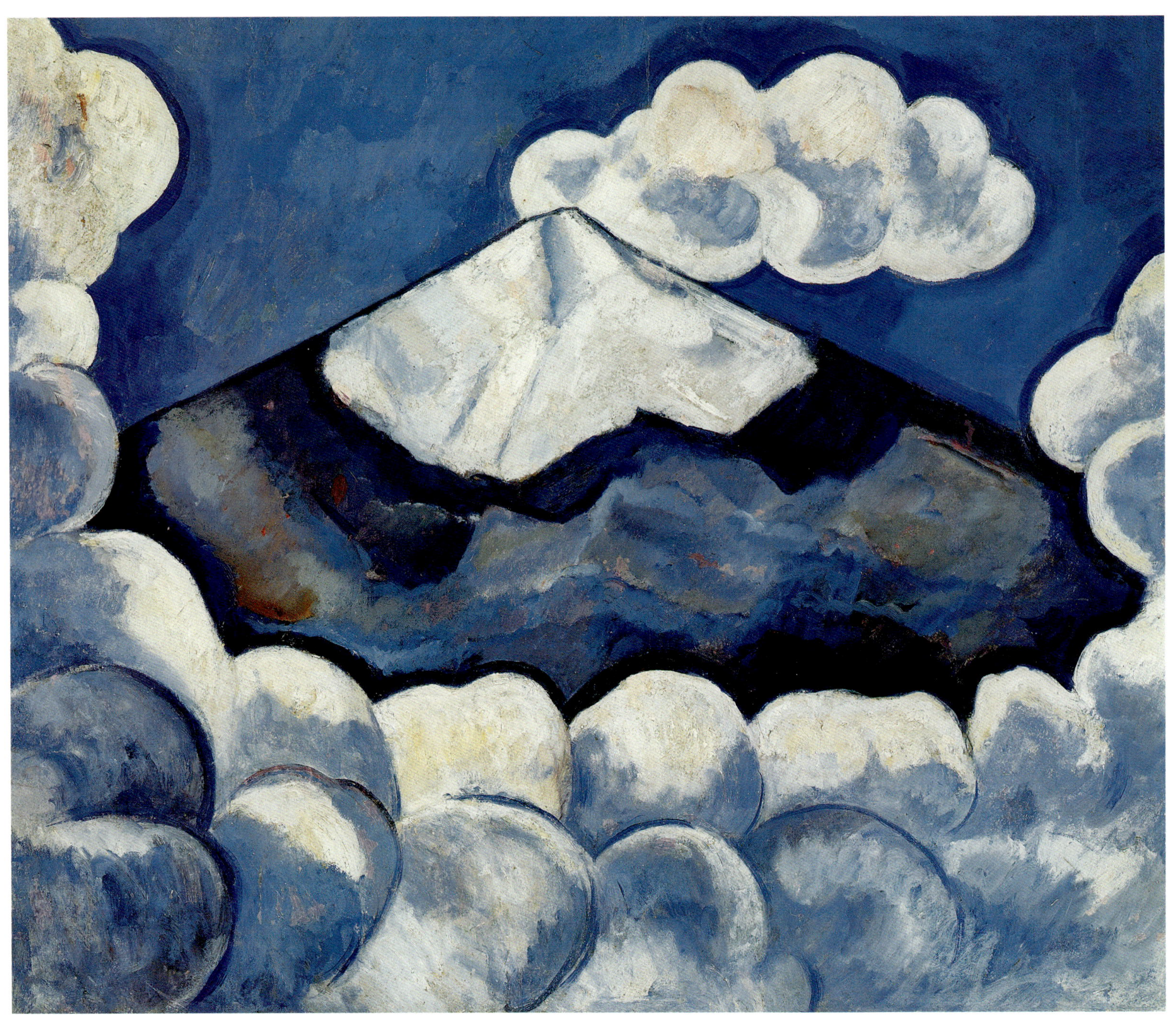

53
Popocatépetl, Spirited Morning—Mexico, 1932
Oil on academy board, 25 × 29 in.
Private Collection
Courtesy of Gerald Peters Gallery, New York

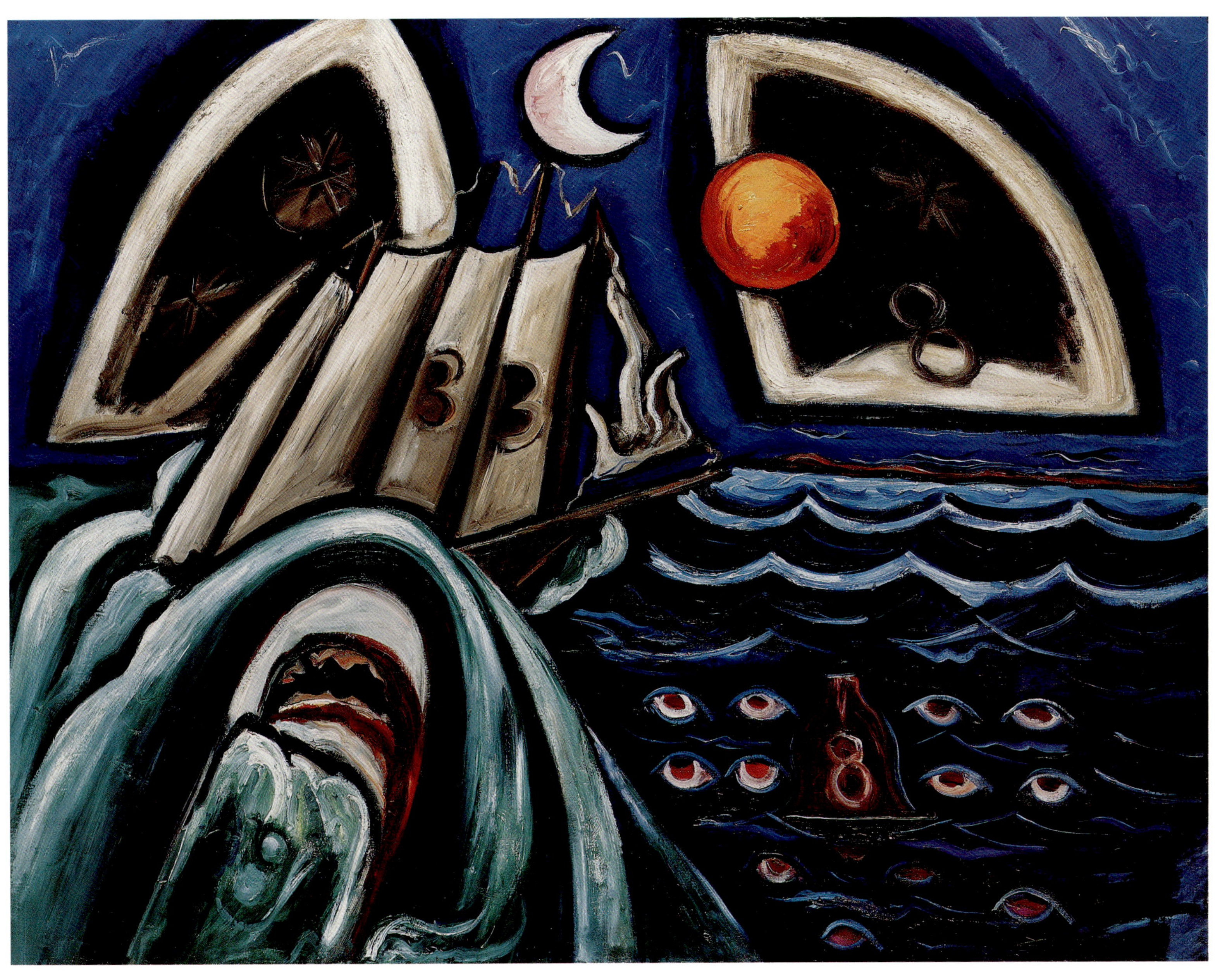

54
Eight Bells Folly, Memorial for Hart Crane, 1933
Oil on canvas, 31⅝ × 39½ in.
Frederick R. Weisman Art Museum, University of Minnesota, Minneapolis
Gift of Ione and Hudson Walker

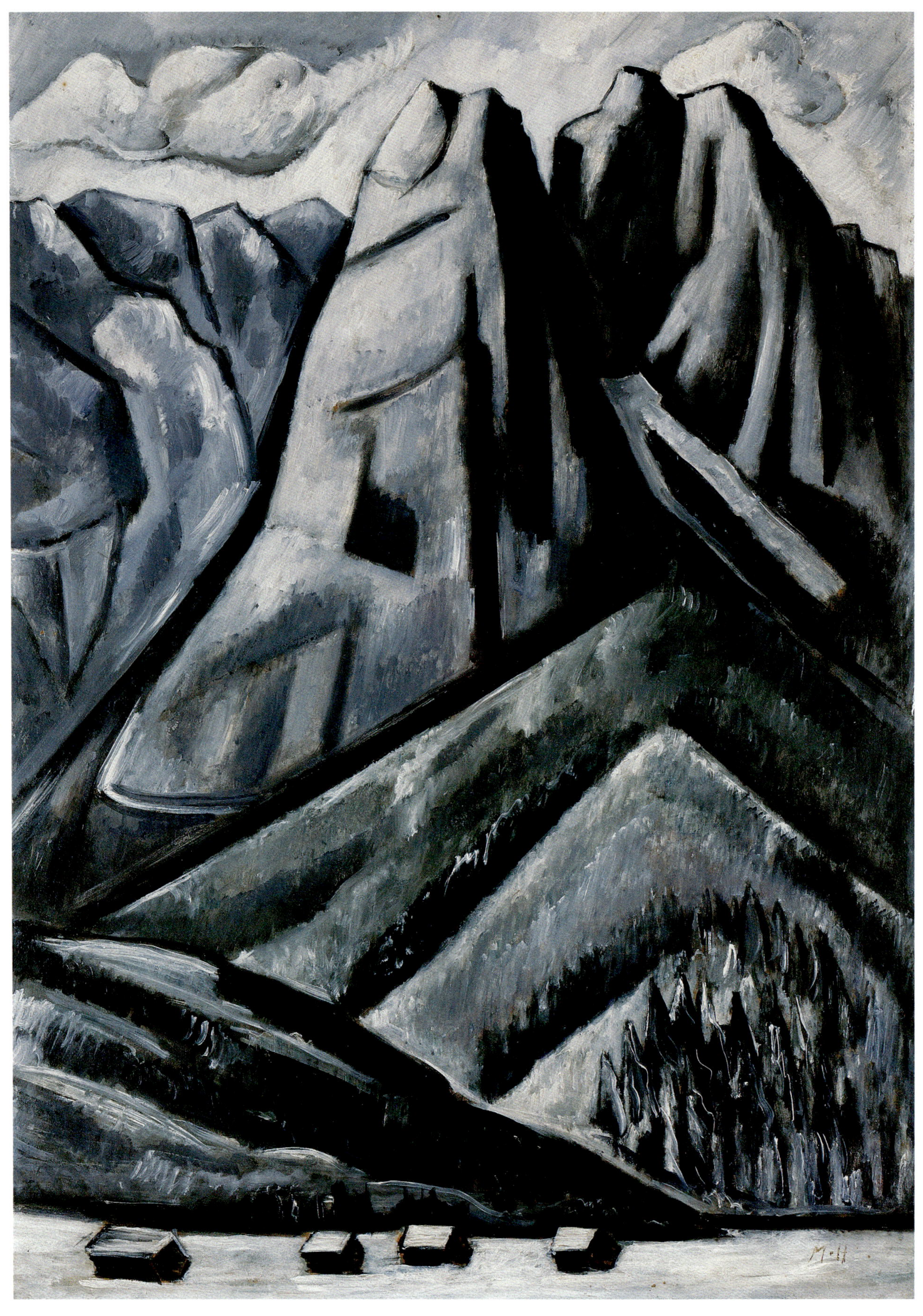

55

Waxenstein at Hamarsbach, Garmisch, Bavaria, 1933–34

Oil on cardboard, 29¾ x 20¾ in.

Private Collection

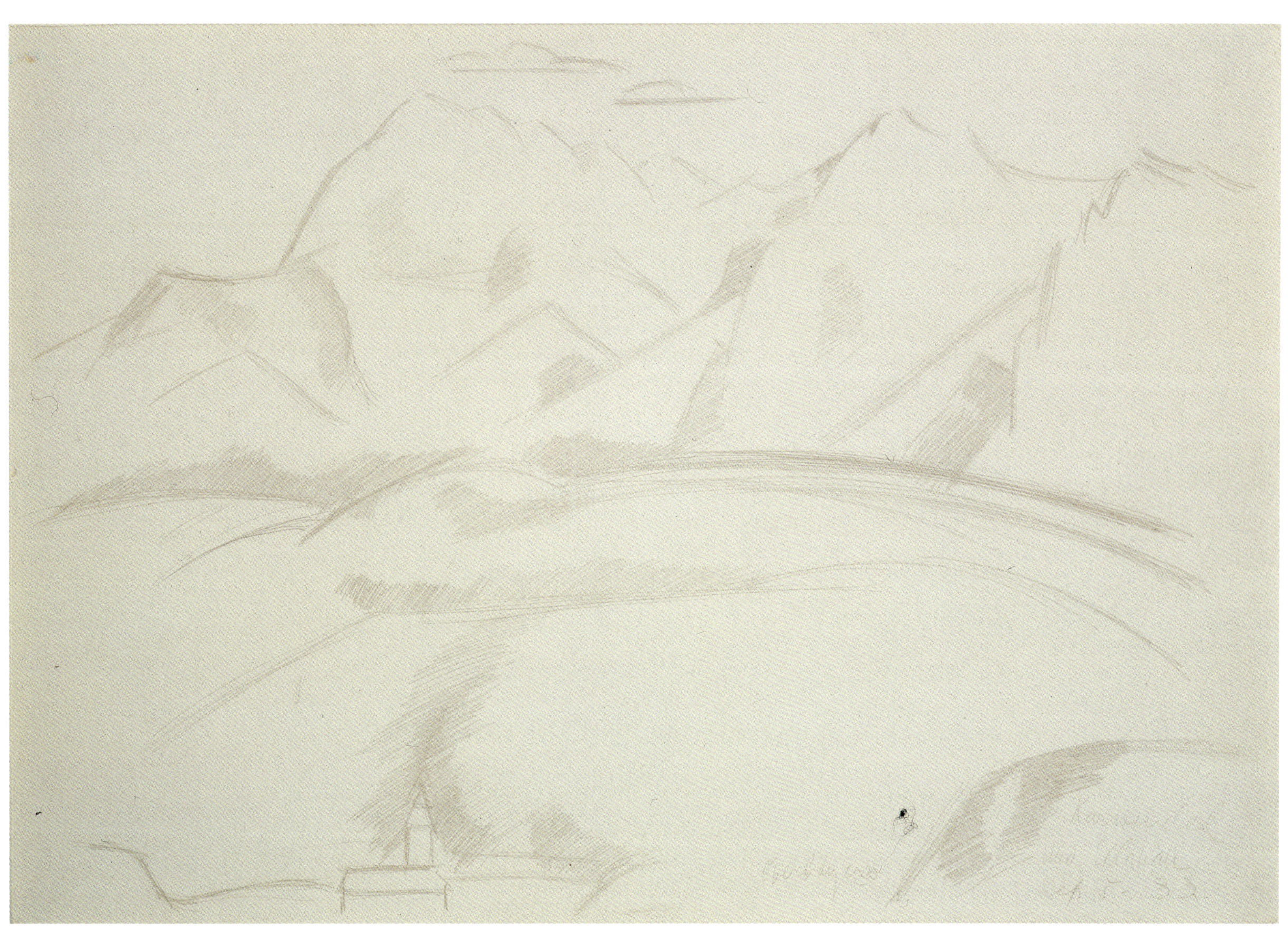

56

Mountain Landscape, Church Steeple in Foreground, 1933
Silverpoint drawing on paper, 10⅝ × 14⅞ in.
The Huntington Library, Art Collections, and Botanical Gardens,
San Marino, California
Gift of Michael St. Clair

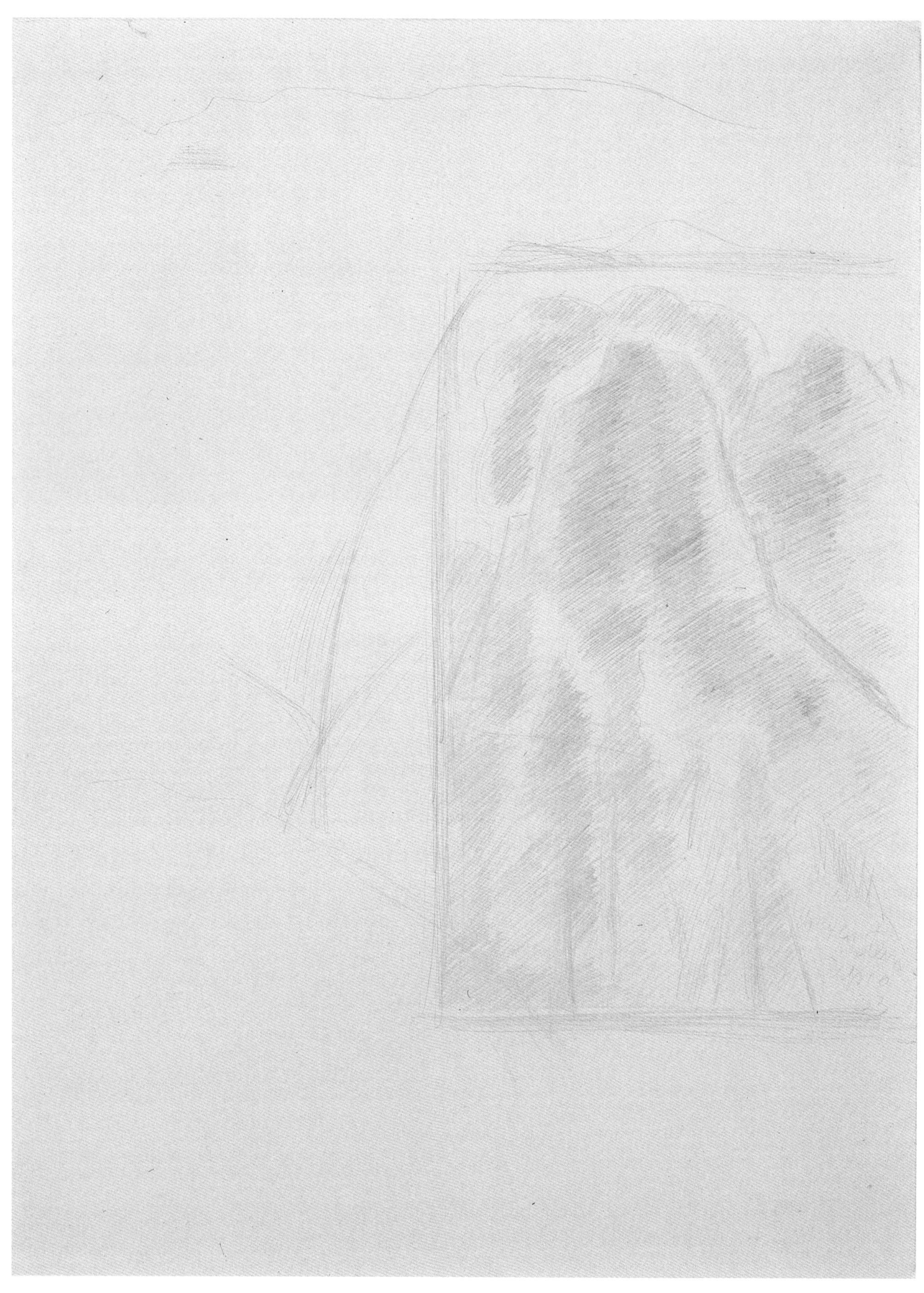

57

Mountain Landscape with Pine Trees, 1933
Silverpoint drawing on paper, 14⅞ × 10⅝ in.
The Huntington Library, Art Collections, and Botanical Gardens,
San Marino, California
Gift of Michael St. Clair

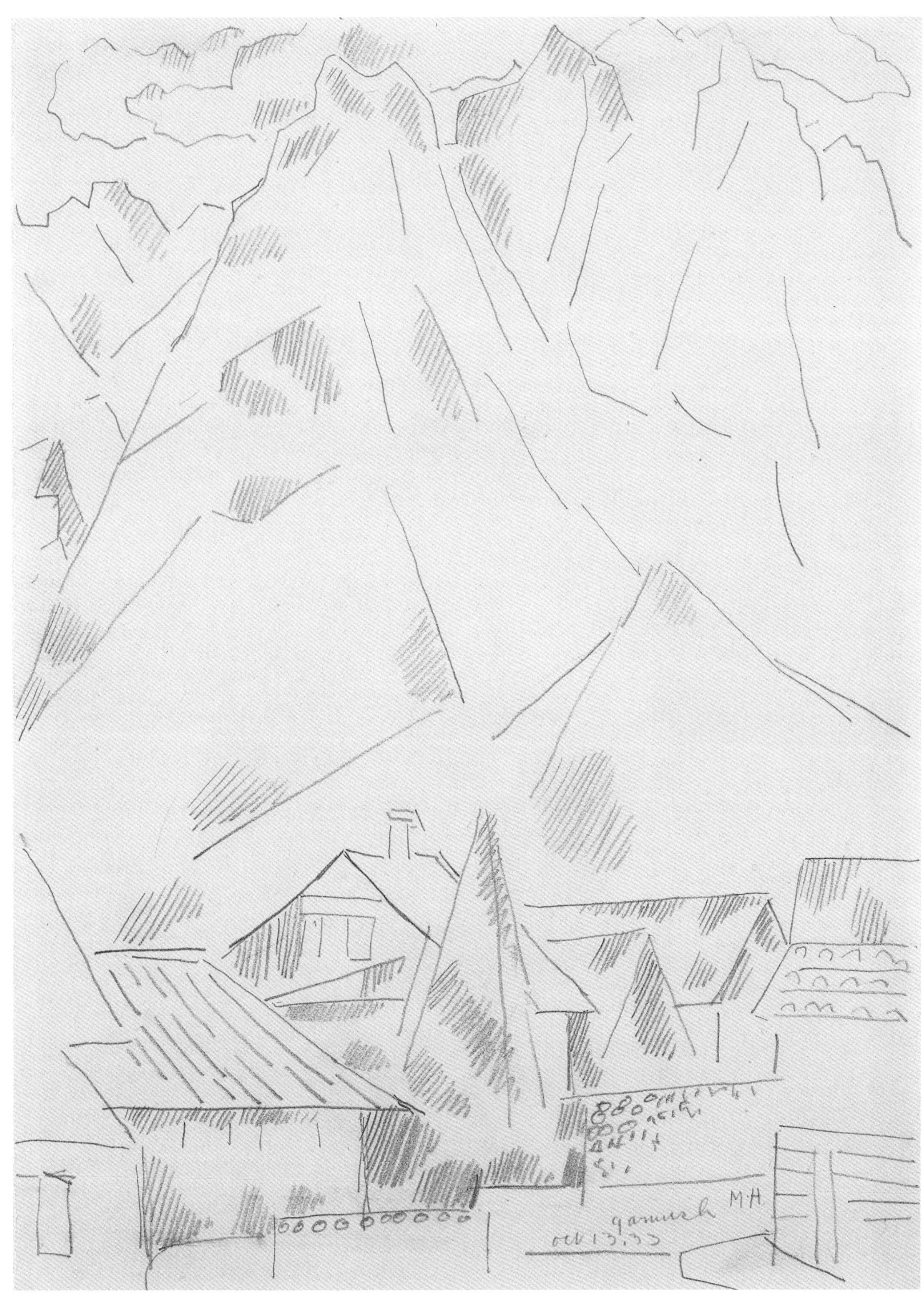

58

Garmisch, 1933

Pencil on beige paper, $9\frac{7}{8} \times 7$ in.

Bates College Museum of Art, Lewiston, Maine

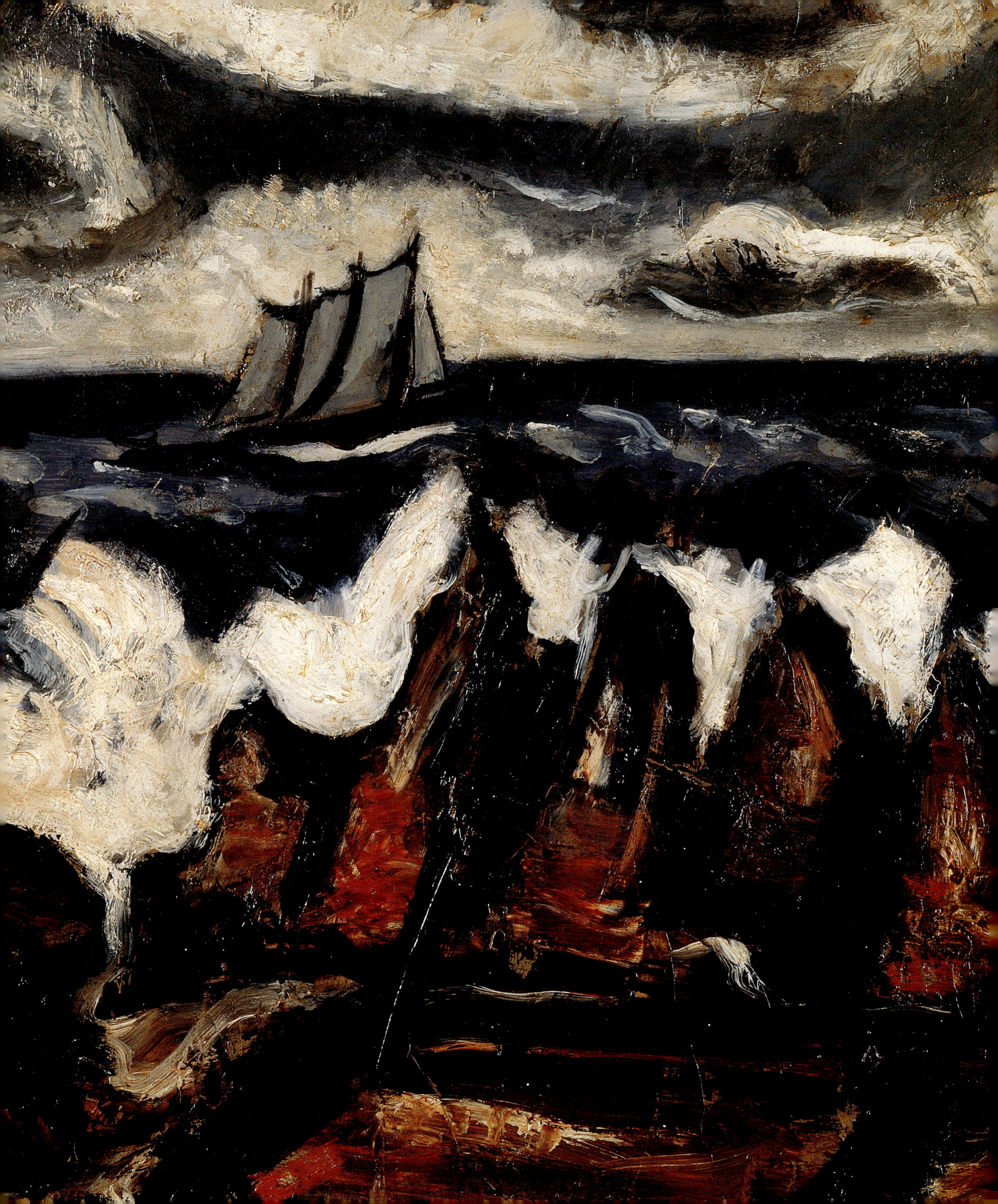

Localized Glory: Marsden Hartley as New England Regionalist

Donna M. Cassidy

Since I went back to Maine and have drawn the power of
Maine's force and grandeur to me I have taken
another spurt and my glory has become localized which
delights me beyond words—as everyone knows
of me in Maine now and is so kind and welcoming—
the State of Maine itself having sent me a
letter of "official" recognition as Maine's #1 artist—
and I am so proud of all that.[1]

Marsden Hartley to Norma Berger, April 16, 1940

Marsden Hartley's return to his native state in 1937 signaled a new phase of his career and the formation of a fresh artistic identity as "the painter from Maine." He had begun this campaign to shed the label of expatriate and to publicize himself as a regional artist with his 1930 and 1931 painting trips to New Hampshire and Gloucester and his 1932 exhibition, *Pictures of New England by a New Englander,* organized by Edith Halpert for the Downtown Gallery in New York. This campaign was stepped up in the mid-1930s owing to the worsening Depression art market and heightened Americanist discourse in the arts. Hartley recognized that Henry McBride's praise of the New England paintings in his 1936 American Place exhibition helped promote him as a native artist, and he took this powerful critic's words to heart, vowing to have a "100% Yankee show next year."[2] While the paintings on view at his 1937 exhibition did not fulfill this promise, the catalogue essay, "On the Subject of Nativeness—A Tribute to Maine," served as Hartley's regionalist manifesto. After this exhibition, he was determined to have "an all Maine show" the following year "for purposes of publicity" and planned to paint "only Maine and put Maine really on the art map as is my right."[3] This agenda shaped much of Hartley's work from 1937 until his death in 1943.

Although often interpreted as being motivated by a personal quest for home, the last in his lifelong series of restless wanderings following the childhood break-up of his family, Hartley's Maine homecoming was not driven solely by individual pursuits but by broader cultural concerns of the 1930s, particularly a newfound regionalism. A widespread identification with region emerged as part of the conservative isolation after World War I and as a way of dealing with social and cultural upheavals—urbanization, industrialization, and standardized mass culture on the one hand, and the Depression and its dislocations on the other.[4] Like many Americans, artists and writers of diverse aesthetic and political persuasions left the cities to settle in rural areas, including those in New England. Having

Detail, Plate 48

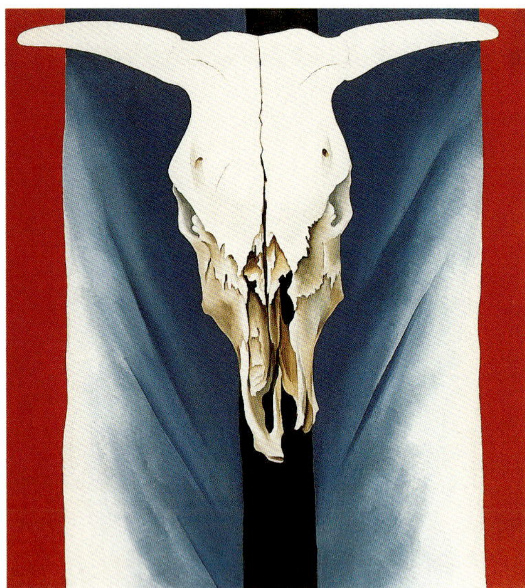

Figure 1
Georgia O'Keeffe
Cow's Skull: Red, White, and Blue, 1931
Oil on canvas, 39⅞ × 35⅞ in. (101.3 × 90.8 cm)
The Metropolitan Museum of Art, New York
The Alfred Stieglitz Collection, 1952 (52.203)
Photograph © 1994
The Metropolitan Museum of Art
© 2003 The Georgia O'Keeffe Foundation/Artists Rights Society (ARS), New York

moved to Vermont and New Hampshire respectively, Norman Rockwell and Robert Frost, for example, represented the northern rural outposts of the region as the heart of New England, the "authentic" New England, in their work. Hartley joined this migration to these northern climes in 1937 and contributed in his own fashion to this New England regionalism until his death. During this time he redefined the image of this locale in his paintings and adapted his expressionist style to subjects bound to the region, its history, and its image in the tourist culture and regional art and literature. These Maine paintings, especially those of the folk, were shaped not only by New England culture and regionalism in the United States, but by the folk cultures that Hartley experienced in both Nova Scotia and Germany as well.

In the visual arts, 1930s regionalism has long been epitomized by the American Midwest and the triumvirate Thomas Hart Benton, Grant Wood, and John Steuart Curry. The writings of these artists and their apologist Thomas Craven situated American cultural identity outside the modern and urban and in traditional rural societies.[5] Vociferously opposing modernism, they touted realism as *the* American style and one accessible to a wide audience. Midwestern regionalism, however, was more complex than its reductive rhetoric would lead us to believe.[6]

During the interwar decades, region played a critical role in the work of the Stieglitz circle, who embraced what art historian Wanda Corn has called a soil-and-spirit nationalism, an insistence upon an artist's mystical and deeply personal connection to an American place.[7] In *Port of New York: Essays on Fourteen American Moderns* (1924), for instance, the writer and critic Paul Rosenfeld figuratively located American art and the Stieglitz-circle artists in the native soil, describing Arthur Dove's "root-taking" and John Marin as "fast in American life like a tough and fibrous apple tree lodged and rooted in good ground."[8] For Rosenfeld, Hartley, who possessed an "instinctive refinement" typical of the New England temperament, needed to reconnect with the place of his birth to revitalize his art: "It is to this soil, so it would seem, that he must return."[9] Such metaphors were enlisted again as the battle between modernism and midwestern regionalism raged in the 1930s. Published as a tribute to Stieglitz on his seventieth birthday and challenging Craven's claim that Stieglitz was ill-equipped to guide the formation of an authentic American art,[10] *America and Alfred Stieglitz: A Collective Portrait* (1934) equated both the photographer and his artists with things American. Writing in this volume, critic Elizabeth McCausland argued that Dove, Marin, and Georgia O'Keeffe were continuing an American romantic tradition as they lived "under the American sun, sucking up strength from the American soil, rooted in the American earth."[11]

Indeed, in the post–World War I years, the Stieglitz-circle artists grounded themselves in native places, with Hartley making a short-lived attempt at this in New Mexico in 1918. All (with the exception of Hartley) abandoned European travel by the early 1920s and lived outside the city (at least for part of the year) in rural or natural settings. As Corn has pointed out, O'Keeffe, like the midwestern regionalists, advanced the idea that a modern American art could be created outside the urban Northeast, in her case by establishing ties to the American Southwest after her first trip to New Mexico in 1929 and building on both regional and national art traditions in such works as *Cow's Skull: Red, White, and Blue* (fig. 1).[12] Maine became identified with Marin and his art (fig. 2). Privately published for An American Place in 1931, *Letters of John Marin* portrayed the artist as both an American and a Mainer, and critics, particularly those reviewing his 1936 Museum of Modern Art retrospective, hailed him as a true Yankee (that is, a Mainer and New Englander) and heir to Winslow Homer.[13] This commentary did not go unnoticed by

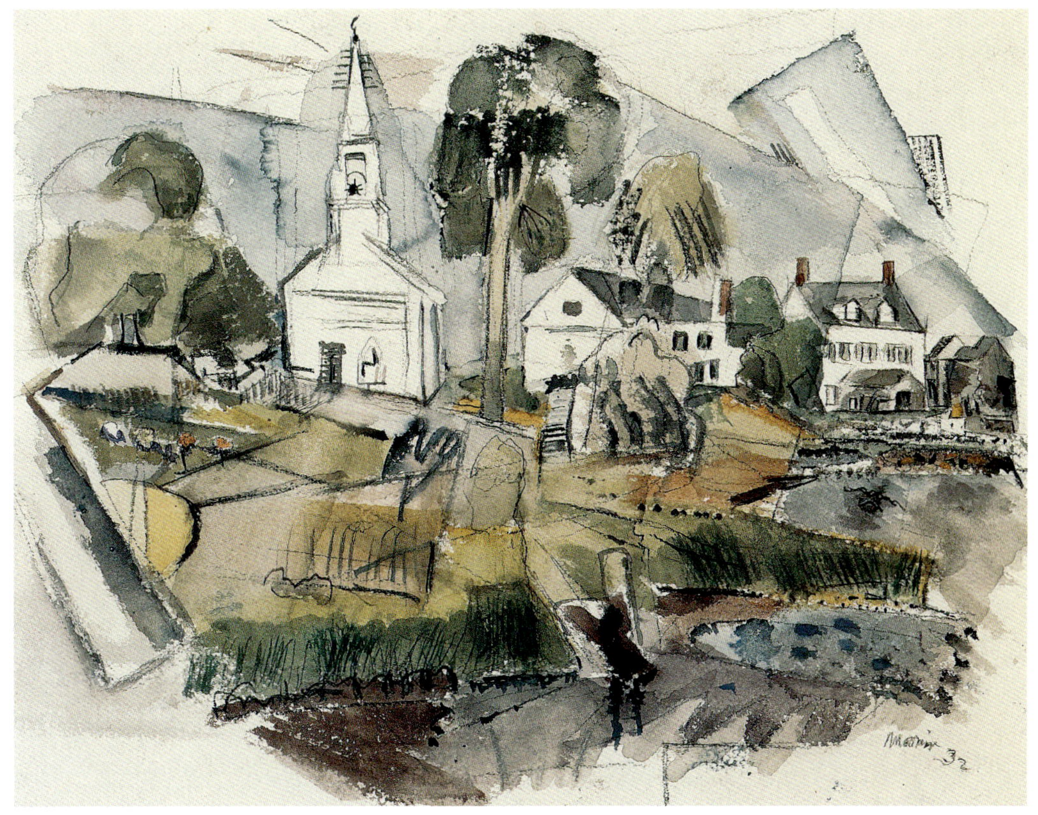

Figure 2
John Marin
Phippsburg, Maine, 1932
Watercolor on paper, 15¼ × 19⅞ in. (38.7 × 50.5 cm)
The Metropolitan Museum of Art, New York
The Alfred Stieglitz Collection, 1949 (49.70.145)
Photograph © 1981
The Metropolitan Museum of Art
© 2003 Estate of John Marin/Artists Rights Society (ARS), New York

Hartley, who resented Marin's acclaim as a regional painter as a result of this exhibition and grumbled to Stieglitz about not receiving due recognition himself as a New England artist: "Now I have the feeling everybody sees my Maine but me—and I kind of regret it— . . . well I don't know yet but a strong feeling comes over me of late to go up to Lewiston [Maine] and float some publicity on after all I am as far as I know the outstanding painter from Maine."[14] It is no coincidence that Hartley set out to play up his own Yankeeness, his own New England identity, the following year.[15]

Yankeeness had high value in the 1930s America as writers, artists, and critics sought to define the distinctiveness of New England and challenge the common perception of the region as bankrupt and in decline.[16] New England had a unique history that formed a distinctive character and that could prove edifying for Depression-era Americans. Post-1929 post office murals—Charles Anton Kaselau's *Battle at the Bridge* (1941, Concord, Massachusetts), for example, which illustrated the first skirmish of the American Revolution—reminded viewers of New England's key role in the founding of the nation,[17] while books like Lewis Mumford's *The Golden Day* (1926), Van Wyck Brooks's Pulitzer Prize–winning bestseller *The Flowering of New England* (1936), and F. O. Matthiessen's *American Renaissance* (1941) praised antebellum New England with its shipbuilding, trade, and literary achievements, especially transcendentalism, as the region's "golden age." For these authors, the region's literature—that of Ralph Waldo Emerson, Henry David Thoreau, Nathaniel Hawthorne, and Herman Melville—served as the height of New England and American literary expression. In the age of Emerson and Thoreau, as Brooks argued, the region had reached its zenith by exercising economic and cultural power and playing an important part in defining national identity: eminent Bostonians "were determined to carry out, in every sphere in which their interest lay, their duties as American citizens. They meant to make Boston a model town. They meant to make New England a model region."[18]

Transcendentalist Boston was not the only New England held forth as a model in the 1930s. For the critic Bernard DeVoto, New Englanders, especially those who lived in the inhospitable northern reaches, could instruct Americans about survival during tough times: this "almost-perfect" region, divorced from modernization and consumerism, was a society "founded on granite," and its Yankee inhabitants were "free, self-reliant," "unfrightened by the future," and masters of the "conditions of their life."[19]

In the popular and artistic imagination, the "real" New England was located "north of Boston," outside the ethnic diversity and elite Brahminism of urban centers and in rural Vermont, New Hampshire, and Maine.[20] Promoted as a pre-industrial arcadia akin to mid-nineteenth-century New England, this region of small towns, farm kitchens, covered bridges, schooners, steepled meetinghouses, traditional customs, and stone walls was pictured in the pages of *Yankee* magazine, photographs of the Farm Security Administration's Small Town Project (1938–43), and paintings by both traditional and avant-garde artists.[21] In 1939 Norman Rockwell and his new wife retreated from divorce and fear of the Depression to a farm in Arlington, Vermont, where he subsequently drew from the local community in his art.[22] Paul Sample pictured the rituals, customs, and pastoral flavor of Vermont country life in paintings such as *Beaver Meadow* (fig. 3), reminiscent of Grant Wood, while Charles Sheeler and Marguerite Zorach, in images like *Maine Landscape* (fig. 5), composed modernist visions of the bucolic, white-steepled New England village nestled in a valley surrounded by verdant hills. Pre-modern labor—fishing, lumbering, agriculture—performed by robust New Englanders took center stage in the region's post office murals, from Sample's *Apponaug Fishermen* (1942; Warwick, Rhode Island) to Waldo Peirce's *Woodmen in the Woods of Maine* (fig. 4).

A similar New England was imagined by writers like Robert Frost, who emerged as the region's mythic poet (fig. 6). With the publication of *North of Boston* (1915), Frost

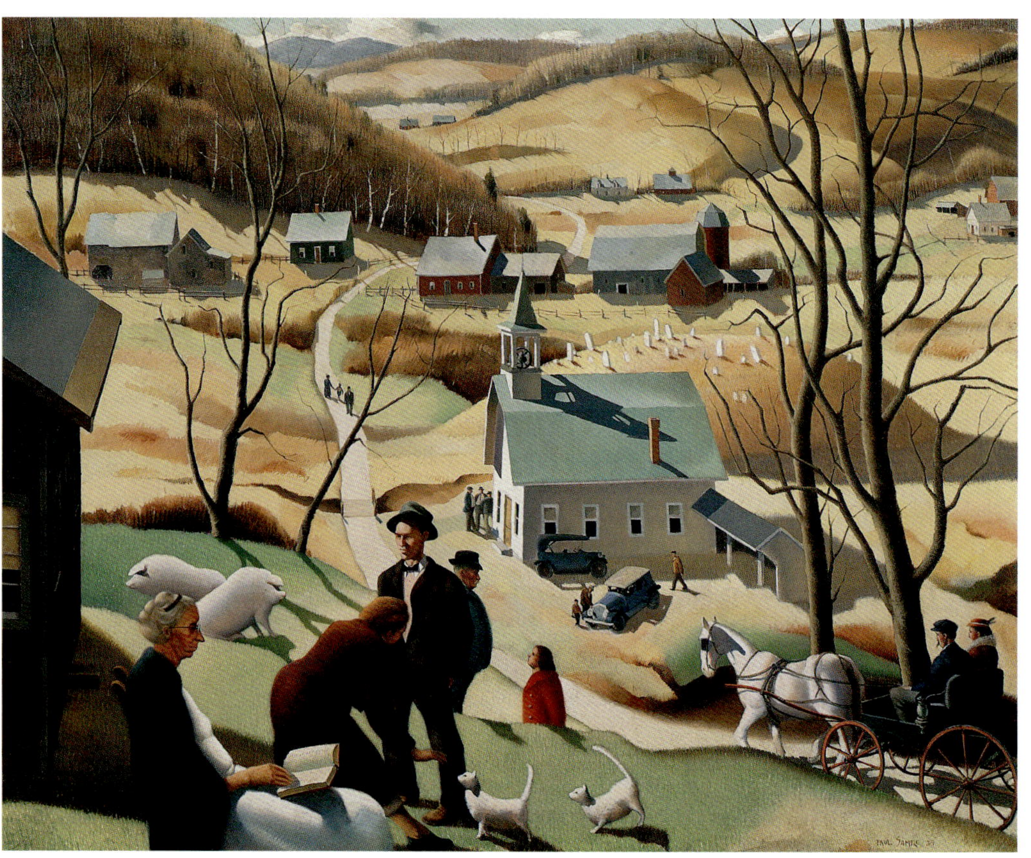

Figure 3
Paul Starrett Sample
Beaver Meadow, 1939
Oil on canvas, 40 × 48¼ in. (101.6 × 122.6 cm)
Hood Museum of Art, Dartmouth College, Hanover, New Hampshire
P.943.126.1
Gift of the artist, Paul Sample, Class of 1920, in memory of his brother, Donald M. Sample, Class of 1921

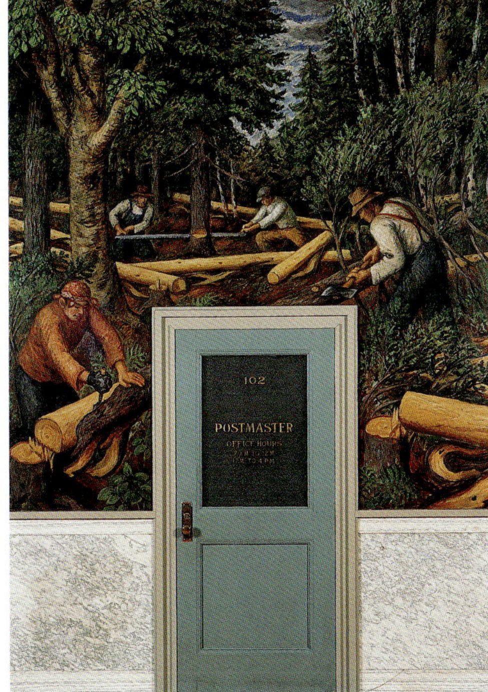

Figure 4
Waldo Peirce
Woodmen in the Woods of Maine, 1937
Oil on canvas, 117 × 110 in. (297.2 × 279.4 cm)
Portland Museum of Art, Portland, Maine
Lent by the United States Postal Service, L185
Photograph by Melville D. McLean

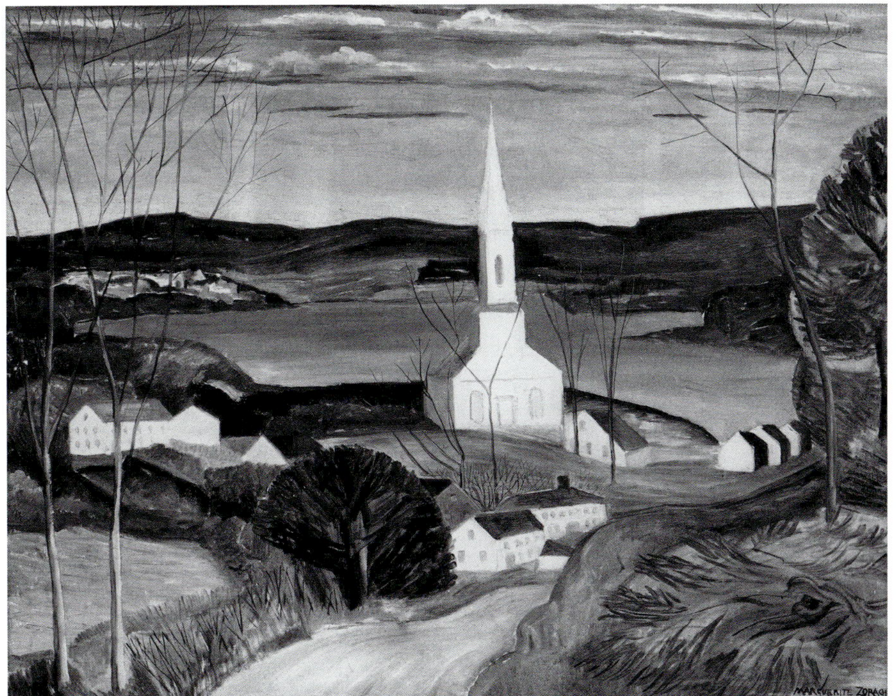

Figure 5
Marguerite Zorach
Maine Landscape, date unknown
Oil on canvas, $25\frac{15}{16} \times 31\frac{15}{16}$ in. (65.9 × 81.1 cm)
Colby College Museum of Art, Waterville, Maine
Gift of the IBM Corporation

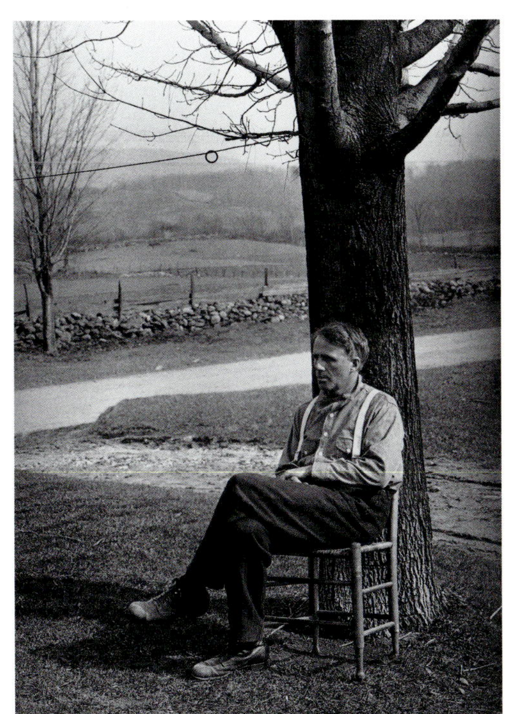

Figure 6
Paul Waitt
The Farmer-Poet at Stone Cottage, 1921
Blackington Collection
Courtesy of Yankee Publishing Inc., Dublin, N.H.

constructed himself as a "farmer-poet," a "Yankee bard," and he expertly advanced this identity in his public readings and lectures and in his poetry featuring stones walls, harsh landscapes, and the local speech of the laconic, down-to-earth, shrewd Yankees of rural northern New England. Frost's reputation flourished during the Depression and the accompanying rise of regional sentiments.[23] In his 1938 book *New Poetry of New England,* Robert P. Tristram Coffin (a writer himself and literary editor of *Yankee* magazine) described Frost and the Maine poet Edwin Arlington Robinson as leaders of a "whole new brood of New England poet."[24] Following their examples, many contemporary writers wielded their pens to craft stories and poems about the region and its exceptionality, as in *The Triad Anthology of New England Verse,* published in Portland, Maine, in 1938. This volume sought, in the words of the compiler, Louise Hall Littlefield, "to mirror New England's people, life, and landscape."[25]

Hartley contributed two poems to the volume—"The Berry House" and "She Went without Telling," which deal with the dark side of New England in the burning of an old square gray house and the quickly forgotten death of an elderly woman—and here and in his other writings and paintings participated in this New England regionalism. He was familiar with the Maine Works Progress Administration projects and regional painters like Peirce and Zorach, knew Coffin, avidly read New England literature, and often invoked the names of Frost and Robinson.[26] Frost may well have been Hartley's model as he tried to promote himself as a Maine painter. Contemporary histories of New England—Brooks's *The Flowering of New England* and Coffin's *Kennebec: Cradle of Americans* (1937), for example—inspired Hartley as he wrote his own commentaries on the region's traditions.[27]

Like Bernard DeVoto, these regionalist writers and others sought to remake the image of New England, to disrupt the association of the region with dour Puritans and deserted farms, and, instead, to tell the world about the "everlasting vigor" of the region and its inhabitants.[28] Similarly, Hartley's late paintings represented the region as potent, vibrant, pre-industrial, as DeVoto's society "founded on granite," through subjects like the manly folk, the rocky coast, and Mt. Katahdin painted in a bold, rugged style. They, moreover, show his desire to engage with the past as a way to define regional identity during the Depression years—a desire Hartley shared with contemporary artists, writers, and filmmakers across New England and the United States.

Upon his arrival in Georgetown, Maine, in 1937, Hartley planned to paint Edwin Arlington Robinson's birthplace along with the nearby church at Head Tide, the "amazing little white church which no one has done and is 'mine' really."[29] *Church at Head Tide No. 2* (plate 89) is constructed from thick, painterly brush strokes, and the perspective is flattened and distorted. With its blackened windows and shaky form, it represents less an ideal white-steepled New England and seems more an artifact of a bygone day. Such images have parallels in Hartley's own poems of the period, as in the abandoned houses in "Mansion" and "The Outcast City on the Kennebec," for example, and in the New England literature he admired, especially that of Robinson, which often described Mainers whose cultural glory as mariners and shipbuilders in the nineteenth century had long passed. His painting of this "little white church" reveals the strategies that he used for representing place at this time: he selected familiar, sometimes marketable, subjects and sites associated with the region and with regional art, literature, and history (in this case Robinson), and painted them in an expressionistic style that he considered to be of a mystical and imaginative New England art tradition associated with the painter Albert Pinkham Ryder.

Born in New Bedford, Massachusetts, a town known for its seafaring history, Ryder served as a powerful inspiration for Hartley throughout his career, but especially in the late 1930s. His portrait of Ryder (plate 71), painted in 1938–39 and based on a memory of seeing the artist in New York decades earlier, was part of Hartley's hero portrait series in which he created an artistic and intellectual family for himself. Its rough paint surface and dark tones emulate Ryder's style, and these qualities can also be seen in Hartley's late seascapes. In *Northern Seascape, Off the Banks* (plate 61) the impastoed white crust of the sea foam, waves crashing against the rocky coast, dark clouds with brightened edges, and small boats sailing on a vast, inhospitable ocean match features in Ryder's *Lord Ullin's Daughter* (fig. 7), which tells the tale of two drowned lovers—a fitting narrative source for Hartley's work dedicated to the Mason brothers and their cousin who drowned off the coast of Nova Scotia. This image of the minute, storm-tossed boat against the expansive, dangerous sea recurred in Ryder's art, and Hartley associated him with this "profound spectacle of the soul's despair in conflict with wind and wave."[30]

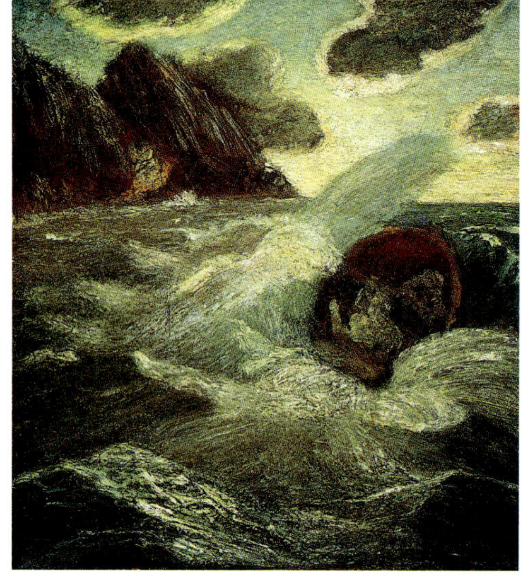

Figure 7
Albert Pinkham Ryder
Lord Ullin's Daughter, before 1907
Oil on canvas mounted on panel, 20½ × 19¾ in.
(52.1 × 49.2 cm)
Smithsonian American Art Museum, Washington, D.C.
Gift of John Gellatly, 1929.6.101

In Hartley's estimation, Ryder's style was affiliated with both an Americanness and a New Englandness. Hartley challenged the midwestern regionalists' claim that realism was the national artistic mode by defining the dramatic mysticism of George Fuller, Homer Dodge Martin, Ralph Blakelock, and Ryder as a "possible and plausible basis for a genuine American art."[31] His two 1937 essays on the history of New England art—"The Six Greatest New England Painters" and "On the Subject of Nativeness—A Tribute to Maine"—argued Ryder's poetical and subjective manner as central to the New England art tradition.[32] The former claimed that Ryder, Fuller, and Winslow Homer did the most to establish a New England art, although Ryder, "the great mystic," was "the greatest of them all because he went deeper into the realities of the imaginative life of New England."[33]

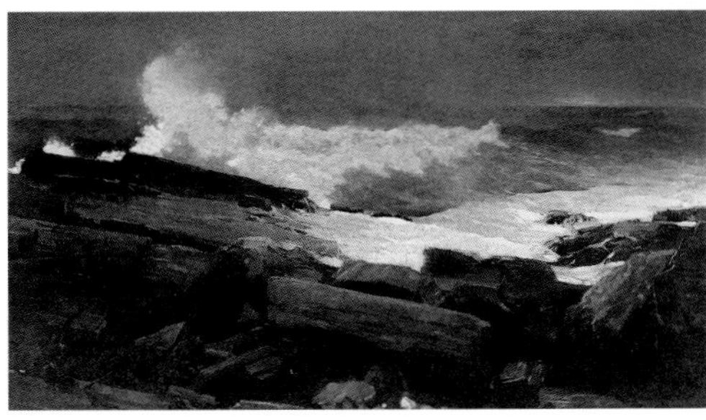

Figure 8
Winslow Homer
Weatherbeaten, 1894
Oil on canvas, 28½ × 48⅜ in. (72.4 × 122.9 cm)
Portland Museum of Art, Portland, Maine
Bequest of Charles Shipman Payson, 1988.55.1

For Hartley, the introspective and spiritual defined the New England character, as these attributes were evident in writers like Ralph Waldo Emerson and Emily Dickinson. He foregrounded the mystical temperament as central to New England art too, claiming that "This quality of abstract yet definite reality appears in the realm of art in its strongest and most powerful degree in the paintings of Albert Ryder, who has said once and for all—all that will ever be known about that country."[34] By emulating Ryder, Hartley asserted his own identity as a New England artist. Written in the 1930s, his autobiography recalls his first viewing of a Ryder seascape as the most crucial moment in his early career, as it brought out all Hartley's "essential Yankee qualities," "stamped" him an American, and "converted him to the field of the imagination" into which he was born.[35] Such associations served to authenticate Hartley as a bona fide regional artist.

Hartley tied his seascapes not only to Ryder but to other New England artists and writers from the past. For him, the "dramatic entities" and "devilish treacheries" of Ryder's sea had an affinity with Herman Melville's novels like *Moby-Dick* (1851), an account of the New England whaling industry (the *Pequod* embarks from New Bedford) and a sea adventure story with storms, lightning, and the white whale overwhelming the vessels and crews (save Ishmael).[36] This power of the sea, which was so essential to Hartley's late seascapes (plates 96, 99), also referred to Homer's paintings of the Maine coast (fig. 8), as Bruce Robertson has shown.[37] Reviews of the Homer 1936 centennial exhibitions at the Whitney Museum of American Art, Knoedler's Galleries, and Macbeth Gallery stressed Homer's status as a Maine artist and his Prout's Neck works as the best of his career—an association that Hartley could not ignore.[38] In "On the Subject of Nativeness" he lists Homer along with Ryder as a foremost New England artist, a "fierce Yankee" who painted in Maine, and elsewhere argues his own bond with Homer: "I have always been proud as a yankee, that Homer's inspiration and his sense of dramatic nature were derived chiefly from my own native rocks, at Prout's Neck, Maine."[39]

Homeresque images of crashing waves along the Maine coast were plentiful in tourist literature as well, and such views were considered not only scenic but replete with historical significance. Tourists were reminded over and over again that the Maine coast was the setting of historical events, particularly during the seventeenth and eighteenth centuries: "One would not be an American if he did not thrill to the historical significance of this region where once five nations vied for supremacy."[40] The coast had other connections with the region's history. Antebellum shipbuilding and trade along the north Atlantic seaboard were presented as the apex of the region's culture in Brooks's *The Flowering of New England* and Coffin's *Kennebec: Cradle of Americans,* and Hartley, impressed by these texts, recorded his own thoughts on this maritime history in his essay "This Country of Maine" (c. 1937–38). In the late eighteenth and early nineteenth centuries, New Englanders acquired wealth through shipping and lumbering, and with their money, Hartley points out, they built mansions from Salem, Massachusetts, to Eastport, Maine, "that still survive and keep up their aristocratic appearances as if times had not changed." But times had changed and these industries were in decline—a situation lamented by Hartley, who singled out the old sailing ships grounded and keeled over in Boothbay Harbor and Wiscasset as reminders of Maine's illustrious history (fig. 9). He thought it would be a "fine regional gesture ... if someone for purposes of appearances and the grand picture these ships make in a harbour, would set them all up on their keels again."[41] Given his fascination with New England's maritime history, Hartley's paintings of ships from the late 1930s and 1940s can be understood as his attempts to recreate "grand pictures" from the past, albeit recast in a bold, modern style.

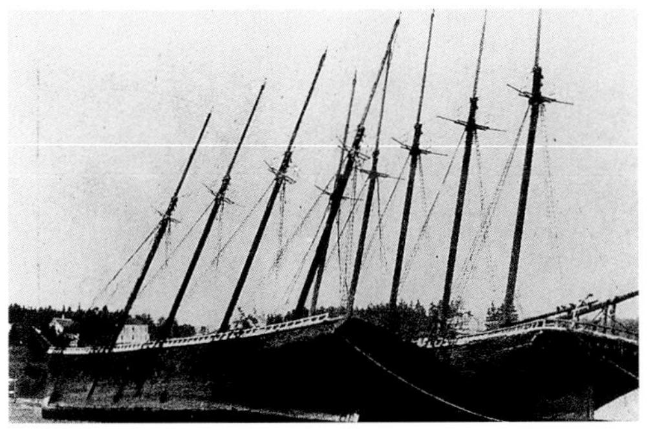

Figure 9
Grounded schooners in Boothbay Harbor
Federal Writers' Project of the Works Progress Administration for the State of Maine, *Maine, A Guide "Down East"* (Cambridge, Mass.: Riverside Press, 1937)

Figure 10
Marsden Hartley
Birds of the Bagaduce, 1939
Oil on board, 28 × 22 in. (71.1 × 55.9 cm)
The Butler Institute of American Art, Youngstown, Ohio

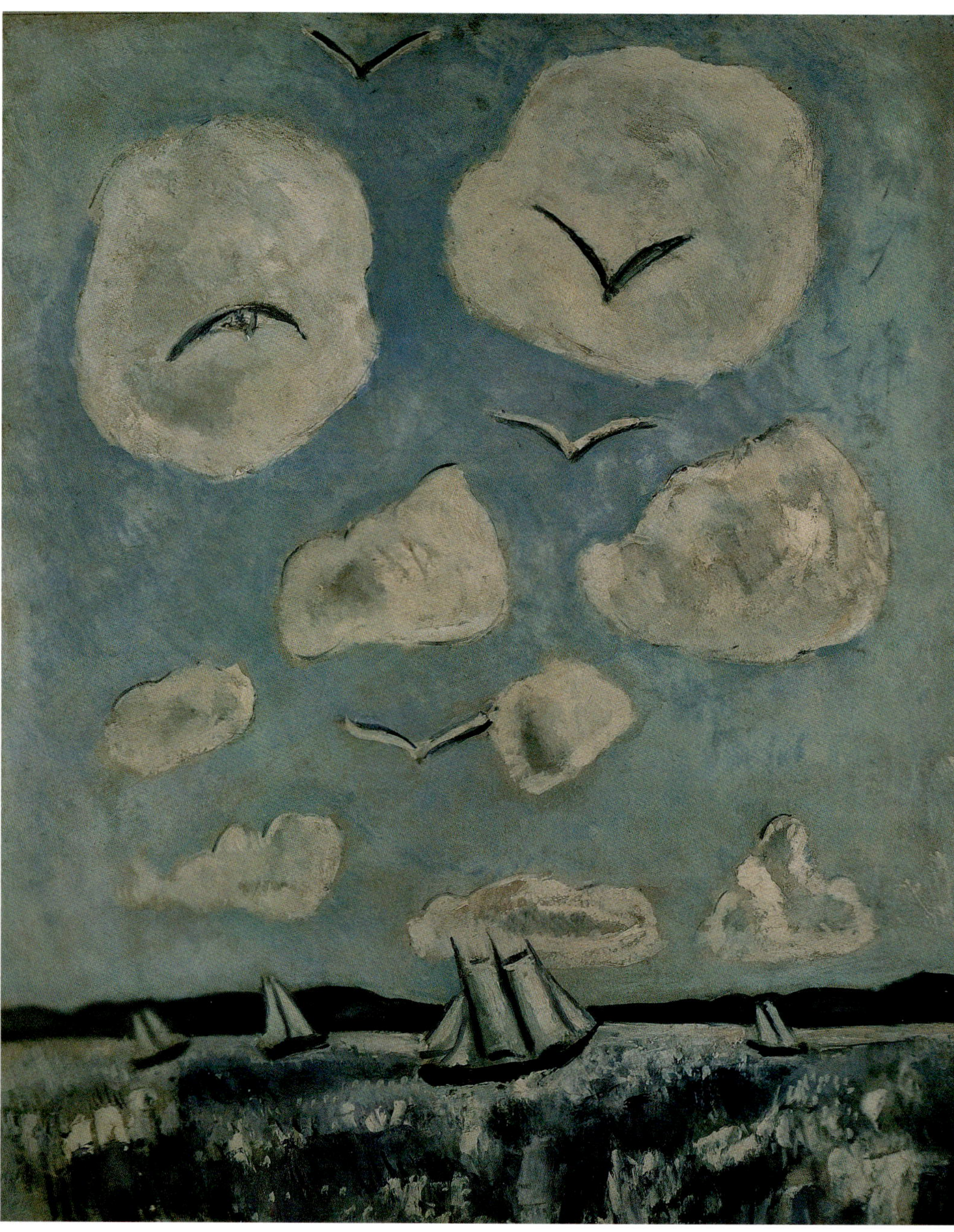

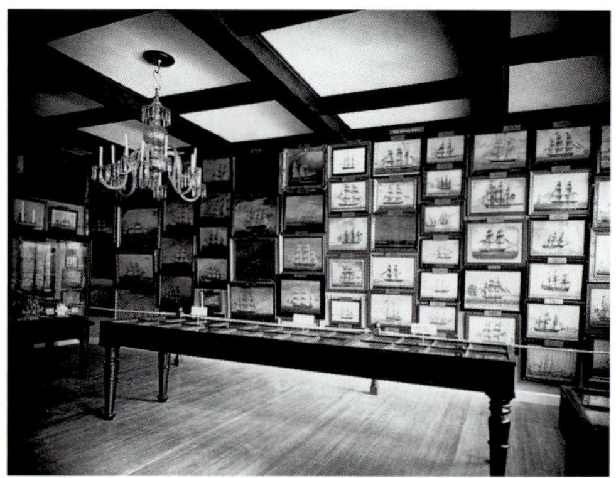

Figure 11
Unknown Photographer
Ship pictures in the Marine Room, c. 1907
View of the East India Marine Museum, Salem, Massachusetts, west side
Photograph courtesy of the Peabody Essex Museum, Salem, Massachusetts

In *Birds of the Bagaduce* (fig. 10) he paints not the downed vessels of a bygone day but four schooners in full sail gliding on a sunlit day and under an expansive blue sky at a location (the Bagaduce River in Castine, Maine) known for its shipping, lumbering, and trade in the nineteenth century.[42] This work drew from Hartley's study of New England maritime art as well. On his frequent visits to the East India Marine Museum in Salem, Massachusetts (fig. 11), he admired the ship paintings, "all done with that touching sense of truth and fidelity to fact that gives them the right to be called good art."[43] While the schooners in *Birds of the Bagaduce* and the one adorning the wall in the 1940–41 *Fishermen's Last Supper* (plate 70) are missing the detailed descriptions of such paintings, they nonetheless make reference to this regional art tradition that Hartley and his contemporaries associated with the height of New England culture, the age of maritime supremacy.

Other sea relics and marine objects figured into Hartley's late still lifes like *Crab, Rope, Seashells* (fig. 12) and *Lobster on Black Background* (plate 101). The sea creatures and objects in these paintings seem timeless, suspended in ether, floating in the ocean's depths, not unlike the effect created by O'Keeffe in paintings like *Shell and Feather* (c. 1940; Colby

Figure 12
Marsden Hartley
Crab, Rope, Seashells, 1936
Oil on panel, 12 × 16 in (30.5 × 40.6 cm)
Private Collection
Courtesy of Babcock Galleries, New York

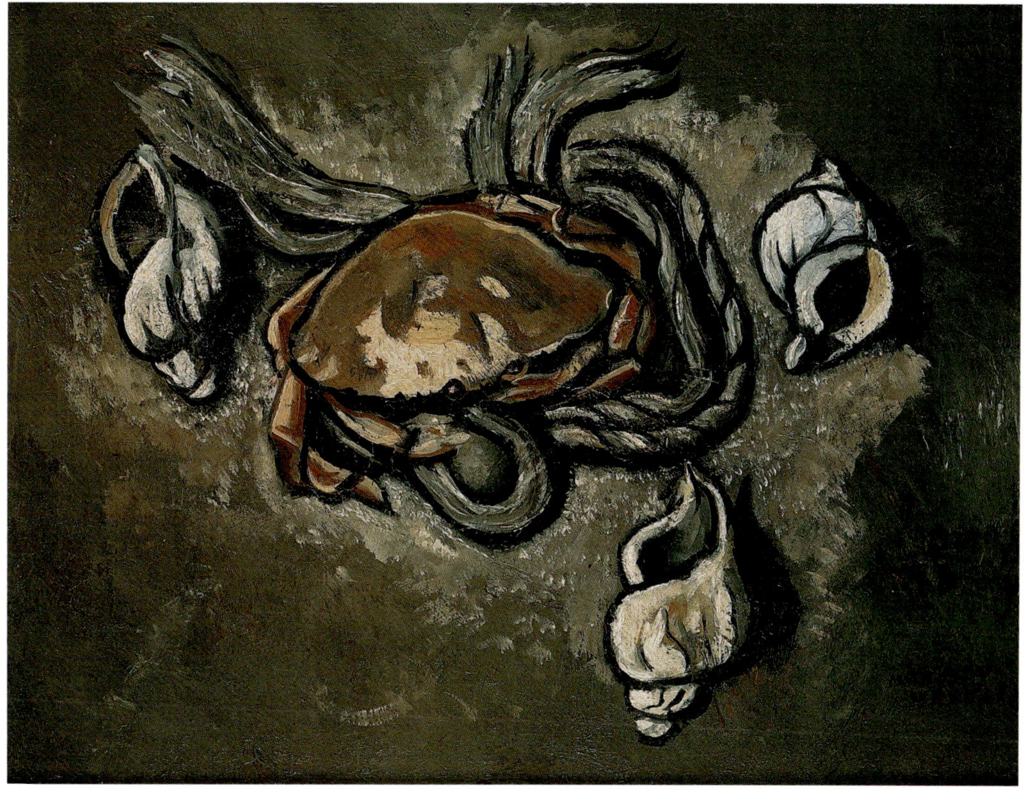

College Museum of Art). The intense focus on the abstract formal qualities of objects evident in these works was essential to the language of American early modernist art, as was the evocative power of these objects. Artifacts in Hartley's *Portrait of a German Officer* (plate 19) and *Insignia and Glove* (1936; private collection) functioned as stand-ins for Karl von Freyburg and the Mason brothers respectively, while those in *Crab, Rope, Seashells* and *Lobster on Black Background* operated as signs of the region. Hartley wrote about the "fragments of rope thrown overboard out on the Grand Banks by the fishermen or shells or other crustaceans driven in from their moorings among matted sea weed and rocks" in the "portraits of objects" in his 1937 exhibition as "representing the visible life of place."[44] Such objects represented place not only in the here and now but in the past. Shells were associated with other times, as Hartley sketched a direct line from these objects to ancient Native American culture in Maine in his poem "Arrowhead and Clamshell."[45]

The lobster was particularly associated with New England history and remains a Maine icon that, by the 1920s, was prevalent in state tourism. One 1939 brochure published by the Maine Development Commission sketched the history of the lobster and even spoke of its "discovery" as food in colonial times.[46] Photographs of visitors eating at lobster pounds were common in this promotional literature, as kettles for boiling live lobsters were set up for motorists along Maine's roadsides, especially Route 1 along the coast. Hartley could not help but be influenced by this visual culture of the tourist's Maine. The lobster in his own *Lobster on Black Background* sits boiled and ready to eat much like the one in the Warren's Lobster House billboard in Kittery, which greeted tourists to the state from 1941 on (fig. 13). The simple, bold form of this work even seems to replicate the billboard style of such popular images, which came to stand for regional identity.[47]

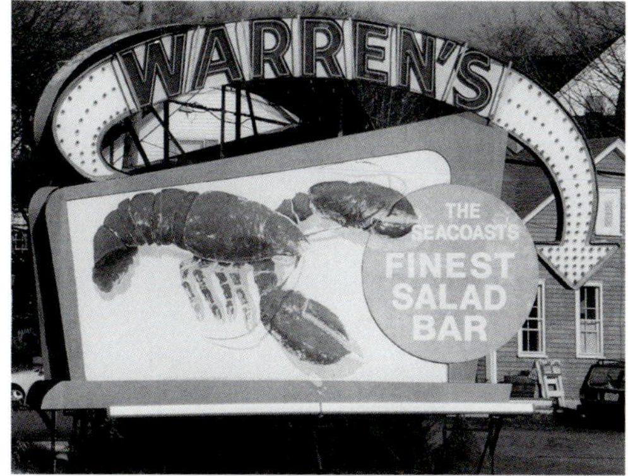

Figure 13
Donna Cassidy
Warren's Lobster House, Kittery, Maine, 2001
Photograph

Hartley often, though, engaged in anti-tourist rhetoric, claiming, for instance, in a 1931 essay that New England was "swinging on the trapeze of modern commerce" and that few spots remained that were "free from exploitation."[48] While in Maine in his late career, he lived largely in places outside the more populated tourist meccas, for example the small fishing village of Corea. It might then seem ironic that Hartley produced a painting like *Lobster on Black Background* so closely allied with tourist iconography. But Hartley was not immune to the appeal of tourism in Maine. Corea is located only a short drive north of the resort area of Bar Harbor, and Hartley himself was drawn to the popular attractions Old Orchard Beach and Mt. Katahdin. Such sites, particularly the latter one, were as much identified with the region's past as with its tourist present.

In 1939, the year that Hartley trekked to Katahdin, the Bangor and Aroostook Railroad's promotional magazine, *In the Maine Woods,* published Myron H. Avery's essay "Katahdin: Its History," which addressed the mountain's many pasts—its place in Native American legends, the period of European explorations and survey mapping, the history of lumber operations, and the more recent establishment of sporting camps and Baxter State Park. The Katahdin landscape offered a picture, "as in a museum, of the most characteristic feature of the Maine Woods," with the ruined dams and decaying lumber camps a "memorial," "a tribute to a glorious past."[49] Katahdin's place in American artistic and literary history was a recurrent topic for commentators too. One article in the 1940 issue of *In the Maine Woods* reported on the visual artists who had ventured to Katahdin, the "great American Landscape School of the last century," including Frederic E. Church, the "master painter of Katahdin." Quoting from an article about Church's 1877 expedition, it speaks of his attraction to the view of the mountain from Katahdin Lake's southern shore and reproduces several of Church's paintings showing this vista.[50] Also frequently mentioned in such literature was Henry David Thoreau, the most famous literary chronicler of the area with *The Maine Woods* (1864), which recorded the author's trips to Katahdin and the Moosehead Lake region in 1846, 1853, and 1857.

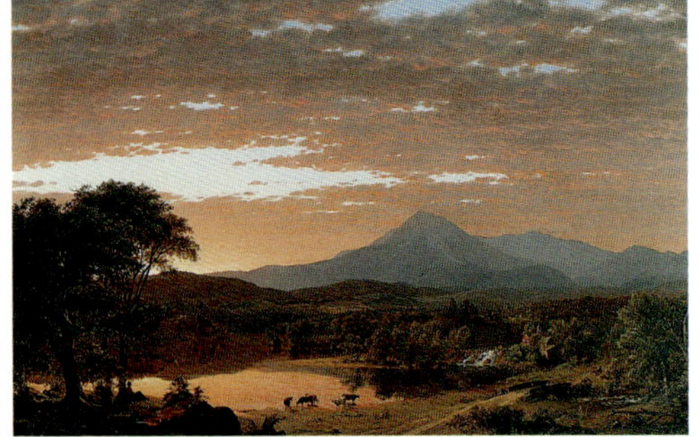

Figure 14
Frederic Edwin Church
Mt. Ktaadn, 1853
Oil on canvas, 36¼ × 55¼ in. (92.1 × 140.3 cm)
Yale University Art Gallery
Stanley B. Resor, B.A. 1901, Fund

This history of Katahdin shaped Hartley's perception of the mountain and its importance in regional identity. He recognized the Native American associations of this mountain. An admirer of the folklorist Fannie Hardy Eckstorm, he undoubtedly knew her *Katahdin Legends* (1924), a collection of the Katahdin myths based on oral histories of the Penobscot Indians, since the Pamola legend—Eckstorm's particular focus in this text—figured in Hartley's essay recounting the adventures of a boy lost on the mountain.[51] Thoreau,

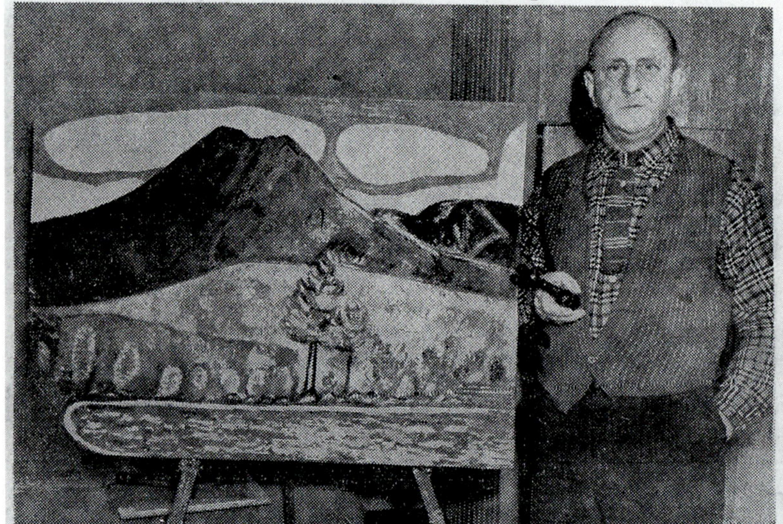

Katahdin As Seen By Bangor Painter

This view of Mount Katahdin was painted by Marsden Hartley, American artist who was born in Lewiston, Maine, and who for the winter months is in Bangor as an instructor for the Bangor Society of Art.

Mr. Hartley, after years in Paris, Munich and New York has returned to his native state and is again painting mountain, shore and forest. He has made a wide reputation as an artist, and the Art society feels fortunate in having him this winter as an instructor in painting and sketch classes.

Mr. Hartley stands beside his canvass.

Figure 15
"Katahdin as Seen by Bangor Painter"
Bangor Daily News, February 8, 1940
Marsden Hartley Scrapbook
Yale Collection of American Literature
Beinecke Rare Book and Manuscript Library
Yale University, New Haven

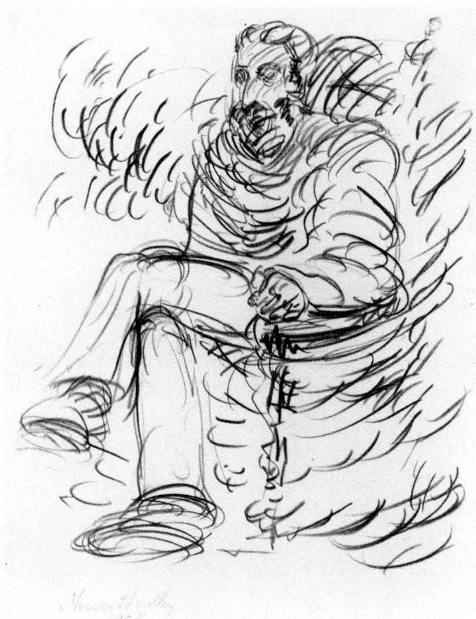

Figure 16
Marsden Hartley
Old Man in a Rocking Chair, 1908
Graphite on paper, mounted on cardboard, 12 × 8 15/16 in. (30.5 × 22.7 cm)
Frederick R. Weisman Art Museum, University of Minnesota, Minneapolis
Bequest of Hudson Walker from the Ione and Hudson Walker Collection

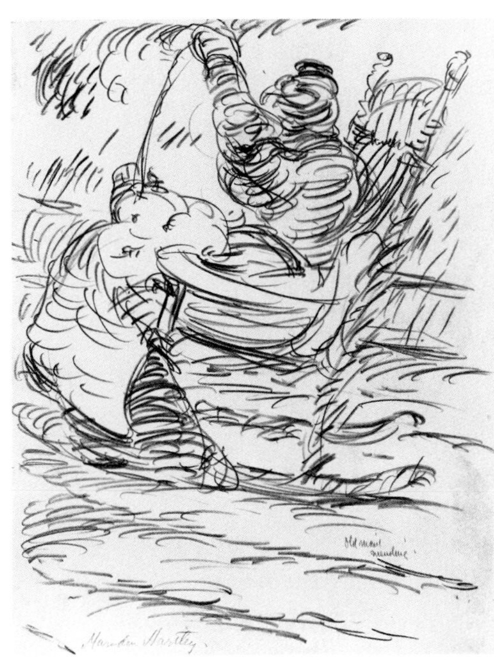

Figure 17
Marsden Hartley
Old Maid Mending, c. 1908
Pencil on paper, 12 × 8 7/8 in. (30.5 × 22.2 cm)
The Brooklyn Museum
Gift of John and Paul Herring in memory of Mr. and Mrs. H. Lawrence Herring

in Hartley's mind, was also tied to Katahdin. Because of *The Maine Woods,* he wrote, "the name of Ktaadn can of course never be spoken alone—because Henry has immortalized himself in relation to that mountain for all time."[52] While Hartley did not speak of Church in the same terms, he was probably aware of his predecessor's Katahdin paintings. Hartley claims his own role as Katahdin recorder by stating that no other artist had portrayed the mountain from the exact spot he had, from Cobb's Camp on the southern shore of Katahdin Lake, a vantage point that took in the dramatic view of Katahdin's pyramidal cone, even though it was similar to the one preferred by Church (fig. 14).[53] Hartley's Katahdin paintings like *Mount Katahdin, Autumn No. 2* (plate 91) compress and flatten the space and simplify the scene into horizontally layered forms—lake, woods, mountain, sky and clouds, with a tall Maine pine at the base. The silhouette of the mountain's granite top stands as a monument of sorts to the region—its ancient geology, Native American myths, Thoreau's great text—just as the boulders did in Hartley's Dogtown paintings (plate 46).

Hartley's Katahdin trip can be attributed to his lifelong attraction to mountains as sacred natural monuments, and, indeed, his pilgrimage was a deeply personal experience. But his Katahdin paintings, like his seascapes, were bound to regional art, literature, and history and, as such, can be understood as part of his campaign to promote himself as a Maine artist. Katahdin's wilds shaped perceptions of Maine; for many, it was Maine. *In the Maine Woods* often characterized Katahdin as the symbol and site of the Maine wilderness, a locale of "rugged beauty," "the mountain of the people of Maine."[54] Hartley saw it as "the great image of our native state" and the "very axis by which the whole of life turns in the north region which it dominates so majestically."[55] He sought to join his identity with the mountain: "I must put myself on record as having [painted Katahdin].... I have elected myself official portrait painter.... I must get that Mt. for future reason of fame and success."[56] Katahdin was essential to Hartley's quest for a new reputation as a regional artist both in New York and in Maine, and he was photographed as a Maine woodsman in a flannel shirt next to one of his Katahdin paintings in the *Bangor Daily News* (fig. 15) to make it clear that, like Thoreau, he had "immortalized" himself in relation to this mountain.

In this photograph Hartley presents himself as a native to his fellow Mainers, as one of the Maine folk, a figure identified with the region and its past. The Maine folk were, in Hartley's words, an "all but vanished race," yet they offered a vision of the future, of a regenerated race and region, as well:

> *There is surface variation in types at this time, since foreigners have come in, the French coming down from Canada have assumed the new movements, there are many Finns and Swedes up and down the coast, some Portuguese, for all or nearly all of these people are of sea origin and so cling to any coast for natural reasons, and the fusion of Yankee with these various bloods produces a fine new type with viking appearances, and Yankee behaviors.*[57]

These new Yankees, pictured in works like *Down East Young Blades* (plate 85) and *Lobster Fishermen* (plate 88), were mostly male, often golden-haired and blue-eyed with suntanned bodies, expansive chests, and large hands signifying their labor. With their looming, blocky, physical forms, they sharply contrast with the feeble, effeminate types that stood for the region in Hartley's earlier figure drawings like *Old Man in a Rocking Chair* (fig. 16) and *Old Maid Mending* (fig. 17) and in his earlier poetic images of the spinster's "wiry hands" and the virginal male bookworm whose white hands were "not made for work" and "never redden[ed] with their own incision in the flesh of proud experience."[58] The rectangular torsos and arms, blunt lines, and chiseled features of the young blades

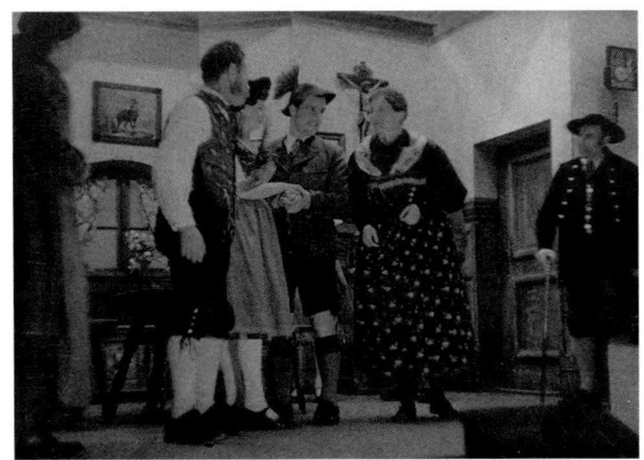

Figure 18
Unknown Photographer
Peasant Theater, Partenkirchen, Bavaria
Bates College Museum of Art, Lewiston, Maine

create the effect that they are part of the granite, rockbound New England landscape. Such paintings of the Maine fisherfolk as masculine, as a new type or race, were shaped by numerous representations of the folk on both sides of the Atlantic and in both the United States and Canada. This subject shows that Hartley's regional imagery was not provincial but drew from sources and experiences both in Maine and beyond.

Ideas about the folk as manly and as the source of racial and national identity were common in early-twentieth-century German culture. In the context of rapid industrialization and rising nationalism in Wilhelmine Germany, the rural peasant was hailed as the embodiment of a traditional, pre-modern culture and of the German nation and race. Julius Langbehn's book *Rembrandt as Educator* (1890), for example, called for the recovery of so-called German virtues—simplicity, subjectivity, individuality—possessed by the *volk* and argued for a new German art grounded in the peasantry and modeled after Wilhelm Leibl's genre paintings.[59] This book was popular among the many artists who flocked to rural colonies throughout Germany, from Worpswede to Nidden, and its theories influenced Nazi politics and aesthetics in the 1930s and 1940s. For the Nazis, Germany had been corrupted by foreigners and their cultural products, and the peasant—genuine, simple, natural—was heralded as the opposite of these external contaminants and the source of racial purity and social regeneration.

Spending time in Germany throughout his career, Hartley encountered these *volkisch* ideas. An admirer of Langbehn's model painter, he saw the Leibl paintings whenever he visited the Hamburg Kunsthalle, and, for him, they had a refreshing wholeness, a conservatism, simplicity, frankness, and authenticity.[60] Hartley was also intrigued by the emergent Nazi culture during his visit to Germany in 1933–34 when the Party was already staging pageants that celebrated the German peasant as the ideal Aryan. Although he was not a Nazi ideologue or strident fascist supporter and later criticized the regime, Hartley's political naïveté along with certain intellectual predilections and discomforts about society—an uneasiness about modernity, an elitist anxiety about the urban lower classes, a concern about racial and national impurities, an admiration for occult mysticism and idealism, and a reverence for the folk—initially made this movement interesting to him.[61]

Based in Garmisch-Partenkirchen in the Bavarian Alps in the early 1930s, Hartley studied the cultural products of the German folk such as the violin-making museum of Mittenwald, the wooden religious shrines along Alpine walkways, the site of the Passion Play in Oberammergau, and the Peasant Theater in Partenkirchen (fig. 18). He worked with the German peasant as subject matter in at least one drawing (fig. 19) and wrote about the people as the primitive Other, as simple and natural.[62] As antimodern ideals, the folk moreover preserved traditional gender roles, and Hartley saw the German peasant in this way, as representing not only a Nordic ideal but an authentic masculinity, as in his description of a young Alpine peasant sitting on a bench in the sun:

> *This young man is of magnificent build, . . . he might satisfy any nordic legend as to his overwhelming golden appearance. He is a champagne blonde, so that you would guess him to be Scandinavia [sic] or Finnish, save that he does not as in the latter have high-cheek bones.*
>
> *He is very wide and thick, . . . he is as brown as a guerrero indian where the sun has burned his creamy flesh and where the sun has not penetrated, the colour is almost girlishly fair.*
>
> *Being spread out like this on the bench, legs spread wide apart is of course narcissistic, and he wants the world to know of his masculinity.*[63]

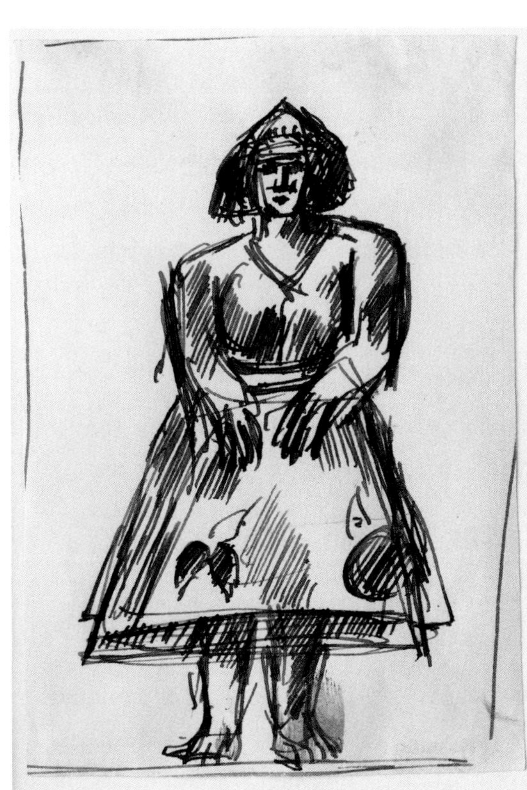

Figure 19
Marsden Hartley
Untitled (Woman in German Peasant Costume),
date unkown
Pen and black ink on paper, 5¾ × 3¾ in. (14.6 × 9.5 cm)
Marsden Hartley Memorial Collection
© Bates College Museum of Art, Lewiston, Maine
Photograph by Melville McLean

Such portrayals of the German folk that eroticize the male body can be seen as expressions of Hartley's homosexuality, but they also helped him appraise his own native region and its inhabitants. While still in Germany, he compared the German and North Atlantic people: Canada had the "warmth of the Bavarian nature and character," and the "Hamburg type" with its "almost Anglo-Saxon style and look" was "quite like my own New England in its outer behavior."[64] In his eyes, Germany was "much the same latitude as that in which I was born, and the racial life of the place here is so much second nature to me that I hardly sense it.... But I am all for the North now as symbol and as actually [*sic*]."[65] Here and elsewhere in his letters and writings, Hartley described a link between the European northerners (Germans) and American northerners (Canadians, Mainers) as all belonging to the northern race.[66] His late paintings of the North Atlantic folk established these bonds too, as the central figure in *Down East Young Blades* wears an Alpine hat and Bavarian boiled wool jacket (not unlike the one in fig. 18) along with typical Maine fishing attire (blue jeans, boots).[67] That he made such connections is undoubtedly due to the fact that German representations of the folk resembled those in Nova Scotia and Maine.

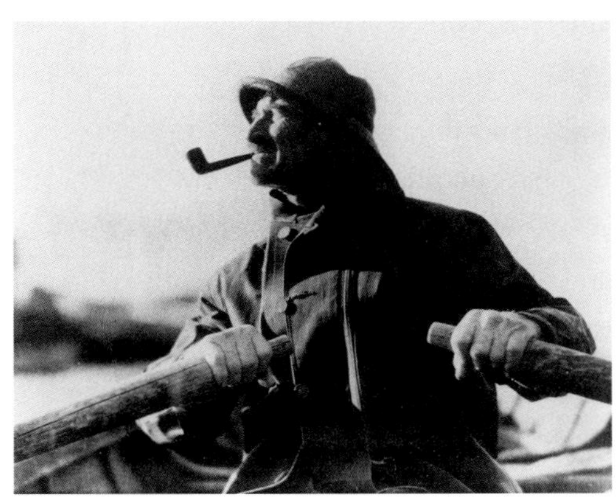

Figure 20
Wallace R. MacAskill
Son of the Sea, 1937
Out of Halifax: A Collection of Sea Pictures (New York: Derrydale Press, 1937)

The Nova Scotia folk, one of the major selling points of the province, were often pictured in tourist literature as having retained "the pleasing simplicity that marked the lives of their ancestors" and "many century-old customs."[68] As historian Ian McKay has demonstrated, by the 1930s, the fisherfolk were "unquestionably the key Nova Scotians in the tourist gaze."[69] Wallace MacAskill's photographs of physically vigorous fishermen were often reproduced in tourist brochures (fig. 20) and, through such pictures, the province came to be seen as a masculine domain. Early-twentieth-century regional literature advanced an identical image. In the 1928 novel *Rockbound* by Frank Parker Day, who wrote about the Lunenburg area close to where Hartley stayed in Nova Scotia in 1935 and 1936, the islanders are courageous, rugged individuals with a masculine power: the main character, David Jung, survives treacherous ocean storms, and Gershom Borg is described as a "blond Viking," a "blue-eyed giant."[70]

Louis Hémon's *Maria Chapdelaine: A Tale of the Lake St. John Country* (1921), a novel Hartley claimed he was never without, portrayed the rural French Canadians in that Québec region as hardy, simple, natural, religious, and in opposition to modern city dwellers, particularly those in the United States.[71] This novel also addressed the preservation of French-Canadian heritage: "So that, it may be, many centuries hence the world will look upon us and say:—These people are of a race that know not how to perish."[72] While western Canada was viewed at this time as an ethnic and racial melting pot, the eastern maritime provinces were considered a locale where the old stock survived and resisted change. Maine possessed similar racial qualities according to many commentators. As early as 1909, one writer for *In the Maine Woods* claimed the northern woods as the "dwelling place of the Anglo-Saxon race," while later publications argued that the state's isolation and resistance to modernity (considered positive qualities by disillusioned urbanites) produced a pure race and helped to retain its Yankee base—the vision of a Maine still dominated by the Yankees that Hartley shared.[73]

Hartley admired Charles C. West's *Sketches of Camp Life in the Wilds of the Aroostook Woods* (1892) and Fannie Hardy Eckstorm's *The Penobscot Man* (1904), both of which documented the lives of the northern Maine woodsmen and presented "real" Mainers like Joe Attien (Thoreau's Indian guide) and the lumberjack Larry Connor as rugged and manly. Eckstorm's book, in Hartley's estimation, had a "wealth of rich data pertaining to Maine life among the indian trappers and lumber folks," the "fine Maine types," who epitomized masculinity with their "stern granite obstinacy."[74] The hardy people who worked in the woods and lived close to the soil and sea were also the focus of the new school of Maine

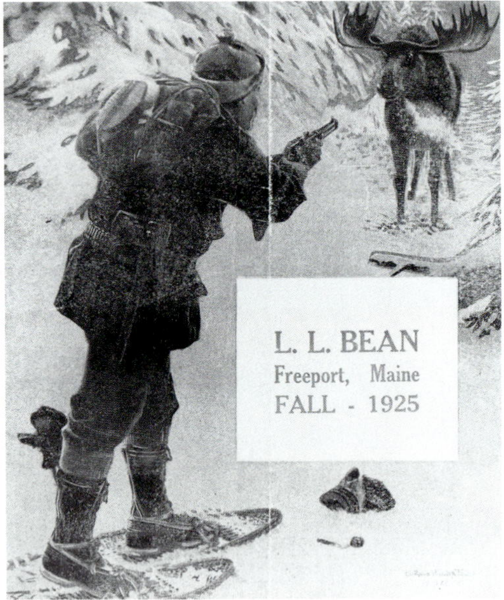

Figure 21
William Harnden Foster
The Moose Hunter, 1921
L. L. Bean Catalogue cover, Fall 1925
Original painting in L.L. Bean, Inc.,
Corporate Collection

writers in the 1930s—Kenneth Roberts, Gladys Hasty Carroll, Rachel Field, Mary Ellen Chase, Robert P. Tristram Coffin—with whom Hartley was familiar.[75] Like West, Eckstorm, and this new school, Hartley wrote about the northern woodsmen in his late essays and poems—"Wesley Adams—Maine Trapper," which describes the "tall and brawny," "broad-boned" woodsman whom Hartley knew when he stayed in the western Maine mountains in the first decade of the century, and "Maine Mountain Man," which imagines a woodsman "one size larger" than Hartley with trees and rock ledges as arms and legs.[76] This sturdy, blocky masculine type also appeared in Hartley's painting *Young Hunter Hearing Call to Arms* (Kornhauser fig. 19), and was featured in the tourist literature as well. Sinclair Lewis's 1922 novel *Babbitt* exemplified the way that the state was perceived in the eyes of outside visitors, in the character of George F. Babbitt, a real estate man, who vacationed in a Maine hunting camp because he wanted to "go off some place and be able to hear [him]self think…Maine…Wear old pants, and loaf, and cuss." He was able not only to escape the modern city in the woods but to recover his masculinity: sitting on a stump and watching his guide Joe Paradise prepare his breakfast, he "felt virile"; he was "free, in a man's world."[77] This manly Maine was aggressively marketed by state tourist agencies and spoke to a male audience, to the Babbitts of America. One brochure boasted that businessmen could return to rural life to escape the city, gain control of their lives and work, and be part of a community, while young college men with their "pioneer spirit" could move to the country "not as cogs in some great industrial enterprise, but as individuals expressing themselves in their own way."[78] L. L. Bean catalogue covers pitched the image of man-against-the-elements and presented Maine as a place for a man to test his mettle, as in William Harnden Foster's *The Moose Hunter,* which appeared on the 1925 catalogue (fig. 21).

The tourist image of the rugged Maine folk, from the manly guides, sportsmen, and woodsmen to the adventurous fishermen, was also pictured by the many artists who came to the state at the turn of the century and into the early decades of the twentieth century. Foremost among them was Winslow Homer, who promoted what Sarah Burns has called a "strenuous life" regionalism in his paintings of the Maine coast and the northern wilderness at the same time that this region was becoming a premier place for summer resorts (a process that Homer himself participated in). Prout's Neck, Maine, in *Winter Coast* (fig. 22), is transformed into a wilderness frontier, a primitive landscape of snow-covered rock ledge and twisted driftwood, inhabited by a lone hunter armed with a rifle and carrying the spoils of his excursion. In such works, Homer created a region of muscular power, vigorous health, and masculine energy that served an audience of urban businessmen in search of renewal.[79]

Following Homer to Maine, the New York realists, led by Robert Henri, translated their anthropological researches of the urban working-class to the rural working-class folk, especially the fishermen on Monhegan Island, who represented something that had been lost by the middle-class urban artists. Rockwell Kent described the Monhegan fishermen as "hardy," "horny-handed sons of toil"[80] and painted them in works like *The Seiners* (fig. 23) engaged in hard physical labor, not the so-called feminine work of the artist or city office workers. Another Henri student, Carl Sprinchorn, who was Hartley's long-time friend and who worked in Maine in the late 1930s and early 1940s, portrayed the Maine woodsmen in a similar manner. For him, lumberjacks on a river drive, with their parti-colored garments, slanted hats, and wet trousers (often slit up the sides for comfort), set "the woods aflame" with "lusty virility."[81] Echoing Babbitt's sentiments, Sprinchorn defined hunting as a male activity, "confined to a circle of 'good' fellows,"[82] and the men in his *Two Hunters* (fig. 24) show off not only their gleaming attire but their sturdy physiques.

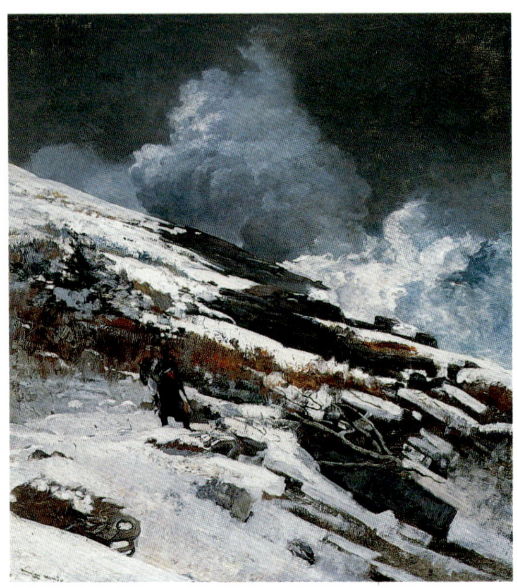

Figure 22
Winslow Homer
Winter Coast, 1890
Oil on canvas, 36⅛ × 31¹¹⁄₁₆ in. (91.8 × 80.5 cm)
Philadelphia Museum of Art
John G. Johnson Collection
Photograph by Eric Mitchell, 1986

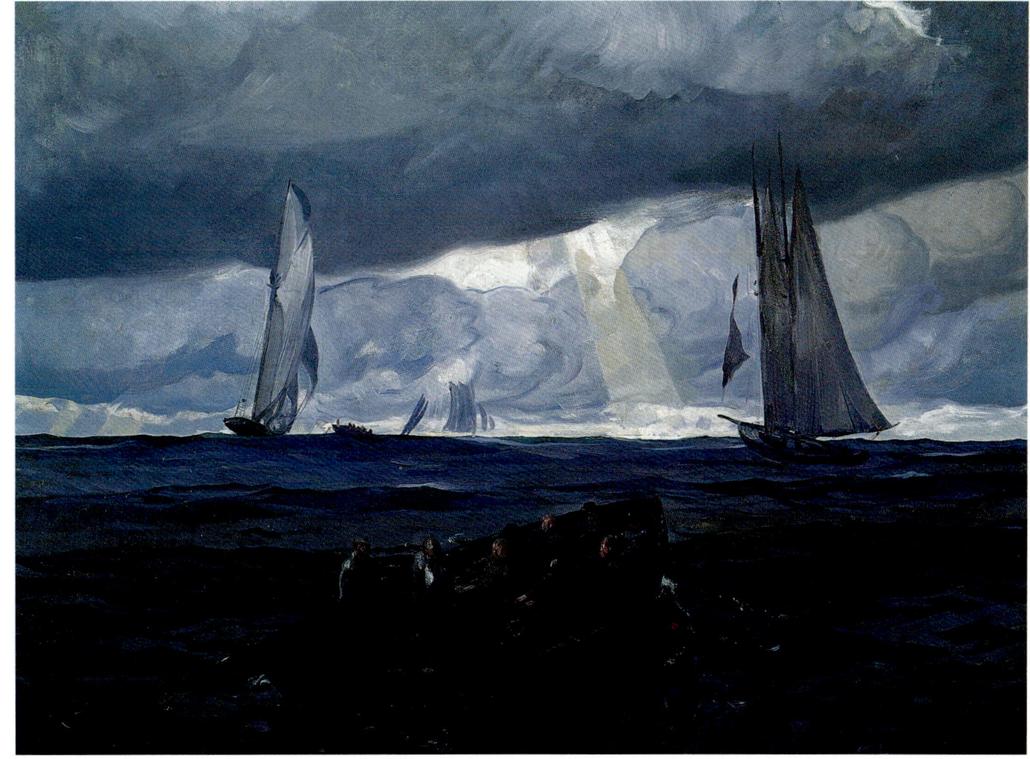

Figure 23
Rockwell Kent
The Seiners, 1910–13
Oil on canvas, 34⅝ × 43½ in. (88 × 110.5 cm)
Hirshhorn Museum and Sculpture Garden
Smithsonian Institution, Washington, D.C.
Gift of the Joseph H. Hirshhorn Foundation, 1966

Hartley's Maine fisherfolk, despite their distinctiveness, are part of this early-twentieth-century artistic lineage. In *Down East Young Blades* (plate 85), Hartley worked in a unique style, rough, sketchy, and expressive, and presented his figures with awkward proportions frontally and iconically, not laboring but holding signs of their labor. This bold technique itself was read as "virile," "all strength and sinew," with a "masculine, well-defined bluntness."[83] One critic explained that Hartley, like Homer before him, painted the "rigorous, relentless, and indomitable" Maine coast and "his idea of [its] formidable strength":

> *The huge granite monoliths which he piles one on top of the other in a mass towering against the sea, are so effectively painted in chalky whites and outlined in contrasting blacks that, were they taken from their particular pictorial content, they should still, by the character of their forms, express the inherent qualities of brutal force.*[84]

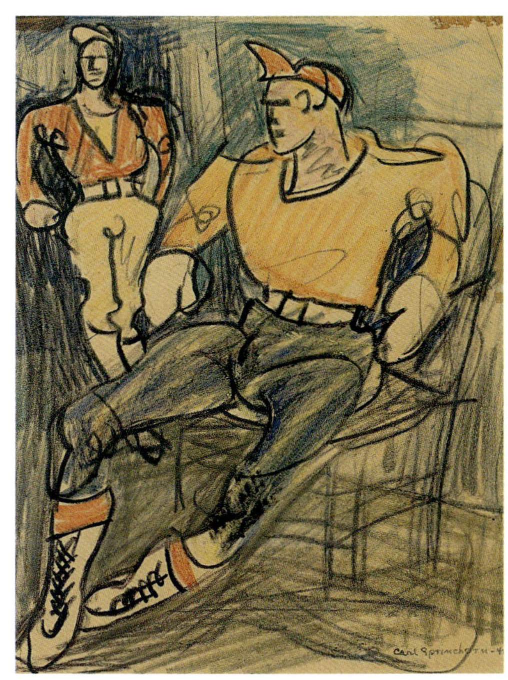

Figure 24
Carl Sprinchorn
Two Hunters (Waiting at Ted Crommett's for Tote Team), c. 1941
Colored crayon on paper, 14⅙ × 9½ in. (36 × 24.1 cm)
Marsden Hartley Memorial Collection
© Bates College Museum of Art, Lewiston, Maine
Photograph by Melville McLean

This masculine style with its force and strength was ideal for Hartley to use in painting the Maine folk—a subject imagined as manly at this time. The figures in *Down East Young Blades* and *Lobster Fishermen* (plate 88) bear a family resemblance to representations of the folk, both written and visual, in Germany, Canada, and Maine, from the manly male figures displaying their bodies in Sprinchorn's painting to the blue-eyed giants in Day's *Rockbound* and the suntanned, sensual German peasant. It was not just the visual qualities but the idea of the folk that Hartley drew from these varied sources. The cultural way of seeing the folk—as masculine, as a vital race—shaped the way that he viewed and represented the Maine fishermen. His Mainers were a "fine new type," a strong race, not the shriveled up Puritan spinsters and old men of an earlier New England. They were new Yankees.

By picturing these new Yankees, Hartley participated in New England regionalism and advanced its goal of recasting the region's image. His paintings of the manly folk, the rockbound coast, and Katahdin gave vision to a fresh regional identity, a vision of a society "founded on granite." It was a region not in decay (as earlier pictured) but vital and populated by those who embodied the physical qualities of place (rocky, rugged). These solid, hardy people were shaped by New England's harsh geography. As Hartley himself wrote, "The opulent rigidity of this north country ... produces a simple unaffected conduct and with it a kind of stark poetry exudes from their behaviours, that hardiness of gaze and frank earnestness of approach."[85] These people survived the trials of their environment but had also survived the trials of their past, and their history is a constant present in Hartley's late work. He did not deal with the region's history in a sentimental or anecdotal fashion but rather poetically evoked this past by selecting subjects and even a style filled with historical regional associations.

Hartley's paintings, moreover, combined both the regional and the modern. Writing in 1940 in the *Boston Globe,* Lucien Price noted this negotiation between the new style and common themes when he proclaimed Hartley a native, "one of our own Yankees painting in extremely modern style landscape and people familiar to us."[86] Indeed, Hartley achieved at the end of his career notoriety as a Yankee artist, a Maine painter—a localized glory within the state and in New York art circles as well. Even as late as 1952, his fame as a regional artist was heralded by *Life* magazine in a posthumous spread entitled "Marsden Hartley: Fame Finally Catches Up to Poet-Painter of Maine." The article emphasized Hartley's identity as a Maine artist, claiming that "his life began and ended [in Maine] and most of his time was devoted to painting and writing about its mountains, gulls, and stormy coastal regions."[87] It is this reputation that still survives among Maine art audiences today as Hartley's paintings of the coast, Katahdin, and the folk remain powerful images of regional identity and the glory of the local.

Notes

1 Hartley to Norma Berger, 16 April 1940, Beinecke/Yale.

2 Hartley to Norma Berger, 20 April 1936, Beinecke/Yale, and Hartley to Adelaide Kuntz, 28 April 1936, McCausland Papers, Archives/Smithsonian, roll X4.

3 Hartley to Norma Berger, 27 May and 31 August 1937, Beinecke/Yale. See Donna M. Cassidy "'On the Subject of Nativeness': Marsden Hartley and New England Regionalism," *Winterthur Portfolio* 29, no. 4 (1994): 227–45, for a discussion of Hartley and regionalism. It is ironic that Alfred Stieglitz, Hartley's longtime patron who had promoted "Americanness" in modern art for years and who had urged Hartley to ground himself in a native locale, no longer represented Hartley in the late 1930s.

4 On regionalism, see Robert L. Dorman, *The Revolt of the Provinces: The Regionalist Movement in America, 1920–1945* (Chapel Hill: University of North Carolina Press, 1993), and Michael C. Steiner, "Regionalism in the Great Depression," *Geographical Review* 73 (October 1983): 430–46.

5 See, for example, Thomas Craven, *Modern Art: The Men, The Movements, The Meaning* (New York: Simon and Schuster, 1934).

6 James M. Dennis, *Renegade Regionalists: The Modern Independence of Grant Wood, Thomas Hart Benton, and John Steuart Curry* (Madison: University of Wisconsin Press, 1998), 173–96, and Erika Doss, *Benton, Pollock and the Politics of Modernism: From Regionalism to Abstract Expressionism* (Chicago: University of Chicago Press, 1991), 10–12, 98.

7 Wanda M. Corn, *The Great American Thing: Modern Art and National Identity, 1915–1935* (Berkeley and Los Angeles: University of California Press, 1999), 3–40. Also see Celeste Connor, *Democratic Visions: Art and Theory of the Stieglitz Circle, 1924–1934* (Berkeley and Los Angeles: University of California Press, 2001), 63, 97–105, on the Stieglitz circle, cultural nationalism, and region.

8 Paul Rosenfeld, *Port of New York: Essays on Fourteen American Moderns* (1924; reprint, Urbana: University of Illinois Press, 1966), 168, 53. See Connor, *Democratic Visions,* 42–50, and Corn, *The Great American Thing,* 4–9, on the importance of this text for the Stieglitz circle.

9 Rosenfeld, *Port of New York,* 89, 100.

10 Craven, *Modern Art,* 312.

11 Elizabeth McCausland, "Stieglitz and the American Tradition," in *America and Alfred Stieglitz: A Collective Portrait,* ed. Waldo Frank, Lewis Mumford, Dorothy Norman, Paul Rosenfeld, and Harold Rugg (New York: Literary Guild, 1934), 229.

12 For a discussion of regionalism, place, and O'Keeffe's art, see Connor, *Democratic Visions,* 188–93; Corn, *The Great American Thing,* 239–91; and Sharyn Rohlfsen Udall, *Carr, O'Keeffe, Kahlo: Places of Their Own* (New Haven and London: Yale University Press, 2000), 47–65.

13 See *Letters of John Marin,* ed. and intro. Herbert J. Seligmann (1931; reprint, Westport, Conn.: Greenwood Press, 1970), and "John Marin, American Artist," *Design* 38 (December 1936): 31, and Rosenfeld, *Port of New York,* 162, for example.

14 Hartley to Alfred Stieglitz, 11 November 1936, Beinecke/Yale. Also see Marsden Hartley, "As to John Marin, and His Ideas," in *John Marin: Watercolors, Oil Paintings, Etchings* (New York: Museum of Modern Art, 1936), 15–18.

15 "Yankee" has a fluid meaning, having variously been used to define Americans (especially in an international context), northerners as during the Civil War, and New Englanders and, more specifically, northern New Englanders as in the 1930s.

16 Bernard DeVoto, "New England: There She Stands," *Harper's,* March 1932; reprinted in

Bernard DeVoto, *Forays and Rebuttals* (Boston: Little, Brown, 1936), 138–39.

17 See Barbara Melosh, *Engendering Culture: Manhood and Womanhood in New Deal Public Art and Theater* (Washington, D.C.: Smithsonian Institution Press, 1991), 237, 243–44, 247, 256, 258, and Marlene Park and Gerald E. Markowitz, *Democratic Vistas: Post Offices and Public Art in the New Deal* (Philadelphia: Temple University Press, 1984), 69–73.

18 Van Wyck Brooks, *The Flowering of New England* (1936; New York: E. P. Dutton, 1952), 7.

19 DeVoto, "New England: There She Stands," 142, 145–46, 156.

20 On this idea of northern New England as the region's center, see Cassidy, "On the Subject of Nativeness," 232, and William H. Truettner, "Small-Town America," in *Picturing Old New England: Image and Memory*, ed. William H. Truettner and Roger B. Stein (New Haven and London: Yale University Press, and Washington, D.C.: National Museum of American Art, 1999), 111–41.

21 See Joseph A. Conforti, *Imagining New England: Exploration of Regional Identity from the Pilgrims to the Mid-Twentieth Century* (Chapel Hill: University of North Carolina Press, 2001), 287–309, on *Yankee* magazine, and William F. Robinson, *A Certain Slant of Light: The First Hundred Years of New England Photography* (Boston: New York Graphic Society, 1980), 186–91, and Truettner, "Small-Town America," 119–22, 129, 135–37, on the Farm Security Administration in New England.

22 See William Graebner, "Norman Rockwell and American Mass Culture: The Crisis of Representation in the Great Depression," *Prospects* 22 (1997): 323–56; Robert L. McGrath, *Paul Sample: Painter of the American Scene* (Hanover, N.H.: Hood Museum of Art, and University Press of New England, 1988); and Truettner, "Small-Town America," 111–41.

23 See Conforti, *Imagining New England*, 267–87, and John C. Kemp, *Robert Frost and New England: The Poet as Regionalist* (Princeton: Princeton University Press, 1979).

24 Robert P. Tristram Coffin, *New Poetry of New England: Frost and Robinson* (1938; reprint, New York: Russell and Russell, 1964), 1.

25 *The Triad Anthology of New England Verse* (Portland, Maine: Falmouth Book House, 1938), 15.

26 See video tape of Dorothy Jenkins (former director of Maine WPA), University of Southern Maine, Gorham; for sample references to Robinson and Frost, see Hartley to Rebecca Strand, October 1928, McCausland Papers, Archives/Smithsonian, roll X3, and Marsden Hartley, "Nothing But Rain and Visitors—The Going Out of Edwin Arlington Robinson," n.d., Beinecke/Yale (Archives/Smithsonian, roll 1368, frames 1124–25); and for references to Coffin, see Hartley to Alfred Stieglitz, 25 July 1937, Stieglitz/O'Keeffe Archive, and Hartley to Norma Berger, 31 August 1937, Beinecke/Yale.

27 See Marsden Hartley, "New England Painting and Painters," c. 1936, Beinecke/Yale (Archives/Smithsonian, roll 1369, frame 1816).

28 Robert P. Tristram Coffin, *Kennebec: Cradle of Americans* (New York and Toronto: Farrar and Rinehart, 1937), 280.

29 Hartley to Rebecca Strand, 18 June 1937, and Hartley to Adelaide Kuntz, n.d. [1937], McCausland Papers, Archives/Smithsonian, roll X3 and roll X4.

30 *Adventures*, 38.

31 Marsden Hartley, "Eakins, Homer, Ryder (1930)," in *On Art*, 171–72.

32 Marsden Hartley, "The Six Greatest New England Painters," *Yankee* 3 (August 1937): 14–16, and idem, "On the Subject of Nativeness—A Tribute to Maine," in *Marsden Hartley: Exhibition of Recent Paintings, 1936* (New York: An American Place, 1937).

33 Hartley, "Six Greatest New England Painters," 15.

34 Ibid., 14–16.

35 Marsden Hartley, "Somehow a Past: Prologue to Imaginative Living," in *Autobiography*, 67.

36 See Marsden Hartley, "A. P. Ryder, 'The sight that never was,'" c. 1929, p. 3, Beinecke/Yale (Archives/Smithsonian, roll 1368, frame 789). Also see Marsden Hartley, "Melville," in *Sea Burial* (Portland, Maine: Leon Tebbetts Editions, 1941), 36. In *The Flowering of New England*, Brooks ranks Melville with Emerson, Thoreau, and Hawthorne as a leading New England author.

37 Bruce Robertson, *Reckoning with Winslow Homer: His Late Paintings and Their Influence* (Bloomington: Indiana University Press, and Cleveland: Cleveland Museum of Art, 1990), 158–64.

38 See, for example, "Philadelphia Shows Homer, the Individualist," *Art Digest* 10 (1 June 1936): 37. There was also a show at Homer's Maine studio from 18 July to 2 August 1936.

39 Marsden Hartley, "New England Painting and Painters," Beinecke/Yale (Archives/Smithsonian, roll 1369, frame 1822).

40 *Maine: The Land of Remembered Vacations* (Augusta: Maine Development Commission, 1935), n.p.

41 Marsden Hartley, "This Country of Maine," c. 1937–38, Beinecke/Yale (Archives/Smithsonian, roll 1371, frame 3444). Also see the poems dedicated to these schooners: "From Wiscasset to Pemaquid," in Marsden Hartley, *Androscoggin* (Portland, Maine: Falmouth Publishing House, 1940), 26; "New Ruins," in *Collected Poems*, 192; and "Forsaken Ships," n.d., Beinecke/Yale (Archives/Smithsonian, roll 1371, frame 3983).

42 Hartley to Helen Stein, 10 September 1939, Stein Papers, Archives/Smithsonian.

43 Marsden Hartley, "New England Notations," after 1936, p. 6, Beinecke/Yale (Archives/Smithsonian, roll 1370, frame 2734). He earlier praised the art at the East India Marine Museum in "The Virtues of Amateur Painting," in *Adventures*, 136.

44 Hartley, "On the Subject of Nativeness," 5. He exhibited a work, *Young Lobster*, at An American Place in 1937. For a discussion of the lobster and regional identity, see George H. Lewis, "The Maine Lobster as Regional Icon: Competing Images over Time and Social Class," *Food and Foodways* 3 (1984): 303–16, and Kathleen Shea, "Regionalism on the Roadside: The Evolution of Route 1, Kittery to Portland, 1925–1947" (M.A. thesis, American and New England Studies Program, University of Southern Maine, forthcoming).

45 Marsden Hartley, "Arrowhead and Clamshell," n.d., Beinecke/Yale (Archives/Smithsonian, roll 1371, frame 3830).

46 *Maine Sea Foods* (Augusta: Maine Development Commission, 1939).

47 See Michele H. Bogart, *Artists, Advertising, and the Borders of Art* (Chicago: University of Chicago Press, 1995), 137–43, on modernism and consumer images.

48 Marsden Hartley, "New England on the Trapeze," *Creative Art* 8 (February 1931): supp. 57.

49 Myron H. Avery, "Katahdin: Its History," *In the Maine Woods* (1939): 25.

50 Myron H. Avery, "Artists and Katahdin," *In the Maine Woods* (1940): 13, 18.

51 See Fannie Hardy Eckstorm, *The Indian Legends of Mount Katahdin* (Boston: Appalachian Mountain Club, 1924), copy in the Maine State Library, Augusta; and Marsden Hartley, "The Story of the Little Boy Lost on Ktaadn," c. late 1930s–early 1940s, Beinecke/Yale (Archives/Smithsonian, roll 1369, frame 2176).

52 Marsden Hartley, "Peter Doyle and the Whitman Group," n.d., Beinecke/Yale (Archives/Smithsonian, roll 1369, frame 2209). He refers to Thoreau's The Maine Woods in several essays—"Ktaadn, or the Love of a Mountain," n.d.; "Fanny [*sic*] Hardy Eckstorm, Penobscot Man," n.d.; and "Camp Life in the Aroostook Woods by Charles C. West," c. 1939, Beinecke/Yale (Archives/Smithsonian, roll 1369, frame 2211; roll 1371, frame 3730; and roll 1369, frames 1394–95). Thoreau's identity as an important New Englander and part of transcendentalism (considered the apex of both regional and national culture) was also advanced in period texts like Mumford's *The Golden Day*, Brooks's *The Flowering of New England*, and Matthiessen's *American Renaissance*.

53 Hartley wrote, for example: "It 'compares' beautifully, especially at the Ktaadn Lake end which is a picture made to order for the painter, and as far as I know I am the only painter who has ever painted it." See Marsden Hartley, "Be That as It May," 1941, Beinecke/Yale (Archives/Smithsonian, roll 1369, frame 2200). He also wrote: "Came out with four paintings of Ktaadn which I am now finishing—the first artist to paint the mountain *there*." See Hartley to Norma Berger, 6 January 1940, Beinecke/Yale.

54 Cecil Johnson, "The Joys of the Maine Woods," *In the Maine Woods* (1935): 116, and Wilfrid A. Hennessy, "Baxter Park at Mt. Katahdin," *In the Maine Woods* (1933): 34.

55 Hartley, "Be That as It May," Beinecke/Yale

(Archives/Smithsonian, roll 1369, frame 2199).

56 Hartley to Helen Stein, 29 September 1939, Stein Papers, Archives/Smithsonian.

57 Marsden Hartley, "This Little City," in *Androscoggin,* 22, and Hartley, "This Country of Maine," Beinecke/Yale (Archives/Smithsonian, roll 1371, frame 3442).

58 Marsden Hartley, *Twenty-Five Poems* (Paris: Contact Publishing Co., 1923), 36, 34. Hartley did not completely abandon the New England woman as subject in his late paintings; see, for example, *Intellectual Niece* (1939; collection of Chris Huntington) and *Ring and Book, Second Version* (1939–40; Hirshhorn Museum and Sculpture Garden). Both of these works are smaller in size than those of the Maine men.

59 On Julius Langbehn, see Fritz Richard Stern, *The Politics of Cultural Despair: A Study in the Rise of the Germanic Ideology* (Berkeley and Los Angeles: University of California Press, 1966), 97–180, and, on the construct of the folk, see Ian McKay, *The Quest of the Folk: Antimodernism and Cultural Selection in Twentieth-Century Nova Scotia* (Montreal and Kingston: McGill-Queen's University Press, 1994).

60 See Marsden Hartley, "Wilhelm Leibl," c. late 1930s, pp. 1–3, Beinecke/Yale (Archives/Smithsonian, roll 1368, frames 1001–3).

61 For a more extensive discussion of Hartley and Nazism, see Donna M. Cassidy, "Marsden Hartley's North Atlantic Folk: Constructing the Northern Race and the New American," in *Ceremonies and Spectacles: Performing American Culture,* ed. Teresa F. A. Alves, Teresa Cid, and Heinz Ickstadt (Amsterdam: VU University Press, 2000), 333–47; Ludington, 226–29; and Weinberg, 173–74.

62 See Hartley to Adelaide Kuntz, 17 and 22 July, 7 September, and 4 November 1933, McCausland Papers, Archives/Smithsonian, roll X4; Marsden Hartley, "The Sleeping Violins of Mittenwald," c. 1933–34, pp. 1–5, Beinecke/Yale (Archives/Smithsonian, roll 1371, frames 3411–15); idem, "The Peasant Theatre of Bavaria," c. 1933–34, Beinecke/Yale (Archives/Smithsonian, roll 1369, frames 1970–71); and idem, "Oberammergau Kept Its Promise Again," c. 1933–34, Beinecke/Yale (Archives/Smithsonian, roll 1369, frames 1618–19). On Hartley's description of the German folk as the primitive Other, see, for example, Hartley to Adelaide Kuntz, 12 and 22 July 1933, McCausland Papers, Archives/Smithsonian, roll X4.

63 Marsden Hartley, "The Eight Capucines," c. 1933–34, p. 3, Beinecke/Yale (Archives/Smithsonian, roll 1368, frame 89).

64 Hartley to Adelaide Kuntz, 19 July 1933, McCausland Papers, Archives/Smithsonian, roll X4, and Hartley to Edith Halpert, 12 July 1933, excerpted in Garnett McCoy, ed., "Letters from Germany, 1933–38," *Archives of American Art Journal* 25, nos. 1–2 (1985): 7–8.

65 Hartley to Adelaide Kuntz, 22–23 July 1933, McCausland Papers, Archives/Smithsonian, roll X4.

66 Hartley wrote, for example, of northerners in "On the Subject of Nativeness," 1.

67 Also see *Young Hunter Hearing Call to Arms* (1939; Carnegie Museum of Art) for this mixing of Maine and German folk dress. I want to thank Carol Dean Krute (curator of costumes and textiles at the Wadsworth Atheneum) and Ingrid Loschek (costume historian) for their help in reading the attire in these paintings.

68 *Nova Scotia, Canada's Ocean Playground* (Halifax: Bureau of Information, Government of Nova Scotia, 1935), 2.

69 McKay, *Quest of the Folk,* 230.

70 Frank Parker Day, *Rockbound* (1928; reprint, Toronto: University of Toronto Press, 1989), 62, 83, 78.

71 Hartley called Louis Hémon's novel "one of the finest in any language" and claimed he was never without it; see Hartley to Adelaide Kuntz, 12 July 1933, McCausland Papers, Archives/Smithsonian, roll X4, and Marsden Hartley, "Marguerite Andoux and her Maire Claire," n.d., Beinecke/Yale (Archives/Smithsonian, roll 1369, frame 1984). Hartley was also familiar with the novels of his friend the Nova Scotian writer Frank Davison/Pierre Coalfleet, and he admired William Henry Drummond's poetry, which portrayed the people of rural Québec.

72 Louis Hémon, *Maria Chapdelaine: A Tale of the Lake St. John Country* (1921; reprint, New York: Modern Library, 1934), 282–83.

73 Dr. J. Madison Taylor, "The Maine Woods as a Health Resort," *In the Maine Woods* (1909): 35. Hartley's description of the "fine new types" in Maine included an admission of ethnic mixing, but it maintained that the Yankeeness (features and behaviors) dominated in the mixing process.

74 Marsden Hartley, "Camp Life in the Aroostook Woods—by Charles C. West," Beinecke/Yale (Archives/Smithsonian, roll 1369, frames 1393–94); Fannie Hardy Eckstorm, *The Penobscot Man* (1904; reprint, La Grosse, Wisc.: Juniper Press, 1978), xi–xii; and Hartley, "Fanny [*sic*] Hardy Eckstorm," Beinecke/Yale (Archives/Smithsonian, roll 1371, frame 3729).

75 Hartley wrote about this new school of Maine writers in his essays "On the Subject of Nativeness" and "This Country of Maine."

76 See Beinecke/Yale (Archives/Smithsonian, roll 1368, frames 1035–38, and roll 1369, frame 2194).

77 Sinclair Lewis, *Babbitt* (1922; New York: Harcourt, Brace, 1961), 64, 238, 241, 115, 121.

78 Thomas Dreier, "The Thunder of New Wings," in *The Transformation of a Maine Farm* (Augusta: Maine Development Commission, and Maine Department of Agriculture, 1934), 8–9.

79 See Sarah Burns, *Inventing the Modern Artist: Art and Culture in Gilded Age America* (New Haven and London: Yale University Press, 1996), 187–217, and idem, "Revitalizing the 'Painted-Out' North: Winslow Homer, Manly Health, and New England Regionalism in Turn-of-the-Century America," *American Art* 9, no. 2 (summer 1995): 21–37. Hartley may well have been directly inspired by Homer's figural works, as they were often reproduced in the late 1930s in the literature surrounding Homer's many centennial exhibitions in 1936. See, for example, the illustrations in "Philadelphia Shows Homer, the Individualist," 37, and "Homer, Artist and Man, Revealed at Show in His Old Studio," *Art Digest* 10 (August 1936): 5.

80 Rockwell Kent, *It's Me O Lord: The Autobiography of Rockwell Kent* (New York: Dodd, Mead, 1955), 120.

81 Carl Sprinchorn, "Cold, Red Wine of Autumn (A Sawtelle Brook Fancy)," in Sprinchorn Papers, Archives/Smithsonian, roll 3014.

82 See Carl Sprinchorn, "Hunting with a Painter," 1939, Archives/Smithsonian, roll 3014.

83 J[ames] W. L[ane], "The Virile Paintings by Marsden Hartley," *Art News* 38 (16 March 1940): 15.

84 Martha Davidson, "The Climax of Hartley's Painting in Powerful Coastal Scenes," *Art News* 36 (26 March 1938): 21.

85 Hartley, "On the Subject of Nativeness," 1.

86 Lucien Price, "New England Art vs. Puritan Hangover," *Boston Globe,* 7 January 1940, clipping in Hartley's press review notebook, Beinecke/Yale.

87 "Marsden Hartley: Fame Finally Catches Up to Poet-Painter of Maine," *Life,* 16 June 1952, 84.

PLATES 59–70

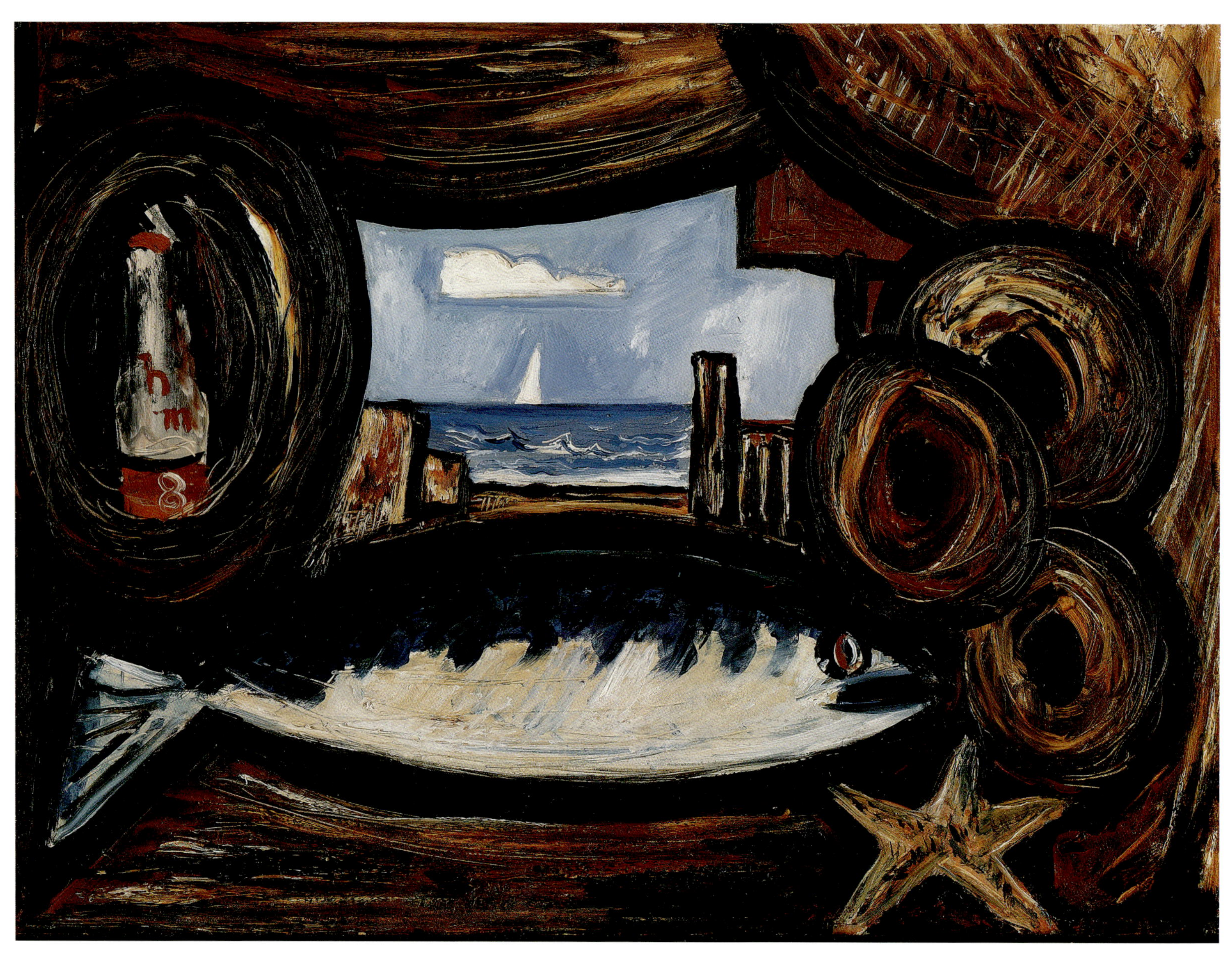

59
Sea View—New England, 1934
Oil on academy board, 12 × 16 in.
The Phillips Collection, Washington, D.C.

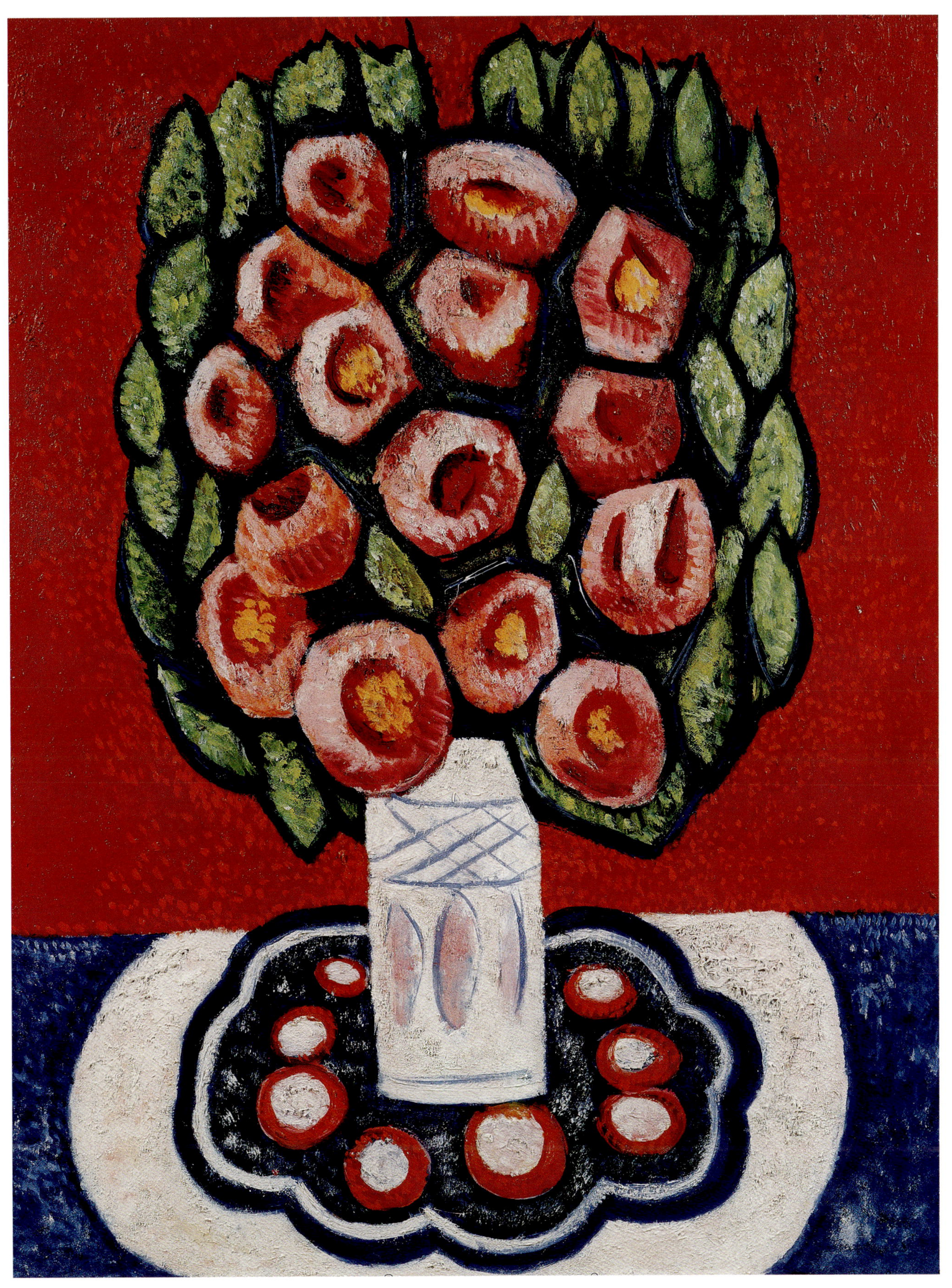

60

(Flowers) Roses from Hispania, 1936
Oil on academy board, 23½ × 17¼ in.
Private Collection
Courtesy of Berry-Hill Galleries, New York

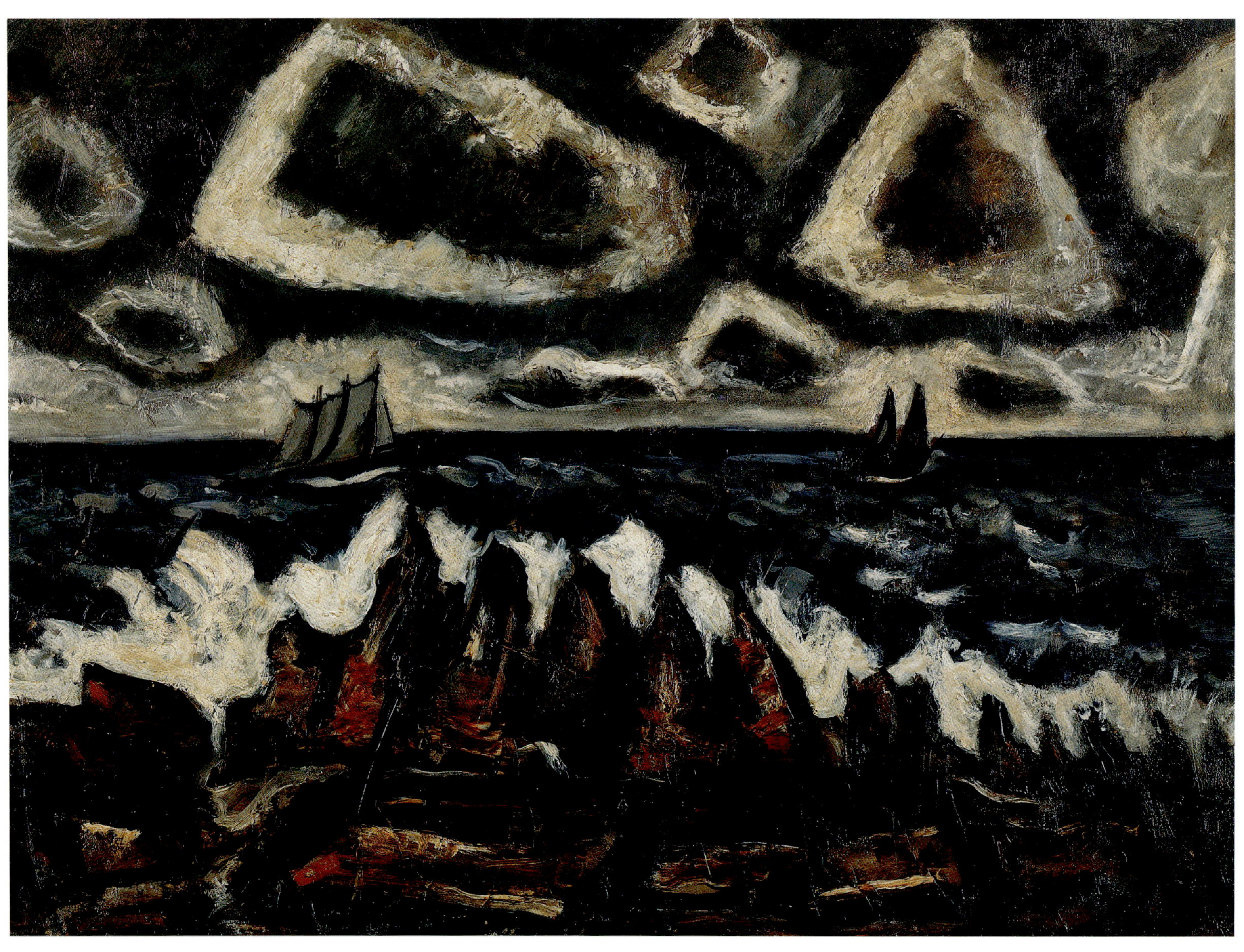

61

Northern Seascape, Off the Banks, 1936

Oil on academy board, 18 1/16 × 24 in.

Milwaukee Art Museum

Bequest of Max E. Friedman

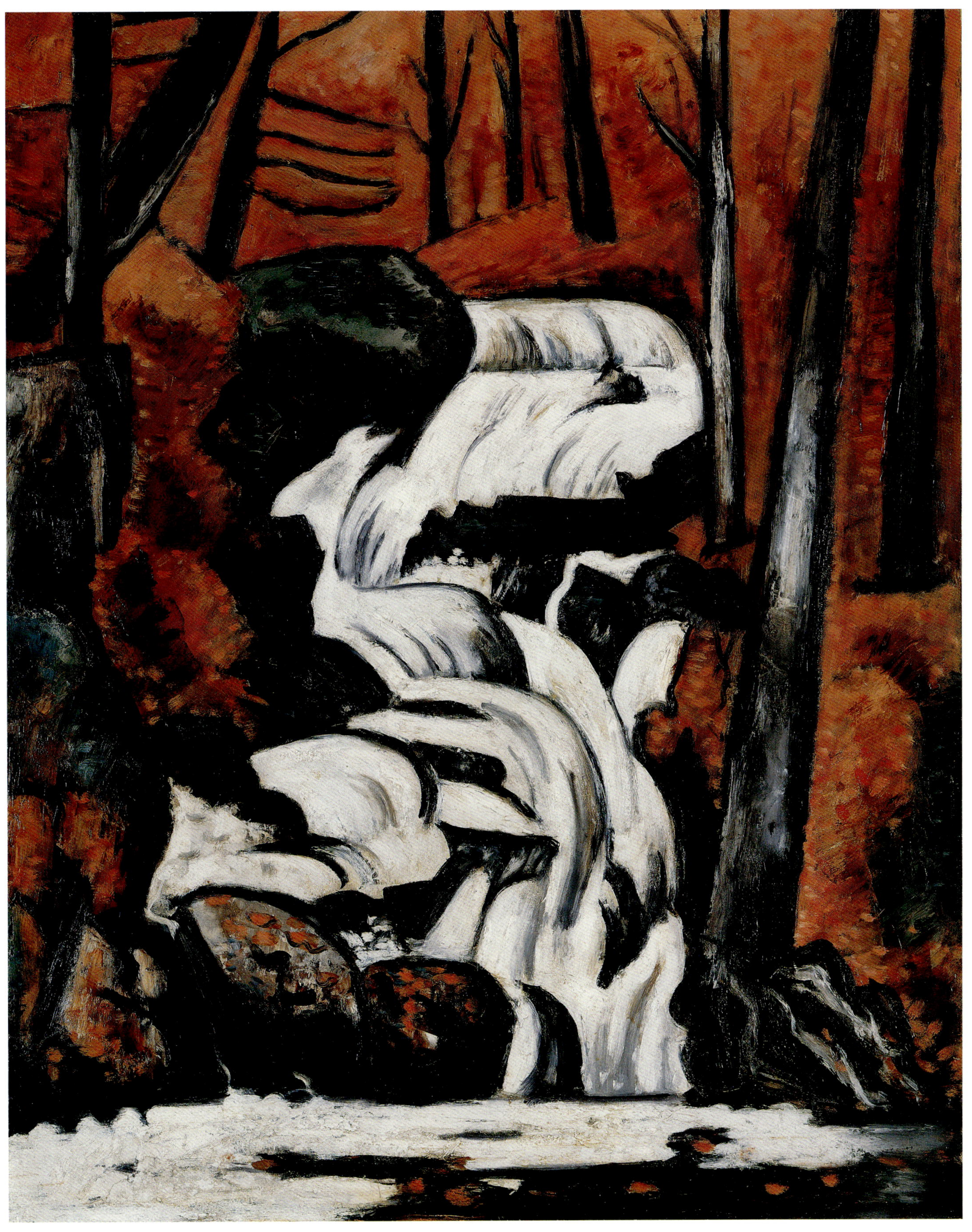

62

Smelt Brook Falls, 1937
Oil on academy board, 28 × 22 in.
The Saint Louis Art Museum, St. Louis, Missouri
Purchase, Eliza McMillan Fund

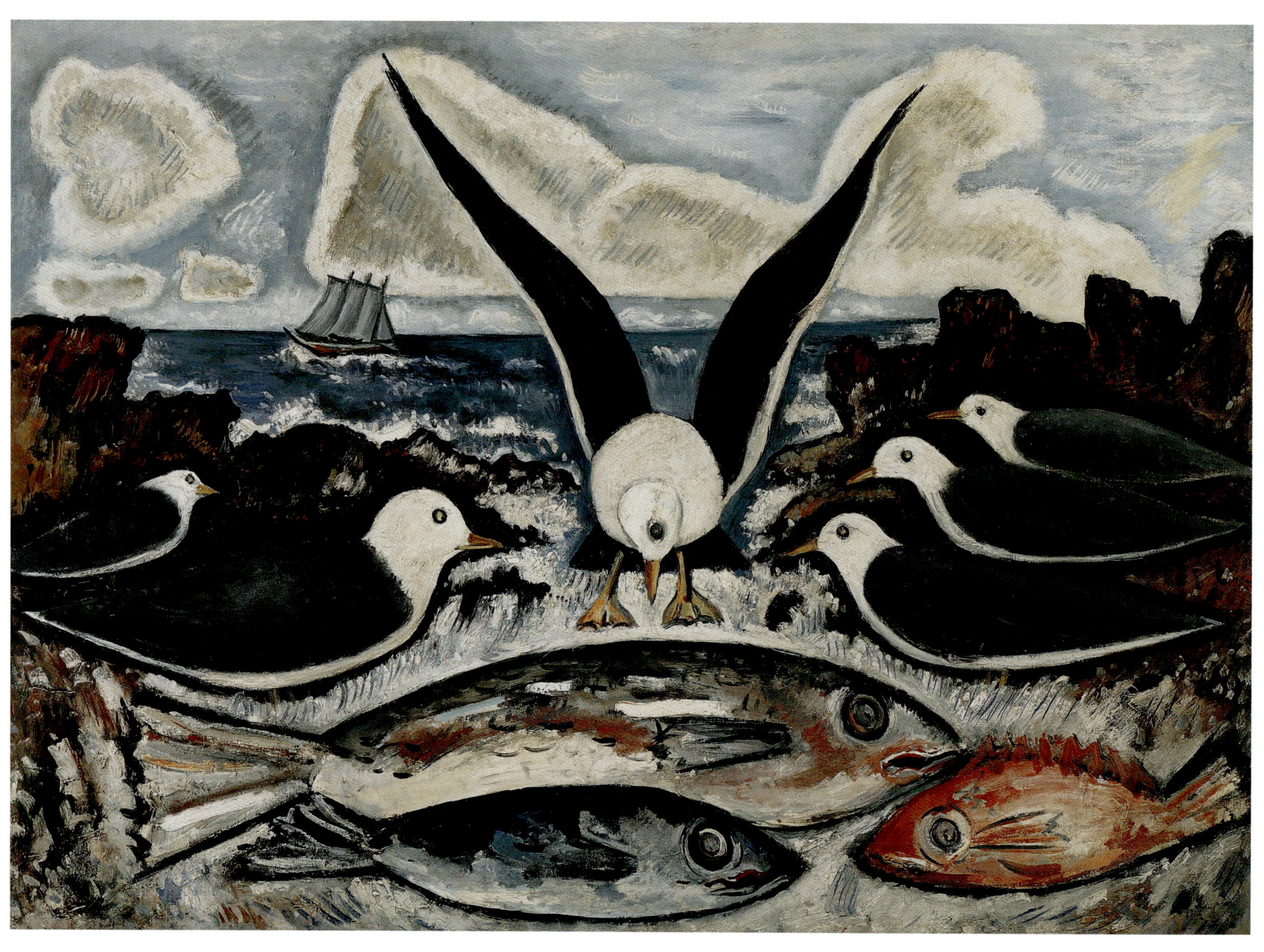

63
Give Us This Day, 1938
Oil on canvas, 30 × 40 in.
Curtis Galleries, Minneapolis, Minnesota

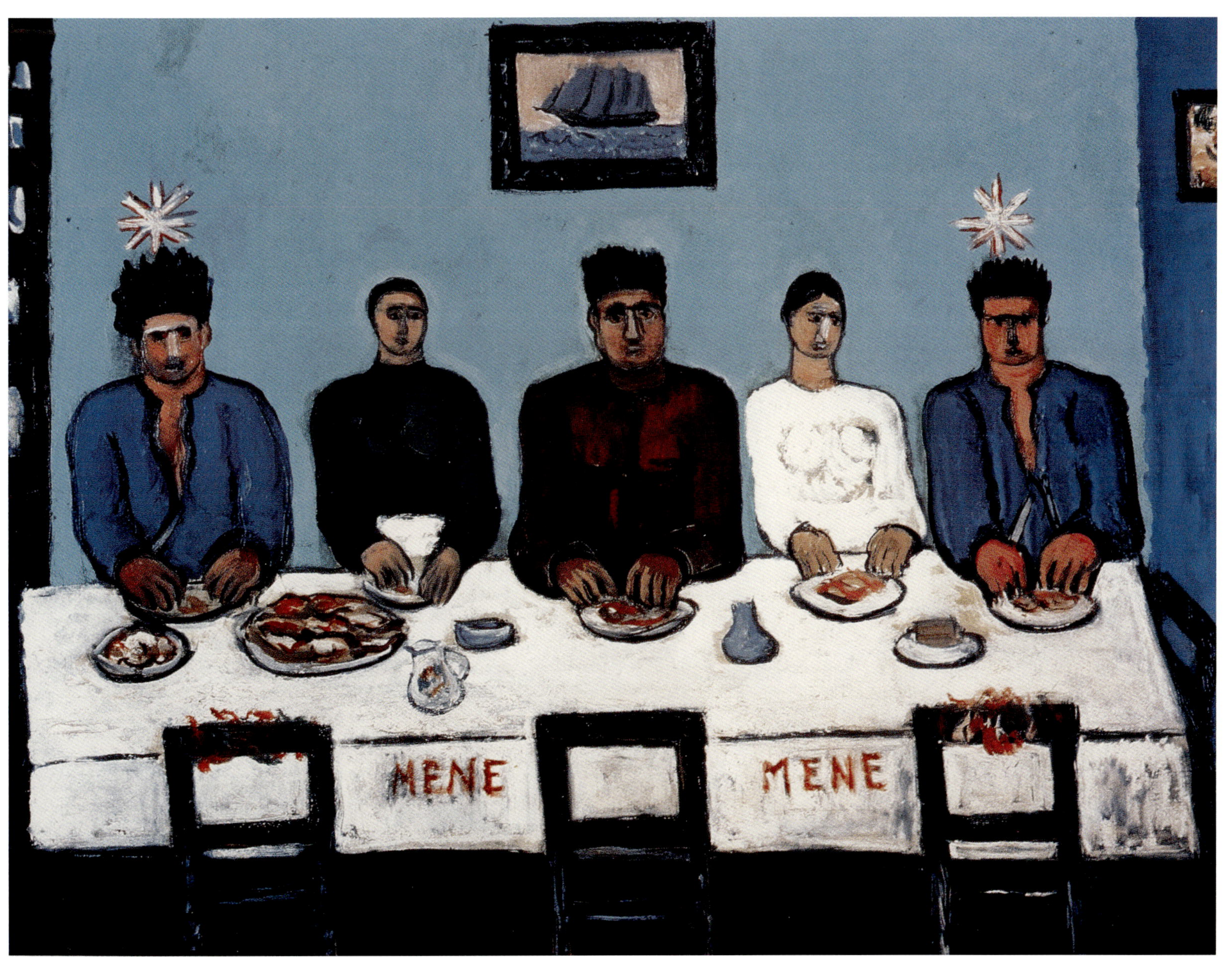

64
Fishermen's Last Supper, 1938
Oil on board, 22 × 28 in.
Private Collection

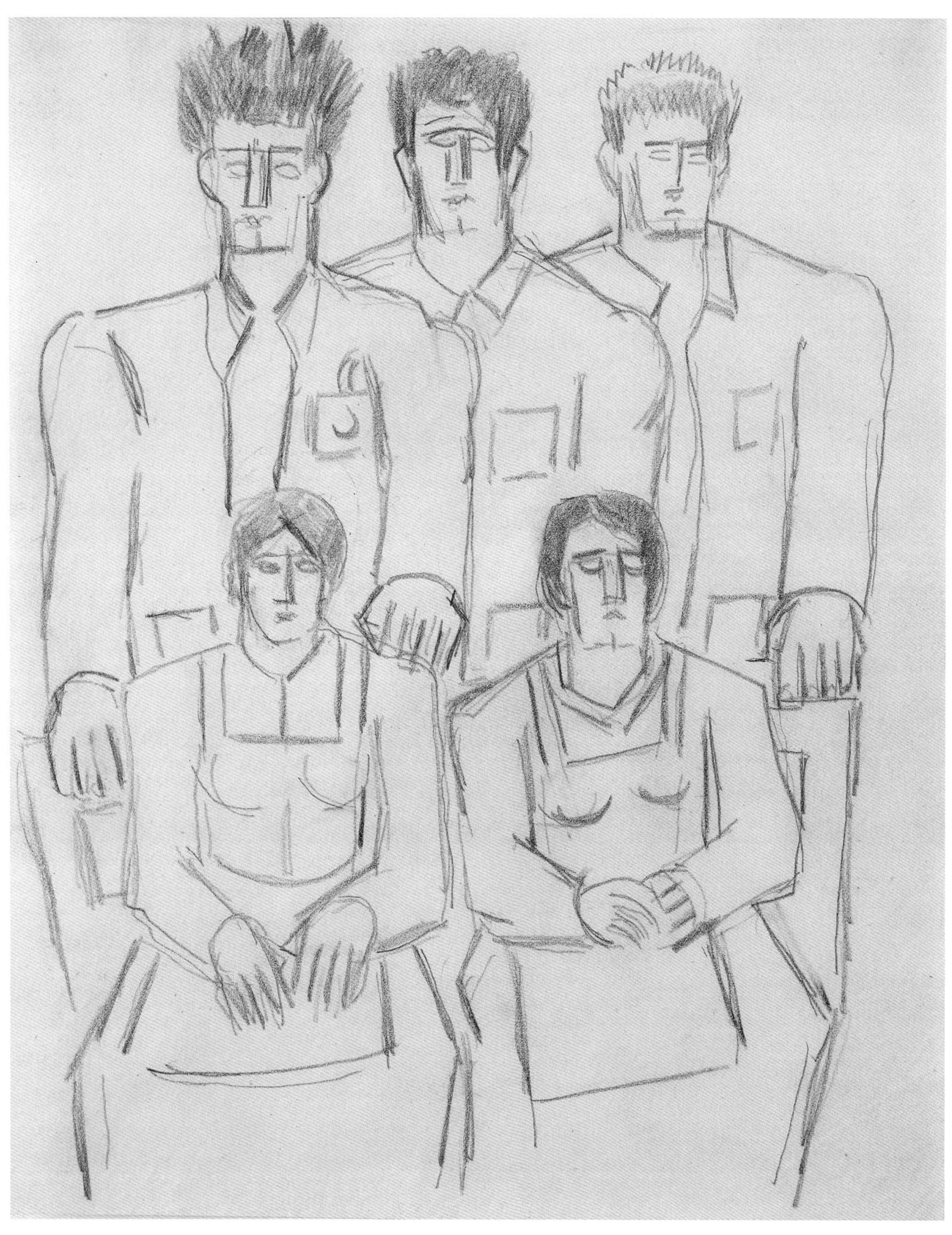

65
Untitled (Three Men Standing Behind Two Women with Aprons)
Pencil on white paper, 10½ × 8 in.
Bates College Museum of Art, Lewiston, Maine

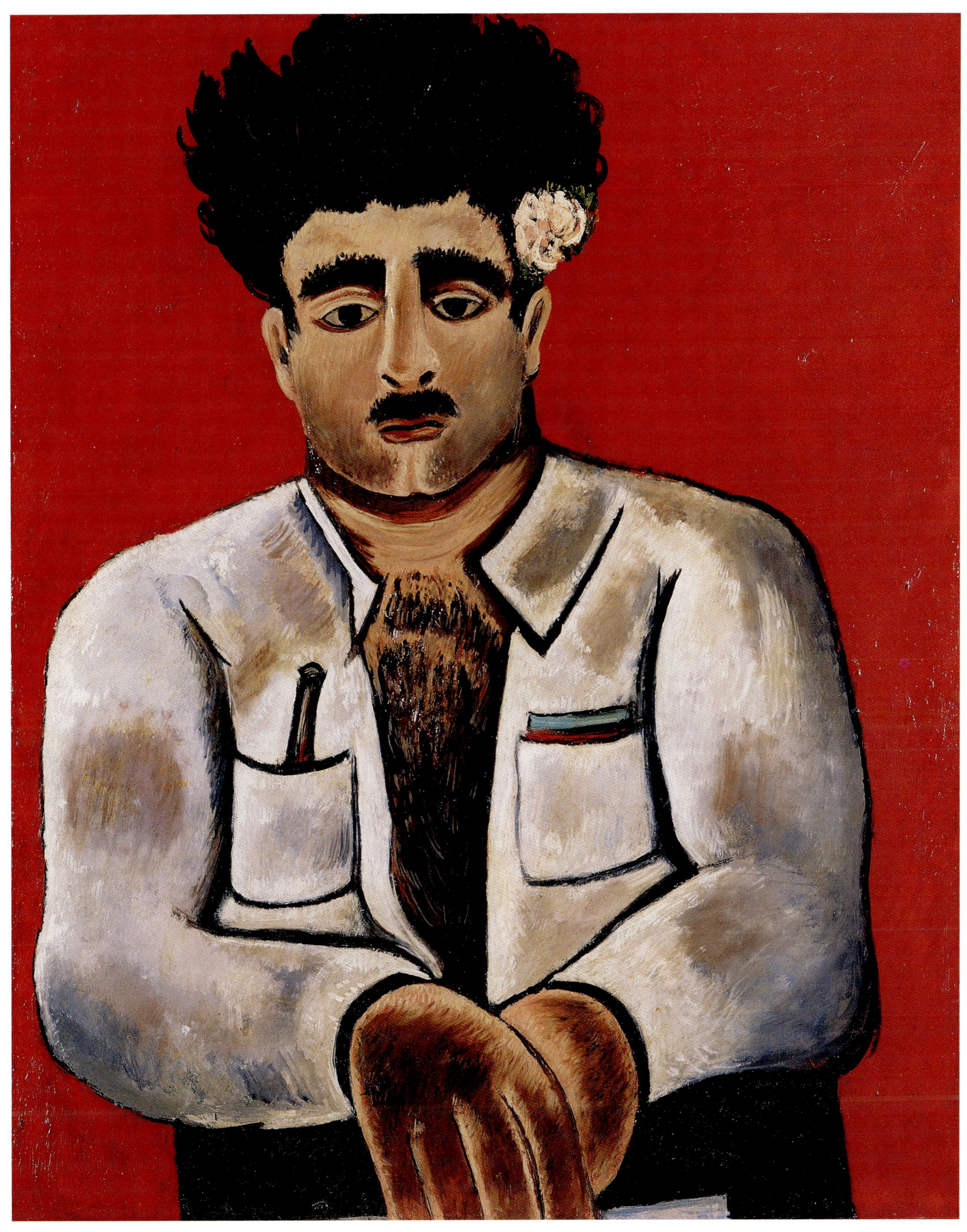

66

Adelard the Drowned, Master of the "Phantom," c. 1938–39
Oil on academy board, 28 × 22 in.
Frederick R. Weisman Art Museum, University of Minnesota, Minneapolis
Bequest of Hudson Walker from the Ione and Hudson Walker Collection

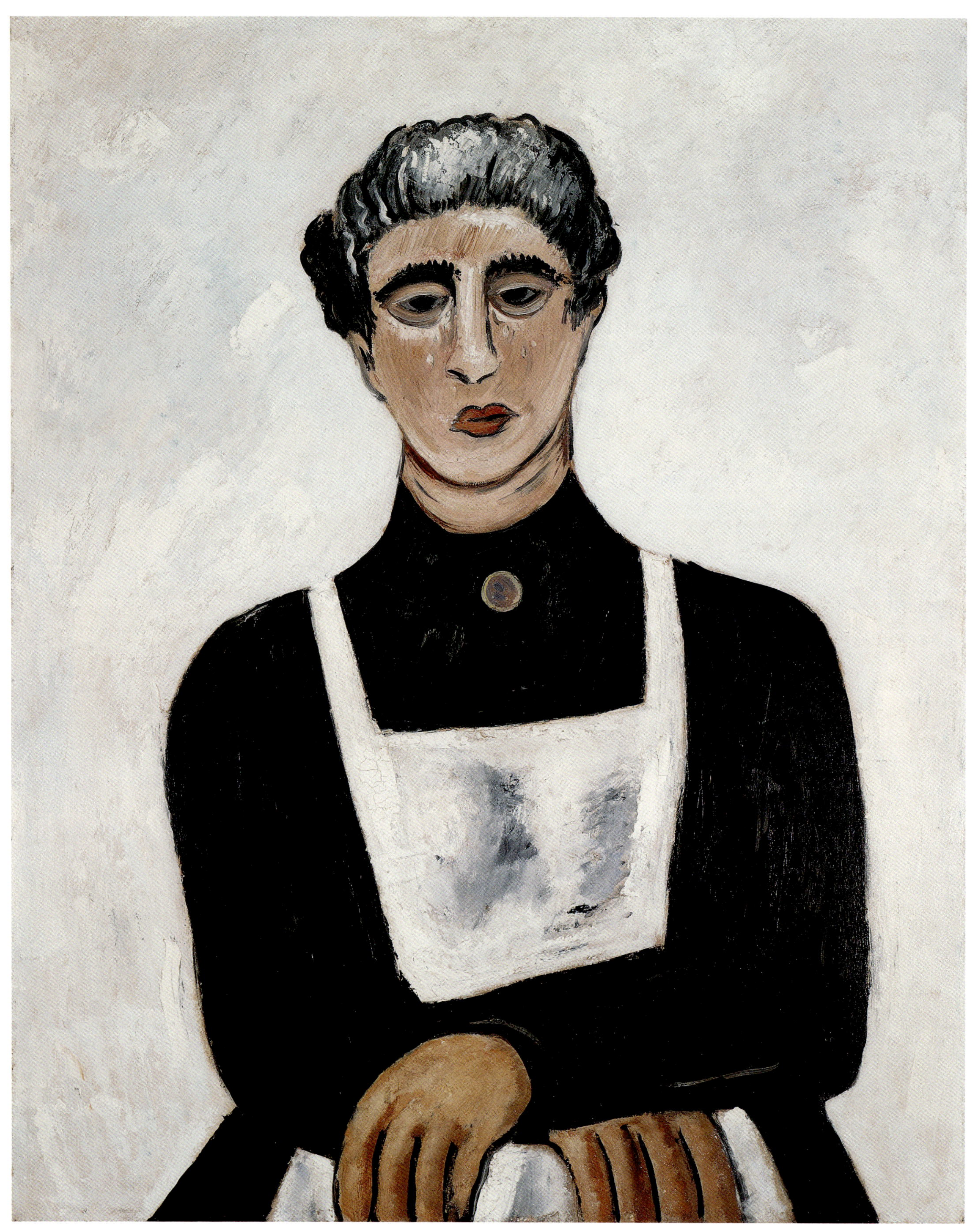

67
Marie Ste. Esprit, 1938–39
Oil on academy board, 28 × 22 in.
Frederick R. Weisman Art Museum, University of Minnesota, Minneapolis
Bequest of Hudson Walker from the Ione and Hudson Walker Collection

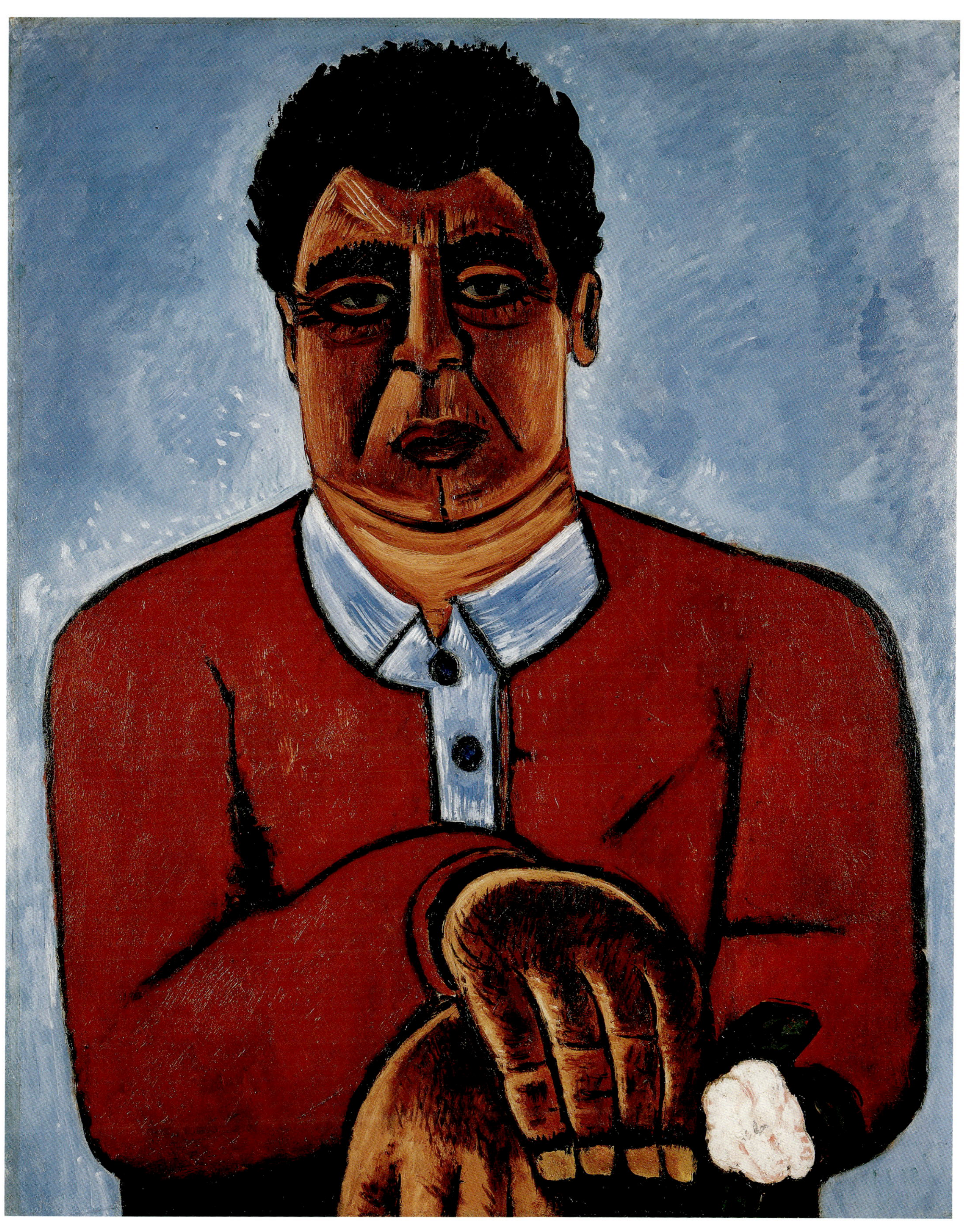

68

Cleophas, Master of the "Gilda Grey," 1938–39
Oil on academy board, 28 × 22 in.
Walker Art Center, Minneapolis, Minnesota
Gift of Bertha H. Walker, 1971

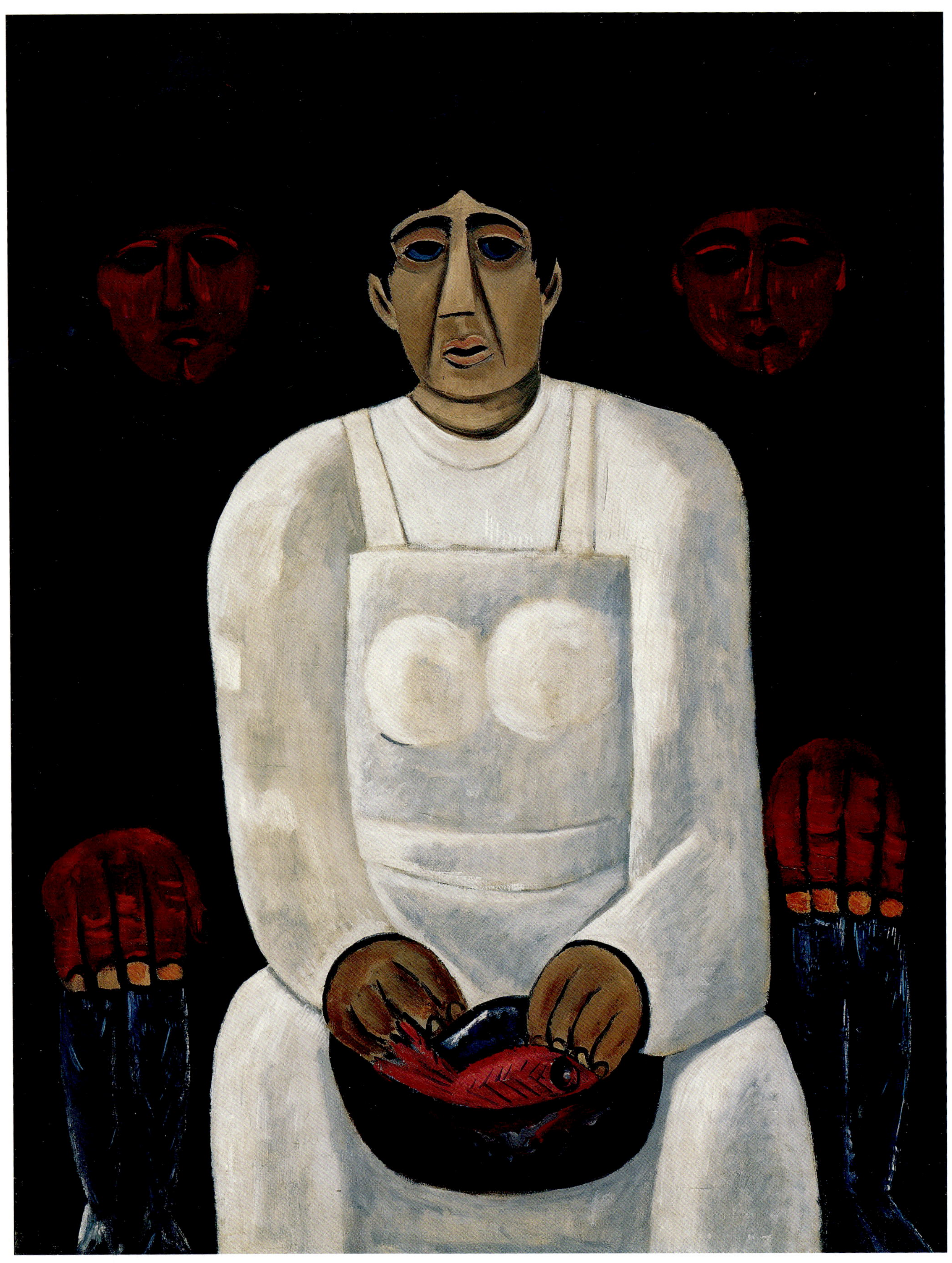

69

The Lost Felice, 1939

Oil on canvas, 40⅛ × 30¹⁄₁₆ in.

Los Angeles County Museum of Art

Mr. and Mrs. William Preston Harrison Collection

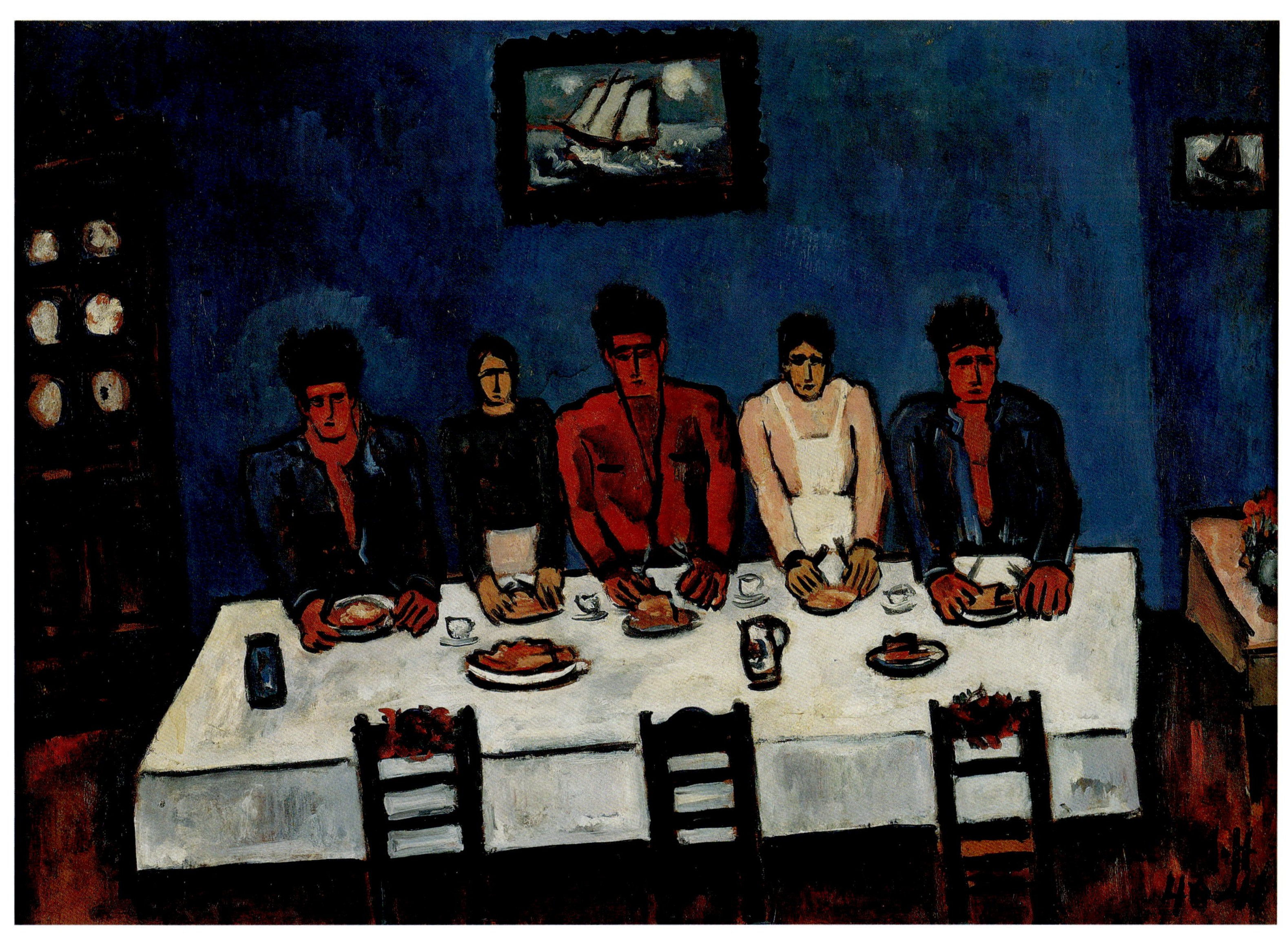

70
Fishermen's Last Supper, 1940–41
Oil on Masonite-type hardboard, 29⅞ × 41 in.
Roy R. Neuberger Collection

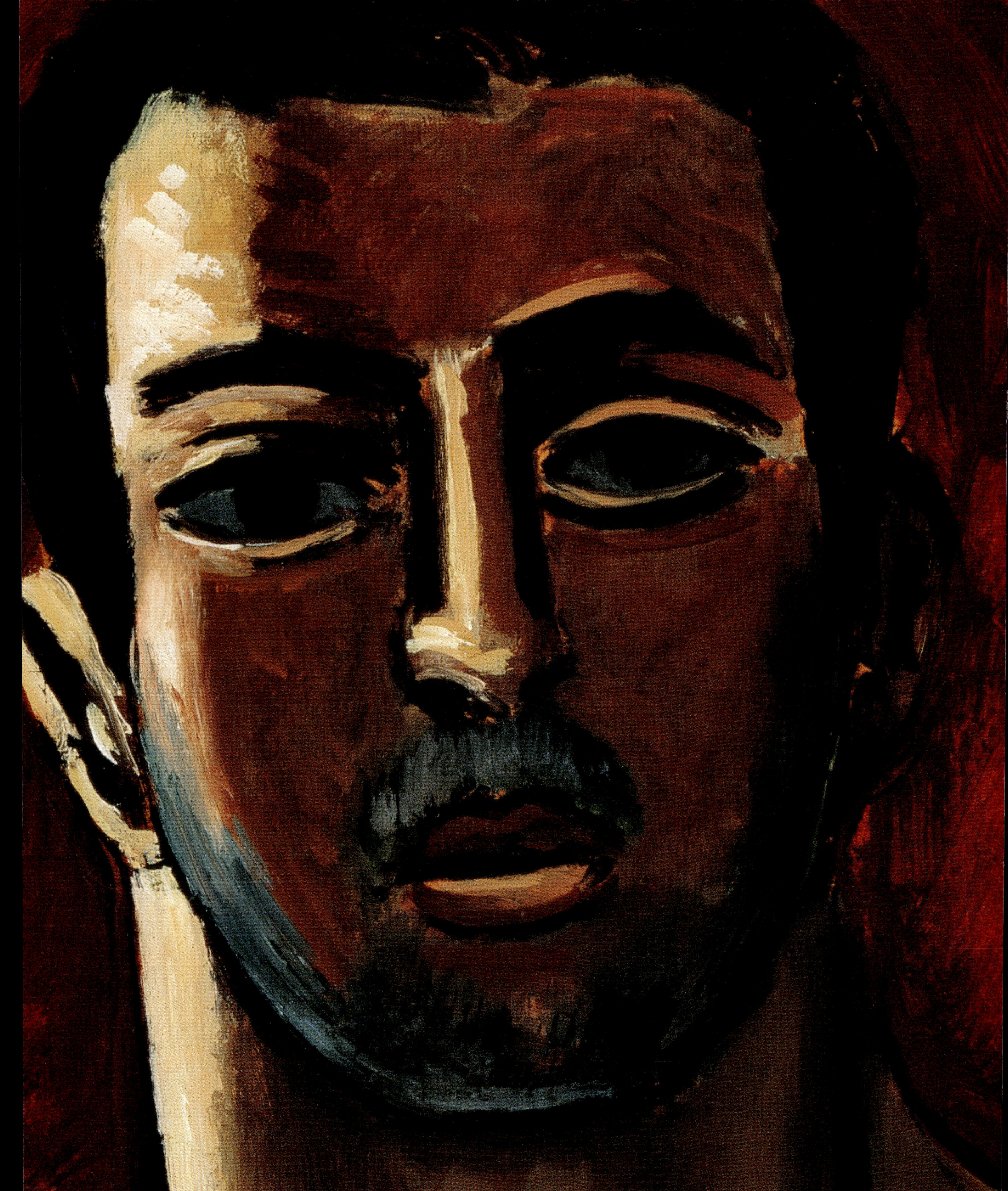

Encoding the Homoerotic: Marsden Hartley's Late Figure Paintings

Randall R. Griffey

Known widely throughout his career as an artist prone to experimentation and reinvention, Marsden Hartley surprised American art critics and audiences once again in 1939, when he unveiled a group of figure paintings at his second exhibition at Hudson Walker's gallery. This group included his portraits of the Francis Mason family in fictional guises (plates 66–69) and his painterly homage to Albert Pinkham Ryder (plate 71), as well as *Finnish-Yankee Sauna,* a highly unusual image featuring four nearly nude men in close quarters striking themselves with switches. Unlike many of his previous artistic experiments, however, Hartley's figure paintings were warmly received by critics. Margaret Bruening, critic for the *Magazine of Art*, reported glowingly about the exhibition: "Mr. Hartley has recently gained a much greater freedom, the ability to express something of the emotion that used to seem to struggle for expression in his painting."[1] Reinvented as a figure painter, Hartley was, in the words of the *Time* magazine art reviewer, "something of a hit."[2]

Undoubtedly encouraged by such an unusually positive reception, the new and improved Hartley unveiled a suite of figure paintings among the twenty-three works he exhibited at Walker's gallery the following year. Along with his first installment of pictures devoted to Mt. Katahdin, Maine's famed geological landmark, and two portraits of Abraham Lincoln, the painter displayed images of semi-nude athletes, including *Madawaska—Acadian Light-Heavy* (plate 76), pictures he identified as mural studies conceived for a gymnasium. In response to Hartley's latest offerings, critics showered the artist with even greater praise. "What endless youthful vitality this man Hartley seems to have," Howard Devree exclaimed in the *Magazine of Art*. "With what galvanizing force he presents his visions! This is distinctly one of the impressive shows of the season."[3] The critic for *Art Digest* concurred: "At sixty, Marsden Hartley may only now be attaining the full realization of his aesthetic powers, and the world appears to be 'catching up.'"[4] Such ringing endorsements of his art set the stage for Hartley's professional success throughout the last few months of his life, as a number of key American art institutions likewise began recognizing his achievements by granting him awards and by acquiring examples of his work for their collections.[5]

Despite the degree to which Hartley's figure paintings were well received by American critics when they were shown and contributed directly to the artist's late rise in the ranks of American art, they fell into a lengthy period of scholarly neglect not long after the painter's death in 1943. The causes for this critical malaise are diverse and difficult to ascertain fully. However, part of the neglect they suffered must be attributed to the rise of abstraction in American art in the 1950s and 1960s, as well as to the concomitant dominance of formalist criticism, which challenged the artistic value of figurative or

Detail, Plate 76

representational imagery in general. In an era that celebrated formal innovation, Hartley's Berlin abstractions were most commonly championed by American critics above all other phases of his career. The bias is perhaps most evident in William Innes Homer's study of Alfred Stieglitz and the artists in his orbit, published in 1977. "At the time of the closing of 291 [in June 1917]," Homer proposed,

> *Hartley's art lacked the definite direction it had shown in Germany in 1913–15. In retrospect, these seem to be the most important years of his career.... When Hartley was forced to abandon the congenial creative ambience of Berlin... his style faltered.... Perhaps a need for relief from the emotional intensity of his experiences in Berlin induced this change, but, whatever the reason, Hartley's most important period was over.*[6]

Another, equally relevant cause for the scholarly neglect of Hartley's late figure paintings has been a prevailing reluctance among critics and historians to engage in issues pertaining to homosexuality. More than any other work he produced over his long and varied career, Hartley's depictions of the male figure beg questions relating to the artist's sexuality and matters relating to homoerotic desire. For years, conditions in the art world and in the Academy discouraged scholars from asking questions related to these taboo and controversial subjects.[7] Such discouragement appears to have stayed the pen of William H. Gerdts, for one, when in 1974 he justly identified Hartley's figure paintings as "perhaps the least studied aspect of Hartley's art," but stopped short of speculating about the possible causes of the oversight. Instead, he simply described the neglected works in general, noting aptly, "the imagery is supermasculine and of heroic scope."[8]

A scholar writing more recently about Hartley's late figure paintings would likely add "homoerotic" to Gerdts's selection of adjectives. Over the last twenty-five years, as the silence regarding Hartley's sexuality has gradually eroded in academic circles, the eroticism of the painter's late pictures has become the subject of increasing interest and examination. Much of the credit in this regard must go to Jonathan Weinberg, who, in his watershed study *Speaking for Vice: Homosexuality in the Art of Charles Demuth, Marsden Hartley, and the First American Avant-Garde* (1993), took a strong stand against the persisting tendency among art historians to desexualize Hartley's late paintings.[9] As one result of Weinberg's groundbreaking analysis, discussions of homoeroticism have more fully entered the common parlance of Hartley studies. This turn of scholarly events is clearly evident throughout the most recent monograph dedicated to the artist, published in 1995. The late figure paintings represent, author Bruce Robertson boldly posits, Hartley's "sexual interests... step[ping] forward into clear light."[10] Once neglected or disregarded by scholars, the homoerotic character of Hartley's late figure paintings has become all but taken for granted.

The recurring feature of Hartley's late figure paintings most commonly identified as homoerotic is the artist's exaggeration of the male anatomy. As Weinberg has emphasized regarding Hartley's *Canuck Yankee Lumberjack at Old Orchard Beach, Maine* of 1940–41 (plate 81) and its relationship to Paul Cézanne's *The Bather* (c. 1885), "Hartley... blatantly eroticizes Cézanne's male figure. He exaggerates the size of the lumberjack's chest and arm muscles. Whereas Cézanne hides the bather's genitals under his bathing suit, Hartley emphasizes the bulge of this subject's crotch, making Cézanne's body overtly sexual."[11] The lumberjack's exaggerated anatomy is, in this instance, interpreted as an indiscreet artistic response to the scopophilic pleasure Hartley derived from seeing rugged men cooling off at Old Orchard Beach. A letter Hartley wrote to friend Helen Stein in 1939 confirms his attraction to such beachside scenery.[12]

Hartley's programmatic exaggeration of male anatomy is even more pronounced in paintings like *Madawaska—Acadian Light-Heavy*, in which a prizefighter confronts the viewer with his imposing, strapping physique. Positioned near the picture plane, he appears within arm's reach. The figure's close proximity, frontal pose, and static posture encourage intense scrutiny and admiration of his exposed muscular frame. The viewer is aided in this regard by a powerful spotlight that streams in from the left and throws his body into dramatic relief against a deep red backdrop, which evokes the nearly palpable body heat generated by his massive, vital physique. Thick black contour lines further accentuate the fighter's anatomy, especially his square jaw, his broad, rock-like shoulders, his wide, almost panoramic pectorals, complete with hard, prominent nipples, and his chiseled obliques and taut abdomen.

Hartley's fixation on youthful male beauty suggested by his exaggerated rendering of the male body is likewise revealed by a private cache of memorabilia that the painter collected over many years.[13] Among his extant personal effects is a group of photographs and news clippings showing beautiful young men and famed athletes of the day, such as Yale football star Larry Kelley, Heisman Trophy recipient in 1936, and boxing champ Arthur Wyns. Featuring heroic male bodies on display, Hartley's late figure paintings seem most closely tied to materials the painter amassed relating to the health and body culture industries, including copies of *Strength and Health* magazine, which featured photographs of scantily clad athletic youths along with articles examining the relationship between manliness and muscularity. Seen in proximity to this private erotica, the figure paintings appear to make public the personal feelings attached to these images he stashed away for safekeeping and delectation.

Such an apparently unrestrained public admission of homoerotic attraction would seem a most ill-advised project for a gay artist working during a conspicuously homophobic period in American history. As historian George Chauncey has observed, the 1930s and 1940s were marked by increasing regulation and criminalization of homosexuality in American society. In New York, for example, police raids on nightclubs featuring "pansy acts" and drag balls increased dramatically, effectively shutting down these entertainment venues, which had gained widespread popularity in the wake of Prohibition. Ironically, Chauncey explains, the repeal of Prohibition in 1933 served only to further suppress gay visibility, as alcohol laws accompanying repeal were "designed . . . not only to control the consumption of liquor per se but also to regulate the public spaces in which people met to drink."[14] Such laws consequently pushed homosexuality further underground and behind closed doors. Nearer the end of the decade, John D'Emilio has additionally emphasized, concerns and debates regarding homosexuality reemerged in response to the militarization of American culture. "In an era when silence most typically characterized society's approach to same-sex eroticism," D'Emilio notes that "the military examination was a significant exception. For gay and nongay men alike, it represented the first and perhaps the only time that they faced such inquiries in a public setting."[15]

Art criticism throughout the 1930s betrays a similarly intense scrutiny of normative masculinity and sexuality. Prominent critics of the period frequently bemoaned endemic "emasculation," a condition that, if detected, cast significant doubt on an artist's sexual identity. Most incendiary was the ongoing commentary of Thomas Craven, an influential columnist for *American Mercury*, who generally attributed the unfortunate state of American art to the overwhelming influence of European modernism. "From time to time," the critic wrote in 1932, *it has been my unpleasant duty to review the general degradation of American painting, and to call the attention of the American artist to the aimlessness and triviality of his performances. Groveling in the emasculated tradition of the French modernists, our painters, as a whole, have been content to contrive their little patterns—to send forth still-life distortions and mutilated figures into which the critics have pumped all sorts of illusory values.*[16]

Three years later, in his extensive survey *Modern Art: The Men, The Movements, The Meaning,* Craven announced even more explicitly that "the artist is losing his masculinity," continuing:

The tendency of the Parisian system is to disestablish sexual characteristics, to merge the two sexes in an androgynous third containing all that is offensive to both. If you doubt the growing effeminacy of the artist, you have only to examine the performances of the modern École de Paris. The school is fundamentally sexless.... In essence, it is an emasculated art, an art of fashions, styles, and ambiguous patterns.[17]

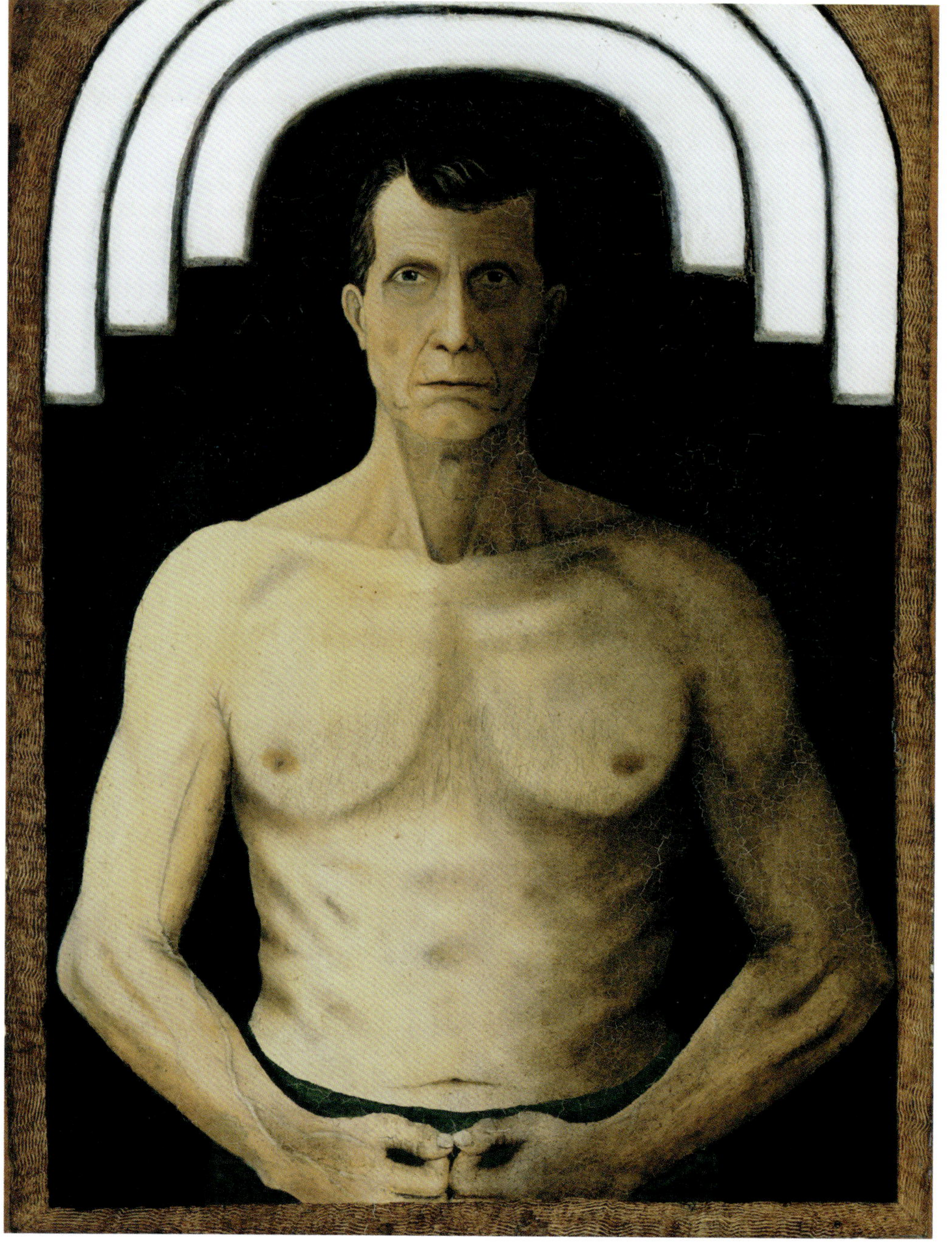

Figure 1
John Kane
Self-Portrait, 1929
Oil on canvas over composition board, 36⅛ × 27⅛ in. (91.8 × 68.9 cm)
The Museum of Modern Art, New York
Abby Aldrich Rockefeller Fund (63.6)
Digital Image © The Museum of Modern Art/Licensed by SCALA/Art Resource, N.Y.

Craven's strident diatribes were matched in tone and tenor by his friend, regionalist painter Thomas Hart Benton, who complained loudly and often about the perceived inordinate influence of gay men in the American art world. Benton launched his all-out homophobic attack in his autobiography, *An Artist in America*, first published in 1938, in which he explained:

> *If young gentlemen, or old ones either, wish to wear women's undergarments and cultivate extraordinary manners it is all right with me. But it is not all right when, by ingratiation or subtle connivance, precious fairies get into positions of power and judge, buy, and exhibit American pictures on a base of nervous whim and under the sway of those overdelicate refinements of tastes characteristic of their kind.... For the most part, the fairies are so deeply involved in their own peculiar sensibilities, so intent on their own jealousies, hysterical animosities, and nursed preferences that they cannot appreciate contemporary forces until these have been consecrated by general acceptance.*[18]

Three years later, with interest in and support of regionalist painting waning considerably, Benton once again turned to homosexuals as the cause of the art world's problems. "Do you want to know what's the matter with the art business in America," the painter asked a room full of reporters. "It's the third sex and the museums. Even in Missouri we're full of them." The typical American museum, he concluded, was "run by a pretty boy with delicate wrists and a swing in his gait."[19]

However seemingly groundless and absurd in retrospect, Craven's and Benton's homophobic rantings were symptomatic of a climate of palpable scrutiny and suspicion that struck fear into the hearts of many American artists. Author Malcolm Cowley shared the paranoia he felt in response to these dreaded circumstances in his 1934 memoir, *Exile's Return: A Narrative of Ideas*. "I had nightmares," Cowley confessed,

> *in which I suffered from the malice directed against contemporary art. Was there a general conspiracy of slander?... I came to believe that a general offensive was about to be made against modern art, an offensive based on the theory that all modern writers, painters, and musicians were homosexual.... I began to feel harried and combative, like Aubrey Beardsley forced to defend his masculinity against whispers.*[20]

Gay artists like Hartley no doubt felt especially vulnerable in the circumstances Cowley described. Hartley had, in fact, already endured the brunt of negative feminizing critique of his art and identity. In 1930 critic Samuel Kootz indicted him on charges of deficient manly expression in his much-publicized survey *Modern American Painters*. Declaring "there are but a few instances of a lusty masculine seeing in modern American art," Kootz identified Hartley as an artist suffering from "hopeless emasculation," whose work up to that point had been generally "informed with taste, a certain daintiness" that thus "never flares with genius."[21] More than just another unfavorable review, Kootz's cutting remarks in 1930 underscored the precarious borders of Hartley's artistic closet and punctuated the lowest critical point in the painter's troubled career.

Despite how personally indulgent and daring Hartley's inflated and immodest hunks might seem to audiences today, they would have found a number of similarly brawny brothers and male cousins in the late 1930s and early 1940s. The muscular athlete featured in *Madawaska—Acadian Light-Heavy*, for instance, shares many striking formal similarities with the most renowned example of folk art of the period, John Kane's *Self-Portrait* (fig. 1), including the frontal pose and exaggerated torso framed by minimal surrounding space. Similar features are exhibited by the heroically proportioned farmer who appears in a Pan

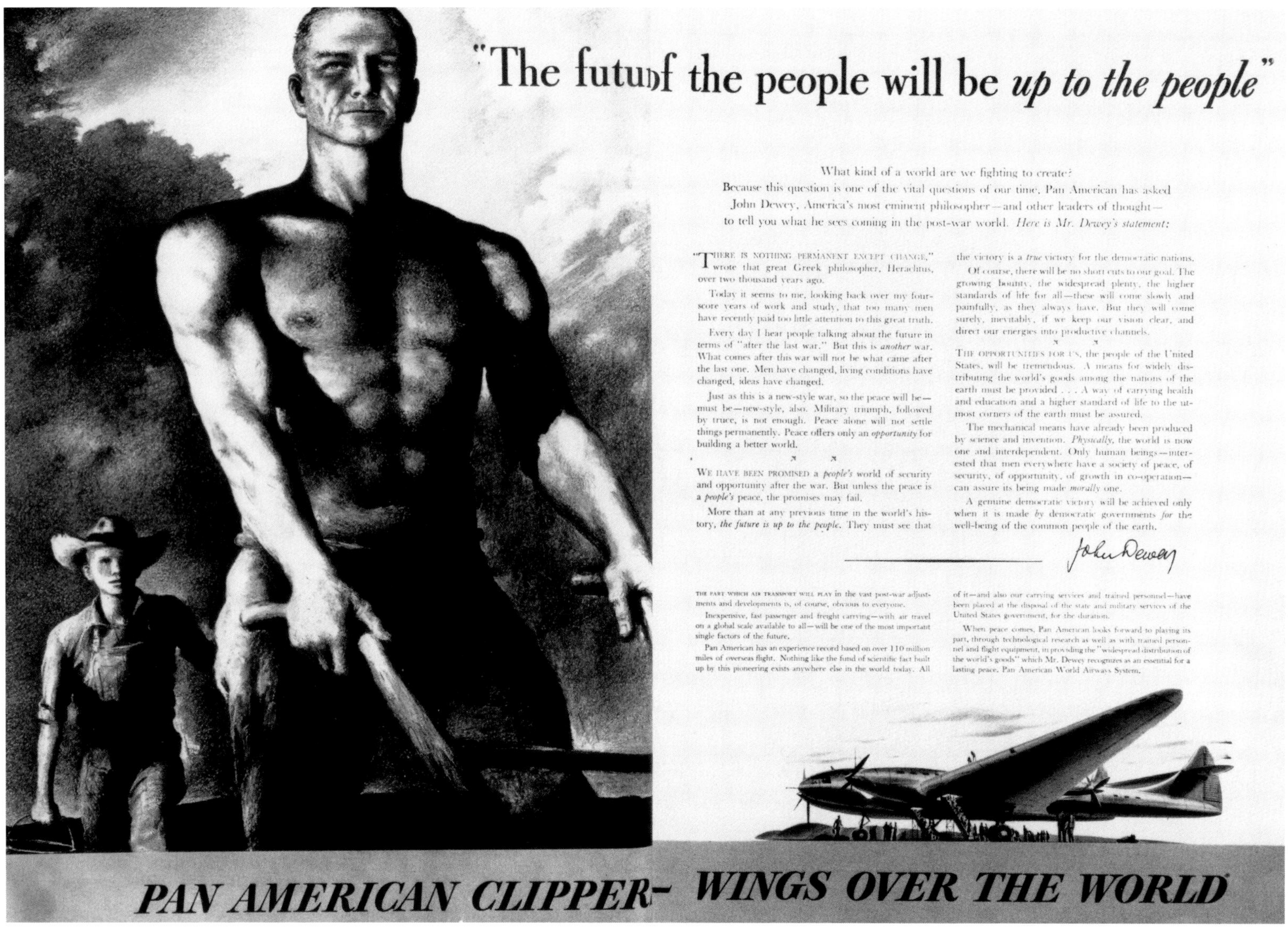

Figure 2
"The future of the people will be *up to the people*" *Life,* September 7, 1942
Photograph by Miller Studios Inc.

American Clipper advertisement from 1942 (fig. 2). The soldier in a promotional campaign by Pennsylvania Railroad from 1944 (fig. 3) might furthermore be considered the fraternal twin of Hartley's Canuck Yankee lumberjack. Nude from the waist up, he too strikes a cocky pose that showcases his massive, muscular torso and creates revealing contours that draw attention to his groin. Wearing only a helmet and fatigues, the soldier also recalls the battalion of anonymous men that appears in *Christ Held by Half-Naked Men* (plate 80) wearing a group uniform inexplicably consisting of merely hats and dungarees.

Reunited with a few of their long-lost relatives of the period, the men featured in Hartley's late figure paintings appear changed considerably in meaning and signification, particularly with regard to their presumed inherent homoeroticism. Viewed from this perspective, their exaggerated physiques no longer appear quite so anomalous, their large, impressive features no longer entirely the byproducts of the artist's private sexual fantasies. Indeed, the muscular company kept by the men in Hartley's late figure paintings points to larger cultural sources that legitimized—*encouraged* even—the production of images that glorified the male body.

Among the most influential forces fostering glorification of the male body was the pervasive cult of the "common man." In the new fight against fascist regimes abroad, American politicians and cultural critics revived the common man as a powerful symbol of the country's democratic ideals of self-governance, national resolve, and continued promise.

Figure 3
"This Fighter Weighs In At 8 Tons On Our Scales"
National Geographic, April 1944
Photograph by Miller Studios Inc.

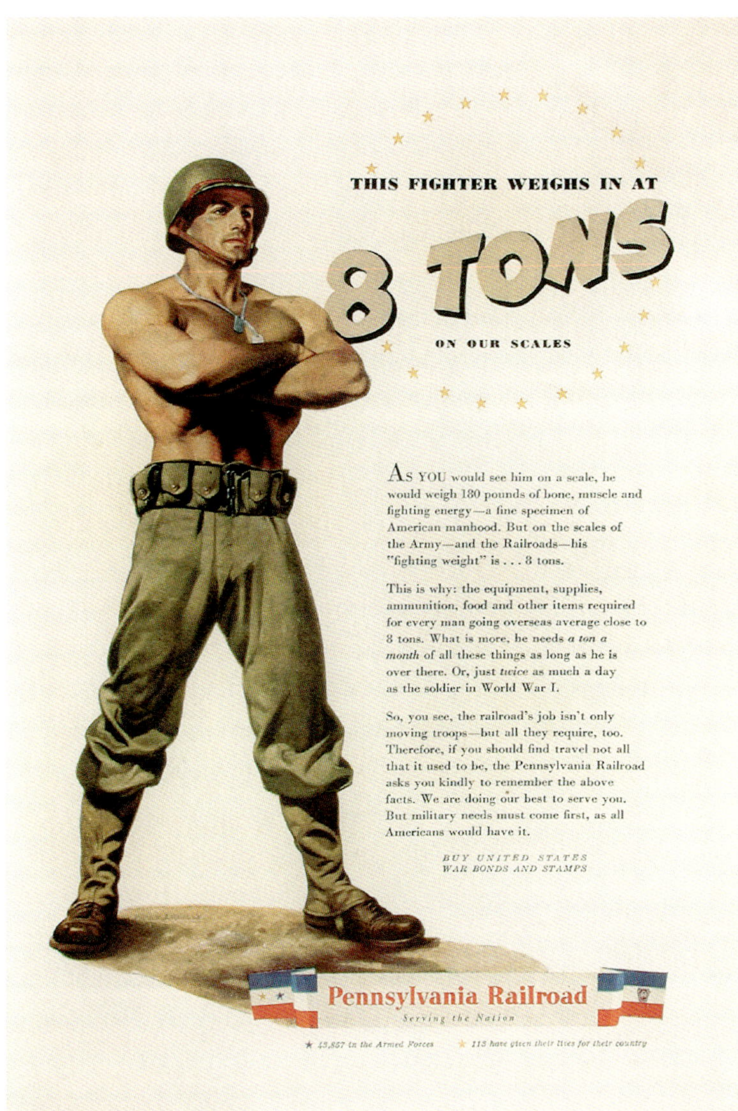

"The fundamental premise of democracy is belief in the common man," George Gallup, director of the American Institute of Public Opinion, announced in a radio broadcast in 1942.[22] Vice President Henry A. Wallace addressed the new and urgent significance of the common man's role in America's history and future in a speech also that year. "The century on which we are entering—the century which will come out of this war," Wallace emphasized to his listeners, "can be and must be the century of the common man."[23]

In response to the revived interest of the common man as an icon of cherished American values, many of America's most prominent writers, composers, and artists offered powerful and moving tributes. Carl Sandburg, for one, published in 1939 the second installment of his multi-volume biography of America's most renowned commoner, Abraham Lincoln. Hartley contributed directly to this particular strain of common man veneration by painting a trio of portraits of Lincoln, including *The Great Good Man* (plate 78), a picture he completed and exhibited in 1942.[24] That same year the best-known tribute of the era—composer Aaron Copeland's triumphal *Fanfare for the Common Man*—debuted before captivated audiences.

Translated into visual terms, the histrionic rhetoric involving the common man frequently imbued depictions of the male body with added bulk and superhuman proportions. Indeed, the amazing physique of the farmer in the Pan American Clipper advertisement attests symbolically to his relevance in light of new threats to national security, a relevance underscored by the accompanying text provided by philosopher John Dewey, who proclaims,

"The future of the people will be *up to the people!*" Even so, the symbolic conflation of nationalism and muscularity was never more widely or popularly recognized than in the form of Superman, who made his debut in June 1938 in *Action Comics #1* and gained his own title the following year. "An immigrant of sorts," historian Les Daniels has written, the legendary creation of Jerry Siegel and Joe Shuster clad in red and blue "became the champion of the American way."[25] Never was the patriotic imperative of Superman's mission clearer than in April 1940, when, as Nazi Germany encroached on Denmark and the Netherlands (after having already conquered Poland), Lex Luthor was introduced as his most dangerous nemesis, one that, not coincidently, threatened to incite war in Europe. Later that fall, Superman's already extraordinarily muscled body assumed even more outrageous proportions, when the hero made his first appearance in flight through Times Square as a helium balloon in Macy's Thanksgiving Day Parade (fig. 4), a spectacular sight that undoubtedly provided holiday revelers hope that the "American way" would prevail in uncertain times.

In addition to adding weight and bulk to the bodies of many of America's best-known male heroes, the cult of the common man sustained and bolstered interest in folk or "primitive" art that had emerged earlier in the century. Among the scores of contemporary folk painters who gained notoriety throughout the 1930s and 1940s, John Kane became the most famous and revered. Eulogized upon his death in 1934 by curator Murdock Pemberton as "one of the few great American painters of this age," the untrained artist enjoyed tremendous posthumous appeal throughout the decade, culminating with the publication of his autobiography, *Sky Hooks*, in 1938.[26] Painted in 1929, Kane's self-portrait became regarded as his masterpiece. More than any other single image Kane created, it was reproduced alongside exhibition reviews and features on the artist, including one that appeared in the May 17, 1937, edition of *Life* magazine.[27] Stripped to the waist, "America's Rousseau," as he was known, reveals courageously his naked torso, representing himself proudly as a common man of art.

Strong and awkward in execution, *Madawaska—Acadian Light-Heavy* betrays Hartley's emulation of the artistic naïveté widely associated with folk art and celebrated as uniquely "American" by prominent art critics, dealers, and museums. In this respect, the picture can most easily be distinguished from the scores of more classically inspired depictions of the male body produced by painters and sculptors working for the Third Reich, bodies similarly invested with nationalist sentiment, including, for example, *Readiness* (fig. 5) by Arno Breker, the Führer's Official State Sculptor.[28] Decidedly unclassical, *Madawaska* betrays Hartley's admiration of Kane, whose memorial exhibition he attended at the Valentine Gallery in 1935.[29] The folk artist's self-portrait would have held special appeal to Hartley on multiple levels. In one respect, the picture presented the image of a fellow aging painter, vital and resolute despite his advanced years. On another, Kane's self-portrait would have offered Hartley an acceptable prototype for the portrayal of the male body, coded and legitimized by American common man ideology.

Turning to Maine's lobstermen, lumberjacks, and athletes, Hartley frequently put a local spin on common man iconography, thereby eliding the regional with the national, as in pictures like *Lobster Fishermen* (plate 88), a leisurely scene of fisherfolk breaking momentarily from their aquatic labors.[30] However, as a national icon intended to be honored and glorified, the common man offered Hartley a useful trope in which he could encode his love and desire for beautiful men without necessarily revealing his homosexuality to the public. These tandem lines of interest are more clearly evident in *Down East Young Blades* (plate 85). More iconic in appearance than *Lobster Fishermen,* the picture features a trinity of hearty bodies arranged symmetrically within a vertically oriented composition, an

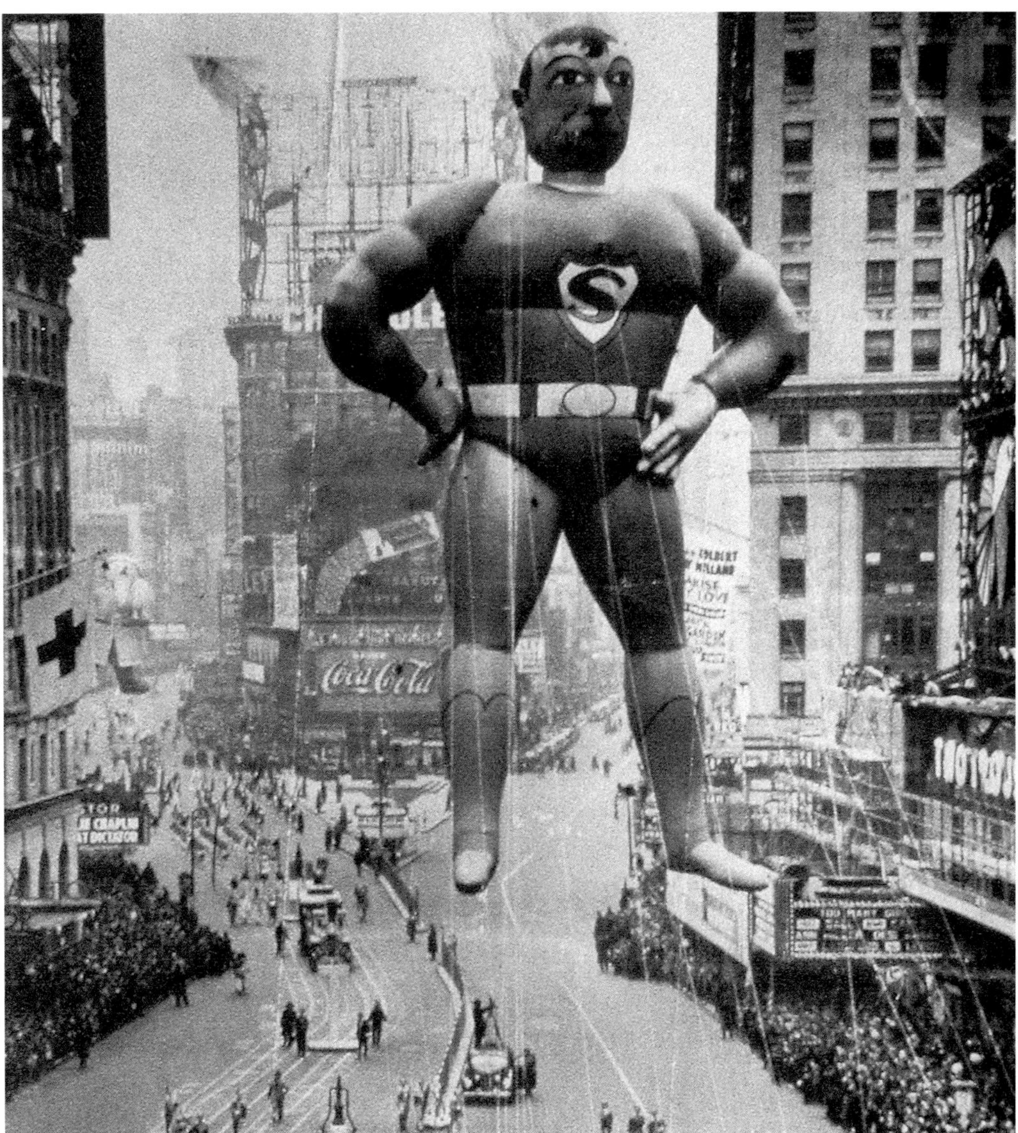

Figure 4
Superman appearing as helium balloon
Macy's Thanksgiving Day Parade, November 1940
Source: *Superman: A Complete History*
Used by permission, D.C. Comics
Photograph by Miller Studios Inc.

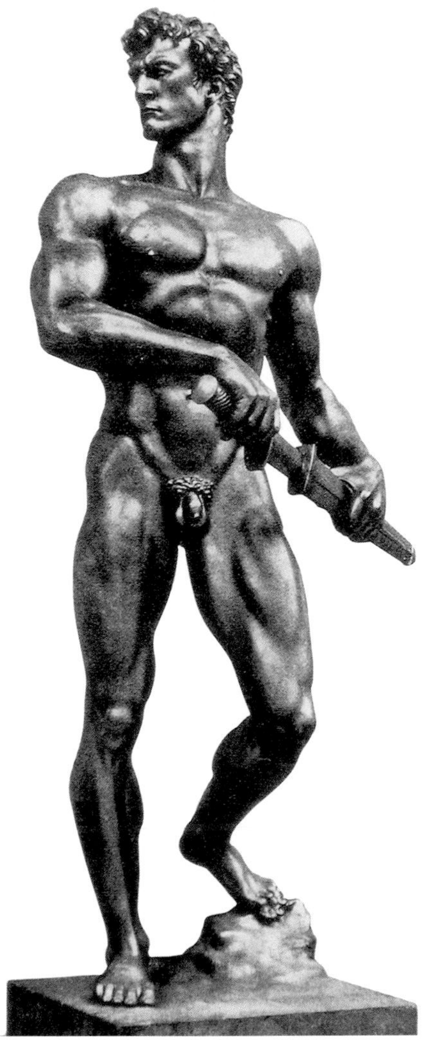

Figure 5
Arno Breker
Readiness
© Arno Breker by Marco Bodenstein, Bonn
Photograph by Miller Studios Inc.

arrangement that causes the image to appear grand and stately despite the plebian subject matter. Hartley here renders three regional deities, each complete with a symbol of his faith: the lobster traps near the man on the left, the fish held by the largest man in the center, and the lobster grasped by the man on the right.

At the same time, Hartley embedded in *Down East Young Blades* many subtle markers pointing obliquely to his own sexuality. These include the cocky swagger of the two men who seem to gaze at each other from either side of the composition and the overall heightened sense of physicality, accentuated by the artist's predominantly warm palette. The title too draws attention to his subjects as dashing young men, attractive and desirable. At once a pictorial tribute to Maine's common men and a gay man's covert admission of same-sex desire, *Down East Young Blades* suggests the means by which Hartley encoded personal desire within public symbolism that authorized glorification of the American male, his outer rugged beauty an indexical sign of his inner strength and goodness, in other words, his Americanness.

Hartley's fixation on the male body in pictures like *Madawaska—Acadian Light-Heavy* or *Christ Held By Half-Naked Men* would have likewise enjoyed considerable cultural legitimacy under the auspices of larger patterns in American society related to World War II. Just as America's entry into war inspired renewed interest in the common man iconography, it ignited intense scrutiny of America's young male population. Particular

Figure 6
"American Soldiers In 1940 Are 2 in. Taller, 15 lb. Heavier Than 1917"
Life, October 21, 1940
Ralph Morse and William C. Shrout/Timepix

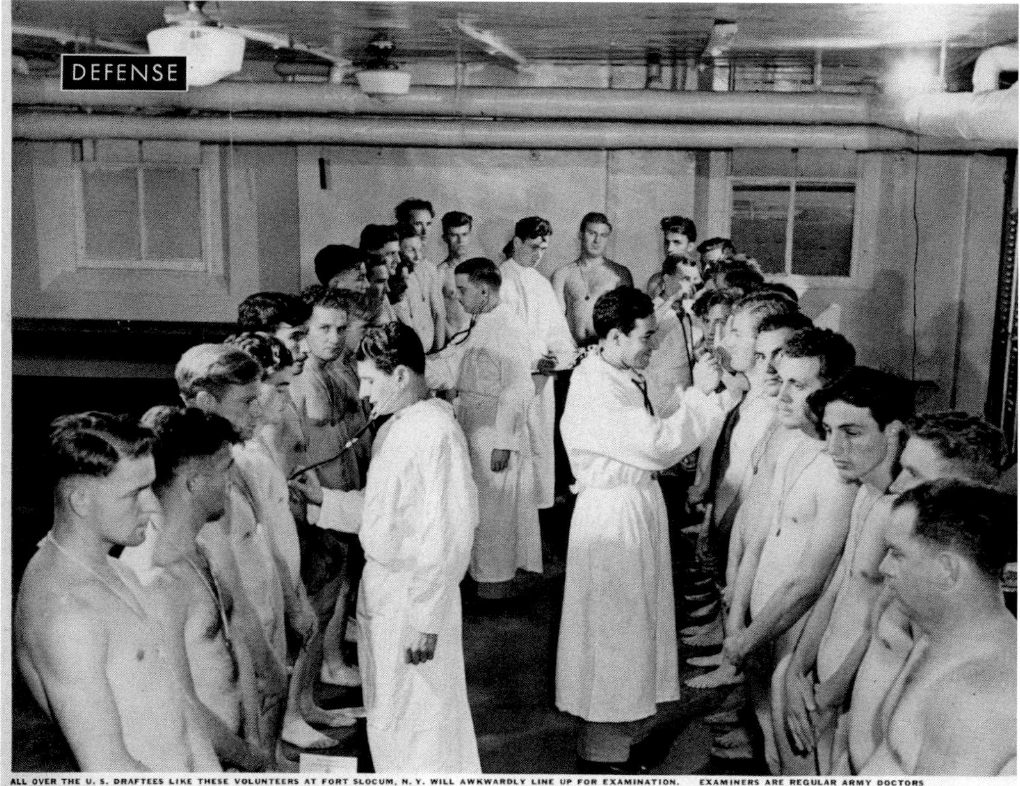

ALL OVER THE U. S. DRAFTEES LIKE THESE VOLUNTEERS AT FORT SLOCUM, N. Y. WILL AWKWARDLY LINE UP FOR EXAMINATION. EXAMINERS ARE REGULAR ARMY DOCTORS

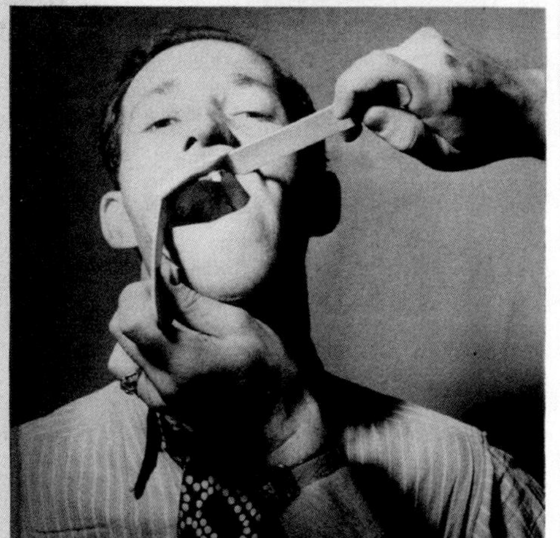

This volunteer was rejected by the Army because he did not have enough teeth. The Army requires that recruits have at least twelve teeth, with three good biting surfaces on each side.

AMERICAN SOLDIERS IN 1940 ARE 2 IN. TALLER, 15 LB. HEAVIER THAN 1917

Next month some 400,000 draftees will troop into recruiting stations throughout the land to receive physical examinations like the one shown above. Doctors will peer down their throats, X-ray their lungs, test their eyes, examine their legs and feet. The results of these examinations should be highly encouraging. They will show that today's soldier is 2 in. taller, 15 lb. heavier, infinitely healthier than the American soldier of World War I. Because of this, he should make a far better fighter.

But the Army still will have plenty to do to improve the health of its draftees. Some 40% of them will be rejected because of bad teeth, defective hearing or eyesight, flat feet, weak lungs, hernias or venereal diseases. Many of the rest will be flabby, undernourished, have poor abdominal muscles. They will be in no condition to take part in strenuous maneuvers or tote a 50-lb. pack 20 miles. To all of them, the Army will first give lessons in sanitation, ordering them to shave, use plenty of soap and water, keep clean, brush their teeth and neatly comb their hair. Then each will be given a thorough shower and outfitted with $90 worth of uniforms.

For the next four weeks, the Army will concentrate principally on health. During that time draftees will do the things that the volunteers shown on these pages are doing now. They will get three good meals a day with as many helpings as they like. On the drill field they will be given setting-up exercises, taught the rudiments of drill. They will be formed into football teams which will play other Army posts. Around camp they will pick weeds, paint fences, indulge in plenty of horseplay. At the end of four weeks they will be physically ready for anything.

CONTINUED ON NEXT PAGE 57

attention was paid to their bodies as repositories of the nation's physical and moral strength and fortitude. Such scrutiny was made most powerfully manifest with the passage of the Selective Training and Service Act in 1940, legislation that recruited more than 16,400,000 males between the ages of twenty-one and thirty-five into the armed forces. The same legislative act set into motion a process that identified and weeded out undesirables, those who were too fat, too short, or too tall.

This rigorous and intrusive physical examination was revealed to a curious American public in the 21 October, 1940 edition of *Life* magazine (fig. 6).[31] One photograph featured in the essay shows naked recruits undergoing examination, a seemingly exclusive Euro-American line-up that exposes indirectly the racial segregation of the armed forces. Another photograph reveals the inside of the mouth of a recruit rejected because he lacked the minimum number of required teeth. Overall, however, there was excellent news to report: "The results of these examinations will show that today's soldier is 2 in. taller, 15 lbs.

heavier, infinitely healthier than the American soldier of World War I. Because of this, he should make a far better fighter." Nevertheless, the article explained, "Some 40% of them will be rejected because of bad teeth, defective hearing or eyesight, flat feet, weak lungs, hernias or venereal diseases. Many of the rest will be flabby, undernourished, have poor abdominal muscles." Like the ancient Greek painter Zeuxis, who rendered the beautiful Helen by painting and combining the most desirable parts of the bodies of multiple maidens, America's military, aided by its team of physicians, created the nation's new male ideal, fit and ready for battle.

The symbolic outcome of the army's intensive physical selection appears in the form of the confident, half-nude soldier in the Pennsylvania Railroad advertisement. He is, the accompanying text assures the reader, "a fine specimen of American manhood," lacking all of the physical defects that caused lesser candidates to be rejected. Bigger and stronger than the men of his father's generation, he embodies America's readiness and willingness to flex its formidable military muscle in efforts to preserve its democratic ideals. The farmer featured in the Pan American Clipper advertisement appears also to have undergone the military's physical examination and to have excelled.

The men Hartley rendered would likewise have passed the military's exam with flying colors. Proudly displaying their large, exaggerated frames, they exhibit external bodily signs that carried larger nationalistic associations in light of America's entry into World War II. On a personal level, Hartley clearly enjoyed the results of the armed services' efforts to gather the nation's finest physical specimens, as suggested by a letter written after a trip to New York, where he delighted in seeing "navies in white duck, and the thighs and arses something to tell mother about—simply wonderful."[32] However, such outwardly erotic longings would likely not have been detected readily by viewers of Hartley paintings, who had been conditioned by other contemporaneous images of muscular male bodies around 1940 and the cultural codes associated with them. As a result of army regulation, the muscular male body possessed signs pertaining not only to national identity, but also to normative sexuality, which would have cloaked in many instances the homoerotic content of Hartley's paintings.

John D'Emilio has pointed out that the selective service examination sought to extract from the ranks of potential recruits not only flat feet, bad teeth, and weak ears. It sought additionally to root out sexual deviancy, particularly homosexuality. "From the beginning of the war," he notes, "psychiatrists examined potential inductees to weed out the unfit. Since a history of homosexual behavior or even tendencies toward it constituted grounds for exclusion, medical personnel interrogated recruits about their sexual inclinations."[33] To ensure that homosexual men did not slip past them undetected, military doctors also adopted quasi-scientific practices dating back to the nineteenth century in which the body was scrutinized for effeminate qualities, which would be interpreted as signs of homosexual inclinations. However, "in general, only the most effeminate," D'Emilio makes clear, along with "those with arrest records [and] those especially worried about the strain of living in an all-male environment with stringent sanctions against homosexual behavior found themselves rejected because of their sexuality."[34] Thus the male body that passed the selective service examination and entered the ranks of the military was coded "masculine" and, by extension, heterosexual.

Similar codes pertaining to normative gender identification and sexuality are evident in contemporaneous images of the male body. Indeed, the "fine specimen of American manhood" featured in the Pennsylvania Railroad advertisement, as the product of the military extraction and idealization, possesses not only broad shoulders and strong legs, but also, the viewer could rest assured, normal sexual drives marking him as "masculine." Likewise, the symbolic heterosexuality of the god-like farmer in the Pan American Clipper advertisement is implied by his muscular frame, in addition to his offspring that follows quite literally in his footsteps, a symbol of the coming generation and, as such, a sign of procreative sex.

Hartley's ultra-masculine male figures would have been received in close proximity to the same cultural codes that governed images of the male body tied to the militarization of American culture. In fact, the painter seems in certain instances to have gone to extra efforts to ensure the reception of his male subjects as heterosexual, most obviously in *On the Beach* (plate 82), in which a male bather is accompanied by a female companion. Saturated with identifiable signs of masculinity, Hartley's late figure paintings could thus pass in spite of their homoerotic content.

That Hartley achieved this remarkable feat is suggested by numerous positive reviews he began receiving near the end of his career. Hartley's late rise in the ranks of contemporary American artists was, in fact, based on the notion prevailing among audiences that the painter had achieved a distinctly "masculine" mode of expression. In his review of Hartley's exhibition at Hudson Walker's gallery in 1940, for instance, *Art News* critic James Lane lauded Hartley's paintings as "virile," noting particularly the artist's "masculine, well-designed bluntness."[35] That same year, Mrs. E. Richardson Cherry of San Antonio, Texas, sent Hartley a fan letter expressing her enthusiastic admiration after seeing his exhibition at the Witte Memorial Museum. "We liked your show here very much," she declared. "So strong and virile. The weight of nature pleased me, for I like that solidity on canvas. How bravely you paint! I wish I had your courage."[36] "Strong and virile," Hartley's late paintings allowed him to operate largely undetected publicly as a homosexual in an era during which normative masculinity was tantamount to great American art.

Hartley's rise in the ranks in American art strikes in this regard a meaningful parallel with the collective experience of the hundreds, if not thousands, of gay men who entered the ranks of the military despite efforts to weed them out. "Although intended in part to keep homosexuals out of the armed forces, psychiatric screening proved relatively ineffective in doing so," D'Emilio emphasizes. "Given the patriotic fervor that the war elicited and the stigma attached to a rejection for neuropsychiatric reasons, few gay men willingly declared themselves in order to avoid service."[37] Like the scores of gay men who passed through the military examination because they possessed sufficiently "masculine" bodies and offered correct responses to questions, Hartley put before his inquisitors appropriate signs of American masculinity, signs that could disguise his own subversive desire and identity even as his paintings bristled with homoerotic appeal.

Notes

The author thanks Patricia Lynagh, Smithsonian American Art Museum library, and Karl Gridley for their respective contributions to this essay.

1 Margaret Bruening, "Exhibition Reviews—Marsden Hartley," *Magazine of Art* 32 (April 1939): 252.

2 "Hartley's Figures," *Time* 33 (20 March 1939): 24.

3 Howard Devree, "Around New York—Marsden Hartley," *Magazine of Art* 33 (April 1940): 257.

4 "The 'New' Hartley Emerges from Down East," *Art Digest* 14 (15 March 1940): 8.

5 A shortlist of Hartley's most notable accomplishments late in his career includes his receipt of the fourth purchase prize for *Lobster Fishermen* (plate 88) at the Metropolitan Museum of Art's exhibition *Artists for Victory* in 1942. Also that year, the influential dealer Paul Rosenberg invited Hartley to join the stable of artists he represented, an invitation the painter took as a sign of undeniable artistic distinction.

6 William Innes Homer, *Alfred Stieglitz and the American Avant-Garde* (Boston: New York Graphic Society, 1977), 233. According to Homer, Arthur Dove's abstract work was most relevant to recent American painters, namely the abstract expressionists and their immediate followers.

7 In an interview published in 1980, art critic John Perreault discussed the silence surrounding issues of homosexuality in the art world in light of the Hartley retrospective concurrently on view at the Whitney Museum of American Art. See "I'm Asking—Does It Exist? What Is It? Whom Is It For?" *Artforum* 19 (November 1980): 74–75.

8 William H. Gerdts, *The Great American Nude*

(New York: Praeger Publishers, 1974): 179.

9 Weinberg.

10 Robertson, 126.

11 Weinberg, 193. Robertson similarly identified Hartley's exaggeration of male anatomy as the primary sign of the artist's homoerotic interest with regard to the same comparison: *"Canuck Yankee Lumberjack*... makes an overt reference to Cézanne's painting of a male bather, but whereas Cézanne's figure is hardly physical, Hartley's is a man, with big muscles, hair, and his penis outlined in his tight trucks." Robertson, 126.

12 Hartley to Helen Stein, 29 September 1939, Archives/Smithsonian. In response to seeing a man bathing at Wingaarsheek Beach, Massachusetts, Hartley recalled: "One of the outstanding visions of that place was an exceedingly well set up bather—standing on his hands—with the little swish of the sea swishing about—perfect in build and all. So fresh and clean and glowing."

13 These materials are housed with the Hartley Papers, Beinecke/Yale.

14 George Chauncey, *Gay New York: Gender, Urban Culture, and the Makings of the Gay Male World, 1890–1940* (New York: Basic Books, 1994), 336.

15 John D'Emilio, *Sexual Politics, Sexual Communities: The Making of a Homosexual Minority in the United States, 1940–1970,* 2d ed. (Chicago: University of Chicago Press, 1998), 24.

16 Thomas Craven quoted in "Vitriol for Murals," *Art Digest* 7 (15 December 1932): 6.

17 Thomas Craven, *Modern Art: The Men, the Movements, the Meaning* (New York: Simon & Schuster, 1935), 29.

18 Thomas Hart Benton, *An Artist in America,* 4th ed. (Columbia: University of Missouri Press, 1983), 265.

19 Benton quoted in "Blast by Benton," *Art Digest* 15 (15 April 1941): 6.

20 Malcom Cowley, *Exile's Return: A Narrative of Ideas* (New York: W. W. Norton, 1934), 198.

21 Samuel Kootz, *Modern American Painters* (New York: Brewer & Warren, 1930), 20. For a sustained discussion of this episode and issues pertaining to the gendered reception of Hartley's late paintings more generally, see Randall R. Griffey, "Marsden Hartley's Late Paintings: American Masculinity and National Identity in the 1930s and '40s" (Ph.D. dissertation, University of Kansas, 1999).

22 George Gallup, "Democracy—And the Common Man: The Quality of Common Sense," reprinted in *Vital Speeches of the Day* 8 (1 September 1942): 687.

23 Henry A. Wallace, "The Price of Free World Victory: The Century of the Common Man," reprinted in *Vital Speeches of the Day* 8 (1 June 1942): 483.

24 For a sustained discussion of Hartley's portraits of Abraham Lincoln, see my "Marsden Hartley's Lincoln Portraits," *American Art* 15 (summer 2001): 34–51.

25 Les Daniels, *Superman: The Complete History* (San Francisco: Chronicle Books, 1998), 18. I have drawn the information about Superman throughout this section from Daniels's illuminating study.

26 Murdock Pemberton quoted in "New York Show Reveals Kane's Greatness," *Art Digest* 9 (1 February 1935): 21.

27 "Pittsburgh Turned House Painter John Kane Into a Major U.S. Artist," *Life,* 17 May 1937, 44–45.

28 On Breker and Nazi art more generally, see Peter Adam, *Art of the Third Reich* (New York: Harry N. Abrams, 1992). More recent studies have been provided by Jonathan Petropoulos: see *Art as Politics in the Third Reich* (Chapel Hill: University of North Carolina Press, 1996) and *The Faustian Bargain: The Art World in Nazi Germany* (New York: Oxford University Press, 2000).

29 Hartley wrote about the folk artist after seeing this exhibition, observing, "the pictures of John Kane... come with a sense of timeliness, joining in the rush towards nationalism in American art." Hartley, "John Kane of Pittsburgh," in *On Art,* 192.

30 On the regionalist aspects of Hartley's late paintings, see Donna Cassidy, "'On the Subject of Nativeness': Marsden Hartley and New England Regionalism," *Winterthur Portfolio* 29 (winter 1994): 227–45.

31 "Defense—American Soldiers in 1940 are 2 in. Taller, 15 lbs. Heavier Than 1917," *Life,* 21 October 1940, 57–58.

32 Hartley quoted in Robertson, 126.

33 D'Emilio, *Sexual Politics,* 24.

34 Ibid., 25. Interestingly, in a letter to Robert McAlmon dated 31 August 1942, Beinecke/Yale, Hartley, utilizing a strikingly homophobic tone, commented on the presence of gay men in the armed services and expressed awareness of psychological methods used to detect them: "As for some that are in the army and navy, well how in the world did they ever let em in and keep em after they got in, but I guess the rigidity of the whole thing scared the piss out of the softies, and they found that even they can act like men. Of course they have psychological analysis when they are called up and if they are too far gone over on the girly side, they tell em so and discard them—as one examiner said to one of them in N.Y.—you would do more harm than good, and dismissed 'her' respectfully."

35 James W. Lane, "The Virile Paintings by Marsden Hartley," *Art News* 38 (16 March 1940): 15.

36 Mrs. E. Richardson Cherry to Hartley, 9 June 1940, Beinecke/Yale.

37 D'Emilio, *Sexual Politics,* 24.

PLATES 71–88

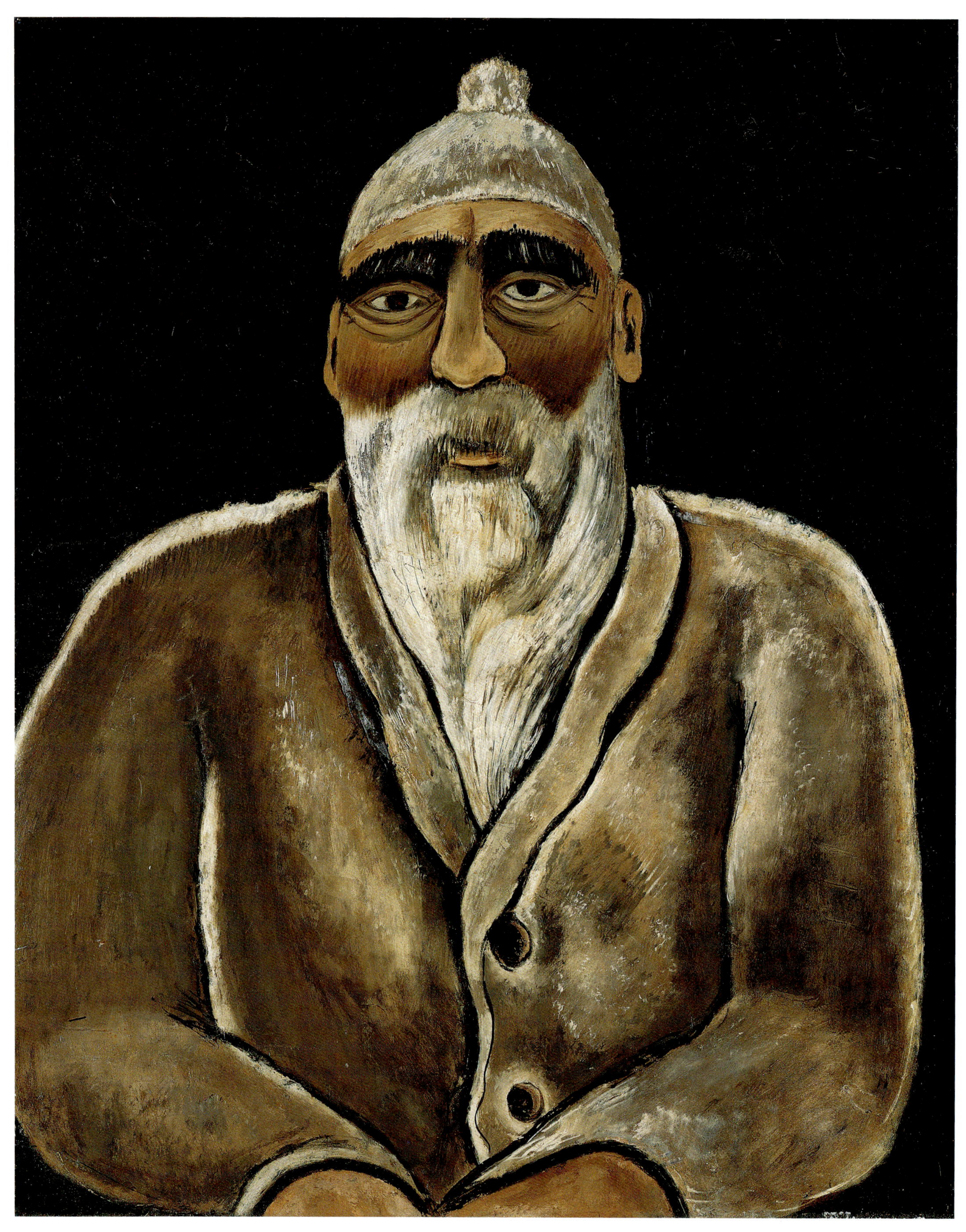

71
Portrait of Albert Pinkham Ryder, 1938
Oil on Masonite board, 28 × 22 in.
The Metropolitan Museum of Art, New York
Edith and Milton Lowenthal Collection
Bequest of Edith Abrahamson Lowenthal, 1991

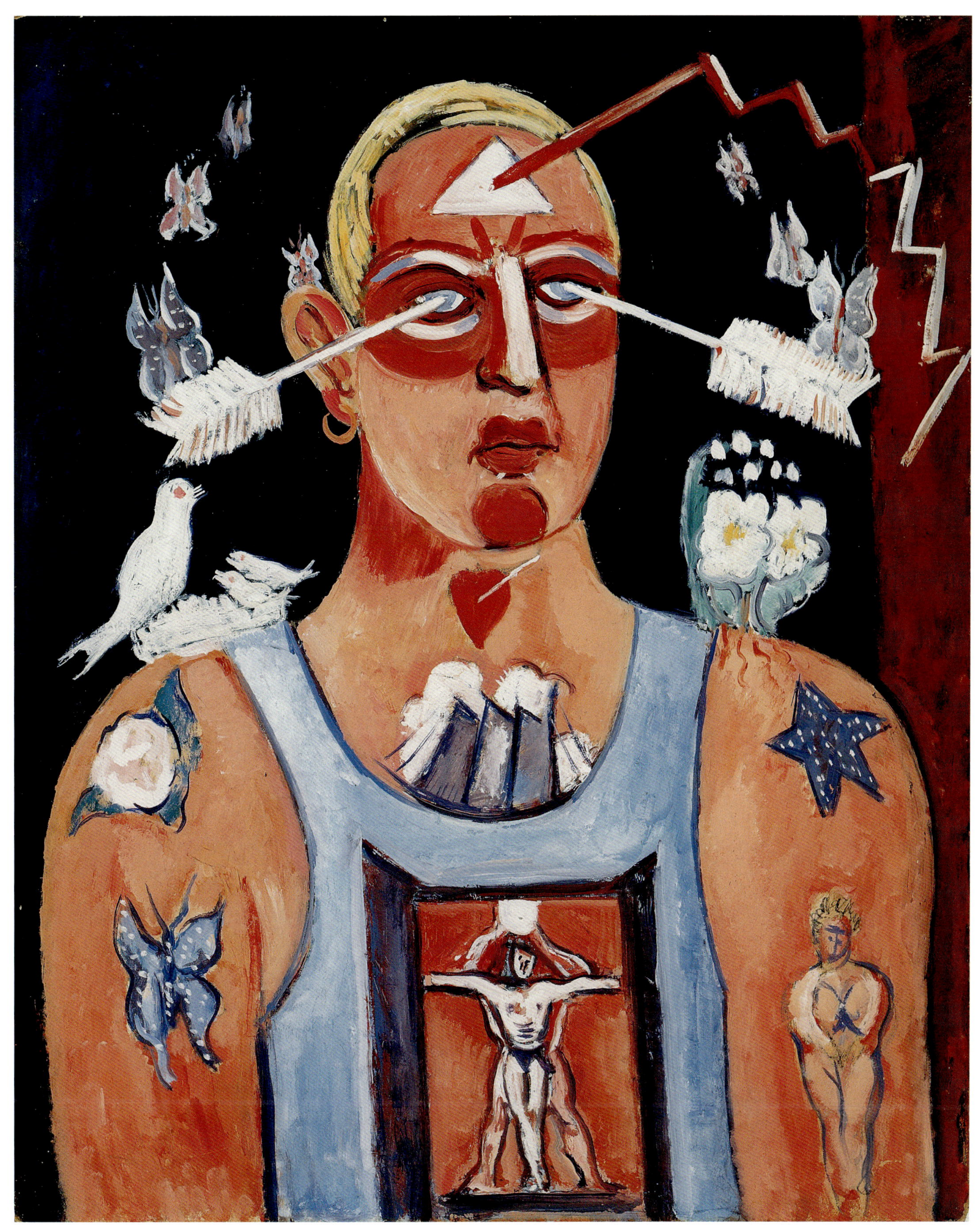

72
Sustained Comedy, 1939
Oil on academy board, 28⅛ × 22 in.
The Carnegie Museum of Art, Pittsburgh
Gift of Mervin Jules in memory of Hudson Walker, 1976, 76.64

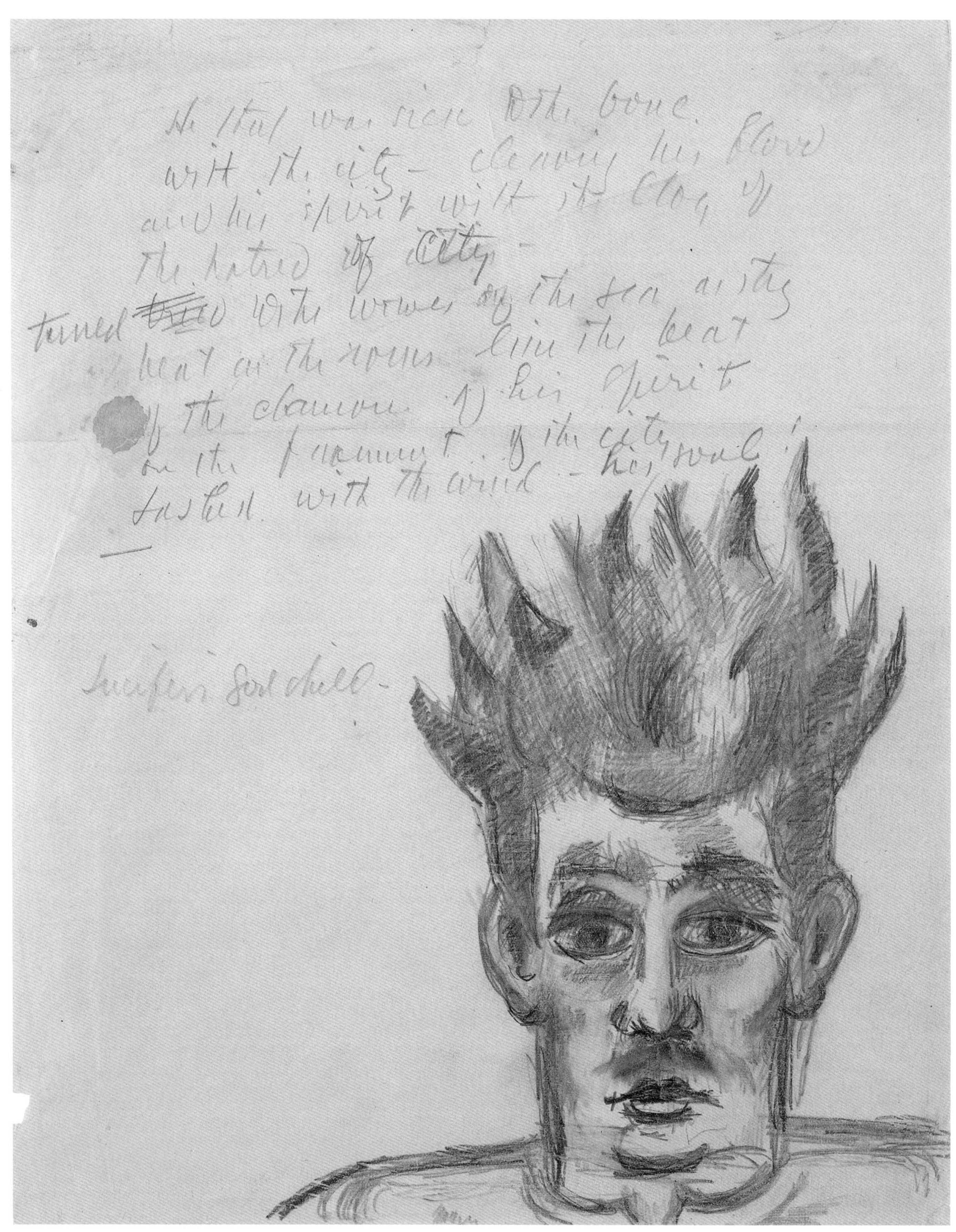

73

Lucifer's God Child

Pencil on beige paper, 10⅜ × 8⅛ in.

Bates College Museum of Art, Lewiston, Maine

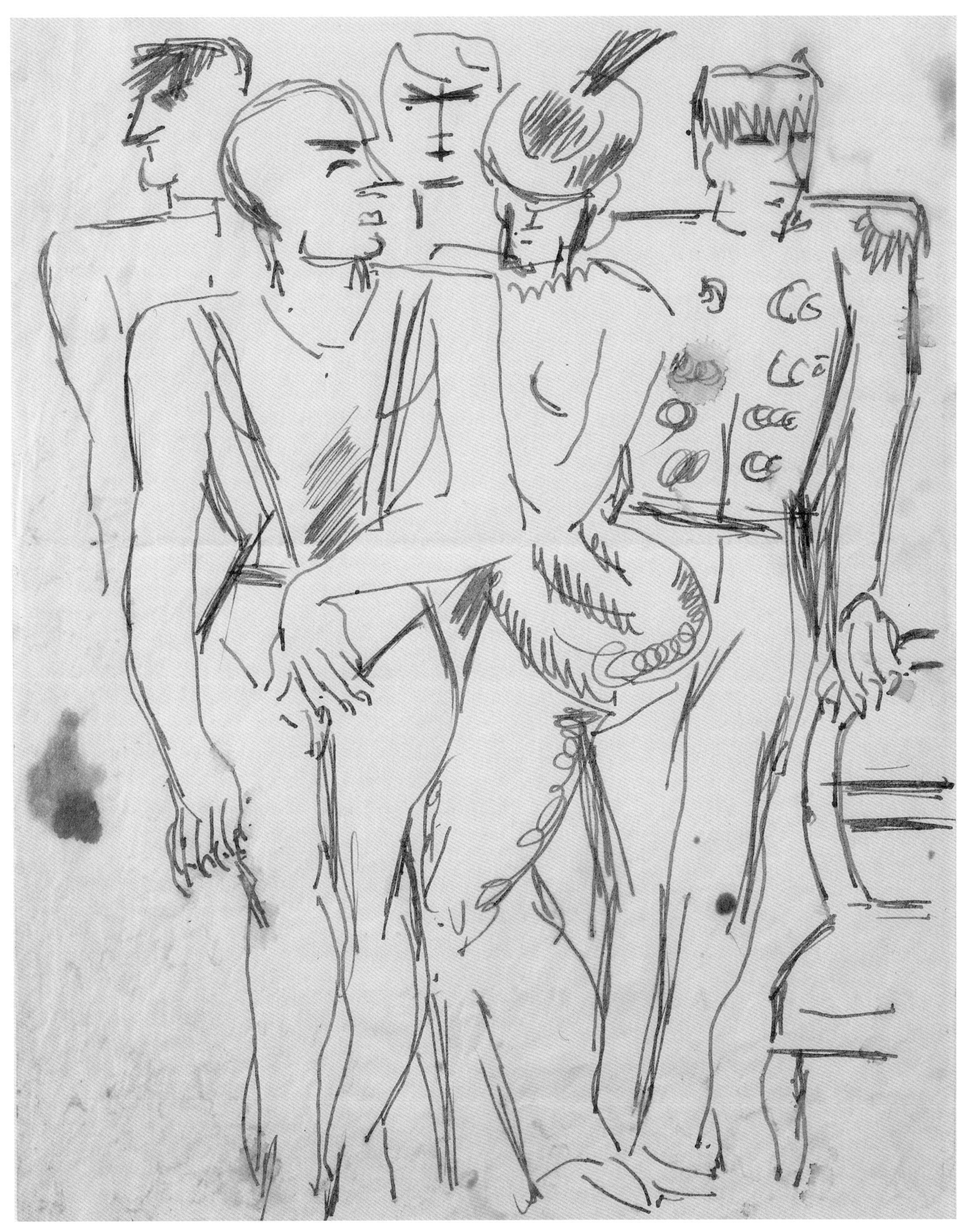

74
Untitled (Five Figures)
Pen and sepia ink on beige paper, 10⅝ × 8¼ in.
Bates College Museum of Art, Lewiston, Maine

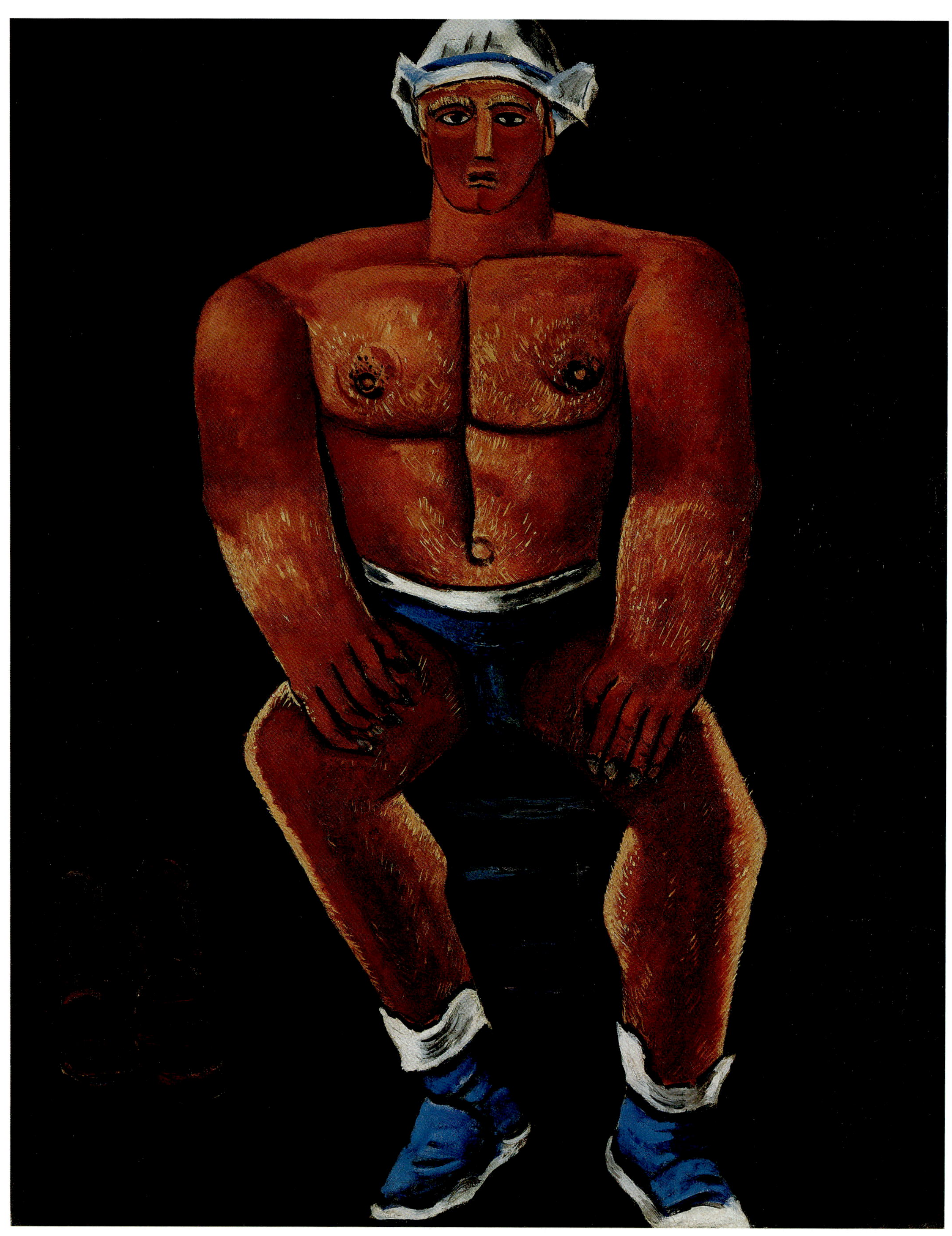

75

Flaming American (Swim Champ), 1939–40

Oil on canvas, $40\frac{1}{8} \times 30\frac{1}{4}$ in.

The Baltimore Museum of Art, Maryland

Edward Joseph Gallagher III Memorial Collection, by exchange

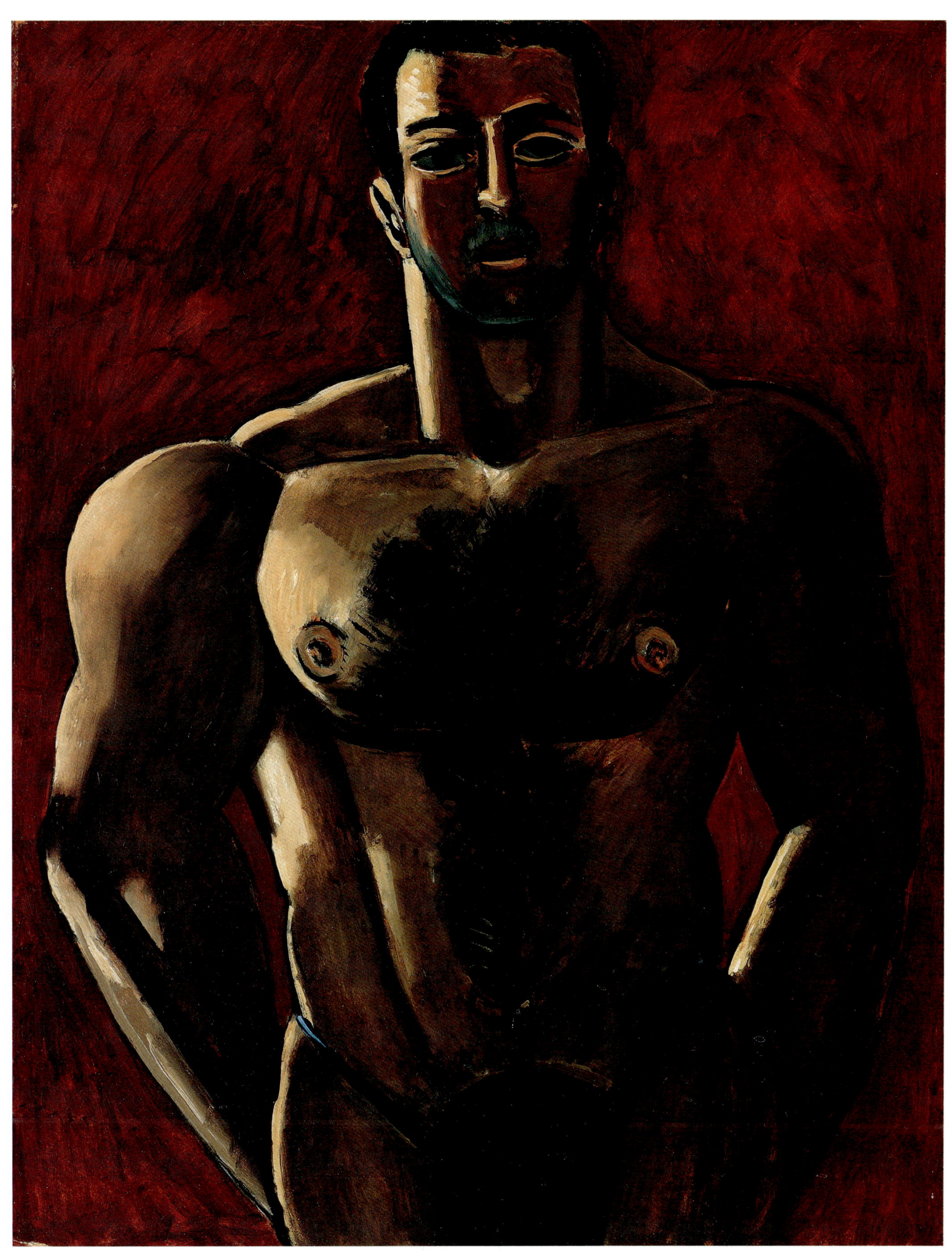

76
Madawaska—Acadian Light-Heavy, 1940
Oil on Masonite-type hardboard, 40 × 30 in.
The Art Institute of Chicago
Bequest of A. James Speyer, 1987.249

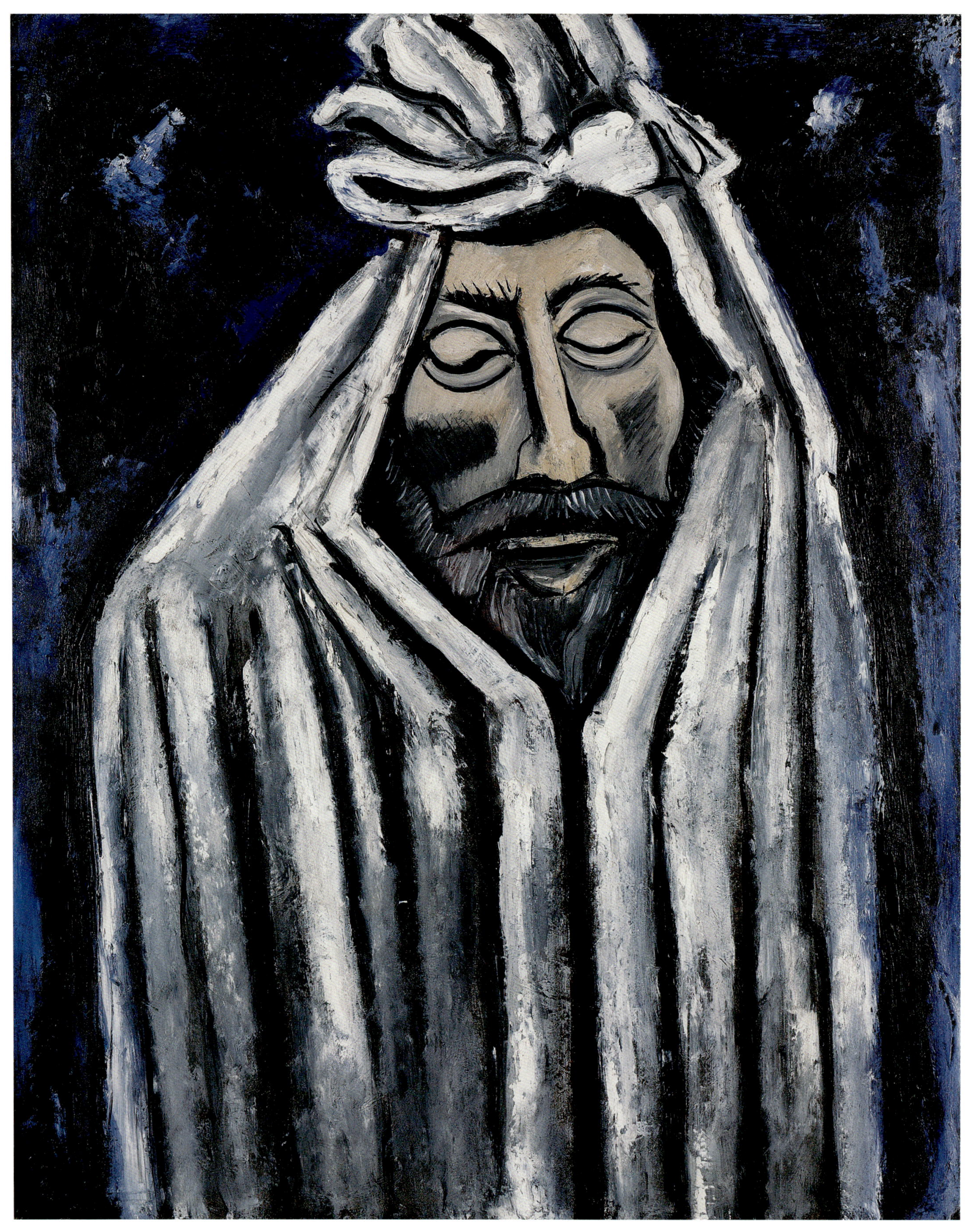

77
The Last Look of John Donne, 1940
Oil on academy board, 28 × 22 in.
Brooklyn Museum of Art, New York
Gift of Mr. and Mrs. Milton Lowenthal, 71.201

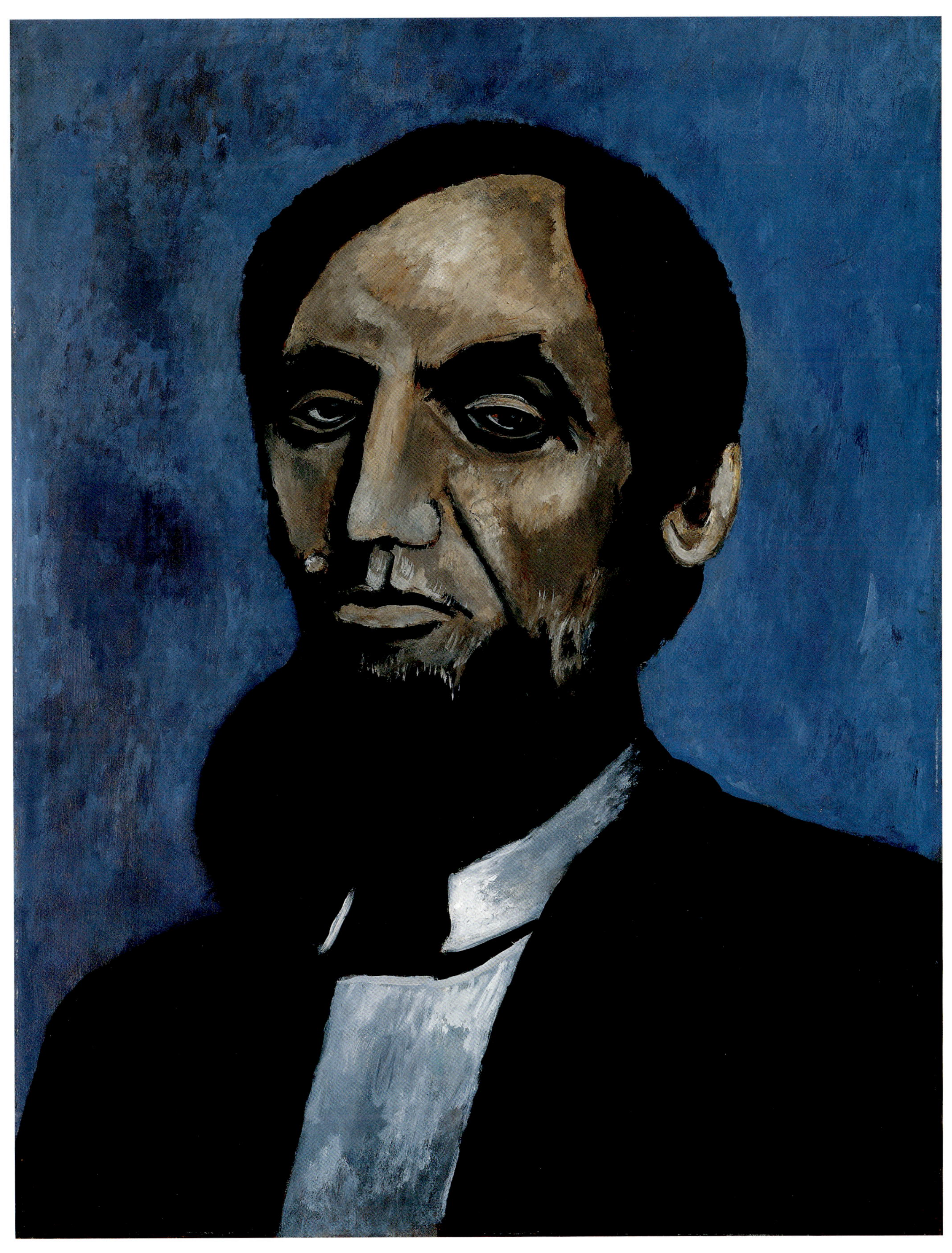

78
The Great Good Man, 1942
Oil on Masonite-type hardboard, 40 × 30 in.
The Museum of Fine Arts, Boston
Gift of William H. and Saundra B. Lane and the Hayden Collection, by exchange, 1990.376

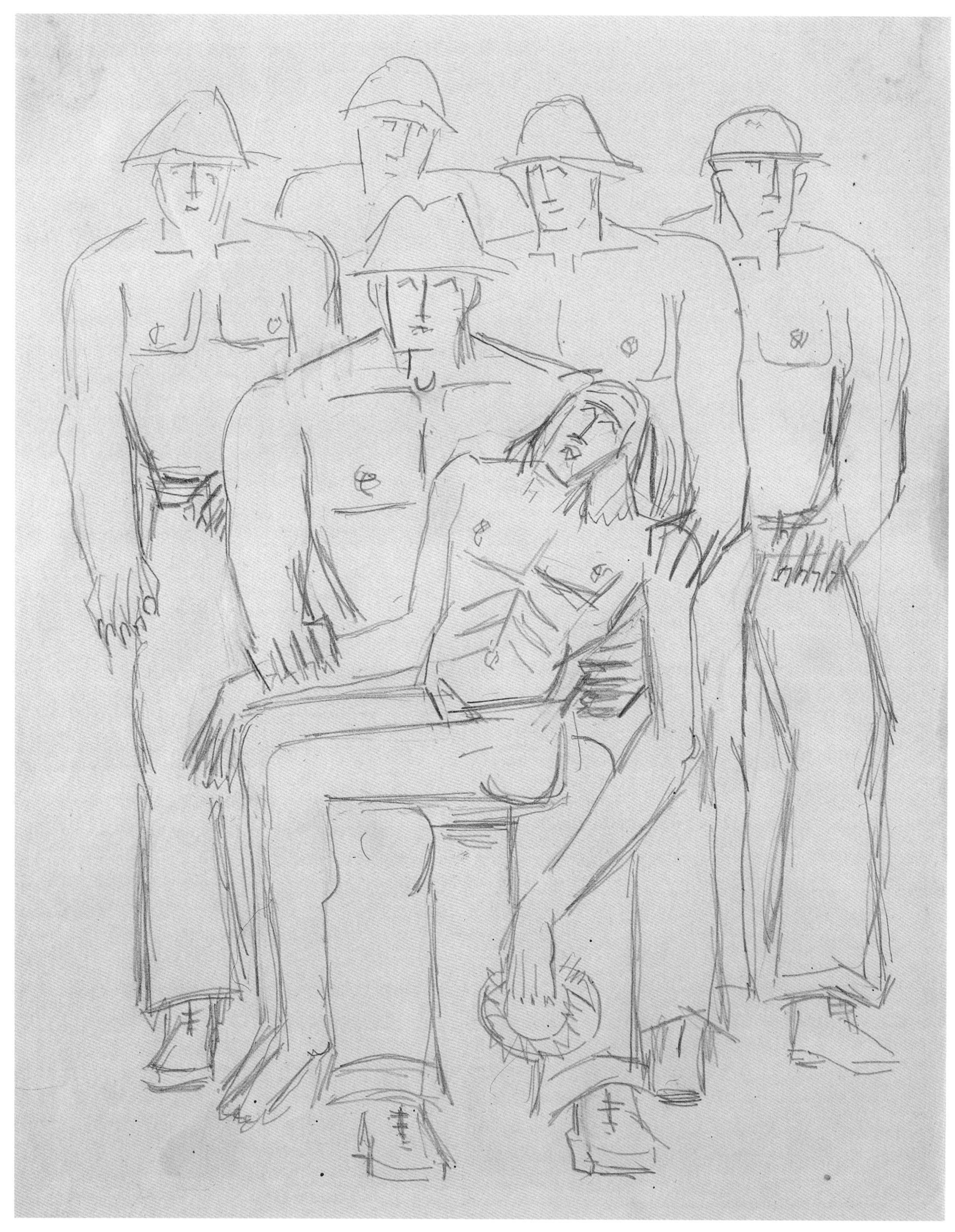

79

Untitled (Five Lobstermen and Christ Figure—Pietà Concept), c. 1940

Pencil on white paper, 10½ × 8 in.

Bates College Museum of Art, Lewiston, Maine

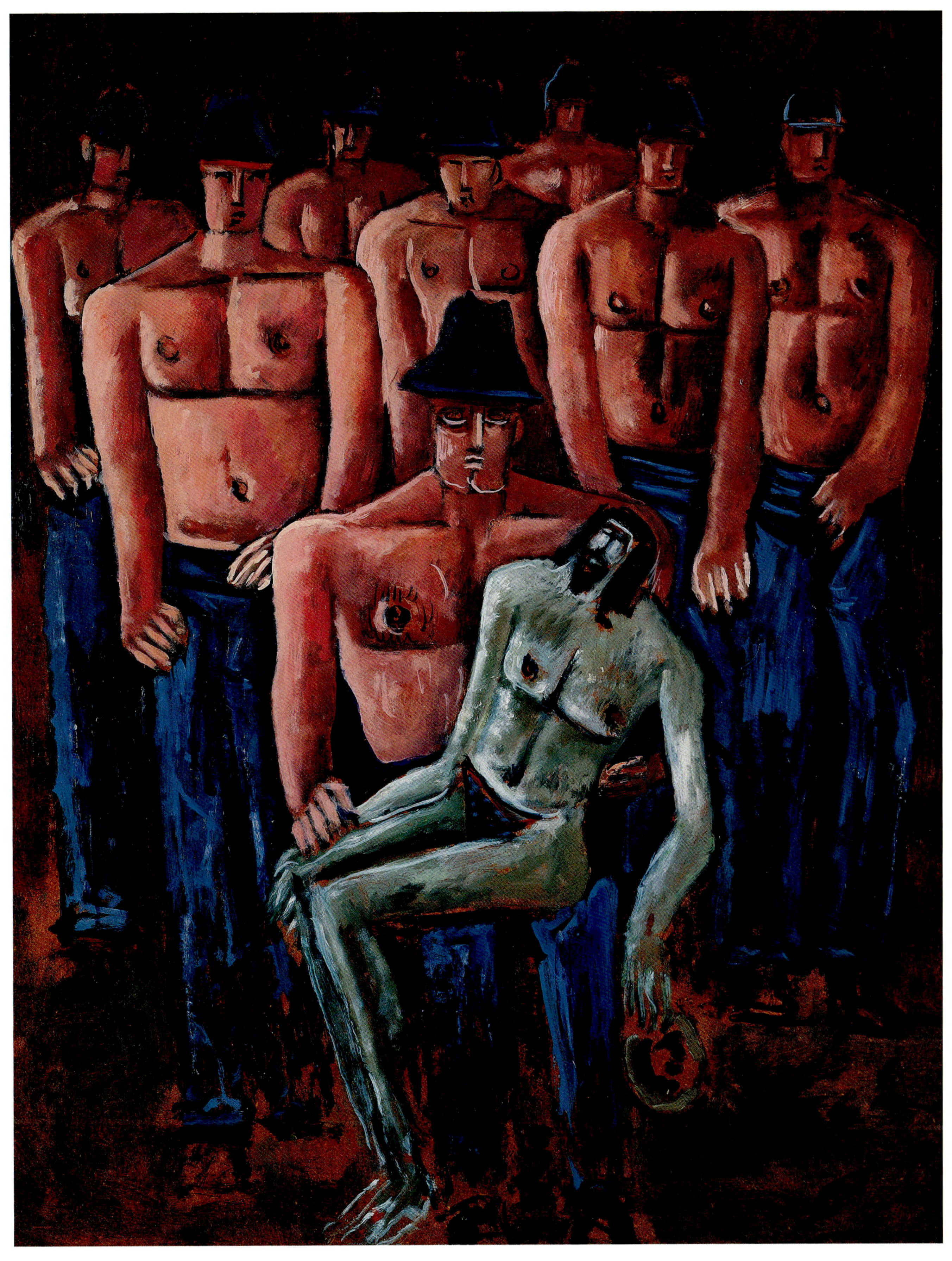

80

Christ Held by Half-Naked Men, 1940–41
Oil on Masonite-type hardboard, 40 × 30 in.
Hirshhorn Museum and Sculpture Garden,
Smithsonian Institution, Washington, D.C.

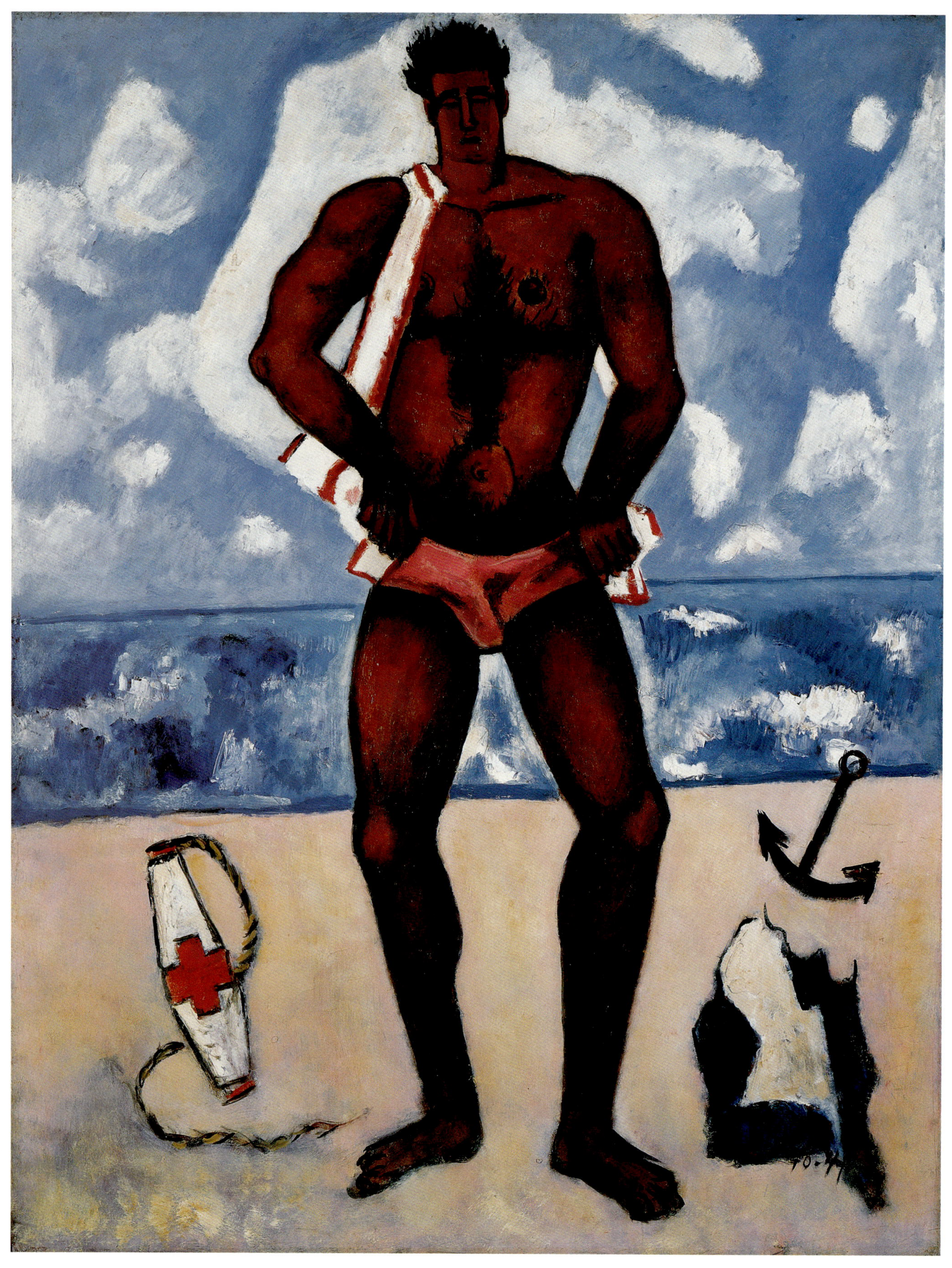

81

Canuck Yankee Lumberjack at Old Orchard Beach, Maine, 1940–41
Oil on Masonite-type hardboard, 40⅛ × 30 in.
Hirshhorn Museum and Sculpture Garden, Smithsonian Institution, Washington, D.C.
Gift of Joseph H. Hirshhorn, 1966

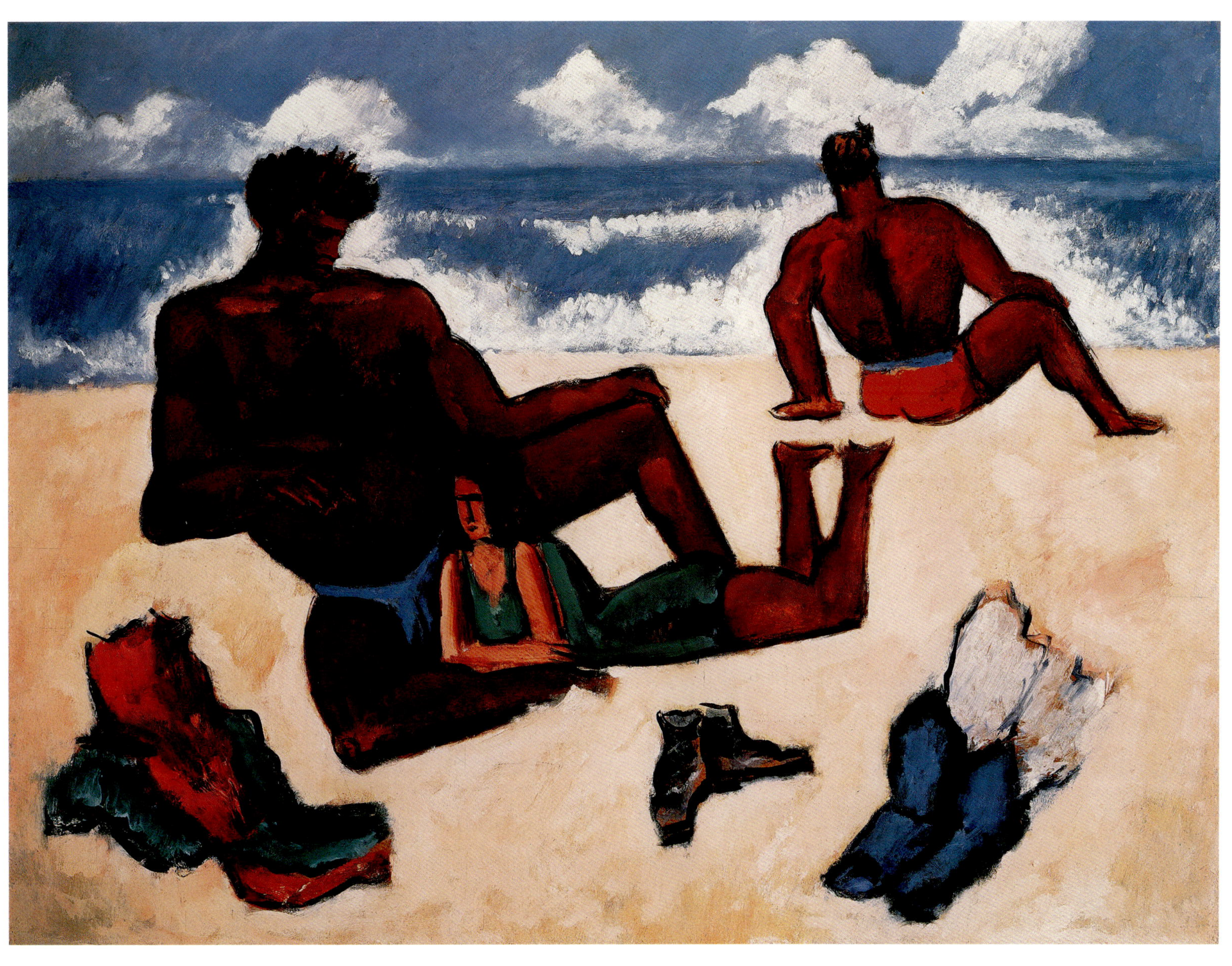

82

On the Beach, 1940

Oil on Masonite-type hardboard, 22 × 28½ in.

Private Collection

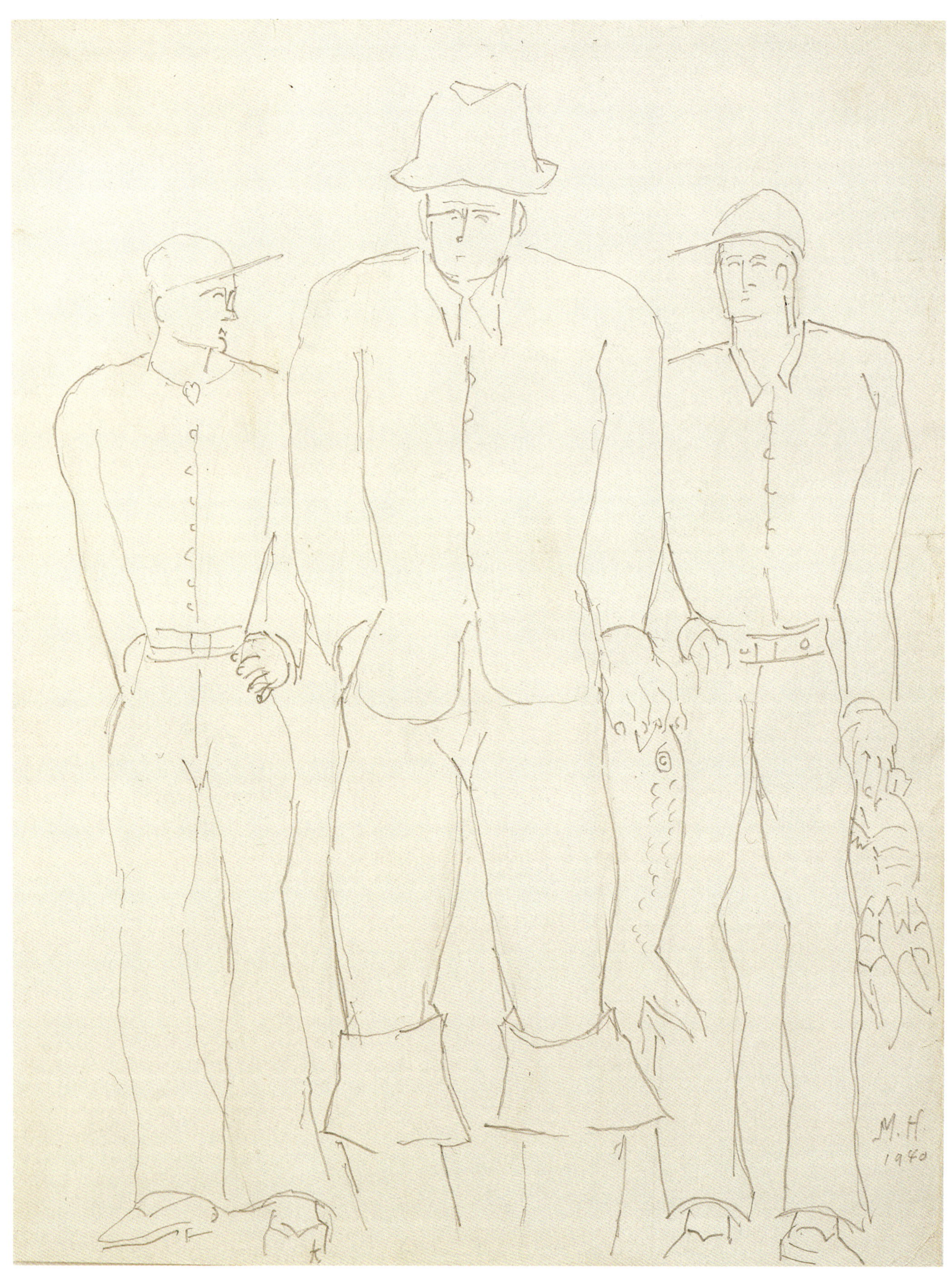

83

Untitled (Three Fishermen with Fish and Lobster), 1940

Pencil on beige paper, 11½ × 8¾ in.

Bates College Museum of Art, Lewiston, Maine

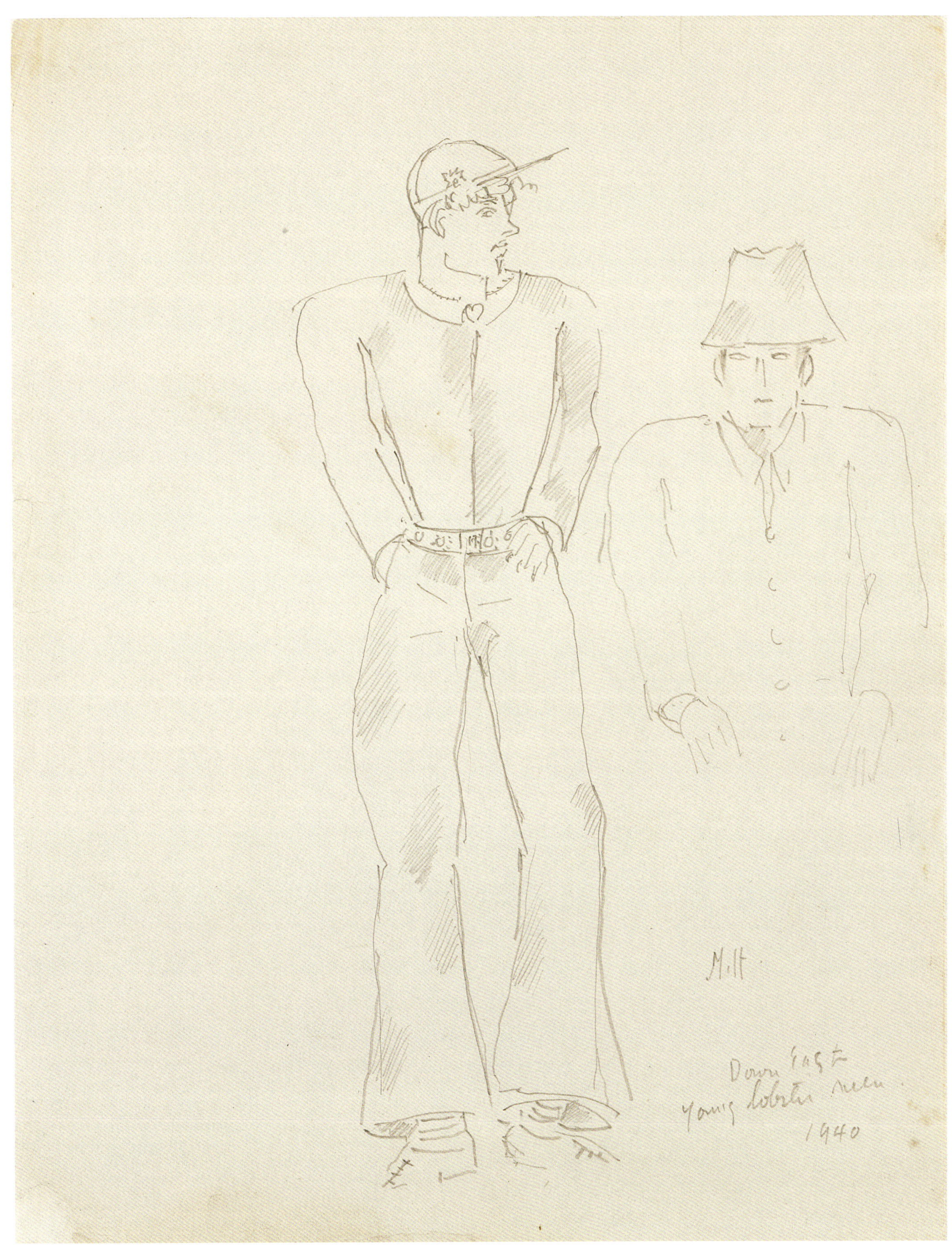

84

Down East Young Lobster Men, 1940

Pencil on beige paper, 11½ × 8⅞ in.

Bates College Museum of Art, Lewiston, Maine

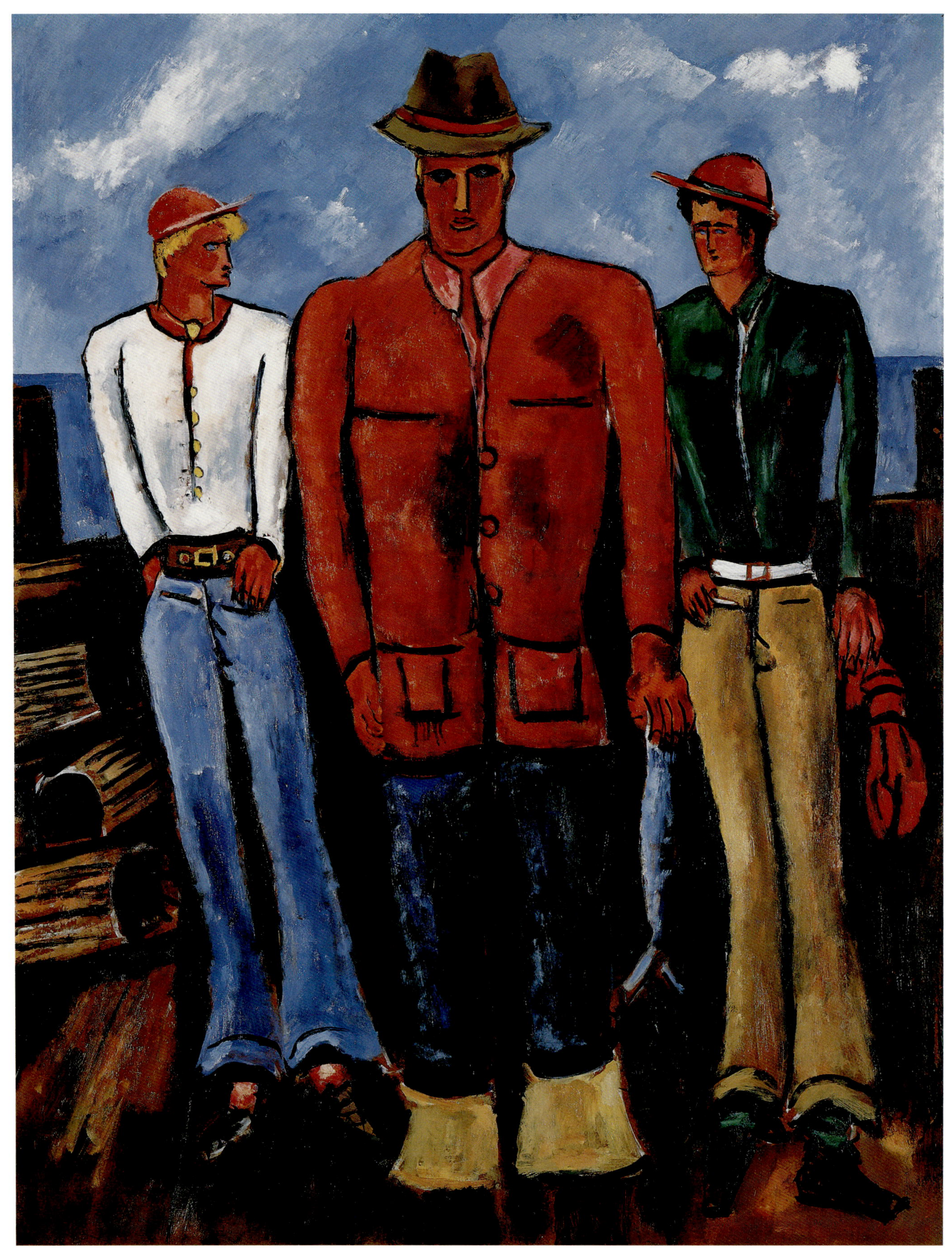

85

Down East Young Blades, c. 1940

Oil on Masonite-type hardboard, 40 × 30 in.

The Wadsworth Atheneum Museum of Art, Hartford

The Douglas Tracy Smith and Dorothy Potter Smith Fund, The Dorothy Clark Archibald and Thomas L. Archibald Fund, the Evelyn Bonar Storrs Trust Fund, The American Paintings Purchase Fund, and The Krieble Family Fund for American Art, 1999.11.1

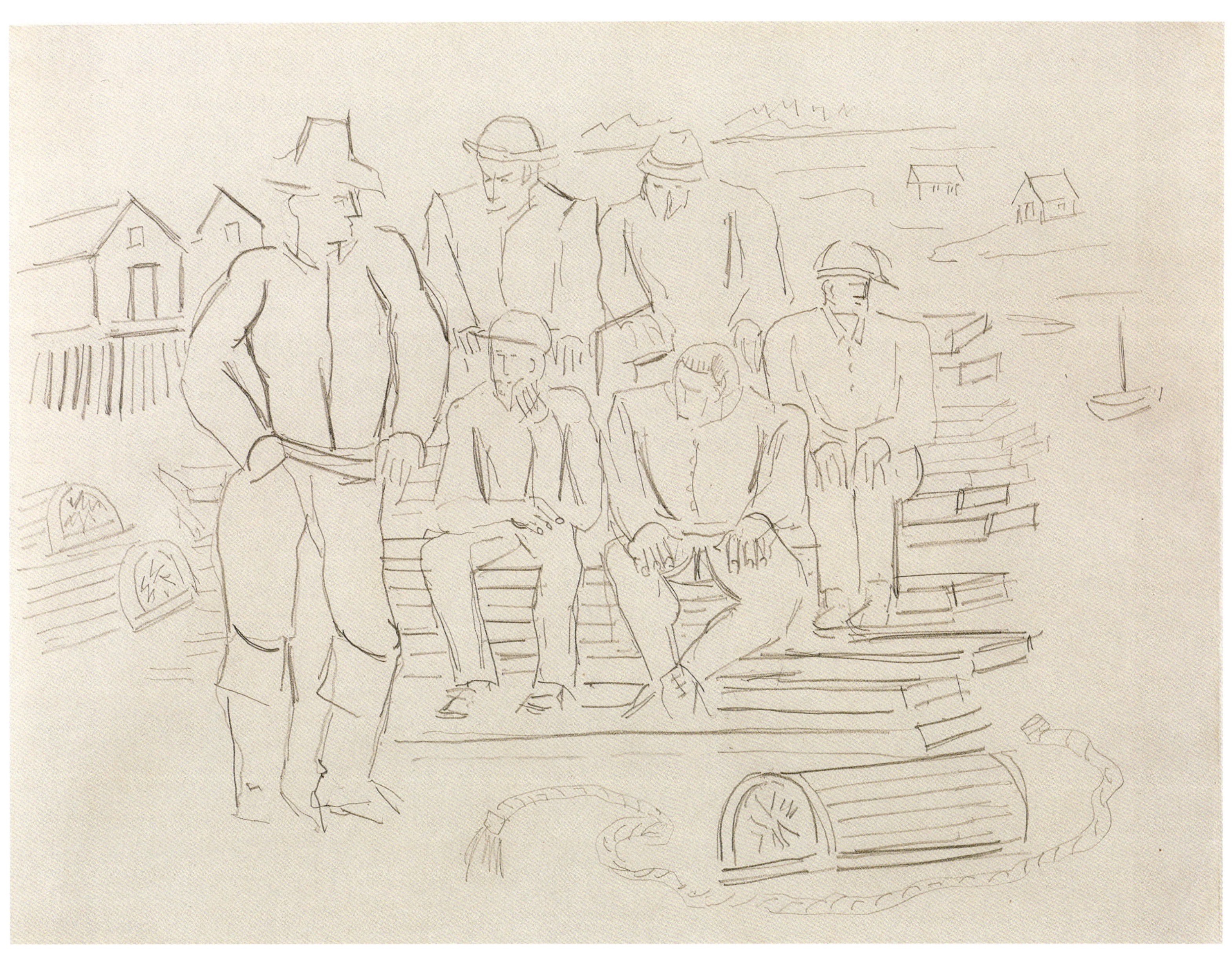

86

Untitled (Six Lobstermen and Lobster Traps), c. 1940
Pencil on white paper, 8 × 10¾ in.
Bates College Museum of Art, Lewiston, Maine

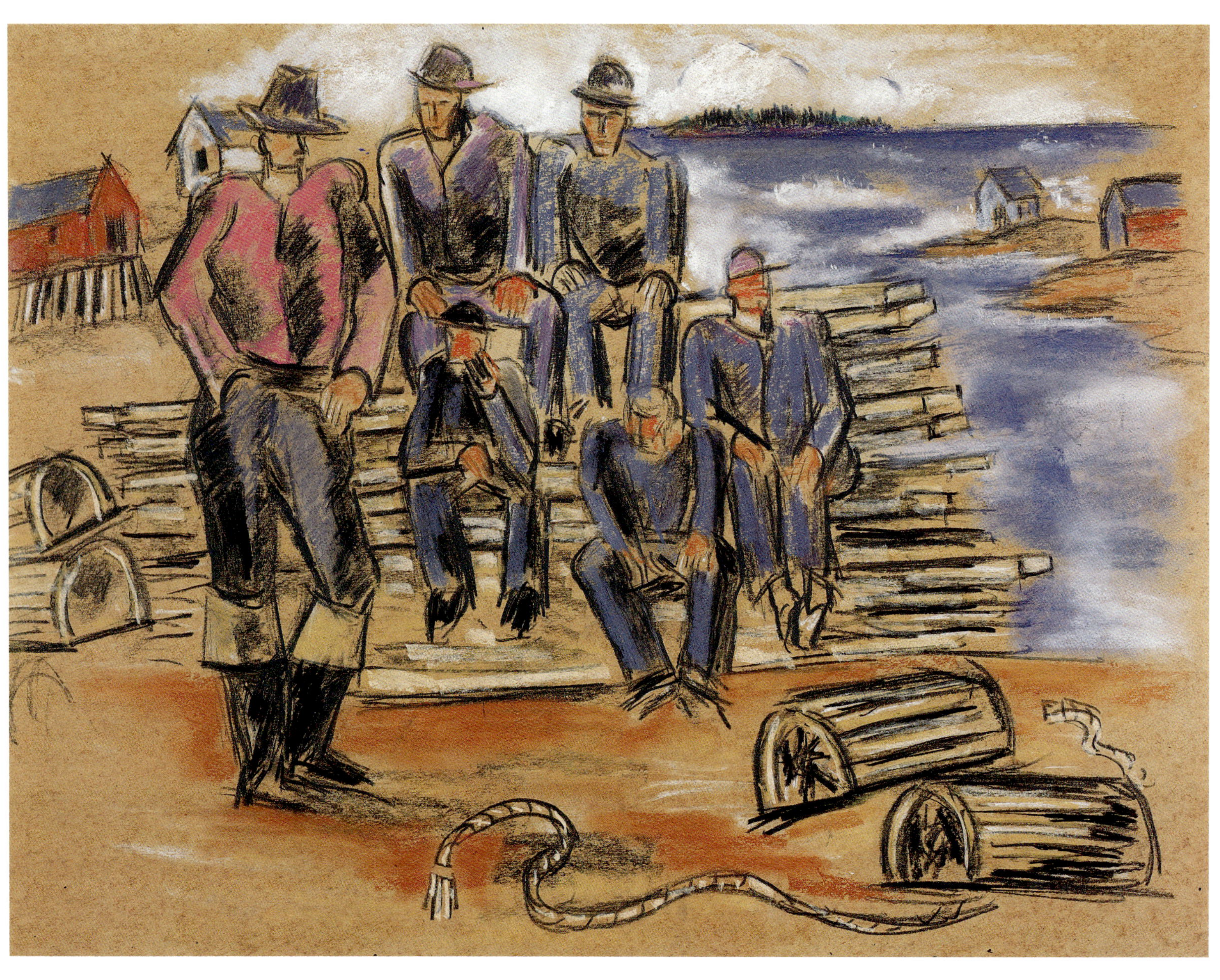

87

Study for "Lobster Fishermen," 1940
Pastel on paper, 21¼ × 27 in.
The Metropolitan Museum of Art, New York
Arthur Hoppock Hearn Fund, 1956

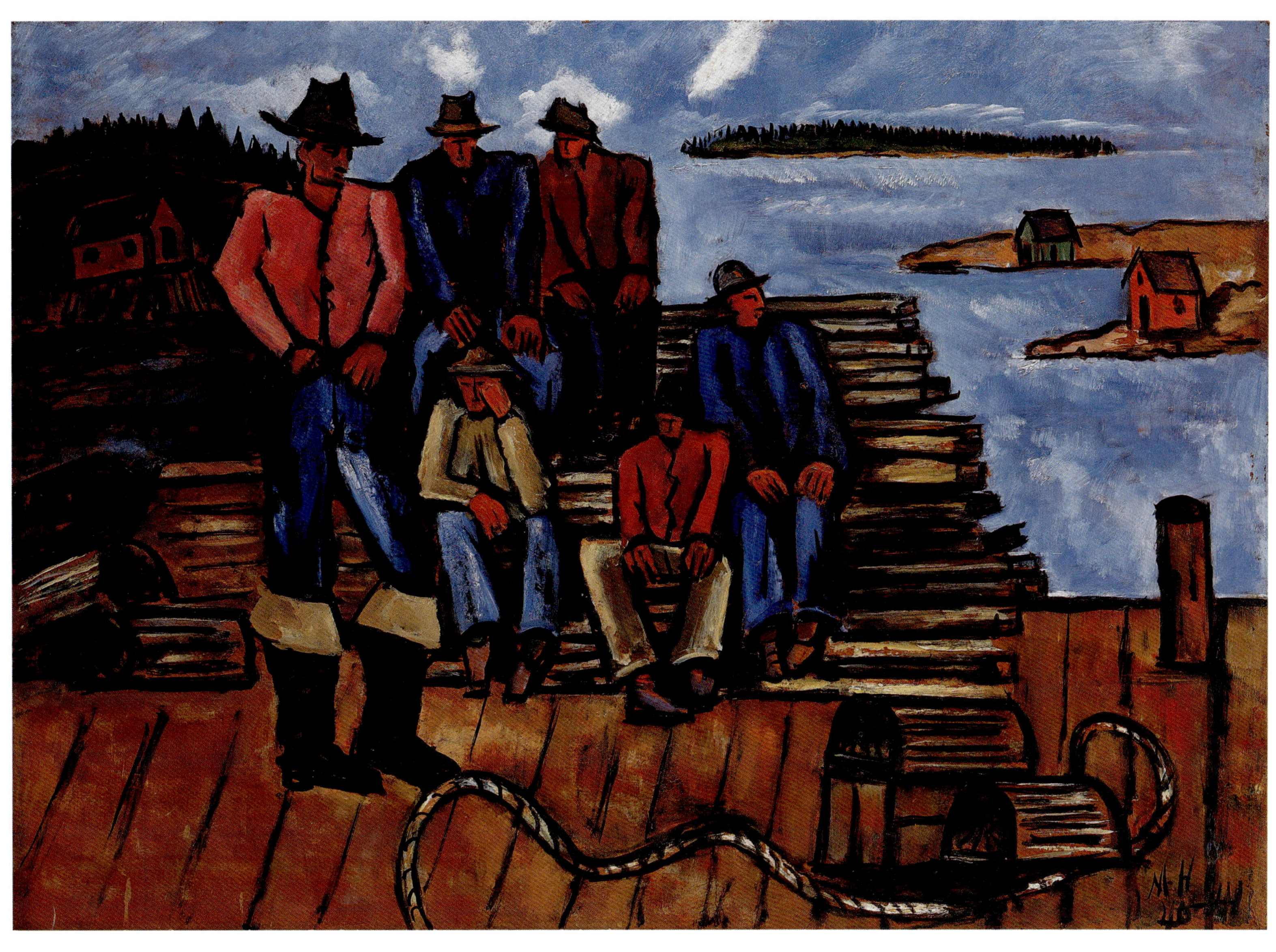

88

Lobster Fishermen, 1940–41
Oil on Masonite-type hardboard, 29¾ × 40 in.
The Metropolitan Museum of Art, New York
Arthur Hoppoch Hearn Fund, 1942

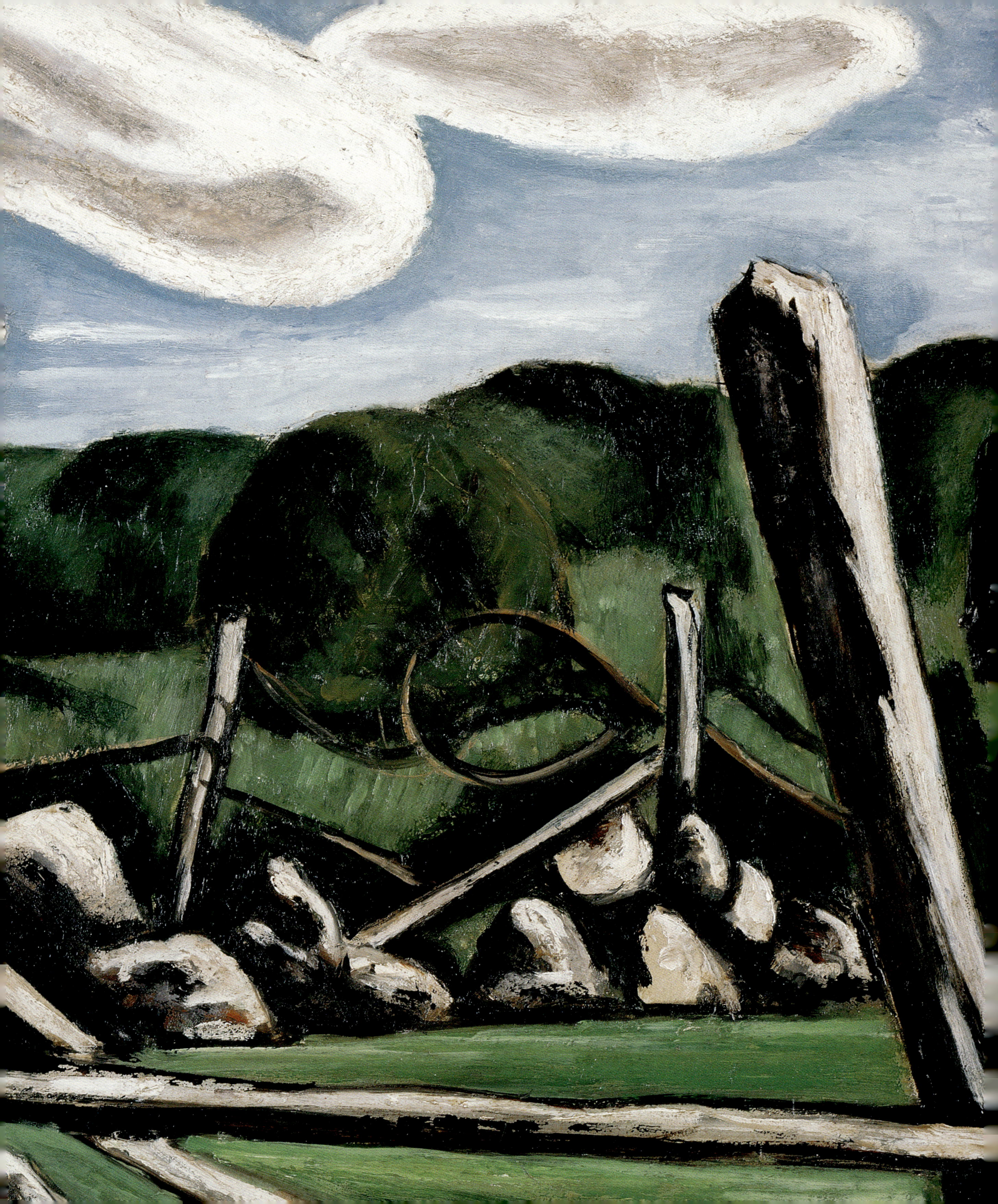

The "Nativeness" of "Primitive Things": Marsden Hartley's Late Work in Context

Carol Troyen

In 1937 Waldo Peirce, Hartley's friend and sometime rival for the honor of calling himself "Maine's greatest painter," produced a self-portrait that became famous, if only briefly. It shows the artist, burly and bearded, wearing a plaid shirt and smoking a pipe, as if to advertise his kinship with the fishermen and lumberjacks who lived around him in Bangor, Maine, and to demonstrate his "honest-to-goodness American spirit."[1] The portrait was featured in Peirce's solo show at the Carnegie Institute in Pittsburgh in 1938. Three years later it was reproduced on an advertisement for Schmincke paints that ran in *Art Digest* and *Art News*, presenting Peirce the working man as the archetypal artist (fig. 1).

In 1943 Milton Avery painted a portrait of Hartley that is no less telling (fig. 2). Although by this time Hartley was spending much of each year in Maine, Avery nonetheless depicted him wearing a mauve jacket, pink shirt, and red bow tie, with a flower in his lapel and a signet ring on his little finger. It is an affecting portrait, an image of an artist both debonair and world-weary.[2] A photograph made by George Platt Lynes in about 1942 (private collection, New York City) similarly shows an elegant Hartley in a tweed suit, silk scarf, felt hat, and double-breasted coat (see Robertson figs. 9-10). Unlike Peirce, who presented himself as a cheerful, friendly type—the artist as working guy next door—Hartley, the self-styled "painter from Maine," rarely elected to appear like one of his neighbors.[3] Rather, his chosen persona was the urban sophisticate, the citizen of the world, the cosmopolitan.

These seemingly contradictory images—man of the world but painter from Maine—are yet another example of Hartley's lifelong search to find a compelling voice that would win public acceptance. Unlike the other artists who had been with Alfred Stieglitz since the early days of 291, Hartley had never been able to maintain a comfortable balance between his drive to be modern and the obligation to express his experiences as an American. Furthermore, by the 1930s, America was racked by the Depression, and in the arts a conservative trend had taken hold. Neither cubist abstraction nor the current chauvinistic manner of painting the American scene held much promise for Hartley.

In the spring of 1936, Hartley was invited to present a lecture at the Museum of Modern Art in New York in conjunction with that institution's exhibition *Cubism and Abstract Art.* At this point Hartley was reasonably well known as a painter and at the height of his powers as a critic. In his remarks, he made no secret of the fact that he was troubled by the show. Cubism, long the touchstone for modernism (he credited it with "qualities and ideas that amazed, confused, and delighted us"), had, in Hartley's view, become respectable. The paintings and collages "wild in their day" had become "settled," "sensible and tame." Even Marcel Duchamp's radical *Nude Descending the Staircase* seemed to Hartley graceful and obvious, over-intellectual, no longer affecting.[4]

Detail, Plate 50

About two years later, Hartley wrote an essay entitled "Is There an American Art?" The essay was never published, nor is it clear what prompted it. What is clear is the author's contempt for the midwestern regionalists, for those he called "corn belt painters." He was irritated by their false optimism and their proprietary nationalism, quoting with some impatience John Sloan's observation, "an American picture is a picture done by an American in America." Hartley found their claim of purity, of being untainted by European art, hypocritical. He pointed out that just like "the polyglot . . . art[ists] east of Chicago" whom they disdained, American scene painters too "got something or other from the international sense of things." Thomas Hart Benton, for example, "has looked well and long at Rubens and Greco." Hartley was also contemptuous of the "utterly illustrative aspect of [Benton's] work."[5] Privately, he maintained that "that American scene stuff" was "tiresome and very common."[6]

Taken together, these statements suggest a concern that would impel Hartley's art for the last decade of his life: how to navigate between the dry intellectualism of the cubist legacy and the triviality of American Scene painting. His solution was to return to his roots—not just to Maine, but to an interest that had animated some of his best early works. In the early 1930s, he set aside the smooth, Cézannesque manner of his Vence landscapes and the

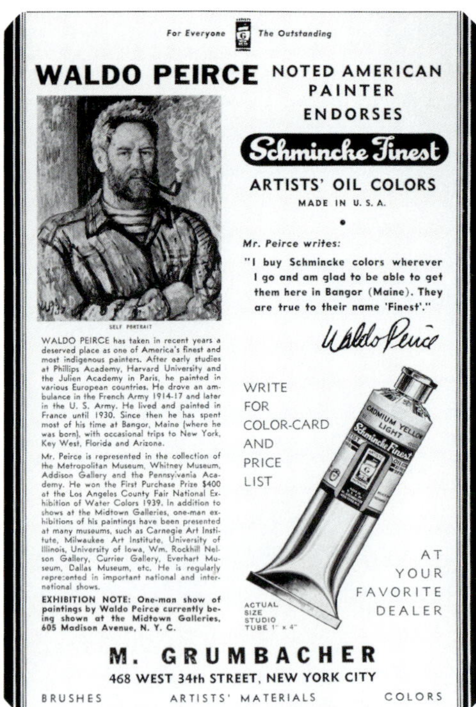

Figure 1
Advertisement
"Waldo Peirce Noted American Painter Endorses Schmincke Finest Artists' Oil Colors"
Art Digest 15 (May 1, 1941): 35

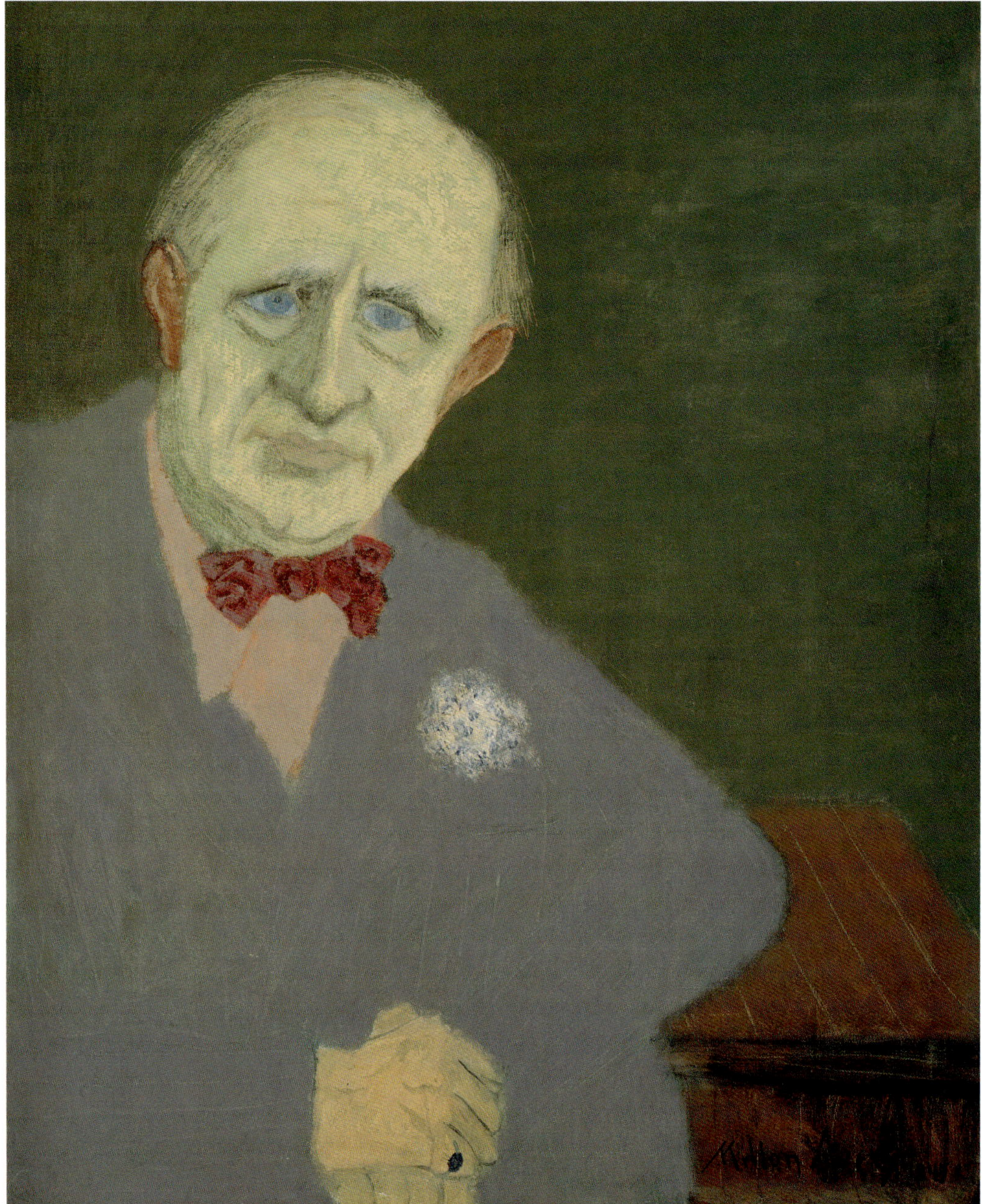

Figure 2
Milton Avery
Marsden Hartley, 1943
Oil on canvas, 36 × 27⅛ in. (91.4 × 68.9 cm)
The Museum of Fine Arts, Boston
The Hayden Collection–Charles Henry Hayden Fund, 65.1293
© 2002 Milton Avery Trust/Artists Rights Society (ARS) New York

mysticism of the pictures from Mexico for an expressionist, primitivizing style. However, he no longer felt the need to include tepees or motifs from Native American pottery in his paintings, as he had in work from the second decade of the twentieth century, to achieve the truthfulness that so-called primitive art represented to him and many other early-twentieth-century modernists. Furthermore, to an artist who had spent most of his working life in sophisticated European art centers, Maine itself was primitive and exotic. It satisfied his romantic yearnings for an uncomplicated, untainted place. And so he began painting it in a style that also aspired to be untainted, uncomplicated. The paintings from Hartley's last decade are rough, awkward, strongly colored, direct, and emotionally intense.

This style first appears in Hartley's paintings of Dogtown. He visited Dogtown, part of Gloucester, Massachusetts, in 1920, 1931, and 1934 and produced three groups of paintings (1931, 1934, 1936) based on sketches made there. Boulder-strewn and barren, with cellar holes, fragments of walls, and fallen-down fences the only remnants of an abandoned eighteenth-century community, Dogtown's vistas were far from the picturesque views afforded by the rest of Gloucester. Hartley called Dogtown "a weird stretch of landscape ... all boulders and scrub," which nonetheless gave him "a creative shot ... a real connection with my native soil."[7]

It also gave him a signature place. While his associates in the Stieglitz stable—Georgia O'Keeffe, John Marin, and Charles Demuth—had long since laid claim to their places and while Gloucester in the 1920s and 1930s was overrun with painters, "no one in all the years of Gloucester painting celebrity had ever done anything about Dogtown."[8] In words that foreshadowed his appropriation of Maine, Hartley wrote to Stieglitz in 1931 that he intended to be *the* painter of Dogtown.[9]

The Dogtown pictures were Hartley's strongest and most original work in years. The first group, from 1931, is marked by high horizons and somewhat glossy skies, with a naturalistic, frequently autumnal, palette. A few of the paintings, for example *Summer Outward Bound* (1931; private collection), retain something of the picturesqueness of the Vence landscapes but are saved from sentimentality by the crude shapes of the rocks and bushes. Other works—such as *Rock Doxology* (1931; private collection) and *Mountains in Stone, Dogtown* (plate 46)—are more abstract, characterized by an all-overness, with boulders and brush piled up on one another. Here Hartley seems to be translating into an expressive idiom the fluctuating spaces of cubist landscape: his boulders recede as they tumble forward, much as in Braque's early views of L'Estaque. Also paralleling cubism are the textured surfaces given to the boulders, which are painted with coarse strokes and scarified with scratchy lines. Yet Hartley's places are organic, animate. The boulders seem to shift and rumble and, despite the sophisticated roots of Hartley's spatial structure, his rough brushwork creates an image that appears unstudied—and as such true to the primeval qualities of the landscape. Hartley clearly saw Dogtown that way: "Dogtown looks like a cross between Easter Island and Stonehenge—essentially druidic in its appearance," a place possessing "the mysticism of nature."[10]

By the 1934 landscapes, especially those depicting the bizarre rock formation known as Whale's Jaw, the coarseness had evolved into an almost brutal style: the boulders are larger and more awkward, their contours are tougher, the scratching is more agitated. Then among the last group (1936–37) are a number in which Hartley discards the cubist-flavored structure in favor of a more legible space. *The Last Stone Walls, Dogtown* (1936–37, Yale University Art Gallery, New Haven) and *The Old Bars, Dogtown* (plate 50) take in a broad swath of the moraine, yet appear compressed and unnatural, like a stage set. Much of the terrain seems impassible, for it is cluttered with civilization's remains. The stones, piled up long ago to form a wall, are oddly aggressive; the falling-down fence posts, arranged like sentinels, have an almost human presence, prohibiting entry. These modest-sized pictures are surprisingly monumental. While Hartley was painting his views of Dogtown, he drafted an essay about John Kane in which he criticized the Pittsburgh artist for "never get[ting] quite down to the bed rock fierceness of the place."[11] Hartley's style in these pictures—the passionate paint handling, the crude drawing, and the cadences established by his fence posts, boulders, and scrubby pines—was ideally suited to the fierceness of Dogtown's bedrock, a primordial fierceness that would characterize his chosen subject matter for the rest of his career.

The Dogtown paintings mark a turning point not just in Hartley's style, but also in his reputation. The third group was shown at An American Place in 1937 in Hartley's final show with Stieglitz. The break afterwards was no doubt distressing to both parties; Hartley had been one of Stieglitz's "first-borns" and had shown with the gallery for nearly thirty years. But the separation also served them both: it allowed Stieglitz to disentangle himself from an extremely needy and frequently ungrateful artist, one who had not always behaved well toward his other painters, and one he had never managed to promote successfully; and the parting freed Hartley to seek representation elsewhere. By this time, the Stieglitz circle had lost much of its aura: the artists were dispersed, and Stieglitz's opinions, though valued, were no longer news.[12] Marin's work was still well received, but O'Keeffe was struggling.[13] By early 1938, Hartley was exhibiting with the young dealer Hudson Walker, who considered him the most important artist on his roster, gave him a well-publicized show every year, placed his paintings in museum annuals and other group exhibitions, and had reasonable success in arranging sales.[14]

Hartley's increased visibility was due to more than his change of dealers. By the mid-1930s, despite the Depression, the New York art scene had become increasingly varied and increasingly international, leaving more room for divergent sensibilities like Hartley's. American Scene painting was still the dominant style. But by the end of the decade that saw Thomas Hart Benton on the cover of *Time* magazine (the first painter ever so featured), the Whitney Annual exhibition's complement of hard-hitting regionalist subjects was outnumbered by derivative anecdotal genre scenes and landscapes from Woodstock, New York—the kind of work one critic called "placid views of pastoral America."[15]

Reinforcing this nationalism was the developing sense of contemporary American art having a worthy American past. Museums dedicated significant portions of their exhibition programs to pre-modern American art, celebrating, among others, Homer, Eakins, Ryder, Copley, American landscape, and, in *Life in America,* American views, events, and heroes of the past 250 years. Even American folk art had begun to be perceived as museum-worthy. The first scholarly monographs of eighteenth- and nineteenth-century American painters were written in this period.[16] Hartley did his part by publishing his essay "The Six Greatest New England Painters" in *Yankee* magazine in 1937.

At the same time, there was a new infusion of energy from Europe, with artists, scholars, critics, and dealers fleeing repression and seeking new inspiration and a more vital market in the United States.[17] Beginning in 1931, the Julien Levy Gallery was a focal point for international surrealism. The Buchholz Gallery, under the aegis of Curt Valentin, exhibited German "degenerate" art through the 1930s. The Brummer Gallery showed Derain, Lipchitz, Villon, Matisse, and Maillol. The main outpost for European art in New York was the newly founded Museum of Modern Art, whose exhibitions of German art (1931), Cubism (1936), Dada and Surrealism (1936), and individual artists promoted international modernism in the 1930s. Nevertheless, art that was in some measure representational—some of it straightforward academic, some expressionist social realism, and much of it supported by the Federal Art Project of the Works Progress Administration—remained the dominant mode in New York. Not until the founding of the Museum of Non-Objective Painting in 1939 did European and American artists pursuing geometric abstraction have a significant public forum. Meanwhile on Eighth Street in New York—invisible to almost all but themselves—a new avant-garde was striving to create an abstract style that was personally expressive yet had a universal, spiritual basis.[18]

In his early years in New York, Hartley had experienced a similar variety and had eagerly embraced it all. He was a member of the Stieglitz circle, secretary of the Société Anonyme, and among the many talented artists and writers who paid court at Mabel Dodge (Luhan's) salon. But as a mature artist, he no longer felt the need to sample everything. He chose carefully from the large menu available on Fifty-seventh Street and responded most enthusiastically to those artists whose work validated his own expressive style.

Perhaps the first corroboration of Hartley's work from the outside came in 1937, when the Whitney Museum paid eight hundred dollars for *The Old Bars, Dogtown* after Hartley's last exhibition at An American Place.[19] This was the exhibition in which he showed pictures from Dogtown and Nova Scotia while proclaiming himself "the painter from Maine." To make good that claim, he spent the summer and fall in Georgetown, Maine, near Bath, with the widow of his old friend Gaston Lachaise. There he embarked on a group of monumental sea- and landscapes that would engage him for the next six years.

Hartley's transfer of attention to Maine was both inevitable and surprising. "The return of the native" had been preordained since 1932, when Edith Halpert of the Downtown Gallery gave him a solo exhibition with that name. For her, the show was one of a series of flagwavers designed to get her cosmopolitan roster of artists on the American Scene bandwagon.[20] Even Hartley, congenitally impractical and obstinate, had to see the wisdom of that marketing ploy—and in Dogtown he had experienced a genuine reconnection with his native soil that was a prelude to his approach to Maine. By autumn 1935, he had settled in with the Masons, a family of rural fisherfolk at Eastern Points on the island of East Point, Nova Scotia. He moved to Maine in the summer of 1937, living in a number of places, finally staying with Katie and Forest Young in Corea, Maine. His moving in with the Masons, while ostensibly a regionalist gesture,[21] was Hartley's attempt to embrace the simple certainties of their community ("all the blackness is gone out of my pictures," he wrote).[22] The return of the native was at least in part a reflection of the escapist heritage of romanticism.

At the same time, Maine was a crowded field. In the late 1930s, Marin, who had been active at Cape Split since 1933 and at Stonington before that, had begun to render coast scenes in oil as well as watercolor. Such lush, exuberant paintings as *Head of the Cape, Ladle and Boats* (1937; private collection) and *Wave on Rock* (fig. 3) tackle themes that parallel Hartley's. But while Hartley was consistently drawn to a dark and moody landscape, Marin saw the coast as scenic; his paintings are about the exhilaration of being in nature.

Among other painters associated with Maine, Hartley's old friend Carl Sprinchorn in 1937 established a pattern that Hartley would soon adopt: Maine in spring, summer, and fall; winters in New York City. The two had tacitly agreed to divide the state; Hartley's domain was to be the seacoast and Sprinchorn's the forests and rivers.[23] Waldo Peirce, whose impressionist-flavored Maine landscapes and genre scenes preceded Hartley's into such collections as the Addison Gallery of American Art, Andover, Massachusetts, and the Metropolitan Museum of Art, New York, in the late 1930s had a number of highly visible exhibitions featuring his Maine scenes.[24] Hartley acknowledged their mutual ownership of Maine: "we are the only two real painters from my at least all beloved country and see you too care. I have gone home." Privately, however, he expressed reservations about Peirce's work: "poor Waldo—such a nice person but not a good artist—one of the best of the not so good ones, or he wouldn't be a

Figure 3
John Marin
Wave on Rock, 1937
Oil on canvas, 22¾ × 30 in. (57.8 × 76.2 cm)
Whitney Museum of American Art, New York
Purchase, with funds from Charles Simon and the Painting and Sculpture Committee, 81.18
Photograph by Roy Elkind, New York

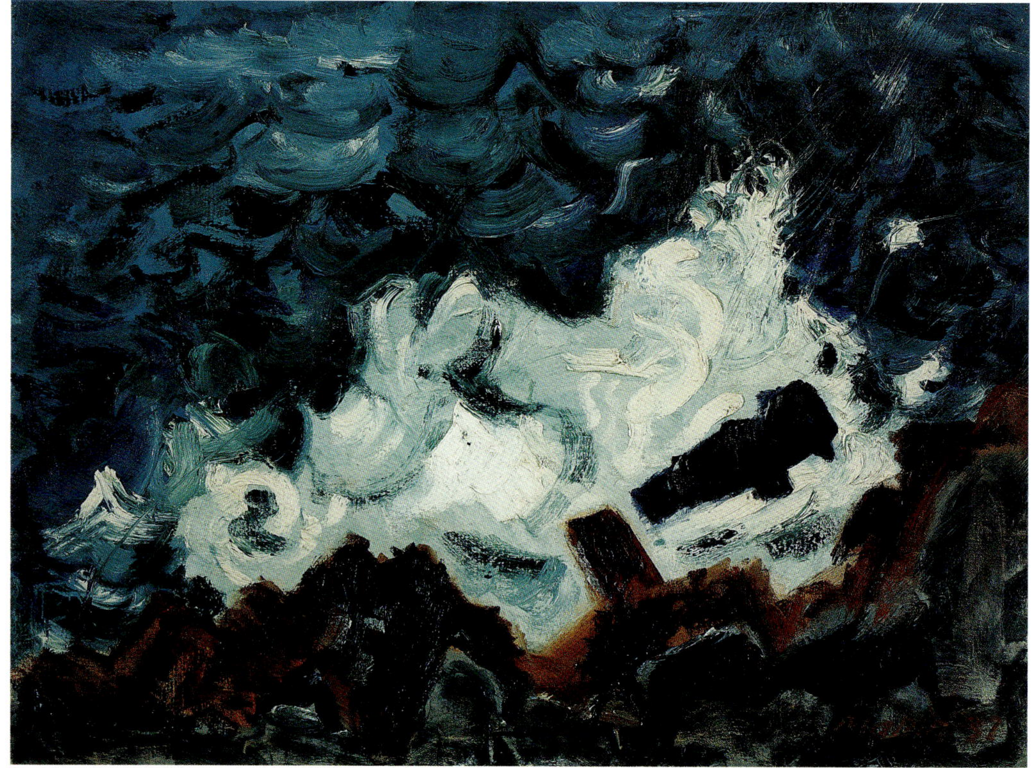

feature of the Midtown Gallery in N.Y., would he? No he wouldn't."[25] Hartley's remarks are no doubt both an honest reaction to Peirce's pleasantly anecdotal, if toothless, work and a reflection of rivalry with a painter whose sales and critical approval outpaced his. And at the end of the decade, up-and-coming painters Andrew Wyeth and Stow Wengenroth exhibited new works that were reviewed under the proprietary title "Wyeth's and Wengenroth's State of Maine" and were credited with "ruggedness and strength of design."[26]

Despite the many artists jockeying to claim a piece of Maine, Hartley's operatic landscapes enabled him to make his mark. The themes of these pictures—crashing waves, storm-tossed boats, the sea after a hurricane, majestic mountain peaks—were straight out of the romantic tradition and were linked by his contemporaries (as well as by more recent scholars) to the subjects and emotions in works by Ryder and Homer.[27] But as Hartley revisited those themes (it was his practice to return to compositions again and again, sometimes—as with the Rising Wave/Spent Wave series—almost immediately, sometimes over several years), they become less traditional. As he had at Dogtown, in his subsequent landscapes Hartley developed a primitivistic vocabulary to express the harshness of the northern coast. For the first time since perhaps the Berlin abstractions of 1914, Hartley's style and subject matter were brilliantly in synch. He had found a voice that both satisfied his restless experimentalism and was acceptable, even appreciated, in the mainstream art world.

Such works as *Northern Seascape, Off the Banks* (plate 61) and *Off to the Banks* (1936–38; Phillips Collection, Washington, D.C.), painted shortly after Hartley left Nova Scotia, are deeply emotional yet almost childlike in their simplicity. Their subject—ships moving through inhospitable seas[28]—had long been a mainstay of romantic art, a metaphor for the vulnerability of humankind in the face of all-powerful nature. The seascapes are full of the presentiment of tragedy. The fang-like rocks in the foreground and the black-centered clouds pressing down on the horizon introduce a vocabulary that Hartley continued to use for the remainder of his career.

When Hartley returned to the subject in 1942, in *Off the Banks at Night* (Phillips Collection), he chose a format nearly twice as large. Although the elements are much the same, down to the identically placed, triangular clouds, they are more stylized and roughly painted. The clouds become flat shapes floating on an oppressive blackness with an eerie red glow beneath. The boulders—truly druidic—seem to dance like licks of flame. The space of *Northern Seascape, Off the Banks,* legible and dense with atmosphere, becomes a series of flat bands. The shoreline is as hostile as the sea, providing no safe haven. The whole takes on a kind of primal rhythm, savage and ritualized.

The majestic wave paintings that resulted from Hartley's visits to Schoodic Point are more distilled, with any vestige of anecdote eliminated and shapes reduced to their basic contours. The first of these, *The Wave* (plate 96), is atmospheric and comparatively naturalistic. In the later variants (*Evening Storm, Schoodic, Maine,* 1942; Museum of Modern Art, New York, and *Evening Storm, Schoodic, Maine No. 2,* 1942; Brooklyn Museum of Art), the sea becomes a thick swath of white cutting through the darks of sky and shore. The rising wave, sculpted with blunt strokes, is a massive presence. The rocks and hovering clouds, thinly painted over a warm ground, resonate in a way that almost anticipates Rothko, while retaining strong ties to the natural world.

In these paintings, Hartley remains true to his roots in the Stieglitz circle. For them, art-making was a romantic enterprise in which a personal vision was used to express spiritual truths. Hartley's technique, however—ponderous, anti-academic, rough, direct—was far from O'Keeffe's delicate, refined brushwork or Marin's animated bravura style. His work was even farther from the mainstream of landscape production. For example, when Hartley painted his *Evening Storm* canvases in 1942, probably the best-known contemporary landscape in America was John Steuart Curry's *Wisconsin Landscape* (fig. 4),[29] a panoramic view painted in 1938–39 of a tidy farm, naturalistically and affectionately observed. Curry's image is as boosterish as Hartley's are foreboding. The snug farmhouse and bounteous fields, stretching beyond our field of vision, promise safety and stability. Even the stormy sky is painted in a vigorous manner that suggests America's resilience, not its vulnerability.

Perhaps because of their obvious American roots and their resonance with Homer and Ryder, Hartley's land- and seascapes were the most frequently exhibited and well received of his late works. Martha Davidson of *Art News* credited the seascapes shown at Hudson Walker's gallery in 1938 with "the nature of bed-rock, solid and enduring"; Alfred Frankfurter admired *The Old Bars, Dogtown,* featured in a 1939 Whitney Museum installation, for its "new druidism." When *Evening Storm, Schoodic, Maine* was shown at the Museum of Modern Art's landmark exhibition *Romantic Painting in America,* Hartley

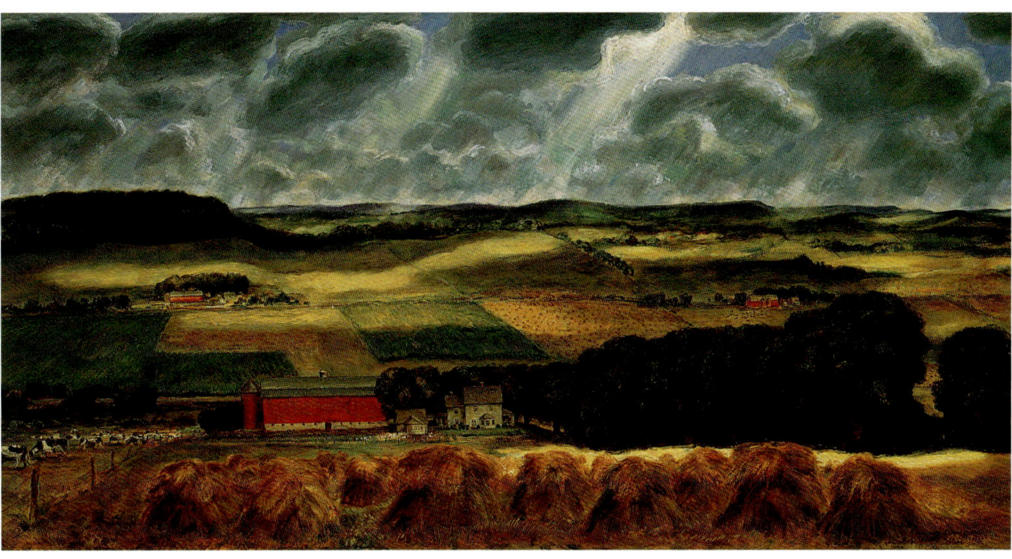

Figure 4
John Steuart Curry
Wisconsin Landscape, 1938–39
Oil on canvas, 42 × 84 in. (106.7 × 213.3 cm)
The Metropolitan Museum of Art, New York
George A. Hearn Fund, 1942 (42.154)
Photograph © 1981
The Metropolitan Museum of Art

was at last assigned a distinguished niche in the pantheon of American landscape painters. James Thrall Soby called him a leader of the "expressionist" side of contemporary landscape, "a magician of summary brushwork" in whose images "abstract patterns of sky and clouds" are organized with "thundering immediacy."[30] Other museums were quick to take notice, and during this period Hartley's work began entering public collections at a gratifying rate. By the time of his death in 1943, his work was owned by the Whitney Museum of American Art, the Metropolitan Museum of Art, the Brooklyn Museum, the Worcester Art Museum, and the Philadelphia Museum of Art, among others. The Museum of Modern Art owned three paintings by Hartley.

Hartley's biggest sale in those years was to his dealer, Hudson Walker, who closed his gallery in 1940 and a few months later paid five thousand dollars for twenty-three of his leading artist's pictures for his own collection.[31] Included in this group were some of Hartley's most personal works—his archaic portraits honoring the Masons (plates 66–68). Created from memory more than a year after he left Nova Scotia, they were Hartley's first attempts at figure painting and were named for the tragic characters of his prose poem "Cleophas and His Own," which recounts the deaths of the Mason sons (as discussed in the essay by Jonathan Weinberg). They were shown in important exhibitions, where they were admired for their strength and their sentiment. Another of Hartley's supporters at the Museum of Modern Art, Monroe Wheeler, described *Adelard the Drowned, Master of the "Phantom"* (plate 66) as "demonstrating the power of tenderness."[32]

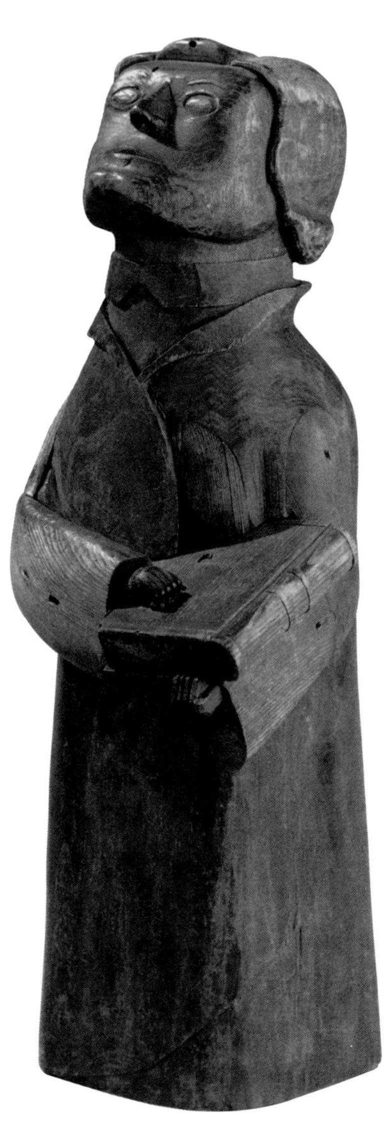

Figure 5
Unknown Artist
The Preacher, c. 1870
Butternut and eastern white pine, 21 × 7½ in.
(53.3 × 19.1 cm)
Colonial Williamsburg Foundation
Abby Aldrich Rockefeller Folk Art Museum,
Williamsburg, Virginia

Like the landscapes of the late 1930s, Hartley's figure paintings—both the portraits of the Masons and the honorific images of Ryder, Donne, and Lincoln (plates 71, 77–78)—are emphatically anti-academic, and are animated by "primitive" techniques and devices. The figures are awkwardly drawn and awkwardly placed. They are positioned uncomfortably high and slightly off center in the picture space, which gives them an edgy presence. A plain, strongly colored background creates a vivid wall from which they project. Some of these figures are rendered in somber tones of black, brown, and white—which makes details like the salmon-hued flower at Adelard's ear all the more startling, and pathetic. They have blocky bodies and squarish heads, like some humble folk carving (see fig. 5). Their hands are crossed in their laps; these massive hands, clearly accustomed not to fine indoor work but to heavy labor, add to the sense of the figures' helplessness.

To distance the personalities of his friends from the archaic portraits he derived from them, Hartley gave them all pseudonyms—Alty Mason became "Adelard," Francis was "Cleophas," and so on. The names he chose were evocative: they are unfamiliar (perhaps French-Canadian), old-fashioned, and with a vague Biblical flavor[33] that imbues the images with a homely piety. Their religious aura was intended: in 1939 Hartley exhibited them under the heading "For a Seaman's Bethel in the Far North." The figures are icons of goodness, possessing a saintly patience.[34]

Hartley's forthright style was well suited to his gentle, tragic figures. His images seem unstudied and sincere, far from painterly suavity or academic contrivance. The archaic portraits also had a contemporary relevance. Just as the Masons' passivity and endurance embodied the Depression-era mood of vulnerability and loss, so Hartley's dispensing with conventions of naturalism in favor of a more expressive manner makes his pictures seem modern.

Even in Hartley's own time, the combination of simple directness and subtle tension in his pictures was recognized as distinct.[35] Hartley's interest in figure painting in the late 1930s was part of a national trend. However, the majority of figure painters—whether regionalists, urban scene painters, or conventional realists such as Eugene Speicher, Leon Kroll, and Walt Kuhn—worked in more or less academic styles. Hartley was well

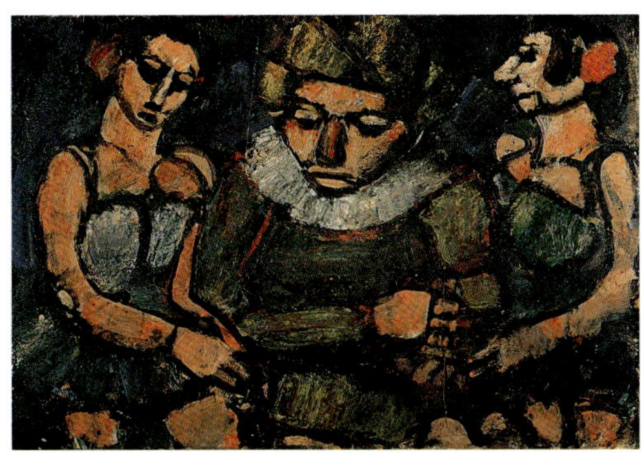

Figure 6
Georges Rouault
Circus Trio, 1924
Oil on paper, 29½ × 41½ in. (74.9 × 105.4 cm)
The Phillips Collection, Washington, D.C.

aware of the dominance of academic painting; in a 1937 review, he predicted that "we are decidedly on the eve of the return to what is called 'academy.'"[36] Although one or two of these artists—notably Kuhn—painted figures with a comparable directness and expressive power, Hartley was by and large indifferent to them, except to resent their commercial success.[37] Rather, he found validation for his roughly painted, mythic figures in other sources, as is apparent from the art he chose to write about.

Hartley's writings served him as a verbal scrapbook in which he gathered art of the past and recent European and American work as inspiration and reference material. For example, after seeing a show of Georges Rouault's early work at Pierre Matisse's gallery in November 1937, Hartley wrote a review that is nothing less than an encomium. Rouault was extremely popular in New York in the late 1930s and early 1940s.[38] His art was seen by many as deeply felt, an antidote to the desiccated intellectualism of cubism and a moral beacon during the Depression and war years.[39] Hartley lauded the "piety and humility" of Rouault's work, its "deep and powerful humanism."[40] His own use of thick outlines, intense color, coarse brushwork, and frontal compositions found confirmation in Rouault's paintings (see fig. 6). Like the French painter's, his secular subjects have a spiritual resonance. He saw in Rouault's figures the sort of fatalism and honesty he wanted to reveal in the Masons.[41]

In other essays written in the 1930s, he lauded the "American primitives" for affording "simple visual pleasure" and relief from the "hocus-pocus intellectualism in art."[42] He admired artists with ties to people like the Masons, claiming, for example, that Ryder's "solid background of fishermen, carpenters, masons and such" was responsible for "the natural forces behind all his pictures."[43] He embraced the piety of the everyday in the humble subjects of Georges de la Tour and the Le Nain brothers. And he identified the direct, sober, truthfulness of these artists with such early Renaissance painters as Piero della Francesca and Masaccio, eschewing the "operatic legerdemain" of "Raphael the gracious."[44] Some of these artists worked in a simple style that provided corroboration for Hartley's own blunt, reductive manner. None were associated with the academic high style and most worked outside the mainstream. Ryder began to be revered as a visionary and an eccentric in the early 1930s.[45] Rouault was characterized as a solitary figure, the "monk of modern art."[46] Hartley clearly took personal solace in the isolation of his heroes. "Walking alone is something of an achievement—perhaps the real solution," he wrote.[47] He regarded these disparate figures—the peasant-painters, the untutored, the prophet, the holy man—as representatives of the same kind of artistic honesty, standing apart from the illustrative, academic art then dominant, and providing reinforcement for his own efforts. Despite the seeming plainness of Hartley's archaic portraits, they are nonetheless rich and allusive. Even more than the landscapes, the figure paintings were the result of a slow process of absorbing countless precedents and influences.

The intensity and toughness of the archaic portraits resonated with another strain of painting in New York that Hartley acknowledged only peripherally but surely knew. Recent German painting had had a significant presence in New York since the early 1930s, when the Museum of Modern Art mounted *German Painting and Sculpture.* The arrival of Curt Valentin and the establishment of the Buchholz Gallery in the mid-1930s meant that an ambitious exhibition program of cutting-edge German art was being offered on Fifty-seventh Street only a few doors away from Hartley's shows at Hudson Walker's. The affinity between Hartley's work and recent German painting—especially that of the expressionist Max Beckmann—was remarked upon by several critics, notably Elizabeth McCausland, who reflected that Beckmann's oils "derive from energies as troubled as those of Hartley's own spiritual crisis."[48]

Though Beckmann's "crisis" stemmed from the horror consuming his native Germany while Hartley's was more internal, certain of their works reveal a shared sensibility. A number of Beckmann's portraits and full-length figure studies (for example, *Self-Portrait as a Sailor,* fig. 7), with their erotic subtexts, can be seen as the sinister analogues of Hartley's prizefighters, swim champs, or lumberjacks on the beach. Hartley's religious images of the early 1940s—his *Christ* (Robertson fig. 2), *Christ Held By Half-Naked Men* (plate 80), and especially *Three Friends* (fig. 8)—come close in their hallucinatory quality to Beckmann's nightmarish visions of the late 1930s.[49] Many of their paintings of that decade also share stylistic traits—rough paint handling; uningratiating color; boldly silhouetted, expressively distorted figures; and compressed, stage-like spaces—that can be labeled expressionist. Both Hartley's self-conscious primitivism and Beckmann's cynical worldliness are strategies to describe an era marked by upheaval and tragedy. Their paintings are dense with personal meaning—an iconography of anguish—that nonetheless has widespread relevance.

The most ambitious of Hartley's personal yet universal images is *Fishermen's Last Supper.* Although described in the press as a memorial to "two drowned companions," the subject—the Mason family at a meal—was apparently on Hartley's mind before the

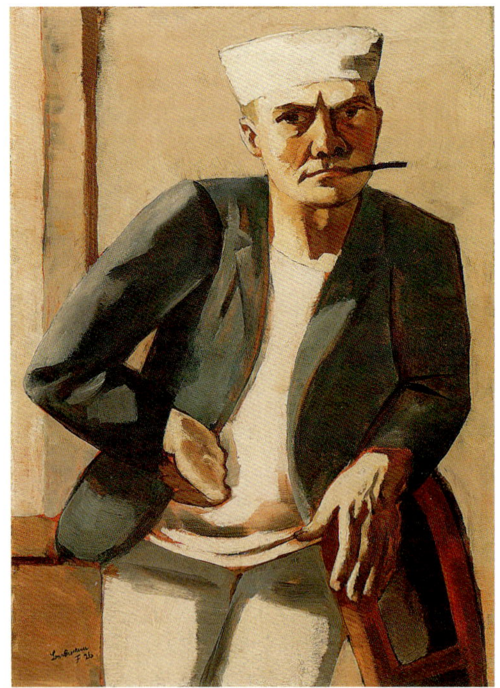

Figure 7
Max Beckmann
Self-Portrait as a Sailor, 1926
Oil on canvas, 39⅜ × 27⅞ in. (100 × 70.8 cm)
Private Collection
Courtesy Richard L. Feigen and
Company, New York

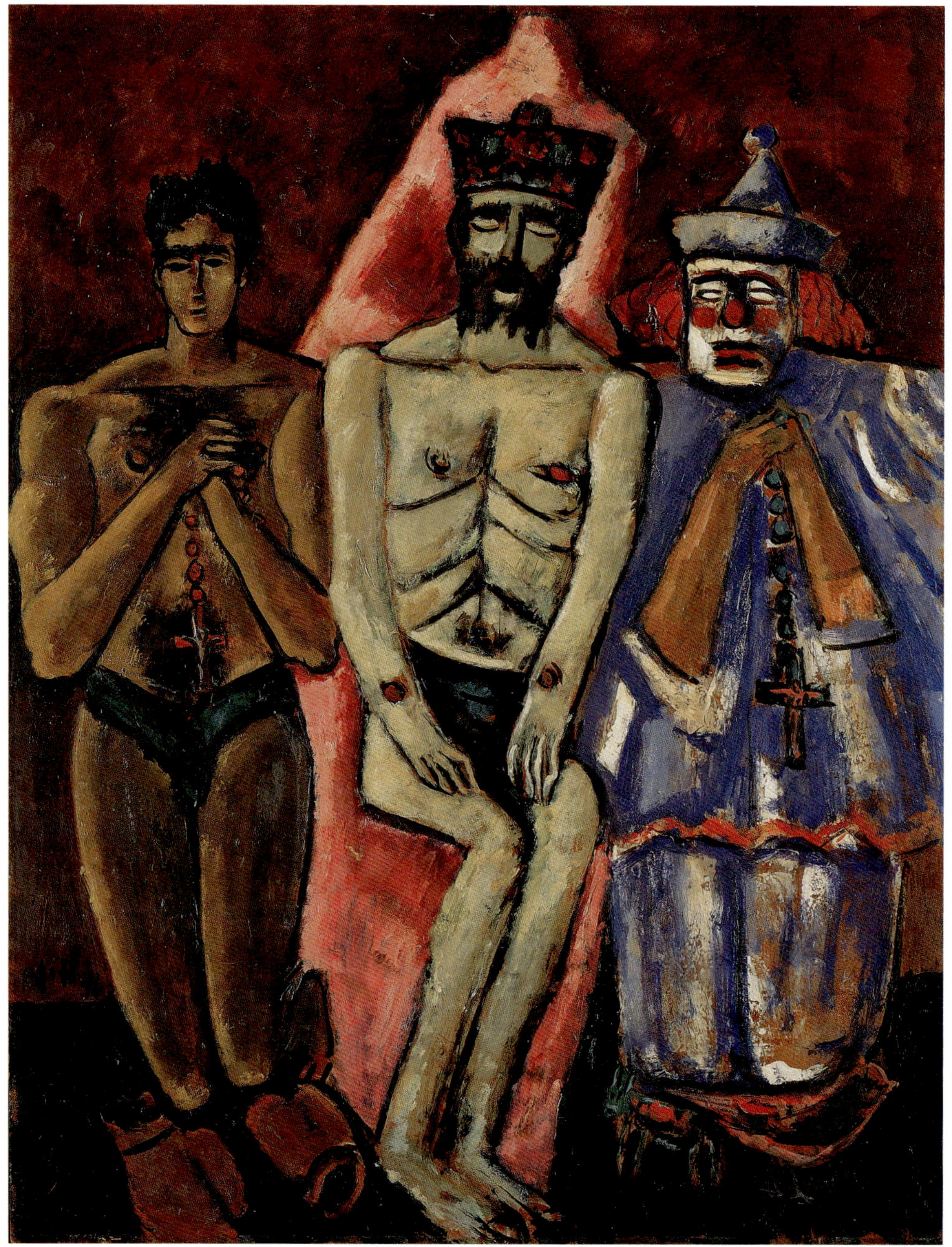

Figure 8
Marsden Hartley
Three Friends, 1941
Oil on Masonite, 51⅝ × 40⅛ in. (131.1 × 101.9 cm)
Indiana University Art Museum, Bloomington
Gift of Sarahanne Adams Hope
in memory of Henry R. Hope
Photograph by Michael Cavanagh
and Kevin Montague
© 2002 Indiana University Art Museum

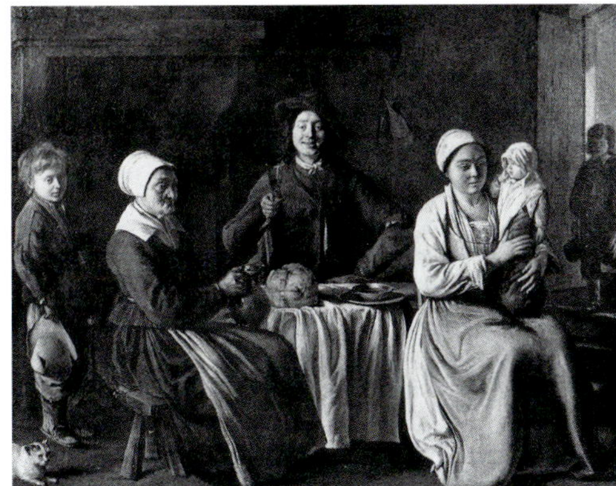

Figure 9
Louis Le Nain
The Return from the Christening, 1642
Oil on canvas, 24 × 30¾ in. (61 × 78.1 cm)
Musée du Louvre, Paris
© CNAC/MNAM/Dist. Réunion des Musées Nationaux/Art Resource, N.Y.

drowning.[50] Like the portraits, it is a memory image, painted after he left Nova Scotia. The first version (plate 64), painted in 1938, was among the group Walker bought in 1941. The second (plate 70), done in 1940–41, was reproduced frequently and purchased by the well-known collector Roy Neuberger in 1943. Hartley was aware of the power of the image and apparently contemplated recreating it "to scale" in the stairwell of the Walker Art Center in Minneapolis, though this plan was never realized.[51]

As with his landscapes, the later version of *Fishermen's Last Supper* is the more intense. The mannerisms and heavy-handed symbolism (the mystical writing on the tablecloth, the stars above the heads of the drowned boys) are eliminated, and the arrangement is more focused. The figures, simply clumsy in the first version, become like folk carvings in the second: blocky, frontal, and compressed. The meal seems less bounteous; the dishes cast no shadows, like the objects in many of Hartley's still lifes, and are isolated from one another so that they attain an almost ritualistic significance. And the pleasant ship portrait on the wall becomes, ominously, a two-master rocked on rough seas, a variant on Hartley's own *Off the Banks at Night.*

Though Hartley's subject stemmed from his own experience, it was reinforced by the memory of the Georges de la Tour and Le Nain brothers exhibition he had seen in 1936. That show included several representations of humble suppers that have the gravity of more sacred events. As in *Fishermen's Last Supper,* in Louis Le Nain's *The Peasant Meal* (1942, Musée du Louvre, Paris) and *Return from the Christening* (also called *The Happy Family;* fig. 9), the compositions are symmetrical, the figures are placed at measured intervals, the interiors are spare. Hartley saw in much the same light the seventeenth-century French peasants who "breathe forth first and last the breath of plain animals and of devout spirits who pause for whatever sublime or ordinary reason" and the people of Nova Scotia "who are pretty much children always."[52] Conscious of the example of the Le Nain, Hartley found in these humble, socially marginalized figures the opportunity to depict emotion at a level of intensity rarely present in everyday events.

Fishermen's Last Supper was also an image that served the needs of late-Depression America. Social commentary is rare in Hartley's work[53] and most likely was not intended here. Nonetheless, Americans' anxieties—about the ability of long-trusted institutions to sustain them, about the seemingly false promises offered by the city and the machine—were addressed by such images of old-fashioned ceremonies of rural life. Possibly for this reason, his subject—country people at a meal—was popular in the 1930s and early 1940s, the most famous of such representations being Grant Wood's *Dinner for Threshers* (fig. 10).

Dinner for Threshers was intentionally old-fashioned. Its plain style, measured composition, and reassuringly recognizable cast of characters create a sense of nostalgia for a faded arcadia. Like *Fishermen's Last Supper,* it evokes traditional religious imagery: its structure recalls the predella of an early Renaissance triptych, and it has been described as

Figure 10
Grant Wood
Dinner for Threshers, 1934
Oil on hardboard, 19½ × 79½ in. (49.5 × 201.9 cm)
Fine Arts Museums of San Francisco
Gift of Mr. and Mrs. John D. Rockefeller 3rd, 1979.7.105
© Estate of Grant Wood/Licensed by VAGA, New York, N.Y.

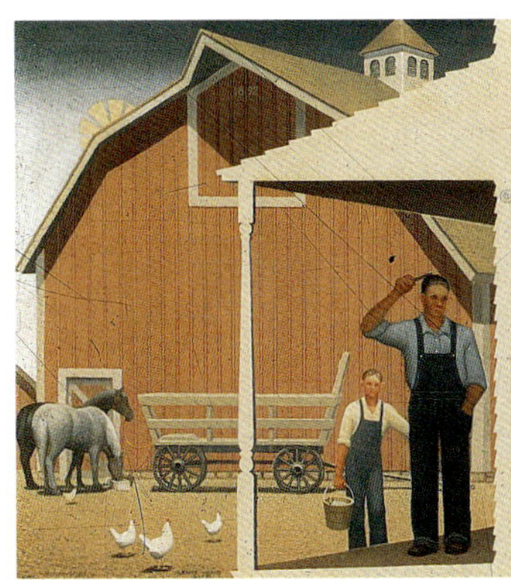
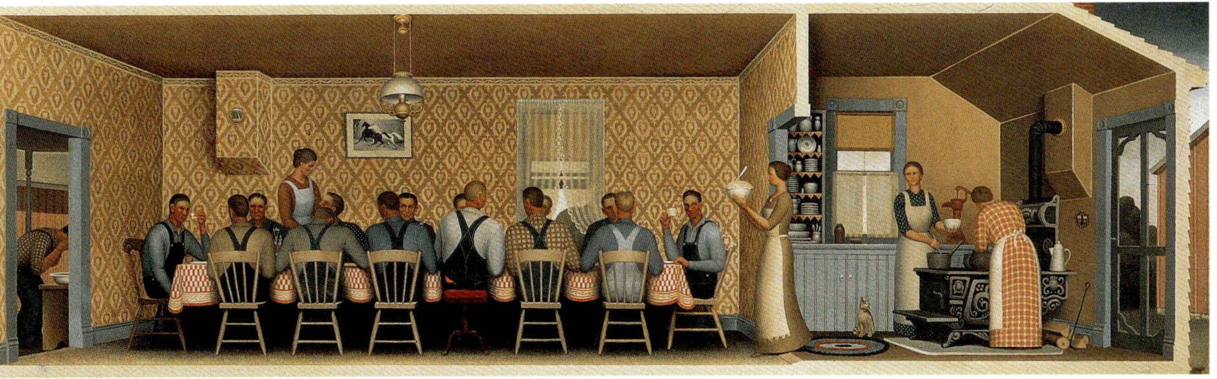

a "midwestern version of the Last Supper."[54] To enhance the familiarity of the scene, Wood filled it with ordinary incidents—a man combs his hair before entering the house, a woman brings in a brimming bowl, a cat waits for scraps. While turning its back on the machine age—work is done by a horse and wagon, not a tractor—Wood's painting promises that honest labor will be rewarded with fellowship and enough to eat. When *Dinner for Threshers* was first shown, at the 1934 Carnegie International, it was voted one of the most popular pictures in the exhibition. It clearly inspired optimism, for it made a secure world feel attainable. It assumed the momentousness of a Last Supper, but without the foreshadowing of tragedy. It is a picture of Christian community without Christian sacrifice.

But if Wood's image offered Americans a fantasy to cling to, Hartley's presented a brutal truth. *Fishermen's Last Supper* is clearly about sacrifice. It is pared down, without specific links to time or place. It too expresses the values of the Depression—of stalwart resolve in the face of great loss, of community as a defense against sorrow—but because of the absence of any moderating incident, and because of the weighty dignity of the figures, its sorrow is unavoidable. It appears awkward and sincere.[55] Its style elevates one family's tragedy to the level of myth, endowing it with perpetuity.

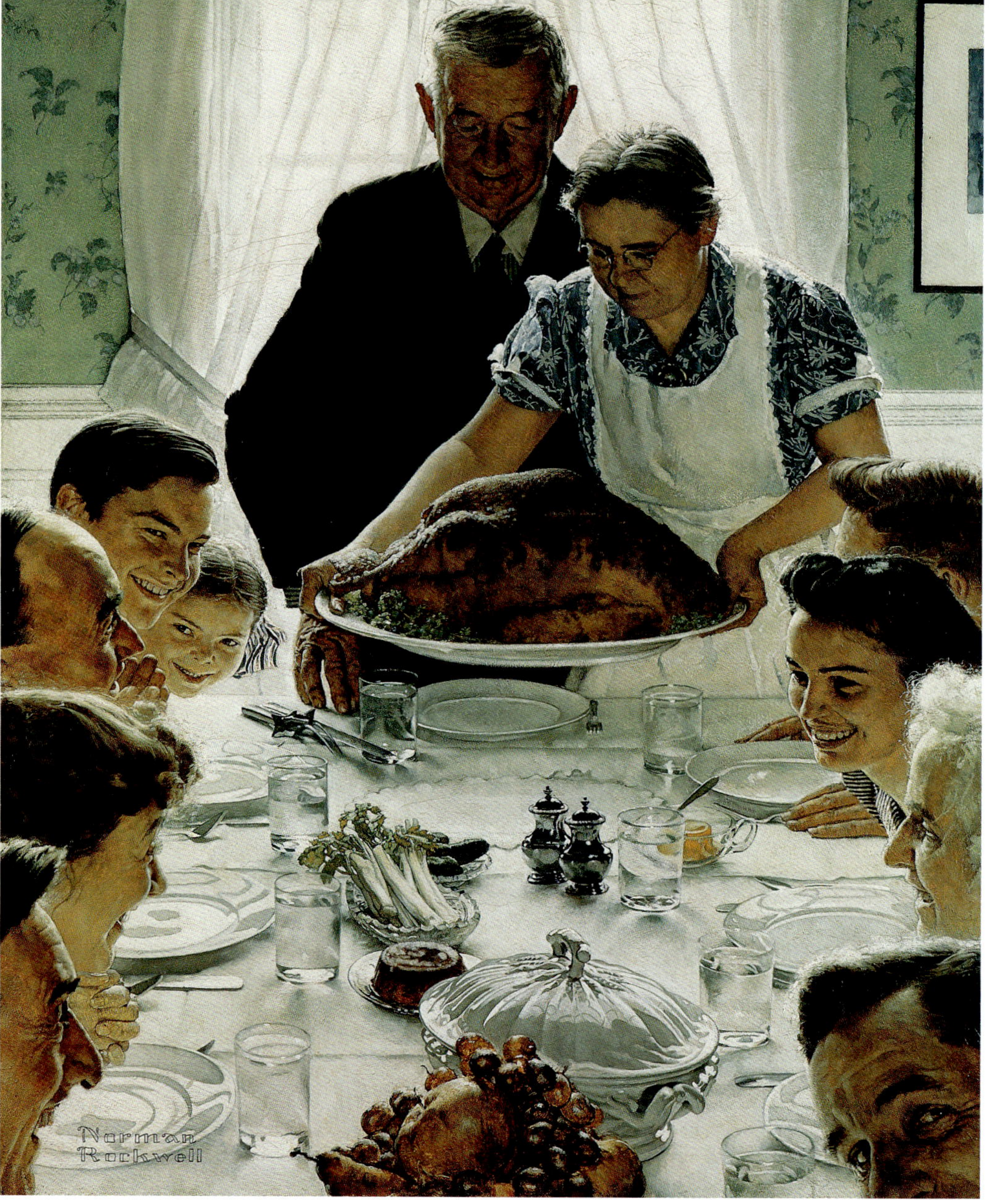

Figure 11
Norman Rockwell
Freedom From Want, 1943
Oil on canvas, 45¾ × 35½ in. (116.2 × 90.2 cm)
Collection of the Norman Rockwell Museum at Stockbridge, Massachusetts
Printed by permission of the Norman Rockwell Family Agency
© 1943 the Norman Rockwell Family Agency

The subject of a ceremonial meal retained its currency during the war years. Hartley's vision of tragedy and sacrifice did not. *Fishermen's Last Supper* gave way to Norman Rockwell's *Freedom From Want* (fig. 11), an image that expresses the optimism necessitated by the war. The scene has changed. The laboring class has been replaced by the middle class, the hardscrabble coastal village by the comfortable small town. The spartan table with its poignantly empty chairs has become a table with every place taken and with cheerful faces urging the viewer to join in the festive meal. This is an image that guarantees wholeness, just as Hartley's foreshadows loss.

Hartley wrote of the "nativeness" of "primitive things,"[56] alluding, presumably, not just to geographic roots but also to values that are innate, inherent, and so common to all. The primitive things he sought in Maine were a way of renewing contact with the most basic human values. At the same time, adopting a self-consciously awkward style enabled him to assert his modernism in response to an art world dominated by narrative and by naturalistic representation. His work, seemingly so straightforward, was enriched by his thoughtful assimilation of myriad sources of inspiration, sources that were no less profound for not being quoted directly. Hartley was equally a cosmopolitan and a homebody, a sophisticated urban stroller creating images from intellect and memory while retaining an almost childlike freshness of vision.

Hartley was also, in his late work, an artist for his own time, reflecting in his powerful seascapes and martyred figures the anxiety and suffering of the Depression. His, however, was a minority voice. The typical artistic response was to manufacture visions of peace and plenty that offered hope.[57] Positive images of stability and community as a defense against despair became even more urgent in wartime, and so Hartley's romantic, expressive, tragic voice had no direct descendants. However, his evocation of mythic places, iconic figures, and ritual events would be followed in just a few years by a similar evocation, but in an abstract language. Hartley never knew the new generation of painters—Gottlieb, Rothko, de Kooning, and so on—who were about to make their mark in New York, nor did they have any particular awareness of him. Yet they were linked by comparable concerns and similar aspirations. As their spokesman Clement Greenberg wrote of Hartley in 1950, "perhaps he anticipated the present mood of American art more clearly than any other American artist of his time.... [His works] have an intensity and are animated by a desire to break through to a fresh and direct reality of pictorial feeling that bring them close somehow to the most recent abstract paintings."[58]

Notes

I am grateful to Karen Quinn, Elizabeth Stillinger, and Elizabeth Turner for sharing information and insightful observations about Hartley with me, and to Gilian Shallcross for her thoughtful reading of this essay.

1 Sibilla Skidelsky, "Peirce: From Maine to Maine via Zuluoga, Matisse, Goya," *Art News* 40 (1–14 May 1941): 27.

2 The portrait was made from a preliminary sketch and completed after Hartley's death. Hilton Kramer described it as "the best of Avery's portraits." "The pasty green face, the intense blue eyes that seem to glow like sapphires in an otherwise tired and ill-used physiognomy, the queer intermingling of foppishness and decadent strength, make this not only a very strong and moving painting but also one of the keenest psychological portrayals in modern portraiture." Kramer, *Milton Avery: Paintings, 1930–1960* (New York: T. Yoseloff, 1962), 15–16.

3 In February 1940 Hartley was photographed in front of one of his paintings of Mt. Katahdin for a story in the *Bangor Daily News* (Cassidy fig. 14). There he did choose to show himself as a Mainer—he wears a plaid shirt and holds an object, perhaps a pipe, in his hand. The photo was undoubtedly meant to underscore Hartley's claim to Maine, but may have been intended as a response to Peirce's popular self-portrait as well.

4 Hartley, "And the Nude has Descended the Staircase," in *On Art*, 268–74.

5 Hartley, "Is There an American Art?" in *On Art*, 200, 197.

6 Hartley to Helen Stein, 13 May 1935, quoted in Ludington 1992, 241. Elsewhere, he writes that Midwesterners "got Thomas Benton stuffing his disguised modern art in the name of pure Americanism up their arses and down their throats." Hartley to Rogers Bordley, 11 August 1939, quoted in Ludington 1992, 268. Hartley could be quite mean-spirited. Hudson Walker was appalled at Hartley's pleasure upon hearing about Grant Wood's death because it meant there could be no more paintings by Wood. See Walker's diary entry for 13 February 1942, Walker Papers, Archives/Smithsonian, quoted in Lyndel King, *Marsden Hartley, 1908–1942: The Ione and Hudson D. Walker Collection* (Minneapolis: University Art Museum, University of Minnesota, 1984), 10.

7 Hartley to Rebecca Strand, undated [1 August 1931], and 27 November 1931, Hartley Papers, Archives/Smithsonian.

8 *Autobiography,* 143. In fact, John Sloan had painted Dogtown in 1916—his images are much sunnier than Hartley's—but none of the North Shore Artists' Association group Hartley so disdained had ever painted there. I am grateful to Karen Quinn for information about painters in Gloucester.

9 Hartley to Alfred Stieglitz, 12 August 1931, Beinecke/Yale.

10 *Autobiography,* 145, and Hartley to Adelaide Kuntz, 22 October 1931, Hartley Papers, Archives/Smithsonian.

11 The essay seems to have been written in response to Kane's January 1935 exhibition at the Valentine Gallery in New York. Hartley, "John Kane of Pittsburgh," in *On Art,* 194.

12 In fact, as the Depression deepened, Stieglitz's pronouncements about the restorative power of art and culture seemed increasingly insensitive even to some of his supporters. See Sarah Greenough, "Alfred Stieglitz, Facilitator, Financier, and Father, Presents Seven Americans," in Greenough, 323–24.

13 If anything, the buoyant Marin's popularity increased throughout the 1930s. In 1935 critic E. M. Benson published a laudatory monograph, and the next year the painter had a triumphant solo show at the Museum of Modern Art that attracted over twenty thousand visitors. O'Keeffe, on the other hand, spent the latter half of the decade shuttling back and forth between New York (where she tended to an increasingly frail Stieglitz) and New Mexico. During this period she traveled much—including an unproductive trip to Hawaii as the guest of Dole Pineapple—but painted little that was new. Her attempts to reconcile her interest in the bones, cliffs, and hills of New Mexico with the popular pressure to paint more flowers were not always successful. In her February 1938 show at An American Place, O'Keeffe was criticized for having "reached the saturation point in the way of subject matter" and for the "lack of experimentation in these works." R. F. [Rosamund Frost], "A Show of the Most Recent Paintings of Georgia O'Keeffe," *Art News* 36 (5 February 1938): 15.

14 "Marsden Hartley" (transcript of interview with Hudson Walker by Elizabeth McCausland and Mary Bartlett Cowdrey), *Journal of the Archives of American Art* 8 (January 1968): 10, 20.

15 M. D. [Martha Davidson], "Some Placid Views of Pastoral America," *Art News* 35 (30 January 1937): 15.

16 Among the exhibitions were *Winslow Homer, Albert P. Ryder, and Thomas Eakins,* Museum of Modern Art, 1930; *John Singleton Copley,* Metropolitan Museum of Art, 1936; *Winslow Homer Centenary Exhibition,* Whitney Museum of American Art, 1936; *A Century of American Landscape Painting, 1800–1900,* Whitney Museum of American Art, 1938; and *Life in America,* Metropolitan Museum of Art, 1939. Of the monographs that appeared in this period, the most significant were Lloyd Goodrich's *Thomas Eakins: His Life and Work* (New York: Whitney Museum of American Art, 1933), and Barbara N. Parker and Anne B. Wheeler, *John Singleton Copley: American Portraits in Oil, Pastel, and Miniature* (Boston: Museum of Fine Arts, 1938).

17 Among the European artists who came to this country beginning in the late 1930s were Tanguy and Ozenfant (1939); Mondrian and Léger (1940); Lipchitz (who produced portraits of Hartley in terra-cotta and bronze in 1942), Ernst, and Chagall (1941). See Sidney Geist, "Prelude: The 1930s," *Arts* 30 (September 1936): 49–55.

18 "Eighth Street between Sixth and Fourth Avenues was the center of the New York art life that I became acquainted with in the late 1930s. There the WPA art project and the Hofmann school overlapped.... Abstract art was the main issue among the painters I knew in the late thirties. Radical politics was on many peoples' minds, but for these particular artists, Social Realism was as dead as the American scene." Clement Greenberg, "The Late Thirties in New York," in *Art and Culture* (Boston: Beacon Press, 1961), 230.

19 This sale apparently came about after Hartley wrote to the Whitney's curator, Lloyd Goodrich, asking him "to help me out in any way you can." Hartley to Lloyd Goodrich, Goodrich Papers, Whitney Museum of American Art, quoted in Haskell, 102.

20 In 1930, for example, she put on *Paint America First,* a show of abstract landscapes by Stuart Davis and others.

21 It was so perceived by several critics. Writing in *Art News,* James W. Lane titled his review of the March 1940 Hudson Walker show, "The Virile Paintings of Marsden Hartley," as though Hartley were Thomas Hart Benton. *Art News* 38 (16 March 1940): 15.

22 Hartley to Alfred Stieglitz, 1 February 1936, quoted in Ludington 1992, 247.

23 See Hartley's introduction to the catalogue of Sprinchorn's 1942–43 exhibition at Macbeth Gallery, reprinted in *Eight Poems and One Essay* (Lewiston, Maine: Bates College, 1976), 29–35, and Gail R. Scott, *Carl Sprinchorn* (Farmington, Maine: Tom Veilleux Gallery, 1994), n.p.

24 The Metropolitan Museum—which did not buy a Hartley until 1942—acquired Peirce's 1934 *Haircut by the Sea* in 1937. The Addison bought Peirce's *The Birches* in early 1936, a year or more before they bought their first Hartley. Peirce had eight solo exhibitions, some of which toured, at the Midtown Gallery beginning in 1938 and the above-mentioned show at the Carnegie in 1938.

25 Hartley to Waldo Peirce, n.d., quoted in Robert F. Brown, "Waldo Observed," in *Waldo Peirce: A New Assessment, 1884–1970* (Orono, Maine: The Art Collection, University of Maine, 1984), 37; Hartley to Helen Stein, 29 September 1939, quoted in Ludington 1992, 268.

26 *Art News* 39 (23 December 1939): 8.

27 See, for example, James Thrall Soby, *Romantic Painting in America* (New York: Museum of Modern Art, 1943), 41; Sanford Schwartz, "A Northern Seascape," *Art in America* 64 (January–February 1976): 72–76; Bruce Robertson, *Reckoning with Winslow Homer* (Cleveland: Cleveland Museum of Art, 1990), 153–61.

28 These seascapes are generally discussed as the first in which Hartley's distress over the Masons' drowning is given visual expression. As Hartley wrote at the end of his poem about the Masons, "Cleophas and His Own: A North Atlantic Tragedy," "'I'll have them both,' said the raging sea, / and took these lovers to his water strategy—." The poem is reprinted in Ferguson, 122.

29 *Wisconsin Landscape* was awarded the first purchase prize in the Metropolitan Museum's 1942 *Artists for Victory* exhibition (Hartley was awarded fourth prize in that show, for *Lobster Fishermen* [1940–41; Metropolitan Museum of Art]). Had also won a medal for best landscape in the 1941 Pennsylvania Academy annual exhibition, and was mentioned prominently in a May 1940 *Life* magazine article on an exhibition in Michigan in which it had been shown. See Patricia Junker, "Twilight of Americanism's Golden Age: Curry's Wisconsin Years, 1936–46," in Junker, *John Steuart Curry: Inventing the Middle West* (New York: Hudson Hills Press, 1998), 206–7.

30 M. D. [Martha Davidson], "The Climax of Hartley's Painting in Powerful Coast Scenes," *Art News* 36 (26 March 1938): 21; Alfred M. Frankfurter, "The Refurbished Whitney Reopens: Show for the Fair," *Art News* 37 (16 September 1939): 10; Soby, *Romantic Painting in America,* 41.

31 Beginning in the spring of 1941, Hartley would be represented by the Macbeth Gallery.

32 Monroe Wheeler, *Twentieth Century Portraits* (New York: Museum of Modern Art, 1942), 25.

33 Cleophas was a New Testament figure, the husband of one of the Marys who stood by Jesus' cross (see John 19:25), a witness to his death and resurrection.

34 Hartley clearly thought these images were inspirational: "the portraits are set in panels for an imagined sea-house perhaps a fisherman's

community house of which these hard working people are much in need." Hartley (from New York) to Elizabeth McCausland, n.d. [after 6 March 1939], McCausland Papers, Archives/Smithsonian, roll D268. Elsewhere, he described the Masons as "veritable rocks of Gibraltar." Hartley (from East Point [Island]) to Adelaide Kuntz, 5 November [1935], McCausland Papers, Archives/Smithsonian.

35 "When Hartley paints these themes, the result is not a wayward pseudo-primitivism, but an expression like that of a child who does not hesitate over considerations of formal pedantry, but says what he wants to say." Elizabeth McCausland, "Marsden Hartley, Max Beckmann and Others," *Springfield Sunday Union and Republican*, 5 March 1939, 6E.

36 Hartley, "Paintings of Harry Watrous," *Magazine of Art* 30 (March 1937): 176.

37 Hudson Walker described Hartley as "fulminating" about Walt Kuhn (Walker's diary entry for 29 February 1942, Walker Papers, Archives/Smithsonian, quoted in King, *Marsden Hartley, 1908–1942*, 11), who was widely regarded as the "leading American painter" of the day. Alfred M. Frankfurter, "Kuhn: Master of the Painting Language," *Art News* 35 (27 February 1937): 11. Kuhn's work has been cited as a source for Hartley's large-scale, frontal figure paintings (see Robertson, 116). In fact, despite Kuhn's connections with the international avant-garde, he remained all his life a fairly conservative painter, working in an academic manner, though employing somewhat rougher paint handling and a brighter palette than most traditional artists of his day. Kuhn worked from models; his art was based on straightforward observation of his subjects. His sad clowns and hardened showgirls, illustrating the loneliness of the entertainer, are in the sentimental, storytelling mood of much 1930s realism.

38 In addition to the show at Pierre Matisse, Rouault had a show of his prints at the Museum of Modern Art in October 1938, and a large-scale retrospective, also at the Museum of Modern Art, in 1945.

39 James Thrall Soby called Rouault's paintings "icons of exceptional strength and conviction." Soby, *Georges Rouault: Paintings and Prints* (New York: Museum of Modern Art, 1945), 26.

40 Hartley, "Georges Rouault," in *On Art*, 213, and "Pictures," in *On Art*, 117.

41 "Men and women have little chance to will anything of their own because they are being too intensely acted upon." Hartley, "Georges Rouault," in *On Art*, 216.

42 Hartley, "American Primitives," in *On Art*, 186. The formal traits of much American folk portraiture—frontality, silhouetting the figure, awkward drawing and proportions, and so on—that contribute to the unselfconsciousness Hartley admired in these pictures are akin to those devices he employed deliberately in the Mason and other "memory" portraits.

43 Hartley, "Albert Pinkham Ryder," in *On Art*, 267.

44 Hartley, "Some Words on Piero and Masaccio," in *On Art*, 227. See also his essay on Rouault, in which he compared that painter's "intellectuality and ... pious directness" with Masaccio and Piero. Hartley, "Georges Rouault," in *On Art*, 215.

45 See, for example, Lewis Mumford, *The Brown Decades: A Study of the Arts in America, 1865–1895* (1931; reprint, New York: Dover Publications, 1971), 99–105.

46 Martha Davidson, "Rouault as Master of Graphic Art," *Art News* 37 (8 October 1938): 11.

47 Hartley, "Georges Rouault," in *On Art*, 217.

48 McCausland, "Marsden Hartley, Max Beckmann," 6E.

49 See, for example, Beckmann's *Departure* of 1932–33 (the most discussed work in his 1938 Buchholz show; now Museum of Modern Art) and *The King* (1937; Saint Louis Art Museum), shown at Buchholz in 1940. Doris Brian, writing for *Art News*, noted that in *Three Friends* the figures are "powerfully welded to the canvas in a manner recalling Beckmann." Brian, "The Passing Shows: Hartley," *Art News* 41 (15–31 March 1942): 27.

50 D. B. [Doris Brian], "New Exhibitions of the Week: Forceful Painting in a Twenty-fifth Show by Marsden Hartley," *Art News* 37 (25 March 1939): 14; Robertson, 114.

51 Hudson Walker interview, *Journal of the Archives of American Art*, 18. See also Hartley to Adelaide Kuntz, 6 November 1935: "if I did murals, I'd do one of the family at supper or noon meal." McCausland Papers, Archives/Smithsonian, roll D268.

52 Hartley, "Georges (Dumesnil) de la Tour," in *On Art*, 276, and "On the Subject of Nativeness—A Tribute to Maine," in *On Art*, 113. Hartley devoted most of his essay on the Knoedler exhibition to de la Tour, whom he described as "amazing"; however, he also singled out Le Nain's *Peasant Meal*, which he described as "a remarkable picture and a remarkable rendering of a common fact" (p. 275).

53 For a superb study linking Hartley's imagery to contemporary concerns, see Randall R. Griffey, "Marsden Hartley's Lincoln Portraits," *American Art* 15 (summer 2001): 34–51.

54 Wanda M. Corn, *Grant Wood: The Regionalist Vision* (New Haven and London: Yale University Press for the Minneapolis Institute of Arts, 1983), 104.

55 For Elizabeth McCausland, *Fishermen's Last Supper* was "painted with a kind of gauche directness ... [and] is powerful because it does not depend on facility or easy statement of cliches for its effect." McCausland, "Marsden Hartley, Max Beckmann," 6E.

56 Hartley, "On the Subject of Nativeness," in *On Art*, 114.

57 Corn, *Grant Wood*, 90.

58 Clement Greenberg, note, *Hartley/Maurer: Contemporaneous Paintings* (New York: Bertha Schaefer Gallery, 13 November–2 December 1950), n.p.

PLATES 89–98

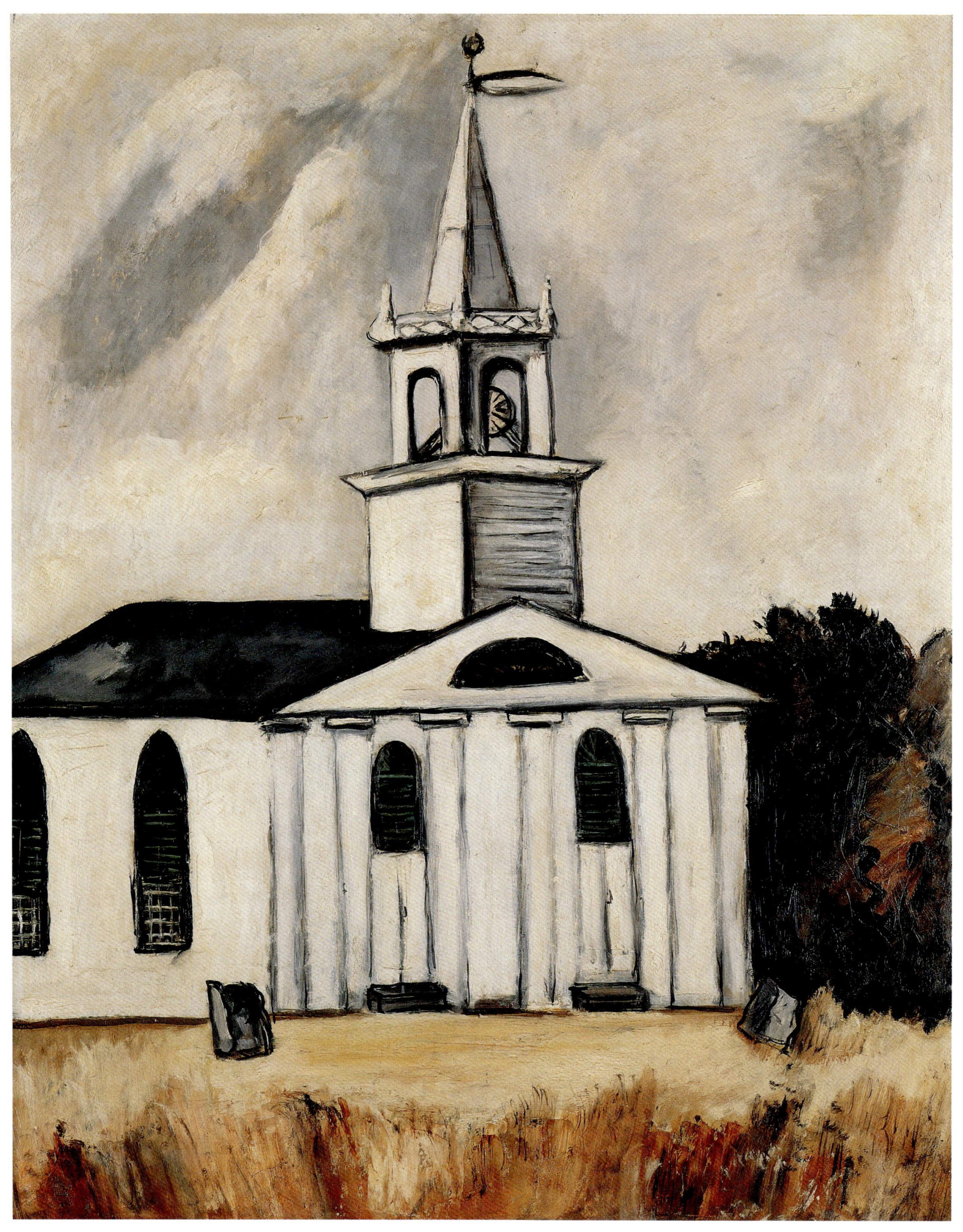

89

Church at Head Tide No. 2, 1938–40
Oil on canvas, 28 × 22½ in.
Minneapolis Institute of Arts
Gift of Mr. and Mrs. John Cowles

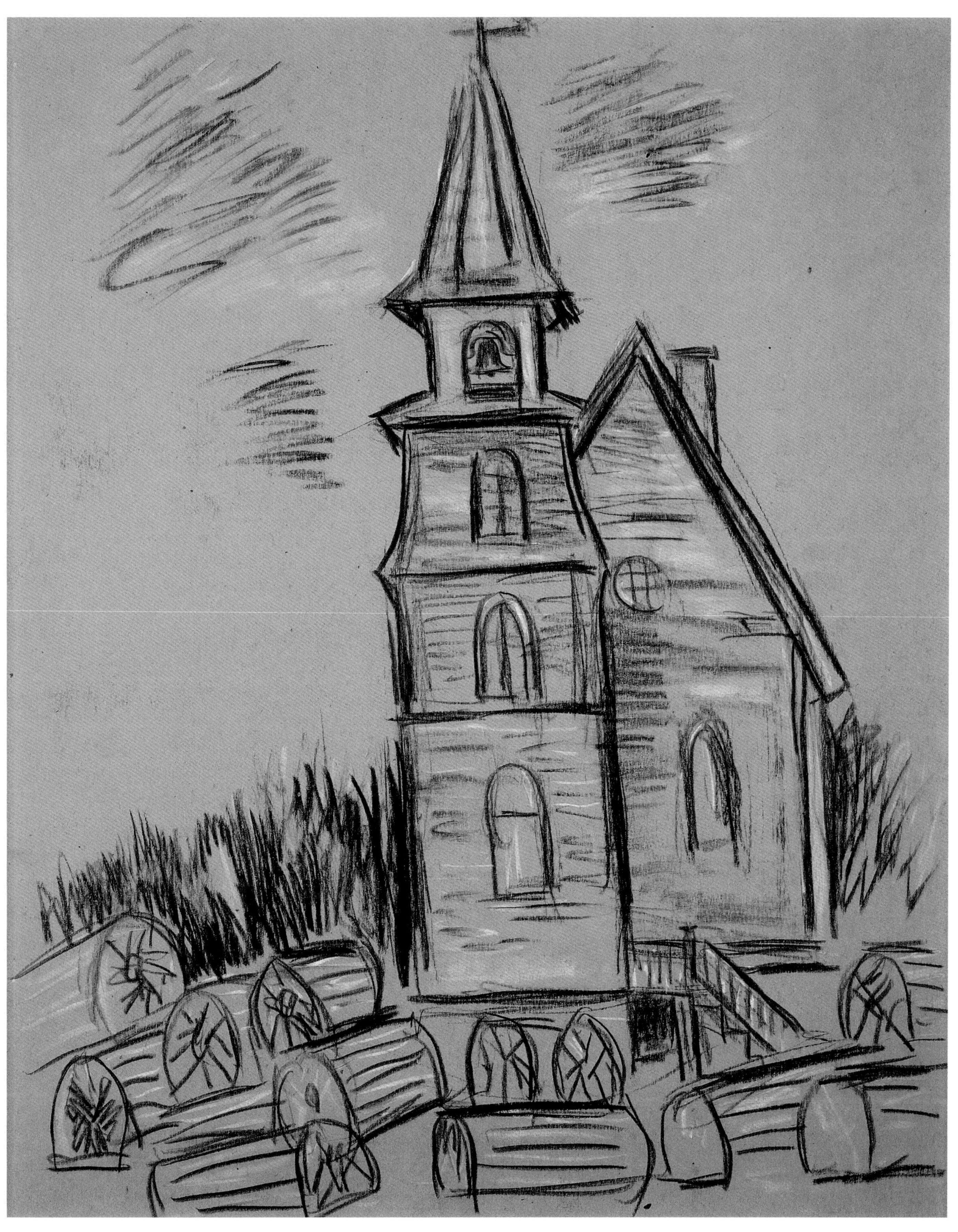

90
Church at Corea, Maine, c. 1940–43
Charcoal and white chalk on paper, 28 × 21¾ in.
Colby College Museum of Art, Waterville, Maine

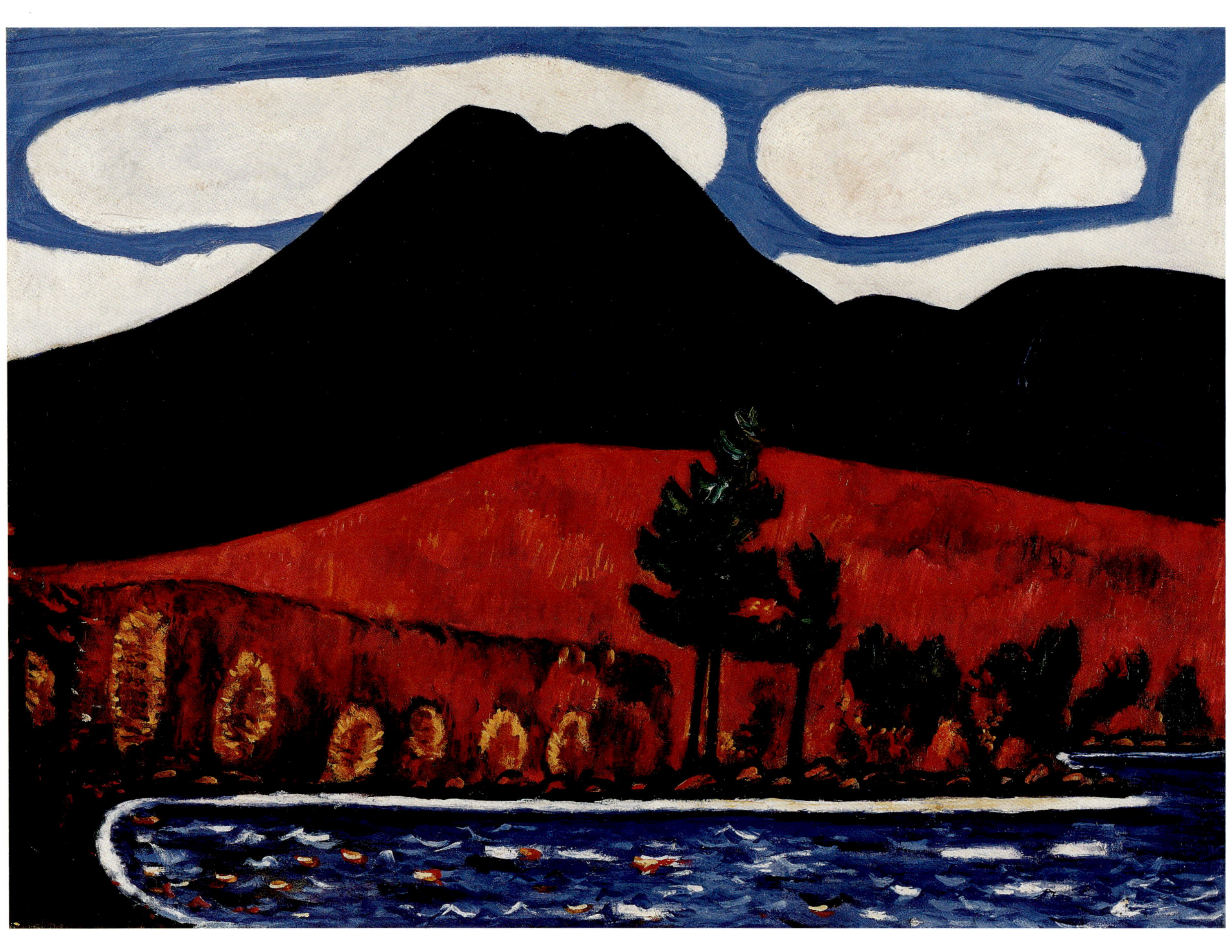

91

Mount Katahdin, Autumn No. 2, 1939–40

Oil on canvas, 30¼ × 40¼ in.

The Metropolitan Museum of Art, New York

Edith and Milton Lowenthal Collection

Bequest of Edith Abrahamson Lowenthal, 1991

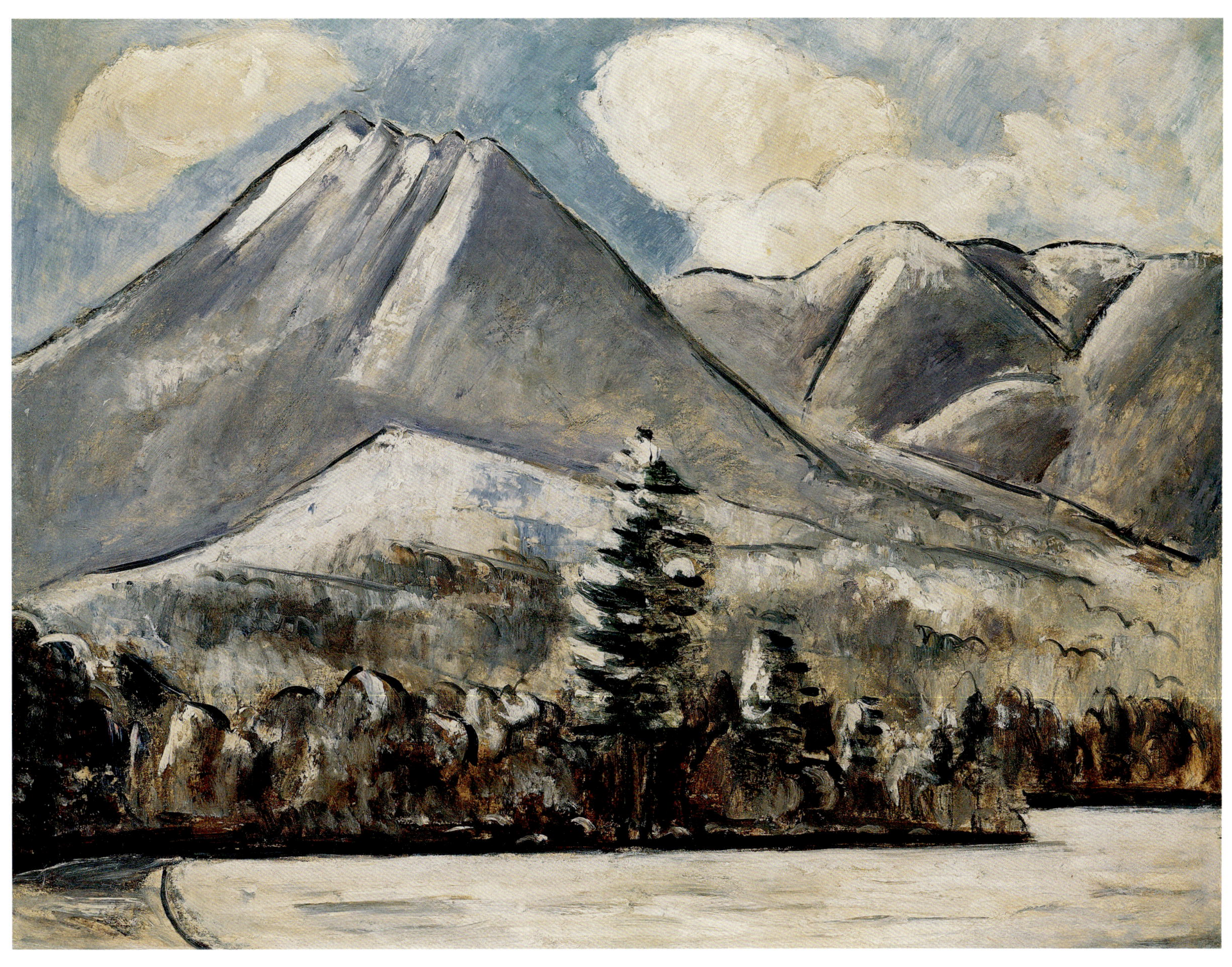

92
Mount Katahdin, Maine, First Snow, No. 1, 1939–40
Oil on academy board, 22 × 28 in.
Private Collection
Courtesy of Salander-O'Reilly Galleries, New York

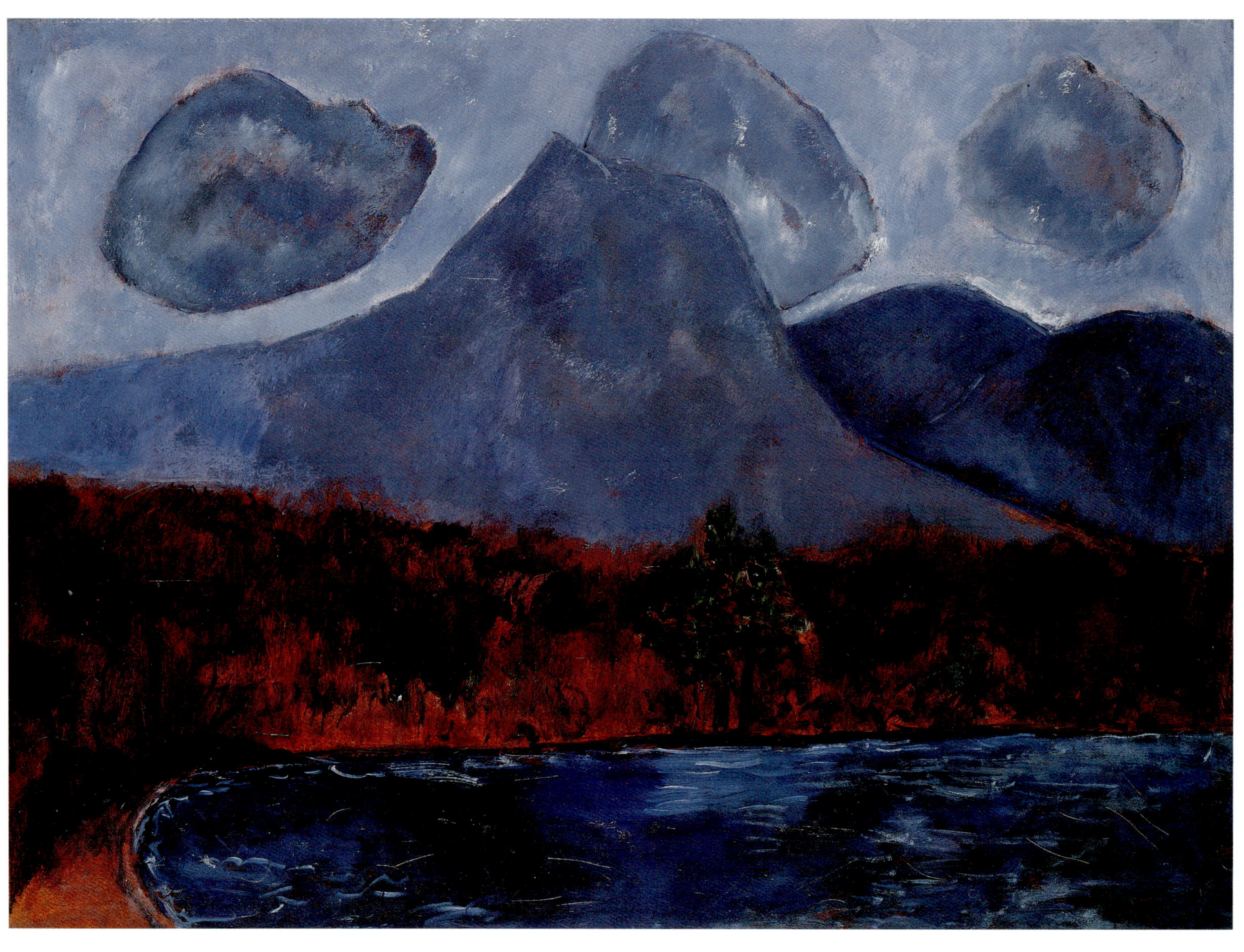

93
Mount Katahdin, 1942
Oil on Masonite-type hardboard, 30 × 40⅛ in.
National Gallery of Art, Washington
Gift of Mrs. Mellon Byers, 1970

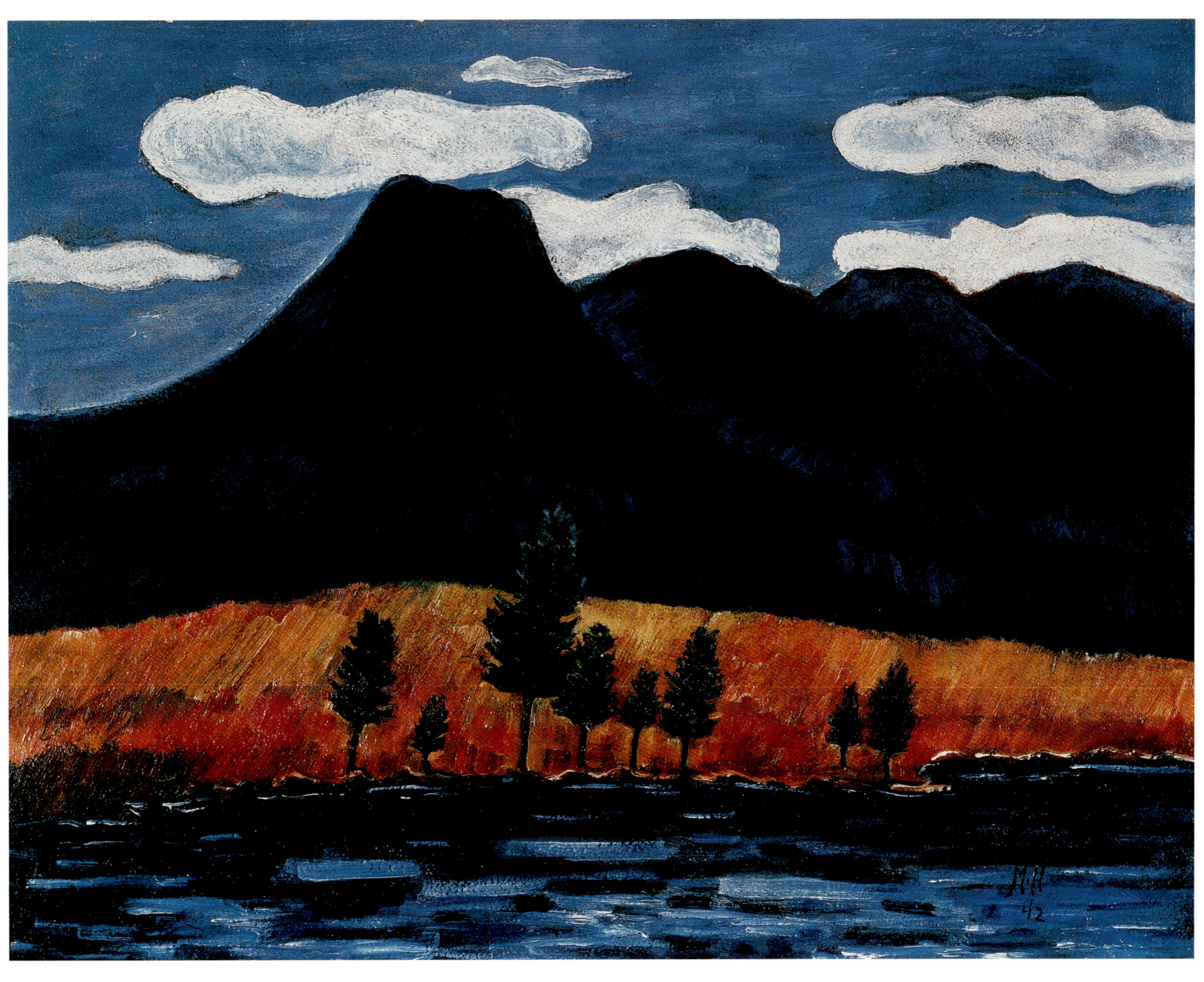

94

Blue Landscape, 1942

Oil on board, 16 × 20 in.

Collection of AXA Financial, Inc., through its subsidiary

The Equitable Life Assurance Society of the United States

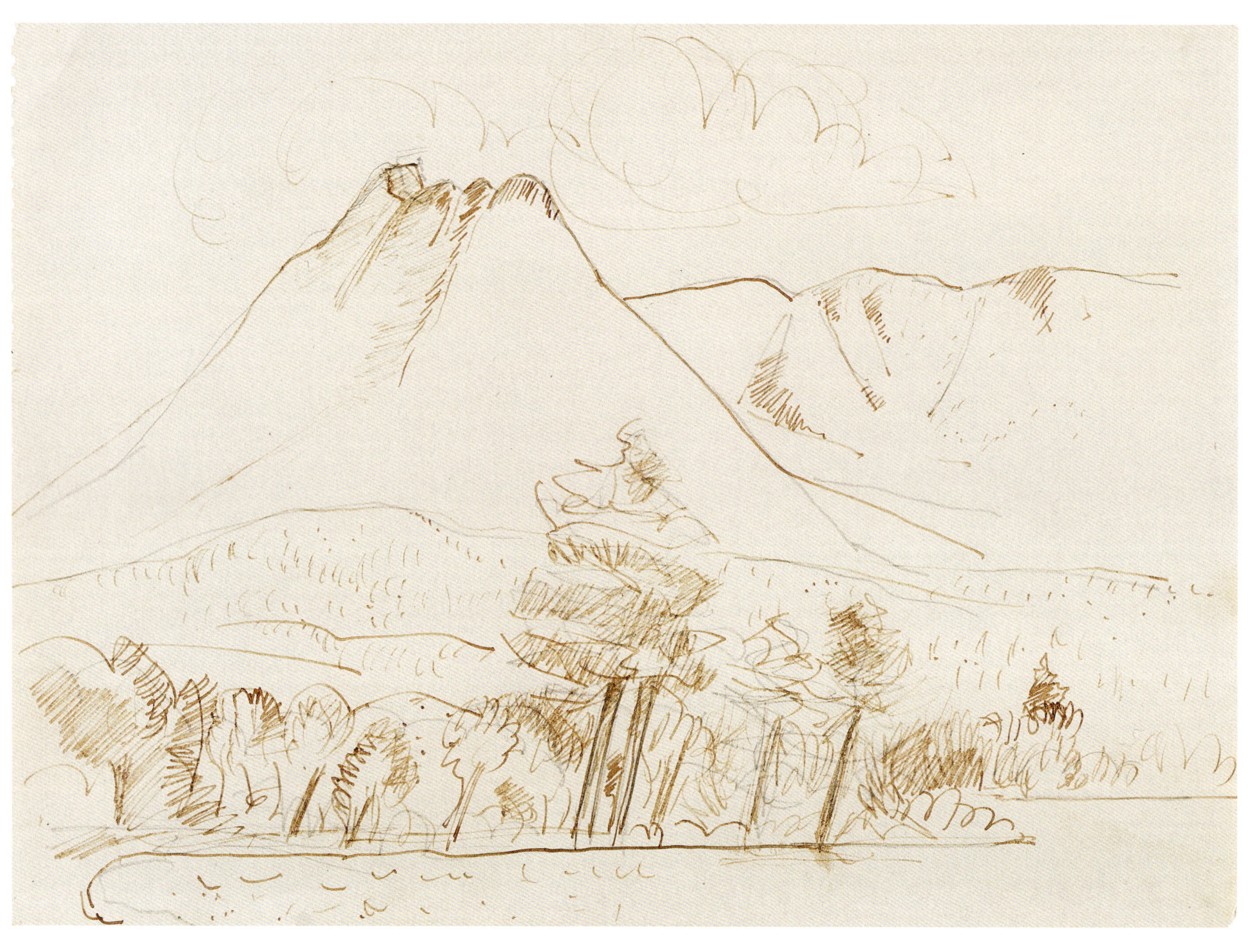

95

Untitled (Mt. Katahdin), c. 1939–40

Sepia ink over pencil on beige paper, 8⅞ × 11¼ in.

Bates College Museum of Art, Lewiston, Maine

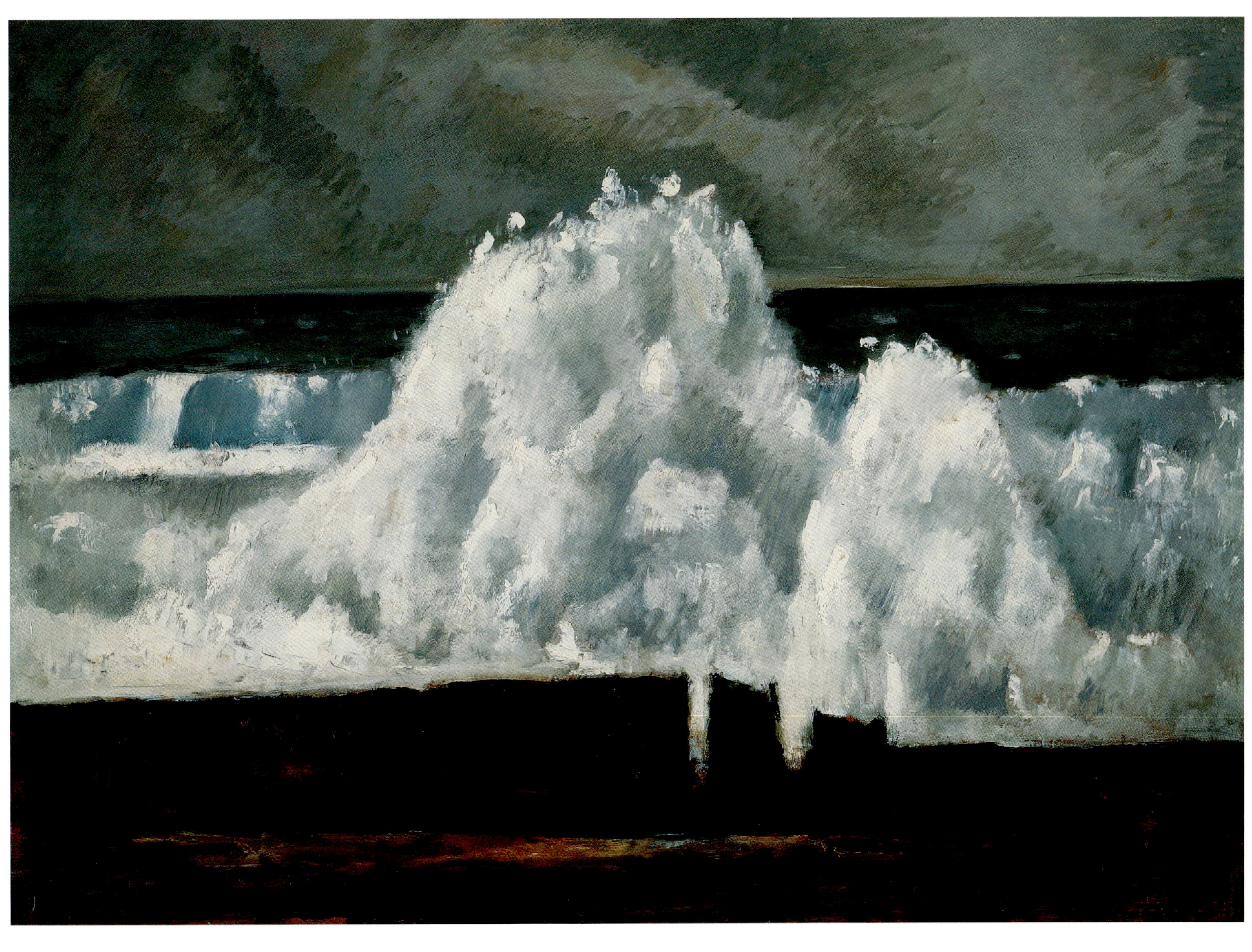

96
The Wave, 1940
Oil on Masonite-type hardboard, 30¼ × 40⅞ in.
Worcester Art Museum, Worcester, Massachusetts
Museum Purchase

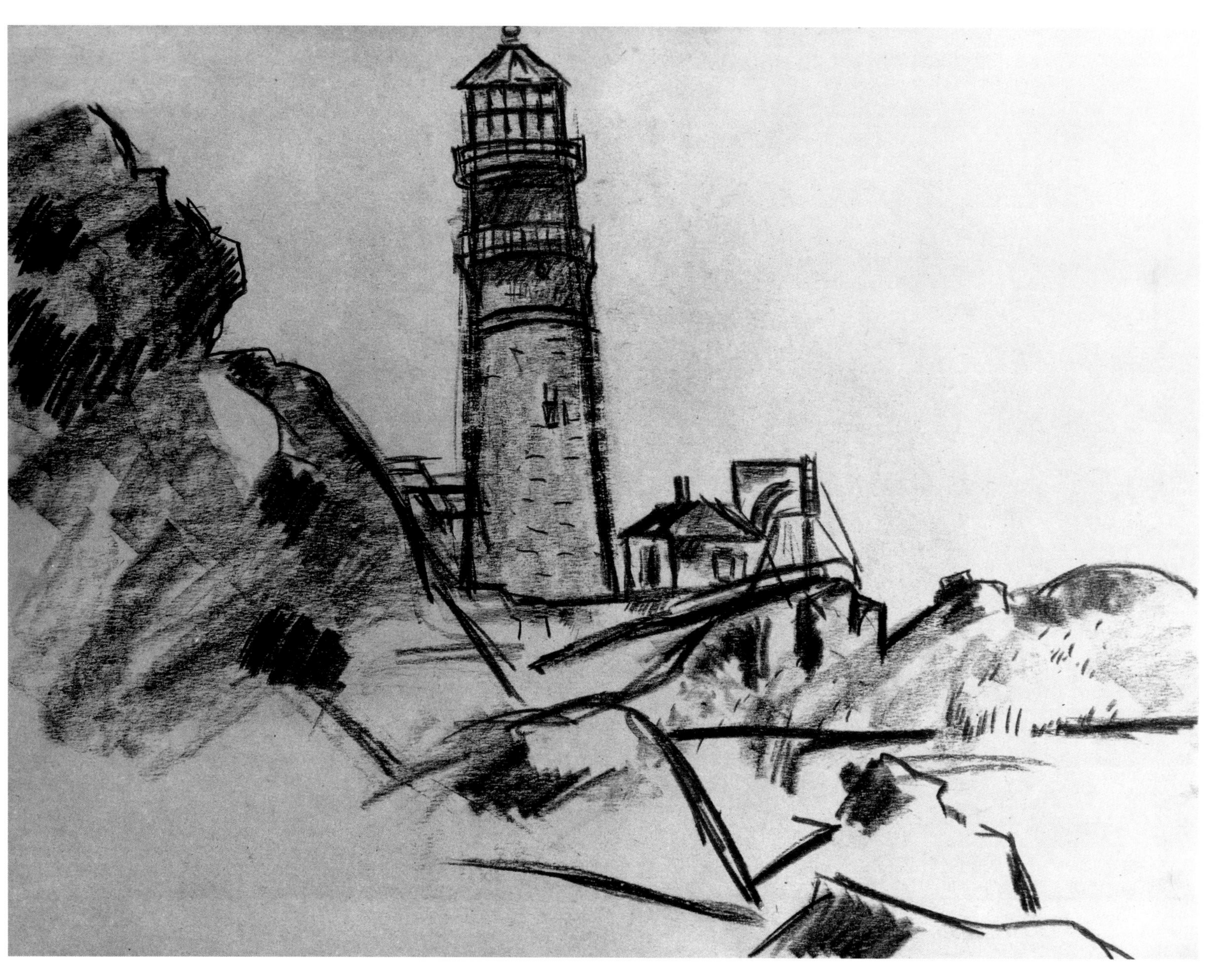

97
The Lighthouse, c. 1940
Charcoal on paper, 22 × 28 in.
Collection of Roy R. Neuberger

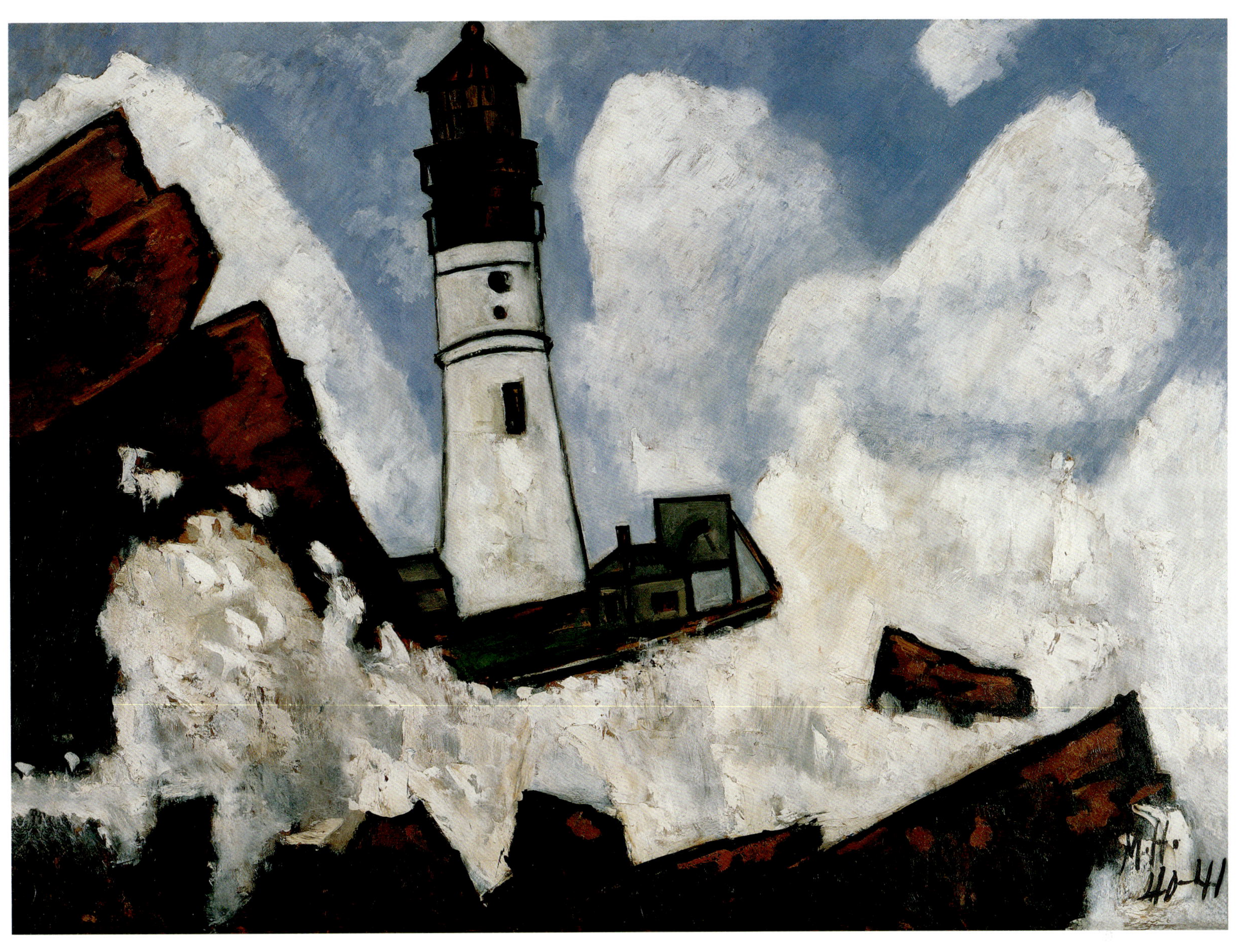

98

The Lighthouse, 1940–41

Oil on Masonite-type hardboard, $30 \times 40\frac{1}{8}$ in.

Private Collection

Courtesy of Martha Parrish & James Reinish, Inc., New York

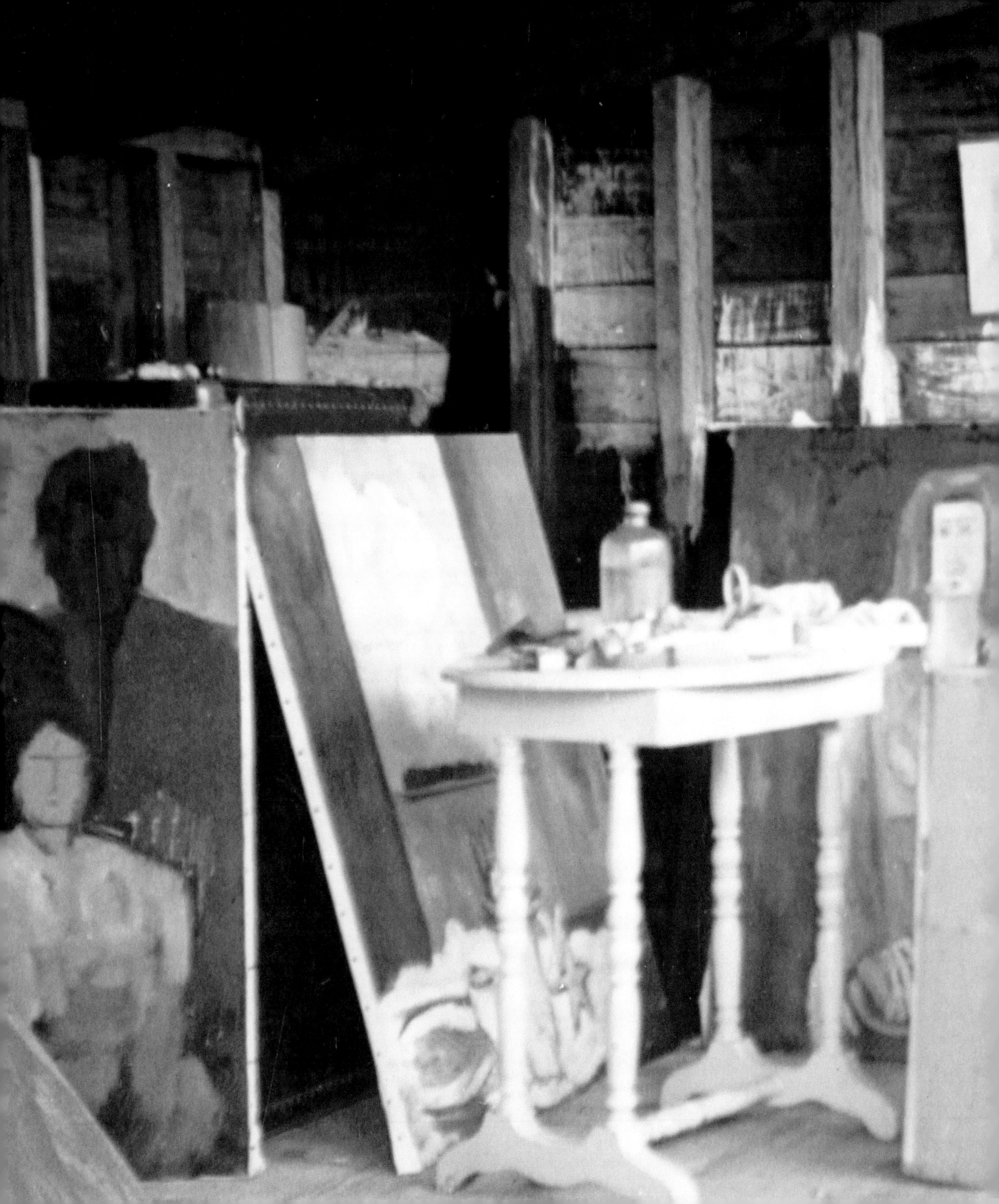

Marsden Hartley's Materials and Working Methods

Stephen Kornhauser
and Ulrich Birkmaier

Materials

Marsden Hartley wrote little about his painting materials, except to complain occasionally of the "difficulties of new canvas" or the fact that he didn't have "material or frame."[1] Descriptive color notations in his correspondence were equally general, such as "black, white, blue and dark red."[2] At his death, an inventory of contents in a New York warehouse merely mentions a "trunk containing paints." The contents of his last studio in Corea, Maine (fig. 1), were left to Bates College, Lewiston, Maine. These, together with the examination of a number of his works, help to reconstruct Hartley's studio practices.

Supports and Grounds

Throughout his career, Hartley painted on a variety of supports for reasons of economy, preference, and availability. Although he never completely abandoned one painting surface for another, some generalizations can be made. Trained in an academic tradition, his large, mostly square-formatted American pictures, painted in or after 1906, are on fabric supports. He continued to use canvas while in Europe. Suppliers' stamps on the reverse of his paintings show that supports were purchased in both Germany and France.[3] When he returned to Europe in 1921 for a second extended stay, he resumed painting on linen. Although he would occasionally paint on linen over the course of his career, he was dissatisfied with the quality or with what he could afford in the United States, and he noted, "so many difficulties new to me—canvas that ate me out of house and home, ruined my brushes . . . its chief distinction being strength and that always appeals but there is no canvas this side of Belgium and Paris that has strength plus intriguing surfaces."[4]

In America, he chose instead to paint on a variety of rigid supports. One type was academy board, a thin paperboard that was commercially primed, usually with a lead and chalk mixture.[5] His small, impressionistic landscapes painted as early as 1906 were usually executed on odd-sized pieces of academy board. But during the late 1930s, he began to rely more on academy boards (fig. 2). Many of his works are on prepared boards manufactured by F. Weber Co.[6] Boards were sold in standard sizes and most of Hartley's paintings were sized either 18 by 24 inches or 22 by 28 inches. The boards were durable enough to take his forceful brush strokes, easy to transport, and less than a quarter of the price of a comparably sized canvas.[7]

In 1917, when Hartley was in Provincetown and Bermuda working on his Movement series, he painted on both a wallboard and a composite board with a core of wooden slats and a pulp paper glued to each side (fig. 3).[8] Because of the war, supplies of artist materials were difficult to find. Hartley wrote the New York framer George F. Of asking him to send

Detail, Figure 1

Figure 1
Unknown Photographer
Hartley's last studio in Corea, Maine, 1943
Archives of American Art
Smithsonian Institution, Washington, D.C.
Photograph by Lee Stalsworth

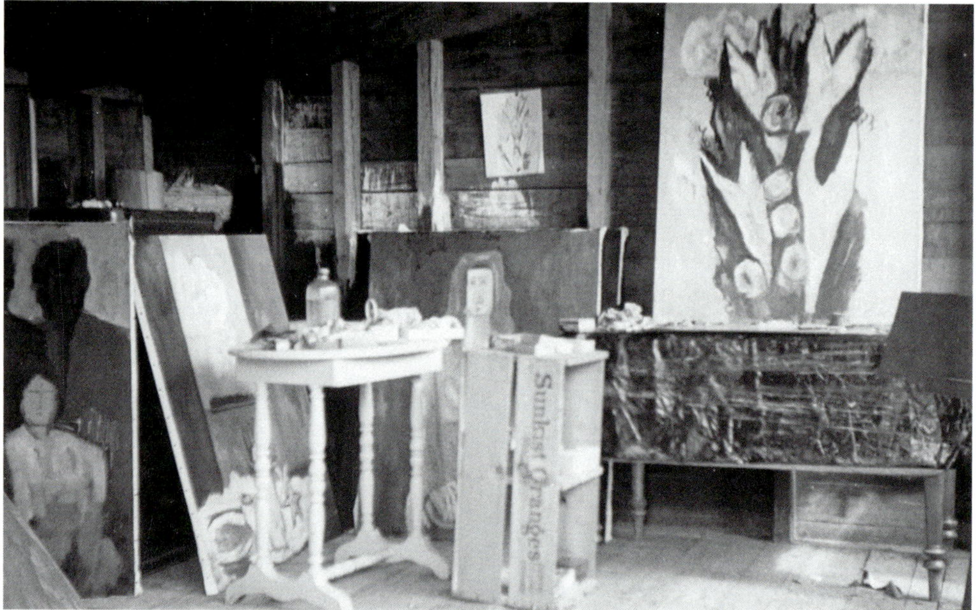

Figure 2
Academy board. Reverse of *Cleophas, Master of the "Gilda Grey"* (plate 68) with Weber label and with the title inscription in Hartley's handwriting

Figure 3
Composite board.
Reverse of Movement No. 8, Provincetown (plate 27)

him "twenty-four composition boards of the same dimensions."[9] The series was painted on two standard formats, 20 by 16 inches and 24 by 20 inches.

Most of Hartley's late works painted after 1939 are on a Masonite-type hardboard.[10] He favored one-quarter-inch tempered boards that had been commercially scored on the reverse with a 4-inch tile-like grid pattern (fig. 4).[11] Most of his paintings of this period were a standard 30 by 40 inches. The larger format was something he felt strongly about: "my thirty by forty is really swell for me, the rest is miniature."[12] Hardboard was fairly common, easily procured, and relatively inexpensive.

Throughout his career, just as he experimented with a variety of styles and drew on a variety of artistic influences, he tested the properties of a range of material. He briefly painted on glass in 1917 but found it was too fragile and caused his paints to crack.[13] Other supports include fine, prepared French panels, French canvas board, and thick, textured wallboard.[14] For a series of still lifes painted in 1921, he painted one on academy board, a second on Beaverboard, and a third on canvas.[15] Throughout his career he also relied on laminated paper boards. While in Germany in 1933, he wrote, "I am even painting on cardboard because I can't afford canvas, but I like cardboard."[16]

For the most part Hartley painted on commercially prepared supports, choosing the standard cooler white grounds that were available containing lead with traces of zinc and barium. Though there are very few examples of non-commercially prepared supports, he was concerned about the consistency of market materials, and he expressed concern with "not knowing [if] the canvas or the panel was absorbent or semi since [he] had not prepared them himself therefore it took forever to build them up."[17] When working on academy boards, he chose a "rough" chalk ground rather than the "smooth" surface that was also available.[18] The few examples of paintings done on hardboard in the mid-1930s are painted on untempered, primed boards. By 1939–40 when he returned to this support, he used the tempered variety unprimed and sealed it with shellac prior to painting.[19] Works done on miscellaneous paper-pulp supports do not appear to have a ground.

Paints

In 1914, when Hartley was in Germany, he wrote to Stieglitz requesting artist materials, and while in Bermuda during the winter of 1917, he sent a shopping list of tube colors to his friend Abraham Walkowitz.[20] These references, together with occasional general color notations on

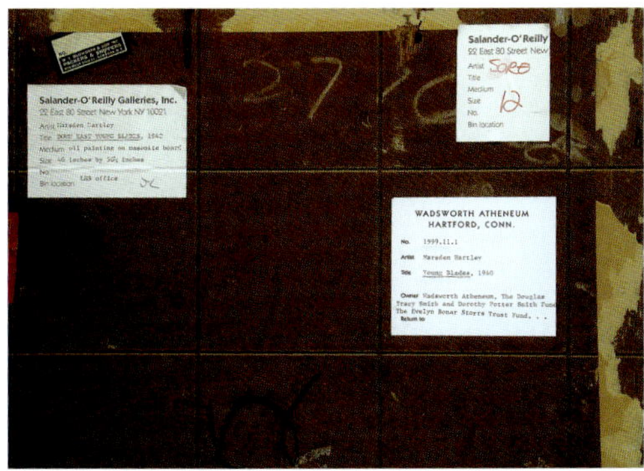

Figure 4
Masonite-type hardboard.
Detail from the reverse of *Down East Young Blades* (plate 85) with tile-like grid pattern

his works or written general comments about a picture, are his only mention of specific paint colors.[21] The contents of Hartley's studio where he painted the final three years of his life, presently at Bates College, contain some of his paints: two glass vials, tube oil colors, and an artist's palette. The vials, one a cadmium yellow pale and the other cadmium yellow light, were manufactured in Germany and presumably bought there.[22] Twenty tubes of oil color were found: eighteen tubes in an "Artist's Thrift Pack" manufactured by Bocour and two tubes of the lesser grade, Bellini oil colors. The wooden artist's palette was left with fresh oil colors matching those on his final painting, *Roses* (plate 106), which he was working on at the time of his death. Paint samples from his palette as well as from three paintings at the Wadsworth Atheneum, *Military* (plate 12) painted in 1913, *Movement No. 8* (plate 27) done in 1916, and *Down East Young Blades* (plate 85) of 1940, were taken and examined with a scanning electron microscope with an energy dispersive X-ray accessory (SEM-EDX).[23] Although samples were taken from only four sources, a few interesting consistencies did turn up. Testing showed that the white used in his *Military* was a traditional ground of white lead, while the white used in *Movement No. 8, Down East Young Blades,* and *Roses* was a less commonly used ground, zinc. The red pigment in his German work was a traditional vermilion, while he used cadmium red for his later works. Samples of his late paintings as well as his palette show the presence of barium sulfate, an extender, used in tube oils. Some of his tube colors are labeled as containing barium.[24]

Varnish

Once again Hartley was silent about his preference for surfaces. What little that can be gleaned from his letters is that his paintings took between "at least ten days to dry" to "a month to dry and can be framed."[25] A note on the reverse of *Silent Expansion* (location unknown) states that the painting "should summer under glass."[26] Elizabeth McCausland's notes mention that in 1943 one of the paintings she saw was "glassed," while also singling out the Art Institute of Chicago's *Dark Mountain* (1908) as being "highly varnished."[27] She also noted that one of the Garmisch-Partenkirchen series is "oil on board [and] looks like a pastel."[28] While Hartley was known to complain about his supports, his grounds, and his paints, he never complained about his "varnish." Could one infer that it was his habit not to varnish his works? More can be learned from looking at the pictures. A surprising number of works painted in Europe are still unvarnished, such as *Portrait of Berlin* (plate 10), *New Mexico Landscape* (fig. 19), and *Movement No. 8* (plate 27). From the Dogtown series to the late works, many of Hartley's paintings have glossy surfaces, characteristic of a varnish film—for example, *Black Duck* (fig. 18), *The Great Good Man* (plate 78), *Down East Young Blades* (plate 85), and *Whale's Jaw, Dogtown Common* (Yale University Art Gallery). When examined under ultraviolet light, which can be used to detect a deteriorated varnish on paintings, the works all show a localized fluorescence. The fluorescence is not haphazard but rather conforms loosely to forms in the paintings, the rocks in *Whale's Jaw* or the darks in *Black Duck*. Samples of the glossy passages of pictures owned by the Wadsworth Atheneum, together with samples of a translucent golden colored gel-like residue from his palette, were analyzed with both FTIR (Fourier Transform Infrared Spectroscopy) and Py-GC/MS (pyrolysis—gas chromatography—mass spectrometry). All samples were principally composed of a drying oil such as a common linseed oil, however the sample from his palette also contained amber. Among Hartley's belongings was an unopened 20 gram vial of Blockx amber varnish. It was sold both in Europe and the United States by various distributors. According to its proponents, as a medium and varnish it was hard, very durable, kept colors brilliant and did not yellow.

Figure 5
Marsden Hartley's palette, 1943
Bates College Museum of Art, Lewiston, Maine

Working Methods

A large number of Hartley's paintings and drawings were examined using a variety of analytical methods[29] to learn more about the composition of specific materials and their effect in the finished painting. A generous loan from Bates College enabled examination and analysis of some of Hartley's painting materials that remained in his studio in Corea, Maine, after his death in 1943. They consisted of the palette (fig. 5) related to his last known painting, *Roses;* a couple of glass vials with pigments of German origin; a glass vial with amber varnish; and most importantly a sketchbook with elaborate color exercises, annotations, and writings on drawing and proportions.

Hartley's complex and evasive personality often makes interpreting his paintings a challenge, but this is not necessarily the case for his working methods. Hartley's studies at the Cleveland School of Art and at the National Academy of Design, New York, provided a traditional art education, which is reflected in the relatively conventional working methods he used through the mid-1930s. After 1934 there was a shift away from traditional materials and methods toward the use of different painting supports (see fig. 4) combined with a much more direct and fast paint application. Stylistically and technically these works marked a departure from everything Hartley had done previously. The following paragraphs attempt to illustrate Hartley's working methods by highlighting key periods throughout his career.

Drawing and Underdrawing

The first step in Hartley's working method was to absorb a place visually and mentally. Hartley considered this the most important phase in the creative process, and he insisted that before he could paint a scene, he needed to process the images mentally, capturing the essence of a location.[30] Preliminary drawings played an important role in this process throughout his career, and Hartley would sometimes make several sketches at a particular site. Despite borrowing stylistically from impressionism in his early years, Hartley was never a "plein-air painter." Once the mental absorption of a place was achieved and preliminary drawings were executed, the actual paintings would be realized in Hartley's studio, often weeks later. In December 1933 Hartley wrote to Norma Berger from Garmisch-Partenkirchen:

> *and I want some more material for subject matter, though I can't do anything outside but make the drawings and then do the rest in my room, which I have done for years, and I don't miss much of the actual facts, even as when I was in Mexico, I absorbed it so well that the one in the Cleveland Museum I did in Berlin and if New Mexico were not so hard to get at and into, I should like to try it again, for I have heard a number of times that I was the only one that ever did get that country, much as years ago I was the one who got Maine and that is the way I get anything, by just getting into it all over.*[31]

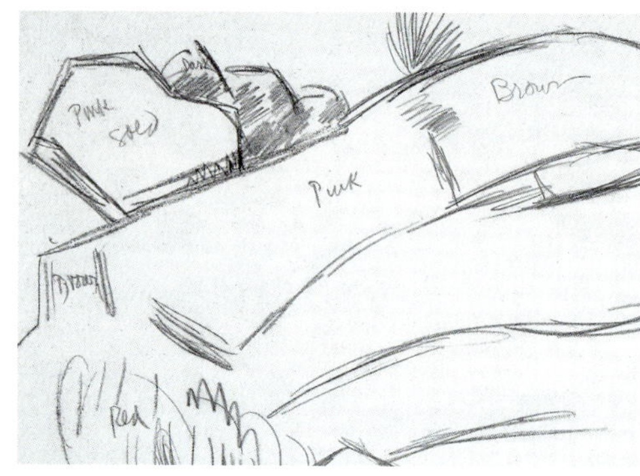

Figure 6
The detail of *Whale's Jaw Rock, Dogtown* (plate 48) illustrates Hartley's use of color annotations to indicate placement and choice of colors for the subsequent paint application.

Hartley was a prolific draughtsman, which is reflected in the large number of surviving drawings. With few exceptions, nearly all the works on paper are directly related to paintings later realized in oil. These drawings not only served as a link from Hartley's initial conception of a scene to the finished work in oil, but they also provide insight into the resolution of compositional problems. The materials used in these drawings include pencil, silverpoint, crayon, and charcoal on a variety of colored papers: white, yellowish, green, gray, pink, wine colored, or black. Hartley's careful choice of different-colored paper for drawings and his notes on drawing, underpainting, and imprimatura[32] in his sketchbook containing color exercises illustrate his keen awareness of the impact that different materials and colored grounds would have on a composition.

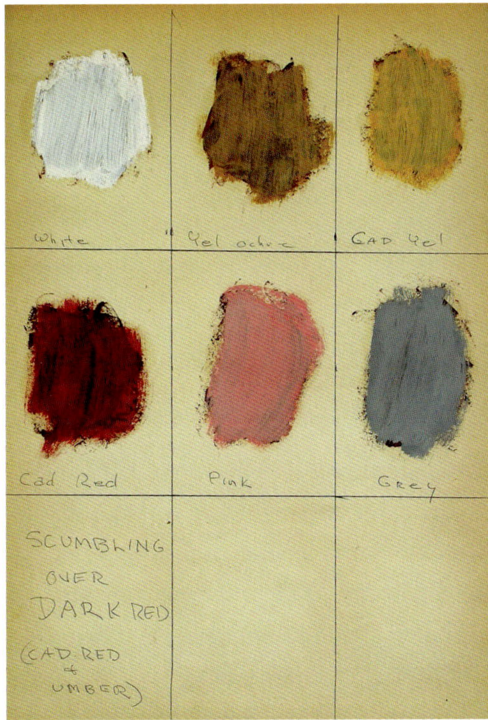

Figure 7
Detail of color exercises from a page from Hartley's sketchbook
Bates College Museum of Art, Lewiston, Maine

After these initial sketches, Hartley often started the painting process with a drawing on the painting support, which could later be covered by paint, but frequently remained visible, becoming an integral part of the finished painting. Some of his early Berlin canvases demonstrate how the meticulous drawing and subsequent sparse application of paint give the work an unfinished appearance (plate 11). Despite their incomplete appearance, we know that Hartley considered the paintings finished, since he exhibited them in Berlin and was always adamant about not showing or leaving any unfinished work.

The Dogtown paintings (plates 46–47, 50) illustrate how the separate steps of drawing and painting could be merged into one. The majority of the Dogtown paintings were done on 18 by 24-inch pre-primed academy boards. Hartley worked out the composition by blocking in shapes with a few, quickly drawn lines. Color annotations within these shapes served as reminders for the placement and choice of colors in the finished painting (fig. 6). These color indicators became particularly important, as much time could pass between the initial drawing and the actual painting realized later in the studio.

Underdrawing remained important during the last years in Maine. Many of the large format works on hardboard show an abbreviated working method, as the paint application became faster and was realized directly onto the unprimed painting support, although Hartley did not skip the crucial step of underdrawing. He usually used what has the appearance of a thick, waxy, black crayon[33] to outline shapes in a quick and generic manner. In these late years, the sole purpose of underdrawing was to indicate shapes,[34] whereas the underdrawing in the Dogtown paintings served the double role of laying out the composition and indicating color selection and placement for subsequent paint application.

Paint Application

When examining Hartley's paintings from very different stylistic periods, such as the early impressionistic landscapes, the Berlin series, New Mexico, Dogtown, and finally the late Maine pictures, it becomes clear that the choice of color and mode of application were important factors in Hartley's work process. The sketchbook with color exercises illustrates his awareness of the complexity and impact of color and how it could be used in various ways to achieve different effects, using simple or complex mixtures, glazes, and scumbles. Numerous large-format pages are covered with these exercises and with notes on painting theory (fig. 7).

The technical execution followed the stylistic influences in the early landscapes, from impressionism to Giovanni Segantini: short brush strokes formed small dabs of multiple colors that created a busy surface with high impasto. Hartley created interesting surface textures in many of the early paintings by changing the orientation of individual brush strokes, matching the juxtapositions of different shapes in the painting. Although impressionistic on the surface, their general appearance is moody and dark, often owing to a layer of black underpaint that can be found in some of the landscapes. This dark, somber mood appears throughout many of the early paintings and reaches a high point in the paintings that Hartley made in homage to Albert Pinkham Ryder. The painting supports are almost entirely covered with paint, but in some small areas the dark layer of underpaint remains visible. It is interesting to note that Hartley achieved this characteristic Ryder style by layering only a couple of paint films, whereas Ryder's paintings often consisted of multiple layers of paint. Stieglitz, who owned these paintings among many others by Hartley, made a dismissive comment to Hudson Walker in 1943: "These paintings wouldn't exist without Ryder, and whereas Ryder worked so deeply into his paintings, Hartley only got a surface quality."[35] Hartley used a wide range of colors for these works, usually in a wet-in-wet application.

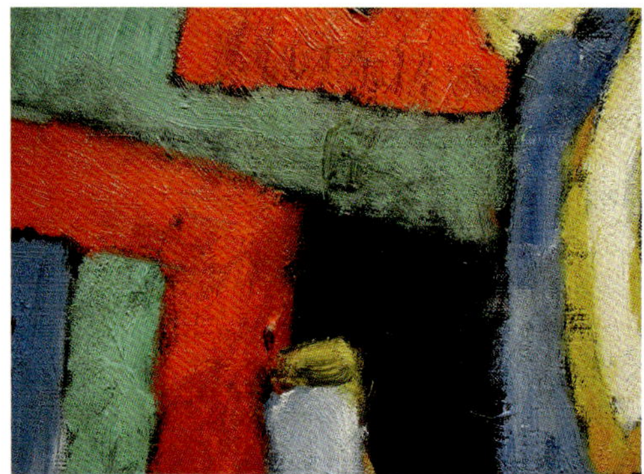

Figure 8
The detail of *Military* (plate 12) illustrates how the bright colors are juxtaposed against the black background.

When examining the works Hartley painted during his first extended stay in Europe, it is as if weight had been lifted off the paintings' surfaces.[36] The greatly reduced palette consisted mainly of red, green, white, blue, and yellow, reminiscent of that of the Blaue Reiter group, in particular Wassily Kandinsky and Franz Marc. Hartley would meticulously draw the composition onto the primed canvas using a soft pencil, and then literally "fill" the drawn shapes with color. The individual oil colors were thinly applied, mostly unmixed, except for additions of white to give the painting a higher key. Very little or no additional oil was used to render the paint liquid, which resulted in a dry, powdery surface. The primed canvas became an integral part of the painting, showing through the surface over large areas.

Starting in November 1914, Hartley created the group of paintings that is today often perceived as the artistic highpoint in his career, the series of War Motif paintings. The overall key, colors, and shapes are similar to the earlier Berlin paintings, but they have an unusual appearance owing to the black ground that is juxtaposed with the bright and colorful shapes. This black imprimatura was applied over the entire paint surface, and the subsequent extremely thin paint application allowed for the underlying black to show through, giving each color depth and saturation. The effect could be compared to seeing a light object in a darkened room as opposed to seeing the same object outside in the bright, glaring sunlight (fig. 8).

It remains unclear how and why Hartley developed the black background. The paintings were a memorial to Karl von Freyburg, suggesting the use of black as a symbol of mourning. However, the Wadsworth Atheneum's *Military* (plate 12), painted in 1913, about one year before von Freyburg's death, already bears the characteristic black background, and it might have been an effect Hartley developed over a period of time. It was not in fact the first time that Hartley used black underpaint; it is reminiscent of the black layer of underpaint in some of his earliest paintings, although the black in the War Motif series assumes a more important role, since it covers large areas of the paint surface.

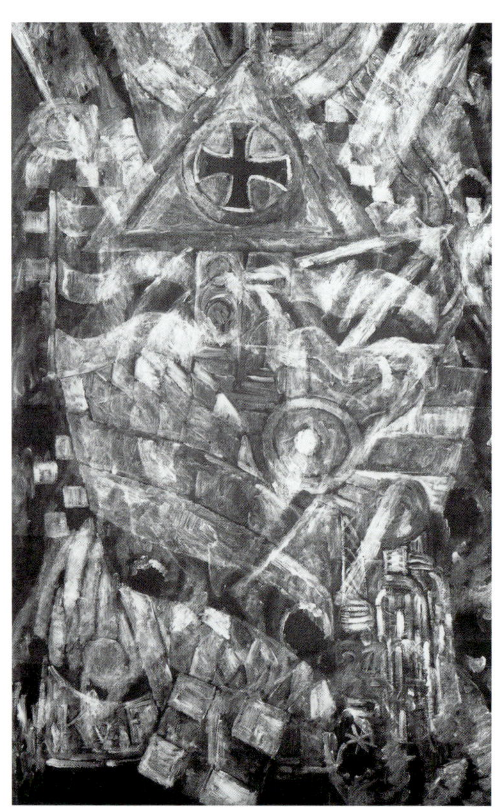

Figure 9
Marsden Hartley
Portrait of a German Officer
Oil on canvas
X-ray photograph
The Metropolitan Museum of Art
Alfred Steiglitz Collection, 1949. (49.70.42)
Photograph courtesy of The Paintings Conservation Department,
The Metropolitan Museum of Art

X-radiography of *Portrait of a German Officer* (fig. 9) shows that the layer of black could also be used to cover pentimenti. The X-ray reveals a complex underlying composition related to a series of paintings that Hartley had made earlier, around 1912. It depicts triangular and circular shapes found in *Portrait of Berlin* (plate 10). With a layer of black paint Hartley then "canceled" and covered the earlier composition, creating the foundation for the present *Portrait of a German Officer.*[37]

In some of the Berlin paintings, Hartley introduced an unusual glazing technique that was an integral part of the painting process and which became an important characteristic of many of the later paintings. Hartley applied a liquid medium locally on top of the paint to modify the appearance of certain areas of the paint surface. This medium consisted mainly of a drying oil and amber resin, and could be used straight or added to the oils on the palette (figs. 10–11).

Upon his return to the United States, Hartley did not abandon canvas as a painting support altogether but predominantly used a variety of alternatives such as academy board or composition board. The works contrast strongly with the Berlin canvases. In Dogtown the paint application became generous, reminiscent of his early impressionistic paintings. Hartley applied paint forcefully and very quickly and shifted his palette to match the colors found in nature, such as ochre, browns, and other earth colors. He started to emphasize shapes by outlining them with dark paint (plate 46), whereas in the Berlin paintings he defined shapes by setting them against a black background. With the Dogtown series, the surface quality of the paint films changes dramatically, owing to the artist's use of the palette knife to modify the paint surface and his scoring of the fresh paint with the back of his brush (fig. 12).

Hartley's last years in Maine were a departure from everything he had done previously, both stylistically and technically. During those last years, the focus was narrow

Figure 10
Detail of *Military* (plate 12)

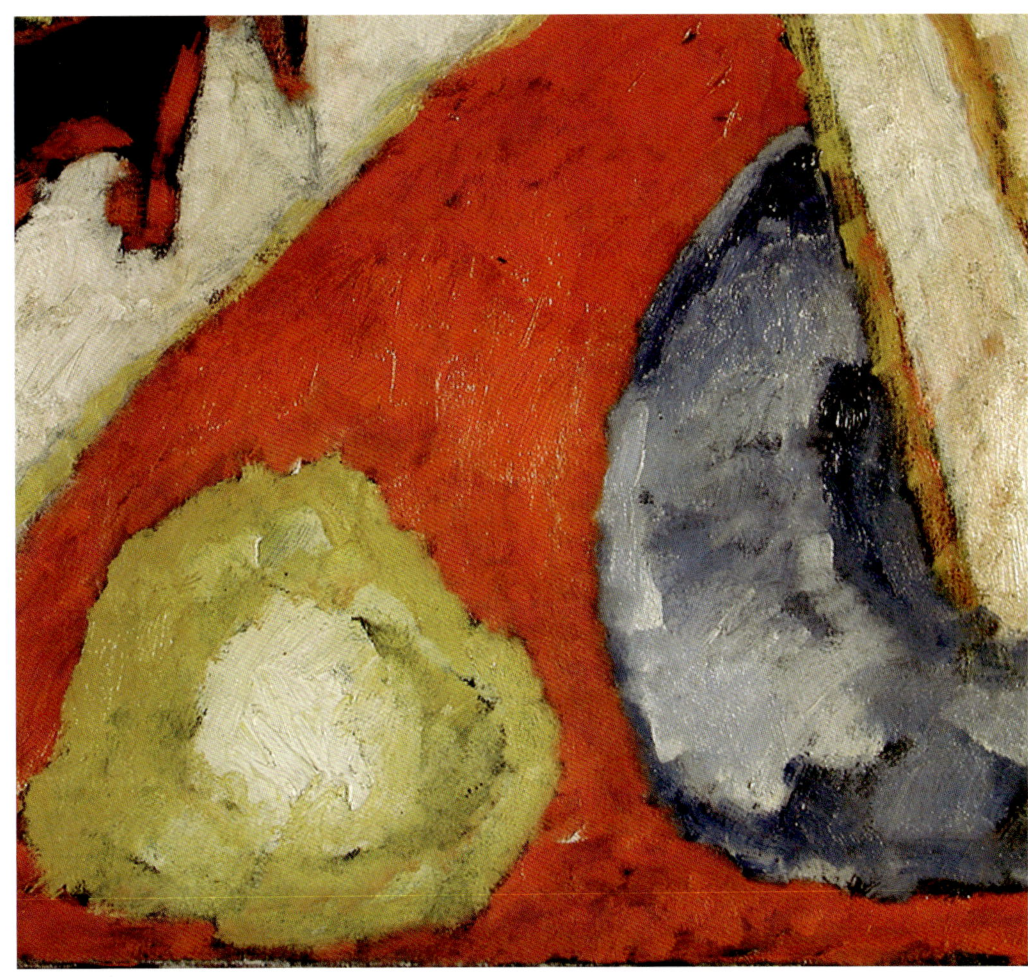

Figure 11
The same detail under ultraviolet illumination shows the presence of a resinous glaze with characteristic greenish fluorescence.

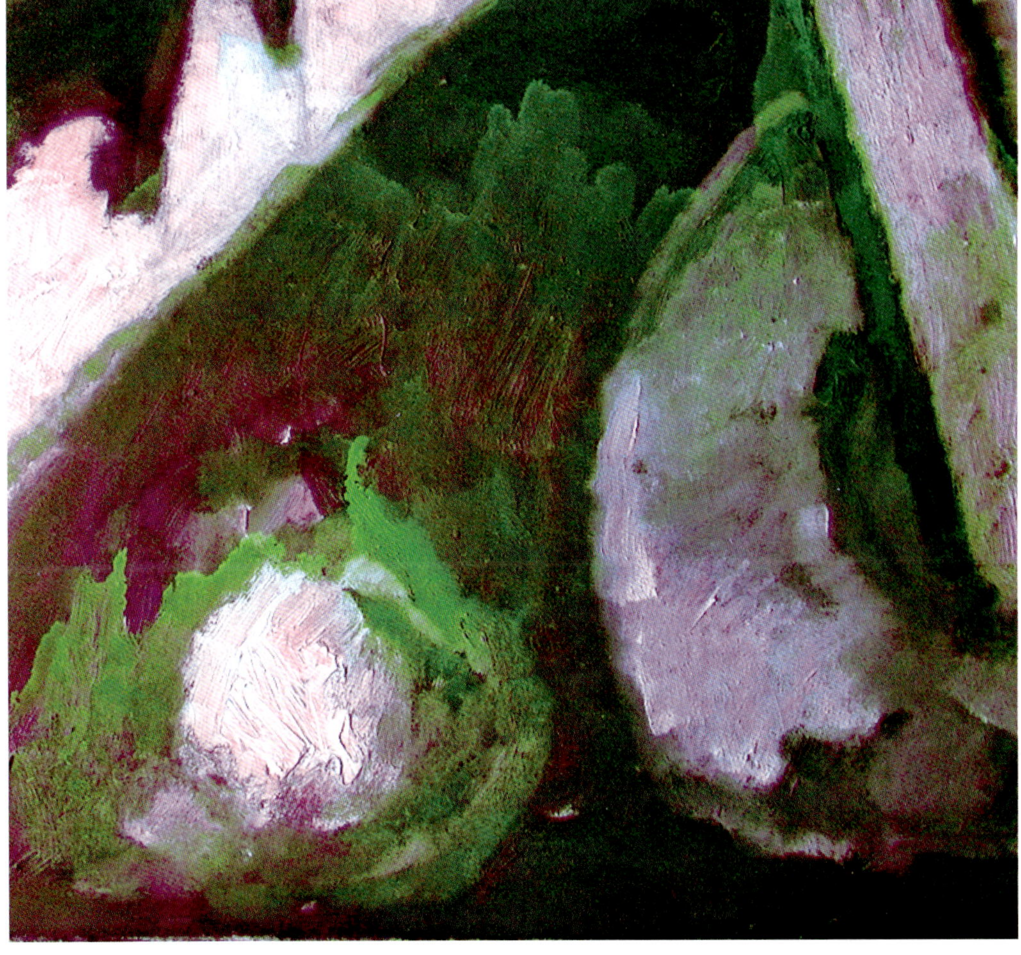

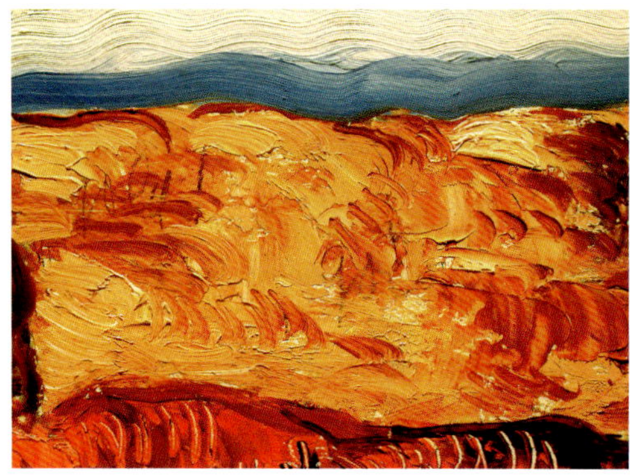

Figure 12
The detail of *Dogtown* (1934; Frederick R. Weisman Art Museum, University of Minnesota, Minneapolis) illustrates surface variations achieved through the use of a palette knife, and by scoring into the wet paint film with the back of a brush. Hartley's drawn color indication *gold*! can be seen in the upper left quadrant of the image.

and concise: most subjects in his paintings were inspired by his immediate surroundings in coastal Maine. The size of the painting supports shifted toward larger formats of Masonite board, frequently used in the construction business. After sealing the slick surface of the tempered hardboard with shellac, Hartley would indicate the composition with a quick, generic drawing using black crayon, which—just as in the early Berlin paintings—was not necessarily covered with paint later.

The paint application itself became very direct, fast, and secure, reduced to the minimum necessary.[38] To achieve this new, faster technique, Hartley began to employ larger brushes of uneven quality, as is evident in the amount of brush hair embedded in the paint film of many of the late paintings. The unprimed, reddish brown colored paint support became an integral part of the finished painting. Figures were often outlined with broad black paint, emphasizing their minimal depth, a two-dimensionality with a focus on flat shapes that has become a trademark in Hartley's paintings.

Surface Appearance

A number of surviving paintings that have never received any conservation treatment appear unvarnished, while paintings that have a surface coating are documented as having been varnished later. The photographer Paul Strand described in a letter to Alfred Stieglitz the Hartley painting *El Santo* (plate 36), which he had seen in 1926 as having "that dry paint quality which he [Hartley] alone has which creates a new fine tactility—paint and not yet paint."[39]

Hartley's early impressionistic works were painted with considerable impasto, and the medium-rich colors right out of the tube provided good surface gloss. The group of paintings from Hartley's first Berlin stay, the War Motif series in particular, stand out not only stylistically, but also for the subtle beauty of their surfaces. The commercially pre-primed canvases from at least two different artist supply stores in Berlin were highly absorbent, and the thin paint application created a matt surface with subtle variations with more or less gloss, depending on the oil-medium content of each individual color and its application. The overall effect is that of an ever-changing appearance in the surface texture of the painting, depending on the light and the angle of observation. The variety of surface textures creates a depth that is in contrast to the otherwise two-dimensional, flat depiction of shapes. This depth is lost when the paintings are uniformly varnished, which appears to affect the black colors in particular.

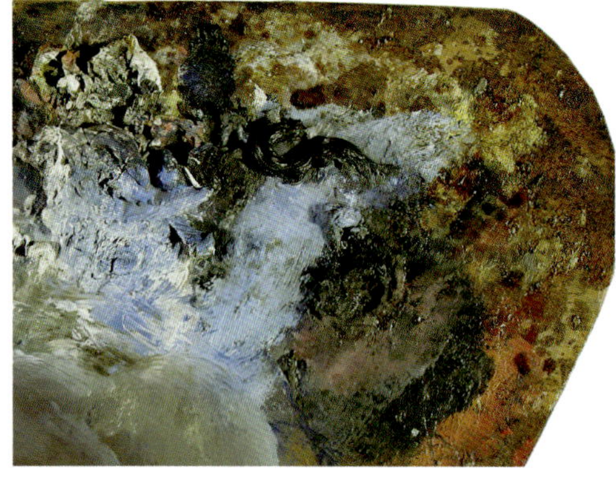

Figure 13
Detail of Hartley's palette

Another group of paintings interesting for their relative surface gloss are the late Maine paintings, realized between 1939 and 1943. The smooth Masonite supports coated with shellac provided a non-absorbent surface, and the subsequent paint application—even thin layers of paint—made for a rich, almost glossy surface. Another material employed by Hartley affected the gloss and general appearance: a number of them show a peculiar, strong fluorescence under ultraviolet illumination. Unlike the fluorescing uniform layer of an aged natural resin, which would suggest a varnish application, this material was found to consist of an oil-resin medium (figs. 13–14).

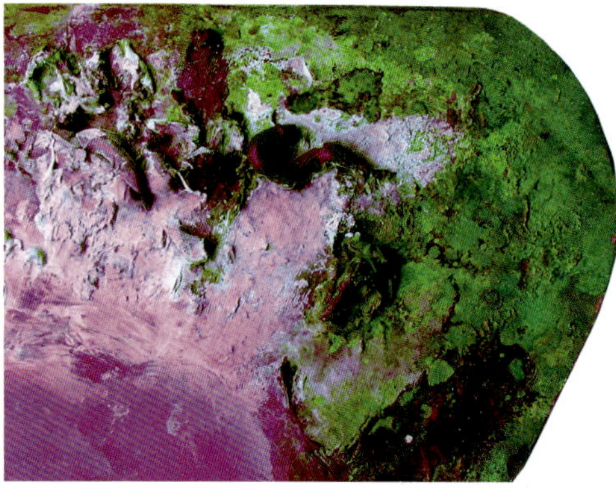

Figure 14
The same detail under ultraviolet illumination shows the greenish fluorescence of a resinous glaze, and illustrates how Hartley mixed the resinous material into his oils on the palette.

Hartley applied this medium in a painterly fashion selectively in some areas of the painting. Most of the time it was applied separately, unmixed, but in one case it was found to be mixed with small amounts of black paint. Examination of Hartley's palette under ultraviolet illumination confirms the presence of the same material found in a number of the paintings. It suggests that the medium could have been added on the palette to individual pigments or pigment mixtures, as found on *Down East Young Blades* (figs. 15–16). In *Black Duck*, the glaze was generously applied throughout the paint surface, with a particular focus on the dark background (figs. 17–18).

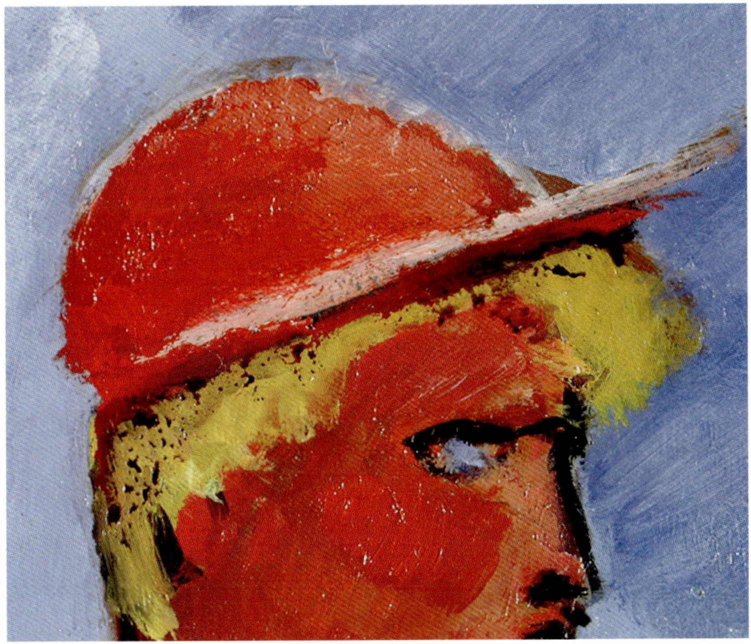

Figure 15
Detail of *Down East Young Blades* (plate 85)

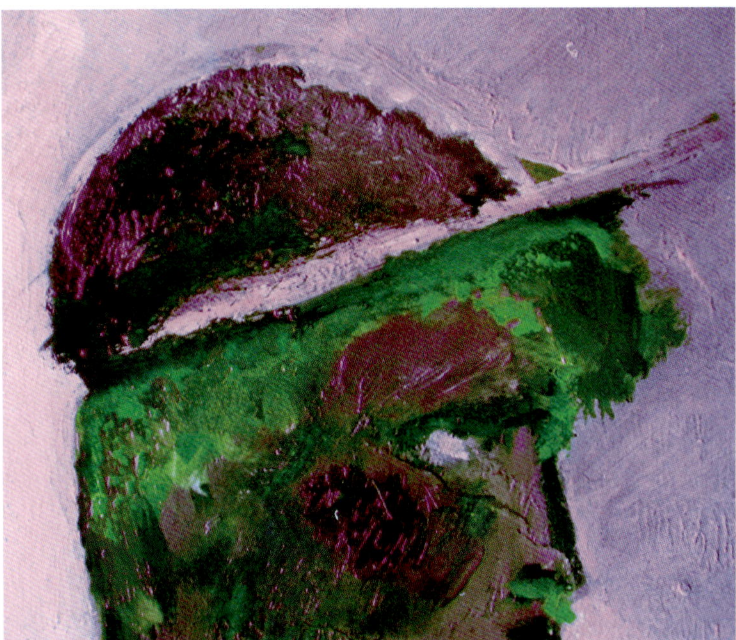

Figure 16
The same detail under ultraviolet illumination shows the presence of the resinous glaze.

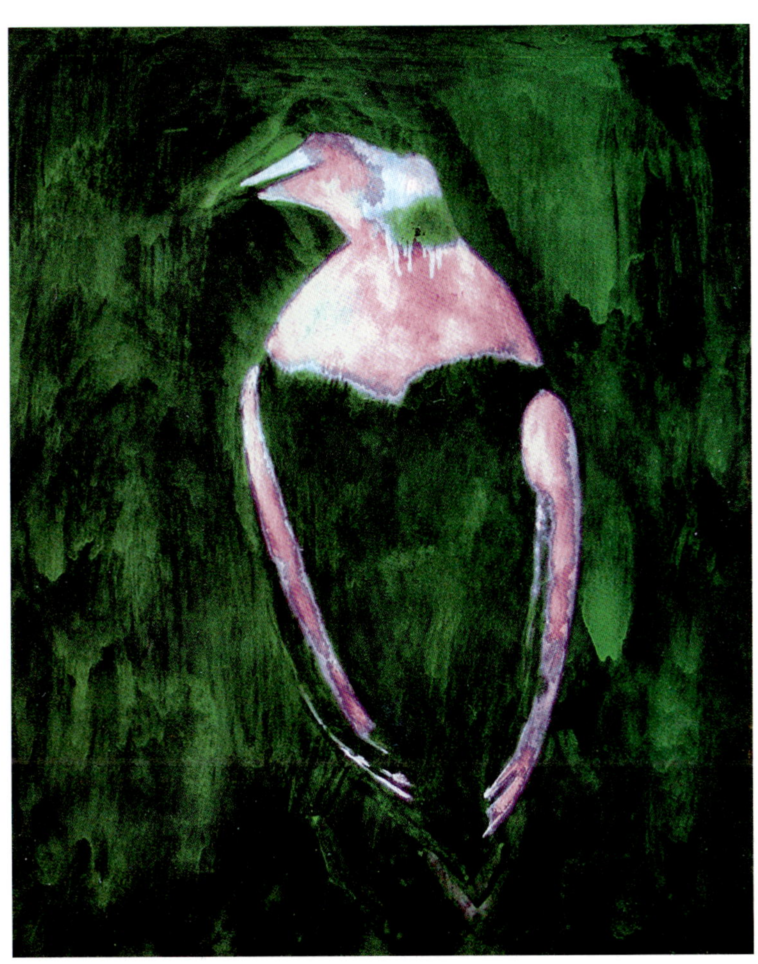

Figure 17
Black Duck under ultraviolet illumination

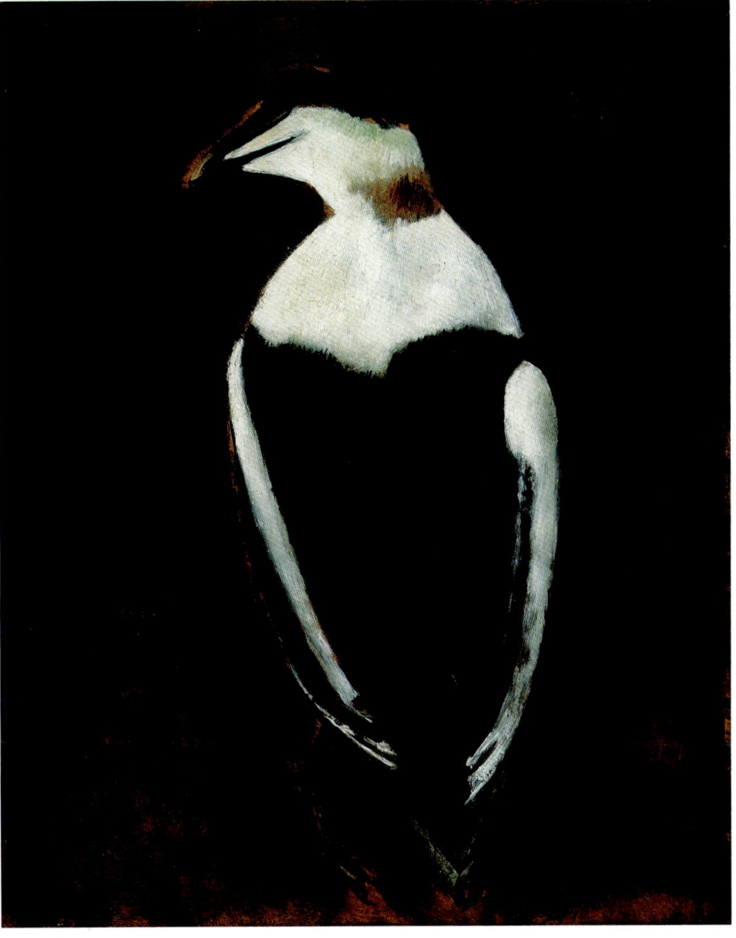

Figure 18
Marsden Hartley
Black Duck, 1940–41
Oil on Masonite, 28¼ × 22 in. (71.75 × 55.88 cm)
The Museum of Fine Arts, Boston
The Hayden Collection—Charles Henry Hayden Fund, 43.32

Stylistically, Hartley's career can be divided into very distinct phases, and the paintings' appearance and working methods employed readily reflect these stylistic changes: every stylistic change is accompanied by a change or modification in Hartley's working methods. Some paintings by Hartley exhibit a tendency to develop flaking in the paint layer as a result of adhesion lacking between painting support and paint film. This appears to be largely due to problematic paint supports rather than shortcomings in technical execution. The works on canvas are generally very stable, but Hartley—like many of his contemporaries—employed a variety of other painting supports, such as Weber academy board, composition board, or cardboard, chosen for practical and economical reasons. The flaking tendency is usually associated with the Weber academy boards. Hartley's thriftiness was legendary, the result of his frequent—perceived or real—financial problems, which forced him to use "inferior" materials such as cardboard and oil thrift packs, but by and large it appears that the occasional choice of cheaper painting materials did not adversely affect the longevity of the paintings.

Notes on Frames

Throughout Hartley's career, his choice of picture frames was rooted in a combination of aesthetics and economics. His early landscape paintings were framed in wide, plain, traditional gilt cove molding, sometimes with a repetitive design such as a bead or egg and dart. A small landscape, *Late Autumn* (1908) for example, is inscribed on the reverse of the academy board in Hartley's hand with "ought to have a gilt frame."[40] *Autumn Lake and Hills, Maine* (1908) was noted in the 1921 Hartley sale as having an "ugly gilt molding on gesso."[41] Hartley's signature moldings are those developed while in Paris and Berlin. The frames are understated, flat, softwood moldings, similar to frame liners, varying in size usually measuring less than 1¾ inches wide and less than 1 inch deep. The thickness of the frame at the site edge is between ⅛ and ¼ inch. The frames are usually finished with either white paint or gesso, such as *Portrait of Berlin* (Plate 10), while the most spectacular ones are polychromed with the continuation of design from the painting, such as *The Aero* (plate 15) and *Berlin Ante-War* (plate 14), similar to what expressionists and futurists were doing. In at least two cases, paintings from the Berlin series are framed in an atypical wide gilt frame with rounded corners.[42] Hartley abandoned these understated yet well-suited moldings in Europe, where he returned to using gilded frames at times for his paintings, especially while he was in France. Unlike those of his early landscapes, the new frames have the thin, clean modernist aesthetic with a variety of stepped profiles, such as *Alps, Martines, Vence* (1925–26; private collection), or a thin scooped molding of *Kinsman Falls* (1929; location unknown). It is difficult to say with certainty if the framing was done abroad or in New York, but in December 1927, Hartley wrote to Stieglitz from Paris that he would have left earlier "but the framers are slow."[43]

A great number of pictures, done in both Europe and America, hung in simple thin moldings and in some cases only strip frames. A general reference to a reverse-glass painting owned by Fisk University, Nashville, states that it was framed in a "plain white wood frame"; paintings in the Movement series were placed in "small flat" frames.[44] Others were framed in thin rounded moldings, either painted or raw wood. According to an interview, Hartley used inserts of about 1 inch because he always felt that his collectors would understand that they needed a frame besides the insert.[45] *New Mexico Landscape* (fig. 19) was noted in the late 1940s as "having a narrow wooden frame about ¼" painted black," a second as having a frame "1½" molded natural wood." Both retain the original frames. *Blueberry Highway, Dogtown* (1932; location unknown) was set in a 1-inch flat

Figure 19
Marsden Hartley
New Mexico Landscape, 1919
The Philadelphia Museum of Art
The Alfred Stieglitz Collection
Photographed with a frame chosen by Hartley

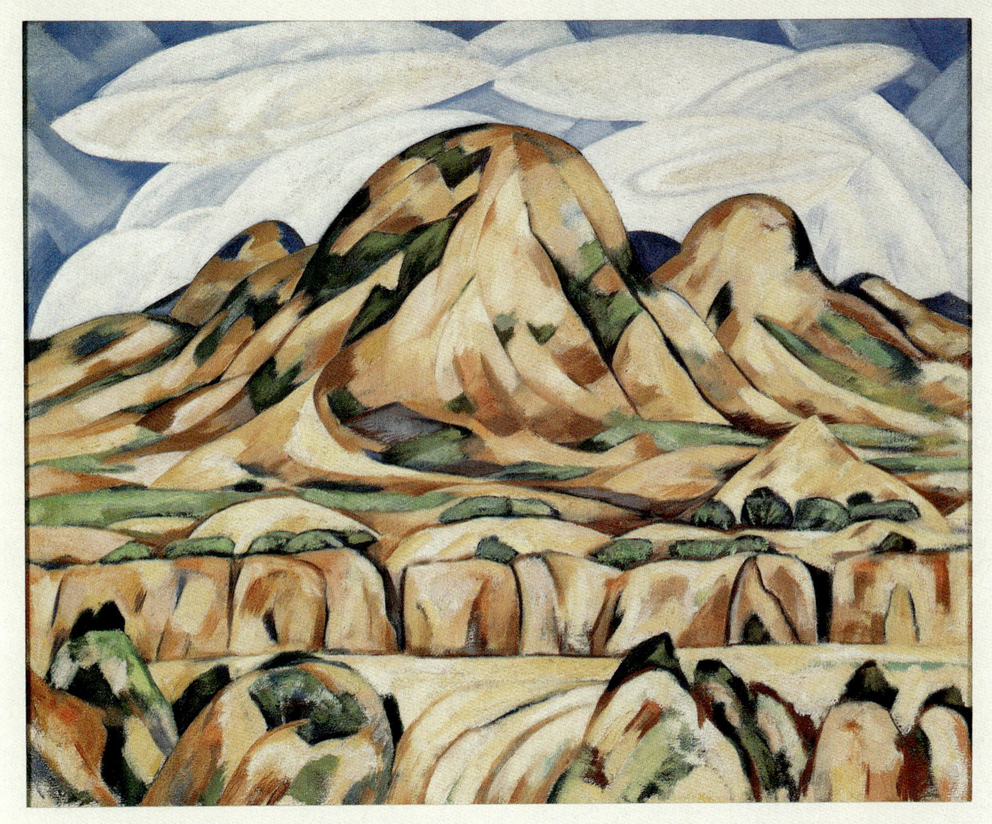

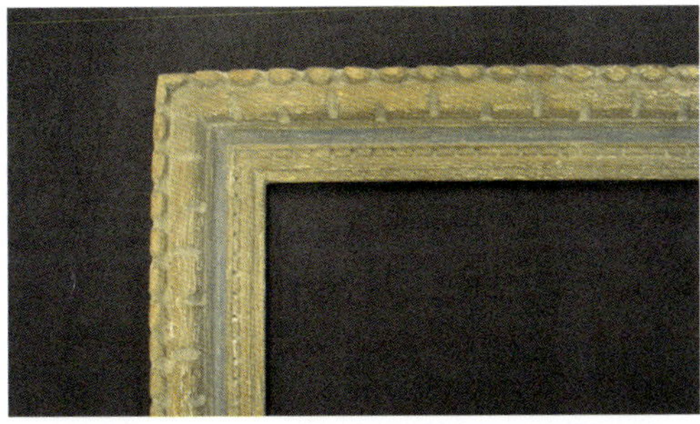

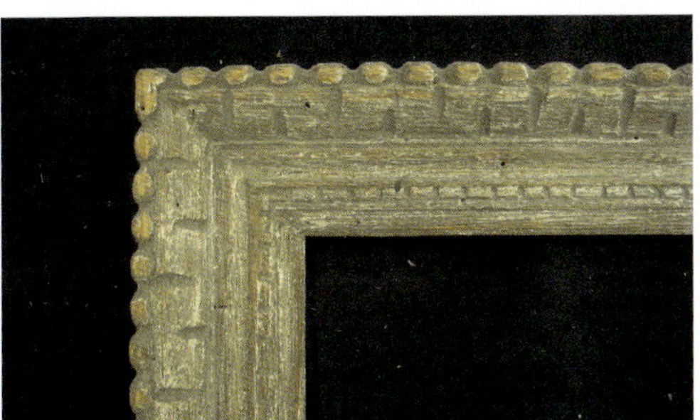

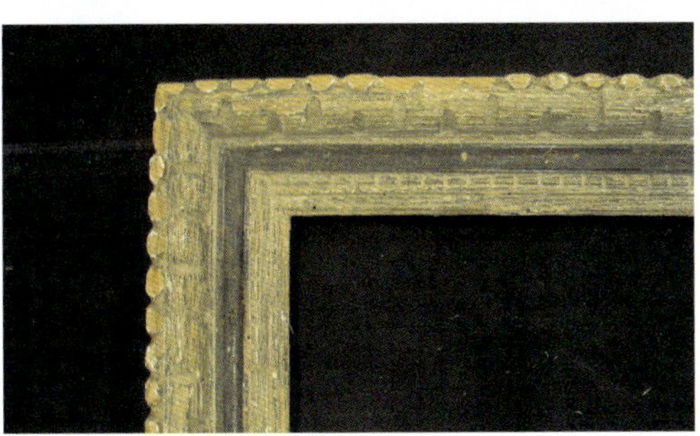

Figure 20
Three types of frame moldings designed by Henry Heydenryk for Hartley
Courtesy of The House of Heydenryk, New York

molding either washed or unpainted. The Garmisch-Partenkirchen paintings were framed rather sparingly. Hartley noted that the frame for *Nova Scotia Fishermen Mending Nets* (formerly IBM Collection) was made by "the local boat builder [who] made me a molding of mahogany—hand rubbed by myself."[46]

Correspondence and interviews suggest that Hartley's contentious personality may have affected his attitudes towards frames. When possible, he would purchase the most inexpensive ones: "the $6.00 ones are excellent and plenty good," he told Macbeth Gallery.[47] For his final showing at An American Place, Hartley bought "sixty, seventy and ninety cent (raw wood moldings) frames," causing Georgia O'Keeffe to refer to them as "a woodpile."[48] To accommodate Hartley, frames were sometimes borrowed for his paintings in an attempt to give them added presence, since he bitterly complained about the cost of a frame supposedly needed to sell a painting: "I can't give a $20 frame without recovering the cost."[49] Although he must have had a number of his European works framed, many pictures sent to his dealers were most likely not framed until they arrived. Both Hudson Walker and Stieglitz mention this.[50]

In 1937 Hartley had his last exhibition with Stieglitz and soon began to show with Hudson Walker. Once Walker became Hartley's dealer, he negotiated with Hartley to have his works framed in more massive frames with more presence. Since Hartley would have no part of paying for the frames, an agreement was reached that Walker would take a thirty percent commission rather than the customary twenty-five and would provide framing. The New York frame dealer Henry Heydenryk was very generous to artists and would lend them simple, standard-size artist exhibition frames. If the works were sold, Heydenryk would be reimbursed. If not, the frames would be returned. Hartley apparently liked the fact that his paintings looked "fully dressed,"[51] and eventually he settled on a molding type (fig. 20) designed for him by Heydenryk that complimented his late, rugged paintings. Most of his late works were framed for the Hudson Walker Gallery in a wormy chestnut

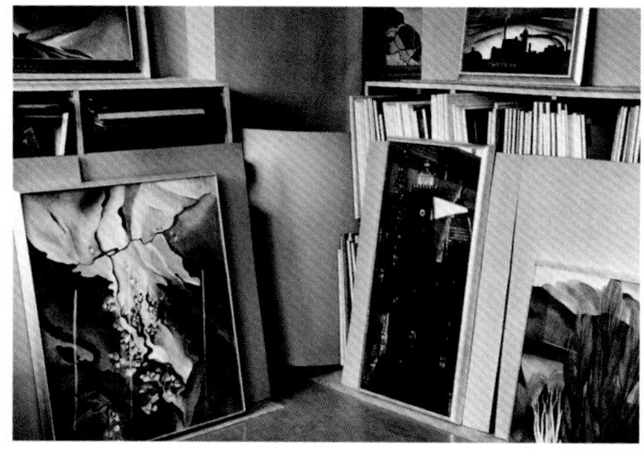

Figure 21
Unknown Photographer
Back room at An American Place
Photograph of the interior of the Stieglitz gallery, showing a variety of simple frame moldings
Yale Collection of American Literature
Beinecke Rare Book and Manuscript Library
Yale University, New Haven

wood, pickled to raise the grain and having a gray antiqued finish that became known as the "Hartley Decape Finish."[52] The rough, unrefined surface went well with his late primitive style. In many cases the frame had a cove molding and toothed edge and the molding was referred to as the model 385 series.[53] It was manufactured in either 3-inch or 5-inch widths and cost about twenty-five dollars for a 30 by 40 inch frame. After Walker closed his gallery in 1940, Hartley showed at the Macbeth Gallery, and eventually with Paul Rosenberg. He continued to use Heydenryk frames but slightly modified the profile to a flat inside rather than a scoop.[54]

Hartley was never opposed to framing but rather to the expense of it. His landmark painted frames reflect his sensitivity to their importance. Fortunately he painted during a time when the minimal, uniform Bauhaus lines of Stieglitz modernism (fig. 21) and his own frugality or stubbornness would allow him to frame in plain, simple moldings and still reflect the prevailing aesthetic. His strip frames were inexpensive versions of O'Keeffe's and Marin's that in many ways were characteristic of him as the "impoverished genius." Three months before Hartley died in 1943, he bought three hundred dollars' worth of frames from Henry Heydenryk. The bill was still outstanding at the time of his death.[55]

Notes

1 Hartley to Alfred Stieglitz, 1928, 1915, McCausland Papers, Archives/Smithsonian.

2 Hartley to Hudson Walker, 8 October 1938, describing *Nova Scotia Fishermen* (formerly IBM Collection). McCausland Papers, Archives/Smithsonian.

3 Hartley purchased pre-primed canvases on both trips from a variety of sources: French sources include Lucien Lefebvre-Foinet / 19 Rue Vavin & 2 Rue Brea; Fourtures D'Artistes / S. France / Nice—19 Rue Fastorelli / Nice; The Paris American Art Co. / 125 Bould. du Montparnasse & 2 Rue Bonaparte, Paris; in Germany, P. PickneFillale / Charlottenburg Hardenberger 13; Doris Ranfft / Genthinerstrasse 14; W. and J. Amler / Charlottenburg / Steinplatz 1339.

4 Hartley to Adelaide Kuntz, 2 February 1940, McCausland Papers, Archives/Smithsonian.

5 Rutherford J. Gettens and George L. Stout, *Painting Materials* (New York: D. Van Nostrand, 1942), 221.

6 F. Weber Co., Philadelphia, Pennsylvania.

7 *Catalogue of Weber Artist and Drawing Material* (New York: 1929), 38. A 22 by 28-inch academy board cost seventy-five cents. Hartley writes that his paintings could easily be transported by putting waxed paper between them when dry.

8 McCausland Papers, Archives/Smithsonian. The wallboard was "Beaver Board / Pure Wood Fibre," a soft laminated pasteboard made of wood pulp and/or waste paper. Alexander Katlin, letter to author, 1 July 2001. The lath laminate was patented as a building material and found limited use as an artist's material. It was sold as A. V. Benoit's / Composite / Artist Board.

9 Hartley to George F. Of, 1916, McCausland Papers, Archives/Smithsonian.

10 Hartley used hardboard, stamped "Genuine Masonite Presswood," as early as 1931–32 in *Masks* (Walker Art Center, Minneapolis) and 1934 in *Dogtown* (Frederick R. Weisman Art Museum, University of Minnesota, Minneapolis).

11 Masonite is made from wood chips separated by high-pressure steam and is made on platens with the aid of heat and high pressure, with the wood lignin acting as adhesive: Gettens and Stout, *Painting Materials*, 223. Tempered Masonite was treated with a water repellant material and did not afford an ideal painting surface.

12 Hartley to Hudson Walker, 8 February 1940, McCausland Papers, Archives/Smithsonian.

13 McCausland Papers, Archives/Smithsonian. Needless to say the glass was quite fragile. Hartley cut the bottom off *Red Chrysanthemum in Blue Vase*, owned by the artist Robert Laurant, when it broke.

14 McCausland Papers, Archives/Smithsonian. *Still Life with Pink Begonia* (1929; location unknown) on a beveled mahogany panel; *Still Life No. 8* (1920; location unknown) painted on a "Troo Tex Canvas / Made by Favoor Ruhl & Co / Grade No. 20—Medium / Pat. March 23, 1920; and *Santos, New Mexico* (plate 35).

15 McCausland Papers, Archives/Smithsonian. *Still Life No. 7* (1920; Weisman Art Museum, Minneapolis) on canvas board, *Still Life No. 9* (1920; location unknown) on Beaverboard, and a third untitled in the series on canvas.

16 Hartley (from Partenkirchen) to Norma Berger, December 1933, McCausland Papers, Archives/Smithsonian.

17 Hartley to Rebecca James, 7 March 1936, McCausland Papers, Archives/Smithsonian. Some non-commercially prepared supports are *Pears* (1911; Weisman Art Museum, Minneapolis), *Masks* (1931–32; Walker Art Center, Minneapolis), and possibly some of his Dogtown series painted on Masonite hardboard.

18 Catalogue from F. Weber and Co. The "rough" surface is really a finely stippled preparation.

19 Edge and reverse drips were examined under ultraviolet light. Shellac gives off a characteristic brilliant orange fluorescence. It was also scientifically tested by Susan Lake, conservator at the Hirshhorn Museum. Tempered hardboards had paraffin on the surfaces giving them a slick, paint-repelling surface. It was recommended that a layer of shellac or nitrocellulose lacquer be used as an isolating layer.

20 Hartley (from Berlin) to Alfred Stieglitz, 19 May 1915, and (from Bermuda) 1917, McCausland Papers, Archives/Smithsonian.

21 Hartley to Carl Sprinchorn, 17 February 1941,

describing a painting as "red jacket, ivory white, soft green." McCausland Papers, Archives/Smithsonian. In at least two paintings of the Dogtown series, one at the Weisman Art Museum and the second at Yale University Art Gallery, color notations are visible. An unfinished work owned by Babcock also has extensive color notes.

22 The bottles were labeled "Dr. Schoenfeld / Dusseldorf."

23 Dr. Henry de Philips, correspondence with author, March 2002.

24 "Artist's Thrift Pack" contains zinc white, cadmium barium red light, cadmium barium red medium, cadmium barium orange, and cadmium barium yellow medium.

25 Hartley to Hudson Walker, 1 February 1940, McCausland Papers, Archives/Smithsonian.

26 Elizabeth McCausland note, McCausland Papers, Archives/Smithsonian.

27 Ibid.

28 Ibid.

29 Paintings were examined using one or several of the following analytical tools: stereomicroscopy, X-radiography, infrared reflectography, UV fluorescence, SEM (scanning electron microscopy), FTIR (Fourier Transform Infrared Spectroscopy), and GC/MS (gas chromatography/mass spectrometry).

30 Gail R. Scott, "In Hartley's Studio," in Scott, 149–55.

31 Hartley to Norma Berger, December 1933, McCausland Papers, Archives/Smithsonian.

32 A colored glaze, size, or wash applied on top of a white ground to provide the initial tone for the design layer.

33 The waxy crayon was an obvious choice, as it was one of the few materials that would adhere to the smooth Masonite support sealed with shellac.

34 Once the composition was indicated by the preparatory drawing, Hartley rarely changed it in the painting process. Pentimenti are rare even in the late Maine paintings, where the underdrawing process was abbreviated.

35 Letter from Hudson Walker, 6 October 1943, McCausland Papers, Archives/Smithsonian, roll D268.

36 Hartley reduced the number of individual colors employed dramatically, and paint application became extremely sparse and dry.

37 Other paintings from the War Motif series show design changes, although X-radiography of the Wadsworth's *Military* (1913) reveals only some brush strokes done in vermilion red, which visually adds depth to the black imprimatura.

38 Between 1939 and 1943 the "new and fast" painting technique resulted in a very large number of paintings accomplished, and Hartley often worked on numerous paintings at the same time.

39 In 1926 Paul Strand described *El Santo* in a letter to Stieglitz. Gail Levin, "Photography's 'Appeal' to Marsden Hartley," *Yale University Library Gazette* 68 (1994): 23.

40 Inscription on academy board noted by Elizabeth McCausland, McCausland Papers, Archives/Smithsonian.

41 Ibid. Hartley sale at the Anderson Gallery.

42 Ibid. McCausland notes frames on *Berlin Series No. 2* (1912; location unknown) and *Indian Symbols* (1914; location unknown). She also notes same frame on *Landscape with Aquaduct, Vence* (1925; location unknown).

43 Ibid.

44 Ibid. Now owned by Fisk University, Nashville. They are presently in thin black frames. When McCausland saw *Movement No. 8*. An early photograph of the Metropolitan Museum's *Movement No. 5* shows it in a thin white frame also.

45 Unpublished interview by William Adair with Henry Heydenryk, 1981.

46 Hartley to Hudson Walker, 8 October 1938, McCausland Papers, Archives/Smithsonian.

47 "Marsden Hartley" (transcript of interview with Hudson Walker by Elizabeth McCausland and Mary Bartlett Cowdrey), *Journal of the Archives of American Art* 8 (January 1968): 19.

48 Ibid.

49 Ibid.

50 Ibid. Stieglitz said his assistant Zola brought out some early Hartleys, most of them not framed. Walker received a number of paintings. "When they arrived, the pictures were set around on the floor in our back gallery" (p. 17).

51 Interview with Charles Schreiber, president, The House of Heydenryk, July 2001. Also mentioned in Walker interview, 19.

52 Heydenryk interview. According to Bill Adair, "decape" derives from "decapitated," describing the breaking of the toothed edges of the frames.

53 Schreiber interview.

54 Ibid.

55 Walker interview, 19. At the time of his death, he also owed George Of four hundred dollars. Both debts were paid out of the Hartley estate.

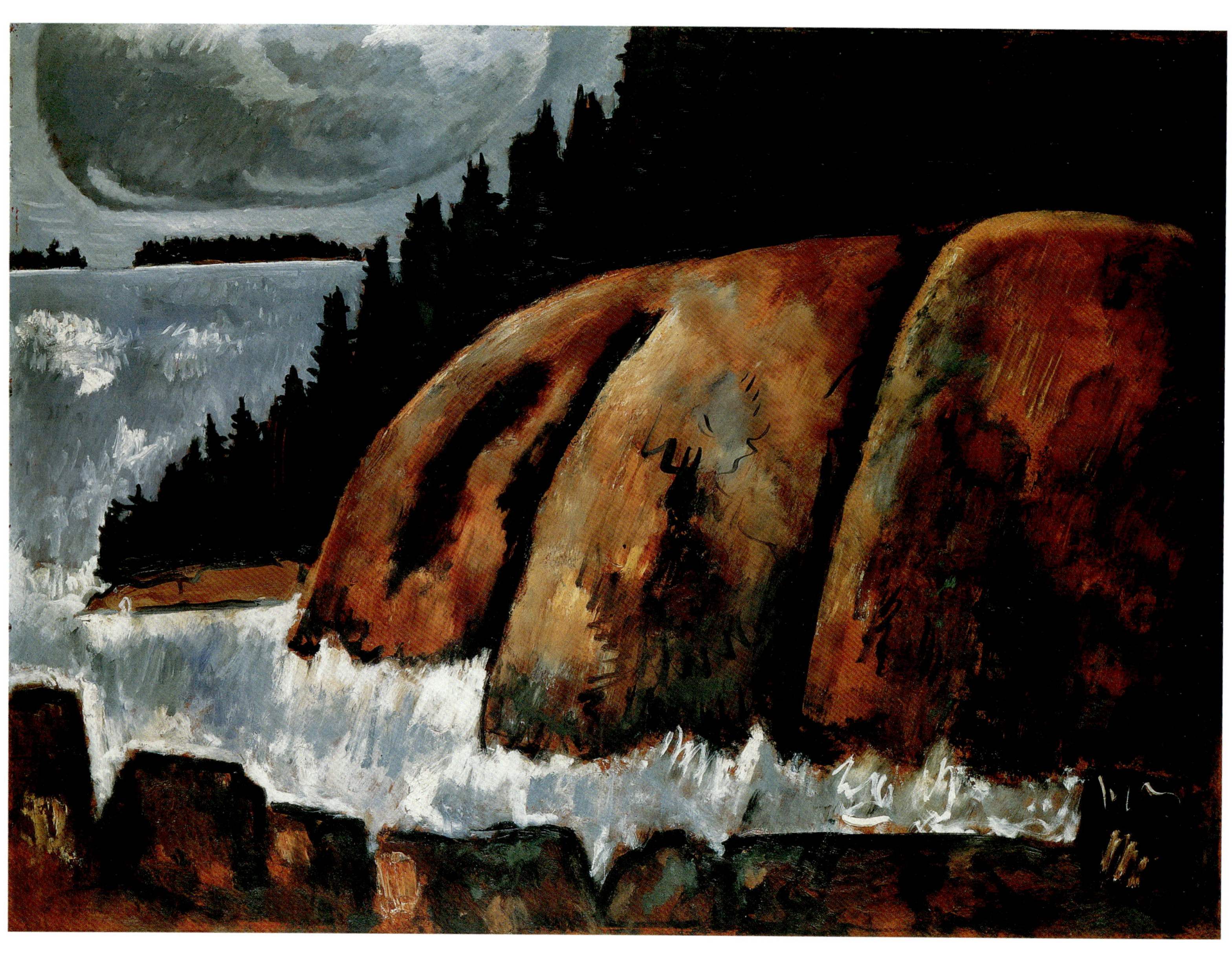

99
Hurricane Island, Vinalhaven, Maine, 1942
Oil on Masonite-type hardboard, 30 × 40¼ in.
Philadelphia Museum of Art
Gift of Mrs. Herbert Cameron Morris

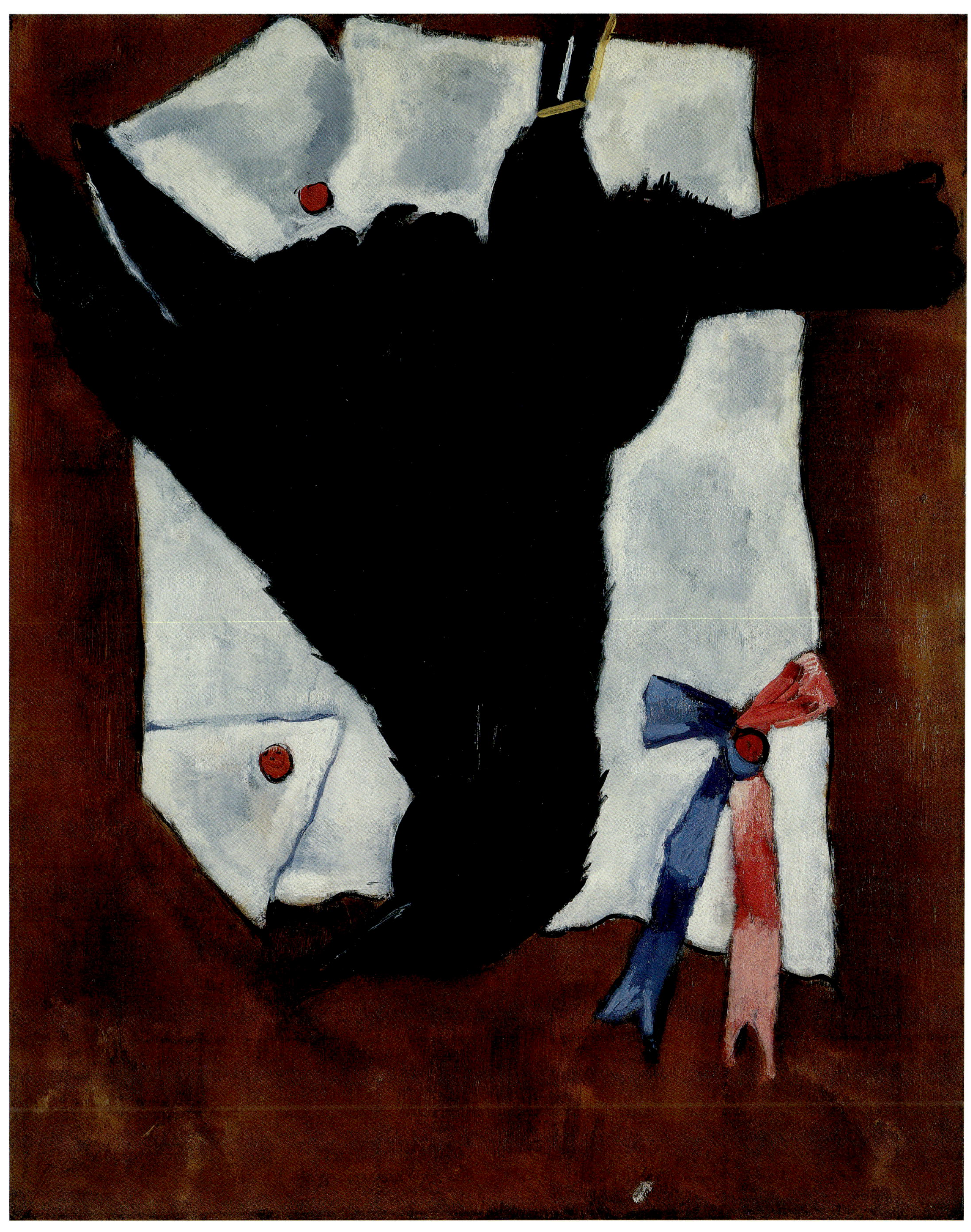

100

Crow with Ribbons, 1941

Oil on Masonite-type hardboard, 28 × 22 in.

Hirshhorn Museum and Sculpture Garden, Smithsonian Institution, Washington, D.C.

Gift of the Joseph H. Hirshhorn Foundation, 1966

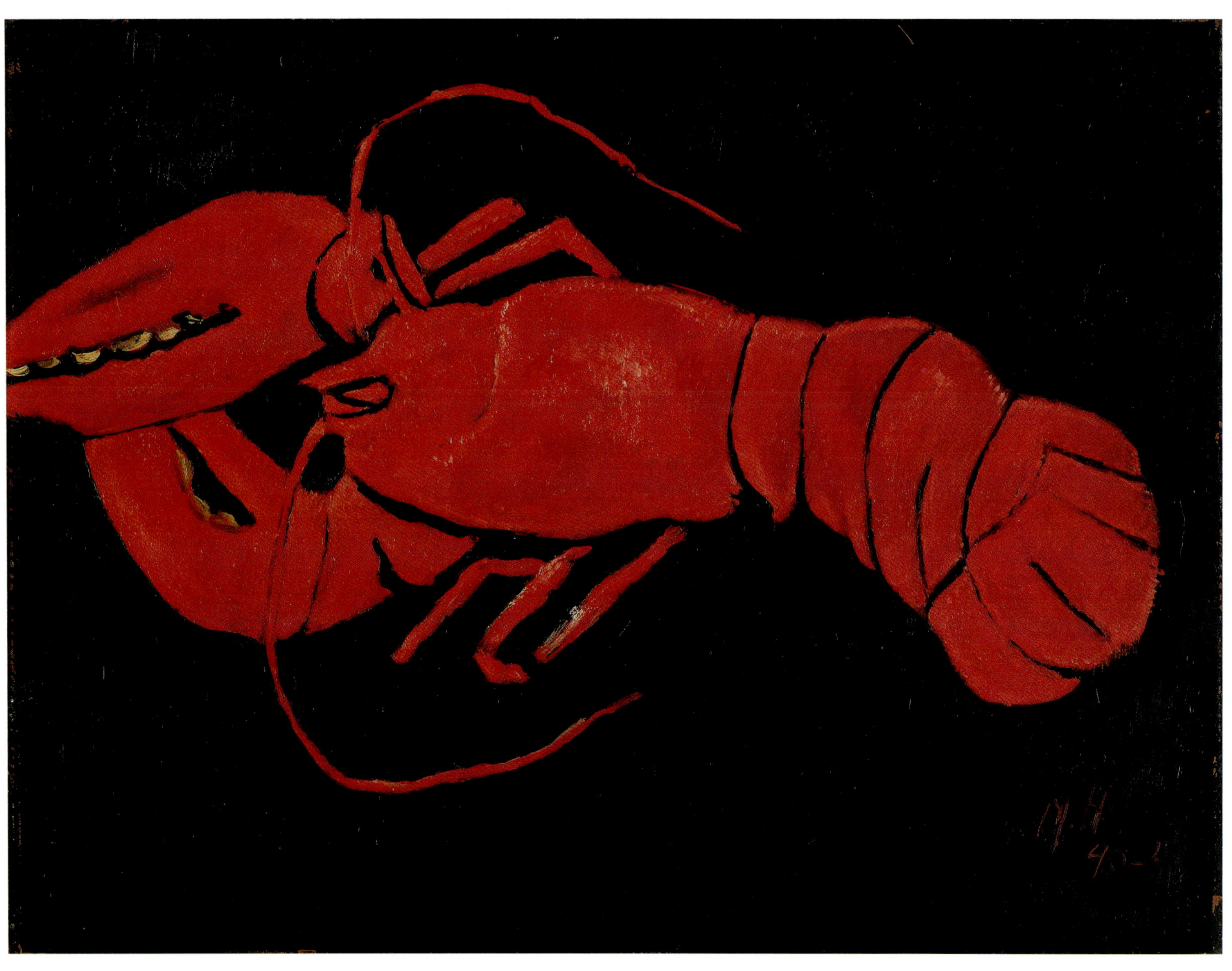

101

Lobster on Black Background, 1940–41
Oil on fiberboard, 22 × 28 in.
Smithsonian American Art Museum, Washington, D.C.
Gift of Mr. Henry P. McIlhenny

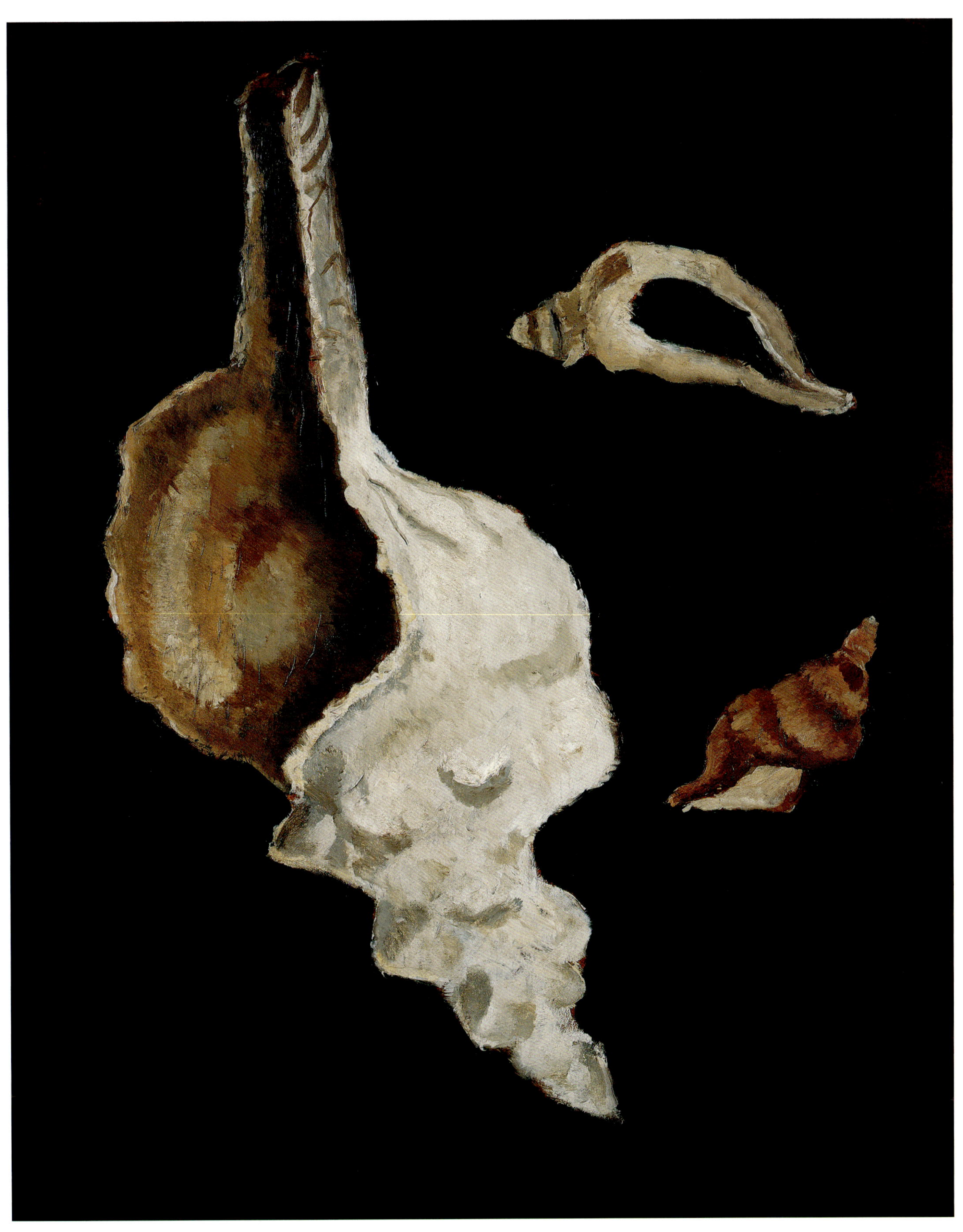

102
Shells by the Sea, c. 1941–43
Oil on Masonite, 28 × 22 in.
Private Collection
Courtesy of Babcock Galleries, New York

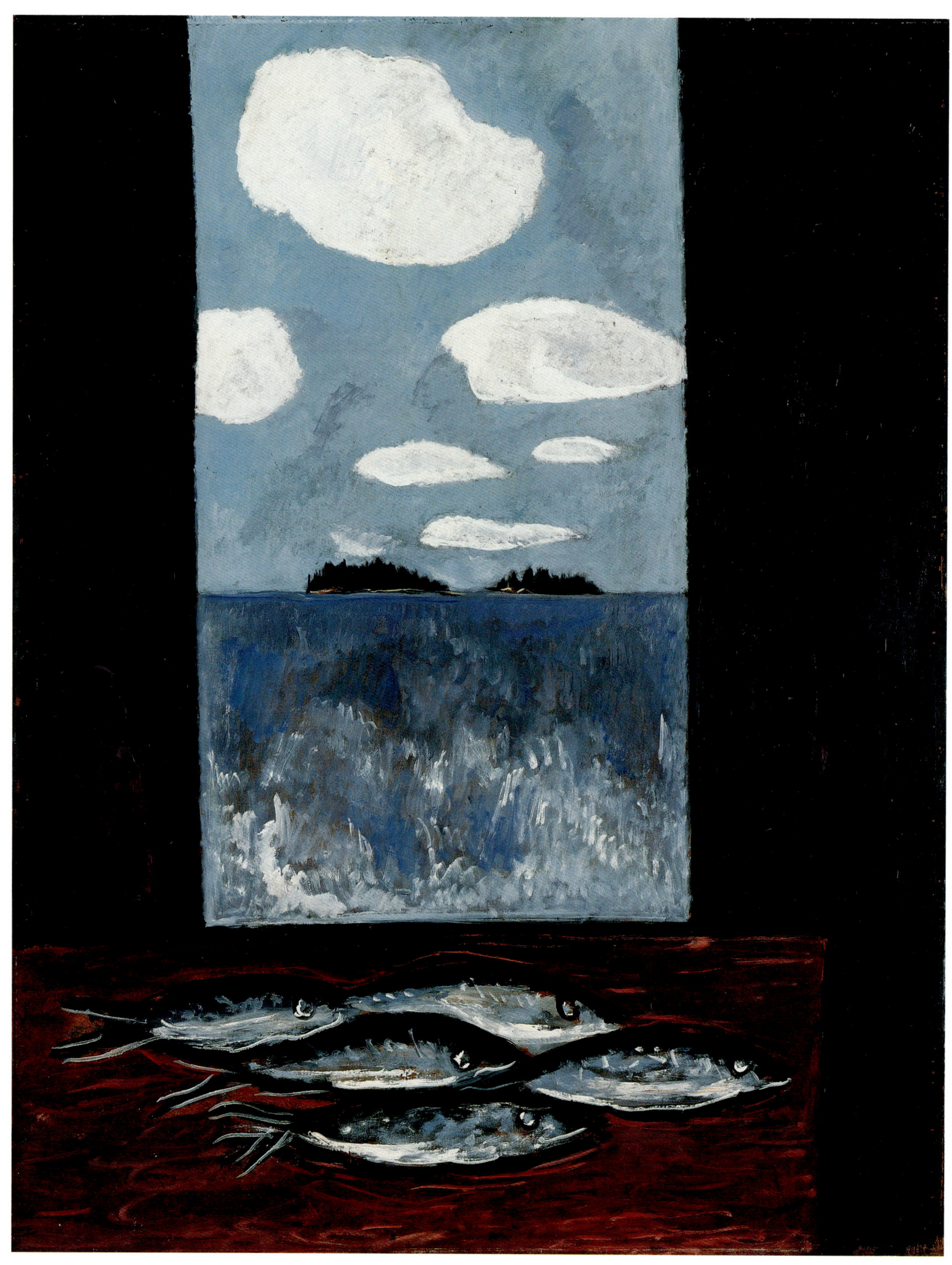

103
Sea Window—Tinker Mackerel, 1942
Oil on Masonite-type hardboard, 40 × 30 in.
Smith College Museum of Art, Northampton, Massachusetts
Purchased with the Sarah J. Mather Fund

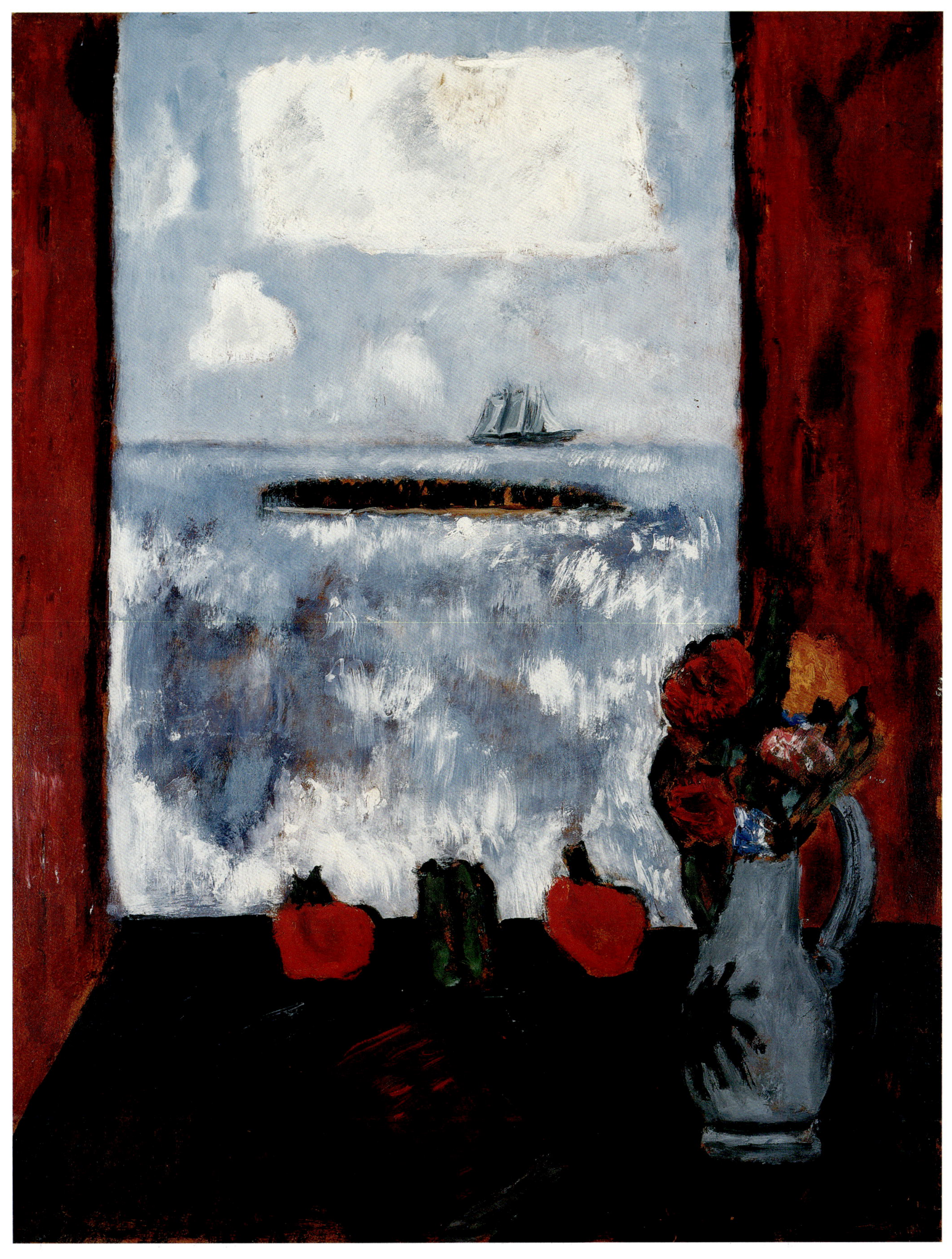

104
Summer, Sea, Window, Red Curtain, 1942
Oil on Masonite-type hardboard, 40⅛ × 30 7/16 in.
Addison Gallery of American Art, Phillips Academy,
Andover, Massachusetts

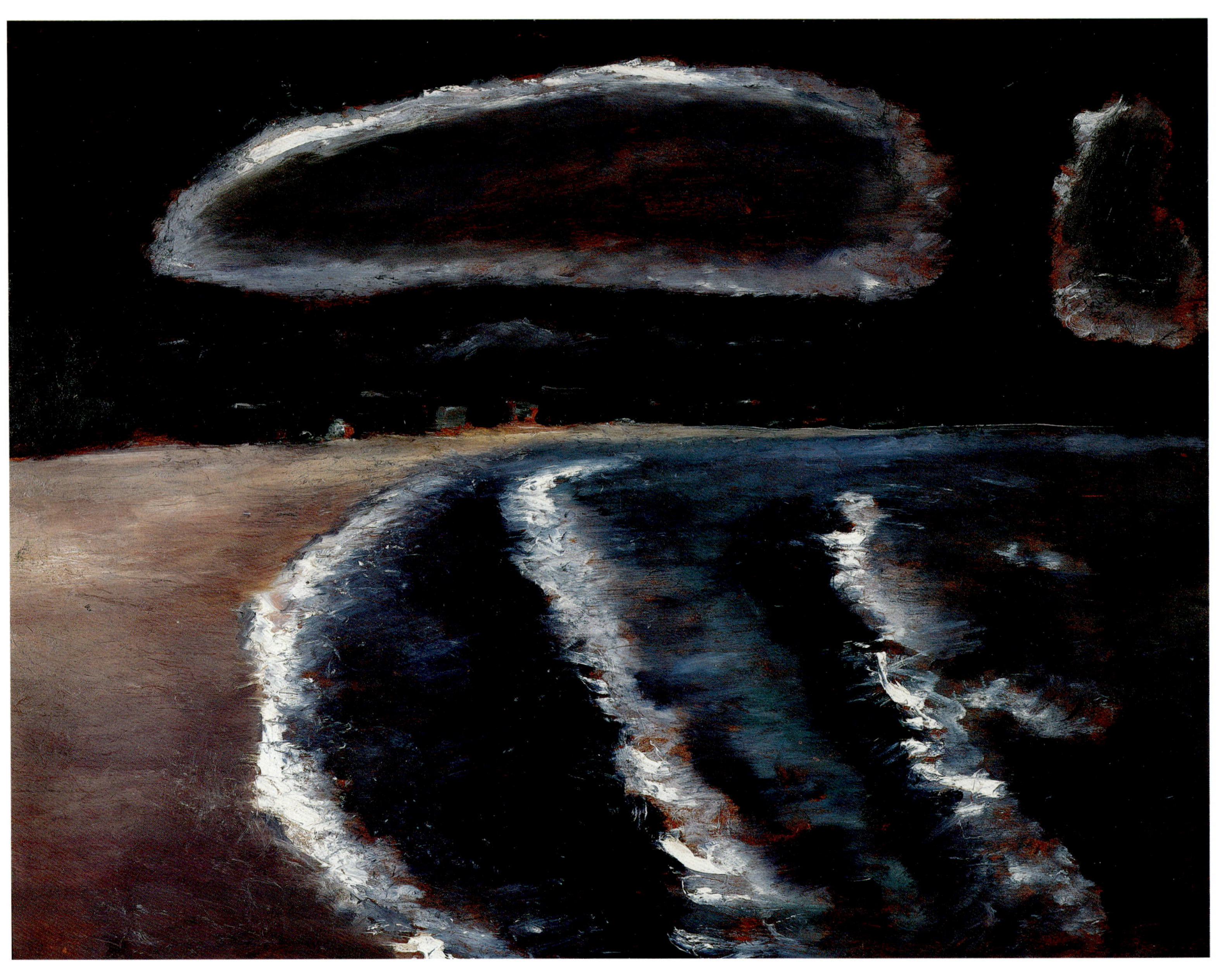

105
Storm Down Pine Point Way, Old Orchard, Maine, 1941–43
Oil on academy board, 22 × 28 in.
Shein Collection

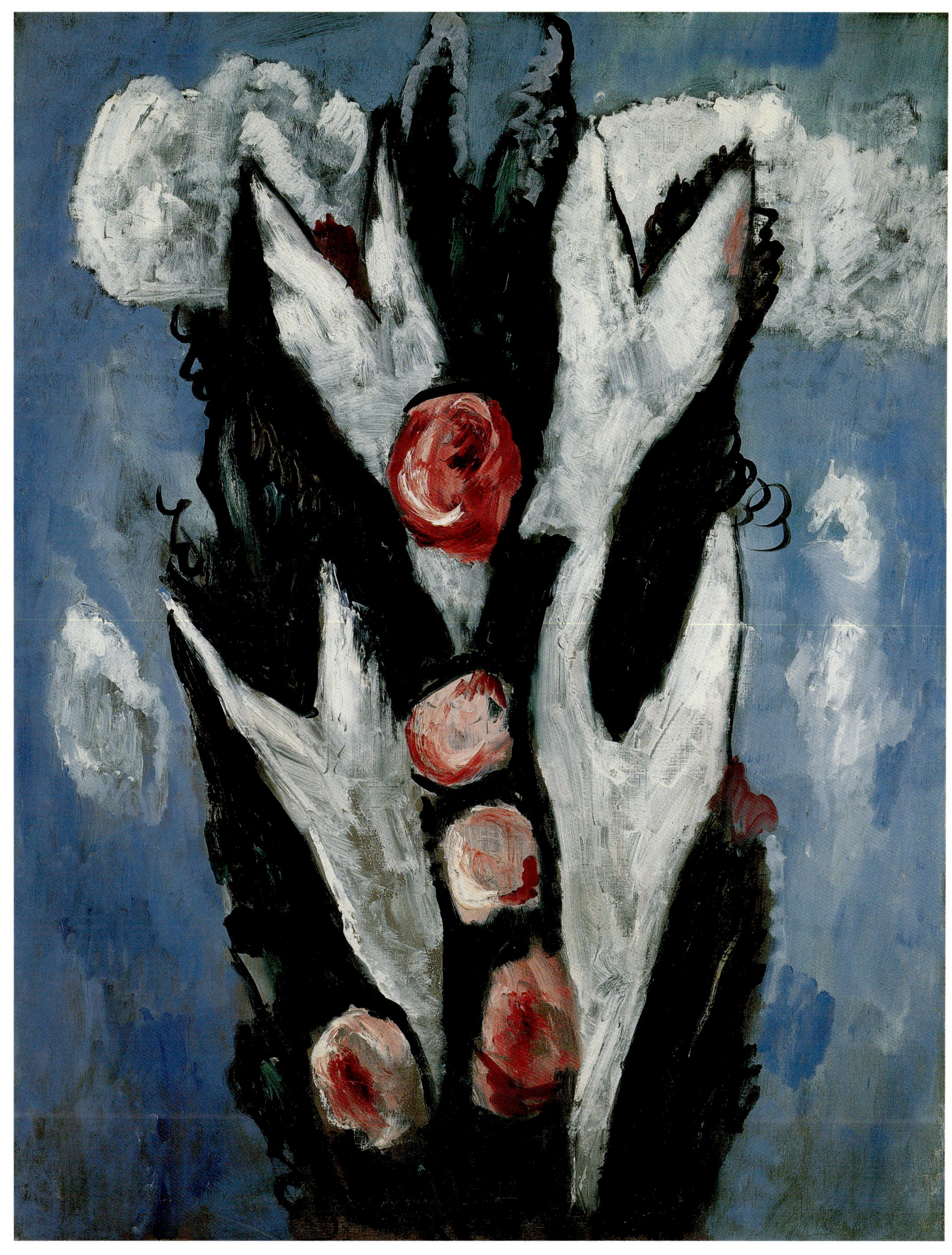

106

Roses, 1943

Oil on canvas, 40⅛ × 30⅛ in.

Walker Art Center, Minneapolis, Minnesota

Gift of Ione and Hudson D. Walker, 1971

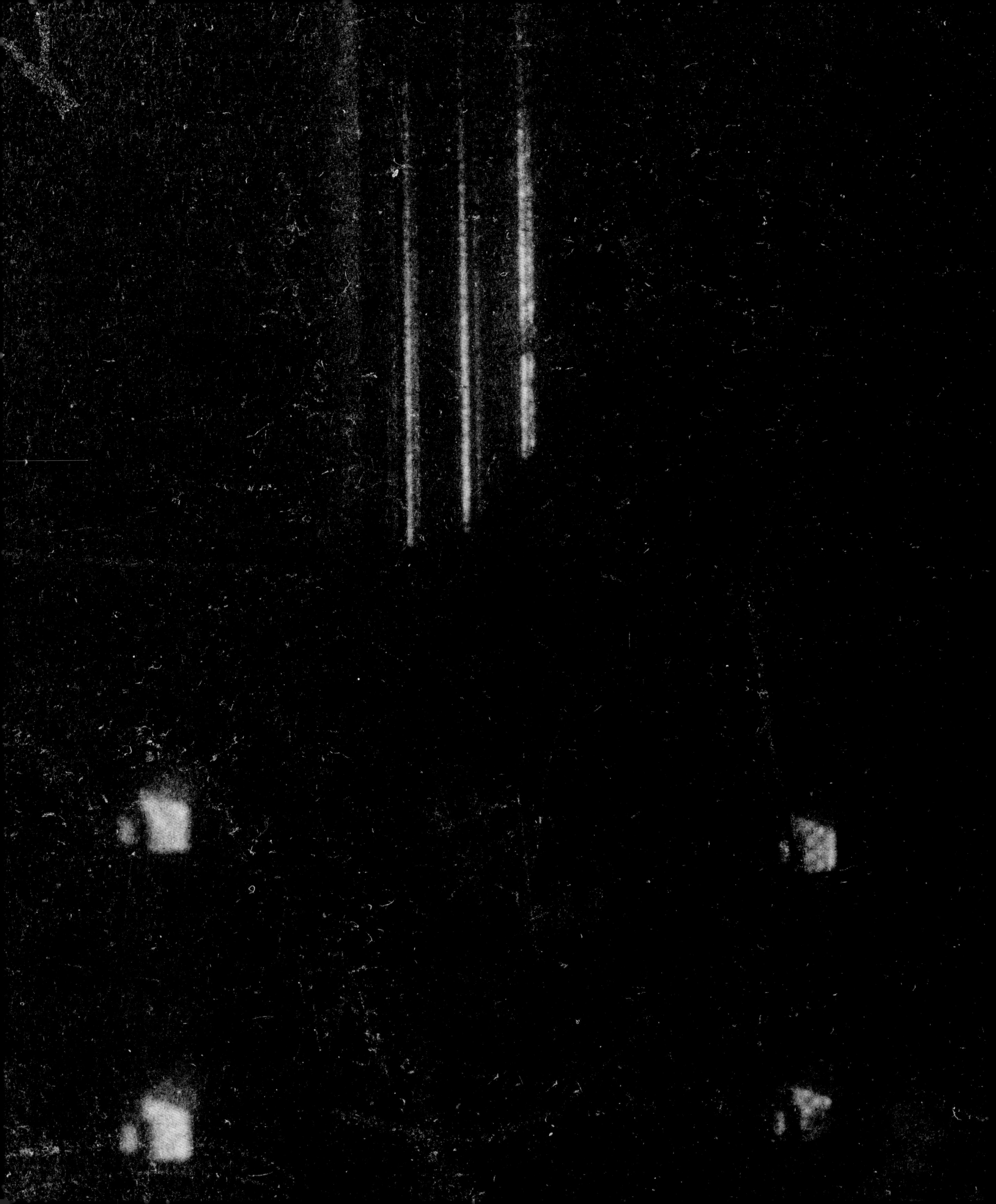

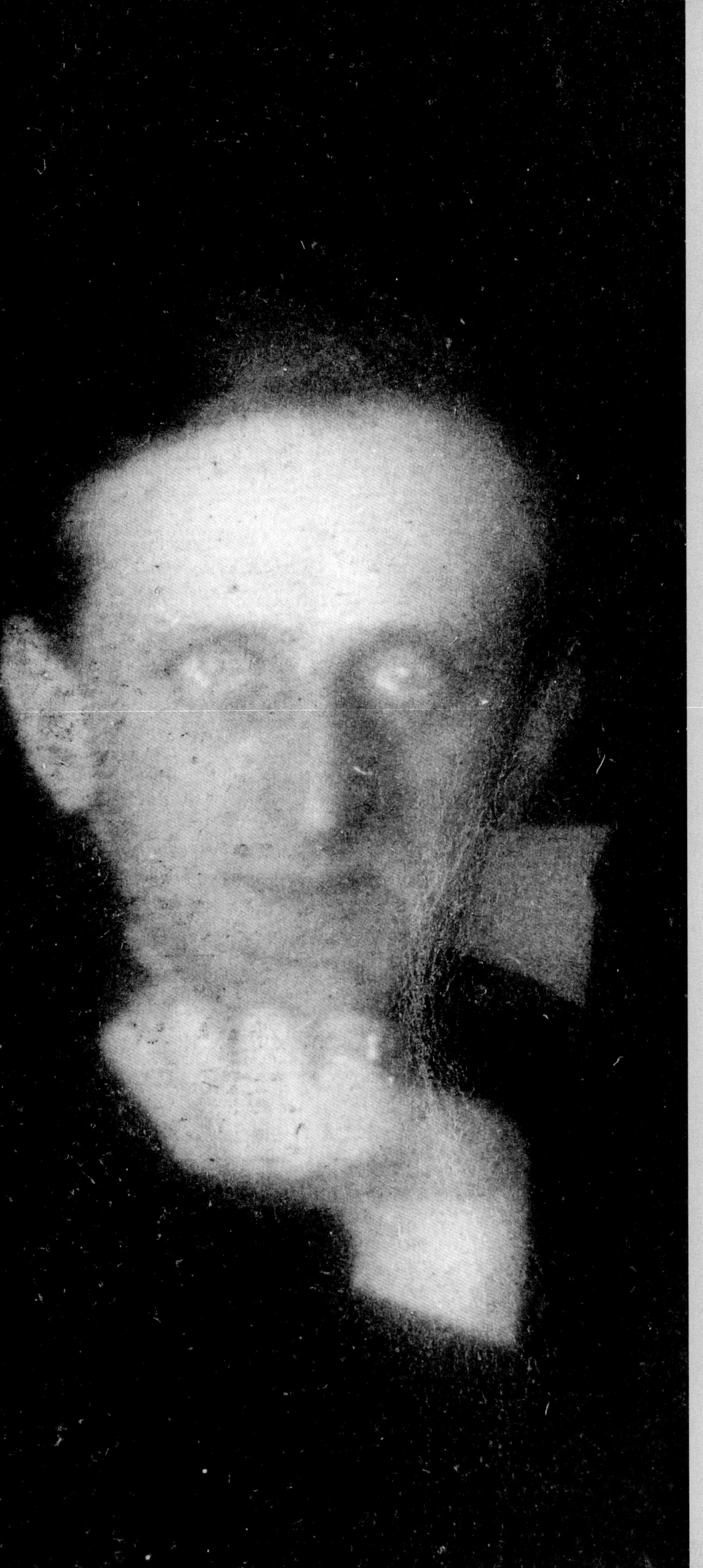

Catalogue Entries

Unknown Photographer
Marsden Hartley, c. 1905–1910
Yale Collection of American Literature, Beinecke Rare Book and Manuscript Library, Yale University

1

Walt Whitman's House, 328 Mickle Street, Camden, New Jersey, c. 1905
Oil on board, 10 × 8 in. (25.4 × 20.3 cm)
Unsigned

PROVENANCE
Mitchell Kennerley (owner Anderson Galleries, New York); Jo Davidson; W. Averill Harriman; private collection (acquired 1960 from Hammer Galleries)

Private Collection

Hartley's early admiration for the writings of Walt Whitman, which he shared with most American artists and writers of his generation, began around 1900 when he read poems from *Leaves of Grass,* and other writings. Hartley's earliest extant painting, *Walt Whitman's House,* honors his idol in a small somber depiction of Whitman's New Jersey town-house. In the second version of his autobiography, Hartley recalled: "I went over to Camden and did a small study of the Whitman house in Mickle Street which was used by Mitchell Kennerley in a frontispiece of a book on Whitman—the story of a woman who knew him—and which portrait is now in the possession of Jo Davidson the sculptor, so he told me when I met him not so long ago."[1]

Hartley was drawn to Whitman and his writings for many reasons including the fact that Whitman's poetry reinforced the transcendentalist beliefs that Hartley had absorbed from Emerson and Thoreau, and for its open expression of homosexuality. At this time, Hartley became a part of a group of Whitman followers, including Horace Traubel, Whitman's private secretary and his most devoted follower. Even at the time of his death, Hartley had a signed photograph of Whitman in his possession.[2] This small painting, which serves as an homage to an early idol, also symbolizes the importance that writing held for Hartley throughout his career. Hartley wrote an unpublished essay about Whitman's influence on a younger generation of artists, entitled "Peter Doyle and the Whitman Group," and wrote the essay "Whitman and Cézanne" for his acclaimed book *Adventures in the Arts* published in 1923.[3] By pairing Whitman with Cézanne, Hartley testified to the enduring importance of Whitman and Cézanne to his art, calling them the "two most notable innovators" in poetry and painting.[4] E.M.K

[1] *Autobiography,* 188. The frontispiece appears in Elizabeth Leavitt Keller, *Walt Whitman in Mickle Street* (New York: Mitchell Kennerley, 1921).
[2] Weinberg, 133.
[3] Marsden Hartley, "Vignettes—Peter Doyle," Hartley Papers, Archives/Smithsonian, reel 1368. In this essay, Hartley indicates that he painted a second version of Whitman's house, which remains unlocated.
[4] *Adventures* (1972), 30.

2

Storm Clouds, Maine, 1906–7
Oil on canvas, 30⅛ × 24¹⁵⁄₁₆ in. (76.5 × 73.3 cm)
Signed lower right: EDMOnD MarsDEN Hartley

PROVENANCE
Rosenberg–Hartley sale at Anderson Galleries, New York, May 17, 1921 (no. 48b); Mr. and Mrs. Otto Steiner, New York (purchased 1921); Mrs. Otto D. (Ruth W.) Steiner, New York (inherited 1925); Bertha Schaefer Gallery, New York (purchased 1948, as "Approaching Storm," then dated before 1909); Ione and Hudson Walker, Forest Hills, N.Y. (purchased 1948); Walker Art Center (gift, 1954, through the T. B. Walker Foundation; dated 1908)

Collection of Walker Art Center, Minneapolis
Gift of the T. B. Walker Foundation, Hudson Walker Collection, 1954

A view of Speckled Mountain in the town of Lovell, *Storm Clouds, Maine* is one of Hartley's earliest mature paintings and demonstrates his indebtedness to the Swiss-born artist Giovanni Segantini (1858–1899). Hartley was familiar with Segantini's work through the Munich periodical *Jugend,* which devoted an entire issue to the artist in January 1903.[1] From reproductions, Hartley discovered Segantini's distinctive "stitch" brush stroke and adopted it as his own in such works as *Storm Clouds, Maine* and *Carnival of Autumn* (plate 3).

The Segantini "stitch" is most easily seen in the trees covering the mountain in *Storm Clouds, Maine.* Short brush strokes placed next to each other create a stitch-like texture across the mountainside. A variation in the color of individual strokes delineates the pattern the sun makes as it shines through a break in the storm clouds.

In 1932 Hartley wrote "On the Subject of the Mountain: Letter to Messieurs Segantini and Hodler," acknowledging the importance Segantini held for him with regard to one of his favorite subjects: "In the beginning of my own negligible career Mons. Segantini, it was you who gave me my first true insight into the mountain in general, and my own mountains in particular.... I have at least felt that you understood so thoroughly the THING-ness of things, causing the mere human soul to penetrate the substance of everything, touching a kind of height which is even almost physical. The geological reality alone of the mountain makes it bear heavily on one's senses, a terrific force pressing down upon one's center and shaking one with its vital energies."[2] Hartley was preoccupied with the mountain as a subject for his painting throughout his career. A.E.

[1] Hokin, 9.
[2] Marsden Hartley, "On the Subject of the Mountain: Letter to Messieurs Segantini and Hodler" (1932), reprinted in Hokin, 136. See also Lucy Flint-Gohlke, catalogue entry for *Storm Clouds, Maine* in Martin L. Friedman, et al., *Walker Art Center: Painting and Sculpture from the Collection* (New York: Rizzoli International Publications, Inc., in association with the Walker Art Center, 1990), 221.

3

Carnival of Autumn, 1908

Oil on canvas, 30¼ × 30⅛ in. (76.8 × 76.5 cm)

Inscribed on verso: Carneval [*sic*] of Autumn—1908 / Marsden Hartley

PROVENANCE

Alfred Stieglitz, New York; Estate of Alfred Stieglitz; Ione and Hudson Walker, Forest Hills, N.Y. (purchased 1949); Museum of Fine Arts, Boston (purchased 1968 through Babcock Galleries, New York)

Museum of Fine Arts, Boston
The Hayden Collection
Charles Henry Hayden Fund, 1968

4

The Ice-Hole, Maine, 1908–9

Oil on canvas, 34 × 34 in. (86.3 × 86.3 cm)

Inscribed on verso in black paint: Marsden Hartley

PROVENANCE

Rosenberg–Hartley sale at Anderson Galleries, New York, May 17, 1921 (no. 31); Mrs. Elsie W. Dewald, New York (purchased 1921); with Bertha Schaefer Gallery, New York (1954); New Orleans Museum of Art

New Orleans Museum of Art
Museum purchase; Ella West Freeman Matching Fund

Carnival of Autumn and *The Ice-Hole, Maine* belong to a group of ten seasonal views of the same mountains near North Lovell, Maine. Alfred Stieglitz showed these two paintings (along with others of the group) at his gallery 291 from 8 to 18 May, 1909. This was Hartley's first exhibition in New York City. The exhibition received good reviews, with one critic commenting: "the plastic modeling and faithful detail, the hardiness and vigor of representation, showed knowledge of form and sincerity of sentiment," and Hartley's use of color "produced a strictly physical sensation. It irritated the retina and exhausted it. After leaving the gallery, Fifth Avenue looked more grey than usual."[1]

The influence of Swiss-born artist Giovanni Segantini is readily apparent in *Carnival of Autumn* and *The Ice-Hole, Maine* (see also plate 2). Hartley had seen reproductions of Segantini's work in the Munich periodical *Jugend.* In his autobiography, *Somehow a Past,* Hartley wrote, "Living as [Segantini] did so close to his Alps in the Engadine up Sils-Maria way, he had invented a new type of impressionistic brush coupled with a graphic application, so that his pictures were peculiarly 'life-like' regardless even of a certain mysticism that invested them—for it was the age of '*les symbolistes.*' It seemed I got to work then after seeing this coloured print and produced a flood of canvases quite large with a direct sense of the topography of the scene which I had studied intimately—sufficiently well for a New York art critic of a later time to say, after he had gone through that country, 'there are Hartley's all over the hills.'"[2]

What is different from Segantini's work, however, is Hartley's composition. Hartley's mountains are close to the picture plane, particularly in a work like *Carnival of Autumn,* and the landscapes are without human presence. Even in a canvas like *The Ice-Hole,* in which there is evidence of human activity, the ice fishermen are absent.[3] A.E.

1 Charles Caffin, "Unphotographic Paint," *Camera Work* 28 (October 1909): 20; quoted in Hokin, 21.
2 *Autobiography,* 187. Paul Rosenfeld was the art critic.
3 Robertson, 22.

5

Self-Portrait as a Draughtsman, 1908–9

Crayon on paper, 12 × 9 in. (30.5 × 22.9 cm)

Signed lower left: Marsden Hartley

PROVENANCE

M. Knoedler and Co., Inc., New York (by 1945); Allen Memorial Art Museum

Allen Memorial Art Museum, Oberlin College, Ohio
Gift of the Oberlin College Class of 1945

Beginning in about 1908, Hartley made many self-portraits that are composed of a series of agitated strokes in pencil or crayon. These expressionistic drawings take the Segantini stitch of his landscape paintings one step further and convey the intense energy and even desperate anxiety he brought to all his creative output.[1]

As Bruce Robertson has noted, Hartley began drawing self-portraits at the same time that he was creating his first mature paintings (see plates 3–4 and essay by Bruce Robertson). That same year, 1908, he settled on his artistic identity, dropping his first name, Edmund, to be known simply as Marsden Hartley, using his stepmother's name that he had previously assumed as his middle name. A.E.

1 See Haskell, 17; Scott, 21; Robertson, 22.

6

Deserted Farm, 1909

Oil on fiberboard, 24 × 20 in. (61 × 50.8 cm)

Signed lower left: Marsden Hartley

PROVENANCE

Charles Daniel Gallery, New York; Robert Laurent, Brooklyn, N.Y., and Ogunquit, Maine; Paul Rosenfeld, New York; Ione and Hudson Walker, Forest Hills, N.Y. (purchased 1945); University Gallery (now Weisman Art Museum; gift, 1962)

Frederick R. Weisman Art Museum,
University of Minnesota, Minneapolis
Gift of Ione and Hudson Walker

Deserted Farm is one of a series of landscapes called the Black or Dark Landscapes exhibited by Alfred Stieglitz in his gallery 291 in 1910. These paintings were inspired by the work of Albert Pinkham Ryder (see plate 71), which Hartley saw at the N. E. Montross Gallery in New York. Hartley wrote about his Dark Landscapes in his autobiography, *Somehow a Past:* "The next pictures I did were solely from memory and the imagination, of which there were only four or five—those which later became known as the 'black landscapes.'"[1]

Hartley's turn from painting the brightly colored, Segantini-inspired landscape *Carnival of Autumn* of the previous year (see plate 3) to the dark palette of the "black landscapes" may also have been due in part to the depressed mood Stieglitz attributed to him.[2] However, Hartley described this time in his life as one of productivity, despite his poverty:

> *Ryder's spirit lived intensely in me—and as I say I did the four or five black landscapes of that year in [the etcher Ernest] Roth's room. I was mourning I had no place to work for I only had a cold hall bedroom. Roth said, "If you think you can work there"—pointing to a chest against the wall—"it's all right with me." I was sure I could because Roth always had a good effect on me. I am sure he never knew it, but it is one of the silent things that make men get together and like each other—and I liked Roth and had great respect for his ardour and his indefatigable gift of industry. And so that winter the dark landscapes were done.*[3]

The mountain dominates the deserted farm at its foot in this painting. As Jeanne Hokin has shown, mountains were a career-long preoccupation for Hartley; he painted many and he painted them often. Hokin points out that while Ryder's subject matter was literary or mythological, Hartley's was personal: he took the bleak Maine landscape of his youth as his subject. However, Hartley was to transform this same landscape yet again, only a year later, in 1910, by reintroducing the vibrant palette of the earlier landscapes (plate 3).[4] A.E.

1 *Autobiography,* 67–68. Stieglitz referred to them as "dark mountain paintings."
2 Haskell, 18.
3 *Autobiography,* 71.
4 Hokin, 23–28. Entries on *Deserted Farm* can be found in Lyndel King, *Marsden Hartley, 1908–1942: The Ione and Hudson D. Walker Collection* (Minneapolis: University Art Museum, University of Minnesota, 1984), 16, and *American Paintings and Sculpture in the University Art Museum Collection* (Minneapolis: University of Minnesota, 1986), 148–50.

7

Still Life, 1912
Oil on fiberboard, 32⅛ × 25⅝ in. (81.6 × 65.1 cm)
Unsigned

PROVENANCE
Alfred Stieglitz, New York; Ione and Hudson Walker, Forest Hills, N.Y. (purchased 1940); University Gallery (now Weisman Art Museum; bequest, 1978)

Frederick R. Weisman Art Museum, University of Minnesota, Minneapolis
Bequest of Hudson Walker from the Ione and Hudson Walker Collection

The critic Gail Levin believes this to be Hartley's first painting after arriving in Paris in 1912.[1] Certainly it is one of his first, reflecting his growing fascination with the work of Cézanne and Matisse, both of whom he had emulated even before traveling abroad. Barbara Haskell has remarked that the painting "fused Cézanne's composition and structural approach with the palette and decorative emphasis of Matisse."[2]

A well-wrought work, it reveals Hartley's ability to draw from other painters as he worked toward his own styles. That he should emulate Cézanne reflects his respect for the French artist and his ideas, which would continue to influence Hartley throughout much of his career. Elements in the painting such as primitive fabrics and the suggestion of an African background suggest his interest in artifacts he would have seen at the Musée de l'Homme, the museum of anthropology in Paris that influenced Picasso. T.L.

1 Gail Levin, "Wassily Kandinsky and the American Avant-Garde, 1912–1950" (Ph.D. dissertation, Rutgers University, 1976), 80.
2 Haskell, 26.

8

Musical Theme (Oriental Symphony), 1912–13
Oil on canvas, 39⅜ × 31¼ in. (100 × 79.4 cm)
Unsigned

PROVENANCE
Alfred Stieglitz, New York (1913–16); John Quinn, New York (1916–24; as "Oriental Symphony"); Estate of John Quinn, New York (1924–27); auction at American Art Association, New York, 1927; Samuel Lustgarten, Chicago, and Sherman Oaks, Calif. (1927–52); Rose Art Museum (from 1952)

Rose Art Museum, Brandeis University, Waltham, Massachusetts
Gift of Samuel Lustgarten, Sherman Oaks, California

In Paris in 1912 Hartley moved quickly toward cubism, influenced by Cézanne, Matisse, and increasingly Picasso. Gertrude Stein, whom he came to know that summer, approved of his first "mystical abstractions," as he called his new work. Equally important were his readings of Wassily Kandinsky's *On the Spiritual in Art* and *Der Blaue Reiter,* the almanac published by several German expressionist artists centered in Munich. He remarked to Alfred Stieglitz about the importance of Picasso's gift of "visualizing his sensations." That and other art he was seeing were causing him to feel "certain spiritual metamorphoses taking place." And he added, "I find growing in me and I think to more purpose—a recurrence of former religious aspirations—taking finer form in personal expression."[1]

Der Blaue Reiter focused on spiritual matters. August Macke, for example, wrote that "form is a mystery to us for it is the expression of mysterious powers. Only through it do we sense the secret powers, the 'invisible God.'" In the almanac was also an essay by Arnold Schoenberg about mystical expression in music.[2]

By late 1912 when he was beginning what came to be referred to as his Musical Theme series, the forces that would produce his first major works had already converged in him. These were the works of various mystics such as R. M. Bucke, Jacob Böhme, and Johannes (Meister) Eckhardt; the philosopher

Henri Bergson; American transcendentalists, particularly Emerson; and of course modern artists such as Cézanne, Matisse, Picasso, and, to a lesser extent, others of the European avant-garde.

He was "trying to express my emotions of the cosmic scene in general," he wrote Rockwell Kent in December 1912. He believed that his new work was a radical departure from cubism. His aim was "to present a sensation of cosmic bodies in harmony with each other by means of color & form." He was certain he diverged from Kandinsky because of the mystical element in his paintings, and he believed that he was "probably the first to contribute this mystical element to the modern movement." When he wrote Kent from Paris, he was looking at the paintings that lay on the floor of his studio. "They look," he explained,

> *like a conclave of universal elements confiding in one another—things that look like stars—birds' wings sun rays—suns themselves at the sundown time—moon shapes and star beams all radiant together. It is a kind of cosmic dictation applied aesthetically to produce a harmony of shapes & colors—with a sense also of the color of sound as I get these feelings out of music.*[3]

The passage is an excellent description of his intentions, although it does not mention the specifically spiritual and musical symbols in *Musical Theme.* While the shapes in the painting are delineated clearly, his thin application of paints keeps any one from dominating another. Musical staffs, clefs, eight-pointed stars, hieroglyphic marks, a sitting Buddha, and three hands folded so as to signify the Indian religious gesture meaning "have no fear" combine to achieve what Hartley termed "intuitive abstraction," the "cosmic cubism" he sought. T.L.

[1] Hartley to Alfred Stieglitz, 31 October 1912, Beinecke/Yale.
[2] *The Blaue Reiter Almanac,* ed. Wassily Kandinsky and Franz Marc; English edition ed. Klaus Lankheit (New York: Viking, 1974), 85 (Macke quotation).
[3] Hartley to Rockwell Kent, 24 December 1912, Kent Papers, Archives/Smithsonian.

9

Portrait Arrangement No. 2, 1912–13
Oil on canvas, 39½ × 31¾ in. (100.3 × 80.7 cm)
Unsigned

PROVENANCE
Babcock Galleries, New York; private collection

Private Collection
Courtesy of Babcock Galleries, New York

This painting might be considered in the same series as *Musical Theme* (plate 8) because in several ways it is so similar: the application of paint, the colors used, some of the shapes, the three overlapping spheres, and the hand forming an Indian religious gesture. But much is different, and *Portrait Arrangement No. 2* can justifiably be seen to be an important transitional work in which Hartley was still drawing from his Musical Theme series but was at the same time moving toward his next paintings such as *The Warriors,* which celebrates the military pomp and circumstance he relished about Berlin shortly before World War I.

In this painting the lines and forms clearly lead the eye upward and toward the small portrait of a soldier in white on a white horse. Some critics have suggested that this might be the young German officer Karl von Freyburg, whom Hartley had first met in Paris shortly after his arrival, and with whom he fell in love during the following months in France and Germany. But rather than being von Freyburg specifically, the figure is more representative of the officer corps generally, whose dress uniforms, order, and masculinity thrilled Hartley. The most elite of the Kaiser's regiments, the Garde du Corps, was the "First Regiment of Christianity." They were the only ones to wear white. Von Freyburg's regiment wore dress black.

Everything in the painting points toward the soldier on horseback, and everything is about Hartley's devout wish that the soldier and all others "have no fear" and that their world be one of harmony—the number 3, symbolized in the foreground by three interlocked spheres inside a larger one, over which are three lines reaching outward symmetrically, symbolizes spiritual unity and harmony. Further up and behind these are the upper parts of seven spheres, counting the one to the extreme right of the painting. Seven, as Hartley knew, symbolizes perfect order and completeness. The hand might be the hand of God made corporeal, an idea that Hartley drew from the German mystic Jakob Böhme, for whom the seventh realm of divine corporeality was where he found himself in the greatest contemplation of joy, hence in the greatest harmony. Hartley would use the idea of the seven spheres and God's hand made corporeal again; his 1932 painting *Morgenrot* (plate 52) vividly renders these same mystical symbols. T.L.

10

Portrait of Berlin, 1913
Oil on canvas, 39¼ × 39⅜ in. (99.7 × 100 cm)
Unsigned

PROVENANCE
Alfred Stieglitz, New York; Mabel Dodge (Luhan), New York (from 1914); Yale Collection of American Literature (from 1951)

Yale Collection of American Literature
Beinecke Rare Book and Manuscript Library
Yale University, New Haven
Gift of Mabel Dodge Luhan to the Collection of American Literature, University Library

11

The Warriors, 1913

Oil on canvas, 47½ × 47¼ in. (120.6 × 120 cm)

Unsigned

PROVENANCE

Estate of the artist (no. 250, dated 1914); Max Zurier, Palm Springs, Calif. (purchased 1959 through Paul Rosenberg & Co., New York); Curtis Galleries, Minneapolis, Minn.; private collection

Private Collection

12

Military, 1913

Oil on canvas, 39¼ × 39¼ in. (99.7 × 99.7 cm)

Inscribed in blue crayon on back of original frame (now lost): Military, 1913 / H 44

PROVENANCE

Rosenberg–Hartley sale at Anderson Galleries, New York, May 17, 1921 (no. 44, as "Pre-War Pageant, 1913"); Alfred Stieglitz, New York (by 1944; as "Brass Band with Numbers"); Estate of Alfred Stieglitz; Ione and Hudson Walker, Forest Hills, N.Y. (purchased 1949); Berta Walker, New York; Babcock Galleries, New York (from 1971); Wadsworth Atheneum Museum of Art (from 1973; purchased through Peter H. Davidson and Co., Inc., New York)

Wadsworth Atheneum Museum of Art, Hartford
The Ella Gallup Sumner and Mary Catlin Sumner Collection Fund

13

Himmel, c. 1914–15

Oil on canvas with painted frame, 47⅜ × 47⅜ in. (120.3 × 120.3 cm) overall

Unsigned

PROVENANCE

Estate of the artist (no. 66, dated 1915–16); Nelson-Atkins Museum of Art (purchased 1956 through Paul Rosenberg & Co., New York)

The Nelson-Atkins Museum of Art, Kansas City, Missouri
Gift of the Friends of Art

These paintings reflect the fascination Hartley felt for the life of Berlin from the moment he first arrived there in early January 1913. Five days after his arrival he declared the city "superb," and a few days after that he told his niece Norma Berger that it was "charming" and "very gay with the handsome officers and soldiers."[1] Power, order, vitality, and pomp were what he enduringly admired about Berlin. Seven months later he wrote Gertrude Stein that the city had an "interesting source of materials...numbers & shapes & colors that make one wonder—and admire—It is essentially mural this German way of living—big lines & large masses—always a sense of the pageantry of living—I like it."[2]

Ordered chronologically, *Portrait of Berlin* might be the earliest, as it picks up some of the shapes and symbols (spheres, triangles, a sitting Buddha) of his Musical Theme series and of *Portrait Arrangement No. 2* (plate 9). But he carried further the image of the warrior on horseback, representing a more clearly delineated mounted figure inside a sphere in the lower right corner of the painting, as well as the backs of military figures and the hind quarters of their mounts woven as a motif through the picture. To this he added the number 8, once inside a triangle and a second time inside a triangle, itself inside a sphere and that within an eight-pointed star. He was very likely to have been referring to *Portrait of Berlin* when in August 1913 he wrote Alfred Stieglitz that he was finishing a large work, "a mystical presentation of the number 8 as I get it from everywhere in Berlin." He refused to interpret the number and the eight-pointed star he noticed constantly, commenting that "There is a real reason for all these signs but it remains mystical—& explanations are not necessary."[3]

Although he did not explain the symbols to Stieglitz, he had studied his mystics well enough to know that the shape of the figure eight stands between the square (terrestrial order) and the circle (eternal order), representing regeneration and the infinite. Significantly, Hartley added a cross in the upper left of the painting, further reflecting the essential unity of eastern and western religions. Behind all these signs is a large white triangle, outlined in blue. That shape—and the number 3—symbolize variously synthesis, the Trinity, and heaven.[4]

Represented thus, the painting is about the *himmel*—heaven—that Hartley thought Berlin to be. Two years later he titled another Berlin painting *Himmel,* but by then the war and its horrors had closed in on him, and he added "holle"—hell—at the bottom of the work, whose brilliant colors literally spill over onto the frame he painted. At the lower right corner of the picture, Hartley set against a yellow background the figure of a static, monumentalized figure on a horse. Both are entirely red. Perhaps he was merely picking up the two colors that dominate the rest of the painting, but it is also reasonable to think that he meant to signify the hellish nature of the war that had caused the deaths of thousands of young warriors by 1915. The black background, like that in the German Officer series, suggests the mourning that everywhere occurred for the dead.

In *Military* and *The Warriors,* Hartley concentrated less on the mystical elements of Berlin—although various shapes and numbers are reminders of his interest in mysticism—and more on the secular pageantry he saw about him. *Military*—also titled "Pre-War Pageant 1913" and "Brass Band with Numbers"—is in a way a Musical Theme painting, although the sounds being represented have a very different tone from a classical symphony. Hartley showed sounds blaring out of a horn. He translated them into vivid, swirling colors, amid which are the numbers 7, symbolic of perfect order; 8, of regeneration; and 9, of tripling the triple, a completion of the three worlds of the infernal, the terrestrial, and the celestial. On the left of the horn are the numbers 2 and 4, symbolic of, among other things, duality, the poles of good and evil, life and death. Very possibly they refer to Karl von Freyburg's age. While Hartley eulogized him in a series of paintings rendered after his death in October 1914, here he could easily have been symbolizing von Freyburg as part of the Berlin gaiety Hartley idealized. As well, the horn is ithyphallic, and out of it spill all that fertilized the city's (gay) culture. "Hartley's memories of the period are characterized by a sexualization of military imagery," Jonathan Weinberg has observed, quoting from Hartley's memoir, *Somehow a Past:*

It was of course the age of iron—of blood and iron. Every backbone in Germany was made of it—or had new iron poured into it—the whole scene was fairly bursting with organized energy and the tension was terrific and somehow most voluptuous in the feeling of power—a sexual immensity even in it, when passion rises to the full and something must happen to quiet it.[5]

The Warriors, one of Hartley's finest achievements during his time in Germany, presents masses of ceremonially dressed soldiers on horseback. More than the other paintings it is specifically a paean to the military splendor he saw during the numerous parades he observed. While there are two, eight-pointed stars at the bottom of the work that recall his mysticism, a warrior has taken the place that Buddha occupied in other Berlin paintings. Weinberg has noted the "militarism and eroticism" that characterize the scene in which Hartley described the inspiration for *The Warriors.* He was enthralled by the "white leather breeches skin tight" and by the tall youths who soon "went out into the sun and never came back."[6] T.L.

1 Hartley to Norma Berger, 8 and 11 January 1913, Beinecke/Yale.
2 Hartley to Gertrude Stein, 7 August 1913, Beinecke/Yale.
3 Hartley to Alfred Stieglitz, August 1913, Beinecke/Yale.
4 Concerning symbols, see J. E. Cirlot, *A Dictionary of Symbols* (New York: Philosophical Library, 1971).
5 Weinberg, 143.
6 Ibid., 147.

14

Berlin Ante-War, 1914
Oil on canvas with painted frame,
41¾ × 34½ in. (106 × 87.6 cm) overall
Unsigned

PROVENANCE
Arthur B. Davies, New York; Davies Estate Sale at American Art Association, New York, April 17, 1929 (no. 436, as "Berlin Anti-War," c. 1914–15); Ferdinand Howald, Columbus, Ohio (purchased 1929); Columbus Gallery of Fine Arts (now Columbus Museum of Art; gift, 1931)

Columbus Museum of Art, Ohio
Gift of Ferdinand Howald

Painted at the outbreak of World War I, *Berlin Ante-War* has often been interpreted as a eulogy for the passing of a peaceful, idyllic Germany. It bears some formal similarities to the Amerika series, particularly in its use of thinly applied, unmodulated swatches of bright colors (see *Indian Fantasy* and *Indian Composition,* plates 16–17). However, while Hartley wove the individual figural elements of *Indian Fantasy* into a larger, decorative whole, in *Berlin Ante-War* he has chosen to emphasize the separateness and distinct identity of each figure and vignette in the painting: the pastoral scenes in the lower portion of the canvas are each framed in green, the white military figure on horseback stands in a separate space, and the sunshine that bathes the kneeling white horse at the top of the canvas is bounded by a gold circle. The result is a painting in which the separate pictorial moments add up to a larger allegorical message, in a fashion similar to the eighteenth- and nineteenth-century Bavarian folk paintings that Hartley (along with the artists of the Blaue Reiter group, such as Franz Marc and Wassily Kandinsky) collected and studied at this time.[1] Indeed, Hartley has encompassed the entire allegorical message of *Berlin Ante-War* within a unique, painted frame, an element he copied from the native German folk art.[2]

The four small, simple landscapes in the lower section of the painting depict an idealized German countryside of steeply pitched roofs, mountains, and sunrises. Between these, a striped and dotted curtain is parted to reveal a cross and a small sun. In the upper section of the canvas a Prussian horseman sits on a blue horse, an emblem of the military pageantry that pervaded pre-war Berlin and to which Hartley was greatly attracted. Above the horseman's head, Hartley has painted a white horse with a figure eight on its flank, surrounded by flowers in a gold circle. In the quasi-mystical science of numerology, which Hartley studied at the time, the number 8 signifies cosmic transcendence; similarly, the abstracted clouds that surround both horse figures are a folkish trope signifying divinity.[3] Thus, in its evocation of the idyllic folk past and the divine splendor of the military present, *Berlin Ante-War* weaves an allegorical tapestry celebrating the beauty and endurance of Germanic culture. K.W.

1 Haskell, 43; Gail Levin, "Marsden Hartley's 'Amerika': Between Native American and German Folk Art," *American Art Review* 5, no. 2 (winter 1993): 120–25ff. See also Hartley's *Tinseled Flowers* (plate 32).
2 For numerous paintings from 1914, including those devoted to more modern subjects, Hartley painted specific frames. See *The Aero* (plate 15); *Forms Abstracted, Berlin* (1914; Whitney Museum of American Art, New York); and *Himmel* (plate 13).
3 Haskell, 43.

15

The Aero, c. 1914

Oil on canvas with painted frame,

42 × 34½ in. (106.7 × 87.6 cm) overall

Unsigned

PROVENANCE

Rosenberg–Hartley sale at Anderson Galleries, New York, May 17, 1921 (probably no. 46, as "Pre-War Pageant"); Hamilton Easter Field, Brooklyn, N.Y., and Ogunquit, Maine (purchased 1921); Robert Laurent, Brooklyn and Ogunquit; Mr. and Mrs. John Laurent, York, Maine; National Gallery of Art (purchased 1970)

National Gallery of Art, Washington
Andrew W. Mellon Fund, 1970.31.1

The Aero takes its name from the flaming red spot in the upper half of the canvas, which is meant to depict the flames at the rear of a dirigible engine. Dirigibles, or zeppelins, were the most common flying machines in the years preceding the war and for many seemed to embody the technological transformation of modern daily life. As Patricia McDonnell discusses in her essay, Hartley noted that zeppelins crossed the Berlin sky with some frequency and that they never failed to amaze him. Although *The Aero* shares a basic compositional structure with canvases from the War Motif series—emanating from its center is a panoply of overlapping, flag-like graphics—it contains few of the military and personal emblems that populate that series. *The Aero* thus might be better understood as a painting of the experience of daily life in the European capital of modernity. In strolling the streets and sitting in the cafés and nightclubs of Berlin, Hartley was continually inundated with a dizzying variety of signs, lights, and bright colors. His cacophonous yellows, reds, and greens evoke both the visual and aural experience of this modern metropolis, ultimately presided over by the firey yet ethereal presence of the zeppelin.[1]

As with *Berlin Ante-War* (plate 14), Hartley painted a frame to accompany *The Aero.* And, as with *Berlin Ante-War,* the frame may be evidence of Hartley's interest in the Bavarian folk painting tradition, to which his friends in the Blaue Reiter group had recently introduced him; in fact, Wassily Kandinsky and others in the group experimented with painting their own frames during this period.[2] The painted frame may also indicate that Hartley was thinking seriously at the time about how his art would be presented to the public: by painting a frame specifically for the canvas, he both extended the boundaries of the "work" itself and ensured that the art would always have a sympathetic visual environment. K.W.

1 See also Bruce Robertson, "Marsden Hartley, 1916: Letters to the Dead," in Greenough, 229–46; and Patricia McDonnell, *Dictated By Life: Marsden Hartley's German Paintings and Robert Indiana's Hartley Elegies* (Minneapolis: Frederick R. Weisman Art Museum, University of Minnesota, 1995).

2 Gail Levin, "Marsden Hartley's 'Amerika': Between Native American and German Folk Art," *American Art Review* 5, no. 2 (winter 1993), 122.

16

Indian Fantasy, 1914

Oil on canvas, 46⅝ × 39⅜ in. (118 × 100 cm)

Unsigned

PROVENANCE

Photo-Secession Gallery, New York; sold to Aline Meyer (Mrs. Charles J.) Liebman, New York (1915); auction at Parke-Bernet Galleries, New York, December 7, 1955 (no. 68); Martha Jackson Gallery, New York (purchased 1955, inv. no. 1394); Nelson-Taylor Consultant Gallery, New York (1959); Dr. & Mrs. Norman Simon, New York (purchased 1959); André Emmerich Gallery, New York (purchased 1974); with Hirschl & Adler Galleries, New York (1974); North Carolina Museum of Art (purchased 1975)

North Carolina Museum of Art, Raleigh
Purchased with funds from the State of North Carolina

17

Indian Composition, 1914

Oil on canvas, 47¾ × 47¾ in. (121.3 × 121.3 cm)

Unsigned

PROVENANCE

Alfred Stieglitz, New York; John Quinn, New York (purchased 1916, as "Indian Tents"); auction at American Art Association, New York: "The John Quinn Collection: Paintings and Sculpture of the Moderns," February 9–11, 1927 (no. 128); Paul Rosenfeld, New York (purchased 1927, as "Indian Encampment"); Frances Lehman Loeb Art Center (gift, 1950, acc. no. 50.1.5)

Frances Lehman Loeb Art Center, Vassar College, Poughkeepsie, New York
Gift of Paul Rosenfeld (through Edna Bryner '07), 1950

Indian Fantasy and *Indian Composition* are two paintings from a larger group that Hartley called his Amerika series.[1] He painted several canvases, including these two, in the late spring and summer of 1914 in Berlin, just after his return from a brief trip to New York; he returned to the series again in 1915. During his 1914 trip to New York, he had sold enough work to support an extended stay in the German capital, but his delight in his financial stability was tempered by the threat of war. Hartley's Amerika series can be seen as a conflicted exploration of both his identity as an American abroad and his love of German culture on the eve of World War I.

Hartley's decision to explore American Indian motifs in paint was undoubtedly the product of several concerns at this time. As some scholars have noted, Hartley interpreted the Native American's harmonious relationship to the natural world as a forebear of the spirituality of Whitman and Emerson.[2] From this perspective, American Indian culture became the primitive, untainted manifestation of a uniquely American concept of spirituality. However, American Indians were also a source of great fascination among Germans, a fact that Hartley could hardly have overlooked. As Wanda Corn discusses in her essay, the "Wild West" shows of Buffalo Bill and the Indian adventure novels of German author Karl May were extremely popular among the German public in the first decades of the twentieth century. In addition, German artists and intellectuals were intrigued by the "primitiveness" of these peoples, as evidenced in the extensive display of American Indian artifacts that Hartley viewed in Berlin's ethnographic museum (Museum für Völkerkunde).[3]

Thus, the Amerika series celebrates the American Indian, but largely through the eyes of a distanced European. For example, their compositions mimic some of the geometric simplicity of Indian decoration—both *Indian Composition* and *Indian Fantasy* are organized around a central triangular tepee—but they also demonstrate a sophisticated tension between two- and three-dimensionality, oscillating between an abstract, tapestry-like pattern of colors and a detailed array of figures from a mythical American Indian world. The fragmented space of *Indian Composition* is particularly complicated. A chieftain sits opposite a sleeping horse outside two tepees along the bottom of the canvas; this scene is enclosed within a larger tepee, behind which other tepees are pitched along the bank of a river. Presiding over the figures on the land is a gold circle of the sun, enclosed within a red circle filled with baby corn plants; this circle, in turn, is flanked on either side by a host of chieftains in profile. Superimposed on this world of land and sky is, on the left, a green circle enclosing a cross, and, on the right, a red, symbol-laden circle. These medallions float against the picture plane, and pull the tepees, river, and sun gods into a flat, obsessively decorated abstract pattern. The multiple layers of symbolism and formal sophistication evident in the Amerika series represented a major stylistic breakthrough for Hartley, one that continued to mature through the subsequent War Motif series. K.W.

[1] Other canvases in the series are *American Indian Symbols* (1914; Amon Carter Museum, Fort Worth, Texas); *Painting No. 50* (1914; Terra Museum of American Art, Chicago); *Painting No. 2 (Arrangement, Hieroglyphics)* (1914; Museum of Fine Arts, Boston); *Schiff* (1915; Staatliche Galerie Moritzburg, Halle, Germany); and *Leuchtturm* (1915; Staatliche Galerie Moritzburg, Halle). The last two paintings were identified and discussed by Gail Levin in "Marsden Hartley's 'Amerika': Between Native American and German Folk Art," *American Art Review*, 5, no. 2 (winter 1993): 120–25ff.

[2] Patricia McDonnell, "*Indian Fantasy:* Marsden Hartley's Myth of *Amerika* in Expressionist Berlin," *North Carolina Museum of Art Bulletin* 16 (1993): 50–64.

[3] Gail Levin, "American Art," in *"Primitivism" in Twentieth Century Art: Affinity of the Tribal and the Modern*, vol. 2, ed. William Rubin (New York: Museum of Modern Art, 1984), 455–61.

18

Military Symbols I, 1914
Charcoal on paper, 24¼ × 18¼ in.
(61.6 × 46.4 cm)
Unsigned

PROVENANCE
The Metropolitan Museum of Art, New York
Rogers Fund, 1962

19

Portrait of a German Officer, 1914
Oil on canvas, 68¼ × 41⅜ in. (173.4 × 105.1 cm)
Unsigned

PROVENANCE
Alfred Stieglitz, New York (as "Portrait of My Friend" and "Portrait of a Young Man"); Estate of Alfred Stieglitz; Metropolitan Museum of Art (gift, 1949)

The Metropolitan Museum of Art, New York
The Alfred Stieglitz Collection, 1949

Portrait of a German Officer is the best known of the War Motif series, begun in the fall of 1914 after Hartley learned of the battlefield death of one of his closest German friends, Karl von Freyburg. Hartley was deeply in love with von Freyburg and wrote to Stieglitz that the news of his death had filled him with "eternal grief" and "unendurable agony."[1] After a brief period of debilitating sorrow, he embarked on the War Motif series, which represents both significant stylistic maturation and a powerful expression of his grief. Hartley called these canvases "subliminal or cosmic cubism": in them, he marshaled a complex array of emblems that, while abstract and graphic, also carried profound personal meaning for him.[2] The result was a series of dynamic compositions that possessed an unprecedented visual and emotional intensity.[3]

Portrait of a German Officer, which introduces several of the series' most potent pictorial elements, is a symbolic portrait of von Freyburg. A collection of checkered and striped flags (including the blue-and-white flag of Bavaria, von Freyburg's home, and the black-and-white checkerboard of von Freyburg's favorite game, chess) form the officer's body, with the triangular tip of a lance emerging behind each shoulder.[4] At the center of his chest, within a gold triangle, is the Iron Cross, the medal of bravery von Freyburg received upon his death. Suspended below the cross is an identification tag with the number 4, von Freyburg's regiment number. On the lower right, the tassels from his dress sash hang at hip level. On either side of the red cross in the lower center, which marks his genitals, are von Freyburg's initials, "Kv.F," and his age at the time of his death, 24. The entire figure lies against a black ground that may represent Hartley's own mourning.[5]

However, Hartley's bright palette and animated brush strokes are far from somber and imbue this non-anatomical portrait with a pulsing vibrancy, as if the body of his friend could be barely contained within the symbols of his public persona. Indeed, the success of this and the other paintings of the series derives from the artist's ability to infuse the accoutrements of public pageantry with the emotional intensity of personal love.[6] K.W.

[1] Quoted in Robertson, 56.
[2] Quoted in Bruce Robertson, "Marsden Hartley, 1916: Letters to the Dead," in Greenough, 229.
[3] Hartley experimented with the compositional possibilities of these symbols in drawings from the period. See *Military Symbols I* (plate 18).
[4] Arnold Rönnebeck, a sculptor friend of Hartley's in Berlin and von Freyburg's cousin, claimed in a letter to Duncan Phillips from c. 1943 that chess was his cousin's favorite game. See Gail Levin, "Hidden Symbolism in Marsden Hartley's Military Pictures," *Arts Magazine* 54, no. 2 (October 1979): 155–56.
[5] An X-ray of *Portrait of a German Officer* has recently revealed an underlying composition on the canvas which has been completely masked by Hartley's dense black paint. Thus the black ground may have served a practical as well as symbolic function. See the essay by Stephen Kornhauser and Ulrich Birkmaier.
[6] For further information on this painting and the War Motif series, see Roxana Barry, "The Age of Blood and Iron: Marsden Hartley in Berlin," *Arts Magazine* 54, no. 2 (October 1979): 166–71; Patricia McDonnell, *Dictated By Life: Marsden Hartley's German Paintings and Robert Indiana's Hartley Elegies* (Minneapolis: Frederick R. Weisman Art Museum, University of Minnesota, 1995); and Weinberg.

20

Painting No. 47, Berlin, 1914–15
Oil on canvas, 39½ × 31⅝ in. (100.3 × 80.3 cm)
Inscribed on stretcher: Hartley, Berlin

PROVENANCE
Estate of the artist (no. 140, dated 1915); Martha Jackson Gallery, New York (purchased 1958); Joseph H. Hirshhorn, Greenwich, Conn. (purchased 1968); Hirshhorn Museum and Sculpture Garden (gift, 1972)

Hirshhorn Museum and Sculpture Garden, Smithsonian Institution, Washington, D.C.
Gift of Joseph H. Hirshhorn, 1972

Painting No. 47, Berlin can be read as a portrait of Karl von Freyburg's head, missing from the full-body *Portrait of a German Officer* (plate 19). In the center of the canvas, Hartley has painted the thick tassels of a helmet cockade which, typically worn as part of a dress uniform, represents the public spectacle of military pageantry that so enthralled the artist. Again, suspended from the helmet's visor are identification tags (the 4 denoting von Freyburg's regiment). Clustered in the painting's lower right corner are other motifs from *Portrait of a German Officer:* the prominent Iron Cross, von Freyburg's initials, his age, and his boot spur. Also like *Portrait of a German Officer,* the vibrant colors of *Painting No. 47* are set against an oppressive ground of black.

Unlike the tightly wrapped composition of *Portrait of a German Officer,* however, the emblems in *Painting No. 47* radiate from behind the helmet cockade and extend to the very edges of the canvas. The gold medallion resting on the helmet visor contains the number 9 and indicates Hartley's studies in numerology.[1] In numerology, 9 signifies constant regeneration, an appropriate anchor for this expansive mourning image of a friend whom Hartley described as "Man in perfect bloom / of six foot splendor / lusty manhood time—all made of youthful fire / and simplest desire."[2] K.W.

[1] Haskell, 43.
[2] Quoted in Robertson, 58.

21

Painting No. 49, Berlin, 1914
Oil on canvas, 47 × 39½ in. (119.4 × 99.7 cm)
Unsigned

PROVENANCE
Estate of the artist (no. 142, dated 1915–16); Babcock Galleries, New York (as "Portrait of a German Officer"); Zabriskie Gallery, New York; Felix Landau Gallery, Los Angeles; Arnold H. Maremont, Chicago; auction at Sotheby Parke-Bernet, New York, May 1, 1974 (no. 12, as "Berlin Abstraction"); Peter H. Davidson and Co., Inc., New York (purchased 1974); private collection (purchased 1977 through Babcock Galleries, New York)

Collection of Mr. and Mrs. Barney A. Ebsworth
Partial and promised gift to the Seattle Art Museum

Painting No. 49, Berlin stands out in the War Motif series for its silver-white background, a stark contrast to the mournful black seen in *Portrait of a German Officer* (plate 19) and *Painting No. 47, Berlin* (plate 20).[1] A few of its elements, not found in other War Motif canvases, recall the imagery of the Amerika paintings, especially the predominant palette of red and yellow and the repeated radiating sun. However, the white ground may also be interpreted as a symbolic reference to Karl von Freyburg, the portrait subject of *Portrait of a German Officer* and *Painting No. 47.*[2] After von Freyburg's death, Hartley dreamt that his beloved friend appeared at his side in a blaze of white light, "in full uniform but the uniform purged of all military significance was white."[3] *Painting No. 49* does contain some symbols of von Freyburg's death, namely the central Iron Cross and the number 24 (both of which appear in *Portrait of a German Officer* and *Painting No. 47*), but it lacks other specific references, such as the deceased's initials. Like *Painting No. 47, Painting No. 49* depicts a helmet cockade and visor and bears a prominent number 9, the numerological symbol of regeneration. However, on the visor in this painting is the number 8, the symbol of cosmic transcendence. Immediately to the right of the helmet is the same cursive *E* that appears in other paintings in the series, which Arnold Rönnebeck, Hartley's friend and von Freyburg's cousin, later claimed referred to him.[4] While there is no corroborating evidence to support Rönnebeck's reading, it opens the possibility that all or some of the "portraits" in the War Motif series can be read as a more generalized portrayal of Germany's valiant soldiers.[5] K.W.

[1] Some scholars have interpreted the white ground as evidence that the painting was done early in the series, perhaps even first, following the Amerika paintings. See Haskell, 44. Other scholars, however, argue that *Portrait of a German Officer* was first in the series. See Patricia McDonnell's essay in this volume.
[2] Jeffrey Weiss, "*Painting No. 49, Berlin,*" in *Twentieth-Century American Art: The Ebsworth Collection,* ed. Bruce Robertson (Washington, D.C.: National Gallery of Art, 2000), 126–28.
[3] Quoted in Robertson, 56.
[4] Rönnebeck explained that the *E* referred to Queen Elisabeth of Greece, the patron of his regiment whose initial was embroidered, red on a yellow ground, on his "full-dress epaulettes." See Gail Levin, "Hidden Symbolism in Marsden Hartley's Military Pictures," *Arts Magazine* 54 (October 1979): 155–56.
[5] Haskell, 45.

22

The Iron Cross, 1914–15
Oil on canvas, 46¾ × 46¾ in. (118.7 × 118.7 cm)
Unsigned

PROVENANCE
Estate of the artist (no. 163, as "The Red Cross," 1915); Washington University Gallery of Art, St. Louis, Missouri (purchased 1952 through Paul Rosenberg & Co., New York)

Washington University Gallery of Art, St. Louis
University Purchase, Bixby Fund, 1952

23

E. (German Officer—Abstraction), c. 1915
Oil on canvas, 47⅛ × 47⅛ in. (119.7 × 119.7 cm)
Unsigned

PROVENANCE
With Paul Rosenberg & Co., New York; University of Iowa Museum of Art

University of Iowa Museum of Art, Iowa City
The Mark Ranney Memorial Fund (1958.1)

The Iron Cross and *E. (German Officer—Abstraction)* are among the latest canvases in the War Motif series. Like other works in the group (see *Portrait of a German Officer; Painting No. 47, Berlin;* and *Painting No. 49, Berlin,* plates 19–21), they feature an assortment of brightly colored flags and emblems against a ground of mournful black. However, there are fewer synecdochic references to the dead figure of von Freyburg in these later paintings, and Hartley seems to have shifted his focus to a formal exploration of abstraction and the flatness of the picture plane. Both paintings contain an Iron Cross, the symbol of von Freyburg's martyrdom: along the top edge of *The Iron Cross* and half hidden behind a red circle in *E.*[1] Both paintings also contain the script letter *E* in red against blue, a symbol of the regiment in which Arnold Rönnebeck, von Freyburg's cousin, served: just below the center of *The Iron Cross* and along the top edge of *E.*[2] However, in neither painting is a surrogate for a soldier's head or body apparent. Furthermore, both canvases have a perfectly square format, which removes the allusion to the human figure typically engendered by a longer, narrower canvas, as in *Portrait of a German Officer.* And, while Hartley maintained a shallow sense of depth in *Portrait of a German Officer,* evoking the sense of a body in space, he greatly compressed the pictorial depth in *The Iron Cross* and *E.*, creating virtually flat planes of decoration. Because of these paintings, scholars have pointed to Hartley as the first American painter to work successfully with synthetic cubism, which, based on Picasso's precedent, concerned the arrangement of planes of color flush against the picture plane.[3] Hartley's cubism is less clinical and strict than the formula, however: his vigorous, visible brushwork and irregular, undulating patterns imbue his abstractions with an emotional intensity akin to German expressionism.

Hartley showed the fruits of his productive stay in Berlin at Stieglitz's New York gallery 291 in April 1916. Perhaps in anticipation of popular anti-German sentiment or perhaps out of reluctance to share the intimate emotions that had fueled the War Motif series, he penned an artist's statement that defended his paintings from over-interpretation: "The Germanic group is but part of a series which I had contemplated of movements in various areas of war activity.... The forms are only those which I have observed casually from day to day. There is no hidden symbolism whatsoever in them.... Things under observation. Just pictures of any day, any hour."[4] While the early paintings in the War Motif series are clearly not about mere casual observation, the later paintings seem to be less iconographically dense. *The Iron Cross* and *E.* are at once echoes of the manifest grief in *Portrait of a German Officer* and a more detached experiment in capturing the vibrancy and color of military Berlin. K.W.

1 See Ruth L. Bohan, "Marsden Hartley: *The Iron Cross*," in *A Gallery of Modern Art* (St. Louis: Washington University Gallery of Art, 1994), 152–53; and Townsend Ludington, *Seeking the Spiritual: The Paintings of Marsden Hartley* (Ithaca: Cornell University Press, 1998), 33.
2 Gail Levin, "Hidden Symbolism in Marsden Hartley's Military Pictures," *Arts Magazine* 54, no. 2 (October 1979): 156.
3 See, for example, Haskell, 44.
4 Quoted in Bruce Robertson, "Marsden Hartley, 1916: Letters to the Dead," in Greenough, 237.

24

Handsome Drinks, c. 1916
Oil on composite board, 24 × 20 in. (61 × 50.8 cm)
Unsigned

PROVENANCE
Charles Daniel, New York (dated 1915); auction at Parke-Bernet Galleries, New York, March 14, 1946 (no. 79, dated 1910); Mr. and Mrs. Milton Lowenthal, New York (purchased 1946); Brooklyn Museum of Art (gift, 1972; dated c. 1912)

Brooklyn Museum of Art, New York
Gift of Mr. and Mrs. Milton Lowenthal

Handsome Drinks is one of a group of three enigmatic still-life canvases (see *A Nice Time* and *One Portrait of One Woman,* plates 25–26) that Hartley painted upon his return to New York in December 1915. He had left Berlin with great reluctance: he seems to have had no sense of the complications that his residence in a de-facto enemy country might create (the United States did not enter the war until 1917) and returned home only when the slow war-time mail prevented his receiving money to live on. Hartley had often complained about New York's crowds and frantic pace of life, and with the rising tide of popular anti-German sentiment, he now felt even less comfortable in the city. He exhibited *Handsome Drinks,* along with *A Nice Time* and *One Portrait of One Woman,* in the large Forum Exhibition of Modern American Painters in March 1916.

Handsome Drinks depicts an assortment of drinks on a black café table: on the lower right sit a teacup and saucer, in the center stands a martini glass (possibly containing a Manhattan cocktail), and on the far left stands a glass filled with the tell-tale green of absinthe, the potent, hallucinogenic liqueur popular among European artists and usually drunk through a sugar cube (depicted on a spoon resting across the top of the glass). Towering behind these everyday drinks is an incongruously large grail-like chalice. Hartley's café table, with its explicitly European absinthe, follows in a long line of modernist café renderings, from Van Gogh and Toulouse-Lautrec to Picasso, whose cubist café tables Hartley had seen in Paris.[1] Indeed, as Jonathan Weinberg writes in his essay, the nonsensical words Hartley painted on the canvas—"LUS" and "LOGH"—may be a reference to the word fragments Picasso included in paintings such as *The Architect's Table.* Although *Handsome Drinks* does not continue in the abstract mode of the Berlin War Motif series, it does share a basic synthetic cubist structure—volumes flattened into colored shapes and pushed towards the picture plane—and vibrant palette with the earlier paintings. Because *One Portrait of One Woman* is generally understood to be a portrait of Gertrude Stein, scholars speculate that *Handsome Drinks* may also be a portrait. If the four drinks on the table are seen as surrogates for four friends gathered around a café table, the painting may be a portrait of not merely a particular friend, but perhaps a group of friends.[2] K.W.

[1] "Marsden Hartley: *Handsome Drinks*," in *The Edith and Milton Lowenthal Collection* (New York: Brooklyn Museum of Art, 1981), 28; Scott, 59.
[2] Lisa Mintz Messinger, "Marsden Hartley: *Handsome Drinks*," in *American Art: The Edith and Milton Lowenthal Collection* (New York: Metropolitan Museum of Art, 1996), 27.

25

A Nice Time, c. 1916
Oil on board, 24 × 20 in.
(61 × 50.8 cm)
Inscribed on verso: Marsden Hartley

PROVENANCE
An American Place, New York; E. Weyhe Art Books, New York; Mrs. B. Satuloff, Buffalo, N.Y. (purchased 1951); Christie's New York, November 30, 1999 (no. 125); Curtis Galleries

Curtis Galleries, Minneapolis, Minnesota

The profusion of overlapping patterns that characterizes the War Motif series is transposed into a brightly colored café table in *A Nice Time,* another still life from early 1916. Like both *Handsome Drinks* (plate 24) and *One Portrait of One Woman* (plate 26), *A Nice Time* depicts a cup on a table. Hartley may have chosen such a relatively banal subject for these canvases out of fear of the anti-German sentiment that he anticipated would greet his passionate War Motif paintings. However, it is also possible that these still-life paintings contain some personal symbolism for him: a drink on a café table could refer to his community in both Paris and Berlin and the general sociability that made him so happy there, or to specific European friends he had left behind. Bruce Robertson has speculated that these three may be symbolic portraits of individuals dear to Hartley; if so, the identity of only one (Gertrude Stein in *One Portrait of One Woman*) has ever been decoded.[1]

A blue saucer and cup, filled with steaming tea, anchor *A Nice Time.* Around them on the table lie a red banana, a tomato, a flowering camellia, and a folded napkin. The checkerboard from the War Motif series reappears as well on the table, now rendered in yellow and black. As discussed with *Handsome Drinks,* Hartley may have used these paintings to rework the questions of perspective and fragmented space that Picasso had posed in his early analytic cubist paintings and collages. In choosing a café table as his subject, Hartley was therefore painting himself into the most avant-garde canon in European art. It is also possible, as Jonathan Weinberg proposes in his essay, that Hartley's nonsensical words were a gesture to Dadaism, and that as he painted himself into the canon inherited by Picasso, he also laughed at the Spaniard's self-importance: "HAH." K.W.

[1] See Christie's New York, 30 November 1999, no. 125.

26

One Portrait of One Woman, c. 1916
Oil on fiberboard, 30 × 25 in. (76.2 × 63.5 cm)
Unsigned

PROVENANCE
Alfred Stieglitz, New York; Estate of Alfred Stieglitz; Ione and Hudson Walker, Forest Hills, N.Y. (purchased 1949); University Gallery (now Weisman Art Museum; bequest, 1978)

Frederick R. Weisman Art Museum, University of Minnesota, Minneapolis
Bequest of Hudson Walker from the Ione and Hudson Walker Collection

Scholars have long speculated that *One Portrait of One Woman,* the third of Hartley's still-life canvases shown at the Forum Exhibition in March 1916 (see plates 24–25), is a portrait of Gertrude Stein, the expatriate writer, art collector, and host of the famous salon at 27 rue de Fleurus in Paris.[1] Stein was one of the most important and influential friends Hartley made while abroad from 1913 to 1915.[2] At Stein's salon, Hartley met many members of the Parisian avant-garde, including Robert and Sonia Delaunay and Pablo Picasso. While his exposure to the newest ideas and works of such artists was an undoubted benefit of friendship with Stein, more important perhaps were the reassurance and confidence he derived from her interest in his work. Shortly after his introduction to her Saturday evening soirées, Hartley recalled in his autobiography, Stein and Alice B. Toklas visited him in his studio.

Pronouncing his work that of "an original American," Stein then suggested that he "go to their place one day to lunch, bring some of [his] pictures and take down some of the Matisses and Picassos and stick them in their places. 'You will see they hold their own,' said Gertrude—and it was naturally a most edifying experience for me—and helped me greatly then."[3]

The blue teacup and saucer—the recurring motif from *A Nice Time* and *Handsome Drinks*—have often been interpreted as a symbol of the tea Stein served at her salons. The word "MOI" may refer to Stein's (or Hartley's) egocentrism, but more likely is an allusion to a 1913 play written by Stein entitled *IIIIIIIIII* featuring Hartley as a character: as the writer made the painter the subject of a work, so the painter returned the honor.[4] The red-and-white checkerboard tablecloth, reminiscent of von Freyburg's chess board (see *Portrait of a German Officer,* plate 19), combines with the blue teacup to create a vibrant red, white, and blue pattern, the colors of both Stein's original and adopted countries. Behind the tabletop, Hartley has painted a series of smaller and larger mandorlas, the leaf-like shape that traditionally framed the body of Christ and that appeared in his Amerika series of 1914 (see *Indian Fantasy* and *Indian Composition,* plates 16–17). The floating mandorlas, combined with the large candles at either edge of the canvas and the shadowy yellow cross in the teacup, contribute a mystical air to the painting, somewhat out of keeping with its portrait subject. Such enigmatic symbols are further evidence of the elusive meanings that may lurk behind these three still lifes. K.W.

[1] Haskell, 52; Lyndel King, *Marsden Hartley, 1908–1942: The Ione and Hudson D. Walker Collection* (Minneapolis: University Art Museum, University of Minnesota, 1984), 22; Patricia McDonnell, *Marsden Hartley: American Modern* (Minneapolis: Frederick R. Weisman Art Museum, University of Minnesota, 1997), 49.

[2] Donald Gallup, "The Weaving of a Pattern: Marsden Hartley and Gertrude Stein," *Magazine of Art* 41, no. 7 (November 1948): 256–61.

[3] *Autobiography,* 84.

[4] Excerpts from the speeches made by "M-N H-" in the play were reprinted the following year in the pamphlet for Hartley's exhibition at 291. "Marsden Hartley Exhibition at The Little Galleries of the Photo-Secession, January Twelfth to February Fifth, MDCCCCXIV, forewords by Mabel Dodge, Marsden Hartley, and Gertrude Stein," Beinecke/Yale.

27

Movement No. 8, Provincetown, 1916
Oil on composite board, 23¼ × 19¼ in.
(59.1 × 48.9 cm)
Unsigned

PROVENANCE
Alfred Stieglitz, New York; Estate of Alfred Stieglitz; E. Weyhe Gallery, New York (purchased 1949); Wadsworth Atheneum Museum of Art (purchased 1959, as "Movement No. 2," through funds given by Mrs. Robert E. Darling)

Wadsworth Atheneum Museum of Art, Hartford
Gift of Mrs. Robert E. Darling, 1959.5

28

Elsa, 1917
Oil on composite board, 20 × 16 in.
(50.8 × 40.6 cm)
Unsigned

PROVENANCE
Alfred Stieglitz, New York; Estate of Alfred Stieglitz; Ione and Hudson Walker, Forest Hills, N.Y. (purchased 1949); University Gallery (now Weisman Art Museum; bequest, 1978)

Frederick R. Weisman Art Museum, University of Minnesota, Minneapolis
Bequest of Hudson Walker from the Ione and Hudson Walker Collection

29

Trixie, c. 1916–17
Oil on composite board, 24 × 20 in.
(61 × 50.8 cm)
Unsigned

PROVENANCE
Rosenberg–Hartley sale at Anderson Galleries, New York, May 17, 1921 (no. 50a); Robert Laurent, New York (purchased 1921); private collection

Private Collection

During the spring of 1916, Hartley's work was shown in New York in two venues: as one artist among many at the Forum Exhibition in March (see *Handsome Drinks, A Nice Time,* and *One Portrait of One Woman,* plates 24–26) and in a solo show at Stieglitz's 291 (see *The Iron Cross* and *E.,* plates 22–23). Despite the high quality of his work, public response was tepid, and he sold very few paintings. With no money and his hopes of returning to Europe thwarted by the war, he found a rent-free room for the summer in Provincetown, Massachusetts, in the house of radical writer John Reed. In Provincetown, which was already known as a vibrant artistic summer colony, he socialized with a broad spectrum of artists, writers, and actors, including Charles Demuth, William and Marguerite Zorach, Max Eastmann, and Eugene O'Neill (whose plays were first produced by the Provincetown Players that summer). Hartley later referred to it as "the Great Provincetown Summer" (as discussed in the essay by Amy Ellis).[1]

Hartley continued to experiment with synthetic cubism over the summer and fall, developing a series of radical abstractions of which *Movement No. 8, Provincetown* and *Trixie* are two examples.[2] These paintings lack the emotional motivation that underlies the War Motif series, and their comparative coolness and detachment derive not only from the muted palette of pinks, yellows, grays, and blues—evocative of the hazy light at the tip of Cape Cod after a storm—but also from their relatively flat brushwork and their precisely delineated geometries that are pushed flush against the picture plane. Their small size, in contrast to the larger, dramatic canvases of the War Motif series, also contributes to their air of understatement and reserve. The original inspiration for this series was the movements of sailboats on the ocean: in a classic cubist exercise, Hartley observed the play of geometries in nature, then abstracted them and transformed them into a set of formal explorations. (In other paintings in the series, he turned his abstracting eye towards houses and clouds.) Both *Movement No. 8* and *Trixie* are oriented vertically around a central mast, which is adorned with a flag in *Trixie* and reduced to a single striped circle in *Movement No. 8*.[3] However, the geometric forms in *Trixie* more closely resemble the sails and structure of a boat than do the shapes in *Movement No. 8*. The irregular trapezoids of pink, yellow, and black in *Trixie* are pulled in tight to the mast, and the listing stern of the boat, adorned with the bold letters "TRIXIE," puts the entire composition in a state of precarious balance. In *Movement No. 8,* the trapezoids are unfurled with monumental presence, arrayed across the surface in a painstaking collage of two-dimensional shapes.

Michael Taylor has recently argued that Hartley actually continued working on his Provincetown abstractions throughout the following winter in Bermuda (see *Atlantic Window* and *Still Life with Eel,* plates 30–31). *Elsa,* probably painted in February 1917 after Hartley received a new shipment of painting supplies, depicts a Danish ship that docked at St. George's port in Bermuda during the winter of 1916–17.[4] While it includes the name of the ship, as does *Trixie,* the expansive solidity of the composition—into which the Danish flag is deftly woven as an abstract element—bears more in common with *Movement No. 8*.[5] The entire series of paintings, a "radical venture into non-objectivity," was by far the most sophisticated, avant-garde visual expression in America at the time.[6] K.W.

[1] Ludington, 132.
[2] Other canvases from the Provincetown summer are *Provincetown* (1916; Art Institute of Chicago); *Sailboat* (1916; Columbus Museum of Art); *Elsa Köbenhavn* (1916; Frederick R. Weisman Art Museum, University of Minnesota, Minneapolis); and *Boat (Black and White Hull)* (1916; unlocated).
[3] "Marsden Hartley: *Movement No. 8, Provincetown,*" in Elizabeth Mankin Kornhauser, et al., *American Paintings before 1945 in the Wadsworth Atheneum* (New Haven and London: Yale University Press, 1996), vol. 2, 442–44.
[4] Michael R. Taylor, "Marsden Hartley, the 'Movement' Series," lecture, University of Pennsylvania, Philadelphia, 7 December 2000, publication forthcoming. *Elsa* has previously been given the date 1916.
[5] Lyndel King, *Marsden Hartley, 1908–1942: The Ione and Hudson D. Walker Collection* (Minneapolis: University Art Museum, University of Minnesota, 1984), 24–26.
[6] Haskell, 55.

30

Atlantic Window, 1917
Oil on board, 32 × 25¾ in. (81.3 × 65.4 cm)
Inscribed on verso in pencil: Atlantic Window / In the New England Character

PROVENANCE
Sold at Rosenberg–Hartley sale at Anderson Galleries, New York, May 17, 1921, to Paul Rosenfeld, New York; Harvey and Françoise Rambach; with Gerald Peters Gallery, New York (1999); private collection

Private Collection
Courtesy of Gerald Peters Gallery, New York

31

Still Life with Eel, c. 1917
Oil on canvas, 30 × 25 in. (75.7 × 63.5 cm)
Unsigned

PROVENANCE
William Carlos Williams; Ogunquit Museum of American Art

The Ogunquit Museum of American Art
Permanent Collection, 58.4
Gift of Mrs. William Carlos Williams

In the winter of 1916–17, immediately following the "Great Provincetown Summer," Hartley traveled to Bermuda with Charles Demuth in search of inexpensive housing and a warm climate. He was, upon his arrival, thrilled with the warm air and almost tropically luxuriant plants, writing to Stieglitz: "I like it here—I like the suggestion of the orient in the voluptuousness of vegetation about—the large red hibiscus blossoms—full beautiful bell-like things bright [along] every hedge as you walk—and the sensuous banana trees are every where in evidence."[1] Although he quickly became bored with Bermuda's atmosphere of lassitude (he returned to New York after only six months), the voluptuousness and sensuality he found in its flora are manifest in his paintings from the period. In *Still Life with Eel* and *Atlantic Window,* both works from the Bermuda sojourn, Hartley painted with vigorous brush strokes and imbued the phallic shapes of the calla lilies, banana, and eel with a robust, sculptural vibrancy that did not go unnoticed by friends and critics. Demuth later made a sketch for a "poster portrait" of his friend that features a sexualized calla lily on an open windowsill not unlike the elongated, aggressive flower in *Still Life with Eel*[2] (see Weinberg, fig. 1). And Paul Rosenfeld, describing in 1924 a painting that might well be *Atlantic Window,* wrote: "This regal white lily with its wickedly horned leaves, erect between butter-yellow draperies, is felt as a volume against that lustrous purplish-blue sweep of bay."[3]

For Hartley, these paintings[4]—despite their explicit erotic charge—represented a continuing shift away from the intense emotions of the War Motif series towards an art evacuated of all personal "excitement."[5] Like the Provincetown paintings (see *Movement No. 8, Provincetown,* plate 27), the Bermuda paintings depict ostensibly neutral, impersonal subject matter: in the former, sailboats on the sea, in the latter, still-life arrangements on an open windowsill. The Bermuda paintings could even be interpreted as more emotionally vacant than the Provincetown works in their return to conventional pictorial space: the artist abandoned the synthetic cubism that had marked his personal ambition to be a member of the international avant-garde. However, it is important to note that Hartley's Bermuda paintings recall the fauvist windowsill compositions of Henri Matisse from a decade earlier, and thus are not without avant-garde pretensions. The eroticism of Hartley's Bermuda canvases and their echoes of Matisse perhaps indicate a different approach to the personal and professional themes embodied in the War Motif series, and not, as the artist might have claimed, their complete abandonment. K.W.

1 Hartley to Alfred Stieglitz, 26 December 1916, Beinecke/Yale.

2 See Weinberg, 114–20; and Robin Jaffee Frank, *Charles Demuth: Poster Portraits, 1923–1929* (New Haven: Yale University Art Gallery, 1994), 15–22.

3 From Paul Rosenfeld, *Port of New York* (New York: Harcourt and Brace, 1924), 85; noted by Elizabeth McCausland, McCausland Papers, Archives/Smithsonian, reel D269.

4 See also *Movement No. 10* (1917; Art Institute of Chicago); *Still Life No. 9* (1917; Frederick R. Weisman Art Museum, University of Minnesota, Minneapolis); and *A Bermuda Window in a Semi-Tropic Character* (1917; Fine Arts Museum of San Francisco).

5 Haskell, 56.

32

Tinseled Flowers, 1917

Tempera, silver foil, and gold foil on glass, 16⅞ × 9¼ in. (42.9 × 23.5 cm)

Unsigned

PROVENANCE

Alfred Stieglitz; Weyhe Gallery, New York; William H. Lane Foundation (1955); Museum of Fine Arts, Boston (1990)

The Museum of Fine Arts, Boston
Gift of the William H. Lane Foundation

The summer following his productive stays in Provincetown and Bermuda, Hartley resided in Ogunquit, Maine, at an art colony sponsored by Hamilton Easter Field. Field, a wealthy patron and an art critic for the *Brooklyn Daily Eagle,* had recently begun collecting nineteenth-century American folk art, and he encouraged the young modernists at his colony to use the older art as a source for developing a quintessential American aesthetic. Hartley experimented with painting on glass, of which *Tinseled Flowers* is an example, during this summer and the subsequent fall, and cited as his inspiration nineteenth-century American folk paintings on glass and mirrors, and saloon signs.[1] It is also possible that his experiment was influenced in part by nineteenth-century Bavarian folk glass painting, which he had learned about from the Blaue Reiter artists Franz Marc and Wassily Kandinsky while in Berlin. Indeed, a few of Hartley's glass paintings bear similarities to the Bavarian images in their symmetry and meticulous detail.[2] However, for the most part, Hartley's simplified still-life arrangements share more with the hieratic compositions found in American painted signs than with the detailed, often well-sculpted Bavarian images.

Tinseled Flowers depicts a calla lily with a prominent yellow and red stamen, framed by mottled green leaves, in a pale pink vase against a black background. While the composition of the painting is not unusual in Hartley's oeuvre, as a technical exercise, *Tinseled Flowers* (and the other glass paintings) represent a significant departure from standard practice. When painting on glass, one paints "in reverse," that is, on the back side of the glass, so that the viewer sees the painting through the glass from the other side. Thus, the artist must paint all of the finest details and highlights first (the front-most layer of paint), and fill in the background after the figure has dried.[3] Hartley later described the difficulty of the "reverse painting" technique, writing to Rebecca Strand: "it nearly killed me and I never had the courage to take it up again."[4] K.W.

1 Elizabeth McCausland to Hans Huth, 7 September 1953, McCausland Papers, Archives/Smithsonian, reel D270.

2 See, for example, *Vase of Flowers* (1917; Carl Van Vechten Gallery of Art, Fisk University, Nashville, Tennessee). See also Helena Lepovitz, *Images of Faith: Expressionism, Catholic Folk Art, and the Industrial Revolution* (Athens: University of Georgia Press, 1991).

3 Jonathan Weinberg and Carol Troyen provided information about the technique of painting in reverse on glass. See also Mildred Lee Ward, *Reverse Paintings on Glass: The Mildred Lee Ward Collection* (Lawrence, Kansas: Spencer Museum of Art, 1978).

4 Haskell, 57.

33

Pueblo Mountain, New Mexico, 1918

Pastel on paper, 17½ × 27⅞ in. (44.5 × 70.8 cm)

Signed lower right: Pueblo Mountain N.M. / Marsden Hartley / 1918

PROVENANCE

Georgia O'Keeffe; Babcock Galleries, New York (purchased 1969)

Babcock Galleries, New York

Hartley arrived in Santa Fe, New Mexico, on June 12, 1918, and went to Taos just two days later. He was entranced by the landscape, writing to *Poetry* editor Harriet Monroe: "it is of course the only place in America where true colour exists, excepting the short autumnal season in New England."[1]

Hartley's first pictures of the Santa Fe landscape were large pastels, like this one. He wrote to Stieglitz that he "had several good pastels finished," and that he was trying to get his "eye soaked with the colour and form of the place."[2] In September he wrote that pastels are "the only way I can get a line on the qualities [of the landscape], and it is a very important and typical medium for this country which has such wonderful dry quality of colour, and such hardness and brilliancy."[3]

In *Pueblo Mountain, New Mexico,* Hartley captured in vivid purples, blues, greens, terracotta, and yellows what he described as "those great isolated alter-like [sic] forms that stand alone on a great mesa with the immensities of blue around & above & that strange Indian red earth making such almost unearthly foregrounds."[4] This particular pastel was in the collection of Georgia O'Keeffe, who spent much of her life and career painting the landscape and architecture of New Mexico. A.E.

1 Hartley to Harriet Monroe, 13 September 1918, quoted in Haskell, 58.

2 Hartley to Alfred Stieglitz, 20 July 1918, quoted in Ludington, 140.

3 Hartley to Stieglitz, 19 September 1918, quoted in Ludington, 142.

4 Hartley to Stieglitz, quoted in *John Frederick Kensett, Childe Hassam, Marsden Hartley* (New York: Babcock Galleries, 2001), 36.

34

Blessing the Melon: The Indians Bring the Harvest to Christian Mary for Her Blessing, 1918
Oil on cardboard, $32\frac{1}{2} \times 23\frac{7}{8}$ in.
(82.6 × 60.6 cm)
Unsigned

PROVENANCE
Alfred Stieglitz, New York; Estate of Alfred Stieglitz; Philadelphia Museum of Art (gift, 1949)

Philadelphia Museum of Art
The Alfred Stieglitz Collection

In June 1918 Hartley moved from New York, where he had spent the winter, to Taos, New Mexico. He was drawn to the Southwest for several reasons, among them the promise of inexpensive living and the company that salon hostess Mabel Dodge (Luhan) and her circle of acquaintances would provide. Hartley may also, like other artists who had made the pilgrimage before him, have been interested in the region for its folk art, both Hispanic-American and American Indian. The previous summer, at the Ogunquit art colony, he had developed a group of oil and tempera on glass paintings derived from the study of northeastern American folk art (see *Tinseled Flowers,* plate 32). He was attracted to such American folk painting, as well as to the Bavarian folk painting he had seen in Germany, for its perceived primitive qualities.[1] Hartley and others of his generation felt that the simple, untutored forms of folk art represented an untainted, pure account of one's world and life experiences.

During his time in the Southwest, Hartley found inspiration in the artifacts of nineteenth-century Catholic Hispanic-American culture, especially the small-scale, vibrantly colored Mexican-American altarpieces called *santos. Santos* existed in the eighteenth and nineteenth centuries in two forms: a painted wooden panel, known as a *retablo,* and a carved and painted figure, known as a *bulto.*[2] *Blessing the Melon* essentially recreates a *retablo*: the Virgin, crowned with stars, stands on a shallow stage, flanked by yellow curtains, candles, and a vase of flowers, blessing the large melon at her feet (discussed in the essay by Wanda Corn). Hartley emulated the authentic *retablo* style in his flat, schematic rendering of the Virgin's robes, the crude crown of stars, and the incongruous scale of the candles. He did not frame the *retablo* in any way—this is a painting that recreates a *retablo,* not a painting of a *retablo*—and in so doing, he attempted to capture what he felt was the spiritual immediacy and purity of expression of these naïve paintings.

Hartley was also fascinated by the American Indian culture he encountered in both Taos and Santa Fe, and he attended numerous tribal dances.[3] Although he had painted elaborate fantasy canvases about American Indians while in Berlin (see *Indian Fantasy* and *Indian Composition,* plates 16–17), once in the presence of the real-life pageantry, he chose, surprisingly, not to render his impressions in paint.[4] Indeed, Native American culture appears in Hartley's art from this period only as a series of isolated symbols—the watermelon in *Blessing the Melon,* the striped blanket in *El Santo* (plate 36)—as if he were unable to express visually the profound spirituality that he saw in tribal culture. K.W.

[1] Haskell, 59.
[2] Larry Frank, "Santos Celebration," *Art and Antiques* (December 1992): 46–51.
[3] Scott, 66.
[4] He did, however, write articles about his observations of American Indian culture over the next few years. See, for example, "Red Man Ceremonials: An American Plea for American Esthetics," *Art and Archaeology* 9 (January 1920): 7–14.

35

Santos, New Mexico, c. 1918–19
Oil on cardboard, $31\frac{3}{4} \times 23\frac{3}{4}$ in. (80.6 × 60.3 cm)
Unsigned

PROVENANCE
Alfred Stieglitz, New York; Ione and Hudson Walker, Forest Hills, N.Y.; University Gallery (now Weisman Art Museum; bequest, 1978)

Frederick R. Weisman Art Museum, University of Minnesota, Minneapolis
Bequest of Hudson Walker from the Ione and Hudson Walker Collection

Three brightly-colored *bultos,* or painted wooden altar figures (see *Blessing the Melon,* plate 34), anchor the foreground of *Santos, New Mexico.* The figures may well have been among the many at Mabel Dodge (Luhan's) house in Taos, where Hartley often painted during his stay in the Southwest.[1] The *santos* (referring to both *bultos* and *retablos*) that attracted twentieth-century modernists were worshipped originally in individual homes on the barren frontier of eighteenth- and nineteenth-century New Spain and New Mexico. In that Catholic culture, in which personal, emotional relationships with the saints were central, such *santos* provided community, continuity, and solace to isolated desert abodes.[2]

Hartley's rendering of the three *bultos* captures their iconic power: they are peculiarly bright against a field of gray; their disarmingly small bodies are quite solid; and their blank faces thoroughly resist the viewer's inquisitive stare. Hartley has also arranged the *bultos* in a composition that echoes their spiritual significance: the large bearded king and the two smaller figures that flank him form a single triangle, evoking the doctrine of the Holy Trinity. Indeed, if the larger *bultos* represents the Father and Son, missing is only the Holy Spirit. Some scholars have conjectured that the mysterious, grayish, larger-than-life figure lurking in the background is meant to allude to the Holy Spirit.[3] However, others have hypothesized that the gray figure is Mabel Dodge (Luhan) herself[4], a new type of patron saint who has protected the *santos* from extinction in the modern world by collecting them. K.W.

[1] Haskell, 59.
[2] Larry Frank, "Santos Celebration," *Art and Antiques* (December 1992): 46–51.
[3] Lyndel King, *Marsden Hartley, 1908–1942: The Ione and Hudson D. Walker Collection* (Minneapolis: University Art Museum, University of Minnesota, 1984), 26–28.
[4] Robertson, 78.

36

El Santo, 1919
Oil on canvas, 36 × 32 in. (91.4 × 81.3 cm)
Unsigned

PROVENANCE
Museum of New Mexico, Santa Fe (purchased from the artist 1919, through funds given by an anonymous donor)

Museum of New Mexico,
Museum of Fine Arts, Santa Fe
Anonymous Gift of a Friend of Southwest Art

El Santo differs from Hartley's other *santos* paintings (see plates 34–35) in that it depicts a *santo* as one element in a still-life arrangement and does not attempt to replicate the spiritual immediacy of the original icons. Also included on the canvas are a brightly colored, striped American Indian blanket and an Indian *olla* pot, from which spiky yucca leaves protrude.[1] Thus, in *El Santo,* Hartley brought together artifacts from the two vibrant cultures he observed during his time in the Southwest, that of the Hispanic Catholic and that of the American Indian. Although to him both groups represented an emotionally resonant existence and a pure, unmaterialistic lifestyle, in his still life he has carefully framed the relics, stripping them of their spiritual power and transforming them into an exercise in formal objectivity.[2] K.W.

[1] Scott, 66.
[2] Haskell, 59.

37

Calla Lilies, 1920
Pastel on paper, 24½ × 16¼ in. (62.2 × 41.3 cm)
Unsigned

PROVENANCE
Harvey and Françoise Rambach;
with Gerald Peters Gallery, New York (1999)

Gerald Peters Gallery, New York

The calla lily was a favorite subject of Hartley's and, with its phallic stamen, like the anthurium, it undoubtedly had sexual connotations for the artist (see *Atlantic Window,* plate 30). His interest in still life, and particularly in the calla lily, may have had something to do with his close friendship with the painter Charles Demuth. Demuth painted the calla lily often, including one 1926 oil titled *Calla Lilies (Bert Savoy)* (Fisk University, Nashville), an homage to a female impersonator.[1]

Hartley's fresh pastel of the flower demonstrates his dexterity with the medium. A.E.

[1] See Weinberg, 50–51.

38

Landscape, New Mexico, 1923
Oil on canvas, 21¾ × 35¾ in. (55.2 × 90.8 cm)
Unsigned

PROVENANCE
Carl Sprinchorn (as "Mountains with Clouds No. 2," dated 1922); Babcock Galleries, New York; Collection of AXA Financial, Inc.

Collection of AXA Financial, Inc., through its subsidiary The Equitable Life Assurance Society of the United States

39

New Mexico Recollections—Storm, 1923
Oil on canvas, 29 × 41½ in. (73.7 × 105.4 cm)
Unsigned

PROVENANCE
Estate of the artist (no. 135, dated 1922–23); William H. Lane Foundation, Leominster, Mass. (purchased 1958, as "Recollection of New Mexico—Storm," through Babcock Galleries, New York); Shein Collection

Private Collection

By the spring of 1923, when Hartley painted *Landscape, New Mexico* and *New Mexico Recollections—Storm,* he had been living in Berlin for almost eighteen months. His return to Europe had been financed by a record-breaking auction of his paintings held at the Anderson Galleries in New York in May 1921, from which he netted almost five thousand dollars. Although he was thrilled to be living once again in his favorite city, by the winter of 1922–23 he was complaining of a lack of inspiring urban subjects for his painting. He began to contemplate a rejuvenating move to the French or Italian countryside, and, as he explained to Stieglitz, revisited his memories of the vast New Mexican landscape in preparation for his pending change of scenery.

Landscape, New Mexico and *New Mexico Recollections—Storm,* along with the other canvases that comprise Hartley's Berlin-based New Mexico Recollections series, bear little resemblance to his earlier paintings of the Southwest landscape.[1] Hartley had expressed ambivalence towards the land around Taos and Santa Fe when he stayed there in 1918–19, and he was not able to capture his experiences in paint successfully until after he moved to New York in 1920. His New York recollections depict a dense, well-sculpted landscape of sun-bleached orange and green under a vibrant blue sky.[2] In contrast, *Landscape, New Mexico* portrays an almost otherworldly place, the hot, white expanse of desert in the painting's middle ground trapped between the impenetrable black of the mountains in the distance and the cacti in the foreground.[3]

In *New Mexico Recollections—Storm* Hartley has contorted the barren land into an undulating, almost dizzying progression of hills which sweep the sagebrush and cacti along in their wake; rising behind the furthest peak is a pair of massive clouds. In both paintings, Hartley's brush strokes have become longer, almost entirely horizontal, and the paint is more thinly applied, all of which contribute to the effect of a windswept plain cowering under the brewing tempest of a cloudy sky. While scholars have interpreted the apocalyptic air of the New Mexico Recollections as an indication of Hartley's discontent and restlessness in Berlin, he himself, surprisingly, described the works in quite opposite terms.[4] Writing to Stieglitz, he explained: "I have calmed down generally in composition & general effects—I think you'll like the 'simplicity' of the new work—and a certain coming toward repose & thank heaven at least no intervention of private states of personal existence. I think they are for the first time in my life—almost without me in them."[5] K.W.

[1] Other New Mexico Recollections are *Landscape Fantasy* (1923; New York University Art Collection, Grey Art Gallery and Study Center); and *New Mexico Recollections No. 12* (1922–23; Jack S. Blanton Museum of Art, University of Texas at Austin).
[2] See, for example, *Landscape No. 3, Cash Entry Mines, New Mexico* (1920; Art Institute of Chicago); and *New Mexico Landscape* (1919; Philadelphia Museum of Art).
[3] See the essay by Wanda Corn.
[4] Haskell, 72; Robertson, 84.
[5] Hartley to Alfred Stieglitz, 28 April 1923, Beinecke/Yale.

40

Seated Male Nude, 1922
Sanguine pastel on paper, 24 × 17 in. (61 × 43.2 cm)
Unsigned

PROVENANCE
Estate of the artist; private collection

Babcock Galleries, New York

For Hartley, the decade of the 1920s was one of frequent travel and artistic experimentation. While in Berlin in 1923, Hartley returned to the figure, a subject he had not focused on since 1909. Beginning in July, he made more than a dozen pastel drawings of mainly muscular male nude figures, and some robust female nudes. As seen in *Seated Male Nude,* Hartley used sanguine pastel, outlining the figure in black, set against a suffused pastel background. Hartley wrote to Stieglitz that he worked with a twenty-two-year-old wrestler as his model.[1] The muscular figure with bear-like hands is reminiscent of the later male figure paintings that Hartley executed in Maine. E.M.K.

[1] Robertson, 85.

41

Landscape, Vence, 1925–26
Oil on canvas, 25⅝ × 31⅞ in. (65.1 × 81 cm)
Unsigned

PROVENANCE
Adelaide Kuntz, New York; Ione and Hudson Walker, Forest Hills, N.Y. (acquired 1945, in exchange for another Hartley painting); University Gallery (now Weisman Art Museum; bequest, 1978)

Frederick R. Weisman Art Museum, University of Minnesota, Minneapolis
Bequest of Hudson Walker from the Ione and Hudson Walker Collection

After fantasizing about the countryside of southern France for several years, Hartley finally moved to Provence in the summer of 1925. He rented a house in Vence, and although his initial response to his new locale was one of jubilance, his mood, as usual, soon darkened and he began to regret that his year-long lease could not be broken. He spent much of his sojourn avoiding the "dreadful busy-body English & a few not too exciting Americans" and driving through the region searching for vistas to paint.[1] As Barbara Haskell has noted, his restlessness and melancholy seemed to affect his sense of stylistic direction, and the paintings from this unhappy period display little aesthetic or intellectual coherence.[2] In addition to a series of still lifes and a group of sketchy, impressionistic scenes, he produced a collection of highly polished, weighty landscapes of which *Landscape, Vence* is a superlative example.[3]

Landscape, Vence turns the mountains of southern France into a series of sculptural masses that have the incessant, irregular nooks and scars of a human body. Hartley has layered the orange-brown of the land, the green of the vegetation, and the blue-black of the shadowy crevices with repeated short brush strokes, capturing the dense weight of the geography. Human presence is represented by the sweeping road and smaller paths on the hill, but by far the most compelling actors in the painting are the mountains' shadows.[4] Their darkness disrupts and animates the expanses of sun-drenched stone and grass—which Hartley once called "this golden, expanding light"—and a single large shadow with immaculate contours spreads down onto the road and disappears seductively behind the bend.[5] K.W.

[1] Hartley to Alfred Stieglitz, 26 January 1926, Beinecke/Yale.
[2] Haskell, 74.
[3] See also *Vence, Landscape* (1925–26; Tucson Museum of Art).
[4] Lyndel King, *Marsden Hartley, 1908–1942: The Ione and Hudson D. Walker Collection* (Minneapolis: University Art Museum, University of Minnesota, 1984), 32–34; Hokin, 58–59.
[5] Hartley, "Impressions of Provence from An American's Point of View," in *On Art,* 144.

42

Fig Tree, c. 1926–28

Oil on canvas, 24¼ × 20½ in. (61.6 × 52.1 cm)

Unsigned

PROVENANCE

Private collection, Kansas City, Missouri (1980); through Martha Parrish & James Reinish, Inc., New York, to another private collection

Private Collection
Courtesy of Martha Parrish & James Reinish, Inc., New York

It is likely that Hartley painted *Fig Tree* during his sojourn in Aix, in southern France, where he lived on and off from 1926 to 1928.[1] In Aix, Hartley was surrounded by the landscape and vegetation that had inspired Cézanne, and he took the older painter's work and way of seeing as a guide for his own unfocused artistic meanderings. For Hartley, Cézanne's chief accomplishment was the elimination of the painter's own intrusive ego and a complete, absorbing attention to "beauty as it is seen to exist in the real, in the object itself."[2]

Through a series of drawings and oil paintings, Hartley thoroughly explored the physicality of the fig trees that populated southern France, examining the designs made by their intertwining branches and their sculptural presence in the region's glowing light.[3] In *Fig Tree,* Hartley has placed the snaking branches of the fig tree against a dramatic dark sky. The tree itself is realized through a series of layered patches of color, a painterly technique that Hartley adapted from Cézanne and used in other works from this period, such as *Mont Sainte-Victoire, Aix-en-Provence* (plate 43). Here Hartley allows the architecture of the layered paint to convey the volume of the tree. As he painstakingly builds up regions of shadow and light, the physicality of the paint recreates the physicality of the tree; Hartley is indeed painting "the real . . . the object itself." In contrast, he has devoted little detail to the surrounding landscape, choosing to render it in illegible forms of vibrantly contrasting oranges and greens, which compare with the palette of *Mont Sainte-Victoire, Aix-en-Provence.* Against such vivid colors, Hartley's fig tree takes on an otherworldly air: its waving white branches dance through the night sky and seem to bear no connection to the earth beneath them. K.W.

1 The painting has been previously dated c. 1924–25. However, judging from its painterly style and its subject matter, it is likely that it was painted sometime during Hartley's stay in Aix. See dates of the works listed in note 3.

2 Hartley, "Whitman and Cézanne," in *Adventures*, 30. See also Scott, 76.

3 See *Trees and Wall* (c. 1927, pencil on paper; Bates College Museum of Art, Lewiston, Maine); *Tree and Rocks* (1927, silverpoint on prepared paper; University of Michigan Museum of Art, Ann Arbor); and *Fig Tree in Winter, Provence* (c. 1928, oil on canvas; private collection).

43

Mont Sainte-Victoire, Aix-en-Provence, 1927

Oil on canvas, 25½ × 31⅞ in. (64.8 × 81 cm)

Unsigned

PROVENANCE

Estate of the artist (no estate number, dated 1928); Mrs. Herbert C. Morris, Philadelphia (purchased 1945, through Paul Rosenberg & Co., New York); Edward Knox Morris, Gladwyne, Penn. (gift); Mr. and Mrs. Carl D. Lobell, New York (purchased 1979, though Joshua Strychalski, New York); private collection; through Martha Parrish & James Reinish, Inc., New York, to another private collection

Private Collection
Courtesy of Martha Parrish & James Reinish, Inc., New York

After his year in Vence, Hartley headed to Aix-en-Provence, still in pursuit of a profoundly inspiring landscape. Although he preferred the countryside of Aix to that of Vence, he was still restless and his painting unfocused, and he fled to the urban centers from which he had only recently escaped, Paris and Berlin, for several months in early 1927. Upon his return to the south, Hartley seems to have turned to the ghost of Cézanne for guidance. He lived in the French master's second studio, a house named Maison Maria, and set about painting the land that had proved to be the older artist's most potent material. In his group of paintings of Mont Sainte-Victoire, including this canvas, he revisited the specific mountain that Cézanne had explored, even painting it from the same vantage point.[1] Most noticeably, he adopted the short hatch mark strokes of Cézanne's landscapes, building up the architectural presence of the mountain through luminescent patches of color.

Hartley's Mont Sainte-Victoire paintings, for all their intellectual similarity to Cézanne's work, are nonetheless unique aesthetic expressions.[2] Hartley adopted a saturated, almost electric palette of pinks and oranges to render his mountain; in *Mont Sainte-Victoire, Aix-en-Provence,* the mountain's peak has a shimmering, almost hallucinatory quality. The sky behind the peak, in contrast, is rendered in a wash of diffused yellow, and seems to impart to the scene none of the stark, clear light that bathes *Landscape, Vence* (plate 41). In the painting's foreground, a pink road practically falls off the bottom of the canvas, exaggerating the steep and disorienting climb one must make to reach the top of the mountain. Through Hartley's eyes, Mont Sainte-Victoire has become an awe-inspiring, almost blinding jumble of rocks and vegetation. In a poem written the following year, entitled "The Mountain and the Reconstruction," Hartley described his experience before a mountain in Provence in similar terms: "Light poured from it in the passing of the day / . . . and there was the quality / of revelation contained in it, revelation / for the body, the mind, and the spirit."[3]

Hartley showed his French landscapes at Stieglitz's new gallery, The Intimate Gallery, in January 1929. Although critics largely dismissed his newest work as derivative and uninspired, Lee Simonson, writing in the exhibition pamphlet, sympathetically captured the fervor that emanates from a painting such as *Mont Sainte-Victoire, Aix-en-Provence:* "[Hartley] lifted my eyes to the hills and from them, thru my most tormented years, came peace.... I can think of no one...who has expressed with more finality of form and color than Hartley, the meaning of mountains, or so completely revealed the forces that draw our feet to them, lift up our hearts and free our minds in their sight."[4] K.W.

[1] Haskell, 75. Other canvases in this group are *Mont Sainte-Victoire* (1927; Des Moines Art Center); and *Mont Sainte-Victoire* (1927; private collection).
[2] Hokin, 59–64.
[3] Hartley, "The Mountain and the Reconstruction," [1928], in *On Art,* 75. Hartley's belief in the importance of mountain landscapes for both his work and his spiritual well-being is indicated by his numerous writings over the years; in addition to "The Mountain and the Reconstruction," see "On the Subject of the Mountain," [1932], in *The Book of Nature: American Painters and the Natural Sublime* (Yonkers, N.Y.: Hudson River Museum, 1983), 102–4.
[4] Lee Simonson, foreword to *Hartley Exhibition* (exhibition pamphlet, The Intimate Gallery, New York, 1–31 January 1929), Beinecke/Yale.

44

Mont Ste.-Victoire, 1927
Pencil on paper, 21 × 24 in. (53.3 × 61 cm)
Unsigned

PROVENANCE
Babcock Galleries

Babcock Galleries, New York

This drawing by Hartley of Mont Sainte-Victoire is a departure from his paintings of the mountain that Cézanne memorialized in paint (see plate 43). In the profile of the mountain against the sky, the profile of a reclining man can be seen, with the torso along the top-right edge of the mountain. Mme M. Debrol wrote in 1928:

In his mountains, Mr. Hartley sees more than the mass, the outline in the sky, the fusion of granite and of earth.... it is the mountain with its own name, a beautiful French name that sounds clear and very French—Sainte Victoire, the mountain that is part of the universe, that stands sentinel for millenniums and for millenniums to come, the mountain that has its profile, that receives the light, but receives it like a benediction, and gives it back transformed pacified to the valley where human beings move. That is what Marsden Hartley has been the first to show, and to give us—an exact portrait grown into a vision, of that formidable thing, so touching, immovable, tender, intangible, colossal, living—the mountain.[1]

A.E.

[1] Mme M. Debrol, quoted in Hokin, 53.

45

Franconia Notch, 1930
Oil on canvas, 30 × 36 in. (76.2 × 91.4 cm)
Inscribed on verso: Mt. Lafayette / Franconia Notch / N.H / 1930. / Marsden Hartley

PROVENANCE
Mrs. Claire Ornstein; E.C. Group; Jon and Barbara Landau, New York; Curtis Galleries

Curtis Galleries, Minneapolis, Minnesota

Hartley returned to the United States from Europe in March 1930, after having spent fourteen of the past eighteen years abroad. His 1929 exhibition at Stieglitz's Intimate Gallery, in which he had shown his landscapes from Provence (see plates 41–43), had been a critical and financial failure. Many members of the press and his own colleagues, foremost among them Stieglitz himself, felt that Hartley had abandoned American subjects and an American aesthetic sensibility. Their opinions were not unusual for the day: by the late 1920s, a strong nationalistic pride had seized the country at large and the avant-garde artistic community in particular. Among painters and critics, this nationalism was increasingly manifested in realistic images rooted in the unique daily experiences and regional landscapes of the country.

In this changed environment, Hartley not only felt pressured to defend his national identity, but also worried about alienating dealers such as Stieglitz and potential patrons. Although he would not return to Maine for another seven years, in this first summer back in his native country he immersed himself in the mountainous landscape of its neighboring state, New Hampshire. Forever in search of inexpensive lodgings, he rented a deserted house on a farm in the Franconia Valley, at the western foot of the dramatic Franconia Ridge. As he later wrote, he chose the Franconia Valley in part out of a compulsion to see the opposite face of the mountains he had known since childhood: "I had seen Mt. Washington so many years from the Lovell side—and as is always the case with mountains, there is always the other side drawing one over—and I had never gone."[1] He spent much time in the early part of the summer exploring the Ridge trails, scrambling among the rocks, and painting in the outdoors. However, he quickly grew irritated at the incessant tramp of hikers, who often disrupted his work, and the lack of any "social life," as he complained to Rebecca Strand: "All work and no play is turning this Jack into a duller boy than he has been for a long time."[2]

Franconia Notch, painted during this first summer back in New England, belies Hartley's ambivalence about this quasi-homecoming. The short, repeated hatch marks that constitute the painting's foreground and middle ground are a distinct reference to his recent immersion in Cézanne's painterly techniques; in particular, the high-keyed palette of the trees and fields echoes his Mont Sainte-Victoire paintings (see *Mont Sainte-Victoire, Aix-en-Provence,* plate 43). The contours of the blue-violet mountain stand out crisply against the vibrant blue sky, but the mass of the mountain itself is thinly painted, with hardly any articulation or detail. It is almost as if Hartley—haunted by his childhood, misunderstood by his colleagues, and lonely in his native country—cannot quite bring himself to explore the physicality of the mountains that once were, and would become again, a significant source of spiritual and artistic inspiration.[3] K.W.

1 *Autobiography*, 142.
2 Hartley to Rebecca Strand, 30 September 1930, quoted in Haskell, 80.
3 Hokin, 64–73.

46

Mountains in Stone, Dogtown, 1931
Oil on academy board, 18 × 24 in.
(45.7 × 61 cm)
Inscribed on verso:
Dogtown 1931 / Marsden Hartley

PROVENANCE
Mrs. Adelaide (Charles P.) Kuntz (purchased from the artist); Harvey and Françoise Rambach; Barbara R. Palmer

Collection of Barbara R. Palmer
Courtesy of Babcock Galleries, New York

47

Flaming Pool, Dogtown, 1931
Oil on academy board, 18 × 24 in.
(45.7 × 61 cm)
Inscribed on verso: Flaming Pool / Dogtown 1931 / Marsden Hartley / Beethoven (in Dogtown) / Deep chested trills arise— / from organ pipes of juniper / Oboe's throat expands—mezzo cries / of blueberry and sage and ferns prefer / to die among the rocks, nobly perish / mire of torrid green— / Summer's strident blades of damascene / hot tone or here is garish / the vox human swells and dwells / Persistently mid nuances of lapis grey / So much more wonderful this way / than summer in a trance / of chlorophyll or other circumstance

PROVENANCE
The Downtown Gallery, New York; Adelaide Kuntz; Yale Collection of American Literature (from 1952)

Yale Collection of American Literature
Beinecke Rare Book and Manuscript Library
Yale University, New Haven
Gift of Adelaide Kuntz

48

Whale's Jaw Rock, Dogtown, c. 1931–34
Pencil on academy board, 18 × 24 in.
(45.7 × 61 cm)
Inscribed on front with color notations in pencil

PROVENANCE
Salander-O'Reilly Galleries

Salander-O'Reilly Galleries, New York

49

Untitled (Blueberry Patch), c. 1934–35
Pen and black ink on white paper, 6⅞ × 9⅞ in.
(17.5 × 25.1 cm)
Unsigned

PROVENANCE
Estate of the artist; gift to Bates College from Hartley's niece, Norma Berger

Bates College Museum of Art, Lewiston, Maine

50

The Old Bars, Dogtown, 1936
Oil on academy board, 18 × 24 in.
(45.7 × 61 cm)
Unsigned

PROVENANCE
Whitney Museum of American Art (purchased 1937 from An American Place, New York)

Whitney Museum of American Art, New York
Purchase

In the summer of 1931, not at all happy about having had to leave France the previous year and after a relatively unsuccessful year of painting, Hartley traveled to Gloucester, Massachusetts. He remained there through much of the fall, and the time became one of the defining moments of his life. Typically, he scorned the picturesque harbor that most artists painted and hiked back from the port into Dogtown Common, a remote area that had been an agricultural community during the seventeenth and eighteenth centuries. From a visit in 1920, he "remembered the rocks and the name Dogtown—that's a great name—and no one in all the years of Gloucester painting celebrity had ever done anything about Dogtown."[1]

He went to Dogtown every day, he told a friend in mid-July, and "a very strange stretch of landscape it is." It was "full of magnificent boulders driven & left there by the glacial pressures ages ago."[2] He quickly sketched outcroppings such as the Whale's Jaw Rock, which embodied for him the forces of nature. Split apart thousands of years before, the two parts of a boulder looked like the head of a whale as it broke from the sea. In his memoir he recalled

> *A sense of eeriness [which] pervades all the place... and the white ghosts of those huge boulders—mostly granite—stand like sentinels guarding nothing but shore—seagulls fly over it on their way from the marshes to the sea—otherwise the place is forsaken and majestically lonely, as if nature had at last formed one spot where she can live for herself alone....*
>
> *[To paint it] takes someone to be obsessed by nature for its own sake—one with a feeling for the austerities and the intellectual aloofness which lost lonesome areas can persist in—all of a piece—even though another kind of piece it is with those vast spaces of New Mexico where nature is given up majestically to her own freedom.*[3]

Once in Dogtown he would wander about, then sit for a long time absorbing one view or another and briefly sketching it on a board, where he might indicate the primary colors, but the scene he later painted would be largely from memory, landscape distilled to its essences. By mid-August he had five paintings under way, small but intense, he felt certain, and he told Alfred Stieglitz that "It may prove this summer to be a general resurrection-revelation—evolution out of revolution I am wanting to phrase it." He called it "emotion contained—'art condensed not diluted' as Degas puts it."[4]

Mountains in Stone, Dogtown is an excellent example of "art condensed." Hartley held on to elements of Cézanne's still lifes while conveying the vitality and movement he observed. Heavy brushwork and large, distinct blocks of color add force to the painting. Rocks and vivid red and gold bushes are topped by a stylized tree in the shape of a cross that from the viewer's perspective touches a white cloud in a clear blue sky. "I paint rocks & rocks only," he wrote the artist Florine Stettheimer. He told her that he had put some lines from T. S. Eliot's poem "Ash Wednesday" on the back of one painting, explaining that the poem was for him "a kind of biblical motto for it is what I am trying to practice in my life just now. To care magnificently—& equally not to care—in the same [manner]—Precept enough don't you think for one [tame] life."[5]

Dogtown inspired him to write as well as to paint. On the back of *Flaming Pool, Dogtown* he inscribed the poem that he first titled "Beethoven (in Dogtown)." While later he would expand it, change the title to "Soliloquy in Dogtown, Cape Ann," and strengthen its images, the first version catches the sense of calm and closeness to nature that he strove for. Both *Mountains in Stone, Dogtown* and *Flaming Pool, Dogtown* convey a sense of solitude and tranquility, but also of vitality and pleasure because the colors pulsate, the dense texture of the paint gives the paintings a tactile quality, and the designs have movement. Just as the work of the abstract expressionists would later—one thinks of Pollock's action paintings and the blocks of color filling Rothko's canvases—these substantially abstract pictures evoke responses more on their own terms than as representations of literal nature.

For the catalogue to an exhibition of twenty of his Dogtown landscapes at the Downtown Gallery in April and May 1932, Hartley included a poem he had undoubtedly written under the influence of Dogtown:

Rock, juniper, and wind,
And a sea gull sitting still—
All these of one mind.
He who finds will
To come home
Will surely find old faith
Made new again,
And lavish welcome.
Old things breaketh
New, when heart and soul
Lose no whit of old refrain;
It is a smiling festival
When rock, juniper, and wind
Are of one mind;
A sea gull signs the bond
makes what was broken, whole.[6]

Hartley visited Gloucester again in 1934 and 1936, both times making pen and ink sketches from which he executed paintings such as *The Old Bars, Dogtown.* While these convey the sense of the 1931 paintings, the patterning of shapes is more complex, having, as Gail Scott has noted, "a greater depth of field, marked by a rich interplay of diagonals."[7] As a group, the Dogtown paintings mark a breakthrough in his work. He gave all his attention to "this extraordinary stretch of almost metaphysical landscape," he told Adelaide Kuntz. "It cannot appeal to dull painters because it calls for deep contact and study and I am capable of both, and while my pictures are small—they are more intense than ever before, and I have for once (again) immersed myself in the mysticism of nature."[8] T.L.

1 *Autobiography,* 143.
2 Hartley to Adelaide Kuntz, 16 July 1931, Beinecke/Yale.
3 *Autobiography,* 144.
4 Hartley to Alfred Stieglitz, 12 August 1931, Beinecke/Yale.
5 Hartley to Florine Stettheimer, 17 August 1931, Beinecke/Yale.
6 *Collected Poems,* 251.
7 Gail R. Scott, "Marsden Hartley at Dogtown Common," *Arts Magazine* 54, no. 2 (October 1979): 163.
8 Hartley to Adelaide Kuntz, 22 October 1931, Beinecke/Yale.

51

Earth Cooling, Mexico, 1932
Oil on cardboard, mounted on Masonite, $24\frac{1}{2} \times 33\frac{7}{8}$ in. (62.2×86 cm)
Inscribed on verso in blue paint: EARTH-COOLING / MEXICO / MARSDeN / HARTLEY / 1932

PROVENANCE

Estate of the artist (no. 34); The Downtown Gallery, New York (from 1958); Dr. and Mrs. Michael Watter, Philadelphia; auction at Parke-Bernet Galleries, New York, October 19, 1967 (no. 27); Amon Carter Museum (purchased 1967)

Amon Carter Museum, Fort Worth, Texas

52

Morgenrot, 1932
Oil on canvas, 25×23 in. (63.5×58.4 cm)
Inscribed on verso in blue paint: Morgenrot / Marsden Hartley / Mexico / 1932

PROVENANCE

Estate of the artist; private collection

Private Collection
Courtesy of Babcock Galleries, New York

53

Popocatépetl, Spirited Morning—Mexico, 1932
Oil on academy board, 25×29 in. (63.5×73.6 cm)
Inscribed on verso in blue paint: Popocatápetl / —Spirited Morning / Marsden / Hartley / Mexico / 1932

PROVENANCE

Estate of the artist; Elizabeth B. Blake; Gerald Peters Gallery, New York; private collection

Private Collection
Courtesy of Gerald Peters Gallery, New York

Early in 1932 Hartley traveled to Mexico on a Guggenheim Fellowship. At first he was infatuated with the land and the people, but soon he felt overpowered: "Grandeur of scene, splendour of race, smoldering volcanoes, fire coloured birds, the most amazing light eye has ever encountered ... pestilence, miasmas, crocodiles, aigrettes, lizards, flame consuming the whole aspect of life" was how he described Mexico in his memoir.[1] He never became acclimated to the country, so after moving from Mexico City to Cuernavaca, where he read in the large collection of books on mysticism that belonged to friends there, he began "pictures of mystical import."[2] Eventually he would have an exhibition in Mexico City of twenty paintings, including *Earth Cooling, Morgenrot,* and *Popocatépetl, Spirited Morning.* The elemental shapes and colors of *Earth Cooling* and *Popocatépetl, Spirited Morning* are reminiscent of what he attempted in the Dogtown works.

Morgenrot is the most complex of the three, incorporating the strong tones he found everywhere in Mexico with the mysticism of Paracelsus and his follower Jakob Böhme, for whom the materialized word of God was to be found in the seventh realm of divine corporeality where perfect order and completeness are found. In *Morgenrot* the seventh sphere is on the materialized hand of the Lord. The red is a reminder of the Indians, the land, the brilliant sun, and the blood of man, all aspects of God made corporeal in the *morgenrot,* the red morning of the seventh day when all was in harmony. Hartley's subtitle for the painting is "The hand of the morning born from the triumphant night," revelation and light, that is, after darkness. As the *Exposicion Marsden Hartley* was about to open in late February 1933, he wrote Adelaide Kuntz that he was "happy that I have risen to [the] field of sensation and experience, and that I have realized the desire of years to really enter the field of true fancy and imagination, and that I don't think that even Blake would laugh at my fantasias if he were to see them."[3] T.L.

1 *Autobiography,* 146.
2 Hartley to Adelaide Kuntz, 28 July 1932, Beinecke/Yale.
3 Hartley to Adelaide Kuntz, 17 February 1933, Beinecke/Yale.

54

Eight Bells Folly, Memorial for Hart Crane, 1933
Oil on canvas, 31⅝ × 39½ in. (80.3 × 100.3 cm)
Inscribed on verso in black paint: Eight Bells' / Folly. Memorial / for Hart / Crane Marsden / Hartley Mexico / 1933

PROVENANCE
Adelaide Kuntz, New York (from 1946, acquired through The Downtown Gallery, New York); Bertha Schaefer Gallery, New York; Ione and Hudson Walker, Forest Hills, N.Y.; University Gallery (now Weisman Art Museum; from 1961)

Frederick R. Weisman Art Museum, University of Minnesota, Minneapolis
Gift of Ione and Hudson Walker

Shortly after arriving in Mexico City, Hartley renewed his friendship with the poet Hart Crane, which he had forged in France several years before. In Mexico they saw a lot of each other before Crane departed aboard ship for the United States at the end of April 1932. During the voyage Crane committed suicide by throwing himself overboard. His death was a severe blow to Hartley, who in the succeeding months wrote prose and a long poem, "Un Recuerdo—Hermano—Hart Crane R.I.P.," and painted *Eight Bells Folly* in tribute to the poet.

He did not begin the painting immediately after Crane's death, but by December he wrote Adelaide Kuntz that he had six paintings under way, among them a "marine fantasy symbolic of Hart Crane's death by drowning." It had a "very mad look" about it, and he explained that

> *There is a ship foundering—a sun, a moon, two triangles, clouds—a shark pushing up out of the mad waters—and at the right corner—a bell with "8" on it—symbolizing 8 bells—or noon when he jumped off—and around the bell are a lot of men's eyes—that look up from below to see who the new lodger is to be—on one cloud will be the number 33—Hart's age—and according to some occult beliefs [that] is the dangerous age of a man—for if he survives 33 he lives on—Christ was supposed to be 33—on the other cloud will be 2—the sum of his poetic product.*[1]

To this he added two, eight-pointed stars on the left cloud, not the number 2, and one eight-pointed star to the right cloud, signifying cosmic transcendence (see plates 14, 21). Hartley placed 33 on the ship's sail, added an 8 to a cloud, and set the number 9, representing body, mind, and spirit, in front of the devouring shark. The painting when completed was without doubt one of his most complex, thoroughly symbolic works which nevertheless is visually satisfying because of its form and color. T.L.

1 Hartley to Adelaide Kuntz, 5 December 1932, Beinecke/Yale.

55

Waxenstein at Hamarsbach, Garmisch, Bavaria, 1933–34
Oil on cardboard, 29¾ × 20¾ in. (75.6 × 52.7 cm)
Signed lower right: M·H

PROVENANCE
Vanderwoude Tananbaum Gallery, New York (1993); private collection

Private Collection

Hartley was relieved to depart the spiritually tempestuous Mexico for his beloved Germany in April 1933. After a stay in Hamburg he settled in Partenkirchen, nestled in the Bavarian Alps. By early September he was "alpining," as he called his long walks, and he reveled about being "next to rocks & mountains again." The Waxenstein peaks to the south were glorious, and he immediately began making detailed studies of them and recognized that for him painting mountains meant understanding "the meaning of space the significance of rhythm and the quality of time in appearances." Mountains to him were symbols of power and potential destructiveness, but also of beauty and stability.

He believed that painting in the Alps was a "proud preparation for recovering the 'eye' for the native scene," the New England landscape, which was very like the Alps "in structure & repetition." He quickly observed the closeness of the mountains, which because there was "almost no intervening atmosphere, as nothing is more than a mile from the eye, and as it is all shut in here, the play of light is very small or limited, so they just stand like monuments, a cross between Blake and the Chinese."[1] The mountains he painted in the Alps are foregrounded and flattened out so that the viewer is brought directly up to them. What Gail Scott has written about another painting of the peak holds true for *Waxenstein at Hamarsbach* as well: "the lessons of Cézanne come home: from the perfect harmonizing of color comes precise design. Even though the architectonics of the mountain dominate, the viewer is not overwhelmed by a picturesque alpine panorama but rather embraced by the shadow of its somber presence."[2] "What I am doing here now," Hartley asserted to Adelaide Kuntz in November, "is the work of the rest of my life." And as the year ended he told her that "I have never painted like I am doing now."[3] T.L.

1 Hartley to Adelaide Kuntz, 7 September 1933, Beinecke/Yale.
2 Scott, 101.
3 Hartley to Adelaide Kuntz, 4 November and 25 December 1933, Beinecke/Yale.

56

Mountain Landscape, Church Steeple in Foreground, 1933
Silverpoint drawing on paper, 10⅝ × 14⅞ in. (27 × 37.8 cm)
Inscribed lower right: Oberbayern, Karwendel und Ellmau Sep 5, 33

PROVENANCE
From A Bavarian Sketchbook; Michael St. Clair, New York; Huntington Library, Art Collections, and Botanical Gardens (purchased 1996)

The Huntington Library, Art Collections, and Botanical Gardens, San Marino, California
Gift of Michael St. Clair

57

Mountain Landscape with Pine Trees, 1933
Silverpoint drawing on paper, 14⅞ × 10⅝ in. (37.8 × 27 cm)
Signed lower right: MH Waxenstein Sep 10–33

PROVENANCE
From A Bavarian Sketchbook; Michael St. Clair, New York; Huntington Library, Art Collections, and Botanical Gardens (purchased 1996)

The Huntington Library, Art Collections, and Botanical Gardens, San Marino, California
Gift of Michael St. Clair

58

Garmisch, 1933
Pencil on beige paper, 9⅞ × 7 in. (25.1 × 17.8 cm)
Signed lower right: garmisch / M.H. / oct 13.33

PROVENANCE
Estate of the artist; gift to Bates College from Hartley's niece, Norma Berger

Bates College Museum of Art, Lewiston, Maine

Hartley spent the autumn and winter of 1933–34 in the Bavarian Alps with his sketchbook, making studies for paintings, pastels, and prints of the Alpine scenery (see plate 55). This was a shift toward realism for Hartley, who had been painting fantasy pictures in Mexico. In November, when heavy snowfall made hiking through the mountains difficult, Hartley used his sketches such as this pencil *Garmisch* to create paintings that were often simpler and sometimes amalgams of the drawings they were based on. He called his beautiful, delicate silverpoint drawings mountain skeletons.[1] A.E.

1 Scott, 100–101.

59

Sea View—New England, 1934
Oil on academy board, 12 × 16 in. (30.5 × 40.6 cm)
Inscribed on verso: Sea View—New England / Marsden Hartley. / 1934

PROVENANCE
Phillips Collection (purchased 1939 from the artist through Hudson Walker Gallery, New York)

The Phillips Collection, Washington, D.C.

60

(Flowers) Roses from Hispania, 1936
Oil on academy board, 23½ × 17¼ in. (59.7 × 43.8 cm)
Unsigned

PROVENANCE
Estate of the artist; Berry-Hill Galleries, New York; private collection

Private Collection
Courtesy of Berry-Hill Galleries, New York

During the period 1934–36 Hartley faced his most difficult time financially. (When in November 1934 he was presented with a bill for $184 for storage of his paintings, he became desperate and in January 1935 destroyed more than one hundred paintings and drawings to reduce his storage costs.) Knowing that his Dogtown works were not likely to be very saleable, while he was in Gloucester in the summer of 1934 he painted still lifes in the hope of having some commercial success.

But he was his own worst enemy. He could not make himself paint slick scenes of Gloucester harbor. Rather, he made works such as *Sea View—New England,* which, although Bruce Robertson has termed them "very polished and commercial still lifes,"[1] have Hartley's stamp too much on them for them to be simply "polished and commercial." Gail Scott, discussing a slightly larger "sea view," *New England Sea View—Fish House* (1934), which is nearly identical to *Sea View—New England,* pointed out that it is a motif of his own invention, a still life "in front of [a] telescopic seascape vista."

Scott recognized intricacies that Hartley had employed earlier in works such as *Atlantic Window* (plate 30) and would use in powerful late paintings such as *Summer, Sea, Window, Red Curtain* (plate 104). *Sea View* is a painted collage of symbols of the New England coast: a star fish and perhaps a cod, nets, lobster buoys, dock pilings, beach, the ocean, and what was becoming Hartley's signature symbol, the sail of a ship heading out to sea. In *Sea View* he added his reversed initials to a lobster buoy in the upper left, and under that he placed the symbolic number 8. As in *New England Sea View,* in the smaller seascape "opposites of near and far, closed and open, mesh in a tightly controlled web of shape, line, and color."[2] These paintings are homages to the northern coast of the Atlantic Ocean, which played a major role in the remainder of Hartley's life.

Hartley began *Flowers (Roses from Hispania)* in Bermuda during the summer of 1935. There he worked at small paintings—"pure spirit" he termed them—as well as some flower pieces and fish arrangements. Late in the summer he traveled to Nova Scotia, settling quickly in Blue Rocks, near the fishing town of Lunenburg. He immediately felt embraced by the people and the setting, and when he made the acquaintance of the Francis Mason family, he asked them if he might stay with them on East Point Island, where they lived. "I fell in love with a most amazing family of men & women the like of which I have never in my life seen—veritable rocks of Gibraltar in appearance the very salt of salt," he wrote Adelaide Kuntz in November.[3] Having made plans to visit the Masons the following summer, he returned to New York, where during the early months of 1936 he prepared for an exhibition that opened at An American Place on March 22, finishing *Flowers* and others of the paintings he had begun in Bermuda. *Flowers* was one of what in the catalogue for the show he termed "Six Romantic Intervals," its vivid colors and ordered design reflecting something of the contentment Hartley felt about his intimate friendship with the Masons.[4] T.L.

[1] Robertson, 105.
[2] Scott, 104.
[3] Hartley to Adelaide Kuntz, 4 November 1935, Beinecke/Yale.
[4] The "Six Romantic Intervals" were, in the words of the 1936 exhibition catalogue, "intended for use as focus motives in a convalescent pavilion, chiefly neurotic." See An American Place, *Marsden Hartley* (New York: An American Place, 1936), 7.

61

Northern Seascape, Off the Banks, 1936
Oil on academy board, 18³⁄₁₆ × 24 in.
(46.2 × 61 cm)
Unsigned

PROVENANCE
Sold by Hudson Walker to Karl Freund; Max E. Friedman, Milwaukee (from 1939); Milwaukee Art Museum (bequest 1954)

Milwaukee Art Museum
Bequest of Max E. Friedman

On the night of September 19, 1936, the two Mason sons, Alty and Donny, and their cousin Allen were drowned when they attempted to return to East Point Island in a fierce storm. The Mason family and Hartley were devastated. He offered to leave, but they urged him to stay, and until he departed, he wrote extensively and painted more than twenty pictures and made numerous drawings. While the island itself did not offer him spectacular landscapes or seascapes in a literal fashion, the associations he made with them and the terrible intensity of his experiences fueled his imagination. One of his first responses to the boys' drowning was *Northern Seascape, Off the Banks,* a dark, Ryderesque scene of jagged, tooth-like rocks with surf smashing against them, and on the gray-black ocean beyond, two wave-tossed sailing ships driving toward a black horizon line. Lowering clouds and a threatening sky complete the scene, a stark, even violent, reminder of a natural world that could be savagely cruel. T.L.

62

Smelt Brook Falls, 1937
Oil on academy board, 28 × 22 in.
(71.1 × 55.9 cm)
Unsigned

PROVENANCE
Hudson Walker Gallery, New York; City Art Museum of St. Louis (now Saint Louis Art Museum; purchased 1939)

The Saint Louis Art Museum, St. Louis, Missouri
Purchase, Eliza McMillan Fund

For the last exhibition Hartley ever had with Alfred Stieglitz, he wrote a catalogue introduction in which he declared that he wanted to be known as "the painter from Maine." During the summer of 1937 he set about accomplishing that, taking on Maine with notable success, as with *Smelt Brook Falls.* Here he demonstrated his awareness of cubism and his Cézannesque insistence upon rendering elemental forms drawn from the woods of Maine. The painting is flattened out, nearly two-dimensional, and it has a monumentality about it, but also a dedication to exact shape and detail that celebrates the natural world that Hartley knew could seem ordered, certainly graceful, even as it could be harshly destructive. T.L.

63

Give Us This Day, 1938
Oil on canvas, 30 × 40 in. (76.2 × 101.6 cm)
Unsigned

PROVENANCE
Ione and Hudson Walker, Forest Hills, N.Y. (by 1939); Fine Arts Work Center, Provincetown, Mass. (bequest); Babcock Galleries, New York; Shaklee Corporate Art Collection, San Francisco; Curtis Galleries

Curtis Galleries, Minneapolis, Minnesota

64

Fishermen's Last Supper, 1938
Oil on board, 22 × 28 in. (55.9 × 71.1 cm)
Inscribed on verso in pencil: Fisherman's Last Supper—/ Marsden Hartley / 1938

PROVENANCE
Ione and Hudson D. Walker, Forest Hills, N.Y.; Estate of Ione Walker; Salander-O'Reilly Galleries, New York; private collection

Private Collection

65

Untitled (Three Men Standing Behind Two Women with Aprons) c. 1938–39
Pencil on white paper, 10½ × 8 in. (26.7 × 20.4 cm)
Unsigned

PROVENANCE
Estate of the artist; gift to Bates College from Hartley's niece, Norma Berger

Bates College Museum of Art, Lewiston, Maine

66

Adelard the Drowned, Master of the "Phantom," c. 1938–39
Oil on academy board, 28 × 22 in. (71.1 × 55.9 cm)
Inscribed on verso: Adelard—The Drowned— / Master of the "Phantom"— / Marsden Hartley / 1938–9

PROVENANCE
Ione and Hudson Walker, Forest Hills, N.Y. (purchased 1941); University Gallery (now Weisman Art Museum; bequest, 1978)

Frederick R. Weisman Art Museum, University of Minnesota, Minneapolis
Bequest of Hudson Walker from the Ione and Hudson Walker Collection

67

Marie Ste. Esprit, 1938–39
Oil on academy board, 28 × 22 in. (71.1 × 55.9 cm)
Unsigned

PROVENANCE
Ione and Hudson Walker, Forest Hills, N.Y. (purchased 1941); University Gallery (now Weisman Art Museum; bequest, 1978)

Frederick R. Weisman Art Museum, University of Minnesota, Minneapolis
Bequest of Hudson Walker from the Ione and Hudson Walker Collection

68

Cleophas, Master of the "Gilda Grey," 1938–39
Oil on academy board, 28 × 22 in. (71.1 × 55.9 cm)
Inscribed on verso in pencil: Cleophas— / Master of the "Gilda Grey" / Marsden Hartley / 1938–39

PROVENANCE
Ione and Hudson Walker, Forest Hills, N.Y. (purchased 1941); Bertha H. Walker (by 1971); Walker Art Center (1971)

Walker Art Center, Minneapolis, Minnesota
Gift of Bertha H. Walker, 1971

69

The Lost Felice, 1939
Oil on canvas, 40⅛ × 30 1/16 in. (101.9 × 76.4 cm)
Inscribed on verso across top: THE LOST / FELICE. / Marsden / Hartley / 1939–40.

PROVENANCE
With Mabeth Gallery, New York (1941–42); Estate of the artist (1943); with Paul Rosenberg & Co., New York (1942–46); Mr. and Mrs. Walter Bareiss, Greenwich, Conn. (1946–c. 1960); with Paul Kantor Galleries, Beverly Hills, Calif. (to 1963); Los Angeles County Museum of Art (1963)

Los Angeles County Museum of Art
Mr. and Mrs. William Preston Harrison Collection

70

Fishermen's Last Supper, 1940–41
Oil on Masonite-type hardboard, 29⅞ × 41 in. (75.9 × 104.1 cm)
Signed lower right: M.H / 40–41

PROVENANCE
Macbeth Gallery, New York; Paul Rosenberg & Co., New York; acquired from the artist in 1943 by Roy R. Neuberger

Roy R. Neuberger Collection

All of these paintings refer to the Mason family. In mid-spring of 1938 Hartley moved to Vinalhaven, off the coast of Maine, for a long summer of painting. It seemed ideal to him at first, a place which might inspire him with its views of the ocean and where he could observe the population, nearly all "fishermen up from the sea—picturesque men of course—quiet, gentle—and all say 'hi' or hello here—so you can't escape a friendly recognition."[1] The setting and the people on the island created the right atmosphere for the work he had in mind: highly symbolic pictures, memory portraits of Albert Pinkham Ryder and of the Mason family, and powerful seascapes—coastal scapes, really—which were also symbolic, picking up images of a rugged, rocky shoreline pounded by waves, very much like *Northern Seascape, Off the Banks* (plate 61), which he had painted shortly after the deaths of Alty and Donny Mason in September 1936.

He painted with great energy, noting after he had been on Vinalhaven only a short while that he already had seven paintings under way. One, *Give Us This Day* (plate 63), is an obviously symbolic piece about community and communion, in which five seagulls (the Mason family), with a sixth somewhat further back and off to one side (Hartley), are poised behind three fish in the foreground—representing the livelihood of fishermen as well as the parable of the loaves and fishes and even the Holy Trinity. The background is the familiar rocky coastline, ocean, and sky, with Hartley's trademark, a single schooner, outbound. The harmony of the painting's forms and colors and the stillness of the gulls themselves convey the sense of calm that Hartley most admired about the Mason household.

The memory portraits that he began in 1938 of Alty and his father and mother, Francis and Martha, are, as Hartley called them, "archaic." Barbara Haskell has noted that, "although individualized, these portraits are not intended to be naturalistic. Rather, as with other artists, like Georges Rouault and Gauguin, who attempted to depict religious faith and renewal in contemporary terms, Hartley was inspired by pre-Renaissance sources." The figures were meant to be icons, and in these paintings Hartley picked up on the "abstract rigidity and mannered, stylized effect [of] his Mexican paintings."[2] To protect the privacy of the Masons he gave them French-Canadian names: Alty became Adelard; Martha, Marie Ste. Esprit; Francis, Cleophas; and for a painting he did later than the first three, Alice, a Mason daughter, became Felice.

His newfound interest in the human figure marked his deepening involvement in the idea of community, which had culminated for him during his two stays with the Masons. Through them he had discovered new meaning and a deeper faith. The primitive, archaic quality of his portraits did not spring from an inability to paint the human figure well; rather, he made a conscious effort to render the figures as direct, simple icons. He loved Ryder, the Masons, and Abraham Lincoln, whom he would paint as *The Great Good Man* (plate 78) in 1942, for their elemental natures. Sophisticated, naturalistic portraits would have conveyed his emotion less well.

Repeatedly he described his feelings for the burly Alty. A poem, "Encompassed," conveys Hartley's passion for him:

Encompassed me in arms
Concentric—
Took kin and left me happy
free
eyes burned like flames in burning
tree
tongue clogged with exquisite fury.

Hair stood on end like fury-fire
mouth blowing steam of thick desire
we will go, you will go, you will
not go, without me.
I will be thunder in your stride
I will be terror in your thickening
eyes—wide
with stricken wonder.

I will be love
you never heard of
and shoots of everlasting fear-
lessness
will break from your engendered
breast
ere sun go to west
you will be utterly encompassed.

I walked along
Beaten with the song.

In a long prose poem entitled "Cleophas and His Own: A North Atlantic Tragedy," Hartley described each member of the family while recounting his experiences in Nova Scotia that ended with his departure in late November. Essentially completed before he left the Masons, it consists of a long threnody describing his life among the Masons and a group of "Postludes," prose and poetic pieces about the time after the death of the young men and his eventual poignant departure. "Si tu n'avais pas connu [If I hadn't known you—a line from a French sailor song]— / So long, my five beauties, whose lives enlarged my own," he ended the entire work, referring to the Mason family.

Francis (Cleophas) was "six feet one or two in his stocking feet and his powerful words seem[ed] to have an upraising quality and gave him for me a monumental quality." He had "no angular slant to any of his thoughts, he never resorted to the abuses of oblique conduct." With a body "as hard as rocks" and huge hands, he was a veritable giant in Hartley's eyes, but a gentle one, kind to the admiring painter and "a natural mystic of the sea, which has taught him to be brave, fearless, trusting, full of faith—all simplicity." His wife Martha (Marie Ste. Esprit) had about her a "mystical splendour" that was "of an entirely practical quality." Gentle, beautiful, the mother of seven children, she managed every aspect of the household. "She was the appointed Mother of us all," Hartley wrote in admiration.

Alty (Adelard) was "tall, huge, giantesque, and his smoke black hair [stood] six inches above his low forehead, making him seem all the taller, almost spectral, he—the most Norman looking of them all." Powerful, emotional, uninhibited, in love with men as with women, Alty had "a heart as tender as that of a young girl." His sister Alice (Felice) was dutiful, proud of her work that was "all given to the mother and father, and the giant sons." But for all that, she was "solemn because there [was] no love coming into her life"; hence when Hartley painted her portrait in 1939 she became *The Lost Felice,* deeply saddened and lonely after the deaths of her brothers.[3] The painting is of her "sitting staring out of the picture and dark visions of the two brothers in the background offering her blue fish at either side."[4]

"Cleophas and His Own" concludes with a short poem, "Fishermen's Last Supper":

For Wine, they drank the ocean—
for bread, they ate their own despairs;
counsel from the moon was theirs
for the foolish contention.

Murder is not a pretty thing
yet seas do raucous everything
to make it pretty—
for the foolish or the brave,
a way seas have.[5]

The poem was the seed for Hartley's climactic painting about the Masons, the second version of *Fishermen's Last Supper* painted in 1940–41. On Vinalhaven in 1938 he told Adelaide Kuntz of his intention to do a large painting of "the N. S. family at table—never have I seen such an epic sight as it was three times a day—such a sense of unity—as they all loved and admired each other & were so gracious to each other at all times & that is what love & harmony can bring forth when two parents are perfectly joined."[6] The next year when the art critic Elizabeth McCausland enthusiastically reviewed Hartley's second show with his dealer Hudson Walker, he immediately responded: "I want you to know that I am *most pleased* with your report of my show in the Springfield Republican." He was impressed that she could "go into the 'new pieces' with such a sympathetic understanding. It is quite my purpose to get out of the scale of 'chichi' which a lot of good painting sometimes displays." "Simplification," he continued, "is not easy—but I felt I had accomplished it to a respectable degree, and the people with whom I lived in the north taught me that to an encouraging degree by their profoundly simple & humble behavior concerning all things.... The Fishermen's Last Supper is of course but the preliminary study for a proposed large—very large canvas and the portraits are set in panels for the imagined sea-house perhaps a fishermen's community house of which these hard working people are much in need."[7]

In the first version of *Fishermen's Last Supper* (plate 64), the five Masons are seated at a dining table. On the wall behind Francis, at the center, is a picture of a schooner; seated at either end of the group are the two boys, with eight-pointed stars above their heads, symbolizing regeneration. In the immediate foreground are three empty chairs, the two outer ones wrapped at the top with wreaths to mark the drowned boys, the center chair being symbolic either of Hartley himself or of Allen, the third boy who drowned. On the front edge of the tablecloth between the chairs is written "Mene Mene," a reference to the Old Testament tale of the proud and defiant King Belshazzar, whose doom God warned of by His handwriting on the wall, which said, in effect, "You have been judged and found wanting." Alty's proud defiance of the elements was believed to have been the cause of the three boys' deaths.

In 1940 Hartley began the second and larger version of the same scene (plate 70). More brilliantly colored—a deep-blue wall instead of a pale-blue one serves as the background—the painting is more forceful not only because of that but also because it is less overtly symbolic. Hartley removed the eight-pointed stars and the "Mene Mene," and the figures of the family, while still archaic in style, are more fully rendered and dominate the painting as they do not in the first version. T.L.

1 Hartley to Adelaide Kuntz, n.d. [spring 1938], Beinecke/Yale.
2 Haskell, 115.
3 The quotations from "Cleophas and His Own" come from Ferguson, 94–98, 122; Gail Scott discusses the creation of the piece in her essay "'Cleophas and His Own': The Making of a Narrative," in Ferguson, 55–73.
4 Hartley to Elizabeth Sparhawk Jones, 23 October 1939, Beinecke/Yale.
5 Ferguson, 132.
6 Hartley to Adelaide Kuntz, 19–20 July 1938, Beinecke/Yale.
7 Hartley to Elizabeth McCausland, [April] 1939, McCausland Papers, Archives/Smithsonian, reel 270. Her review is "Marsden Hartley, Max Beckmann and Others," *Springfield Sunday Union and Republican*, 5 March 1939.

71

Portrait of Albert Pinkham Ryder, 1938
Oil on Masonite board, 28 × 22 in.
(71.1 × 55.9 cm)
Inscribed on verso: ALBERT RYDER SEEN ONLY AT NIGHT / 8th AVE & 15th ST. NEW YORK.

PROVENANCE
Estate of the artist (no estate no.); Paul Rosenberg & Co., New York; Edith and Milton Lowenthal, New York (from 1946); Metropolitan Museum of Art (1991)

The Metropolitan Museum of Art, New York
Edith and Milton Lowenthal Collection
Bequest of Edith Abrahamson Lowenthal, 1991

In 1938 Hartley wrote to Hudson Walker:

I have a memory portrait of Albert Ryder nearly finished and that will cause a "stir" because I am one of the few left who remember him—or saw him evenings on 8th Avenue—but I never saw him but once in daylight—as he was never out. Hayes Miller painted a dry formal portrait from him years ago but Ryder insisted on "dressing up"—but I have him exactly as he was every day in his woolen jacket and his woolen skull cap—and I am proud of the memory feat since I saw him last around nineteen seventeen, or eighteen—and besides interesting many people and surely it ought to interest this generation—it will be a valuable document and if sold must have a high price for it.[1]

Hartley painted a group of memory portraits in the mid-1930s and early 1940s, including his posthumous portrait of Alty Mason (plate 66) and his portraits of Abraham Lincoln (plate 78) and John Donne (plate 77), these last painted from photographs or engravings. His portrait of Ryder, however, is strictly from memory—he did not work from an image of any sort, other than that in his mind.

As Hartley himself asserted in his letter to Walker, he presents Ryder in the knitted skullcap and jacket he habitually wore. Like the portraits of the Masons and some of the other late figurative works, the figure of

Ryder nearly fills the composition. His frontal pose and his direct gaze also recall Hartley's other "archaic" portraits.[2]

Hartley first encountered Ryder's work in 1909 at the gallery of Mr. N. E. Montross, located at 550 Fifth Avenue, New York. In his autobiography, Hartley recalled the marine by Ryder he saw at Montross's: "It was a picture that so affected me that I in all truth was never the same after the first moment—for the power that was in it shook the rafters of my being and left me sort of shaking in the force of the wind."[3] In 1909 Hartley painted a group of paintings identified by Alfred Stieglitz as "dark mountain" paintings (see plate 6), characterized by a dark palette and a melancholy mood, and clearly influenced by Ryder's work,[4] which Hartley himself described as "dramatic mysticism."[5]

Hartley wrote extensively about Ryder, including essays "Albert P. Ryder"[6] and "Eakins, Homer, Ryder" (1930),[7] and the poem "Albert Ryder—Moonlightist."[8] A.E.

1 Hartley (from Vinalhaven, Maine) to Hudson Walker, 8 October 1938, quoted in McCausland Papers, Archives/Smithsonian, roll D270.
2 Coptic textiles, Fayum portraits, and early Renaissance masters were important influences on Hartley's archaic portraits. See Robertson, 114.
3 *Autobiography,* 67.
4 See Ludington, 64–65.
5 Hartley, "Eakins, Homer, Ryder," reprinted in *On Art,* 168.
6 In *Adventures,* 37–41.
7 Reprinted in *On Art,* 168–268.
8 Reprinted in *Collected Poems,* 224.

72

Sustained Comedy, 1939
Oil on academy board, 28⅛ × 22 in. (71.4 × 55.9 cm)
Signed lower left: M.H.
Inscribed on verso: Marsden Hartley / 1939 / Sustained / Comedy—[*crossed out*] / Portrait of an object [*crossed out*] / "O Big Earth"— / or—the sustained travesty

PROVENANCE
Hudson Walker, Forest Hills, N.Y. (c. 1939); Mervin Jules, Northampton, Mass. (by 1976); Carnegie Museum of Art (1976)

The Carnegie Museum of Art, Pittsburgh
Gift of Mervin Jules in memory of Hudson Walker, 1976, 76.64

Marsden Hartley explored self-portraiture in his writing and in his visual art (as discussed in the essay by Bruce Robertson), but only a single self-portrait has been identified as such by one of Hartley's contemporaries, and that painting is *Sustained Comedy.*[1] This painting, contemporaneous with and yet unlike the so-called archaic portraits (see plates 66–69), is highly symbolic. A number of scholars have pointed out that Hartley employed Christian imagery in *Sustained Comedy.* For example, the arrows through the figure's eyes suggest martyrdom in general and Saint Sebastian in particular, and on his chest is an image of the crucified Christ.[2]

Other symbols include the ambiguous make-up on the face of the figure, which suggests either a Native American in war paint or a clown, and the earring and dress of the figure, which evokes a sailor's costume. Some of the tattoos on his arms, chest, and throat seem to refer to other paintings or writings by Hartley. The ship on his chest recalls the ship in *Northern Seascape, Off the Banks* (plate 61) and the 1938 *Fishermen's Last Supper* (plate 64) and looks ahead to the ship in the painting on the wall in the later version of *Fishermen's Last Supper* (plate 70), all three paintings connected with the tragic deaths of the Masons. Sometime in the late 1930s, Hartley wrote "He Too Wore a Butterfly," a poem that names some of the same symbols that appear in *Sustained Comedy.*[3] It begins: "He wore a butterfly upon his flanks, / upsetting the woman and the ship in their angles, / and down his midrib the image of Christ, the feet / and the nails, touching his navel."[4] A.E.

1 It was Hartley's dealer Hudson Walker who said that *Sustained Comedy* is a self-portrait. See Weinberg, 185.
2 See ibid., 188–90, and Diana Strazdes, *American Paintings and Sculpture to 1945 in the Carnegie Museum of Art* (New York: Hudson Hills Press in association with the Carnegie Museum of Art, 1992), 230–31.
3 See Strazdes, *American Paintings and Sculpture,* 231.
4 Marsden Hartley, "He Too Wore a Butterfly," reprinted in *Collected Poems,* 171.

73

Lucifer's God Child, c. 1938–39
Pencil on beige paper, 10⅜ × 8⅛ in. (26.3 × 20.6 cm)
Inscribed on front with poem: He that was sick to the bone, / with the city cleansing his blood / and his spirit with the clog of / the hatred of the city— / turned with waves of the sea as they / beat on the rocks like the beat / of the clamor of his spirit / on the firmament of the city / lashed with the wind his—soul! / Lucifer's God Child—

PROVENANCE
Estate of the artist; gift to Bates College from Hartley's niece, Norma Berger

Bates College Museum of Art, Lewiston, Maine

Lucifer's God Child is one of a number of drawings of men that Hartley made throughout his career. Its enigmatic title and accompanying poem suggest Hartley's own dual affinity with the city and the sea. The drawing itself, however, bears a strong resemblance to Hartley's portrait of Alty Mason, *Adelard the Drowned* (plate 66). Not only is the hair, standing on end, similar to that of Alty's portrait, but the expression and facial features compare as well. With this in mind, the *sturm und drang* of the poem inscribed on the drawing reminds the reader of Hartley's tribute to Alty in "Cleophas and His Own: A North Atlantic Tragedy." There, the artist writes:

What a spectacle is Adelard, if I hadn't known he was a human being, I should have thought him some devouring beast from the caverns and the caves, all of his thoughts emotionalized and dramatized by magnificent, opulent, voluminous body action. He is tall, huge, giantesque, and his smoke black hair stands six inches above his low forehead, making him seem all the taller, almost spectral, he—the most Norman looking of them all.

His eyes have the famished look of one never to be appeased, of an under-eaten, over-ravenous wolf, sniffing at the mouth of dungeons, or at the edges of forest fires, loving the pungence of the burning vegetation, sniffing it all in with lustful eagerness, for Adelard, life must literally burn to mean anything at all.[1]

A.E.

[1] Marsden Hartley, "Cleophas and His Own: A North Atlantic Tragedy," reprinted in Ferguson, 98.

74

Untitled (Five Figures)

Pen and sepia ink on beige paper,

10⅝ × 8¼ in. (27 × 21 cm)

Unsigned

PROVENANCE

Estate of the artist; gift to Bates College from Hartley's niece, Norma Berger

Bates College Museum of Art, Lewiston, Maine

Hartley had a lifelong fascination with performance, including vaudeville, theater, the circus, and the pageantry of a military parade. Three related drawings—of which this is one—in the Bates College collection, feature groups of figures apparently in costume.[1] Here, a woman in a hat is flanked by a man in what looks to be the dress of an acrobat at the left and a man in military uniform at the right. Not enough is visible of the two figures in the background to make a guess at their roles.

Hartley wrote a great deal of published and unpublished material on the performing arts, including *Adventures in the Arts* (published in 1921) and "Elephants and Rhinestones" (unpublished manuscript on the circus).[2] A.E.

[1] See William J. Mitchell, *Ninety-nine Drawings by Marsden Hartley (1877–1943) from Its Marsden Hartley Memorial Collection, Treat Gallery* (Lewiston, Maine: Bates College Art Department, 1970), nos. 2–3, for reproductions of the other two drawings.

[2] Manuscript in Hartley Papers, Beinecke/Yale.

75

Flaming American (Swim Champ), 1939–40

Oil on canvas,

40⅜ × 30¾ in. (102.6 × 78.1 cm)

Inscribed on verso: Marsden Hartley 1939/40 / Flaming / American / (Swim-Champ)

PROVENANCE

Paul Rosenberg & Co., New York (until November 1966); Mr. Robert Brady (purchased 1966); Christie's, New York, Important American Paintings, Drawings and Sculpture, May 23, 1990 (no. 228A)

The Baltimore Museum of Art, Maryland
Edward Joseph Gallagher III Memorial Collection, by exchange

In 1937 Hartley declared himself "the painter from Maine," and in that year he completed his first series of figure paintings featuring the Francis Mason family. These were followed by a group of iconic male figure paintings of plain fishermen, Maine backwoodsmen, and Acadian heavyweights. He used a primitive style for these masculine works, which were presented to the public as the United States readied itself to enter World War II.

Flaming American (Swim-Champ) and *Madawaska—Acadian Light-Heavy* (plate 76) were first shown at the Hudson Walker Gallery in 1940, and were identified in the exhibition catalogue as wall panels for a gymnasium.[1] By providing a specific program for these paintings, not unlike the programs that Thomas Hart Benton and other American regionalists defined for their murals of the American scene, Hartley was able to imbue these works with homoerotic imagery that was not seen as such at the time. As Randall Griffey has written: "The masculine space of the gymnasium would… keep the erotic content of the work in check… the visual and physical embodiment—of the good, strong, natural, and healthy masculinity that characterized the gymnasium's clientele."[2]

Hartley's blond haired and blue-eyed swimmer is a bear-like figure wearing a swimming cap and skimpy swimsuit. He confronts the viewer directly and is seated on a barrel with his massive arms and claw-like hands resting on his thighs. Hartley explained that this work was intended for a "junior gym," and described it as "a large one of a champ swimmer at Yale—Claire [Evans]'s nephew & my God! Is he handsome—wonderful body—& so clean and nice."[3] He met the young swimmer and painted him during the summer of 1939, when he stayed with John and his wife Claire Spencer Evans, the son and daughter-in-law of Mabel Dodge [Luhan], in West Brooksville, Maine.

There is one drawing that relates directly to *Flaming American (Swim-Champ)* in the Bates College Museum of Art in Lewiston, Maine. It is pen and black ink drawing of the swimmer, untitled, which shows the figure seated on a barrel, But in the drawing the figure has bare feet and his shoes are placed to the right.[4] E.M.K.

[1] *Recent Paintings of Maine: Marsden Hartley*, Hudson Walker Gallery, New York, March 11–30, 1940.

[2] Randall R. Griffey, "Marsden Hartley's Late Paintings: American Masculinity and National Identity in the 1930s and 1940s" (diss., University of Kansas, 1999), 127–28.

[3] Hartley to Adelaide Kuntz, 1 August 1939, quoted in Ludington, 266.

[4] See no. 43 in William J. Mitchell, *Ninety-nine Drawings by Marsden Hartley (1877–1943) from Its Marsden Hartley Memorial Collection, Treat Gallery* (Lewiston, Maine: Bates College Art Department, 1970).

76

Madawaska—Acadian Light-Heavy, 1940
Oil on Masonite-type hardboard, 40 × 30 in. (101.6 × 76.2 cm)
Inscribed on verso: Madawaska—Acadian / Light-Heavy / Marsden Hartley / 1940.

PROVENANCE
Estate of the artist (no. 94); Eva Lee Gallery, Great Neck, N.Y. (1960); Alan Gallery, New York; A. James Speyer, Chicago (purchased 1962); Art Institute of Chicago (1987)

The Art Institute of Chicago
Bequest of A. James Speyer, 1987.249

Madawaska—Acadian Light-Heavy is one of a series of paintings that Hartley intended for a gymnasium. Hartley wrote to a friend praising this particular model: "My model last year at the art school in Bangor and who posed for me privately God what a magnificent corps—is a Madawasca boy of Acadian descent . . . a prizefighter . . . and is such a sweet lad—22."[1] He wrote to Adelaide Kuntz on February 2, 1940: "I have for the first time since 1922 a real live model a magnificent young feller a light heavy weight French Canadian and his body is so fine and dear I could work almost without end from him."[2]

Although Hartley seems to have been working from a live model for this painting, he collected a variety of photographs and postcards of men, some of them boxers, standing in similar stances. He also took photographs himself of men, nude or half nude, standing with arms akimbo, as does the figure in *Madawaska.*[3]

There is at least one other version of this composition, called *Madawaska—Acadian Light-Heavy (2nd Arrangement),* and also dated 1940, in the Curtis Galleries, Minneapolis, Minnesota.[4] The Minneapolis version differs from the first in that the figure rests his hands on the tops of his thighs, instead of behind his back, and the figure wears briefs rather than the more revealing support featured in the Chicago painting.[5]

There is at least one drawing that relates directly to *Madawaska.* It is an untitled pencil on paper of a male torso and is in the Bates College Museum of Art in Lewiston, Maine.[6] Hartley wrote a poem titled "Light-Heavy at Prayer" that describes the workout routine of the prizefighter.[7] A.E.

1 Hartley to Frank Davison, n.d., quoted in Robertson, 126.
2 Hartley (from Bangor, Maine) to Adelaide Kuntz, 2 February 1940, transcribed in McCausland Papers, Archives/Smithsonian, roll D268.
3 Gail Levin, "Photography's 'Appeal' to Marsden Hartley," *Yale University Library Gazette* 68 (1994): 35–36.
4 Elizabeth McCausland notes a third version, a bust-length portrait of this figure. It is oil on Masonite and measures 28 by 22 inches, location unknown. See McCausland Papers, Archives/Smithsonian, roll D270.
5 See Robertson, 127, for a reproduction of this work.
6 See no. 53 in William J. Mitchell, *Ninety-nine Drawings by Marsden Hartley (1877–1943) from Its Marsden Hartley Memorial Collection, Treat Gallery* (Lewiston, Maine: Bates College Art Department, 1970). See also nos. 74–76, which may also be related to *Madawaska.*
7 *Collected Poems,* 162–63.

77

The Last Look of John Donne, 1940
Oil on academy board, 28 × 22 in. (71.1 × 55.9.cm)
Unsigned

PROVENANCE
Paul Rosenberg & Co., New York;
Edith and Milton Lowenthal, New York (1950);
Brooklyn Museum of Art (1971)

Brooklyn Museum of Art, New York
Gift of Mr. and Mrs. Milton Lowenthal, 71.201

John Donne (1572–1631) was one of the greatest English metaphysical poets and is one of the most famous of those poets even today. It is easy to see why Hartley might have been drawn to Donne's poetry—the combination of passion and reason mirrors Hartley's own work. Hartley captures something of this in his poem "John Donne in His Shroud," in which he talks of "fierce passion turned to ice / and frozen light."[1]

Donne was also the dean of St. Paul's Cathedral, London. Hartley found his pictorial source for *The Last Look of John Donne* in the engraved frontispiece for the poet's last sermon, titled *Death's Duell.* Very close to the end of his life, Donne commissioned the drawing on which this engraving and a marble effigy now in St. Paul's are based. Donne delivered the sermon *Death's Duell* at St. Paul's, but it was not published until after his death.[2]

The frontal pose of Hartley's *John Donne* differs from the oblique pose in the engraving. Lisa Mintz Messinger has suggested that *The Last Look of John Donne* is a companion piece to Hartley's archaic memory portrait of Albert Pinkham Ryder (plate 71).[3] A.E.

1 *Collected Poems,* 195.
2 See *Modernist Art from the Edith and Milton Lowenthal Collection* (Brooklyn: Brooklyn Museum, 1981), 31, and Lisa Mintz Messinger, *American Art: The Edith and Milton Lowenthal Collection* (New York: Metropolitan Museum of Art, 1996), 28, for catalogue entries on this painting. I'd like to thank Barbara Dayer Gallati, curator of American art at the Brooklyn Museum, for generously sharing information from the curatorial file on this painting.
3 See Messinger, *American Art,* 28.

78

The Great Good Man, 1942
Oil on Masonite-type hardboard, 40 × 30 in. (101.6 × 76.2 cm)
Signed lower right: MH / 42

PROVENANCE
Babcock Galleries, New York; William H. and Saundra B. Lane (from 1958); Museum of Fine Arts, Boston (1990)

The Museum of Fine Arts, Boston
Gift of William H. and Saundra B. Lane and the Hayden Collection, by exchange, 1990.376

Marsden Hartley painted three portraits of Abraham Lincoln: *Young Worshipper of the Truth* (1940; Sheldon Memorial Art Gallery and Sculpture Garden, University of

Nebraska, Lincoln); *Weary of the Truth* (1940; Yale University Art Gallery); and, two years later, *The Great Good Man.* He wrote two poems, "A Lincoln—Odd, or Even," and "American Ikon—Lincoln," around the time of the first two portraits.[1] The portraits of Lincoln are part of a group of "archaic" portraits that Hartley painted near the end of his career. These portraits (plates 66–69, 71) are characterized by a "raw immediacy" and exhibit a severity and primitivism meant, in part, to suggest strength of character.[2]

Just after painting *The Great Good Man,* Hartley wrote to his friend the artist Carl Sprinchorn: "[Lincoln's] is the one great face for me and I never tire of looking at it, he was photoed so often . . . each time so different."[3] Hartley cut at least four photographs of Lincoln from the newspaper and owned a print titled *Lincoln as He Appeared directly after his Nomination in 1860.*[4] *The Great Good Man* is based on a photograph by Mathew Brady dated 1862. As Randall Griffey has observed, Hartley took some liberty with Brady's portrait, simplifying and hardening the former president's likeness so that a reviewer was able to refer to the "granite-like head of Lincoln."[5] A.E.

1 Both poems are published in *Collected Poems.*
2 Haskell, 115.
3 Quoted in Randall R. Griffey, "Marsden Hartley's Lincoln Portraits," *American Art* 15, no. 2 (summer 2001): 41. This excellent article informs much of this catalogue entry and should be consulted for a complete discussion of Hartley's Lincoln portraits. An excerpt of Hartley's letter to Sprinchorn, dated November 1942, can be found in the McCausland Papers, Archives/Smithsonian, roll D268.
4 Gail Levin, "Photography's 'Appeal' to Marsden Hartley," *Yale University Library Gazette* 68 (1994): 38.
5 Griffey, "Marsden Hartley's Lincoln Portraits," 43. See "Marsden Hartley Shows Rugged Paintings," *Art Digest* 17, no. 8 (15 February 1943) for the review.

79

Untitled (Five Lobstermen and Christ Figure—Pietà Concept), c. 1940
Pencil on white paper, 10½ × 8 in.
(26.7 × 20.3 cm)
Unsigned

PROVENANCE
Estate of the artist; gift to Bates College from Hartley's niece, Norma Berger

Bates College Museum of Art, Lewiston, Maine

80

Christ Held by Half-Naked Men, 1940–41
Oil on Masonite-type hardboard, 40 × 30 in.
(101.6 × 76.2 cm)
Unsigned

PROVENANCE
Joseph H. Hirshhorn; Hirshhorn Museum and Sculpture Garden

Hirshhorn Museum and Sculpture Garden, Smithsonian Institution, Washington, D.C.
Gift of Joseph H. Hirshhorn, 1966

Several scholars have linked this painting to the deaths of the Masons (plates 63–70), suggesting that it is both a portrayal of a Christian subject and a memorial to the Masons.[1] Barbara Haskell, for one, suggested that Hartley was connecting the recovery of a Mason boy's body from the ocean with the carrying of Christ to the tomb.[2] In this "all-male pietà," as Jonathan Weinberg described it, a hulking, shirtless lobsterman assumes the role of the Virgin Mary, cradling the diminutive dead Christ, while seven more lobstermen, clad only in jeans and the Nova Scotia fishermen's hats, look on. The homosexual content of the painting is pointed up through the absence of women and the emphasis on male physique.[3]

The untitled drawing in the Bates College Museum of Art, described as *Five Lobstermen and Christ Figure—Pietà Concept,* compares with the painting in that the figures are dressed as they are in the painting, and a single figure holds the dead Christ. What is different in the drawing is that there are four lobstermen behind the seated figure as opposed to the seven in the painting, and, in the drawing, the figure of Christ is larger in proportion to the other figures than in the finished painting.

There are at least three other drawings related to this painting: two in pen and ink on paper (10½ × 8¼ in. and 10 × 8 in.), both circa 1940 and in the Bates College collection, and *Christ Held by Men* (lithographic crayon on board, 27 × 21½ in.) from 1940–41 in a private collection.[4] The central group of the lobsterman cradling Christ is related to *O Bitter Madrigal* (c. 1942, lithographic crayon on board, 27 × 21½ in.; private collection) and a related poem of the same title by Hartley.[5]

The title of the painting, *Christ Held by Half-Naked Men,* was assigned to the work after the artist's death.[6] The painting was not exhibited during Hartley's lifetime. A.E.

1 See, for example, Haskell, 122; Ludington, 271–72; and Weinberg, 29–32, 180–85.
2 Haskell, 122.
3 Weinberg, 31.
4 Reproductions of these drawings can be found in Ferguson, 158–60.
5 Scott, 138–39. The poem can be found in *Collected Poems,* 235–36.
6 Ferguson, 160.

81

Canuck Yankee Lumberjack at Old Orchard Beach, Maine, 1940–41
Oil on Masonite-type hardboard,
40⅛ × 30 in. (101.9 × 76.2 cm)
Signed lower right: M.H. / 40–41
Inscribed on verso in chalk: Moment in Duration / Old Orchard / Maine / July 1940

PROVENANCE
Joseph H. Hirshhorn; Hirshhorn Museum and Sculpture Garden

Hirshhorn Museum and Sculpture Garden, Smithsonian Institution, Washington, D.C.
Gift of Joseph H. Hirshhorn, 1966

Hartley divided his time between Corea and Bangor, Maine, in 1940–41. He visited Old Orchard Beach often, where he found subject matter for a number of sketches and oil paintings, including *Canuck Yankee Lumberjack.* Gail Scott, among others, compared Hartley's French-Canadian lumberjack with Paul Cézanne's *Bather* (c. 1885; Museum of Modern Art, New York). As in Cézanne's composition, Hartley's figure looms large and, although grounded, is positioned in front of rather than *in* the landscape.[1]

Bruce Robertson has noted, however, a difference between Hartley's and Cézanne's figures. Hartley's bather "is a man, with big muscles, hair, and his penis outlined in his tight trunks."[2] Hartley's sketches include a study for the painting, at one time in the collection of Hartley's friend the photographer Alfred Valente, a photograph of which was labeled "Hartley self-portrait" in an unknown hand.[3] A.E.

[1] Scott, 136–38. See also Robertson, 126–28.
[2] Robertson, 126.
[3] McCausland Papers, Archives/Smithsonian, roll D272. Elsewhere, Elizabeth McCausland noted a study for *Canuck Yankee Lumberjack* that appears to be the same as the one in the aforementioned photograph, and she described it as "crayon & white chalk on heavy cardboard, 27⅞ × 21⅞, no signature," and noted that on the reverse of this drawing was "Another study of same figure, less finished & no anchor, etc." These notes were taken in November 1945. See McCausland Papers, Archives/Smithsonian, roll D270.

82

On the Beach, 1940
Oil on Masonite-type hardboard, 22 × 28½ in.
(55.9 × 72.4 cm)
Unsigned

PROVENANCE
Estate of the artist; Wright Ludington, Santa Barbara, Calif. (purchased 1946 through Paul Rosenberg & Co., New York); auction at Sotheby Parke-Bernet, New York, April 29, 1976 (no. 183); Suzanne Vanderwoude, Great Neck, N.Y. (purchased 1976); private collection

Private Collection

On the Beach is one of a group of figurative paintings Hartley created in Maine (see plate 81, for example). This particular composition stands out in that it includes the figure of a woman, along with two of the more characteristic brawny men Hartley loved to depict.[1] The woman, significantly smaller than the two men, lies propped up on her elbows, sheltered by one of the men gazing down at her.

Hartley used a strong palette, as he did in his other figurative beach scenes from this period, and strong brushwork to delineate the landscape of pink beach, blue sea, white waves, and white clouds. Related drawings are *Couple at Old Orchard Beach* (c. 1940, pencil on white paper, 4½ × 7 in.; Bates College Museum of Art, 55.1.58) and, for the male figure at the right, *Wrestler* (c. 1940, pencil on white paper, 4½ × 7¼ in.; Bates College, 55.1.60).[2] A.E.

[1] See Peter Selz, *Marsden Hartley* (San Francisco: Hackett-Freedman Gallery, 2002). Little else has been written on this painting.
2. See William J. Mitchell, *Ninety-nine Drawings by Marsden Hartley (1877–1943) from Its Marsden Hartley Memorial Collection, Treat Gallery* (Lewiston, Maine: Bates College Art Department, 1970), nos. 58, 60, for reproductions.

83

Untitled (Three Fishermen with Fish and Lobster), 1940
Pencil on beige paper, 11½ × 8¾ in.
(29.2 × 22.2 cm)
Signed lower right: M.H. / 1940

PROVENANCE
Estate of the artist; gift to Bates College from Hartley's niece, Norma Berger

Bates College Museum of Art, Lewiston, Maine

84

Down East Young Lobster Men, 1940
Pencil on beige paper, 11½ × 8⅞ in.
(29.2 × 22.5 cm)
Signed lower right: M·H / Down East / Young lobster men / 1940

PROVENANCE
Estate of the artist; gift to Bates College from Hartley's niece, Norma Berger

Bates College Museum of Art, Lewiston, Maine

85

Down East Young Blades, c. 1940
Oil on Masonite-type hardboard, 40 × 30 in.
(101.6 × 76.2 cm)
Unsigned

PROVENANCE
Estate of the artist; Paul Rosenberg & Co., New York; Armand G. Erpf (acquired 1957); Babcock Galleries, New York; Contemporary Paintings, Inc., New York; Mrs. Gerrit P. Van de Bovenkamp; John and Barbara Landau, New York; Gerald Peters Gallery, New York; Wadsworth Atheneum (1999)

Wadsworth Atheneum Museum of Art, Hartford
The Douglas Tracy Smith and Dorothy Potter Smith Fund, The Dorothy Clark Archibald and Thomas L. Archibald Fund, the Evelyn Bonar Storrs Trust Fund, The American Paintings Purchase Fund, and The Krieble Family Fund for American Art, 1999.11.1

In 1937 Hartley moved to his home state, Maine, and wrote "On the Subject of Nativeness—A Tribute to Maine." In that essay, Hartley described the character of the people of Maine as a product of the landscape itself: "Maine is . . . a strong, simple, stately and perhaps brutal country, you get directness of demeanor, and you know where you stand, for lying is a detestation, as it is not in the cities."[1] These two drawings and the final canvas, *Down East Young Blades,* are of lobstermen and fishermen, Maine "types" that Hartley admired and painted often (see plate 88, for example).

A striking composition, *Down East Young Blades* is of three lobstermen or fishermen. One central figure, dressed in a red jacket over a pink shirt, and wearing an Alpine-looking hat (traditionally worn by

Nova Scotia fishermen), dominates the composition. This figure, with his blond hair and piercing blue eyes, has at times been identified as a possible self-portrait of Hartley (see the essay by Bruce Robertson). The two flanking figures, much slighter in build, look toward him. The figure at the left, dressed in a white shirt unbuttoned nearly to his waist and wearing a necklace and red cap, wears red socks. The figure at the right also wears a red cap but is dressed in a green shirt and green socks. They stand on a dock or boardwalk with lobster traps behind them at the left.

The two flanking figures' dress, their poses, and their slight physique suggest a boyishness or effeminacy in contrast to the hyper-masculinity of the central figure. In addition, the red socks on the left (or port side) and the green socks on the right (or starboard side) relate not only to conventions of the sea but may also hint at their wearers' homosexuality.[2] In New York during the 1930s and 1940s, the colors red and green were used specifically to signal homosexual orientation to others familiar with the code. Other significant apparel included tight-cuffed trousers and necklaces.[3] As in other figural paintings from this period, such as *Canuck Yankee Lumberjack at Old Orchard Beach, Maine* (plate 81), Hartley emphasized the physical sexuality of the figures (see the essay by Randall Griffey). A.E.

[1] Marsden Hartley, "On the Subject of Nativeness—A Tribute to Maine," in *On Art*, 113.
[2] For this information, I am grateful to Carol Dean Krute, curator of costume and textiles at the Wadsworth Atheneum.
[3] George Chauncey, *Gay New York: Gender, Urban Culture, and the Making of the Gay Male World, 1890–1940* (New York: Basic Books, 1994), 52. See also Richard Martin, "Identity: George Platt Lynes's Photograph of Carl Carlsen," *Dress* 22 (1995): 78–84, for more information on clothing associated with homosexual identity. Thanks again to Carol Dean Krute for this reference.

86

Untitled (Six Lobstermen and Lobster Traps), c. 1940
Pencil on white paper, 8 × 10⅜ in.
(20 × 26.3 cm)
Unsigned

PROVENANCE
Estate of the artist; gift to Bates College from Hartley's niece, Norma Berger

Bates College Museum of Art, Lewiston, Maine

87

Study for "Lobster Fishermen," 1940
Pastel on paper, 21¼ × 27 in. (54 × 68.6 cm)
Unsigned

PROVENANCE
Paul Rosenberg & Co., New York; Lieutenant Richard S. Davis (purchased by 1945); Metropolitan Museum of Art

The Metropolitan Museum of Art, New York
Arthur Hoppock Hearn Fund, 1956

88

Lobster Fishermen, 1940–41
Oil on Masonite-type hardboard; 29¾ × 40 in.
(75.6 × 101.6 cm)
Signed lower right: M.H. / 40–41

PROVENANCE
Purchased from the artist by The Metropolitan Museum of Art (1942)

The Metropolitan Museum of Art, New York
Arthur Hoppoch Hearn Fund, 1942

The oil *Lobster Fishermen* won fourth purchase prize ($2,000) in the Artists for Victory exhibition at the Metropolitan Museum in 1942.[1] The exhibition opened on December 7, Pearl Harbor Day, and was organized by Artists for Victory, Inc., "the emergency wartime agency representing the twenty-three leading art societies in New York," in the words of Francis Henry Taylor, then director of the museum.[2] In the press, Hartley's prizewinning painting was described by one critic as "tightly designed," and by another as "more…American." The last writer continued, "There is something irrevocably of this shore of the North Atlantic about the blue water here, in the artist's sturdy, salty way of emphasizing the essentials and being taciturn about the details."[3]

Hartley's lobstermen wear the Alpine hat that appears in other paintings, such as *Down East Young Blades* (plate 85) and *Christ Held by Half-Naked Men* (plate 80). Hartley connected the North Atlantic people with Germans, describing Canadians as possessing the "warmth of the Bavarian nature and character" and the "Hamburg type" as "almost Anglo-Saxon" in appearance and dress and "quite like my own New England in its outer behavior" (as discussed in the essay by Donna Cassidy).[4]

Gail Levin has shown that Hartley employed photography as a basis for elements—and sometimes compositions in their entirety—of his paintings. She discovered prints in the Hartley Papers at Beinecke Library, Yale University, that related to the docks, lobster traps, and buoys, among other things, in pictures such as *Lobster Fishermen.*[5]

Although the original owner of the pastel, Lieutenant Richard S. Davis, believed that it was a study for the oil painting, the size and finish of the pastel suggest that it was meant to stand on its own as a work of art.[6] The drawing, on the other hand, appears to be a working out of the ultimate composition. A.E.

[1] McCausland Papers, Archives/Smithsonian, roll D270.
[2] Francis Henry Taylor, quoted in Alfred M. Frankfurter, "Artists for Victory Exhibition: The Winning Paintings," *Art News* 41, no. 16 (1–14 January 1943): 9.
[3] The first quote, "tightly designed," appears in "Artists for Victory Score Victory in Metropolitan Exhibition," *Art Digest* 17, no. 6 (15 December 1942): 6. The next two comments were made by Frankfurter, "Artists for Victory," 12.
[4] Hartley to Adelaide Kuntz, 22–23 July 1933, Hartley Papers, Archives/Smithsonian, reel X4.
[5] See Gail Levin, "Photography's 'Appeal' to Marsden Hartley," *Yale University Library Gazette* 68 (1994): 34.
[6] Lieutenant Richard S. Davis to Elizabeth McCausland, 15 September 1945: "Except for size and difference in intensity of color resulting from the difference in medium, it is exactly like the

Metropolitan's large oil called Lobster Fishermen, Corea, Maine, dated 1940–41. My picture is no doubt the study, for its proportions and composition are essentially the same. It is the most colorful pastel by Hartley I have seen." Quoted in McCausland Papers, Archives/Smithsonian, roll D270.

89

Church at Head Tide No. 2, 1938–40
Oil on canvas, 28 × 22½ in. (71.2 × 57.2 cm)
Inscribed on verso in pencil: Church at Head Tide No. 2 / M.H. 35 / 8/1/40
Inscribed on verso in blue ink: To Mathilde with devotion. Marsden Hartley

PROVENANCE

Paul Rosenberg & Co., New York; Mr. and Mrs. Kalman Greenhill, New York; The Downtown Gallery, New York (sale, June 19, 1961); Mr. and Mrs. John Cowles, Minneapolis, Minn.; Minneapolis Institute of Arts (gift, 1964)

Minneapolis Institute of Arts
Gift of Mr. and Mrs. John Cowles

Since 1932 Hartley had tried to emphasize his ties to New England and his love of the American landscape; in that year, an exhibition of his work at Edith Gregor Halpert's Downtown Gallery had been entitled *Pictures of New England by a New Englander.* Although he traveled constantly throughout the mid-1930s to places far removed from New England (to Mexico, Germany, Bermuda, and Nova Scotia, among others), he finally returned to Maine in the summer of 1937 and embarked upon an exploration of the state that would consume the final years of his life. During his first summer in Maine, he stayed with Mme. Lachaise in the small coastal town of Georgetown. Although the precise date of *Church at Head Tide No. 2* is unknown, Hartley probably painted it during his first few seasons back in the state, when he made several visits to Head Tide, a small community inland from Georgetown.[1]

The white clapboard church depicted in *Church at Head Tide No. 2*, with its steeple and Greek-revival portico, is a quintessential New England icon. Hartley, in his effort to establish his identity as the "first painter of Maine," may have chosen to paint the building precisely because of its archetypal imagery.[2] The church also represents, of course, the role of religion in American life. Hartley had been inspired as a young man by the anti-establishment spirituality of the transcendentalists, and scholars have speculated that his decision to portray the church at Head Tide as a deserted institution with its doors closed reflects his own dismissal of organized religion.[3]

If the church itself was readily recognizable as a traditional New England institution, however, Hartley's painterly style was highly untraditional. He intentionally distorted the structure of the building so that its façade stands parallel with the picture plane, while the body of the church recedes at an angle. The disjointed perspective gives the painting a studied awkwardness that is similar to the self-consciously primitive figures that populate Hartley's other canvases in these years (see, for example, *Adelard the Drowned, Master of the "Phantom"* and *Cleophas, Master of the "Gilda Grey,"* plates 66, 68). In addition, Hartley's manipulation of white against black—the thick, white impasto of the church walls against the black windows and roof—gives the building a tactile solidity that is similar to the effects achieved in other landscapes of this period.[4] Indeed, in the weight of his brushwork, Hartley has conveyed the strength and tenacity of the institution which, like the hearty rural Maine residents he admired, will endure the changes in the seasons and the passing of time. K.W.

1 Hartley had first visited Head Tide in the summer of 1928 with Paul and Rebecca Strand and Gaston and Isabel Lachaise; Strand had photographed the painter there. Gail Levin has discovered a picture postcard of the church at Head Tide in Hartley's papers at Beinecke/Yale. She posits that the postcard was an aide-mémoire for Hartley as he painted *Church at Head Tide No. 2*. See Gail Levin, "Photography's 'Appeal' to Marsden Hartley," *Yale University Library Gazette* 68 (1994): 24, 31. In Elizabeth McCausland's research notes on Hartley, she reported that Hudson Walker thought it possible that *Church at Head Tide No. 2* was painted in 1937–38, and repainted in 1940. See McCausland Papers, Archives/Smithsonian, reel D270.

2 Hartley to Rogers Bordley, 1939, quoted in Haskell, 111. Hartley also made several sketches of New England churches, including *Church at Corea, Maine* (plate 90).

3 Scott, 141–42.

4 See for example: *Granite by the Sea, Sequin Light, Georgetown* (1937–38; Neuberger Museum of Art, Purchase College, State University of New York); and *Fox Island, Georgetown, Maine* (1937; Addison Gallery of American Art, Phillips Academy, Andover, Mass.).

90

Church at Corea, Maine, c. 1940–43
Charcoal and white chalk on paper, 28 × 21¾ in. (71.1 × 55.3 cm)
Unsigned

PROVENANCE

Estate of the artist; Babcock Galleries, New York (1959); Joseph H. Hirshhorn, New York (1959–66); Hirshhorn Museum and Sculpture Garden, Washington, D.C. (1966–88); private collection; Salander-O'Reilly Galleries, New York; private collection; Gerald Peters Gallery, Santa Fe; Colby College Museum of Art

Colby College Museum of Art, Waterville, Maine

In the summer of 1940, Hartley moved to Corea, Maine, where he boarded with Forest and Katie Young. Forest Young was a lobster fisherman. Hartley sometimes used the abandoned church in Corea, captured here in charcoal and white chalk, as a studio (also see essay by Kornhauser, fig 18). Gail Scott has suggested Hartley's depiction of an empty church signifies his belief that spirituality was not to be found in organized religion, but in nature, as the American transcendentalists thought. Hartley's poem "Reflex" probably describes this church.[1] A.E.

1 Scott, 141–42. Hartley's poem is quoted on p. 141. See also *Collected Poems*, 210.

91

Mount Katahdin, Autumn No. 2, 1939–40
Oil on canvas, 30¼ × 40¼ in. (76.8 × 102.2 cm)
Inscribed on verso: MT. KTAADN (Maine) / Autumn #2 / Marsden Hartley / 1939–40

PROVENANCE
Paul Rosenberg & Co., New York; Edith and Milton Lowenthal, New York (purchased 1944); Metropolitan Museum of Art (bequest, 1991)

The Metropolitan Museum of Art, New York
Edith and Milton Lowenthal Collection
Bequest of Edith Abrahamson Lowenthal, 1991

Since at least 1930, when he first returned to the mountains of New England, Hartley had longed to visit Mt. Katahdin, Maine's remote, tallest peak.[1] It had served as an inspiration not only for older generations of American painters (Frederic Church among them), but also for the quintessential American philosopher Henry David Thoreau. To Hartley, visiting the mountain and capturing it in paint was essential to cementing his identity as "the painter of Maine."

The remoteness of Katahdin, for the older generation as for Hartley, was part of its mystical appeal—it was a site that required dedication to reach. In September 1939, Hartley, on the advice of his friend Carl Sprinchorn, contacted a state game warden named Caleb Schriber to help him reach the famed mountain. Schriber met him at the train station in Millinocket, and drove him to the base of the mountain. From there, Hartley walked four miles in the growing darkness to Cobb's Camp. He spent a week at the camp, in awe of both the mountain and the effort he had expended to reach it.[2]

Over the next three years, Hartley painted about eighteen works based on his Katahdin experience, capturing the mountain in all seasons and moods.[3] In *Mount Katahdin, Autumn No. 2,* painted soon after his trip, Hartley has rendered the mountainscape in a bright, strong palette using simplified contours and figures, reminiscent of his memorial portraits of the Mason family (see *Adelard the Drowned, Master of the "Phantom"; Cleophas, Master of the "Gilda Grey";* and *Fishermen's Last Supper,* plates 66, 68, 70). The massive, ridged mountain has been simplified into an unmodulated, dark blue silhouette that looms against the deep blue sky and rounded white clouds. The flat blue of the sky is reflected in the choppy waters of Katahdin Lake, which stretches across the foreground of the scene. The middle ground is a riot of flaming orange: short brush strokes of varying shades create an undulating field of color, broken only by the small yellowed trees on the water's edge and the towering green pines.[4] The mass of the mountain itself, inscrutable and silent amidst the surrounding carnival of color, could well be the "nonchalant" God that Hartley described in a letter to Adelaide Kuntz in the winter after his trip: "I have achieved the 'sacred' pilgrimage to Ktaadn [*sic*]. I feel as if I had seen God for the first time—I find him so nonchalantly solemn."[5] K.W.

[1] Robertson, 119.
[2] Hokin, 110–11.
[3] See *Mount Katahdin, Maine, First Snow, No. 1* (plate 92); *Mount Katahdin* (plate 93); and *Blue Landscape* (plate 94). Others in the series include *Mount Katahdin, Autumn No. 1* (1939–40; Sheldon Memorial Art Gallery and Sculpture Garden, University of Nebraska–Lincoln); *Mount Katahdin, First Snow, No. 2* (1939–40; Newark Museum, N.J.); and *Mount Katahdin* (1941; Hirshhorn Museum and Sculpture Garden, Washington, D.C.). Hartley also made numerous sketches of the mountain, including *Untitled (Mt. Katahdin)* (plate 95).
[4] Conservation analysis has revealed that the current layer of varnish on *Mount Katahdin, Autumn No. 2* was applied after Hartley's death and has caused a saturation of color that he did not intend. For a further discussion of Hartley's use of varnish, see the essay by Stephen Kornhauser and Ulrich Birkmaier.
[5] Hartley to Adelaide Kuntz, 2 February 1940, quoted in Haskell, 117.

92

Mount Katahdin, Maine, First Snow, No. 1, 1939–40
Oil on academy board, 22 × 28 in. (55.9 × 71.1 cm)
Inscribed on verso: Mt. Ktaadn—(Maine) / First Snow #1 / Marsden Hartley / 1939–40

PROVENANCE
Hudson Walker Gallery, New York (shown at Museum of Modern Art, New York, 1944, as "Mount Katahdin, Winter No. 1"); Mr. and Mrs. Arnold Hutcheson, New York; private collection, New York

Private Collection
Courtesy of Salander-O'Reilly Galleries, New York

Hartley painted *Mount Katahdin, Maine, First Snow, No. 1* during the same fevered rush of inspiration that produced *Mount Katahdin, Autumn No. 2* (plate 91), in the winter of 1939–40 after his trip to the heart of Katahdin. Although the two paintings obviously depict the same view of the mountain, their moods are strikingly different. Whereas the mountain in *Mount Katahdin, Autumn No. 2* occupies a vibrantly colored, almost abstract world of raw energy, in the later, wintry view it sits in a delicately realized scene of soft shadows and hazy sun. Hartley witnessed the season's first snowfall during his week at Cobb's Camp in September 1939, and his memory of the after-effects of the storm is revealing.[1] Although he complained about the lack of heat in the camp's cabins, his view of his snowy surroundings is bathed in a gentle light and has an air of quietude. The snowfall has made the mountain's contours more legible, and Hartley has captured them in shades of gray and brown. The lake in the foreground of the scene appears to be iced over, and the trees along its edge are sketchy, almost impressionistic forms. Unlike the trees in *Mount Katahdin, Autumn No. 2,* these almost melt into the foothills of the great mountain, mimicking the effects of a blanket of snow across a landscape.

In these dramatically differing depictions of Katahdin, Hartley had found a way to explore the multiple faces of Maine's wilderness. His series also announced a kind of spiritual ownership of the site: the pictures, with their shifting palettes and styles, demonstrate an intimate understanding of the mountain's constantly changing atmosphere. As he wrote to Roger Bordley, with no small degree of self-importance, in October 1939: "Came back from Mt. Katahdin, our 'sacred' mountain of Maine.... I now know my own beloved Maine as I have never known it before, and I shall immortalize that mountain, as no one else has or likely will, as it is *my* mountain and I the 'official' portraitist of it."[2] K.W.

1 Hokin, 110–11.
2 Hartley to Roger Bordley, 22 October 1939, McCausland Papers, Archives/Smithsonian, reel D268.

93

Mount Katahdin, 1942
Oil on Masonite-type hardboard, 30 × 40⅛ in. (76.2 × 101.9 cm)
Signed lower right: M·H· / 42.

PROVENANCE
Estate of the artist (no. 74); Paul Rosenberg & Co., New York (as "Katahdin, Autumn Rain"); Ione and Hudson Walker, Forest Hills, N.Y. (purchased 1951); American Federation of Arts (gift, May 1970); Babcock Galleries, New York; National Gallery of Art (purchased 1970, through funds given by Mrs. Mellon Byers)

National Gallery of Art, Washington
Gift of Mrs. Mellon Byers, 1970

94

Blue Landscape, 1942
Oil on board, 16 × 20 in. (40.6 × 50.8 cm)
Signed lower right: M.H. / 42

PROVENANCE
AXA Gallery

Collection of AXA Financial, Inc., through its subsidiary The Equitable Life Assurance Society of the United States

95

Untitled (Mt. Katahdin), c. 1939–40
Sepia ink over pencil on beige paper, 8⅝ × 11¼ in. (21.8 × 28.6 cm)
Unsigned

PROVENANCE
Estate of the artist; gift to Bates College from Hartley's niece, Norma Berger

Bates College Museum of Art, Lewiston, Maine

Hartley painted *Mount Katahdin* and *Blue Landscape* during the summer of 1942, almost three years after his only visit to the mountain and a year before his death.[1] In the years since his stay at Cobb's Camp, his memory had transformed the mountain into a simpler shape and cloaked it in a more nuanced, mystical atmosphere.[2] Few of the ridges and shadows visible in *Mount Katahdin, Maine, First Snow, No. 1* (plate 92) remain, and the mountain's rambling highest peak, Baxter Peak, has been narrowed into a more compact pyramid shape, flanked on the right by a collection of lower, indistinct peaks. In both paintings Hartley uses only slightly modulated blues to render the mountain, the sky, and the water; in *Blue Landscape* the blues are brighter and more intense, and in *Mount Katahdin* they are a deeper, more subtle gray-indigo.[3] The only contrasting color is in the middleground swath of fall-colored trees and underbrush: in *Blue Landscape* a ribbon of fiery orange cuts across the lower portion of the canvas, while in *Mount Katahdin* the deeper rust color of the foliage hugs the edge of the lake and, at the bottom of the painting, swings in the direction of the viewer's perch. Rather than being limited by the absence of the mountain before him as he painted, Hartley seems to have been liberated by the wealth of his memories. In 1932 he had written about mountains: "To understand the mountain one must have a feeling for it, one must know it, sense it in all its moods and aspects, the affirmation and the negation."[4] In these two paintings, the moods of the mountain become an index for his own moods late in life: an almost religious awe of the majesty of nature in the saturated blues of *Blue Landscape,* and absorbed introspection in the muted, subtle palette of *Mount Katahdin.*

Hartley painted these two canvases the summer he learned that the prestigious Paul Rosenberg Gallery wanted to represent him, giving him the confidence and professional satisfaction that had eluded him for so long. While these two paintings convey the quiet solitude of the aged artist, they also reveal an exacting, intent focus that no doubt was inspired by the prospect of future respect and acclaim that Rosenberg's offer represented. K.W.

1 A preparatory drawing exists for *Mount Katahdin: No. 50 (Mount Katahdin)* (1939, ink and pencil on paper, 8½ × 11¼ in.; Bates College Museum of Art, Lewiston, Maine).
2 Hokin, 112–17; Scott, 130–32.
3 Some scholars have argued that Hartley's shift towards a more muted palette, in paintings such as *Mount Katahdin* and *Summer, Sea, Window, Red Curtain,* was a product of his failing eyesight in his last years. See Haskell, 123.
4 Marsden Hartley, "On the Subject of the Mountain," [1932], reprinted in *The Book of Nature: American Painters and the Natural Sublime* (Yonkers, N.Y.: Hudson River Museum, 1983), 102.

96

The Wave, 1940
Oil on Masonite-type hardboard, 30¼ × 40⅞ in. (76.8 × 103.8 cm)
Signed lower right: M-H

PROVENANCE
Worcester Art Museum (purchased 1941 through Macbeth Gallery, New York)

Worcester Art Museum, Worcester, Massachusetts
Museum Purchase

In the summer of 1940, Hartley moved to the isolated lobstering town of Corea, further north on the Maine coast past Georgetown and Vinalhaven, on a raw, windswept peninsula. He lived in Corea, renting a room in the house of a lobster fisherman's family, for a substantial part of each year from 1940 until his death in 1943. The barren, brutal landscape appealed to Hartley initially because it reminded him of Nova Scotia. However, as was typical of the painter, he craved Corea's isolation when he was not there, and, upon returning to the town for the last few summers of his life, complained bitterly about the unenlightened townspeople and the oppressiveness of his loneliness.

It was out of this desperate ambivalence that some of Hartley's most elegiac seascapes emerged. In *The Wave,* the painter has eliminated all references to human habitation (see, in contrast, *The Lighthouse,* plate 98) and makes the overwhelming, angry energy of the sea his sole subject.[1] Although Hartley has captured, in the broad sweep of his horizon, the openness of the sky over the ocean, it is a murky and gray sky that smothers the viewer with its dark weight. The wave itself is animated with a restless energy, achieved through Hartley's thick application of white paint and subtle modulations of gray, blue, and lavender. His unfaltering focus on the bulk of the stormy sea recalls the late seascapes of Winslow Homer, which Hartley admired.[2] In an essay about the older artist, Hartley wrote that Homer "was essentially on the ground, and wanted to paint the very grip of his own feet on the rocks."[3] In the turbulent immediacy of *The Wave,* Hartley has succeeded in capturing the grip of his own feet on the foreground rocks. K.W.

1 See also *Evening Storm, Schoodic, Maine* (1942; Museum of Modern Art, New York).
2 Vivian Endicott Barnett, "Marsden Hartley's Return to Maine," *Arts Magazine* 54, no. 2 (October 1979): 174.
3 Marsden Hartley, "Winslow Homer," in *Adventures* (1972), 44.

97

The Lighthouse, c. 1940
Charcoal on paper, 22 × 28 in. (55.9 × 71.1 cm)
Unsigned

PROVENANCE
A.P. Rosenberg & Co., Inc., New York; Roy R. Neuberger (purchased 1952)

Collection of Roy R. Neuberger

98

The Lighthouse, 1940–41
Oil on Masonite-type hardboard, 30 × 40⅛ in. (76.2 × 101.9 cm)
Signed lower right: M·H·/ 40–41

PROVENANCE
Macbeth Gallery, New York; Mr. and Mrs. William A. M. Burden, New York (purchased 1943); private collection (purchased through Martha Parrish & James Reinish, Inc., New York)

Private Collection
Courtesy of Martha Parrish & James Reinish, Inc., New York

The Lighthouse was one of a group of paintings that Hartley began during his first sojourn in Corea and completed during the winter of 1940–41 in Bangor, Maine.[1] The lighthouse depicted, however, is in neither Corea nor Bangor, but rather in Portland, where Hartley had stayed during previous winters. Hartley owned a picture postcard of the Portland lighthouse standing above a calm sea, which bears certain compositional similarities to his own painting, and it is possible that the postcard served as an aide-mémoire for this work.[2]

In Hartley's scene, the sea is possessed of the same turbulent energy that animated *The Wave* (plate 96). He has chosen to tilt the horizon line—like a skewed photograph, snapped midst the storm's gusting winds—and the lighthouse juts out from the rock at a precarious angle. The waves and spray are painted, as in *The Wave,* with thick, white brush strokes, as if Hartley were trying to mimic the structure and weight of the water in the viscosity of the paint. As the waves swell and burst against the small houses grouped around the lighthouse, they also blend imperceptibly into the thick white of the cloudy sky, and thus surround the human habitation on all sides. In this battle of civilization against nature, the unrestrained power of the stormy sea conquers all. K.W.

1 Haskell, 122.
2 Hartley also made at least two drawings that relate to the finished painting. Both are charcoal on paper and date to around 1940; one is in this exhibition (plate 97). The postcard is in the Hartley Papers, Beinecke/Yale. See Gail Levin, "Photography's 'Appeal' to Marsden Hartley," *Yale University Library Gazette* 68 (1994): 33.

99

Hurricane Island, Vinalhaven, Maine, 1942
Oil on Masonite-type hardboard, 30 × 40¼ in. (76.2 × 102.2 cm)
Signed center right: MH / 42

PROVENANCE
Paul Rosenberg & Co., New York; Mrs. Herbert Cameron Morris, Philadelphia; Philadelphia Museum of Art (gift, 1943)

Philadelphia Museum of Art
Gift of Mrs. Herbert Cameron Morris

Hartley had spent the summer and fall of 1938 on Hurricane Island, where he embarked on a group of dramatically colored figure paintings that he called his "archaic portraits" (see *Adelard the Drowned, Master of the "Phantom"* and *Cleophas, Master of the "Gilda Grey,"* plates 66, 68) and a series of landscapes that featured heavy layers of white paint against black (see *Northern Seascape, Off the Banks,* plate 61). Several years later, in the summer of 1942, he revisited his Vinalhaven memories and painted *Hurricane Island, Vinalhaven, Maine.*[1]

In contrast to the turbulent energy and vibrant colors that infused his paintings from Vinalhaven, *Hurricane Island* depicts cliffs of subtly blended browns, yellows, and reds, and an ocean of animated energy that yet remains contained by the surrounding land.

Hartley painted *Hurricane Island* the same summer that he revisited Katahdin in paint for the last time (see *Mount Katahdin* and *Blue Landscape,* plates 93–94), and common to all of these landscapes is an interest in the blending of rich, saturated colors, inspired in part by the artist's fascination with a few Coptic textiles he had recently acquired.[2] The cliffs in *Hurricane Island,* while not infused with the same quiet mysticism of the late Katahdin scenes, reveal the painter's close, absorbed attention to the subtle effects of color: blended hues recede and emerge across the board, and the calligraphic surface application of a dark green is balanced against the glowing undertones of red, orange, and yellow. The gray sky, just visible beyond the trees, is almost entirely consumed by a single large cloud itself formed of varying grays. The sea, unlike the dramatic, attention-getting forms in *The Wave* (plate 96) or *The Lighthouse* (plate 98), froths at the base of the cliffs in a series of animated but indistinct brush strokes. This seascape is less a celebration of bracing physical experience than a contemplative study of the muted colors and diffused light of the Maine coast. K.W.

1 *Hurricane Island, Vinalhaven, Maine* bears a close resemblance to an earlier painting, *End of Storm, Vinalhaven, Maine* (1937–38; William Benton Museum of Art, Storrs, Conn.).
2 Haskell, 125.

100

Crow with Ribbons, 1941
Oil on Masonite-type hardboard, 28 × 22 in. (71.1 × 56.5 cm)
Unsigned

PROVENANCE
Joseph H. Hirshhorn; Hirshhorn Museum and Sculpture Garden

Hirshhorn Museum and Sculpture Garden, Smithsonian Institution, Washington, D.C.
Gift of the Joseph H. Hirshhorn Foundation, 1966

Crow with Ribbons, like *Lobster on Black Background* (plate 101) and *Shells by the Sea* (plate 102), was among the many penetrating still-life studies Hartley completed during his last summers in Corea, Maine. Hartley actually painted several portraits of single birds, but *Crow with Ribbons* is unique in the series for several reasons.[1] While in the other paintings he posed the birds naturally, with no props, against a dark ground (thus making it difficult to determine whether they were alive or dead), the crow in the present painting is unmistakably dead, hung upside-down from its tied feet.[2] It is framed against a piece of sailcloth, to which are tacked red and blue ribbons. The sailcloth provides a dramatic contrast with the blackness of the crow's body, which Hartley has rendered with such dense brushwork and dark pigment that few details of its anatomy are legible. Indeed, it is only along the edges of the crow's body, where Hartley's brush strokes imitate the bird's feathers against the white ground, that the creature's physicality and weight can be felt.

Hartley was pleased when audiences, upon seeing his bird paintings, recalled Albert Pinkham Ryder's famous painting *The Dead Bird.*[3] Ryder's delicate work is a still life of death itself, a painting that forces the viewer into intimate confrontation with mortality. *Crow with Ribbons* is likewise a still life of death. The sailcloth, the tacks, the ribbons are each carefully arranged, and in the opacity of the bird's body, which the viewer studies in the vain attempt to discern detail and life, is found the blankness of death. K.W.

1 See, for example, *Black Duck No. 1* (1941; Detroit Institute of Arts) and *Gull* (1942–43; private collection).
2 Scott, 144–45; Haskell, 125.
3 1890–1900; Phillips Collection, Washington, D.C. Robertson, 111.

101

Lobster on Black Background, 1940–41
Oil on fiberboard, 22 × 28 in. (55.9 × 71.1 cm)
Signed lower right: M.H. / 40–41

PROVENANCE
Estate of the artist (no estate number); Paul Rosenberg & Co., New York (sold December 1944); Henry P. McIlhenny, Philadelphia; National Collection of Fine Arts (now Smithsonian American Art Museum; gift, 1978)

Smithsonian American Art Museum, Washington, D.C.
Gift of Mr. Henry P. McIlhenny

102

Shells by the Sea, c. 1941–43
Oil on Masonite, 28 × 22 in. (71.1 × 55.9 cm)
Unsigned

PROVENANCE
Estate of the artist (1943–59); Paul Rosenberg & Co., New York (1959); Joseph H. Hirshhorn, New York (purchased 1959); Hirshhorn Museum and Sculpture Garden (gift, 1969); private collection, New York (purchased 1987)

Private Collection
Courtesy of Babcock Galleries, New York

During his last few summers staying with the Young family in Corea, Maine, Hartley complained that he no longer found the raw wilderness of the coastal town inspiring. Struggling with failing health (due, in part, to high blood pressure), he turned to landscapes based on memories (see *Mount Katahdin* and *Blue Landscape,* plates 93–94), figure paintings, and still lifes. Among the latter are a group of absorbing studies of individual objects suspended against a dark ground, including *Lobster on Black Background* and *Shells by the Sea.*[1] Neither painting includes any props that might lend narrative interpretations—a trap for the lobster, for example, or rocks and sand to accompany the seashells. Instead, each of these paintings is simply an intense study of an individual object, rendered in such detail and with such tactile sophistication that the work has a potent, almost iconic immediacy.

Hartley's lobster occupies a precarious state that seems to be equal parts life and death. The painting is, on the one hand, imbued with a latent animation, conveyed partly by its brilliant red, the artist's own recognizable, vigorous brushwork, and the claw reaching just beyond the left edge of the frame. Bruce Robertson has interpreted this image as an icon of the stereotypical New England virtues of steadfastness, strength, and endurance; as an icon, it is not merely a symbol, but rather an image that makes incarnate the spirit of endurance and constancy.[2] On the other hand, the red of the lobster's shell indicates that it has been boiled, and the painting's black background recalls the funereal tone of the War Motif series (see, for example, *Portrait of a German Officer,* plate 19). The lobster may also refer to the occupation of Hartley's landlord and adopted family in Corea, lobster fishing. Thus this portrait of both animation and death may refer to the struggle of daily life in the harsh climate of Corea.

In *Shells by the Sea,* Hartley has turned his gaze towards three inanimate objects, which appear to be located in intimate proximity to his easel. The tightly cropped composition reflects Hartley's interest in photography during these years, and his desire to recreate in paint the immediacy that Paul Strand achieved through his lens. He wrote to Strand in 1940: "I have always cherished my nearness to good photography—and have wished for a long time to emulate its veracities & so have tried to develop my approach to myopic visions."[3] In *Shells by the Sea,* he has carefully explored each curve and bump of the shells, and they appear to the viewer as both intricately contoured bodies and an abstract meditation on light and shadow. The spiny surface of the large shell is conveyed through the layering of lighter and darker tones of yellow and brown, so that the texture of the paint, as well as the hue, recreates its physicality. Indeed, in as much as these paintings are a record of the intimate, consuming observation of an object, they are also quite simply a record of physical presence, a painterly demonstration of human creation and existence. K.W.

[1] Scott, 143–45; Townsend Ludington, *Seeking the Spiritual: The Paintings of Marsden Hartley* (Ithaca: Cornell University Press, 1998), 78.

[2] Bruce Robertson, "Yankee Modernism," in *Picturing Old New England: Image and Memory,* ed. William H. Truettner and Roger B. Stein (Washington, D.C.: National Museum of American Art, Smithsonian Institution, 1999), 174.

[3] Hartley to Paul Strand, postmarked 12 September 1940. Hartley also experimented with photographing shells in the late 1930s; the images are in the Hartley Papers, Beinecke/Yale. Gail Levin, "Photography's 'Appeal' to Marsden Hartley," *Yale University Library Gazette* 68 (1994): 29, 34.

103

Sea Window—Tinker Mackerel, 1942

Oil on Masonite-type hardboard, 40 × 30 in. (101.6 × 76.2 cm)

Signed lower right: M / H / 42

Inscribed on verso: Sea Window—Tinker Mackerel

PROVENANCE

Estate of the artist (no estate number); Smith College Museum of Art (purchased 1947 through Paul Rosenberg & Co., New York)

Smith College Museum of Art, Northampton, Massachusetts

Purchased with the Sarah J. Mather Fund

104

Summer, Sea, Window, Red Curtain, 1942

Oil on Masonite-type hardboard, 40⅛ × 30 7/16 in. (101.9 × 77.4 cm)

Signed lower right: M / H / 42

PROVENANCE

Paul Rosenberg & Co., New York (as "Sea Windows, Red Curtain"); Addison Gallery of American Art (purchased 1944)

Addison Gallery of American Art, Phillips Academy, Andover, Massachusetts

In addition to the portrait-like studies of individual objects done during his last summers in Corea, Maine (see *Shells by the Sea, Lobster on Black Background,* and *Crow with Ribbons,* plates 100–102), Hartley also painted a group of more conventional still-life arrangements against an open window, such as *Sea Window—Tinker Mackerel* and *Summer, Sea, Window, Red Curtain.* Hartley had first experimented with the windowsill still life in Bermuda in 1917, where he painted a series of sensuous, brightly colored compositions such as *Atlantic Window* (plate 30) and *Still Life with Eel* (plate 31). The present two works were painted during Hartley's last full season in Corea, from July to December 1942. In August of that year, the prestigious Paul Rosenberg Gallery of New York and Paris had offered to represent him, an opportunity that not only promised income but also represented the apogee of critical respect. Hartley was profoundly gratified by his belated recognition, and was inspired, despite his ill health, to continue painting in preparation for a solo show in the winter.

Sea Window—Tinker Mackerel and *Summer, Sea, Window, Red Curtain* share a basic compositional organization consisting of a foreground arrangement of objects on a sill, behind which a window, framed on either side by dark panels, opens out to a view of the sea with pine tree–studded islands and a blue sky full of billowing clouds. In choosing this compositional schema, Hartley undoubtedly recalled the windowsill still life paintings of Henri Matisse, which had perhaps been an inspiration for his earlier Bermuda paintings (see the discussion for *Atlantic Window*). Despite their similarities, however, these two pictures cultivate different atmospheres. In the foreground of *Sea Window—Tinker Mackerel,* Hartley has flattened the sill almost entirely, so that it appears in a plane parallel to the window. The fish are rendered in blues and grays, in profile against the brown sill. With their bold black outlines they echo the isolated object studies of shells and fish (see *Lobster on Black Background* and *Shells by the Sea,* plates 101–2) that Hartley was painting simultaneously.

The bracing turquoise blues and grays of the sea and sky are the same colors as those of the fish; in using the same hues above and below the sill's dark edge, Hartley further distorts the foreshortened space into a collage-like flattened pattern.[1] *Summer, Sea, Window, Red Curtain,* in contrast, has a perspectivally correct foreground sill, on which sit familiar elements of Hartley still lifes, including flowers in a vase, tomatoes, a green pepper, and a book.[2] The painting hints at abstraction only in its upper portion, where the almost rectangular cloud is framed by the indistinct masses of the deep red curtains.[3] Hartley has used a richer, more mellow palette in *Summer, Sea, Window, Red Curtain* than in *Sea Window—Tinker Mackerel.* Its lavender-tinted water and dark red curtains recall the searching, almost mystical renderings of Katahdin done in these last years (see *Mount Katahdin,* plate 93). In neither of these windowsill scenes, however, does Hartley probe the experiences or memories that made his contemporaneous works—the remembered landscapes of Mount Katahdin and isolated object portraits—so emotionally resonant. Rather, these still-life paintings quite simply demonstrate the artist's tireless, straightforward love of the paint itself. K.W.

[1] Elizabeth C. Evans-Iliesiu, "*Sea Window—Tinker Mackerel,* 1942," in *Masterworks of American Painting and Sculpture from the Smith College Museum of Art,* ed. Linda Muehlig (New York: Hudson Mills Press, 1999), 186.

[2] Debra Bricker Balken, "Marsden Hartley: *Summer, Sea, Window, Red Curtain,*" in *The Addison Gallery of American Art: 65 Years* (Andover, Mass.: Addison Gallery of American Art, 1996), 386–87.

[3] Ronald Paulson has suggested that the abstract masses of the clouds, sky, and curtains in this painting set the stage for Mark Rothko's mature canvases. Ronald Paulson, "Marsden Hartley's Search for the Father(land)," in Ferguson, 28–29.

105

Storm Down Pine Point Way, Old Orchard, Maine, 1941–43
Oil on academy board, 22 × 28 in. (55.9 × 71.1 cm)
Unsigned

PROVENANCE
Salander-O'Reilly Galleries, New York; Clyde B. Hurt, South Carolina; Mr. and Mrs. George Perutz, Dallas (1965); Curtis Galleries, Minneapolis; Babcock Galleries, New York; Shein Collection

Shein Collection

This late landscape, along with *Summer, Sea, Window, Red Curtain* (plate 104), suggests the degree to which Hartley's late work anticipated the work of the abstract expressionists (see the essay by Carol Troyen). Hartley's large clouds floating in the sky have been compared with Mark Rothko's mature paintings of rectangles of color set against a differently colored ground.[1] In 1950 Clement Greenberg compared Hartley's works with those of the New York school, writing that Hartley's works "have an intensity and are animated by a desire to break through to a fresh and direct reality of pictorial feeling that bring them close somehow to the most recent abstract paintings."[2]

Storm Down Pine Point Way also indicates the influence Hartley had on his contemporary Milton Avery, whose beach scenes with blocks of color are direct descendants of Hartley's nearly abstract seascapes. K.W.

[1] Ronald Paulson, "Marsden Hartley's Search for the Father(land)," in Ferguson, 28.

[2] Clement Greenberg, note, in *Hartley/Maurer: Contemporaneous Paintings* (New York: Bertha Schaefer Gallery, 1950), n.p., quoted by Carol Troyen in her essay in this volume.

106

Roses, 1943
Oil on canvas, 40⅛ × 30⅛ in. (101.6 × 76.5 cm)
Unsigned

PROVENANCE
Estate of the artist; Paul Rosenberg & Co., New York (by 1944); Hudson D. Walker, New York (purchased 1948); Walker Art Center (gift, 1971)

Walker Art Center, Minneapolis, Minnesota
Gift of Ione and Hudson D. Walker, 1971

Hartley returned to Corea, Maine, in July 1943, just two months before his death on September 2. The preceding winter had been the most professionally gratifying in over two decades: in December 1942 he had won fourth purchase prize in an exhibition, *Artists for Victory,* sponsored by the Metropolitan Museum of Art in New York; and in February, the Paul Rosenberg Gallery had shown his work in a solo show that garnered substantial critical acclaim and generated numerous sales. Hartley returned to Corea partly out of habit (he had spent the latter six months of 1940, 1941, and 1942 in Corea) and partly because his ill health had left him exhausted amidst the busy pace of the city. However, he found the remote, coastal fishing village far too quiet after his satisfying winter, and focused himself with anticipation on the upcoming season, writing to a friend: "I can't tell you how I suffered since I came back here—nothing but rocks—the ocean—seagulls. I just hated to leave the beautiful scene of Broadway at night... knowing it was the last I should see of the white splendor until next spring and summer."[1]

Hartley set to work on a few canvases during this last, short summer of 1943; *Roses* was on his easel when he died.[2] As some scholars have pointed out, Hartley used roses as symbols of mourning and death several times in his later career, most notably in a poem about gulls lost at sea.[3] However, little else in the painting intimates the melancholy or introspection that characterized some of the artist's other late works (see, for example, *Mount Katahdin; Hurricane Island,*

Vinalhaven, Maine; and *Shells by the Sea,* plates 93, 99, 102). The flowers and leaves of the arrangement are rendered with his typical dense, vigorous, highly tactile brushwork, which imparts to them an aura of teeming, animated energy. The deep green of the foliage contrasts boldly with both the interspersed, forked white leaves and the brilliant blue of the surrounding sky; its vibrant palette is significantly different from the subtle, rich hues that predominate in such works as his 1942 portrait of Katahdin (plate 93) or *Summer, Sea, Window, Red Curtain* (plate 104). Indeed, as Gail Scott has written, Hartley's arrangement of roses, "with its upward thrust of organic life, is surely a work of triumph and joy, not of a dying man."[4] K.W.

1 Hartley to Richard Sisson, 3 August 1943, quoted in Haskell, 126.

2 A preparatory drawing exists for *Roses: Roses* (c. 1943, pencil on paper, 10⅛ × 7 in.; Bates College Museum of Art, Lewiston, Maine). This drawing appears in a frequently reproduced photograph of Hartley's Corea studio: it is tacked to the wall near his easel, on which the finished oil painting rests.

3 Lucy Flint-Gohlke, "*Roses,* 1943," in *Walker Art Center: Painting and Sculpture from the Collection* (Minneapolis: Walker Art Center and Rizzoli International, 1990), 237.

4 Scott, 147.

Photographic Credits

All images provided by the owner unless otherwise noted.

© Addison Gallery of American Art, Phillips Academy, Andover, Massachusetts, All Rights Reserved, pl. 104

Reproduction © Art Institute of Chicago, All Rights Reserved, pl. 76

© AXA Financial Inc., New York, pl. 38, 94

Courtesy of Berta Walker Gallery, Provincetown, Massachusetts, pl. 1

Carnegie Museum of Art, Pittsburgh, PA (photographer, Richard A. Stoner), pl. 72

Hirshhorn Museum and Sculpture Garden, Smithsonian Institution, Washington, D.C. (photographers Lee Stalsworth and Ricardo Blanc), pl. 20, 80, 81, 100

Los Angeles County Museum of Art, Photograph © 2003 Museum Associates/LACMA, pl. 69

© Marsden Hartley Memorial Collection, Bates College Museum of Art, Lewiston, Maine, pl. 49, 58, 65, 73, 74, 79, 83, 84, 86, 95

The Metropolitan Museum of Art, New York.

All Rights Reserved. © pl. 18; © 1985, pl. 19; © 1992 pl. 71, 91; © 2002 pl. 87, 88

Courtesy Museum of Fine Arts, Boston. Reproduced with Permission. © 2002, All Rights Reserved, pl. 3, 32, 78

National Gallery of Art, Smithsonian Institution, Washington, D.C. © 2001 Board of Trustees, pl. 15, 93

Courtesy of the Neuberger Museum, Purchase College, State University of New York, Roy R. Neuberger Collection (photographer, Jim Frank) pl. 70; (photographer, Geoffrey Clements) pl. 97

Courtesy of Salander-O'Reilly Galleries, New York, pl. 64, 82

Index

Page numbers in bold italics indicate the exhibit paintings. Page numbers in italics indicate other illustrations and photographs. Paintings, photographs, books, poems, and plays are listed under artist, photographer, or author.